Kaccāyana Pāli Vyākaraṇaṁ

कच्चायन पालिवेयाकरणम

Kaccāyana Pāli Grammar

Volume 2

Translated into English with additional notes, simple explanations and tables

By

A. Thitzana

Pariyatti Press

Pariyatti Press
an imprint of
Pariyatti Publishing
867 Larmon Road, Onalaska, WA, 98570, USA
www.pariyatti.org

First edition

ISBN: 978-1-68172-037-1
LCCN: 2016906544

Printed in China

DEDICATION

Yo me upajjāyo āsi, Asokā'rāmamāpako
Aggamahā panditā'bhi-dhajamahāraṭṭhaguru.
Chaṭṭasaṅgīti-ukkaṭṭho, Sūriyo guṇabāṇumā
Ta'mahaṁ abhipūjemi, Vyākaraṇena iminā.

Contents

Preface 1

Introduction 7

Pronunciation Guide 49

Guide to Conjuncts 53

Key to Entries 57

List of Abbreviations 59

Frequently Found Words 65

Suttakkama (Order of Suttas) 69

1. Sandhi Kappa 117

2. Nāma Kappa 183

3. Kāraka Kappa 373

4. Samāsa Kappa 443

5. Taddhita Kappa 495

6. Ākhyāta Kappa 575

7. Kibbidhāna Kappa 685

8. Uṇādi Kappa 763

Appendices 829

Index 881

Preface

A Wholesome Pursuit

This work of translation was carried out with an aim and a noble desire to bridge the gap which naturally exists between the contemporary man and an ancient sacred language known as "Pāli". The language of Pāli is like a gateway to the treasury of profound wisdom called "Tipiṭaka Pāli canon" expounded by Buddha. The study of Pāli, the spoken language of Buddha, is a worth-while and wholesome pursuit for anyone with a sincere heart and an inquiring intellectual mind whose apparent aim and purpose is to explore and understand Buddha's spoken words. By being able to understand His words, it will enrich knowledge and deepen one's wisdom thus leading to a much nobler and more meaningful life. Understanding the words of Buddha will surely bring a person much closer to the noble message of Buddha in its original tone, on the first-hand basis of the speech as it was originally spoken by Him more than almost two thousand six hundred years ago.

When I first taught Pāli to some foreign students from 1997 to 2005, using some well-written guide books on the Pāli study, I found out that they can progress quite smoothly in the reading and understanding of the Pāli passages. However, they usually make a number of recurrent mistakes in their writing exercises. Though most serious students are able to understand what they have learnt to some degree, they still find it quite challenging to write correctly and flawlessly.

The areas of weakness for the majority of students is in using the correct form of words with the right inflection, verb forms in the right place and the usage of participles and gerunds in the correctly arranged sentences. Pāli, as a matter of fact, is a highly inflective language based on its case and the role each word plays in a sentence of a contextual structure. Various word-formations such as nouns, verbs and other essential parts of the sentence too are quite variable based mainly on the case, tense and syntactical role of the word. Unless one clearly understands how each word is structured and how they are syntactically related according to the role they play, one will not be able to gain mastery of the language and necessary skills in spite of making the best efforts in learning it.

A Long-felt Need

An earnest student with serious interest needs a very basic, thorough understanding and careful study about the structural patterns of words and their morphological process. This can be achieved only through studying its original grammatical text along with detailed explanations on the rules known as Suttas and the accompanying word-examples shown alongside in the Suttas. In other words, there is no replacement for an original ancient text with a ready-made, short-cut guide though it may fill some language-learning need but not in such a way as an original text can certainly do. An original grammar text written at a distant time when the ancient grammatical concepts and rules were conceptualized and formulated by the ancient sages, can clearly explain all aspects of the language and its grammar.

The oldest Pāli grammar widely used and still extant is the one supposedly written by the most Venerable Kaccāyana. His grammar is a very-well written book, concise but lucid, compact with only six hundred and seventy-five Suttas[1]. It is complete as

---

[1] There are **673** Suttas in most versions. In the earliest-known publications such as Emile Senart's edition (1871) and Kaccāyana grammar published by Mahābodhi society(1901), Kaccāyana and Kaccāyana-vutti edited by Ole Holten Pind(published by Pāli Text Society in 2013), there are **675** Suttas with two more Suttas in the fourth section, Nouns chapter.

They are: (a) *Obhāvo kvaci yosu vakārassa* (b) *Bhadantassa bhaddanta, bhante* which are also found in Rūpasiddhi text. In light of this finding, it has

it covers all areas of the grammatical importance, ideally suited for any serious students of Pāli to study and master it within a short span of time. It is still used as a major popularly used grammatical text in countries such as Thailand, Myanmar and Sri Lanka where Buddhist scriptures are studied.

To date, there have been two translations of the text. One is a French translation by M.E. Senart published in 1871. The other is an English translation of the Kaccāyana's original Pāli grammar text translated by Satis Chandra Ācharyya Vidyābhūshana, the Professor, Sanskrit College, Calcutta and published by the Mahābodhi Society in 1901. Each Suttas of the text were shown in archaic Devanāgari-Pāli characters along with French or English translation of the Suttas and a few word examples. Both were nonetheless inaccessible to those who cannot read nor understand the French and the old-style Devanāgari characters.

Although both translations are neither a thorough translation nor a detailed treatment of the complete text, they were indeed helpful in providing some basically needed insights into grammar and served as useful guides and references for the students of Pāli for many years since.

There is a long-felt need to have a more thorough and complete English rendering of the great grammarian's work so that it can benefit all those studying Pāli. This book is the first-ever attempt not only to translate all of the whole text but also to contemporize an ancient grammar and its contents for the contemporary world. I fervently hope that through such a

---

to be logically assumed that there must have been 675 Suttas in the original text. The translation of these two Suttas are also shown in the footnote of this book in the fourth section of the Nouns chapter.

detailed translation, it would surely be much more easier and more accessible to any student, regardless of various language backgrounds with the aid of a translated grammatical text such as this.

An Eternal Tribute

Although this work is a not a groundbreaking work nor laying of a new foundation in the matters of Pāli grammar, it is nevertheless an important milestone in the Pāli grammatical literature. I humbly hope that this translation work will take the study of Pāli to a more higher dimension of advanced, in-depth study for all serious international students of Pāli. It will thus greatly benefit the students of Pāli in their study in many ways either as a basic companion guide or as an academic reference text at all times as long as their association with the Pāli study is concerned.

I had started this work of translation as a token of eternal tribute to my great preceptor, the most Venerable Sayādaw Bhaddanta Sūriyābhivaṁsa (1879-1975), the founder of two great Masoeyein (Asokārāma) monasteries in Mandalay. He was also the chief presiding patriarch chairman of the great sixth Buddhist Synod held in 1954-56, as well as the founder of Pañcanikāya Sāsana Beikman monastery, Yangon, who has had nurtured me even while I was just a young novice. It is also a memorial tribute of the deep gratitude to my late Pāli teachers venerable Kan-oo Sayādaw U Kondañña, (Lhaw-gar, Pale township, Monywa) and Sayādaw U Nāyakābhivaṁsa, (Masoeyein Taik-thit Monastery, Mandalay), to whom I feel greatly indebted for all the grammatical knowledge I had acquired. It is through dedicated care and guidance of such great teachers that I am able to share this translation work of an ancient sacred language with others. I feel that all the immense amount of energy, time and effort put into this important work will not be in vain, if this translated ancient grammatical text would surely and greatly benefit all serious students of Pāli in providing strong grammatical insights and skills they earnestly wished for. It will even be like receiving the greatest reward and abundant blessings for me if all earnest students pursuing the study of Pāli would one day become competent and accomplished Pāli scholars of great goodwill who would selflessly serve the common interests and well-being of many in the human society.

Acknowledgement

While this translation work is being carried out, some people have graciously rendered unstinted support and compassionate help in many ways. Among such gracious people are the most Venerable Si-shin Sayādaw Bhaddanta Aggañāṇābhivaṁsa (Mahāvisuddhārāma Monastery, Mandalay), Shwe-tu-wan Sayā daw U Saddhiyābhivaṁsa (Yangon), Sayādaw U Ñeyadhammā bhivaṁsa & U Vicittābhivamsa of Masoe Yein Monastery (Mandalay), Sayādaw U Rājinda (Satipaṭhāna Meditation Center) & Ms.Yap Siew Choo (Singapore) who ran errands and did all the necessary things tirelessly, Phrakru Vara Paññā Khun (Wat Mahā That, Bangkok), Phra Ñāṇakusala, Jamroon Damatā (Mahā Chulalongkorn Rājavidyālaya University, Bangkok, Thailand), Rob Moult who helped in reformatting of the book with great dedication, Dr.Wong & Flora Wong, Sister L.C., Ms. Elaine Lew Mee Ling, Yennifer Low, (all from Kuala Lumpur, Malaysia), Mrs. Genny Chee Family, Brother Li Chum family (Singapore), David Berry (Dharma Centre of Canada), Donald Altman (Moonlake media & Mindful Practices USA), Ms.Yin Yin Aye (Corona Hills, USA) Brihas Sarathy & U Tin Htoon (Pariyatti, USA), Nyan Lin Aung (La Puente, USA), Ms. Khin Mar Kyi & Ms. Khin Myo Kyi, Ms. Myint Myint Than & Hnin Hnin Aye(All from Mandalay), M. Thet Naing Kyaw (General formatting), K. Kyaw Han, Nalin Ariyarathne (Cover design), Ms. Moe Moe & Ms. Soe Moe Lwin (Final proof-reading), K. Kyaw Lwin of Dhamma download, all well-wishers not mentioned by name but who generously contributed to this project. To all of them, I feel greatly indebted. Their generous help and goodwill are forever appreciated. May their goodwill and generosity enrich them in material abundance and spiritual wisdom to lead a blessed and fulfilled life. May their devotion to the triple gem bring them countless blessings.

Patthanu'yyojanā

Englisāya bhāsāya, Anuvuttaṁ Kaccāyanaṁ.
Sādhavo viciya sukhaṁ, Sikkhe Pālivyākaraṇaṁ.

Ya'miha suṭṭhu ni'dditthaṁ, anvī'ritañ'ca sabbaso
Sū'padhāriya sabbaṁ taṁ, Pāliniruttisa'ññhitaṁ

Paññāya somanassena, saddhāpubbena chandasā
Vyākaraṇamhi kusalā, Buddhavacanamāmakā

Saddhammagarukā hontu, saddhammavuḍḍhikārino
Saparahitakārī ca, amatayāyino bhave.

With boundless Metta and goodwill for all,

A. Thitzana
February 21, 2016
USA

Introduction

Historical Background
The relationship of Sanskrit, Pāli and Prakrit

It is quite obvious that Pāli, Sanskrit and Prakrit have indeed common linguistic traits and close parallels to each other. These ancient languages, which belong to the Indo-Aryan language family of the Indus civilization, are linked not only in terms of geographic, cultural and close societal conditions, but also through some shared grammatical elements and inherent linguistic patterns. The intimate contact through daily interaction among people might have played a greater part in the development of such shared linguistics which resulted in somewhat interfused grammatical system. It can be logically assumed that the grammar of each respective language might have had appeared alongside since many centuries prior to or around the time of Buddha. None of them, however, were put into any record in the form of the written manuscripts but were rather passed through generations as orally transmitted grammatical trends. This might be the reason why the great grammarian Pāṇinī had made references in some of his Suttas to his predecessor grammarians. Amazingly enough, with the emergence of various belief-systems in the ancient Indian society, each language has come to play as the sacred languages of three main religious ideas among which Sanskrit became the sacred language of Hinduism and Vedic texts, while Pāli being the sacred media for all Buddhist texts and Prakrit being the sacred language of Jains and their religious texts.

Pāli Grammar vs. Sanskrit Grammar

The grammar or the science of language, had occupied high and honorable place in the ancient civilization of India. Having much grammatical skill and expertise is one of the virtues of being a respectable man of dignity among high social elites. The pursuit of grammatical study was thus a very respected trend of learning those days.

Though there have been ancient grammars previously, the only extant and oldest Sanskrit grammar still in use is the one written by Pāṇini which is referred to as "ashṭadhyāyī". As the name suggests, it has eight chapters, with numerous Suttas (aphorisms or brief grammatical rules) totaling 3995 in all. Both Sanskrit and Pāli grammars have similar grammatical models as all have the same format of having eight chapters although the contents of each are distinctive and different in their own various aspects. The Pāli Grammar, the one traditionally believed to have been written by the great Pāli grammarian Kaccāyana is not totally based on the Pāṇinīan-system but an independent work which has its own style and character. Thus, there is significant difference and an independent way of presentation of the grammar.

The Grammarians of Ancient India

In ancient Indian society, the tradition of learning any branch of knowledge including the grammar, is usually based on the oral tradition transmitted by teacher to student for many generations until modern printing machine was introduced into India at the turn of fifteenth century by the Christian missionaries. The study of grammar, even before Buddha's time, is pursued by social elites especially those belonging to the high Brāhmin caste. The Sanskrit, Pāli and Prakrit are the languages interwoven and intertwined into the ancient Indian society as linguistic threads in the matters of daily communication and learning among diverse communities. It is no wonder that the grammar of each language, as a result, have certain things in common despite having some distinctive features of their own in many respects. The following verses mention the name of ancient grammarians:

(1) इन्द्रश्चन्द्रः काशकृत्स्नापिशली शाकटायनः ।
पाणिन्यमरजैनेन्द्राः जयन्त्यष्टादिशाब्दिकाः ॥
(2) इन्द्रं चान्द्रं काशकृत्स्नं कोमारं शाकटायनम
सारस्वतं चापिशलं शाकल्यं पाणिनीयकम ॥

According to these verses, there have been eight earlier grammarians (ādisabdikā) such as Indra, Candra, Kāsakrtsna, Apisāli, Sākatāyana, Pāṇini, Amara and Janendra. In the second verse, Komāra(usually referred to as Kātantra or Kalāpa Vyākaraṇa), Sārsvata and Sākalya are extra names cited as grammarians. All those Indian grammarians are a mixed breed of scholars from different religious backgrounds. Among them, Candra(Circa 400-480 A.D), Janendara(Circa 8th century A.D), for example, are the disciples of Buddha. There was a verse of salutation to Buddha by the author Candra Gomin at the beginning of his grammar text which reads:

सिद्धं प्रणाम्य सर्वज्ञं ।सर्वीयं जगतो गुरुम ।
लधु विश्वस्तसम्पुर्णं । मुच्यते शब्दलक्षणम ॥

Those grammarians had lived in different timelines though some of them might have been quite possibly co-eval. However, it is beyond the capacity of anyone to deconstruct or reconstruct the past incidences which happened many centuries ago. As such, it is quite problematic to establish the exact order of timeline of these ancient grammarians and establish the correct biographic profile and the earliest seniority of one over another.

Of those grammarians, Pāṇinī is the most eminent as his grammar is still extant and occupies the highest place of honor and respect among the grammarians of ancient India. In both aspects of linguistics and grammar, Pāṇinī's grammar is indisputably an outstanding treatise as it details the areas of word-formation, morphology, philology, sound system and various grammatical rules. Despite unique attributes of linguistic ingenuity, Pāṇinī had undoubtedly adapted or incorporated the grammatical concepts of his predecessors in one way or the other. This fact is clearly noticeable through references he used to make in some Suttas of his grammar text to his predecessor grammarians such as Kāsakrtsna, Apisāli and Sākatāyana.

Pāṇinī's "ashṭadhyāyī" grammar served as a seminal ground in which attempts either to gloss over his text or to reformat or to improve on his grammar are pursued by later grammarians.

This had led to the development of rich grammatical literature of ancient India. Among such notable grammatical treatises written within the premises of Pāṇinīan concepts are: (A) a monumental commentary work titled "Mahā Bāshya" by Patanjali, (B) a more improved thematic treatment of Pāṇinī titled "Vaiyākaraṇa Siddhanta Kaumudi" by Bhaṭṭoji Dikṣetā and (C) Kāshikā Vritti(still an extensive commentarial work on Pāṇinī).

Also, another grammarian named Varadarāja, who is the disciple of Bhaṭṭoji Dikṣetā, wrote three grammar texts. They are: (1) Madhyakaumudī, (2) Laghukaumudī, (3) Sārakaumudī, (an abridged, but well-presented version of Laghukaumudī). His grammars are arranged in a manner which is more thematic and easy to study, yet simple to understand even for the beginners.

Kaccāyana

Kaccāyana, like Pāṇinī, is a pioneer, the earliest-known Pāli grammarian whose work too either adapted or absorbed some terminology and fundamental grammatical concepts from the preceding grammatical sources he is well-conversant with. Even though his work cannot be said as a grammar solely based on the Pāṇinīan system and model, there are quite a number of Suttas whose physical structures or functions share some similarities with those found in Pāṇinī's "ashṭadhyāyī" grammar. This does not mean that all those supposedly similar Suttas are totally identical in terms of both structure and function. Upon closer observation and careful analysis, some of the Suttas are found only to have structural resemblances to some degree but quite different in terms of functions. Some Suttas, as a matter of objective analysis, are found to have similar functions although the ratio of such Suttas are quite marginal in relation to voluminous numbers of Suttas contained in Ashṭadhyāyī.

Kaccāyana and his identity

The term Kaccāyana (कच्चायन or कात्यायन Katyāyana[2], a somewhat differently spelt name due mainly to different morphological procedures which exists in Pāli & Sanskrit grammars) is a name of highly regarded disciple of Buddha. According to the descriptions in Buddhist texts, he was born in Ujjenī, into an educated wealthy Brāhmin family, whose father is royal advisor (Purohita) to the king. He is highly educated in all ancient Vedic and Upanishad texts and also highly skilled in the grammar. He later became a disciple of Buddha and well-known for his wonderful capacity to explain any brief sayings of Buddha in a way either to be in tune with or completely agrees with Buddha's original view. Therefore, Lord Buddha praised him and placed him in a special position of honor known as **Eta'dagga** (The most outstanding position) among disciples in a

---

[2] See page vii, the preface to Prakrita Prakāsa (1868 Edition) by Professor E.B. Cowel, The University of Cambridge. Also the same spelling of this name (कात्यायन) is seen in the initial verse of Kita section of the Kātanta Vritti written by Durga simha(दुर्ग सिंह) which reads:

वृक्षादिवदमी रूढाः । कृतिना न कृाः कृतः ।
कात्यायनेन ते सृष्टा । विबुद्धिप्रतिवृद्धये ॥

particular field of excellence in being able to correctly elucidate Buddha's short sayings into detail.

In Apādāna'ṭṭhakaṭhā, II (the commentary to Apādāna texts which is like the biographic accounts about special deeds in the past lives of eminent disciples of Buddha), there is some remarkable account regarding Venerable Mahā Kaccāyana which reads:

Attano Pubbapatthanāvasena Kaccāyanapakaraṇaṁ, Mahāniruttipakaraṇaṁ, Nettipakaraṁan'ti Pakaraṇattayaṁ Saṁghamajje Vyākāsi.

Atha Santuṭṭhena Bhagavatā "Etada'ggaṁ Bhikkhave Mama Sāvakānaṁ Saṁkhittena Bhāsitassa Vitthārena Atthaṁ Vibhajantānaṁ Ya'didaṁ Mahākaccāno"ti Etada'ggaṭhāne ṭhapito Aggaphalasukhena Vihāsi. (Mahākaccāyana'tthera apādānavaṇṇanā, 54 Kaccāyana vagga, pp 213, Chaṭṭha saṅgā yanā Edition)

[Translation] By virtue of his own aspirations in times of previous Buddhas, he (**i.e.** Kaccāyana) was able to outline and declare three monologues (texts) at an assembly of Saṁgha, namely, **Kaccāyana text**, **Mahā Nirutti** and **Netti** texts.

Being satisfied on his intellectual prowess, Lord Buddha then honored him with the **"etadagga"** honor, a highest, outstandingly exalted position by making the following statement:

"Of all my disciples who can explain whatever I have said briefly, Kaccāyana is the most outstanding of all".

Having placed in such an exalted position, Venerable Mahā Kaccāyana, mostly lived a quiet and unfettered life enjoying the noble peaceful fruit (**i.e.** the benefit) of his enlightenment.
Also, there are some discourses such as Madhupiṇḍika Sutta, Madhura Sutta and Mahākaccāna Badde'karatta Sutta in the Majjima Nikāya and Uparipaṇṇāsa texts where Venerable Mahā Kaccāyana's detailed explanations won Buddha's unreserved praise.

In the light of such accounts from Buddhist texts, the author of earliest Pāli grammar can still possibly be assumed as a well-known personality from the viewpoint of scriptural records despite some later academic opinions of different views. However, the two grammatical texts, **(Kaccāyana text & Mahānirutti)** which he was supposed to have authored, may have actually existed in the form of grammatical principles and relevant knowledge handed down and preserved through successive generations of monastics by means of the oral tradition only.

In one ancient Pāli record named **Sutta-niddesa**, the legend has it that the first Sutta of Kaccāyana's grammar **"Attho Akkharasaññāto"** which had served as the most important initial statement regarding the principle of grammatical necessity of a language, is attributed to Lord Buddha Himself. Those words which form as the first Sutta were supposed to have been said by Buddha as the brief outline of advice and reminder to two meditating monks who were meditating by the river bank, but whose minds were being distracted and wrongly uttering the words "*Udakabaka*-water and egret" instead of the right word "*Udayabbaya*-the arising and passing". Those initial words of Buddha, according to Sutta-niddesa, were further elaborated by venerable Kaccāyana. Thus, that elaboration and exposition process has led to the development of such a detailed grammatical work which commonly referred to as "Kaccāyana Vyākaraṇa".

Netti and Peṭakopadesa

Although the Mahā Nirutti text is no longer extant, **The Netti** (Annotative Exegesis) which is attributed to Kaccāyana's authorship is still extant. Besides these texts, The **Peṭakopadesa** (the conspectus summary of the canonical principles) is likewise attributed to his bright authorship evidently traceable through Pāli records contained in both *ganthārambha* (the beginning section) and *Nigama*(the concluding verses) at the end of both texts with his name specifically cited as shown below:

(a) *Soḷasa Hārā Netti Pañcakanayā Sasanassa Pariyeṭṭhi Aṭṭhārasamūlapadā* ***Mahākaccānena*** *Niddiṭṭhā*
(The Beginning verse. 3 of Netti Pāli text)
(b) *Ettāvatā Samattā Netti Yā Āyasmatā* ***Mahākaccāyanena*** *Bhāsita Bhagavatā Anumoditā Mūlasaṅgītiyaṁ Saṅgītā'ti*
(The concluding words, the Netti Pāli text)

(a) *Aṭṭhārasamūlapadā* ***Mahākaccāyana****-gotta-niddiṭṭhā*
(Uddāna Gāthā, Peṭakopadesa Pāli Text)
(b) *Peṭakopadese* ***Mahākaccāyanena*** *bhāsite Paṭhabhūmi Ariyasaccapakāsanā nāma*
(c) *Therassa* ***Mahākaccāyanassa*** *Jambuvanavāsino Peṭakopadeso Samatto* (At the end of each section called "*Bhūmi*" and also at the conclusion of Peṭakopadesa PāliTexts)

The Netti and Peṭakopadesa Pāli texts are replete with the most brilliant analytical exegesis and encyclopedic wisdom of the author. The texts themselves serve as the clear testament to the linguistic ingenuity and extraordinary broad level of wisdom of Kaccāyana. The grammar which he was supposed to have been elaborated is also unique in many ways. It bespeaks itself about the simplicity of Pāli grammatical system without any hint of delicate technical complexities. It was in fact concisely written

to explain the basic grammatical concepts, the relevant terms and simple morphological procedures.
Due to incomplete fragments of the records and lack of exactly coherent chronological stratification in such a remote time, it is nevertheless impossible to draw an exclusive conclusion on the true identity of the author. The fact that the author may be a reputed personality such as the one found in the scriptural records or just an obscure person of the same name who might have been much earlier or coeval with the author of Kātantra grammar or a much later one is an unsettled issue. It is still open for unbiased scholarly opinion and intellectual analysis. It is nonetheless beyond the capacity of anyone to exactly point out in a more conclusive manner by reconstructing incoherent and unreliable fragments of the past records and events which happened in such a long span of time except on vague terms of intellectual speculation and inferential hypothesis.

It is almost logically as well as historically tenable to hold a factual view not based on inveterate bias. Among such views, is a possibility that there must have already been a Pāli grammar of some sort which might have existed not in the form of a complete text but in an oral tradition over such a long period of 1800 years' time spanning from the birth of Lord Buddha in B.C. 624 to the close of 1200 A.D, a timeline when Buddhism had flourished in the Indian sub-continent.

According to the "Indica" written in Arabic by Persian scholar Al-Bīrūnī (Circa 973-1048) and translated by Edward Sachau, some mention is made regarding the popular grammars used then among Buddhist communities. They were the one written by Candra Gomin and another non-Pāṇinīan grammar named Kātantra written by Sarvavarman, both of which were known to have been widely used among Buddhist communities. Candra Gomin authored Candra Vyakaraṇa, a Sanskrit grammar somewhat similar to the Pāṇinīan system but a distinctive grammatical work which has about 3099 Suttas. The author himself was a disciple of Buddha which he had indicated by the beginning verse of the text.

Kātantra and Kaccāyana

Some Western scholars, such as [3]Arthur A. Macdonell had opined that Kaccāyana's work must have been based mainly on the grammatical model of **Kātantra** vyākaraṇa also known as Kalāpa or Komāra (authored by Sarvavarman) as the striking similarities, especially similar naming of the chapters, the names of Ākhyāta verbs and some similar Suttas are found in the Kaccāyana's work. To put such similarity in a clear perspective, it could be simply and obviously **a matter of shared fundamentals** of the Sanskrit and Pāli. Both languages have had inherent affinity to each other since the early days of their inception as the spoken languages as far as the Indian civilization is concerned. This nature of affiliation along with interfusion of the grammatical thoughts of successive generation of grammarians had resulted in such apparent grammatical similitude to a certain degree.

Supposedly, Kātantra could had been a widely used grammatical text among Buddhist communities in India and Tibet for many years. Most scholars such as Sri Patidatta(श्री पति दत्त), Trilocanadāsa(त्रिलोचनदास, the author of Kalāpa Piñjikā) and Durgasimha(दुर्ग सिंह, the author of Kātantra Vritti Ṭikā), an important commentary on the Kātantra grammar, were assumed to be Buddhist disciples in the light of the following verse written by Durgasimha at the beginning of his text "Kātantra Vritti". The verse clearly attest to it. Here is the verse:

---

[3] See the introduction, A Sanskrit Grammar for students by Arthur A. Macdonell.

देवदेवं प्रणम्यादौ । सर्वज्ञं सर्वदशिनम ।
कातन्त्रस्य प्रवक्ष्यामि । व्याख्यनं शार्ववमिकम ॥

If seen from the viewpoint of a broader intellectual position and unbiased objectivity, the nature of some fundamental similarity found in Pāṇinī, Kaccāyana and Kātantra can also be viewed **as a kind of relative symbiosis, not as complete similarity**. Most similar Suttas, with the exception of a few identical ones found in the Pāṇinī, Kātantra and Kaccāyana, are not totally identical with regard to the functions they enjoined or the meanings implied by those supposedly similar Suttas. This fact is very clearly noticeable and self-evident when one carefully delves into Kaccāyana's grammar and make a comparative juxtaposition and objective analysis. **The list of such seemingly similar Suttas,** albeit being different in terms of contents and enjoined functions, **are shown separately in the appendices section of this book** in order of Suttas as found in the "ashṭadhyāyī" of Pāṇinī and Kātantra grammars.

The Talent and Skill

Regardless of various views with respect to the exact authorship, the Kaccāyana's Pāli Grammar text is a living testament to the linguistic talent, the grammatical skills and intellectual caliber of the author. He had deftly charted his own grammatical path by defining a more clearly distinctive presentation of the grammar uniquely independent of ubiquitous Pāṇinīan influences.

There is no doubt regarding the fact that he is an accomplished as well as a competently talented grammarian who have had unquestionable mastery in both Sanskrit and Pāli languages and in relevant matters of the grammar. His grammatical work simply stands out of the shadow of predecessors and shines in his own intellectual light and in a class by itself. His linguistic acumen, the highest level of caliber and ingenuity as a skillful grammar- ian are clearly noticeable. Had Kaccāyana followed all which he had known in the Sanskrit grammarian models, even the initial preliminary section (संज्ञाप्रकरणम) alone would have become a sort of repetition. He had skillfully drawn the clear and fine line of a very important Pāli-grammatical core principle which he has formally termed as "**Jinavacanayutta** (the principle of conformity to the relevant usage in Buddhist Pāli texts) ".

He had formulated this important principle in Sutta number 52 so as to steer clear of the procedures and linguistic nuances which used to be generally applied in the Sanskrit grammars. He had dexterously distinguished the natural physiology of Pāli words and its grammar by formulating new relevant rules, numbers, tense and moods, verb and noun terminations and simple morphological procedures. These facts are distinctive from the Sanskrit although he had adapted or integrated some aspects of the Sanskrit grammatical models. He had thus masterfully laid out a very simple, yet markedly different grammatical model quite uniquely exceptional in its own way though not totally dissimilar from that of the fraternal Sanskrit models.

These facts are self-manifest by the grammatical text itself. He clearly sees a very fine and delicate line which inherently exists between what is Sanskritized and what is not. This becomes even more noticeable when one goes into all the length, width, and depth of his grammatical text. One will, in the course of studying his text, clearly understand how difficult and delicate it will be for a grammarian to draw a very subtle demarcation between the two languages which have shared, though not totally identical, grammatical frameworks and linguistic norms. Unless he is a very consummate grammarian, it will certainly be impossible to formulate the rules and procedures applicable and relevant to the natural linguistic patterns of the Pāli. Instead, it will be a rebranding of the same packet with the same contents.

The Distinctive Pāli Grammars

There are a number of Pāli grammars which were written by eminent scholars. Among such treatises, the **Moggalāna** Pāli grammar written by the great scholar monk named Moggalāna of Sri Lanka (Circa 11-12 A.D), is a distinctively unique Pāli grammar. With 1037 Suttas thematically arranged in seven differently named chapters, he had authored one of the most brilliant Pāli grammatical texts, unique in its own style. His text was supposed to have been mainly based on the Candra Vyākaraṇa[4] of Candra Gomin. It was in fact a different grammatical work independent of Kaccāyana but seemed a bit Sanskritized in the physical structure of some Suttas and distinctive terminology of some functions, affixes and usage of anuvandha (conjoined tech-terms). The great grammarian Kaccāyana can rightly be said as a pioneering grammarian whose seminal work had served as a foundation from which various grammatical treatises of the Pāli language had later emerged. Among such ones is the **Saddanīti** written by the great Pāli scholar named Aggavaṁsa of Burma in the ancient city of Bagan (Circa 1157 A.D). The author of Saddanīti, could be coeval with Moggalāna. Saddanīti is indeed a very extensive grammatical treatise which is almost encyclopedic in terms of topic and contents written within the premises of Kaccāyana.

---

[4] Though the old original manuscript of Candra Vyākaraṇa did not not survive to date, the one still accessible for modern day researchers is a copy of the grammatical text named "Candra Vyākaraṇa of Candra Gomin" edited by Kshitish Chandra Chatterji, Sastri M.A., D.Lit. There are 3099 Suttas in it. The arrangement of Suttas and portioning of the chapters are non-thematic in Candra grammar while in Moggalāna it is more thematic, more methodical and well-assigned. After careful research, it is found that there are only about 330 Suttas in the Moggalāna's text which have similarities to varying degrees. In the light of this, the degree of similarity between the two grammatical texts is quite marginal.

Another grammar is **Rūpasiddhi** Vyākaraṇa (also known as Pada rūpasiddhi). It is a very unique grammatical text written by the great Pāli scholar monk named Buddhappiya of Sri Lanka (Circa 13 A.D). There are 672 Suttas with the exception of three Suttas viz. *Samāse ca vibhāsa, Arahasakkādihi tuṁ, Sacajānaṁ kagā ṇānubandhe*, found in Kaccāyana. It is a very extensive, broad treatment of the Kaccāyana's work with a more systematic explanation of thematically arranged Suttas, a unique aspect of his grammatical text which proves the talent and wisdom of a true scholarly capacity of the author. A wider variety of relevant examples in each Suttas drawn from the scriptures as well as from various sources also added up to its uniqueness. His text, although he had said as being based on Kaccāyana's work, is in fact an outstanding work of the applied grammar written within the confines of Kaccāyana's grammar and had as such received much popularity. The style and presentation of grammatical lessons such as proceeding from the previous Sutta to the next Sutta, explaining the meaning of Sutta and elucidating the word structure and the relevant morphology of an example in a very pithy way, are innovative and informative which is not found in other Pāli grammar texts. Thus, it is much easier to understand and accessible for both teachers and the students alike.

Following the style of Rūpasiddhi, is a concise grammar superbly written by Dhammakitti of Sri Lanka (Circa 1390-1410 A.D) which is called **Bālāvatāra**. The term Bālāvatāra means "the beginner's easy access". [**bāla**-the young person, **i.e.** uninitiated beginner+**ava**-down, being inside+**tara**-to swim, **i.e.** to access]. It is an abridged grammar arranged in a very systematic order of relevant chapters with about 420 Suttas, making it much more compact and concise in the structural design of grammatical text. The text has remarkable brevity and simplicity in imparting necessary grammatical knowledge and presentation of it in a more effectively brief style. Despite its small size, it covers all the essential aspects of grammar for beginners thus making it quite suitable for the beginners.

In addition, there is another grammar which deserves respectful mentioning. It is **Nirutti Dīpanī** written by the eminent scholar monk Ñāṇadhaja Mahāthera, popularly known as the great Ledi Sayādaw of Burma (1846-1923 A.D). His text is based on the Moggalāna's grammar as mentioned in the beginning verses of the text. In fact, it can even be said as an improvement on Moggalāna's grammatical text as there are some complex points in some Suttas of the original text. It is an outstanding grammatical masterpiece written in a very simple and understandable manner.

As a matter of fact, there are considerable numbers of grammatical treatises written by the successive generations of Pāli scholars of Sri Lanka and Burma from 11 century A.D to the close of 19 century A.D. periods. Most of them can be classified into two Pāli grammatical schools as either of Kaccāyana or Moggalāna. However, not all of those written treatises are focused on grammatical aspects. A few ones, such as **Sadda'tthabhedacintā** and **Kaccāyanasāra** etc., mostly dealt with some of the delicate points of the grammar and grammatical polemics. One can only be amazed and inspired by the development of such a rich Pāli grammatical literature in the history of Buddhism.

The Study of Pāli
Advantage and Disadvantages

Learning an ancient language such as Pāli has more advantages than disadvantages. The reasons are quite obvious. Firstly, it is no longer a daily spoken language. Therefore, it has not expanded over a long period of time spanning two and half millennium. No new words nor any circumstantially emerged new terms are added through the passage of such a long time of

Buddhism in its daily contact with the changing social, cultural and language patterns of everyday world. This does not mean that Pāli is a completely dead language which remains static. It can nevertheless be active and progressive like its cousin language Sanskrit when it is being revived and renewed by means of the relevant coinage of appropriate words and more added loan-words by the forward-looking academics.
Secondly, Pāli, especially the canonical Pāli in the Buddhist scriptures, has a more fixed pattern of the style and usage in its coherent structure and modes of expression. Anyone with serious interest and determination, supported by the reliable source of guidance, such as a good book or a good teacher along with an effective learning method can progress quite smoothly and successfully within a short span of two to three years. There is no appreciable disadvantage in the learning process of Pāli for anyone. These two facts, that it is no longer a living language with an ever-expanding vocabulary and having fixed patterns of the structure, are wonderful advantages for a keen and serious student in his learning journey.

Why the Romanized Pāli?

When translating the grammar text, a common linguistic platform of the Romanized Pāli is deliberately chosen, instead of the traditional oriental languages such as either Devanāgari or Burmese scripts. The choice of the Romanized Pāli is genuinely for the sake of reaching out to a wider base of the international students, not out of disregard for the tradition, nor based on any biased views and language preferences.

All of the grammatical text has been translated along with detailed explanations, footnotes and tables added wherever necessary. Some grammatical points, which may seem quite complex to students, are carefully explained and simplified by means of a more simple yet easy to understand clarification and elucidation process. Detailed care is given to interpret and elucidate the essential meanings of each Sutta so that the students will easily understand the function and the rules each Sutta implies in addition to clearly highlighting the applied function on the examples. Sometimes one may come across some of the redundant phrases and easily understandable sentences in its original text. Such instances of repeated texts are left as it is, in order to avoid pleonastic renderings. Of any translation work on the Kaccāyana's grammar, it is humbly hoped that this is by far a thorough and complete work as all the original text of each Sutta, along with its main examples, the split-Sutta functions, some additional expositions regarding the component words of the Sutta and related examples thereof, are translated and explained in a more simple and understandable manner.

Dialectics and Simple Exegesis

The students will even find that studying and reading such an ancient grammatical text, which may be seemingly boring and monotonous, becomes quite lively and enlightening when they go through the question and answer sessions which used to begin with **"Kima'tthaṁ?** (For what purpose is this word, this function or this procedure?) and **Kva'ttho?** (What benefit is there?) etc. It is clear that the ancient grammarians did not lack common sense, tact or talent in imparting the grammatical knowledge to the students. They clearly knew what they needed to do in the process of teaching a language to enliven the interest of the students and keep them engaged in the learning process by means of including such a system of dialectics. Therefore, simple explanatory answers are given to each question in a detailed, understandable manner as it was traditionally taught by teachers. Thus, it becomes more clearer and understandable by practically pointing out the relevant examples shown in the Sutta. As a matter of fact, translating such an ancient text complete with complex linguistic concepts and some subtle grammatical technicalities through the medium of another language, is not an easy task. Needless to say, it surely requires resourcefulness, a lot of hard work, strong determination and an extensive research and references along with the relevant information from various sources. During the entire period of translating and preparing this book, various grammatical texts and other related literature written in Pāli, Sanskrit as well as in Hindi were extensively researched.

It is a daunting project fraught with challenges and pitfalls. Every effort has been made to avoid any inadvertent error or misrepresentations throughout the translation process although it can not be said as a perfect work. It is nonetheless humbly assumed as a thorough work which has been done in a more detailed manner as far as possible and to the extent of pertinent necessity. Any phrase or word of the grammatical significance is never left untranslated nor remain unexplained throughout.

Traditional Pāli Script Vs. Romanized Pāli

Traditional Pāli written in Devanāgari or any Asian alphabet system poses some evident challenges for a beginner as there is no clear and visible separation of the vowel and consonant in its writing style. It is generally written by means of diacritical marks, add-on ligature and sometimes a dot. A dot represents "a niggahita" in the Pāli grammar which is also called "anusvara" in the Sanskrit grammars. The grammars of ancient Indo-Aryan languages such as Sanskrit and Pāli, teach about a detailed system of metamorphosis of the words which occur among vowels and consonants. A student of such grammars needs to have the basic knowledge on the rudiments of such languages, a process which takes some considerable amount of time before the actual learning process can practically start.

In order to easily understand this, the following basically differing writing styles of the Devanāgari Pāli, Burmese Pāli and Romanized Pāli are shown alongside. [Please note that there is no representation of an "a" as it is traditionally assumed hidden in the basic form of every consonant without any mark. Read left to right. **Left will be referred to as "the front" while the right will be referred to as "behind, after or the next"** in explaining the morphological procedures and application of a Sutta's function in this book].

[Devanāgari] क का कि की कु कू के को कं

[Diacritical marks which symbolizes vowels & dot]

n/a ा ि ी ु ू े ो ं

[Burmese] က ကာ ကိ ကီ ကု ကူ ကေ ကော ကံ

[Diacritical marks which symbolizes vowels & dot]

n/a ာ ိ ီ ု ူ ေ ေ+ာ ံ

[Romanized Pāli] Ka Kā Ki Kī Ku Kū Ke Ko Kaṁ

In Devanāgari and Burmese characters, **"a"**, the first vowel, is totally invisible. **ā, i, ī, u, ū, e, o** are shown by diacritical marks while **"ṁ** or **ṃ"** is **shown by a dot** on top or below the consonant "m".

Besides, the way of writing conjunct-consonants is quite a challenge for a beginner as it is written either horizontally or vertically. In Devanāgarī, it is written in either horizontal or vertical style using a truncated half-form of the syllable and add-on symbols. For example,

(Horizontal) क्क(kka) क्ख(kkha) ग्ग(gga) ग्घ(ggha)

च्च (cca) ज्ज(jja) ल्ल(lla)

(Vertical) ङ्क(ṅka) ङ्ग(ṅga) ट्ट(ṭṭa) द्ध(ddha) ह्न(hna) and so on.

In Burmese writing style, it is also either in horizontal or vertical style. For example,

(Horizontal) ကာ (Kā) ကေ (Ke) ကော (Ko)

(Vertical) ကိ(Ki), ကီ(Kī), ကု(Ku), ကူ(Kū), ကံ(Kaṁ),

က္က(kka), က္ခ(kkha), ဂ္ဃ(ggha), တ္တ(tta), န္ဒြိ (ndri),

In the Romanized Pāli, the vowel after each consonant it accompanies, is clearly visible in a non-conjunct single combination of one consonant and one vowel. In the writing style of conjuncts, it is quite clear and simple without any vowel between two or three cluster-formation of the consonants. There is no need to use any vertical style writing nor any diacritical mark. **This makes it far more easier for the student to understand** some minute details in the process of morphological changes being taken place in a word as per the function of a Sutta's rule. Such ease of understanding will further make it even more interesting to learn the grammatical evolution process of Pāli words for the students.

The Rules and Role of Grammar

When one starts learning a new language, grammar is a first step to begin with. **The rules of grammar are consistently established patterns of a language** discovered by the grammarians of sharp linguistic insight. As such, **they do neither invent nor stipulate these rules but expound those rules** in such a way that it would make a coherently understandable text for the student. The majority of modern Pāli learning guides written by the scholars, usually adopt a more brief, efficient, and abridged-form of the teaching method which may contain, if not all, necessary rules with the practical exercises. They may not cover all the minute nuances and some essential aspects which play more important roles in the development of grammatical insight and subsequent mastery of the language. They may not be able to offer more in-depth, detailed insight into the structural patterns of words in a way an original text of the Pāli grammar can possibly do. Take a look at the following sentences to clarify this.

For example,

(a) Namo Tassa Bhagavato Arahato Sammāsambuddhassa.
Salutation to that Lord Buddha, who has infinite glories, worthy of respect and perfectly enlightened.

Namo(Re:Sutta 104) Tassa (Re: Sutta 61) Bhagavato(Re:Sutta 127) Arahato(Re:Sutta 187, 127) Sammāsambuddhassa(Re:Sutta 61)

(b) Buddhaṁ Saraṇaṁ Gacchāmi .
To the Buddha, I go (as) refuge.

Buddhaṁ (Re:Sutta 297) Saraṇaṁ(Re:Sutta 297) Gacchāmi (Re: Sutta 423, 476, 478)

(c) Ekaṁ Samayaṁ Bhagavā Sāvatthiyaṁ Viharati Jetavane.
At one time, Lord Buddha stays at the city of Sāvatthi, in the prince Jeta's grove.

Ekaṁ Samayaṁ (Re:Sutta 307) Bhagavā (Re: Sutta 124,)
Sāvatthiyaṁ(Re:Sutta 216) Viharati(Re:Sutta 423) Jetavane(Re:Sutta 108)

Note: The underlined points indicate the grammatical aspects. The numbers indicate the relevant Suttas whose rules affect such word-forms & structures.

Although one may roughly understand the meaning of each sentence, one may not yet thoroughly understand with respect to the structural patterns or the specific mode of inflection shown underlined as to why it is shaped like such and what it means etc. An ancient grammar such as this Pāli grammar can give all the necessary instruction and insight into the fundamental aspects of the word structure and thereby leading to the development of strong grammatical skills firmly established in the students. It will take the student far beyond superficial level of the words to a more deeper understanding of how each word is built and evolved to play their individual roles and convey necessary meanings. To simply put, it will provide the students with a more in-depth understanding of the individual words so that they gain mastery of the Pāli words in the long term. This will further help them firmly settle in the good stead of the Pāli language.

The Style of Translation

Translating an ancient academic text is quite different from translating a simple narrative. It has to be simple and to the point so that it is easily understandable. Therefore, a more informal non-literary style of translation is applied for the most part of this translation although some literal "word for word" translations are added wherever necessary in order to elucidate some of the delicate and complex points. In addition, notes, some detailed explanations, tables and footnotes are added for the purpose of easy understanding and clarification wherever it is called for. For some Pāli-terms with ambiguous meanings, an equivalent Sanskrit word is shown alongside. Every reasonable effort has been made to translate almost every part of the grammatical text without making any exception to its contents.
The purpose is to make students aware that a standard ancient grammatical text is a very broad and a very rich presentation of the linguistics and grammar conceptualized by the most bright and talented sages of the ancient times. There is a very visible element of dynamics in the whole text where the evolution of a word, or words as part of a complete language, are brought to coherent completion by means of injunctive rules of each Sutta and due morphological procedures. This way, each different Pāli word of various evolving patterns becomes ready to be used in a group of words known grammatically as a sentence. Moreover, a grammatical text also explains on genders, nouns, verbs, voices, persons and all the necessary rules regarding the applicable grammatical norms and standards though it may not be quite identical with today's contemporary grammars.

The Grammatical Codes

When translating the meaning of each individual word, whether it be an example word without context, or a word with different structural components such as the plain nouns, compound nouns, Taddhita-nouns, Kita-affixed nouns or Ākhyāta verbs along with their relevant case-endings, **a standardized, yet easy-to-understand grammatical codes of abbreviations is devised and added wherever deemed necessary.** Without the use of such improvised codes, it would be rather futile and impossible to render a meaningful translation of such an ancient text. **It is therefore advisable to refer to the list of abbreviations section and necessary information** prior to studying this book.

Some Notes on the Romanized Pāli Alphabets

"ṁ" or **"ṃ"** or **"ŋ"**?

When representing some Pāli words, especially **"Niggahita**, the so-called **dot"**, it is used to be shown either as **"ṁ"** or **"ṃ"** or **"ŋ"**. In view of the grammatical norms regarding the "Niggahita", **"ṁ"** is more preferable as it is rather in line with its inherent nature of having a symbolic "upper dot" aptly positioned on top of the three short (rassa) vowels, such as **"aṁ, iṁ** and **uṁ"**, not with its symbolic "dot" down below. In the earlier publications of Pāli-related books, **ṁ** or **ṃ** are used to show it. Sometimes, **"ŋ"** is also found to be used by some scholars in the case-endings of words or wherever a niggahita is needed to be represented. All three styles are correct in its own way as it represents nasalized nature of the Niggahita, but it tends to be a bit confusing for the uninitiated beginner. In order to have a more standardized, uniform representation of the niggahita dot, only "**ṁ**" is chosen throughout this book so that the students will find it much easier to understand. As a matter of fact, a niggahita-dot can remain unchanged when the word ending in it is either an independent word by itself in a sentence, or the word itself has an integral dot as part of its structure such as **vaṁsa**-race, **saṁgha**-community (**saṅgha** is also applicable writing in case of a vagganta-function), **aṁsa**-shoulder, portion etc. However, when it is used as non-independent word such as the one being conjoined in a Sandhi-combination, it will have to change into any of **ṅ, ñ, ṇ, n** or **m** depending on any specific vagga-group of the letter it precedes.

Another confusable word is **"b"** which is interchangeable with **"v"**. Please keep in mind that both can be assumed as the same as they are morphologically interchangeable though they have different sources of the sound. ["b" is labial, *oṭṭhaja* while "v" is denti-labial, *danto'ṭṭhaja*]

Similarly, **l** and **ḷ** can be assumed quite similar as well as interchangeable although they have different origins of the sound as **l** is dental *dantaja*, while **ḷ** is palatal *muddhaja* (cerebral, also called retroflex).

Other syllables of somewhat similar sounds, such as **ṭ** and **t**, **ṭha** and **tha**, **ḍ** and **d, ḍha** and **dha, ṇ** and **n** are also morphologically interchangeable although they have different origins of the sound.

The Steps of Effective Learning

The study of Pāli language is to be pursued systematically so that the student will progress smoothly and successfully. The first step is called "**Padasikkhā**-learning about the physiology of the words". The next second step is called "**Vākyasikkhā**-the study of sentences". These two important steps, when methodically followed, will surely set the student in a firm foundation of the grammar, leading him to develop the skills and ability to use the correct words in the right place in actual sentence writing and understanding of it.

The first step of Padasikkhā, studying the physiology of words involves learning the Suttas, its meaning and the enjoined function and example words as explained in the relevant Suttas, along with studying their structural evolution through applicable morphological procedures.

When this is sufficiently done, the **noun groups** which have similar make-ups through similar morphological procedures, classified in the same gender and declension, are to be familiarized both orally and grammatically. This process is called **"Nāma padamālā** (the garland of Nouns festooned together) " study. Then, the **Verb groups** which share similar kind of affix, conjugation and the same shared morphological procedures are to be studied likewise. This is called **"Ākhyāta padamālā"** study. Having thoroughly and proficiently trained in these steps, it will lead the student to a firm grasp of the Nouns and Verbs and will further lead to the development of strong understanding, reading and writing skills gradually and effectively.

Sub-units of the Grammar Study

In addition, all other sub-branches of grammar study, such as **(a)** word-analysis (abbreviated as WA), **(b)** Etymological Definition (ED) and **(c)** the study of structural morphology (SM) are to be included in this important process of Padasikkhā. Those wishing to have a more scholarly grasp of the language should include these sub-branches in their study so that the study itself becomes a multi-faceted and multi-disciplined approach for a more advanced, skill-oriented, in-depth learning. This approach of study is very effective in the development of scholarly skills and a thorough understanding of Pāli in its entirety.

Vākyasikkhā, The study of sentences

The next step "Vākyasikkhā", the study of sentences, should be done progressively by studying suitable minor readings and a small collection of easy texts and verses from the scriptural sources. This will immerse the student in the actual language, keeping him in touch with the vocabulary of new words, various usages of both literary and figurative styles in addition to rich structural pattern of the sentences. With strong determination and persistent effort, the student should proceed studying the whole length of some selectively chosen short Suttas. It is recommended to start with the following: (a) Bodhikathā (It is a very inspiring account on the early days of Buddha's enlightenment) (b) Dhamma cakka pavattana Sutta, (c) Anattalakkhaṇa Sutta, (these are from Mahāvagga Pāli, Vinaya Piṭka) (d) Mahāsati patṭhāna Sutta, (e) Dhammapada verses etc.

How to study the Kaccāyana's text?

There are eight chapters in the Kaccāyana text. The core of each chapter which forms the important part are a collection of 673 grammatical rules. The rules are further clarified by the Vutti and word-examples whose structural patterns are to be brought to completion by means of applying those rules. The rules are short and pithy descriptions of injunctions enclosed in a short sentence-structure called Sutta. It literally means "the thread" used as a measurement tool by the carpenters of ancient times for cutting the wood in the prescribed measures.

The Components of a Sutta

A Sutta mainly consists of three components. They are: **(a)** Sutta (a brief and concise rule), **(b)** Vutti (explanatory sentences clarifying the rule) and **(c)** Udārharaṇa (applicable examples drawn from the scriptures) and Paccudārharaṇa (inapplicable examples). See the kinds of Suttas and the roles of each Sutta explained in the table below:

No.	Sutta Type	Sutta Rule Classification
1	Saññā Sutta	Outlines the formal terms and some basic preliminaries of the grammar
2	Adhikāra Sutta	Influences the nature of other related Suttas
3	Paribhāsā Sutta	general announcements on the grammatical outline serving as a general directive.
4	Vidhi Sutta	enjoins various kinds of rules and procedures to be applied in the Pāli morphology showing the evolution of actual word-formation and structural linguistics.

Of these four kinds of Sutta, **Vidhi** Suttas play quite important roles as they enjoin the rules to perform various specific functions and morphological procedures. The term "vidhi" means function to be carried out for completing the word. It is classified into eight groups according to the functions they perform. See the table below to understand clearly.

Types of Vidhi (functions)

No	Name of Vidhi	Function
1	**Lopa** (means to elide, to delete)	Elides a vowel, or consonant or a niggahita or an affix or a vibatti or even the whole word.
2	**ādesa** (to change or to substitute)	Transforms either of above (vowels etc.,) into different syllables. These kind of Suttas usually have various functions, such as changing the whole word into another word-form, Vuddhi, Vipriyāya, Pakati, Atidesa and so on, are also included.
3	**āgama**(to come and insert)	Inserts a new syllable into a word to become a complete word.
4	**dīgha** (to lengthen)	Lengthens the short vowel of a word.
5	**rassa** (to shorten)	Shortens a long vowel.
6	**patisedha** (to debar)	Debars a specific function of a Sutta as it is inapplicable.
7	**paccaya** (an affix)	Applies an affix.
8	[5]**vibatti** (a vibatti)	Applies a vibatti after a noun or a verb.

The Recommended Order of the Study

As a beginner, it is **not necessary to go through all the passages of the grammatical text in the arranged order of the chapters** although one may do so for the purpose of orientation and familiarization with each chapter. Begin the practical learning guide shown in the table by order of numerical sequence. Try to understand the meanings of various Suttas in the recommended order of chapters. Learn to recognize the

[5] The term "vibatti" refers to noun case-endings and verb-terminations.

enjoined rules and relevant examples. Then check how the enjoined function of a Sutta matches the way selected example words are being structured to become a complete word. **Priority should be given to the recommended chapter sequence** when studying Pāli grammar using this practical reference guide.

Pāli Grammar Study Guide

Chapter	Explains about:
1	Grammar Fundamentals & Sandhi
2	Nouns
6	Verbs
7	Kita-affixed nouns and some verbs
8	Uṇādi-affixed nouns and a few verbs (Can skip this chapter to study after all chapters)
4	Compound nouns
5	Taddhita-affixed nouns
3	Case-endings of nouns specifically termed as Kāraka and non-Kāraka.

Chapter One

In this chapter, Sandhi (euphonic combination of words) will provide the student with some fundamentals of grammatical terms and concepts. Sandhi is one specific feature of the ancient Indo-Aryan languages such as Sanskrit and Pāli. It is somewhat similar to the contracted word-forms in the English such as *He'll, I've,* etc. Sandhi is formed by combining two different words into one, so that verbal expressions are smooth and concise. Sometimes it may occur in one single word where multiple upasagga (prefixes) particles are present in its structure.

Types of Sandhi

Sandhi is usually formed through the union of vowels of two different words or one single word. Sometimes it may occur at the union of an end-vowel of the front word and the initial consonant of the next word. Sometimes it may occur at the

union of a niggahita dot of the front word and an initial vowel or the consonant of the next word. In order to better understand this, one needs to know about different types of Sandhi. See the table below:
According to Rūpasiddhi, there are four types of Sandhi:

No.	Sandhi Type	Sandhi Formation
1	**Sara**-sandhi	union of two vowels, one being the end-vowel of the preceding word, the other being the initial vowel of the second word to be united.
2	**Vyañjana**-sandhi	union of the end-vowel of the preceding word and an initial consonant of the next word in a would-be combination.
3	**Niggahita**-sandhi	union of niggahita in the initial word with either a vowel or consonant of the next following word
4	**Pakati**-sandhi.	retaining the status quo of the structural pattern of two or more words without performing any specific procedure.

In the initial stage of study, unless one is a highly intelligent, sharp learner with a good memory, one need not try to understand everything. Just go through all Suttas, meanings, enjoined rules and relevant examples. One may test one's understanding by separating and combining the separated examples into a Sandhi on one's own. For the ease and convenience, a practical workshop shown as SM is provided in the first chapter.

Chapter Two

A more intense and focused study should be made on nouns and verbs, which are like major building blocks of the language. In this Chapter, all information regarding word structure and declension rules of the nouns are clearly explained through relevant Suttas. There is an apt saying: "If you have understood nouns in their entirety, then you have grasped half of the grammar" which is particularly relevant as the subsequent chapters of Samāsa, Taddhita, Kita, Uṇādi and Kāraka explain more about different noun patterns.

Chapter Six

After studying nouns in the chapter two, students should proceed to the chapter six regarding main Pāli verbs called "Ākhyāta". The two chapters are complementary as they deal with nouns and verbs which constitute the fundamentals of sentence construction. The additional notes at the end of the first section of the chapter six are really quite important as they explain fundamental aspects of the Pāli verbs in clear detail.

It can be said or safely assumed that as soon as the second and the sixth chapters are thoroughly studied, the student may have now understood some important facts on the plain nouns and basic Pāli verbs fundamental to a more comprehensive understanding of the language and its grammar.

Chapter Seven

One should then proceed to study chapter seven on Kita-affixed nouns. In this chapter, the basic structure and morphological procedures of all Kita-affixed verbal nouns and words are clearly explained in more detail. Priority and more careful focus should be given to study Sutta Nos. **540, 555, 556, 557, 560, 561, 562, 563, 564 and 565,** to learn about the affixes which can be used sometimes either as main verbs or some auxiliary verbs such as the absolutive (also called gerund), the present participle and past participle. The majority of Kita-affixed words, except the example words shown in above Suttas, are just nouns structured with roots and affixes. Though a student may not at first understand the roles played by all these kita-affixes, one will slowly and firmly understand about them later on.

Next Important Step

After one had made a firm grasp of understanding on the nouns and Ākhyāta verbs and some Kita-affixed words as explained in those chapters, one should start studying all those nouns and verbs together in a more practical mode of application. For this, Dr. Lily De Silva's book, "The Pāli Primer", or "The New Pāli course" by Venerable A.P. Budhadatta and A.K. Warder's "Introduction to Pāli" are quite suitable ones to start with. These books will surely complement and reinforce the basic grammatical knowledge a student has acquired through the study of recommended chapters in the ancient Kaccāyana grammar text thus far.

Chapter Eight

Chapter eight, **the uṇādi section,** is like an extension or expansion of the chapter seven which further explains some more about words having affixes similar to Kita-affixed words of the previous chapter. This time, however, with a different rubric known as **"uṇādi-affixes"**. The word "uṇādi" refers to the initial affix **"ṇu"** which has an ṇ-joined "u". [Re: Sutta 624, example words with this affix such as Kāru, Kāruko]. All the affixes shown in this chapter are collectively known as "uṇādi-affixes". That is the reason why there are some Suttas with similar functions as those shown in the previous chapter.

Priority and focused attention should be given to Suttas 625, 626, 635, 636, 637 and 655 as there are explanations regarding some affixes which can be used as either verbs or auxiliary verbs or future participles. Most of the remaining Suttas are usually about nouns structured with root and affixes. The study of this chapter is quite easy if one had done a thorough study of the Kita chapter as both are interrelated.

There, the student may even find quite a few interesting affixes such as **"kta"** and **"ghiṇ"** which may seem somewhat

Sanskritized. In the Sanskrit grammar texts, the affix "**ta**" is termed as "**kta** (क्त) ". The affix "**tvā**" is termed in Sanskrit "**ktvā** (क्त्वा) " while "**ṇī**" is termed as "**ghiṇ** (घिनुण) ". Also, the affix "**ṇa**" is sometimes differently termed "**ghañ** (घञ) ". These are just a few examples. Actually, the Sanskrit and Pāli grammars have different grammatical systems, morphological procedures and terminology even though they have some shared fundamentals occurred through long periods of affiliation, synthesis and shared ancestry in the ancient Indo-Aryan civilization.

Chapters Four and Five

A keen student, if he may wish so, can still decide to continue chapter eight or skip it to go back to study the chapter four on compound nouns and then chapter five on Taddhita-affixed nouns. **These two chapters too explain about nouns of different structure,** the former being two or more nouns conjoined in a process called "Samāsa, the compound noun", while the latter, instead of being joined with another noun, is affixed with a suffix expressive of distinctive meanings and consequently have some distinctive structural patterns.

Order of Suttas to study in the Samāsa

When studying the Samāsa chapter, students should begin with Sutta 316, 317 and 318 to understand the nature of Samāsa. Then 319, 320, 341, 342 and 343 together to learn all about abyayībhāva. Then proceed to study 325 and 321 together to learn about Digu. Afterwards, proceed to study 329, 322, 323 and 339 to learn about Dvanda compound. Then, begin with 324, 330 and 332 to learn about Kammadhāraya compound. Then continue 327, 326, 333, 334, 335 and 336 to learn about Tappurisa compound. After all this is thoroughly done, one can start with Sutta 328 (Skip all the long compound structures at first go), 331, 338 and 340 to learn about Bahubbīhi compound. Later on, one should round off all the remaining Suttas to cover all of the chapter. This way, it will be more effective and quicken the learning process in a short time.

As for the chapter five, just follow the Suttas as shown in this book under each individual heading of a Taddhita. No specific further recommendation is required. Actually, the study of uniquely-structured nouns in these two chapters is quite a fascinating learning-experience which can further enrich the grammatical knowledge of the student in many ways.

A quick study guide of Samāsa:

Step	Sutta No	Learning objective
1	316, 317 and 318	Understand the nature of Samāsa
2	319, 320, 341, 342, 343	Abyayībhāva (Adverbial Compound)
3	325, 321	Digu(Numeral Determinative Compound)
4	329, 322, 323, 339	Dvanda (Copulative Compound)
5	324, 330, 332	Kammadhāraya (Appositional Compound)
6	327,326,333,334,335,336	Tappurisa (Determinative Compound)
7	328, 331, 338, 340	Bahubbīhi (Attributive Compound)
8	337	Some general aspects on the inflection of Determinative and Attributive Compounds.

Chapter Three

When sufficient amount of time and effort is being made to study the chapters four and five, one should start studying chapter three. In it, all the grammatical terms of noun case-endings called "Kāraka" and their implied meaning and usage, are explained in detail. Although it is termed as Kāraka-chapter, it also explains about non-Kārakas and unique case-endings which have exceptionally special senses along with the relevant examples.

Both Kāraka & non-Kārakas form parts of a complete sentence. They are syntactically related to verbs as well as to each other in a language structure formally known as "the sentence" and play their respective roles such as the subject (Kattā), the object(Kamma) or the possessive (Sāmi) and so on. It is not necessary to memorize but only required to familiarize with grammatical concepts, their relevant roles and practical application in the actual expression of verbalized or written language. To simply put, the chapter three, after all, is like a continuation of the chapter two regarding nouns.

Sub-Units of the Grammar Study

There are other sub-units of Pāli grammar study as outlined below:

No	Sub-Unit Title	Abbreviation Used
1	Etymological Definition: *Viggaha-vākya*	ED
2	Word Analysis: *Pada-vicaya*	WA
3	Structural Morphology: *Rūpasiddhi*	SM

The ED, which stands being abbreviated for the **Etymological Definition**, called **"Viggaha-vākya"** in Pāli (similarly termed विग्रहवाक्य in Sanskrit) is a process of expansion and explanation of the original example words shown in some Suttas. In chapters 4, 5, 7 and 8, the students will have to go through some form of grammatical sub-unit of the study termed EDs. This ED is an important feature which forms part and parcel of a complete grammatical text. **The student, as a beginner does not yet need to study EDs in the initial phase of learning** except a casual light-reading through all those translated examples of

EDs and try to get some familiarity with it, so that one will get used to it later on. This will help a lot in smoothly moving through all the chapters without bumping into any hard-to-understand word or phrases which may pose unnecessary challenge to the beginner.

Knowing and understanding the ED as well as being able to write a relevant ED of a word, is in fact one special characteristic of a true Pāli scholar. One cannot develop this skill in the beginning as it takes considerable amount of time and study. A student only needs to be able to understand its basic meaning and the resultant structure of a word by examining its ED. Therefore, it is not yet at all necessary to prioritize the study of EDs in the initial phase of learning.

Three Kinds of EDs

There are three different categories of EDs classified as per the respective chapters. They are:

(1) **Samāsa-Viggaha,** compound EDs for those examples shown in the Samāsa-chapter,

(2) **Taddhita Viggaha,** the ED of Taddhita-affixed nouns for the examples shown in the Taddhita-chapter,

(3) **Kita-Viggaha,** the ED of Kita-affixed words in the Kita chapter and the Uṇādi chapters.

Of these three,

(a) **The compound ED explains** how each relevant noun is conjoined in a compounding process, using any applicable case-ending of nouns, Upasagga or Nipāta particles, according to a specific category of the compound a word belongs to. Once a student can clearly understand its ED, he will then be instantly able to tell what kind of a particular compound the example word belongs to.

(b) **Taddhita-viggaha, the ED of Taddhita-affixed nouns, usually explains** the base word and the implied meaning of its component affix by means of using relevant explanatory words or phrases. By understanding it, one will be able to dissect the complete make-up of a Taddhita-affixed noun in a very simple way. The student will also understand what specific kind of Taddhita-class it belongs to.

(c) The last is Kita-viggaha, the ED of Kita & Uṇādi-affixed nouns. This kind of **Kita-ED explains** the meaning of the root of example word, together with the respective "Sādhana-meaning" of the affix comprised in an example. It is in the ED of Kita-affixed words where so-called seven **Sādhana** are originated. Usually a Kita-ED may employ an Ākhyāta verb or a Kita-verb which is synonymous with the root's meaning in one of three voices to signify the relevant Sādhana of Kita-affixed-word, either it be a Kattu or Kamma or Bhāva. Sometimes, a substitute verb with approximate meaning may also be employed in the ED.

If an example word belongs to other four Sādhanas such as Karaṇa, Sampadāna, Apādāna or Adhikaraṇa, it may use additional Sabbanāma-nouns such as **tena, etena, yena** (Instrumental case for Karaṇa Sādhana examples), **Tassa, assa** (Dative for Sampadāna Sādhana), **Tasmā, yasmā, asmā, yato,** (Ablative for Apādāna Sādhana), **Ettha, Yasmim** (Locative for Adhikaraṇa Sādhana) and so on. These additional words are called "**Sādhana-indicators**". It is quite interesting to learn about EDs and their role in exposing the structural dynamics of a word and its relevant semantics although one may at first find it a bit confusing and challenging. In consideration of the benefits a student can acquire through the study of EDs, it does not need to further emphasize nor overrate on its role. It is up to the personal capacity and convenience of the student either to pay some amount of focused attention or just pass it by through cursory glance. It should be noted that some examples may have an ED, while some words may be without it. If a student has made a thorough study and possess some degree of comprehensive knowledge of the chapter two, six and seven, studying different kinds of EDs will not pose a problem.

WA (Word Analysis)

The next important part is to have a firm grasp of Pāli words by clearly understanding its complete make-up (for Ākhyāta & Kita-affixed words), and the related name of Samāsa and Taddhita (for compound and Taddhita-affixed nouns). One can acquire this skill by studying WA, an acronym abbreviated for the word analysis.

This, in fact, is not an original sub-branch of the grammatical study included in the text, but a latter-day development devised by the wise, far-sighted teachers of the grammar in ancient times for easy development of the necessary word-analysis skill of the students.

If truth be told, a well-trained grammatical student should have this "WA skill" known in Pāli as "Padavicayañāṇa [**Pada**-word+**vicaya**-analysis+**ñāṇa**-knowledge]" or "pada vicāraṇa [**pada**+**vicāraṇa**-analysis]". Having this skill greatly helps the student to gain a high level of mastery on the Pāli words. It will also help the student to be able to build any form of correct and suitable word in the language with much efficiency and skill.

Therefore, this word analysis feature(WA) is included in almost every Sutta of the chapters 5, 6, 7 and 8. **The students do not need to memorize them** at all but make some careful study of it so that necessary grammatical skills will gradually increase as the student proceeds through various chapters.

[6]Rūpasiddhi or Payogasiddhi

(The Structural Morphology, SM)

Another equally important part of the grammar study is understanding the structural morphology of words known as "Rūpa siddhi or Payogasiddhi". This is also a sub-branch of the grammatical study which can be said as already included in the Suttas but not in a complete detail under any formal name.

As a matter of fact, Pāli grammar, like its cousin Sanskrit grammars, explains about the grammatical rules and brief morphological procedures with an aim to show how each word is basically structured and how it is brought to completion to become a coherent word by means of applying the functions of relevant Suttas. If seen from the perspective of objective analysis, the study of Kaccāyana grammar or other similar grammatical texts of the Indo-Aryan Languages, is the science of pure linguistics which may be seemingly quite different from the way modern-day contemporary grammars are structured and designed.

This branch of SM study is a very beneficial process as it can strengthen the understanding of a Sutta and its related functions. It can also reinforce the knowledge and skill of understanding on the gradual evolution process of a word till it finally becomes a complete word. This feature abbreviated as SM is included in the first chapter of Sandhi but not in the remaining chapters for the sake of making this translation work less bulky and less challenging for the students.

---

[6] **Rūpa**-word+**siddhi**-mode and method of completion, **Payoga**-example.

Through this feature, the grammatical information as to how a separated Sandhi-example is recombined into a perfect Sandhi by applying the relevant function of each applicable Sutta, is clearly explained in a step-by-step detail. The study of Rūpasiddhi may not be possible without the aid of a truly competent teacher or a reliable guidebook, such as the one written by the late *Tha-bye-kan* Sayādaw Bhaddanta Ukkaṁsācāra, a very well-known, highly respected, Pāli, Hindi, and Sanskrit scholar of Burma. In the days gone-by in countries where the study of Pāli is pursued in a more strict systematic manner, this step along with memorization of the whole of Kaccāyana text, is a necessity and always emphasized. Those who have had included this sub-branch in their study, become very competent Pāli students and scholars.

Footnotes

There are important additional notes inserted in the form of footnotes wherever necessary. They are intended to be part of the required readings for all keen students as they contain essential information for the development of overall grammatical knowledge and the skills. Therefore, it need not be further emphasized to be part of an inclusive study regimen for all serious students.

Appendix

There is also an appendix section at the end of the book which provides some essentially necessary grammatical information for the serious student. The sample morphology, the Kāraka & Sādhana and the Pāli-root index are some of the subtle areas of grammatical skills and study. Proceeding through those sections will not only enrich but also broaden the scope of understanding and the grammatical knowledge. Therefore, it is encouraged to read the appendices section.

Generalized Understanding

When studying an ancient language such as Pāli, it is quite necessarily important to have a balanced as well as relaxed attitude toward the subject of study. One should neither push oneself too much nor be inert. So, there are two scenarios and choices. One is a casual student whose aim and purpose is only to be able to read and understand Pāli to some degree. The other is a serious student with keen interest, whose aim is not only to be able to read and understand, but also to be able to write the flawless Pāli by gaining some substantial amount of mastery on it. For both of them, having a generalized understanding of the subject is the first necessary step and an important key to further progress which one has to decide for a more intensive and progressively detailed study.

Therefore, students should start their study by going through various Suttas in the recommended order of the chapters, try to understand their meanings, the enjoined rules and relevant examples as shown in each translation. Then check how the enjoined function of a Sutta matches the way example words are accordingly structured and completed. If the student finds that what one has learned is as it is explained in the Sutta, then it can be assumed that one has been coming along well and made some progress in the first step. The students will surely have some degree of understanding of whatever is read and studied and thus be ready to progress much further. It is not at all necessary to understand everything in the text even though having a more substantial way of understanding is far more preferable than having a vague understanding. It is sincerely and firmly hoped that with strong determination, consistent efforts combined with graduated steps of the study, students will certainly progress in the learning process of Pāli in a minimum span of two to three years. This is what this English translation work is specifically and mainly intended for.

Pronunciation Guide

The Eight vowels

Except a few special ones unique to Pāli, the majority of ordinary Pāli alphabets are pronounced like basic normal sound of English words. The following are the sample sounds of individual vowels. Please take only the sound of underlined words, not of the whole word nor of any consonant.

(1) **a** to be pronounced as in amid, about

(2) **ā** to pronounce as in far

(3) **i** as in meet, eat

(4) **ī** as in we, he

(5) **u** as in shoot

(6) **ū** as in you, beauty

(7) **e** as in way

(8) **o** as in all, auto

The Consonants

There is an "a" after each consonant which is added for easy utterance or producing an articulate sound of the respective consonants. There are five groups comprising five consonants in each which is called "vagga". On the other hand, there are non-vagga consonants comprising seven consonants and one niggahita.

Ka-group

This group of consonants are velar (guttural).

Note: In each group, every **second and fourth** consonants are aspirated. As a physical sign, there is an "h" which symbolizes the stress. So, it has to be pronounced with the stress and a puff of air being released.

The first and the third are unaspirated. So, they are pronounced normally without stress. **The fifth** ones in each vagga-group are nasals.

(1) **Ka** as in Kab

(2) **Kha** as in khaki, khmer

(3) **Ga** as in glad

(4) **Gha** as in ghat

(5) **Ṅa** as in sing, John Ng

Ca-group

This group of consonants are palatal.

(1) **Ca** as in cell, Sarah
(2) **Cha** as in Charge, charity
(3) **Ja** as in jab
(4) **Jha** as in jack

Note: There is a slight variation of sound for both "**J and Jh**" which are pronounced as "**za**" and "**zha**" in Burmese.

(5) **Ña** as in Lasagna, signor, signora (It is a nasal sound)

Ṭa-group

This group of consonants are retroflex, to be pronounced with the tongue being pulled backward away from the teeth and slightly touching the upper palate.

(1) **Ṭa** as in tea
(2) **Ṭha** as in train
(3) **Ḍa** as in disc
(4) **Ḍha** as in dart
(5) **Ṇa** as in Nagoya

Ta-group

This group of consonants are dental, to be pronounced with the tip of tongue touched against upper teeth or the ridge behind the upper teeth.

(1) **Ta** as in tachometer
(2) **Tha** as in try or train
(3) **Da** as in daffodil
(4) **Dha** as in dark
(5) **Na** as in nab

Pa-group

This group of consonants are labial, to be pronounced with lips gently touched against each other and then quickly opened.

(1) **Pa** as in pacific
(2) **Pha** as in Facility, phacelia

(3) **Ba** as in basalt
(4) **Bha** as in bath
(5) **Ma** as in macau

Seven Non-Vagga group consonants

(1) **Ya** as in yacht, yak
(2) **Ra** as in rabbit
(3) **La** as in lab (to be pronounced with the tip of tongue gently touching the upper teeth.)
(4) **Ḷa** as in lasagna (Actually, this is very much the same as ordinary "la"). To be pronounced with the mouth being slightly opened, with the tip of tongue slightly touching the upper palate.
Note: This is one special "Ḷ" with a different dot down below which is unique only to Sanskrit and Pāli. In the grammatical texts, it is mentioned as being homogenous and interchangeable with ordinary "L" despite having slight physical difference.
(5) **Wa** as in warp, vat (Both sounds of **w & v** are permissible)
Note: In the grammatical text, there will be more of "v" such as "kvaci, vā and so on" though it is rather pronounced as "w" in majority of cases. For example, the word "Kvaci" is pronounced as **Kuaci** or **kwaci**, while "vā" as sounded as **wā**. In Asian syllabary such as Devanāgari and Burmese, there are only two representations of "v & w". For example, "v" is shown as "ब-ဗ" while "w" is written as "व-ဝ". However, in Romanized Pāli, "v" is sometimes represented as "b" while "w" is shown by both ways either as "v" or "w". Therefore, keep in mind that all these three of "**b, v & w**" are basically as well as morphologically homogenous to each other. This fact will become even clearer when studying the morphological procedures of the Pāli words which comprise either "v" or "w".

One Sibilant

(6) **Sa** as in sabbath

One Aspirate sound

(7) **Ha** as in habit, half

Niggahita dot

This Niggahita "upper-dot" is semi-vowel as well as a semi-consonant though it is classified as a byañjana, (**i.e.** consonant in the grammatical text)

(1) **ṁ** as in <u>am</u>

Note: This "**ṁ**" is interchangeable with all the fifth syllables "**ṅ, ñ, ṇ, n, m**" of the five vagga-groups through applicable morphological procedure. This means that "ṁ" can change into any consonant form of "ṅ, ñ, ṇ, n, m". These fives are called "vagganta" which means the group-endings [**vagga**-group+ **anta**-ending]. Sometimes, it is also referred to as "five nasal stops".

Guide to Conjuncts

A conjunct is a cluster of consonants combined together by being based on a single vowel. Such a structure is technically called "saṁyoga" in grammatical term. Most conjuncts in Asian languages are written either in horizontal or vertical structure (Refer to the preface of this book). Depending on how it is written, one has to read it from left to right or up to down. In Romanized Pāli, it is written in horizontal style which is much easier to read from left to right. [saṁyoga=**saṁ**-together+**yoga**-to bind, to join, **i.e.** being joined together, conjunct]

There are two types of conjuncts:
(a) conjuncts of similar consonants,
(b) conjuncts of dissimilar consonants.

Of the two, conjuncts of similar consonants usually occur:
(1) in the first and third consonants of five vagga-groups,
(2) also in the last four **"ñ, ṇ, n, m"** of five vagga-group with the exception of "**ṅ**" of Ka-group. Of non-vagga consonants, conjuncts also occur in **y, l, w, s**. There are **no conjuncts of similar consonants found to be combined with** the four consonants **"ṅ, r, ḷ, h"**. This kind of conjunct is formed due mainly to:
(a) the rule of Sutta No.28,
(b) other applicable morphological procedures, and
(c) the natural structure of the word itself. **Onc of these three causes lead to the formation of conjuncts of similar consonants.**

Conjuncts of similar consonants
Vagga-group similar conjuncts

(Ka-group) kka, gga,
(Ca group) cca, jja, ñña,
(Ṭa group) ṭṭa, ḍḍa, ṇṇa,
(Ta group) tta, dda, nna,
(Pa group) ppa, bba, mma,

Non-vagga group similar conjuncts

yya, lla, vva, (Being morphologically homogenous and interchangeable, it is also sometimes written as bba), ssa,

Conjuncts of Dissimilar Consonants

As for the conjuncts of dissimilar consonants, it used to occur in the second, fourth and the fifth of vagga-group consonants. However, this explanation is only about general patterns from the grammatical perspective, not a complete description. There are diverse varieties of anomalous conjunct-formation of dissimilar consonants found in the Pāli texts caused and mainly influenced by:
(a) the rule of Sutta No.29,
(b) other relevant applicable morphological procedures, and
(c) the natural structure of the word itself. **One of these three causes may lead to the formation of such conjuncts of dissimilar consonants.** The following is a list of such dissimilar conjuncts found in various Pāli literature. By studying the list carefully, one will easily understand how these conjunct-words are formed.

Vagga Conjuncts

(1st vagga) kkha, ggha (2nd Vagga) ccha, jjha (3rd Vagga) ṭṭha, ḍdha (4th Vagga) ttha, ddha (5th Vagga) ppha, bbha (Refer to function of Sutta No.29)

The following conjuncts are formed by joining the last of vagga with its own group. Please carefully study so that it becomes much easier to understand some of the fixed pattern of such dissimilar conjuncts. Actually, this pattern is as what is described in the rule of Sutta number 31.

(Conjuncts with the last alphabet **"ṅ"** of 1st Vagga) ṅka, ṅkha, ṅga, ṅgha

(Conjuncts with the last alphabet **"ñ"** of 2nd Vagga) ñca, ñcha, ñja, ñjha

(Conjuncts with the last alphabet **"ṇ"** of 3rd Vagga) ṇṭa, ṇṭha, ṇḍa, ṇḍha

(Conjuncts with the last alphabet **"n"** of 4th Vagga) nta, ntha, nda, ndha

(Conjuncts with the last alphabet **"m"** of 5th Vagga) mpa, mpha, mba, mbha

Non-vagga Conjuncts

1.Dissimilar conjuncts with non-vagga "ya"(This type of conjuncts with "ya" are usually found in the grammatical texts)

(1st) kya, khya, gya, (2nd) cya, (3rd) ṭya, ḍya, ṇya (4th) tya, thya, dya, dhya, nya (5th) pya, phya, bya & vya, bhya, mya (non-vagga) lya, sya,

Dissimilar conjuncts with non-vagga "ra"

(1st) kra, kri, (4) tra, tri, dra, dri (5) bru

(with non-vagga "sa" & "ta") stra

3.Two dissimilar conjuncts with non-vagga "la"

(1st) kla (5th) pla

4.Eight dissimilar conjuncts with non-vagga "va"

kva, khva, ṇva, tva, dva, nva (Non-vagga) sva, hva

5.One dissimilar conjuncts with non-vagga "sa"

sta as in Usto-shocked.

5.Nine Dissimilar conjuncts with non-vagga "ha"

ñha, ṇha, nha, mha,

(Non-vagga) yha, rha, lha, vha, ḷha,

Triple conjuncts

Note: Triple conjuncts are quite rarely found except a few words.

(1) ndri as in Indriya-faculty.

(2) ntvā as in Gantvā-having gone

Note: There is no quadri-conjuncts found in the texts. Keep in mind that these shown above are only a common list of conjuncts which used to be found in a wider source of Pāli literature, not a limitation of other possible forms of conjuncts. As a general rule of grammar, any acceptable conjunct coined within the confines of grammatical logic and relevant morphological applicability is still possible depending on the skill and discretion of the author. "Paṭādīhyalaṁ, Cyādīhi Īvaro, Sasvādīhi tudavo (See the underlined conjuncts) " are such examples among applicable possibilities found in this gammatical text.

Vowel Conjuncts?

In Sanskrit, there are some vowels such as ऐ , औ, classified as diphthongs. But in Pāli, there are absolutely no such vowels. The vowels are like foundations where generally one or two or three consonants are based to produce a clear, well-articulated sound. In order to produce such sound of an individual consonant or two to three consonants in a cluster-formation, one vowel alone is sufficient. The rules of Suttas 12 & 83 clearly indicate this fixed linguistic pattern of morphology as stipulated in the Pāli grammatical texts.

Key to Entries

THE NUMBER OF SUTTA

THE NUMBER OF THIS SUTTA IN RŪPASIDDHI GRAMMAR

TRANSLATION

THE SUTTA (THE GRAMMATICAL RULE)

VUTTI PĀLI

THE PARSING OF SUTTA AND THE AMOUNT OF WORDS CONTAINED IN SUTTA ARE SHOWN INSIDE BRACKET

140, 232. **Tva'mahaṁ simhi ca.**

[Tvaṁ, ahaṁ+simhi+ca. 3]

[V] Sabbesaṁ **tumha, amha**saddānaṁ savibhattīnaṁ **tvaṁ, ahaṁ,** icce'te ādesā honti yathāsaṅkhyaṁ **si**mhi vibhattimhi.

The whole words "**tumha** and **amha**" changes into " **tvaṁ, ahaṁ**" respectively along with vibatti "**si**" applied after them.

(Tumha+si=**tvaṁ,** Amha+si=**ahaṁ**) ← SIMPLIFIED EXPLANATION OF FUNCTION

• Tvaṁ-you. • Ahaṁ-I. ***ns.*** ← CASE-ENDING CODE

Simhīti kimatthaṁ?

What is the word "simhi" for?

To show that in the examples below, the function of Sutta is inapplicable as they are not of "si", but of "smiṁ".

* Tayi. * Mayi. (Refer to Sutta 139) ← INAPPLICABLE EXAMPLES

Caggahaṇena **tuvaṁ** ca hoti.

By means of "Ca" in the Sutta, tumha also changes into "**tuvaṁ**" (together with vibatti) when "si" is applied after it.

• Tuvaṁ-you. ***ns.*** satthā-(are) teacher. ***nv.*** **i.e.** You are teacher.

EXAMPLES OF SPLIT-SUTTA

SIMPLIFIED MEANING

EXTRA FUNCTION APPLICABLE VIA PART OF SUTTA (ALSO CALLED SPLIT-SUTTA FUNCTION)

DIALECTIC

EXAMPLES OF THE SUTTA

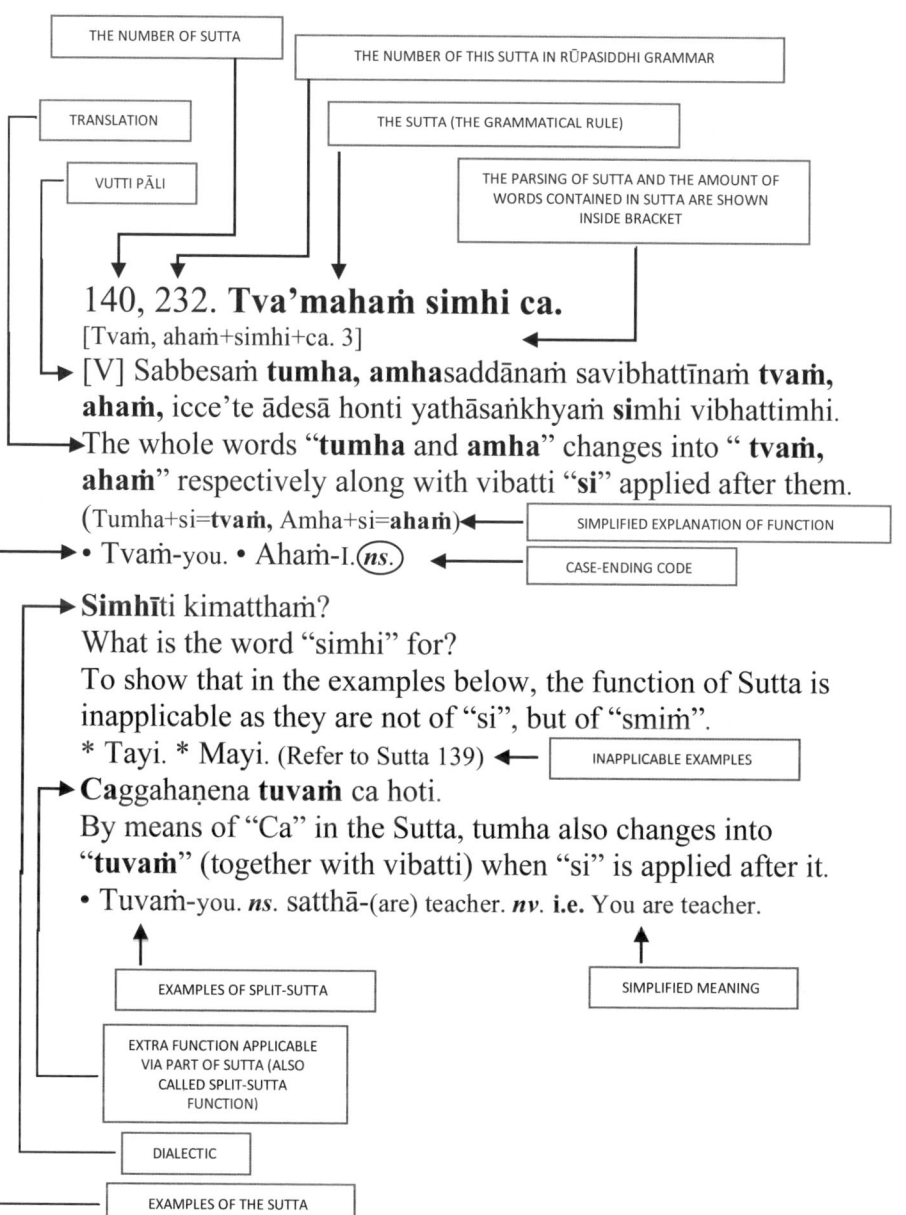

List of Abbreviations
(The Grammatical Codes)

Case-endings
(Shown in order of cases)

ns..Nominative singular
np..Nominative plural
vs..Vocative singular
vp..Vocative plural
as..Accusative singular
ap..Accusative plural
is..Instrumental singular
ip..Instrumental plural
ds..Dative singular
dp..Dative plural
abs..Ablative singular
abp..Ablative plural
gs..Genitive singular
gp..Genitive plural
ls.Locative singular
lp..Locative plural

Specialty Case-endings in the Extraordinary Senses

Nominative:

***nas, nap*..**Nominative in Accusative. This type of case-ending plays the role of an object (Vutta-Kamma, principal object) in a passive voice sentence.

Accusative:

als*..**Accusative in Locative sense singular which means "at, in" **e.g.** ekaṁ samayaṁ, pubbaṇhasamayaṁ, ekamantaṁ (Only singular is commonly found in the Pāli texts. Therefore, plural case in this sense is inapplicable) ***aas,aap..Accusative of ***accantasaṁyoga***(on-going condition) which means "till, until, for a period of, for a certain distance of".

Instrumental:
iss, isp..Instrumental Subject singular or plural which means "by". This type of case-ending plays the role of non-principal Subject (avutta-kattā) in a passive voice sentence.

irs, irp..Instrumental of Reason singular or plural which means "by means of, due to".

Ablative:
abrs, abrp..Ablative of Reason. It means "for reason of, due to".

Genitive:
gns, gnp..Genitive in Nominative, also ***ags, agp***..Agent Genitive (Kattvattha-chaṭṭhī). It means like an ordinary nominative but plays "the role of a subject". This type of case-ending is usually found in wider areas of Pāli texts in the context of either a passive participle kita-noun or a passive-voiced Ākhyāta verb.
gas, gap..Genitive in Accusative, also called Patient-Genitive or Kammattha Chaṭṭhī. It means "to" like an ordinary Kamma but plays "the role of an object".

This type of case-ending is also found in the Pāli texts in the context of a passive participle kita-noun or an Ākhyāta verb of passive voice structure.

gsp..Genitive of Selection plural, also called ***niddhāraṇa chaṭṭhī.*** It means "among, amid, out of".
Note: Singular-case is inapplicable in such usage.

cgs..Concurrent-Genitive singular

cgp..Concurrent Genitive plural
(Also referred to as **anādara** or **absolute *Chaṭṭhī***)
Note: This case-ending is usually an ***anādara*** expression depending on the context.

Locative:
cls..Concurrent Locative singular

clp..Concurrent Locative plural.
(Also referred to as **absolute *Sattamī*** *or* ***lakkhaṇa sattamī,* but in some cases, it can be an *anādara sattamī* too**)

lr, Locative of Reason, also called ***nimitta sattamī.***
Note: This case-ending is frequently found in the majority of Suttas as well as throughout all grammatical text. It is usually a reason-descriptive Locative-case called ***Nimitta-sattamī*** in the grammatical terms. However, sometimes it may be an ***anādara*** or a ***Lakkhaṇa*** expression depending on the contextual aspect.

Examples of ***nimitta sattamī*:**
Sare pare (Sutta No.12), pubbasare lutte(14) se vibhattimhi(61) saṁ,sāsu ekavacanesu vibhattādesesu(62)

lss, lsp..Locative of Selection also called ***niddhāraṇa sattamī***.
lss is seldom found in the Pāli texts though applicable.

Specific terms based on the structure or syntactic context:
ab..Absolutive (also called gerund).
adj..Adjective
adv..Adverb
āv..ākhyāta verb
cn..Compound noun
ger..Gerund
ind..Indeclinable
inf..Infinitive
kn..Kita noun
kv..Kita verb
ni..Nipāta particle
n..Noun
nn..Numerical noun

prp..Present participle
pp..Past participle
sn..Sabbanāma noun
tn..Taddhita noun
up..Upasagga particle

Other Abbreviations
A: Answer
B. Bahubbīhi
CS..Combination of Sandhi
ED..Etymological Definition also called *Viggaha.*
e.g. for example.
Function means the application of the Sutta's rule to be applied on the example as stipulated by the rule of Sutta.
MA..Morphological Analysis.
Q: question
S..Sutta, short aphorisms which concisely explains a grammatical
rule or principle.
SS..Separation of Sandhi
SM..Structural morphology
V..Vutti, explanatory words of a Sutta
WA..Word analysis
' ' This apostrophe is a sign of Sandhi, euphonic combination. It shows a hidden Sandhi procedure in the combined words which will be found throughout this grammatical text.
>becomes. Therefore.
<reversed.
=(a) equals to. (b) Sometimes it indicates an ED in front of an example
word in Taddhita, Ākyāta, Kita and Uṇādi sections.
(c) Sometimes it indicates WA of an example such as parsing into
various parts and showing the meaning of each component.
√ preceded by (as by an *Upasagga* or *nipāta* prefix)

● example word applicable by the function of Sutta or any of split-Sutta function or a component word of Sutta.

* Inapplicable example word by the rule of the Sutta.

(...) The words inside parenthesis are not translations from the original texts but complementary and explanatory words intentionally included for the purpose of easy understanding.

Note: These codes are devised and used for the ease and convenience of grammar study. Without the aid of such codes, the students will find it difficult to understand the important syntactical relation of words and their implied meaning in a sentence. Only a few essential ones are chosen and improvised after careful analysis and research.

Frequently Found Words

ādeso-to change, **i.e.** the function applicable by the rule of Sutta.

āpajjate, āpajjante-literally it means "to reach a morphologically changed state of". ***āv.***

Icce'vam'ādī-etc, [iccevamādī=iti+evaṁ+ādī. **ādi**-means "etc., so on". **iti** and **evaṁ** are indeclinable particles, redundant usage of two *indicatives*]

Iccevamadī yojetabbā-and so on, should be applied. [yuja+tabba, ***kv***]

Iccete, Iccanena, Iccetassassa, Iccetesaṁ, also of the same meaning in different case-endings. All these words are *dual indicatives* which comprise "**iti**-as+**ima**-this". They emphatically mean "such this word", an equivalent of English expression such as "this very man" "that very day".

Iti-This word serves as:

(a) indicative, which means "as, thus". Usually found after the very word it emphatically indicates.
e.g. *Yutte'ti Kasmā?* [yutte+iti kasmā, Sutta No.11]
Why is this word as "Yutte" said here?

(b) a disjunctive which is expressive of the end of a section, usually found at the end of a section or a chapter.
e.g. *Iti sandhikappe paṭhamo kaṇḍo*
the first section of Sandhi ends. ***ind.***

Evaṁ-thus, similarly, in the same manner. [a nipāta particle, ***ind.***]

Bhāvaniddesena-by a component part of Sutta structured in an abstract *taddhita* affix "tta" such as **anattaṁ** (See Sutta 211), **kāsattaṁ** (Sutta 491). [**bhāva**-in abstract formation+**niddesa**-statement, ***cn.***]

Dhātu-Root, **Dhātva'ntassa** (Sutta 615) [**dhātu**-root+**anta**-parts+**ssa**-of *gs*]
Part of the root such as vowel or consonant contained in the root is called **dhātvanta**]

Hoti-is, **Honti-**are. ***āv.***[hū+a+ti or anti.].

Kasmā-why, for what reason. [**ka**-what+**smā**-is an ablative case-ending. See Sutta No.55 to understand this suffix. Both **ko** and **ka** derived from **kiṁ**. See Sutta No.229 to understand this morphological change.]

Kāro-sometimes it refers to **a certain syllable** if used after alphabets such as **a-kāro-**the syllable "a", **ya-kāro-**the syllable "ya" etc. Sometimes it means "to change into **a, ya**" etc.,. In the latter sense, it is an equivalent of "ādeso".

Kārā'deso-this means to change, to be substituted with, to transform into, which implies the function applicable by the rule of Sutta. It also has the same meaning as the word "ādesa". A compound noun [**kāra+ādesa, *cn***].

Kima'tthaṁ-For what purpose? This usage is also the same as **kva'ttho**. [**kiṁ**-what+**atthaṁ**-purpose, result, **kva'ttho**-ko+attho, ***cn.***]

Kvaci-at some instances, optionally. ***ind.***.[kiṁ+va+ci, dual suffixed kiṁ]

Kva'ttho-what benefit? [**kva'ttho**=**ko**-what+**attho**-benefit, result. ***cn.***]

Navā, Vibhāsā (also of the same meaning like "kvaci". ***ind.***)

Nipajjate, Nipajjante-completed, finished. ***āv.***[ni√pada+ya+te or ante.]

Puna-again. ***ind.***

Suttavibhāgena-by splitting part of Sutta. [**Sutta**+**vibhāga**-splitting, ***cn, is***]

Taṁ Yathā? For example. [**Taṁ**-that. It is a Sabbanāma noun "ta" in nominative case "si" which have been transformed into an "aṁ" as it belongs to neuter at this point of usage. See Sutta No.219 to understand this change. **Yathā**-is a Nipāta particle which indicates question. It is more like a question mark? and also ***ind.***]

Tāva-first. Usually this word serves as an introductory to the next phase of statement or explanation though being interpreted as "first". [an indeclinable Nipāta particle. ***ind.***]

Tena-by that. [It is a Sabbanāma noun "ta" in instrumental case "nā" which have been transformed into "ena". See Sutta No.103.]

Yathājinavacanā'nuparodhena-not contravening the words of Buddha. **i.e.** according to usage in Pāli canon.[**Yathā**-according to. *ind*+**jina**-Buddha+**vacana**-word+**anuparodhena**-by not going against. An *abyayībhāva* compound in instrumental case which serves as an adverb.]

Yathāsaṅkhyaṁ-according to the order of number and sequence. **i.e.** respectively. [**Yathā**-according to. *ind*+**saṅkhyaṁ**-number or sequence. An *abyayībhāva* compound in accusative case which serves as an adverb.]

Yathāsambhavaṁ-according to possible applicability. ***adv***. [**Yathā**-according to+ **sambhavaṁ**-possibility. The same *abyayībhāva* compound, ***cn***]

Yogavibhāgena-by splitting part of Sutta. [**yoga**-Sutta+**vibhāga, *cn.***]

Vā-optionally, not always, as other possible method of the example, ***ind.***

Vacanaṁ, vacanena, gahaṇaṁ, gahaṇena, All refer to a certain word or case-termination included in a Sutta or in a Vutti of it. **Vacana** or **gahaṇa** means a word. ***n.***

e.g. (a) **Si**vacanassa, (b) **Nā**vacanassa, (c) **Smā**vacanassa, (d) **Ca**ggahaṇena
All refer to **"si" "nā" "smā"** noun case-endings in a, b and c.

It refers to the nipāta particle **"Ca"** in (d).
(a) **ādi**ggahaṇena, (b) **anta**ggahaṇena, (c) **vibhatti**ggahaṇaṁ.
All refer to the word **"ādi", "anta" "vibhatti"** etc,.

Namo Tassa Bhagavato Arahato Sammāsambuddhassa

Suttakkama (Order of Suttas)

1. Sandhi

Sandhi (Euphonic Combination)

Note: Of the two numbers shown before each Sutta, **the first** refers to the serial sequence of Kaccāyana grammar text while **the second** refers to the numerical order applied in the Rūpasiddhi grammar.

1, 1. Attho akkharasaññāto.
2, 2. Akkharā'pādayo ekacattālisaṁ.
3, 3. Tattho'dantā sarā aṭṭha.
4, 4. Lahumattā tayo rassā.
5, 5. Aññe dīghā.
6, 8. Sesā byañjanā.
7, 9. Vaggā pañcapañcaso mantā.
8, 10. Aṁ-iti niggahitaṁ.
9, 11. Parasamaññā payoge.
10, 12. Pubba'madhoṭhita'massaraṁ sarena viyojaye.
11, 14. Naye paraṁ yutte.

Iti sandhikappe paṭhamo kaṇḍo.

12, 13. Sarā sare lopaṁ.
13, 15. Vā paro asarūpā.
14, 16. Kvacā'savaṇṇaṁ lutte.
15, 17. Dīghaṁ.
16, 18. Pubbo ca.
17, 19. Ya'me'dantassā'deso.
18, 20. Va'mo'du'dantānaṁ.
19, 22. Sabbo caṁ ti.
20, 27. Do dhassa ca.
21, 22. Ivaṇṇo yaṁ navā.
22, 28. Evā'dissa ri pubbo ca rasso.

Iti sandhikappe dutiyo kaṇḍo.

23, 36. Sarā pakati byañjane.
24, 35. Sare kvaci.
25, 37. Dīghaṁ.
26, 38. Rassaṁ.
27, 39. Lopañ'ca tatrā'kāro.
28, 40. Para dvebhāvo ṭhāne.
29, 42. Vagge ghosā'ghosānaṁ tatiyapaṭhamā.

Iti sandhikappe tatiyo kaṇḍo.

30, 58. Aṁ byañjane niggahitaṁ.
31, 49. Vaggantaṁ vā vagge.
32, 50. Ehe ñaṁ.
33, 51. Sa ye ca.
34, 52. Ma, dā sare.
35, 34. Ya, va, ma, da, na, ta, ra, lā cā'gamā.
36, 47. Kvaci o byañjane.
37, 57. Niggahitañ'ca.
38, 53. Kvaci lopaṁ.
39, 54. Byañjane ca.
40, 55. Paro vā saro.
41, 56. Byañjano ca visaññogo.

Iti sandhikappe catuttho kaṇḍo.

42, 32. Go sare puthassā'gamo kvaci.
43, 33. Pāssa ca'nto rasso.
44, 24. Abbho abhi.
45, 25. Ajjho adhi.
46, 26. Te na vā ivaṇṇe.
47, 23. Atissa ca'ntassa.
48, 43. Kvaci paṭi patissa.
49, 44. Puthassu'byañjane.
50, 45. O avassa.
51, 59. Anu'padiṭṭhānaṁ vuttayogato.

Iti sandhikappe pañcamo kaṇḍo.

Sandhisuttaṁ niṭṭhitaṁ.

2. Nāma

(Nouns)

52, 60. Jinavacanayuttaṁ hi.
53, 61. Liṅgañ'ca nippajjate.
54, 62. Tato ca vibhattiyo.
55, 63. Si, yo, aṁ, yo, nā, hi, sa, naṁ, smā, hi, sa, naṁ, smiṁ, su.
56, 64. Ta'danuparodhena.
57, 71. Ālapane si gasañño.
58, 29. Ivaṇṇu'vaṇṇā jhalā.
59, 182. Te itthikhyā po.
60, 177. Ā gho.
61, 86. Sā'gamo se.
62, 206. Saṁsāsve'kavacanesu ca.
63, 217. Eti'māsa'mi.
64, 216. Tassā vā.
65, 215. Tato sassa ssāya.
66, 205. Gho rassaṁ.
67, 229. No ca dvā'dito naṁmhi.
68, 184. A'mā pato smiṁ, smā, naṁ vā.
69, 186. Ādito o ca.
70, 30. Jha, lāna'miyu'vā sare vā.
71, 505. Ya,va,kārā ca.
72, 185. Pasaññassa ca.
73, 174. Gā'va se.
74, 169. Yosu ca.
75, 170. Ava'ṁmhi ca.
76, 171. Āvassu'vā.
77, 175. Tato na'maṁ patimhā'lutte ca samāse.
78, 31. O sare ca.
79, 46. Tabbiparītū'papade byañjane ca.
80, 173. Goṇa naṁmhi vā.
81, 172. Su,hi,nā,su ca.
82, 149. Aṁ,mo niggahitaṁ jha,la,pehi.

83, 67. Saralopo'mādesapaccayā'dimhi saralope tu pakati.
84, 144. Agho rassa'mekavacanayosva'pi ca.
85, 150. Na si, smima'napuṁsakāni.
86, 227. Ubhā'dito na'minnaṁ.
87, 231. Iṇṇa'miṇṇannaṁ tīhi saṅkhyāhi.
88, 147. Yosu katanikāralopesu dīghaṁ.
89, 87. Su, naṁ, hisu ca.
90, 252. Pañcā'dīna'mattaṁ.
91, 194. Patissi'nīmhi.
92, 100. Ntussa'nto yosu ca.
93, 106. Sabbassa vā aṁsesu.
94, 105. Simhi vā.
95, 145. Aggissi'ni.
96, 148. Yosva'katarasso jho.
97, 156. Ve, vo, su lo ca.
98, 189. Mātulā'dīna'mānatta'mīkāre.
99, 81. Smā, hi, smiṁ, naṁ mhābhimhi vā.
100, 214. Na ti'mehi katā'kārehi.
101, 80. Suhisva'kāro e.
102, 202. Sabbanāmānaṁ naṁmhi ca.
103, 79. Ato ne'na.
104, 66. So'.
105,... So vā.
106, 313. Dīgho'rehi.
107, 69. Sabbayonīna'mā-e.
108, 90. Smā, smiṁ, naṁ vā.
109, 304. Āya catutthe'kavacanassa tu.
110, 201. Tayo ne'va ca sabbanāmehi.
111, 179. Ghato nā'dīnaṁ.
112, 183. Pato yā.
113, 132. Sakhato gasse' vā.
114, 178. Ghate' ca.
115, 181. Na ammā'dito.
116, 157. Akatarassā lato yvā'lapanassa ve, vo.
117, 124. Jha, lato sassa no vā.

118, 146. Gha, pato ca yonaṁ lopo.
119, 155. Lato vokāro ca.

Iti nāmakappe paṭhamo kaṇḍo.

120, 243. Amhassa mamaṁ savibhattissa se.
121, 233. Mayaṁ yomhi paṭhame.
122, 99. Ntussa'nto.
123, 103. Ntassa se vā.
124, 98. Ā simhi.
125, 198. Aṁ napuṁsake.
126, 101. Avaṇṇā ca ge.
127, 102. To, ti, tā sa, smiṁ, nā, su.
128, 104. Naṁmhi taṁ vā.
129, 222. Imassi'da'maṁsisu napuṁsake.
130, 225. Amussā'duṁ.
131,... Itthipumanapuṁsakasaṅkhyaṁ.
132, 228. Yosu dvinnaṁ dve ca.
133, 230. Ti, catunnaṁ tisso, catasso, tayo, cattāro, tīṇi, cattāri.
134, 251. Pañcā'dīna'makāro.
135, 118. Rājassa rañño rājino se.
136, 119. Raññaṁ naṁmhi vā.
137, 116. Nāmhi raññā vā.
138, 121. Smiṁmhi raññe, rājini.
139, 245. Tumha'mhākaṁ tayi, mayi.
140, 232. Tva'mahaṁ simhi ca.
141, 241. Tava, mama se.
142, 242. Tuyhaṁ, mayhañ'ca.
143, 235. Taṁ, mama'ṁmhi.
144, 234. Tavaṁ, mamañ'ca na vā.
145, 238. Nāmhi tayā, mayā.
146, 236. Tumhassa tuvaṁ, tva'mamhi.
147, 246. Padato dutiyā, catutthī, chaṭṭhīsu vo no.
148, 247. Te, me'kavacanesu ca.
149, 248. Na aṁmhi.

150, 249. Vā tatiye ca.
151, 250. Bahuvacanesu vo, no.
152, 136. Puma'ntassā' simhi.
153, 138. A'mālapane'kavacane.
154,... Samāse ca vibhāsā.
155, 137. Yosvā'no.
156, 142. Āne smiṁmhi vā.
157, 140. Hivibhatthimhi ca.
151, 143. Susmi'mā vā.
159, 139. U nāmhi ca.
160, 197. A Kamma'ntassa ca.

Iti nāmakappe dutiyo kaṇḍo.

161, 244. Tumha'mhehi na'mākaṁ.
162, 237. Vā yva'ppaṭhamo.
163, 240. Sassaṁ'.
164, 200. Sabbanāmakārate'paṭhamo.
165, 208. Dvandaṭṭhā vā.
166, 209. Nā'ññaṁ sabbanāmikaṁ.
167, 210. Bahubbīhimhi ca.
168, 203. Sabbato naṁ saṁ, sā, naṁ.
169, 117. Rājassa rāju su, naṁ, hisu ca.
170, 220. Sabbassi'masse' vā.
171, 219. Ani'mi nāmhi ca.
172, 218. Anapuṁsakassā'yaṁ simhi.
173, 223. Amussa mo saṁ.
174, 211. Eta, tesaṁ so.
175, 212. Tassa vā nattaṁ sabbattha.
176, 213. Sa, smā, smiṁ, saṁ, sāsva'ttaṁ.
177, 221. Ima-saddassa ca.
178, 224. Sabbato ko.
179, 204. Gha, pato smiṁ, sā, naṁ saṁ, sā.
180, 207. Ne'tāhi, smi, 'māya, yā.
181, 95. Manogaṇā'dito smiṁ, nā, na'mi, ā.

182, 97. Sassa co’.
183, 48. Etesa’mo lope.
184, 96. Sa sare vā’gamo.
185, 112. Santasaddassa so bhe bo ca’nte.
186, 107. Simhi gacchantā’dīnaṁ nta-saddo aṁ.
187, 108. Sesesu ntu’va.
188, 115. Brahma’tta, sakha, rājā’dito a’mānaṁ.
189, 113. Sy’ā ca.
190, 114. Yona’māno.
191, 130. Sakhato cā’yo no.
192, 135. Smi’me.
193, 122. Brahmato gassa ca.
194, 131. Sakhantassi’no, nā, naṁ, sesu.
195, 134. Āro himhi vā.
196, 133. Suna’maṁsu vā.
197, 125. Brahmato tu smiṁni.
198, 123. Uttaṁ sa, nā, su.
199, 158. Satthupitā’dīna’mā sismiṁ silopo ca.
200, 159. Aññesvā’rattaṁ.
201, 163. Vā naṁmhi.
202, 164. Satthunattañ’ca.
203, 162. U sasmiṁ salopo ca.
204, 167. Sakkamandhātā’dīnañ’ca.
205, 160. Tato yona’mo tu.
206, 165. Tato smi’mi.
207, 161. Nā ā.
208, 166. Āro rassa’mikāre.
209, 168. Pitā’dīna’masimhi.
210, 239. Tayā, tayīnaṁ takāro tva’ttaṁ vā.

Iti nāmakappe tatiyo kaṇḍo.

211, 126. Atta’nto hismi’manattaṁ.
212, 129. Tato smiṁ ni.
213, 127. Sassa no.

214, 128. Smā nā.
215, 141. Jha,la,to ca.
216, 180. Ghapato smiṁ yaṁ vā.
217, 199. Yonaṁ ni napuṁsakehi.
218, 196. Ato niccaṁ.
219, 195. Si'ṁ.
220, 74. Sesato lopaṁ gasi'pi.
221, 282. Sabbāsa'māvuso'pasagganipātā'dīhi ca.
222, 342. Pumassa liṅgā'dīsu samāsesu.
223, 188. Aṁ yam'īto pasaññato.
224, 153. Naṁ jhato katarassā.
225, 151. Yonaṁ no.
226, 154. Smiṁ ni.
227, 270. Kissa ka ve ca.
228, 272. Ku hiṁ, haṁsu ca.
229, 226. Sesesu ca.
230, 262. Tra, to, the-su ca.
231, 263. Sabbasse'tassā'kāro vā.
232, 267. Tre niccaṁ.
233, 264. E to, the-su ca.
234, 265. Imassi'thaṁ, dāni, ha, to, dhe-su ca.
235, 281. A dhunāmhi ca.
236, 280. Eta rahimhi.
237, 176. Itthiya'mato āpaccayo.
238, 187. Nadā'dito vā ī.
239, 190. ṇava, ṇika, ṇeyya, ṇantuhi.
240, 193. Pati, bhikkhu, rājī'kārantehi inī.
241, 191. Ntussa ta'mīkāre.
242, 192. Bhavato bhoto[7].
243,110. Bho ge tu.

---

[7] After this Sutta, there are two more Suttas found in the Rūpasiddhi text and earlier versions of the text. They are **1.Obhāvo yosu kvaci vakārassa, 2.Bhadantassa Bhaddanta, bhante.**

244, 72. Akārapitā'dya'ntāna'mā.
245,152. Jha,la,pā rassaṁ.
246,73. Ākāro vā.

Iti nāmakappe catuttho kaṇḍo.

247, 261. Tvā'dayo vibhattisaññāyo.
248, 260. Kvaci to pañcamya'tthe.
249, 266. Tra, tha, sattamiyā sabbanāmehi.
250, 268. Sabbato dhi.
251, 269. Kiṁsmā vo.
252, 271. Hiṁ, haṁ, hiñcanaṁ
253, 273. Tamhā ca.
254, 274. Imasmā ha, dhā ca.
255, 275. Yato hiṁ.
256,... Kāle.
257, 276. Kiṁ, sabba'ññe'ka, ya, ku, hi dā, dācanaṁ.
258, 278. Tamhā dāni ca.
259, 279. Imasmā rahi, dhunā, dāni ca.
260, 277. Sabbassa so dāmhi vā.
261, 369. Avaṇṇo ye lopañ'ca.
262, 391. Vuḍḍhassa jo iyi'ṭṭhesu.
263, 392. Pasatthassa so ca.
264, 393. Antikassa nedo.
265, 394. Bāḷhassa sādho.
266, 395. Appassa kaṇ.
267, 396. Yuvānañ'ca.
268, 397. Vantu, mantu, vī, nañ'ca lopo.
269, 41. Yavataṁ ta, la, ṇa, da, kārānaṁ byañjanāni ca, la, ña, ja, kārattaṁ.
270, 120. Amha, tumha'ntu, rāja, brahma'tta, sakha, satthu, pitā'dīhi smā nā'va.

Iti nāmakappe pañcamo kaṇḍo.

Nāmasuttaṁ niṭṭhitaṁ.

3. Kāraka

(Parts of the Sentence & their Case-endings)

271, 88. Yasmā'dapeti, bhaya'mādatte vā ta'dapādānaṁ.
272, 309. Dhātunāmāna'mupasaggayogā'dīsva'pi ca.
273, 310. Rakkhaṇa'tthāna'micchitaṁ.
274, 311. Yena vā'dassanaṁ.
275, 312. Dūra'ntika'ddhakāla, nimmāna, tvālopa, disā yoga, vibhattā'rappayoga, suddha'ppamocana, hetu, vivitt'ppamāṇa, pubbayoga, bandhana, guṇavacana, pañha, kathana, thokā'kattūsu ca.
276, 302. Yassa dātukāmo rocate dhārayate vā taṁ sampadānaṁ.
277, 303. Silāgha, hanu, ṭhā, sapa, dhāra, piha, kudha, duhi'sso'ssūya, rādhi'kkha, paccā'suṇa, anupatigiṇa, pubbakattā'rocanattha, ta'dattha, tuma'tthā'lamattha, maññā'nādarappā'ṇini, gatya'tthakammani āsisattha, sammuti, bhiyya, sattamya'tthesu ca.
278, 320. Yo'dhāro ta'mokāsaṁ.
279, 292. Yena vā kayirate taṁ karaṇaṁ.
280, 285. Yaṁ karoti taṁ kammaṁ.
281, 294. Yo karoti sa kata.
282, 295. Yo kārehi sa hetu.
283, 316. Yassa vā pariggaho taṁ sāmī.
284, 283. Liṅga'tthe paṭhamā.
285, 70. Ālapane ca.
286, 291. Karaṇe tatiyā.
287, 296. Sahā'diyoge ca.
288, 293. Kattari ca.
289, 297. Hetva'tthe ca.
290, 298. Sattamya'tthe ca.
291, 299. Yen'aṅgavikāro.
292, 300. Visesane ca.
293, 301. Sampadāne catutthī.
294, 305. Namoyogā'dīsva'pi ca.

295, 307. Apādāne pañcamī.
296, 314. Kāraṇa'tthe ca.
297, 284. Kamma'tthe dutiyā.
298, 287. Kāla'ddhāna'maccantasaṁyoge.
299, 288. Kamma'ppavacanīyayutte.
300, 286. Gati, buddhi, bhuja, paṭha, hara, kara, sayā'dīnaṁ kārite vā.
301, 315. Sāmismiṁ chaṭṭhī.
302, 319. Okāse sattamī.
303, 321. Sāmi'ssarā'dhipati, dāyāda, sakkhī, patibhū, pasuta, kusalehi ca.
304, 322. Niddhāraṇe ca.
305, 323. Anā'dare ca.
306, 289. Kvaci dutiyā chaṭṭhīna'matthe.
307, 290. Tatiyā, sattamīnañ'ca.
308, 317. Chaṭṭhī ca.
309, 318. Dutiyā, pañcamī nañ'ca.
310, 324. Kamma, karaṇa, nimitta'tthesu sattamī.
311, 325. Sampadāne ca.
312, 326. Pañcamya'tthe ca.
313, 327. Kāla, bhāvesu ca.
314, 328. Upa'dhyā'dhikissaravacane.
315, 329. Maṇḍitu'ssukkesu tatiyā ca.

Iti nāmakappe kārakakappo chaṭṭho kaṇḍo.

Kārakasuttaṁ niṭṭhitaṁ.

4. Samāsa

(Compound Nouns)

316, 331. Nāmānaṁ samāso yutta'ttho.
317, 332. Tesaṁ vibhattiyo lopā ca.
318, 333. Pakati ca'ssa sara'ntassa.
319, 330. Upasagganipātapubbako abyayībhāvo.
320, 335. So napuṁsakaliṅgo.
321, 349. Digusse'kattaṁ.
322, 359. Tathā dvande pāṇi, tūriya, yogga, sena'ṅga, khuddajantuka, vividha viruddha, visabhāga'tthādīnañ'ca.
323, 360. Vibhāsā rukkha, tiṇa, pasu, dhana, dhañña, janapadā'dīnaṁ ca.
324, 339. Dvipade tulyā'dhikaraṇe kammadhārayo.
325, 348. Saṅkhyāpubbo digu.
326, 341. Ubhe tappurisā.
327, 351. A'mā'dayo parapadebhi.
328, 352. Aññapada'tthesu bahubbīhi.
329, 357. Nāmānaṁ samuccayo dvando.
330, 340. Mahataṁ mahā tulyā'dhikaraṇe pade.
331, 353. Itthiyaṁ bhāsitapumi'tthī pumā'va ce.
332, 343. Kammadhāraya saññe ca.
333, 344. Attaṁ nassa tappurise.
334, 345. Sare an.
335, 346. Kad kussa.
336, 347. Kā'ppa'tthesu ca.
337, 350. Kvaci samāsanta gatāna'makāranto.
338, 356. Nadimhā ca.
339, 358. Jāyāya tu daṁ, jāni patimhi.
340, 355. Dhanumhā ca.
341, 336. Aṁ vibhattīna'makārantā abyayībhāvā.
342, 337. Saro rasso napuṁsake.
343, 338. Aññasmā lopo ca.

Iti nāmakappe samāsakappo sattamo kaṇḍo.

Samāsa sutthaṁ niṭṭhitaṁ.

5. Taddhita

(Nouns in Affixes)

244, 361. Vā ṇā'pacce.
345, 366. Ṇāyana, ṇāna, vacchā'dito.
346, 367. Ṇeyyo kattikā'dīhi.
347, 368. Ato ṇi vā.
348, 371. Ṇavo'pakvā'dīhi.
349, 372. Ṇera vidhavā'dito.
350, 373. Yena vā saṁsaṭṭhaṁ, tarati, carati, vahati, ṇiko.
351, 374. Ta'madhīte, te nakatā'di, sannidhāna, niyoga, sippa, bhaṇḍa, jīvika'tthesu ca.
352, 376. Ṇa rāgā, tasse'da'mañña'tthesu ca.
353, 378. Jātā'dīna'mimi'yā ca.
354, 379. Samūha'tthe kaṇ, ṇā.
355, 380. Gāma, jana, bandhu, sahāyā'dīhi tā.
356, 381. Ta'dassa ṭhāna'miyo ca.
357, 382. Upamatthā'yitattaṁ.
358, 383. Tan'nissitatthe lo.
359, 384. Ālu tabbahule.
360, 387. Ṇya, tta, tā bhāve tu.
361, 388. Ṇa visamā'dīhi.
362, 389. Ramaṇīyā'dito kaṇ.
363, 390. Visese tara, tami'siki'yi'ṭṭhā.
364, 398. Ta'dassatthī'ti vī ca.
365, 399. Tapā'dito sī.
366, 400. Daṇḍā'dito ika, ī.
367, 401. Madhvā'dito ro.
368, 402. Guṇa'dito vantu.
369, 403. Satyā'dīhi mantu.
370, 405. Saddhā'dito ṇa.
371, 404. Āyussu'kārā'sa mantumhi.
372, 385. Tappakativacane mayo.
373, 406. Saṅkhyāpūraṇe mo.
374, 408. Sa chassa vā.

375, 412. Ekā'dito dasassī'.
376, 257. Dase so niccañ'ca.
377,… Ante niggahitañ'ca.
378, 414. Ti ca.
379, 258. La, da, rānaṁ.
380, 255. Vīsati, dase, su bā dvissa tu.
381, 254. Ekā'dito dassa ra saṅkhyāne.
382, 259. Aṭṭhā'dito ca.
383, 253. Dve'ka'ṭṭhāna'mākāro vā.
384, 407. Catu'cchehi tha, ṭhā.
385, 409. Dvi,tīhi tiyo.
386, 410. Tiye du, tā'pi ca.
387, 411. Tesa'maḍḍhūpapadena aḍḍhuḍḍha, divaḍḍha, diyaḍḍha'ḍḍhatiyā.
388, 68. Sarūpāna'mekasesva'sakiṁ.
389, 413. Gaṇane dasassa dvi, ti, catu, pañca, cha, satta, aṭṭha, navakānaṁ vī, ti, cattāra, paññā, cha, sattā'sa, navā yosu yonañ'cī'sa'māsaṁ ṭhi, ri, tī, tuti.
390, 256. Catū'papadassa lopo tu'ttarapadā'dicassa cu, co'pi navā.
391, 423. Ya'danu'papannā nipātanā sijjhanti.
392, 418. Dvā'dito ko'nekatthe ca.
393, 415. Dasa dasakaṁ sataṁ dasakānaṁ sataṁ sahassañ'ca yomhi.
394, 416. Yāva ta'duttari, dasaguṇitañ'ca.
395, 417. Sakanāmehi.
396, 363. Tesaṁ ṇo lopaṁ.
397, 420. Vibhāge dhā ca.
398, 421. Sabbanāmehi pakāravacane tu thā.
399, 422. Ki'mimehi thaṁ.
400, 364. Vuddhā'disarassa vā'saṁyogantassa saṇe ca.
401, 375. Mā 'yūna'māgamo ṭhāne.
402, 377. Āttañ'ca.
403, 354. Kvacā'dimajjhu'ttarānaṁ dīgha, rassā, paccayesu ca.
404, 370. Tesu vuddhi, lopā'gama, vikāra, viparitā'desā ca.

405, 365. A'yuvaṇṇānañ'cā'yo vuddhi.

Iti nāmakappe taddhitakappo aṭṭhamo kaṇḍo.

Taddhitasuttaṁ niṭṭhitaṁ.

6. Ākhyāta

(Verbs)

406, 429. Atha pubbāni-vibhattīnaṁ cha **parassapadāni.**
407, 439. Parāṇy'**attanopadāni.**
408, 431. Dve dve paṭhama, majjhimu'ttamapurisā.
409, 441. Sabbesa'mekā'bhidhāne paro puriso.
410, 432. Nāmamhi payujjamāne'pi tulyā'dhikaraṇe paṭhamo.
411, 436. Tumhe majjhimo.
412, 437. Amhe uttamo.
413, 427. Kāle.
414, 428. Vattamānā pacc'uppanne.
415, 451. Āṇatyā'siṭṭhe'nuttakāle pañcamī.
416, 454. Anumati, parikappa'tthesu sattamī.
417, 460. Apaccakkhe parokkhā'tīte.
418, 456. Hiyyopabhuti'paccakkhe hiyyattanī.
419, 469. Samīpe'jjatanī.
420, 471. Māyoge sabbakāle ca.
421, 473. Anā'gate bhavissanti.
422, 475. Kriyā'tipanne'tīte kālātipatti.
423, 426. **Vattamānā** ti-anti, si-tha, mi-ma, te-ante, se-vhe, e-mhe.
424, 450. **Pañcamī** tu-antu, hi-tha, mi-ma, taṁ-antaṁ, ssu-vho, e-āmase.
425, 453. **Sattamī** eyya-eyyuṁ, eyyāsi-eyyātha, eyyāmi-eyyāma, etha-eraṁ, etho-eyyāvho, eyyaṁ-eyyāmhe.
426, 459. **Parokkhā** a-u, e-ttha, aṁ-mha, ttha-re, ttho-vho, iṁ-mhe.
427, 455. **Hiyyattanī** ā-ū, o-ttha, aṁ-mhā, ttha-tthuṁ, se-vhaṁ, iṁ-mhase.

428, 468. **Ajjatanī** ī-uṁ o-ttha, iṁ-mhā, ā-ū, se-vhaṁ, aṁ-mhe.

429,472. **Bhavissanti** ssati-ssanti, ssasi-ssatha, ssāmi-ssāma, ssate-ssante, ssase-ssavhe, ssaṁ-ssāmhe.

430,474. **Kālātipatti** ssā-ssaṁsu, sse-ssatha, ssaṁ-ssāmā, ssatha-ssiṁsu[8], ssase-ssavhe, ssaṁ-ssāmhase.

431, 458. Hiyyattanī, sattamī, pañcamī, vattamānā **sabbadhātukaṁ.**

Iti ākhyātakappe paṭhamo kaṇḍo

432, 362. Dhātuliṅgehi parā paccayā.
433, 528. Tija, gupa, kita, mānehi kha, cha, sā vā.
434, 534. Bhuja, ghasa, hara, su, pā'dīhi tu'miccha'tthesu.
435, 536. Āya nāmato kattū'pamānā'dācāre.
436, 537. Īyū'pamānā ca.
437, 538. Nāmamhā'tticcha'tthe.
438, 540. Dhātūhi ṇe, ṇaya, ṇāpe, ṇāpayā kāritāni hetva'tthe.
439, 539. Dhāturūpe nāmasmā ṇayo ca.
440, 445. Bhāvakammesu yo.
441, 447. Tassa cavagga, yakāra, vakārattaṁ sadhātvantassa.
442, 448. Ivaṇṇā'gamo vā.
443, 449. Pubbarūpañ'ca.
444, 511. Tathā kattari ca.
445, 433. Bhūvā'dito a.
446, 509. Rudhā'dito niggahitapubbañ'ca.
447, 510. Divā'dito yo.
448, 512. Svā'dito ṇuṇā uṇā ca.
449, 513. Kīyā'dito nā.
450, 517. Gahā'dito ppa,ṇhā.
451, 520. Tanā'dito o, yirā.
452, 525. Curā'dito ṇe, ṇayā.

---

[8] In the earlier versions, it is found "ssiṁsu-स्सिंसु " which is more relevant in the light of practical usage in the canonical texts.

453, 444. Attanopadāni bhāve ca kammani.
454, 440. Kattari ca.
455, 530. Dhātuppaccayehi vibhattiyo.
456, 430. Kattari parassapadaṁ.
457, 424. Bhū'vā'dayo dhātavo.
Iti ākhyātakappe dutiyo kaṇḍo.

458, 461. Kvacā'divaṇṇāna'mekassarānaṁ dvebhāvo.
459, 462. Pubbo'bbhāso.
460, 506. Rasso.
461, 464. Dutiya,catutthānaṁ paṭha,matatiyā.
462, 467. Kavaggassa cavaggo.
463, 532. Māna,kitānaṁ va,tattaṁ vā.
464, 504. Hassa jo.
465, 463. Antassi'vaṇṇākāro vā.
466, 489. Niggahitañ'ca.
467, 533. Tato pā,mānānaṁ vā,maṁ sesu.
468, 492. Ṭhā tiṭṭho.
469, 494. Pā pivo.
470, 514. Ñāssa jā, jaṁ, nā.
471, 483. Disassa passa, dissa, dakkhā vā.
472, 531. Byañjana'ntassa co chappaccayesu ca.
473, 529. Ko khe ca.
474, 535. Harassa gī se.
475, 465. Brū, bhūna'māha, bhūvā parokkhāyaṁ.
476, 442. Gamissa'nto ccho vā sabbāsu.
477, 479. Vacassa'jjatanimhi'makāro o.
478, 438. Akāro dīghaṁ hi, mi, mesu.
479, 452. Hi lopaṁ vā.
480, 490. Hotissare'ho'he bhavissantimhi sassa ca.
481, 524. Karassa sappaccayassa kāho.
Iti ākhyātakappe tatiyo kaṇḍo.

482, 508. Dā'dantassaṁ' mi,mesu.
483, 527. Asaṁyogantassa vuddhi kārite.

484, 542. Ghaṭā'dīnaṁ vā.
485, 434. Aññesu ca.
486, 543. Guha, dusānaṁ dīghaṁ.
487, 478. Vaca, vasa, vahā'dīna'mukāro vassa ye.
488, 481. Ha vipariyayo lo vā.
489, 519. Gahassa ghe ppe.
490, 518. Halopo ṇhāmhi.
491, 523. Karassa kāsatta'majjatanimhi.
492, 499. Asasmā mi, mānaṁ mhi, mhā'ntalopo ca.
493, 498. Thassa tthatthaṁ.
494, 495. Tissa tthitthaṁ.
495, 500. Tussa tthuttaṁ.
496, 497. Simhi ca.
497, 477. Labhasmā ī, iṁnaṁ ttha, ttaṁ.
498, 480. Kusasmā 'dī cchi.
499, 507. Dā-dhātussa dajjaṁ.
500, 486. Vadassa vajjaṁ.
501, 443. Gamissa ghammaṁ.
502, 493. Yamhi dā, dhā, mā, ṭhā, hā, pā, maha, mathā'dīna'mī.
503, 485. Yajassā'dissi'.
504, 470. Sabbato uṁ iṁsu.
505, 482. Jara, marānaṁ jīra, jiyya, miyyā vā.
506, 496. Sabbatthā'sassā'dilopo ca.
507, 501. Asabbadhātuke Bū.
508, 515. Eyassa ñāto iyā, ñā.
509, 516. Nāssa lopo ya-kārattaṁ.
510, 487. Lopañ'ce'tta'makāro.
511, 521. Utta'mokāro.
512, 522. Karassā'kāro ca.
513, 435. O ava sare.
514, 491. E aya.
515, 541. Te āvā'yā kārite.
516, 466. Ikārā'gamo asabbadhātukamhi.
517, 488. Kvaci dhātuvibhattippaccayānaṁ dīgha, viparītā'desa, lopā'gamā ca.

518, 446. Attanopadāni parassapadattaṁ.
519, 457. A-kārā'gamo hiyyatthanī, ajjatanī, kālātipattīsu.
520, 502. Brūto ī timhi.
521, 425. Dhātussa'nto lopo'nekasarassa.
522, 476. Isu, yamūna'manto ccho vā.
523, 526. Kāritānaṁ ṇo lopaṁ.

Iti ākhyātakappe catuttho kaṇḍo.

Ākhyāta-suttaṁ niṭṭhitaṁ.

7. Kibbidhāna

(Verbal Nouns & Nouns in Kita Affixes)

524, 561. Dhātuyā kammā'dimhi ṇo.
525, 565. Saññāya'ma,nu.
526, 567. Pure dadā ca iṁ.
527, 568. Sabbato ṇvu, tvā'vī vā.
528, 577. Visa, ruja, padā'dito ṇa.
529, 580. Bhāve ca.
530, 584. Kvi ca.
531, 589. Dharā'dīhi rammo.
532, 590. Tassīlā'dīsu ṇī, tvā'vī ca.
533, 591. Sadda, kudha, cala, maṇḍa'ttha, rucā'dīhi yu.
534, 592. Pārā'digamimhā rū.
535, 593. Bhikkhā'dito ca.
536, 594. Hanatyā'dīnaṁ ṇuko.
537, 566. Nu niggahitaṁ pada'nte.
538, 595. Saṁhanāñ'ñāya vā ro gho.
539, 558. Ramhi ra'nto rā'di no.
540, 545. Bhāva, kammesu tabbā'nīyā.
541, 552. Ṇyo ca.
542, 557. Karamhā ricca.
543, 555. Bhūto'bba.
544, 556. Vada, mada, gamu, yuja, garahā'kārādīhi jja, mma, gga, yhe'yyā gāro vā.

545, 548. Te kiccā.
546, 562. Aññe kitā.
547, 596. Nandā'dīhi yu.
548, 597. Kattu, karaṇa, padesesu ca.
549, 550. Ra, hā'dito ṇa.

Iti kibbidhānakappe paṭhamo kaṇḍo.

550, 546. Ṇā'dayo tekālikā.
551, 598. Saññāyaṁ dādhāto i.
552, 609. Ti kiccā'siṭṭhe.
553, 599. Itthiya'matiyavo vā.
554, 601. Karato ririya.
555, 612. Atīte ta, tavantu, tāvī.
556, 622. Bhāva, kammesu ta.
557, 606. Budha, gamā'ditthe kattari.
558, 602. Jito ina sabbattha.
559, 603. Supato ca.
560, 604. Īsaṁ, du, sū, hi kha.
561, 636. Iccha'tthesu samānakattukesu tave, tuṁ vā.
562, 638. Arahasakkā'dīsu ca.
563, 639. Pattavacane ala'matthesu ca.
564, 640. Pubbakāle'kakattukānaṁ tuna, tvāna, tvā vā.
565, 646. Vattamāne mānan'tā.
566, 574. Sāsā'dīhi ratthu.
567, 575. Pātito ritu.
568, 576. Mānā'dīhi rātu.
569, 610. Āgamā tuko.
570, 611. Bhabbe ika.

Iti kibbidhānakappe dutiyo kaṇḍo.

571, 624. Paccayā'daniṭṭhā nipātanā sijjhanti.
572, 625. Sāsa, disa, to tassa riṭṭho ca.
573, 626. Sā'disanta puccha, bhanja, hansā'dīhi ṭṭho.
574, 613. Vasato uttha.
575, 614. Vasa vā vu.

576, 607. Dha, ḍha, bha, hehi dha, ḍhā ca.
577, 628. Bhanjato ggo ca.
578, 560. Bhujā'dīna'manto no dvi ca.
579, 629. Vaca vā vu'.
580, 630. Gupā'dīnañ'ca.
581, 616. Tarā'dīhi iṇṇo.
582, 631. Bhidā'dito inna, anna, īṇā vā.
583, 617. Susa, paca, sakato kkha, kkā ca.
584, 618. Pakkamā'dīhi nto ca.
585, 619. Janā'dīna'mā timhi ca.
586, 600. Gama, khana, hana, ramā'dīna'manto.
587, 632. Rakāro ca.
588, 620. Ṭhā, pāna'mi-ī ca.
589, 621. Ha'ntehi ho hassa ḷo vā adaha, nahānaṁ.

Iti kibbidhānakappe tatiyo kaṇḍo.

590, 579. Ṇamhi ranjassa jo bhāva, karaṇesu.
591, 544. Hanassa ghāto.
592, 503. Vadho vā sabbattha.
593, 564. Ākārantāna'māyo.
594, 582. Pura, sa'mupaparīhi karotissa kha, kharā vā tappaccayesu ca.
595, 637. Tave, tunā'dīsu kā.
596, 551. Gama, khana, hanā'dīnaṁ tuṁ, tabbā'dīsu na.
597, 641. Sabbehi tunā'dīnaṁ yo.
598, 643. Ca, na'ntehi raccaṁ.
599, 644. Disā svāna, svā'ntalopo ca.
600, 645. Ma, ha, da, bhehi mma, yha, jja, bbha, ddhā ca.
601, 334. Taddhita, samāsa, kitakā nāmaṁ'vā'tavetunā'dīsu ca.
602, 6. Dumhi garu.
603, 7. Dīgho ca.
604, 684. Akkharehi kāra.
605, 547. Yathā'gama'mikāro.
606, 642. Da, dha'ntato yo kvaci.

Iti kibbidhānakappe catuttho kaṇḍo.

607, 578. Niggahita saṁyogā'di no.
608, 623. Sabbattha ge gī.
609, 484. Sadassa sīdatthaṁ.
610, 627. Yajassa sarassi'ṭṭhe.
611, 608. Ha, catutthṁna'mantānaṁ do dhe.
612, 615. Ḍo ḍhakāre.
613, 583. Gahassa ghara ṇe vā.
614, 581. Dahassa do ḷaṁ.
615, 586. Dhātva'ntassa lopo kvimhi.
616, 587. Vidante Ū.
617, 633. Na, ma, ka, rāna'mantānaṁ ni'yuttatamhi.
618, 571. Na, ka, gatthaṁ cajā ṇvumhi.
619, 573. Karassa ca tattaṁ tusmiṁ.
620, 549. Tuṁ, tuna, tabbesu vā.
621, 553. Kāritaṁ viya ṇā'nubandho.
622, 570. Ana'kā yu ṇvūnaṁ.
623, 554. Ka, gā ca, jānaṁ.

Iti kibbidhānakappe pañcamo kaṇḍo.

Kibbidhānasuttaṁ niṭṭhitaṁ.

8. Uṇādikappa

(Nouns in Uṇādi-Affixes)

624, 563. Kattari kitā.
625, 605. Bhāva,kammesu kicca,kta,kkha'tthā.
626, 634. Kammani dutiyāyaṁ kto.
627, 652. Khyā'dīhi man ma ca to vā.
628, 653. Samā'dīhi tha, mā.
629, 569. Gahassu'padhasse'vā.
630, 654. Masussa sussa, cchara, ccherā.
631, 655. Āpubbacarassa ca.
632, 656. Ala, kala, salehi la, yā.
633, 657. Yāṇa, lāṇā.

634, 658. Mathissa thassa lo ca.
635, 559. Pesā'tisagga, pattakālesu kiccā.
636, 659. Avassakā'dhamiṇesu ṇī ca.
637,... Araha, sakkā'dīhi tuṁ.
638, 668. Vajā'dīhi pabbajjā'dayo nippajjante.
639, 585. Kvi lopo ca.
640,... Sa, ca, jānaṁ ka, gā ṇā'nubandhe.
641, 572. Nudā'dīhi yu ṇvūna'manā'nanā'kā'nanakā sakāritehi ca.
642, 588. I, ya, ta, ma, kiṁ, esāna'mantassaro dīghaṁ kvaci disassa guṇaṁ do raṁ sa, kkhī'ca.
643, 635. Bhyā'dīhi mati, budhi, pūjādī'hi ca kto.
644, 661. Vepu, sī, dava, vamu, ku, dā, bhū, hvā'dīhi thu, ttima, ṇimā nibbatte.
645, 662. Akkose na'mhā'ni.
646, 419. Ekā'dito sakissa kkhattuṁ.
647, 663. Sunassu'nasso'ṇa, vānu, vānū'nū'nakhu'nā'nā.
648, 664. Taruṇassa susu ca.
649, 665. Yuvassu'vassu'vu'vānu'nū'nā.
650, 651. Kāle vattamānā'tīte ṇvā'dayo.
651, 647. Bhavissati gamā'dīhi ṇī, ghiṇ.
652, 648. Kriyāyaṁ ṇvu, tavo.
653, 306. Bhāva vācimhi catutthī.
654, 649. Kammani ṇo.
655, 650. Sese ssaṁ, ntu, mānā'nā.
656, 666. Chadā'dīhi ta, traṇ.
657, 667. Vadā'dīhi ṇitto gaṇe.
658, 668. Midā'dīhi tti, tiyo.
659, 669. Usu, ranja, daṁsānaṁ, daṁsassa daḍho ḍha, ṭhā ca.
660, 670. Sū, vu'sāna'mū'vusāna'mato tho ca.
661, 671. Ranju'dā'dīhi dha, di'dda, ki'rā kvaci jadalopo ca.
662, 672. Paṭito hissa heraṇ hīraṇ.
663, 673. Kaḍhyā'dīhi ko.
664, 674. Khādā'ma, gamānaṁ khandha'ndha, gandhā.
665, 675. Paṭā'dīhya'laṁ.

666, 676. Puthassa puthu, pathā'mo vā.
667, 677. Sasvā'dīhi tu, davo.
668, 678. Cayā'dīhi īvaro.
669, 679. Munā'dīhi ci'.
670, 680. Vidā'dīhyū'ro.
671, 681. Hanā'dīhi nu, ṇu, tavo.
672, 682. Kuṭā'dīhi ṭho.
673, 683. Manu, pūra, suṇā'dīhi ussa, nusi'sā.

Iti kibbidhānakappe uṇādikappo chaṭṭho kaṇḍo.

Uṇādisuttaṁ niṭṭhitaṁ.

सुत्तक्कम

१. सन्धि

१, १. अत्थो अक्खरसञ्ञातो
२, २. अक्खरापादयो एकचत्तालिसं
३, ३ तत्थोदन्ता सरा अट्ठ
४, ४. लहुमत्ता तयो रस्सा
५, ५. अञ्ञे दीघा
६, ८. सेसा ब्यञ्जना
७, ९. वग्गा पञ्चपञ्चसो मन्ता
८, १०.अंइति निग्गहितं
९, ११.परसमञ्ञा पयोगे
१०, १२. पुब्ब मधोठितमस्सरं सरेन वियोजये
११, १४. नये परं युत्ते

इति सन्धिकप्पे पठमो कण्डो

१२, १३. सरा सरे लोपं
१३, १५. वा परो असरूपा
१४, १६. क्वचासवण्णं लुत्ते
१५, १७. दीघं
१६, १८. पुब्बो च
१७, १९. य मेदन्तस्सादेसो
१८, २०. व मोदुदन्तानं
१९. २२. सब्बो चं ति
२०, २७. दो धस्स च
२१, २१. इवण्णो यं नवा
२२, २८. एवादिस्स रि पुब्बो च रस्सो

इति सन्धिकप्पे दुतियो कण्डो

२३, ३६. सरा पकति ब्यञ्जने
२४, ३५. सरे क्वचि
२५, ३७. दीघं

२६, ३८. रस्सं
२७, ३९. लोपञ्च तत्राकारो
२८, ४०. पर द्वेभावो ठाने
२९, ४२. वग्गे घोसाघोसानं ततियपठमा

इति सन्धिकप्पे ततियो कण्डो

३०, ५८. अं ब्यञ्जने निग्गहितं
३१. ४९. वग्गन्तं वा वग्गे
३२, ५०. एहे ञं
३३. ५१. स ये च
३४, ५२. मदा सरे
३५, ३४. य व म द न त र ला चागमा
३६, ४७. क्वचि ओ ब्यञ्जने
३७, ५७. निग्गहितञ्च
३८, ५३. क्वचि लोपं
३९, ५४. ब्यञ्जने च
४०, ५५. परो वा सरो
४१, ५६. ब्यञ्जनो च विसञ्ञोगो

इति सन्धिकप्पे चतुत्थो कण्डो

४२, ३२. गो सरे पुथस्सागमो क्वचि
४३, ३३. पास्स चन्तो रस्सो
४४, २४ अब्भो अभि
४५, २५. अज्झो अधि
४६, २६. ते न वा इवण्णे
४७, २३. अतिस्स चन्तस्स
४८, ४३. क्वचि पटि पतिस्स
४९, ४४. पुथस्सु ब्यञ्जने
५०, ४५. ओ अवस्स
५१, ५९. अनुपदिट्ठानं वुत्तयोगतो

इति सन्धिकप्पे पञ्चमो कण्डो
सन्धिसुत्तं निट्ठितं।

२. नाम

५२, ६०. जिनवचनयुत्तं हि
५३, ६१. लिङ्गञ्च निप्पज्जते
५४, ६२. ततो च विभत्तियो
५५, ६३. सि यो, अं यो, ना हि, स नं, स्मा हि, स नं, स्मिं सु
५६, ६४. तदनुपरोधेन
५७, ७१. आलपने सि गसञ्ञो
५८, २९. इवण्णुवण्णा झला
५९, १८२. ते इत्थिख्या पो
६०, १७७. आ घो
६१, ८६. सागमो से
६२, २०६. संसास्वेकवचनेसु च
६३, २१७. एतिमास मि
६४, २१६. तस्सा वा।
६५, २१५. ततो सस्स स्साय।
६६, २०५. घो रस्सं
६७, २२९. नो च द्वादितो नंम्हि
६८, १८४. अमा पतो स्मिंस्मानं वा
६९, १८६. आदितो ओ च
७०, ३०. झलान मियुवा सरे वा
७१, ५०५. यवकारा च
७२, १८५. पसञ्ञस्स च
७३, १७४. गाव से
७४, १६९. योसु च
७५, १७०. अवंम्हि च
७६, १७१. आवस्सु वा
७७, १७५, ततो नमं पतिम्हालुत्ते च समासे
७८, ३१. ओ सरे च
७९, ४६. तब्बिपरीतूपपदे ब्यञ्जने च
८०, १७३. गोण नंम्हि वा
८१, १७२. सुहिनासु च
८२, १४९. अंमो निग्गहितं झलपेहि
८३, ६७. सरलोपो मादेसपच्चयादिम्हि सरलोपे तु पकति

८४, १४४. अघो रस्समेकवचनयोस्वपि च
८५, १५०. न सिस्मि मनपुंसकानि
८६, २२७. उभादितो नमिन्नं
८७, २३१. इण्णमिण्णन्नं तीहि सङ्ख्याहि
८८, १४७. योसु कतनिकारलोपेसु दीघं
८९, ८७. सुनंहिसु च
९०, २५२. पञ्चादीन मत्तं
९१, १९४. पतिस्सिनीम्हि
९२, १००. न्तुस्सन्तो योसु च
९३, १०६. सब्बस्स वा अंसेसु
९४, १०५. सिम्हि वा
९५, १४५. अग्गिस्सिनि
९६, १४८. योस्वकतरस्सो झो
९७, १५६. वेवोसु लो च
९८, १८९. मातुलादीन मानत्त मीकारे
९९, ८१. स्माहिस्मिंनं म्हाभिम्हि वा
१००, २१४. न तिमेहि कताकारेहि
१०१, ८०. सुहिस्वकारो ए
१०२, २०२. सब्बनामानं नंम्हि च
१०३, ७९. अतो नेन
१०४, ६६. सो
१०५, ०. सो वा
१०६, ३१३. दीघोरेहि
१०७, ६९. सब्बयोनीन माए
१०८, ९०. स्मास्मिंनं वा
१०९, ३०४. आय चतुत्थेकवचनस्स तु
११०, २०१. तयो नेव च सब्बनामेहि
१११, १७९. घतो नादीनं
११२, १८३. पतो या
११३, १३२. सखतो गस्से वा
११४, १७८. घते च
११५, १८१. न अम्मादितो
११६, १५७. अकतरस्सा लतो य्वालपनस्स वेवो
११७, १२४. झलतो सस्स नो वा

११८, १४६. घपतो च योनं लोपो
११९, १५५. लतो वोकारो च

इति नामकप्पे पठमो कण्डो

१२०, २४३. अम्हस्स ममं सविभत्तिस्स से
१२१, २३३. मयं योम्हि पठमे
१२२, ९९. न्तुस्स न्तो
१२३, १०३. न्तस्स से वा
१२४, ९८. आ सिम्हि
१२५, १९८. अं नपुंसके
१२६, १०१. अवण्णा च गे
१२७, १०२. तो तिता सस्मिंनासु
१२८, १०४. नंम्हि तं वा
१२९, २२२. इमस्सिद मंसिसु नपुंसके
१३०, २२५. अमुस्सादुं
१३१, ०. इत्थिपुमनपुंसकसङ्ख्यं
१३२, २२८. योसु द्विन्नं द्वे च
१३३, २३०. तिचतुन्नं तिस्सो,चतस्सो,तयो,चत्तारो,तीणि,चत्तारि
१३४, २५१. पञ्चादीन मकारो
१३५, ११८. राजस्स रञ्ञो,राजिनो से
१३६, ११९. रञ्ञं नंम्हि वा
१३७, ११६. नाम्हि रञ्ञा वा
१३८, १२१. स्मिंम्हि रञ्ञे राजिनि
१३९, २४५. तुम्हम्हाकं तयि मयि
१४०, २३२. त्वमहं सिम्हि च
१४१, २४१. तव मम से
१४२, २४२. तुय्हं मय्हञ्च
१४३, २३५. तंममंम्हि
१४४, २३४. तवंममञ्च न वा
१४५, २३८. नाम्हि तया मया
१४६, २३६. तुम्हस्स तुवंत्वमम्हि
१४७, २४६. पदतो दुतियाचतुत्थीछट्ठीसु वो नो
१४८, २४७. तेमेकवचनेसु च
१४९, २४८. न अंम्हि

१५०, २४९. वा ततिये च
१५१, २५०. बहुवचनेसु वो नो
१५२, १३६. पुमन्तस्सा सिम्हि
१५३, १३८. अमालपनेकवचने
१५४, ०. समासे च विभासा
१५५, १३७. योस्वानो
१५६, १४२. आने स्मिंम्हि वा
१५७, १४०. हिविभत्तिम्हि च
१५१, १४३. सुस्मि मा वा
१५९, १३९. उ नाम्हि च
१६०, १९७. अकम्मन्तस्स च

इति नामकप्पे दुतियो कण्डो

१६१, २४४. तुम्हम्हेहि नमाकं
१६२, २३७. वा य्वप्पठमो
१६३, २४०. सस्सं
१६४, २००. सब्बनामकारते पठमो
१६५, २०८. द्वन्दट्ठा वा
१६६, २०९. नाञ्ञं सब्बनामिकं
१६७, २१०. बहुब्बीहिम्हि च
१६८, २०३. सब्बतो नं संसानं
१६९, ११७. राजस्स राजु सुनंहिसु च
१७०, २२०. सब्बस्सिमस्से वा
१७१, २१९. अनिमि नाम्हि च
१७२, २१८. अनपुंसकस्सा यं स्मिम्हि
१७३, २२३. अमुस्स मो सं
१७४, २११. एततेसं सो
१७५, २१२. तस्स वा नत्तं सब्बत्थ
१७६, २१३. सस्मास्मिंसंसास्वत्तं
१७७, २२१. इमसद्दस्स च
१७८, २२४. सब्बतो को
१७९, २०४. घपतो स्मिं सानं संसा
१८०, २०७. नेताहि स्मि मायया
१८१, ९५. मनोगणादितो स्मिंनान मिआ

१८२, ९७. सस्स चो
१८३, ४८. एतेस मो लोपे
१८४, ९६. स सरे वागमो
१८५, ११२. सन्तसद्दस्स सो भे बो चन्ते
१८६, १०७. सिम्हि गच्छन्तादीनं न्तसद्दो अं
१८७, १०८. सेसेसु न्तुव
१८८, ११५. ब्रह्मत्त सख राजादितो अमानं
१८९, ११३. स्या च
१९०, ११४. योन मानो
१९१, १३०. सखतो चायो नो
१९२, १३५. स्मि मे
१९३, १२२. ब्रह्मतो गस्स च
१९४, १३१. सखन्तस्सि नोनानंसेसु
१९५, १३४. आरो हिम्हि वा
१९६, १३३. सुनमंसु वा
१९७, १२५. ब्रह्मतो तु स्मिंनि
१९८, १२३. उत्तं सनासु
१९९, १५८. सत्थुपितादीन मा सिस्मिं सिलोपो च
२००, १५९. अञ्ञेस्वारत्तं
२०१, १६३. वा नंम्हि
२०२. १६४. सत्थुनत्तञ्च
२०३, १६२. उ सस्मिं सलोपो च
२०४, १६७. सक्कमन्धातादीनञ्च
२०५, १६०. ततो योनमो तु
२०६, १६५. ततो स्मिमि
२०७, १६१. ना आ
२०७, १६६. आरो रस्समिकारे
२०९, १६८. पितादीन मसिम्हि
२१०, २३९. तयातयीनं तकारो त्वत्तं वा

इति नामकप्पे ततियो कण्डो

२११, १२६. अत्तन्तो हिस्मि मनत्तं
२१२, १२९. ततो स्मिं नि
२१३, १२७. सस्स नो
२१४, १२८. स्मा ना
२१५, १४१. झलतो च
२१६, १८०. घपतो स्मिं यं वा
२१७, १९९. योनं नि नपुंसकेहि
२१८, १९६. अतो निच्चं
२१९, १९५. सिं
२२०, ७४. सेसतो लोपं गसिपि
२२१, २८२. सब्बास मावुसो पसग्गनिपातादीहि च
२२२, ३४३. पुमस्स लिङ्गादीसु समासेसु
२२३, १८८. अं यमीतो पसञ्ञतो
२२४, १५३. नं झतो कतरस्सा
२२५, १५१. योनं नो
२२६, १५४. स्मिं नि
२२७, २७०. किस्स क वे च
२२८, २७२. कु हिं हंसु च
२२९, २२६. सेसेसु च
२३०, २६२. त्र तो थेसु च
२३१, २६३. सब्बस्सेतस्साकारो वा
२३२, २६७. त्रे निच्चं
२३३, २६४. ए तोथेसु च
२३४, २६५. इमस्सि थं दानि ह तो धेसु च
२३५, २८१. अ धुनाम्हि च
२३६, २८०. एत रहिम्हि
२३७, १७६. इत्थिय मतो आपच्चयो
२३८, १८७. नदादितो वा ई
२३९, १९०. णव णिक णेय्य णन्तुहि
२४०, १९३. पतिभिक्खुराजीकारन्तेहि इनी
२४१, १९१. न्तुस्स त मीकारे
२४२, १९२. भवतो भोतो
२४३, ११०. भो गे तु
२४४, ७२. अकारपिताद्यन्तान मा

२४५, १५२. झलपा रस्सं
२४६, ७३. आकारो वा

इति नामकप्पे चतुत्थो कण्डो

२४७, २६१. त्वादयो विभत्तिसञ्ञायो
२४८, २६०. क्वचि तो पञ्चम्यत्थे
२४९, २६६. त्रथ सत्तमिया सब्बनामेहि
२५०, २६८. सब्बतो धि
२५१, २६९. किंस्मा वो
२५२, २७१. हिंहंहिञ्चनं
२५३, २७३. तम्हा च
२५४, २७४. इमस्मा हधा च
२५५, २७५. यतो हिं
२५६, ०. काले
२५७, २७६. किंसब्बञ्ञेकयकुहि दादाचनं
२५८, २७८. तम्हा दानि च
२५९, २७९. इमस्मा रहिधुनादानि च
२६०, २७७. सब्बस्स सो दाम्हि वा
२६१, ३६९. अवण्णो ये लोपञ्च
२६२, ३९१. वुड्ढस्स जो इयिट्ठेसु
२६३, ३९२. पसत्थस्स सो च
२६४, ३९३. अन्तिकस्स नेदो
२६५, ३९४. बाळ्हस्स साधो
२६६, ३९५. अप्पस्स कण
२६७, ३९६. युवानञ्च
२६८, ३९७. वन्तुमन्तुवीनञ्च लोपो
२६९, ४१. यवतं तलणदकारानं ब्यञ्जनानि चलञजकारत्तं
२७०, १२०. अम्ह तुम्ह न्तु राज ब्रह्मत्त सख सत्थु पितादीहि स्मा नाव

इति नामकप्पे पञ्चमो कण्डो।
नामसुत्तं निट्ठितं।

३. कारक

२७१, ३०८. यस्मा दपेतिं भयमादत्ते वा तदपादानं
२७२, ३०९. धातुनामान मुपसग्गयोगादीस्वपि च
२७३, ३१०. रक्खणत्थान मिच्छितं
२७४, ३११. येन वा दस्सनं
२७५, ३१२.दूरन्तिकद्धकाल निम्मान त्वालोप दिसायोग विभत्तारप्पयोग सुद्धप्पमोचन हेतु विवित्तप्पमाण पुब्बयोग बन्धन गुणवचन पञ्ह कथन थोकाकत्तूसु च
२७६, ३०२. यस्स दातुकामो रोचते धारयते वा तं सम्पदानं
२७७, ३०३. सिलाघ हनु ठा सप धार पिह कुधदुहिस्सोस्सूय राधिक्खपच्चासुण अनुपतिगिण पुब्बकत्तारोचनत्थ तदत्थ तुमत्थालमत्थ मञ्ञा नादरप्पाणिनि गत्यत्थकम्मनि आसिसत्थसम्मुति भिय्य सत्तम्यत्थेसु च
२७८, ३२०. योधारो तमोकासं
२७९, २९२. येन वा कयिरते तं करणं
२८०, २८५, यं करोति तं कम्मं
२८१, २९४. यो करोति स कत्ता
२८२, २९५. यो कारेति स हेतु
२८३, ३१६. यस्स वा परिग्गहो तं सामी
२८४, २८३. लिङ्गत्थे पठमा
२८५, ७०. आलपने च
२८६, २९१. करणे ततिया
२८७, २९६, सहादियोगे च
२८८, २९३. कत्तरि च
२८९, २९७. हेत्वत्थे च
२९०, २९८. सत्तम्यत्थे च
२९१, २९९. येनङ्गविकारो
२९२, ३००. विसेसने च
२९३, ३०१. सम्पदाने चतुत्थी
२९४, ३०५. नमोयोगादीस्वपि च
२९५, ३०७. अपादाने पञ्चमी
२९६, ३१४. कारणत्थे च
२९७, २८४. कम्मत्थे दुतिया

२९८. २८७. कालद्धान मच्चन्तसंयोगे
२९९, २८८. कम्मप्पवचनीययुत्ते
३००, २८६. गति बुद्धि भुज पठ हर कर सयादीनं कारिते वा
३०१, ३१५. सामिस्मि छट्ठी
३०२, ३१९. ओकासे सत्तमी
३०३, ३२१. सामिस्सराधिपति दायाद सक्खी पतिभू पसुत कुसलेहि च
३०४, ३२२. निद्धारणे च
३०५, ३२३. अनादरे च
३०६, २८९. क्वचि दुतिया छट्ठीन मत्थे
३०७, २९०. ततियासत्तमीनञ्च
३०८, ३१७. छट्ठी च
३०९, ३१८. दुतियापञ्चमीनञ्च
३१०, ३२४. कम्मकरणनिमित्तत्थेसु सत्तमी
३११, ३२५. सम्पदाने च
३१२, ३२६. पञ्चम्यत्थे च
३१३, ३२७. कालभावेसु च
३१४, ३२८. उप'ध्याधिकिस्सरवचने
३१५, ३२९. मण्डितुस्सुक्केसु ततिया च

इति नामकप्पे कारककप्पो छट्ठो कण्डो
कारकसुत्तं निट्ठितं।

४. समास

३१६, ३३१. नामानं समासो युत्तत्थो
३१७, ३३२. तेसं विभत्तियो लोपा च
३१८, ३३३. पकति चस्स सरन्तस्स
३१९, ३३०. उपसग्गनिपातपुब्बको अब्ययीभावो
३२०, ३३५. सो नपुंसकलिङ्गो
३२१. ३४९. दिगुस्सेकत्तं
३२२, ३५९. तथा द्वन्दे पाणि तूरिय योग्ग सेनङ्ग खुद्दजन्तुक विविधविरुद्ध विसभागत्थादीनञ्च
३२३, ३६०. विभासा रुक्ख तिण पसु धन धञ्ञ जनपदादीनञ्च
३२४, ३३९. द्विपदे तुल्याधिकरणे कम्मधारयो

३२५, ३४८. सङ्ख्यापुब्बो दिगु
३२६, ३४१. उभे तप्पुरिसा
३२७, ३५१. अमादयो परपदेभि
३२८, ३५२. अञ्ञपदत्थेसु बहुब्बीहि
३२९, ३५७. नामानं समुच्चयो द्वन्दो
३३०, ३४०. महतं महा तुल्याधिकरणे पदे
३३१, ३५३. इत्थियं भासितपुमित्थी पुमाव चे
३३२, ३४३. कम्मधारयसञ्ञे च
३३३, ३४४. अत्तं नस्स तप्पुरिसे
३३४, ३४५. सरे अन
३३५, ३४६. कद कुस्स
३३६, ३४७. का’प्पत्थेसु च
३३७, ३५०. क्वचि समासन्त गतान मकारन्तो
३३८, ३५६. नदिम्हा च
३३९, ३५८. जायाय तु दं जानि पतिम्हि
३४०, ३५५. धनुम्हा च
३४१, ३३६. अंविभत्तीनमकारन्ता अब्ययीभावा
३४२, ३३७. सरो रस्सो नपुंसके
३४३, ३३८. अञ्ञस्मा लोपो च

इति नामकप्पे समासकप्पो सत्तमो कण्डो
समाससुत्तं निट्ठितं

५. तद्धित

२४४, ३६१. वा णा’पच्चे
३४५, ३६६. णायन णान वच्छादितो
३४६, ३६७. णेय्यो कत्तिकादीहि
३४७, ३६८. अतो णि वा
३४८, ३७१. णवोपक्वादीहि
३४९, ३७२. णेर विधवादितो
३५०, ३७३. येन वा संसट्ठं तरति चरति वहति णिको
३५१, ३७४. तमधीते तेनकतादि सन्निधाननियोग सिप्प भण्ड जीविकत्थेसु च
३५२, ३७६. ण रागा तस्सेद मञ्ञत्थेसु च

३५३, ३७८. जातादीन मिमिया च
३५४, ३७९. समूहत्थे कण णा
३५५, ३८०. गाम जन बन्धु सहायादीहि ता
३५६, ३८१. तदस्स ठान मियो च
३५७, ३८२. उपमत्थायितत्तं
३५८, ३८३. तन्निस्सितत्थे लो
३५९, ३८४. आलु तब्बहुले
३६०, ३८७. ण्य,त्त,ता भावे तु
३६१, ३८८. ण विसमादीहि
३६२, ३८९. रमणीयादितो कण
३६३, ३९०. विसेसे तरतमिसिकियिट्ठा
३६४, ३९८. तदस्सत्थीति वी च
३६५, ३९९. तपादितो सी
३६६, ४००. दण्डादितो इक ई
३६७, ४०१. मध्वादितो रो
३६८, ४०२. गुणादितो वन्तु
३६९, ४०३. सत्यादीहि मन्तु
३७०, ४०५. सद्धादितो ण
३७१, ४०४. आयुस्सुकारास मन्तुम्हि
३७२, ३८५. तप्पकतिवचने मयो
३७३, ४०६. सङ्ख्यापूरणे मो
३७४, ४०८. स छस्स वा
३७५, ४१२. एकादितो दसस्सी
३७६, २५७. दसे सो निच्चञ्च
३७७, ०. अन्ते निग्गहितञ्च
३७८, ४१४. ति च
३७९, २५८. ल द,रानं
३८०, २५५. वीसति दसेसु बा द्विस्स तु
३८१, २५४. एकादितो दस्स र सङ्ख्याने
३८२, २५९. अट्ठादितो च
३८३, २५३. द्वेकट्ठान माकारो वा
३८४, ४०७. चतुच्छेहि थ ठा
३८५, ४०९. द्वितीहि तियो
३८६, ४१०. तिये दु,तापि च

३८७, ४११. तेस'मड्ढूपपदेन अड्ढुड्ढ,दिवड्ढ,दियड्ढ' ड्ढतिया
३८८, ६८. सरूपान'मेकसेस्वसकिं
३८९, ४१३. गणने दसस्स द्वितिचतुपञ्चछसत्तअट्ठनवकानं वीतिचत्तार पञ्ञाछसत्तासनवा योसु योनञ्चीसमासंठिरितीतुति
३९०, २५६. चतूपपदस्स लोपो तु'त्तरपदादिचस्स चु चोपि नवा
३९१, ४२३. यदनुपपन्ना निपातना सिज्झन्ति
३९२, ४१८. द्वादितो को'नेकत्थे च
३९३, ४१५. दसदसकं सतं दसकानं सतं सहस्सञ्च योम्हि
३९४, ४१६. याव तदुत्तरि दसगुणितञ्च
३९५, ४१७. सकनामेहि
३९६, ३६३. तेसं णो लोपं
३९७, ४२०. विभागे धा च
३९८, ४२१. सब्बनामेहि पकारवचने तु था
३९९, ४२२. किमिमेहि थं
४००, ३६४. वुद्धादिसरस्स वा'संयोगन्तस्स सणे च
४०१, ३७५. मा यून मागमो ठाने
४०२. ३७७. आत्तञ्च
४०३, ३५४. क्वचादिमज्झुत्तरानं दीघरस्सा पच्चयेसु च
४०४, ३७०. तेसु वुद्धि लोपागम विकार विपरितादेसा च
४०५, ३६५. अयुवण्णानञ्चायो वुद्धि

इति नामकप्पे तद्धितकप्पो अट्ठमो कण्डो

तद्धितसुत्तं निट्ठितं

६. आख्यात

४०६, ४२९. अथ पुब्बानि विभत्तीनं छ परस्सपदानि
४०७, ४३९. पराणुत्तनोपदानि
४०८, ४३१. द्वे द्वे पठममज्झिमुत्तमपुरिसा
४०९, ४४१. सब्बेसमेकाभिधाने परो पुरिसो
४१०, ४३२. नामम्हि पयुज्जमानेपि तुल्याधिकरणे पठमो
४११, ४३६. तुम्हे मज्झिमो
४१२, ४३७. अम्हे उत्तमो

४१३, ४२७. काले
४१४, ४२८. वत्तमाना पच्चुप्पन्ने
४१५, ४५१. आणत्यासिट्ठे'नुत्तकाले पञ्चमी
४१६, ४५४. अनुमतिपरिकप्पत्थेसु सत्तमी
४१७, ४६०. अपच्चक्खे परोक्खा'तीते
४१८, ४५६. हिय्योपभुति पच्चक्खे हिय्यत्तनी
४१९, ४६९. समीपे'ज्जतनी
४२०, ४७१. मायोगे सब्बकाले च
४२१, ४७३. अनागते भविस्सन्ती
४२२, ४७५. क्रियातिपन्ने'तीते कालातिपत्ति
४२३, ४२६. वत्तमाना ती अन्ति, सि थ, मि म, ते अन्ते, से व्हे, ए म्हे
४२४, ४५०. पञ्चमी तु अन्तु, हि थ, मि म, तं अन्तं, स्सु व्हो, ए आमसे
४२५, ४५३. सत्तमी एय्य एय्युं, एय्यासि एय्याथ, एय्यामि एय्याम, एथ एरं, एथो एय्याव्हो, एय्यं एय्याम्हे
४२६, ४५९. परोक्खा अ उ, ए त्थ, अं म्ह, त्थ रे, त्थो व्हो, इं म्हे
४२७, ४५५. हिय्यत्तनी आ ऊ, ओ त्थ, अं म्हा, त्थ त्थुं, से व्हं, इं म्हसे
४२७, ४६८. अज्जतनी ई उं, ओत्थ, इं म्हा, आ ऊ, से व्हं, अं म्हे
४२९, ४७२. भविस्सन्ती स्सति स्सन्ति, स्ससि स्सथ, स्सामि स्साम, स्सते स्सन्ते, स्ससे स्सव्हे, स्सं स्साम्हे
४३०, ४७४. कालातिपत्ति स्सा स्संसु, स्से स्सथ, स्सं स्साम्हा, स्सथ स्सिंसु, स्ससे स्सव्हे, स्सं स्साम्हसे
४३१, ४५८. हिय्यत्तनी सत्तमी पञ्चमी वत्तमाना सब्बधातुकं

इति आख्यातकप्पे पठमो कण्डो

४३२, ३६२. धातुलिङ्गेहि परा पच्चया
४३३, ५२८. तिजगुपकितमानेहि खछसा वा
४३४, ५३४. भुजघसहरसुपादीहि तुमिच्छत्थेसु
४३५, ५३६. आय नामतो कत्तूपमाना दाचारे
४३६, ५३७. ईयू'पमाना च
४३७, ५३८. नामम्हा'त्तिच्छत्थे
४३८, ५४०. धातूहि णे णय णापे णापया कारितानि हेत्वत्थे
४३९, ५३९. धातुरूपे नामस्मा णयो च
४४०, ४४५. भावकम्मेसु यो
४४१, ४४७. तस्स चवग्गयकारवकारत्तं सधात्वन्तस्स

४४२, ४४८. इवण्णागमो वा
४४३, ४४९. पुब्बरूपञ्च
४४४, ५११. तथा कत्तरि च
४४५, ४३३. भूवादितो अ
४४६, ५०९. रुधादितो निग्गहितपुब्बञ्च
४४७, ५१०. दिवादितो यो
४४८, ५१२. स्वादितो णुणा उणा च
४४९, ५१३. कीयादितो ना
४५०, ५१७. गहादितो प्प,ण्हा
४५१, ५२०. तनादितो ओयिरा
४५२, ५२५. चुरादितो णे णया
४५३, ४४४. अत्तनोपदानि भावे च कम्मनि
४५४, ४४०. कत्तरि च
४५५, ५३०. धातुप्पच्चयेहि विभत्तियो
४५६, ४३०. कत्तरि परस्सपदं
४५७, ४२४. भूवादयो धातवो

इति आख्यातकप्पे दुतियो कण्डो

४५८, ४६१. क्वचादिवण्णानमेकस्सरानं द्वेभावो
४५९, ४६२. पुब्बो' ब्भासो
४६०, ५०६. रस्सो
४६१, ४६४. दुतियचतुत्थानं पठमततिया
४६२, ४६७. कवग्गस्स चवग्गो
४६३, ५३२. मानकितानं वतत्तं वा
४६४, ५०४. हस्स जो
४६५, ४६३. अन्तस्सिवण्णाकारो वा
४६६, ४८९. निग्गहितञ्च
४६७, ५३३. ततो पामानानं वामं सेसु
४६८, ४९२. ठा तिट्ठो
४६९, ४९४. पा पिवो
४७०, ५१४. ञास्स जाजंना
४७१, ४८३. दिसस्स पस्स दिस्स दक्खा वा
४७२, ५३१. ब्यञ्जनन्तस्स चो छप्पच्चयेसु च
४७३, ५२९. को खे च

४७४, ५३५. हरस्स गी से
४७५, ४६५. ब्रूभून माहभूवा परोक्खायं
४७६, ४४२. गमिस्सन्तो च्छो वा सब्बासु
४७७, ४७९. वचस्स'ज्जतनिम्हि मकारो ओ
४७८, ४३८. अकारो दीघं हिमिमेसु
४७९, ४५२. हि लोपं वा
४८०, ४९०. होतिस्सरे' हो'हे भविस्सन्तिम्हि सस्स च
४८१, ५२४. करस्स सप्पच्चयस्स काहो

इति आख्यातकप्पे ततियो कण्डो

४८२, ५०८. दादन्तस्सं मिमेसु
४८३, ५२७. असंयोगन्तस्स वुद्धि कारिते
४८४, ५४२. घटादीनं वा
४८५, ४३४. अञ्ञेसु च
४८६, ५४३. गुहदुसानं दीघं
४८७, ४७८. वच वस वहादीन मुकारो वस्स ये
४८८, ४८१. ह विपरियियो लो वा
४८९, ५१९. गहस्स घे प्पे
४९०, ५१८. हलोपो ण्हाम्हि
४९१, ५२३. करस्स कासत्त मज्जतनिम्हि
४९२, ४९९. असस्मा मिमानं मिम्हा'न्तलोपो च
४९३, ४९८. थस्स त्थत्तं
४९४, ४९५. तिस्स त्थित्तं
४९५, ५००. तुस्स त्थुत्तं
४९६, ४९७. सिम्हि च
४९७, ४७७. लभस्मा ईइंनं त्थ,त्थं
४९८, ४८०. कुसस्मा दी च्छि
४९९, ५०७. दाधातुस्स दज्जं
५००, ४८६. वदस्स वज्जं
५०१, ४४३. गमिस्स घम्मं
५०२, ४९३. यम्हि दा धा मा ठा हा पा मह मथादीन मी
५०३, ४८५. यजस्सादिस्सि
५०४, ४७०. सब्बतो उं इंसु
५०५, ४८२. जरमरानं जीर जीय्य मीय्या वा

५०६, ४९६. सब्बत्था'सस्सादिलोपो च
५०७, ५०१. असब्बधातुके भू
५०८, ५१५. एय्यस्स ञातो इया ञा
५०९, ५१६. नास्स लोपो यकारत्तं
५१०, ४८७. लोपञ्चेत्त मकारो
५११, ५२१. उत्त मोकारो
५१२, ५२२. करस्साकारो च
५१३, ४३५. ओ अव सरे
५१४, ४९१. ए अय
५१५, ५४१. ते आवाया कारिते
५१६, ४६६. इकारागमो असब्बधातुकम्हि
५१७, ४८८. क्वचि धातुविभत्तिप्पच्चयानं दीघविपरीतादेस लोपागमा च
५१८, ४४६. अत्तनोपदानि परस्सपदत्तं
५१९, ४५७. अकारागमो हिय्यत्तनी अज्जतनी कालातिपत्तीसु
५२०, ५०२. ब्रूतो ई तिम्हि
५२१, ४२५. धातुस्सन्तो लोपो' नेकसरस्स
५२२, ४७६. इसुयमून मन्तो च्छो वा
५२३, ५२६. कारितानं णो लोपं

इति आख्यातकप्पे चतुत्थो कण्डो
आख्यातसुत्तं निट्ठितं

७. किब्बिधान

५२४, ५६१. धातुया कम्मादिम्हि णो
५२५, ५६५. सञ्ञाय म नु
५२६, ५६७. पुरे ददा च इं
५२७, ५६८. सब्बतो ण्वुत्वा'वी वा
५२८, ५७७. विस रुज पदादितो ण
५२९, ५८०. भावे च
५३०, ५८४. क्वि च
५३१, ५८९. धरादीहि रम्मो
५३२, ५९०. तस्सीलादीसु णी त्वा वी च
५३३, ५९१. सद्द कुध चल मण्डत्थ रुचादीहि यु
५३४, ५९२. पारादिगमिम्हा रू

५३५, ५९३. भिक्खादितो च
५३६, ५९४. हनत्यादीनं णुको
५३७, ५६६. नु निग्गहितं पदन्ते
५३८, ५९५. संहना'ञ्ञाय वा रो घो
५३९, ५५८. रम्हि रन्तो रादि नो
५४०, ५४५. भावकम्मेसु तब्बा'नीया
५४१, ५५२. ण्यो च
५४२, ५५७. करम्हा रिच्च
५४३, ५५५. भूतो'ब्ब
५४४, ५५६. वद मद गमु युज गरहाकारादीहि ज्जम्मग्गय्हेय्यागारो वा
५४५, ५४८. ते किच्चा
५४६, ५६२. अञ्ञे कित
५४७, ५९६. नन्दादीहि यु
५४८, ५९७. कत्तुकरणपदेसेसु च
५४९, ५५०. रहादितो ण

इति किब्बिधानकप्पे पठमो कण्डो

५५०, ५४६. णादयो तेकालिका
५५१, ५९८. सञ्ञायं दाधातो इ
५५२, ६०९. ति किच्चा'सिट्ठे
५५३, ५९९. इत्थिय मतियवो वा
५५४, ६०१. करतो रिरिय
५५५, ६१२. अतीते त तवन्तु तावी
५५६, ६२२. भावकम्मेसु त
५५७, ६०६. बुधगमादित्थे कत्तरि
५५८, ६०२. जितो इन सब्बत्थ
५५९, ६०३. सुपतो च
५६०, ६०४. ईसंदुसूहि ख
५६१, ६३६. इच्छत्थेसु समानकत्तुकेसु तवे तुं वा
५६२, ६३८. अरहसक्कादीसु च
५६३, ६३९. पत्तवचने अलमत्थेसु च
५६४, ६४०. पुब्बकाले'ककत्तुकानं तुन त्वान त्वा वा
५६५, ६४६. वत्तमाने मान'न्ता
५६६, ५७४. सासादीहि रत्थु

५६७, ५७५. पातितो रितु
५६८, ५७६. मानादीहि रातु
५६९, ६१०. आगमा तुको
५७०, ६११. भब्बे इक

इति किब्बिधानकप्पे दुतियो कण्डो

५७१, ६२४. पच्चयादनिट्ठा निपातना सिज्झन्ति
५७२, ६२५. सासदिसतो तस्स रिट्ठो च
५७३, ६२६. सादि सन्तपुच्छभन्जहन्सादीहि ट्ठो
५७४, ६१३. वसतो उत्थ
५७५, ६१४. वस वावु
५७६, ६०७. धढभहेहि धढा च
५७७, ६२८. भन्जतो ग्गो च
५७८, ५६०. भुजादीनमन्तो नो द्वि च
५७९, ६२९. वच वा वु
५८०, ६३०. गुपादीनञ्च
५८१, ६१६. तरादीहि इण्णो
५८२, ६३१. भिदादितो इन्न अन्न ईणा वा
५८३, ६१७. सुसपचसकतो क्खक्का च
५८४, ६१८. पक्कमादीहि न्तो च
५८५, ६१९. जनादीन मा तिम्हि च
५८६, ६००. गम खन हन रमादीनमन्तो
५८७, ६३२. रकारो च
५८८,६२० ठापानमिई च
५८९, ६२१. हन्तेहि हो हस्स ळो वा अदहनहानं

इति किब्बिधानकप्पे ततियो कण्डो

५९०, ५७९. णम्हि रन्जस्स जो भावकरणेसु
५९१, ५४४. हनस्स घातो
५९२, ५०३. वधो वा सब्बत्थ
५९३, ५६४. आकारन्तानमायो
५९४, ५८२. पुरसमुपपरीहि करोतिस्स ख खरा वा तप्पच्चयेसु च
५९५, ६३७. तवेतुनादीसु का
५९६, ५५१. गमखनहनादीनं तुंतब्बादीसु न

५९७, ६४१. सब्बेहि तुनादीनं यो
५९८, ६४३. चनन्तेहि रच्चं
५९९, ६४४. दिसा स्वानस्वान्तलोपो च
६००, ६४५. महदभेहि म्म य्ह ज्ज ब्भ द्धा च
६०१, ३३४. तद्धितसमासकितका नामं वा'तवेतुनादीसु च
६०२, ६. दुम्हि गरु
६०३, ७. दीघो च
६०४, ६८४. अक्खरेहि कार
६०५, ५४७. यथागममिकारो
६०६, ६४२. दधन्ततो यो क्वचि

इति किब्बिधानकप्पे चतुत्थो कण्डो

६०७, ५७८. निग्गहित संयोगादि नो
६०८, ६२३. सब्बत्थ गे गी
६०९, ४८४. सदस्स सीदत्तं
६१०, ६२७. यजस्स सरस्सि ट्ठे
६११, ६०८. हचतुत्थानमन्तानं दो धे
६१२, ६१५. डो ढकारे
६१३, ५८३. गहस्स घर णे वा
६१४, ५८१. दहस्स दो ळं
६१५, ५८६. धात्वन्तस्स लोपो क्विम्हि
६१६, ५८७. विदन्ते ऊ
६१७, ६३३. न म क रानमन्तानं नियुत्ततम्हि
६१८, ५७१. न क गत्तं च जा ण्वुम्हि
६१९, ५७३. करस्स च तत्तं तुस्मिं
६२०, ५४९. तुंतुनतब्बेसु वा
६२१, ५५३. कारितं विय णानुबन्धो
६२२, ५७०. अनका यु ण्वूनं
६२३, ५५४. क गा च जानं

इति किब्बिधानकप्पे पञ्चमो कण्डो

किब्बिधानसुत्तं निट्ठितं

८. उणादिकप्प

६२४, ५६३. कत्तरि कित
६२५, ६०५. भावकम्मेसु किच्चक्तक्खत्था
६२६, ६३४. कम्मनि दुतियायं क्तो
६२७, ६५२. ख्यादीहि मन म च तो वा
६२८, ६५३. समादीहि थमा
६२९, ५६९. गहस्सु'पधस्से वा
६३०, ६५४. मसुस्स सुस्स च्छरच्छेरा
६३१, ६५५. आपुब्बचरस्स च
६३२, ६५६. अल कल सलेहि ल या
६३३, ६५७. याण लाणा
६३४, ६५८. मथिस्स थस्स लो च
६३५, ५५९. पेसातिसग्गपत्तकालेसु किच्चा
६३६, ६५९. अवस्सकाधमिणेसु णी च
६३७, ०. अरहसक्कादीहि तुं
६३८, ६६८. वजादीहि पब्बज्जादयो निप्पज्जन्ते
६३९, ५८५. क्विलोपो च
६४०, ०. सचजानं कगा णानुबन्धे
६४१, ५७२. नुदादीहि यु,ण्वून'मना'नना'का'ननका सकारितेहि च
६४२, ५८८. इ य त म किं एसान'मन्तस्सरो दीघं क्वचि दिसस्स गुणं दो रं स क्खी च
६४३, ६३५. भ्यादीहि मति बुधि पूजादीहि च क्तो
६४४, ६६१. वेपु सी दव वमु कु दा भूह्वादीहि थुत्तिम णिमा निब्बत्ते
६४५, ६६२. अक्कोसे नम्हानि
६४६, ४१९. एकादितो सकिस्स क्खत्तुं
६४७, ६६३. सुनस्सुनस्सो ण वानु'वानू'नुनखु'ना'ना
६४८, ६६४. तरुणस्स सुसु च
६४९, ६६५. युवस्सु'वस्सु'वुवानुनूना
६५०, ६५१. काले वत्तमानातीते ण्वादयो
६५१, ६४७. भविस्सति गमादीहि णी घिण
६५२, ६४८. क्रियायं ण्वु तवो
६५३, ३०६. भाववाचिम्हि चतुत्थी
६५४, ६४९. कम्मनि णो

६५५, ६५०. सेसे स्सं न्तु मानाना
६५६, ६६६. छदादीहि त त्रण
६५७, ६६७. वदादीहि णित्तो गणे
६५८, ६६८. मिदादीहि त्ति तियो
६५९, ६६९. उसुरन्जदंसानं दंसस्स दड्ढो ढठा च
६६०, ६७०. सूवुसान मूवुसान मतो थो च
६६१, ६७१. रन्जुदादीहि धदिद्दकिरा क्वचि जदलोपो च
६६२, ६७२. पटितो हिस्स हेरण हीरण
६६३, ६७३. कढयादीहि को
६६४, ६७४. खादा'मगमानं खन्ध'न्धगन्धा
६६५, ६७५. पटादीह्य'लं
६६६, ६७६. पुथस्स पुथु पथा'मो वा
६६७, ६७७. सस्वादीहि तु दवो
६६८, ६७८. च्या'दीहि ईवरो
६६९, ६७९. मुनादीहि चि
६७०, ६८०. विदादीह्यू'रो
६७१, ६८१. हनादीहि नु णु तवो
६७२, ६८२. कुटादीहि ठो
६७३, ६८३. मनुपूरसुणादीहि उस्सनुसि'सा

इति किब्बिधानकप्पे उणादिकप्पो छट्ठो कण्डो
उणादिसुत्तं निट्ठितं

MAHĀ KACCĀYANA
SADDA PĀṬHA
PĀLI GRAMMAR TEXT

1. Sandhi Kappa
Euphonic Combinations Chapter

Paṭhama Kaṇḍa
The First Section

Yatanattaya Vandanā
Homage to Triple Gem

(a) Seṭṭhaṁ tilokamahitaṁ abhivandiya'ggaṁ,
Buddhañ'ca Dhamma'mamalaṁ Gaṇa'muttamañ'ca,
Satthussa tassa vacana'tthavaraṁ subuddhuṁ,
Vakkhāmi suttahita'mettha Susandhikappaṁ.

Having bowed down to the Buddha,
the most praised, Honored by three worlds
of human, divine beings and Brahmā (Gods),
And the holiest of the world,
To the sacred Dhamma and the noble Saṅgha.

I will expound the grammar (starting with)
the good chapter of Sandhi-section
For easily understanding of the sacred
words of Buddha, to benefit (those studying)
Buddhist scriptures.

(b) Seyyaṁ jine'ritanayena budhā labhanti,
Tañ'cā'pi tassa vacana'tthasubodhanena,
atthañ'ca akkharapadesu amohabhāvā,
seyya'tthiko padamato vividhaṁ suṇeyya.

The wise realize the supreme happiness,
In the way as taught by the Lord Buddha.

That way is to be acquired only through
a good understanding of the meaning
of the sacred words and by being free
from any confusion on the meaning
of the sacred words. Therefore, anyone
aspiring to attain supreme happiness,
should learn the grammar about various words.

१, १. अत्थो अक्खरसञ्ञातो

1, 1. **Attho akkharasaññāto.** [Attho+akkharasaññāto, 2 words]

[V] Sabbavacanāna'mattho akkharehe'va saññāyate.
Akkharavipattiyaṁ hi atthassa du'nnayatā hoti.
Tasmā akkharakosallaṁ bahū'pakāraṁ suttantesu.

The meaning of all words can be understood only by means of letters (words). Verily, in case of corrupt letters, the correct meaning of words is difficult to know. Therefore, having the skilled knowledge of letters, (**i.e.** grammatical knowledge) is of much benefit in (the study of) texts.

२, २. अक्खरापादयो एकचत्तालिसं

2, 2. **Akkharā'pā'dayo ekacattālīsaṁ.**
[Akkharā+api+a-ādayo+ekacattālīsaṁ. 4 words]

[V] Te ca kho akkharā'api akārā'dayo ekacattālīsaṁ suttantesu so'pakārā.

Those "a" and so on, amounting forty-one letters, called "**akkharā-**the alphabets" are of great benefit in (the study of) Pāli texts.

Taṁ yathā? What are those "akkhrās"?
They are:
a, ā, i, ī, u, ū, e, o,
ka, kha, ga, gha, ṅa,
ca, cha, ja, jha, ña,
ṭa, ṭha, ḍa, ḍha, ṇa,
ta, tha, da, dha, na,

pa, pha, ba, bha, ma,
ya, ra, la, va, sa, ha, ḷa, aṁ,
iti **akkharā** nāma. These are called "**akkharā**, the letters".

Tena kva'ttho? Attho akkharasaññāto.
What is the benefit by mentioning akkhrā?
It has the benefit of making easy reference in Suttas such as "Attho akkharasaññāto".
Summary: This Sutta explains and names forty-one Pāli alphabets.

३, ३ तत्थोदन्ता सरा अट्ठ

3, 3. **Tattho'dantā sarā aṭṭha.**

[Tattha+o-antā+sarā+aṭṭha. 4 words]

[V] Tattha akkharesu akārā'dīsu o'dantā aṭṭha akkharā sarā nāma honti.

Of those "forty-one akkhrās", the eight vowels, beginning with letter "a" and ending in "o", are called "**sara,** vowels".

Taṁ yathā?
What are those Saras?
Namely:
A, ā, i, ī, u, ū, e, o, iti **sarā** nāma.
These are called "Sara, vowels".

Tena kva'ttho? Sarā sare lopaṁ.
What is the benefit by naming that "sara"?
It has the benefit of making easy reference in Suttas such as "Sarā sare lopaṁ".
Summary: This Sutta formally names eight Pāli vowels as "**sara**-vowels".

४, ४. लहुमत्ता तयो रस्सा

4, 4. **Lahumattā tayo rassā.** [Lahumattā+tayo+rassā. 3 words]

[V] Tattha aṭṭhasu saresu lahumattā tayo sarā rassā nāma honti.

Of those eight "Saras (vowels) ", the three Saras which have a short duration of utterance are called "**Rassa**-short vowels".

Taṁ yathā?
What are those Rassas?
Namely:
A, i, u, iti **rassā** nāma.
A, i, u, These are called Rassa.

Tena kvattho? Rassaṁ.
What is the benefit by naming that "rassa"?
It has the benefit of easy reference in Suttas such as "Rassaṁ".
Summary: This Sutta terms three short vowels known as "**rassa**-the vowels of short sounds".

५, ५. अञ्ञे दीघा

5, 5. **Aññe dīghā.** [Aññe+dīghā. 2 words]

[V] Tattha aṭṭhasu saresu rassehi aññe pañca sarā dīghā nāma honti.

Of the eight Saras (vowels), the other five saras (vowels) are called "**Dīgha**-Long vowels, **i.e.** the Saras which have a longer duration of utterance".

Taṁ yathā?
What are those Degas?
Namely:
Ā, ī, ū, e, o, iti **dīghā** nāma.
"Ā, ī, ū, e, o", These are called Degas.

Tena kva'ttho? Dirham.
What benefit is there by naming that "dīgha"?
It has the benefit of easy reference in Suttas such as "Dīghaṁ".
Summary: This Sutta terms five long vowels known as "**dīgha**-the vowels of long sound".

६, ८. सेसा ब्यञ्जना
6, 8. Sesā byañjanā. [Sesā+byañjanā. 2 words]
[V] Ṭhapetvā aṭṭha sare sesā akkharā ka-kārā'dayo niggahita'ntā byañjanā nāma honti.

Excluding the eight Saras (vowels), the remaining thirty-three letters beginning with "ka" and ending in Niggahita "aṁ", are called "**Byanñjana**-consonants".

Taṁ yathā?
What are those byanñjana (consonants)?
Namely:
**Ka, kha, ga, gha, ṅa,
ca, cha, ja, jha, ña,
ṭa, ṭha, ḍa, ḍha, ṇa,
ta, tha, da, dha, na,
pa, pha, ba, bha, ma,
ya, ra, la, va,
sa, ha, ḷa, aṁ,**
iti **byañjanā** nāma.
These are called byanñjana (consonants).

Tena kva'ttho? Sarā pakati byañjane.
What is the benefit by mentioning that "byanñjana (consonant)"?
It has the benefit of easy reference in Suttas such as "Sarā pakati byañjane".
Summary: This Sutta terms thirty-three Pāli consonants as "**byanñjana**-those that manifest the meaning".
Note: The vowel "a" after each consonant is included for the purpose of easy utterance. Actually, the consonants are better represented without any vowel such as "**K, kh, g, gh, ṅ, c, ch, j, jh, ñ, ṭ, ṭh, ḍ, ḍh, ṇ, t, th, d, dh, n, p, ph, b, bh, m, y, r, l, v, s, h, ḷ, ṁ,**".

७, ९. वग्गा पञ्चपञ्चसो मन्ता

7, 9. Vaggā pañcapañcaso ma'ntā.

[Vaggā+pañcapañcaso+ma-antā. 3 words]

[V] Tesaṁ kho byañjanānaṁ ka-kārā'dayo ma-kāra'ntā pañcapañcaso akkharavanto vaggā nāma honti.

Of those byanñjana (consonants), the letters beginning with "ka" and ending in "ma" which are grouped together in fives of each, are called "**vaggas**-the groups".

Taṁ yathā?
What are those vaggas (groups) ?
Namely:
Ka, kha, ga, gha, ṅa, (This group is called **Ka-vagga**)
ca, cha, ja, jha, ña, (This group is called **Ca-vagga**)
ṭa, ṭha, ḍa, ḍha, ṇa, (This group is called **Ṭa-vagga**)
ta, tha, da, dha, na, (This group is called **Ta-vagga**)
pa, pha, ba, bha, ma. (This group is called **Pa-vagga**)
iti **vaggā** nāma.
These are called " Vagga" .

Tena kva'ttho? Vaggantaṁ vā vagge.
What is the benefit by mentioning that "Vaggas (groups) "?
It has the benefit of ease of reference in Suttas such as "Vaggantaṁ vā vagge".
Summary: This Sutta names the fives of each group as "**vagga**-the group" being grouped together out of the twenty-five Pāli consonants. There are five vaggas each comprising five consonants. "**ṅ, ñ, ṇ, n, m**" are formally called **Vagganta**-the end consonants of the group, also called "nasal stops" (**Vagga**-group+**anta**-end). Knowing and understanding these vagga-groups and their end-consonants will help in understanding some of the complex morphological procedures which will be explained in this grammar.

८, १०.अंइति निग्गहितं

8, 10. **Aṁ iti niggahitaṁ**[9]**.** [Aṁ-iti+niggahitaṁ. 2 words]

[V] **Aṁ**iti niggahitaṁ nāma hoti.

The letter "**aṁ**" is called "**niggahita**"

Tena kva'ttho? Aṁ byañjane niggahitaṁ.
What is the benefit by mentioning "niggahita"?
It has the benefit of ease of reference in Suttas such as "Aṁ byañjane niggahitaṁ".
Summary: This Sutta names one nasalized "**aṁ**" as the "niggahita". See the footnote.

---

[9] A **Niggahita** is represented by the consonant "ṁ" in the Romanized Pāli. It is called "Niggahita" as it has to be uttered or sounded out through nasal passage by having the necessary parts of the mouth which serve as a mechanism of the speech or spoken sound such as lip etc. are kept gently pressed while at the same time other parts such as tongue, teeth, etc. remain inactive during the enunciation process. [Niggahīta=ni√gaha+ta]
[Reference Text] *Rassasaraṁ nissāya gayhati, karaṇam niggahetvā gayhatī'ti vā niggahitaṁ.*
(Translation) It is called Niggahita as it is uttered being based on short vowels, also because it is spoken with the act of enunciation (karaṇa) the sources of voice (**ṭhāna**) being repressed. Here, the root "gaha" prefixed with an *upasagga* particle "ni" means to press and to restrain.

Karaṇaṁ Niggahetvāna, mukhenā'vivaṭena'yaṁ
Vuccate niggahita'nti, Vuttaṁ Bindhusarā'nugaṁ. (Rūpasiddhi)

(Translation) This sound of dot is said by restrained act of utterance, with mouth (lips) kept unopened. So, this "dot" is called "niggahita" which used to depend on (three) short vowels.
In Thai, Burmese and Devanāgari alphabets, it is usually represented by a small dot on top of the letters it joined. See these following sample words:

Thai อํ, Burmese အံ, Devanāgari अं .

The niggahita is usually found joined on top of only three rassa (short) vowels "**a, i, u**". It is called an "anusvāra" in Sanskrit. Some grammarians view it as a semi-vowel as well as a semi-consonant as it is interchangeable in the morphological procedure of Pāli grammar. Please note that only "ṁ" is called Niggahita while "**a**" is added for the purpose of easy utterance.

९, ११.परसमञ्ञा पयोगे

9, 11. Parasamaññā payoge. [Parasamaññā+payoge. 2 words]

[V] Yā ca pana paresu sakkataganthesu samaññā **ghosā**'ti vā, **aghosā**'ti vā, tā payoge sati etthā'pi yujjante.

Any grammatical term such as "**ghosa** or **aghosa** and so forth, which are used in other Sanskrit grammar texts, can also be applied here in this Pāli grammar as and when appropriate and applicable.

Tattha **ghosā** nāma-
Of those terms, the following are called "**ghosa**-voiced or sonants".
ga gha ṅa, ja jha ña,
ḍa ḍha ṇa, da dha na,
ba bha ma, ya ra la va ha ḷa, (21)
iti **ghosā** nāma.
These are "ghosas".

Aghosā nāma-
Those called "**aghosas**-unvoiced, or surds" are:
ka kha, ca cha, ṭa ṭha, ta tha, pa pha, sa, (11)
iti **aghosā** nāma.
These are "aghosas".

Tena kva'ttho? Vagge ghosā'ghosānaṁ tatiyapaṭhamā.
What is the benefit by mentioning that "ghosa and aghosa"?
It has the benefit of ease of reference in Suttas such as "Vagge ghosā'ghosānaṁ tatiyapaṭhamā".
Summary: This Sutta states permissibility to use some of the relevant grammatical terms such as "Ghosa and Aghosa" etc., which are used in the Sanskrit grammars.

१०, १२. पुब्बमधोठितमस्सरं सरेन वियोजये

10, 12. **Pubba'madhoṭhita'massaraṁ sarena viyojaye.**

[Pubbaṁ+adhoṭhitaṁ+assaraṁ+sarena+viyojaye. 5 words]

[V] Tattha sandhiṁ kattukāmo pubbabyañjanaṁ adhoṭhitaṁ assaraṁ katvā, sarañ'ca upari katvā, sarena viyojaye.

There, when wanting to conduct the grammatical procedure of Sandhi (Euphonic combination of words), the preceding front consonant has to be put below and make it vowel-less by separating it from its attached vowel and keep the separated vowel above. For example, "• Tatrā'ya'mādi"
Summary: This Sutta sets the rule **to separate the consonant from vowel** it is attached to before performing any morphological procedure such as eliding, shortening, lengthening or changing into other forms of syllables etc., can be carried out properly. **The functions prescribed in Sutta 10 and 11 are two important fundamental procedures of the morphology** in the Pāli grammar.

Example: **Tatrā'ya'mādi.**

(Here, three words "Tatra, ayaṁ and ādi", are combined in a Sandhi. See **' the apostrophe marks** shown as **a sign of Sandhi**). In this example, the point of Sandhi is shown by apostrophe mark**'.** Plcase carefully note this mark as all sign of Sandhi will be shown by this mark throughout this book. Note that there are two points of Sandhi in this example, one between **trā'ya** and the other between **ya** and **mā**. Now, it will look like this when all the combined words are separated:

Tatra+ayaṁ+ādi

(3 words. 2 Point of Sandhi being separated are shown by + sign)
[**Tatra-**at that Nibbāna. **ayaṁ-**this four kind of purity. **ādi-**is the beginning]

Note: The separation process of consonant from vowel as prescribed by this Sutta may seem quite irrelevant in Romanized letters as they are already separated. In Pāli written in Devanagari or in Burmese etc., it is quite relevant and necessary as the vowels are usually written by being joined in one single letter comprising both a vowel and a consonant such as कि, की, कु, कू, ကိ, ကီ, ကု, ကူ. In these sample words, the diacritical marks symbolize vowels which need to be separated.

११, १४. नये परं युत्ते

11, 14. **Naye paraṁ yutte.** [Naye+paraṁ+yutte. 3 words]

[V] Assaraṁ kho byañjanaṁ adhoṭhataṁ para'kkharaṁ naye yutte.

The vowel-less consonant being kept below, should be re-attached to the rear (next) letter when appropriate. (**i.e.** after all due morphological procedures have been done).

Summary: This Sutta sets the rule **to re-attach the separated consonant to the next vowel** after any necessary morphological procedure such as eliding, shortening, lengthening have been done.

Below is an example of Sandhi. Note that there are two (') apostrophe marks which show point of Sandhi.

[CS] • Tatrā'bhirati'miccheyya. (3 words, **CS** means combined in Sandhi)
(Meaning) **Tatra-**at that three kind of tranquility. **abhiratiṁ-**joy. **iccheyya**-(one) should prefer. **i.e.** One should prefer enjoying at that three kind of tranquility, peace.

[SS] Tatr**a**+**a**bhirati**ṁ**+**i**ccheyya. (**SS** means **S**andhi **S**eparated, 3 words)

Morphological Explanation of Example [ME]

[ME] Here, Sandhi is between two points where bold-faced letters with a plus sign are shown.

The steps to make these separated words of Sandhi to be recombined into a perfect Sandhi.

Now let's study **the necessary morphological procedures** on the first point of Sandhi:

(1) First the initial "a" in front of the plus sign is to be elided as per Sutta 12. It then looks like this: Tatr+**a**bhirati**ṁ**+**i**ccheyya.

(2) Then the next "a" is to be lengthened by procedure as prescribed in Sutta 15. It now becomes > Tatr+**ā**bhirati**ṁ**+**i**ccheyya.

(3) By procedure of this Sutta 11, the vowel-less "r" is then to be attached to next lengthened "ā" > Tatrābhiratiṁ+**i**ccheyya.

Now let's work on the second point of Sandhi:

(1) "**ṁ**" is to be changed into "**m**" by the procedure as per Sutta 34. It then becomes > Tatrābhirati**m**+**i**ccheyya.

(2) By procedure of this Sutta 11, "m" is to be attached to next vowel "i". Now finally morphed form is > **Tatrābhiratimiccheyya.**

Thus through all due procedures as shown in these Suttas, it becomes a complete word. **The students do not need to remember all this.** They just only need to learn how morphological procedures as said in the Suttas are carried out in the various stages of evolution of the Pāli words. This will help them learn the structural patterns of the word and gain some insight into the language patterns and achieve mastery of language to some degree, which in many ways can greatly benefit in the study of Buddhist texts written in Pāli. Keep in mind that **the role of Sutta 10 and 11 are always necessary as far as the study of morphological procedures of words are concerned** in the Pāli grammar.

Yutte'ti kasmā?

Why the word "yutte" is included in Sutta?

*Akkocchi maṁ, *avadhi maṁ, *ajini maṁ, *ahāsi me.

Akkocchi-(he) reviled. **maṁ**-me, **avadhi-**(he) hurt. **maṁ**-me, **ajini-**(he) conquered. **maṁ**-me, **ahāsi-**(he) took **me**-my (things).

Ettha pana yuttaṁ na hoti.

Here in this example "Akkocchi maṁ etc.,", there is no "yutta", hence no need to re-attach any vowel-less consonant in those phrases. (In such examples, the term "yutte", as a result, is irrelevant and inapplicable.)

Note: **Yutta** means being appropriate, **i.e.** the applicability of Sandhi procedure.

Kasmā-kiṁ-what+**smā**-for, ablative case-ending. **i.e.** Why?.

Iti sandhikappe paṭhamo kaṇḍo.

The First Section of Sandhi ends.

Dutiya Kaṇḍa
The Second Section

१२, १३. सरा सरे लोपं

12, 13. **Sarā sare lopaṁ.** [Sarā+sare+lopaṁ. 3 words]

[V] Sarā kho sare pare lopaṁ papponti.

When a Sara (vowel) follows, the preceding vowel is to be elided.
Summary: The function of this Sutta **elides the front vowel** when two vowels of different words are in a union after the separation of Sandhi, one in the front, and the other next to it.

[CS] (a) • Yass**'i**ndriyāni samathaṅ'gatāni.
(b) • No h**e'ta**ṁ bhante.
(c) • Samet**ā'**yasmā saṅghena.

[SS] (a) Yass**a**+**i**ndriyāni.
Yassa-of whose. indriyāni-faculties.
[Here see union of two vowels, one the last **"a"** of the word Yassa, the other front **"i"** of the word indriyani. The front "a" is to be elided.]
(b) No h**i**+**e**taṁ bhante.
No hi-is not appropriate. **etaṁ**-this fact. **bhante**-Lord Buddha. [Here, union occurs between **"i and e"**.]
(c) Samet**u**+**ā**yasmā saṅghena.
Sametu-let it be harmonious. **āyasmā**-Your venerable. **saṅghena**-with community of Sangha. [Here, union occurs between **"u and ā"**.]

Now look at separations of Sandhi shown above. There is a union of two vowels, one in the front and one next to it in each separated Sandhi, shown by means of a plus+ sign.
The front vowel is to be elided as per this Sutta. Then the vowel-less consonant in front of the elided vowel is to be attached to next vowel after the plus sign as prescribed by Sutta 11. Then it becomes a complete word perfectly combined in Sandhi.
The whole procedure is quite simple and easy to understand though it may at first seem a bit complex process for a beginner.

The Structural Morphology:

(This will be abbreviated as [SM] throughout this book)

[SM] Just elide or wipe out the front vowels **(a) a (b) i (c) u** and attach all front three vowel-less consonants **(a) s (b) h (c) t** to next vowels. It is done! **This means that once it is done, it will be combined into a Sandhi such as those shown in [CS]**

१३, १५. वा परो असरूपा

13, 15. Vā paro asarūpā. [Vā+paro+asarūpā. 3 words]

[V] Saramhā asarūpā[10] paro saro lopaṁ pappoti vā[11].

The next dissimilar vowel from the preceding dissimilar one (in a union of two different vowels) is to be elided sometimes.

(This Sutta **elides next vowel out of a union of two non-homogenous, different vowels.** See the examples)

[CS] (a) • Cattāro'me bhikkhave dhammā.
(b) • Kinnu'mā'va samaṇiyo.

---

[10] **Asarūpa**-**a**-not, **s**-similar, **rūpa**-shape, the vowels which are not the same in shape. They are also called **Asavaṇṇa.** [**a**-not, **s**-same, **vaṇṇa**-shape, **i.e.** akkhara, letter.] Reversely, the similar ones are called **sarūpa** or **savaṇṇa.** ("S" derives from **Samāna**-similar). **a & ā** are **sarūpa** or **savaṇṇa** to each other. So are **i & ī, u & ū** to each other. This is called **sarūpa** or **savaṇṇa.** Reversely, **a , ā** are **asarūpa** or **asavaṇṇa** to **i, ī, u, ū** & **e, o.** So are **i, ī** to the rest, **u, ū** to the rest. **e & o** are themselves **asarūpa or asavaṇṇa** to each other and to the rest of vowels. These terms are to be regarded as formal grammatical terms named in the sense that they are quite homogeneously compatible or interchangeable either as **dīgha or rassa** within themselves, not in the sense of similarity of the physical shape.

[11] Means sometimes or optionally, the function as prescribed in Sutta is inapplicable at some instances due to lack of condition as outlined in Sutta. Also, **Kaci, Nava, vā, vibhāsā** are words with the same meaning. **All these Nipāta words mean optionally, or sometimes** not applied in some instances. They are used by the grammarians to place restriction and limitation regarding the function of Sutta. **It also means the function of Sutta is not applied in some instances.**

[SS] (a) Cattār**o**+**i**me

Cattāro-four. **ime**-these. [Here, union occurs between **"o and i"**.]

(b) Kinn**u**+**i**m**ā**+**e**va (2 points of Sandhi in this example **b.**)

Kinnu-? **imā**-these nuns. **eva**-only. **i.e.** Are these only Bhikkunī (female monks) ? Aren't we? [Here, between **"u and i"** & **"ā and e"**.]

Kinnu=Kiṁ+nu. [This combination of the Sabbanāma noun **"kiṁ"** and nipāta particle **"nu"** is equal to a question mark **"?"**. **"ṁ"** changes into **"n"** by Sutta 31]

[SM] Just elide or wipe out next vowels **(a) i (b) i** & **e.** That is it!

Vā'ti kasmā? Why the word "Vā" is included in Sutta? *Pañci'ndriyāni. *Taya'ssu dhammā jahitā bhavanti. It is to show that the function of this rule is inapplicable in such instances as "Pañci'ndriyāni, Taya'ssu dhammā jahitā bhavanti etc." because it is restricted by "vā"

[CS] (a) * Pañci'ndriyāni.

(b) * Taya'ssu dhammā jahitā bhavanti

[SS] (a) * Pañc**a**+**i**ndriyāni. **Pañca**-five. **indriyāni**-faculties.

(b) * Tay**o**+**a**ssu dhammā jahitā bhavanti.

Tayo-three. **assu**-are. **dhammā**-defilements. **jahitā**-removed. **bhavanti**-are. **i.e.** Three defilements are removed.

(**assu** and **bhavanti** are two different verbs of the same meaning redundantly used).

[SM] Elide the front vowels **(a) a (b) o** and then attach the front vowel-less consonants **(a) c (b) y** to the next **i and a** respectively. It is done.

१४, १६. क्वचासवण्णं लुत्ते

14, 16. **Kvacā'savaṇṇaṁ lutte.**

[Kvaci+asavaṇṇaṁ+lutte. 3 words]

[V] Saro kho paro pubbasare lutte kvaci **asavaṇṇaṁ** pappoti.

When the preceding vowel has been elided, the next one sometimes changes into asavaṇṇa Sara (a dissimilar vowel) which may be either an **"e"** or an **"o"**. [**i** or **ī**>**e** , **u** or **ū**>**o**]

[CS] (a) Saṅkhyaṁ • no'peti vedagū.

Saṅkhyaṁ-to the state of being counted as a commoner. **na-**does not. **upeti-**reach. **vedagū**-The enlightened saint. **i.e.** The enlightened saint does not reach to the state of being counted as a common worldling.

(b) • Bandhusse'va samāgamo.

Bandhussa-of relative. **iva-**is like. **samāgamo**-meeting. **i.e.** The meeting is like that of relatives.

[SS] (a) • n**a**+**u**peti (b) • Bandhuss**a**+**i**va

[SM] Just elide or wipe out the front vowels **(a) a (b) a** by Sutta 12 **.** Then change **(a) u** into "**o**" **(b) i** into "**e**" by this Sutta. Then combine the front vowel-less consonants **(a) n (b) s** to next vowels "**o**" and "**e**" respectively. Now, it is done easily!

Kvacī'ti kasmā?

Why there is the word "Kvaci" in Sutta?

Yassi'ndriyāni. Tathū'pamaṁ dhammavaraṁ adesayi.

It is to show that the function of this rule is inapplicable in the examples shown below as implied by the word "kvaci".

* Yassi'ndriyāni. * Tathū'pamaṁ dhammavaraṁ adesayi.

[CS] (a) * yassi'ndriyāni.

(b) * tathū'pamaṁ dhammavaraṁ adesayi.

[SS] (a) * Yass**a**+**i**ndriyāni.

(b) * Tath**ā**+**u**pamaṁ dhammavaraṁ adesayi.

Tathā-Like that. **upamaṁ-**simile. **dhammavaraṁ-**the noble Dhamma. **adesayi-** (Buddha) taught. **i.e.** Buddha taught the noble Dhamma resembling that simile.

[SM] (a) This example previously explained in Sutta 12

(b) Elide the front vowel "**ā**". Then lengthen next "**u**" as "**ū**" by Sutta 15. Attach "**th**" to that "**ū**"**.** It is done.

१५, १७. दीघं

15, 17. **Dīghaṁ.** [Dīghaṁ. 1 word]

[V] Saro kho paro pubbasare lutte kvaci **dīghaṁ** pappoti.

When the preceding vowel has been elided, the one behind is to be sometimes changed into a Dīgha-Sara, **i.e.** it is to be lengthened. [After the front vowel had been elided, the next one is to be lengthened into **"a>ā, i>ī, u>ū"**]

[CS] (a) • Saddhī'dha vittaṁ purisassa seṭṭhaṁ.
Saddhā-faith. **idha**-in this world. **vittaṁ**-is wealth. **purisassa**-for a person. **seṭṭhaṁ**-the best. **i.e.** Faith is the best possession of a person in this world.
(b) Anāgārehi • cū'bhayaṁ.
Anāgārehi ca-with homeless persons, **i.e.** ascetics also. **ubhayaṁ**-with both.

[SS] (a) • Saddh**ā**+**i**dha (b) • **ca**+**u**bhayaṁ.

[SM] Just elide or wipe out the front vowels **(a) ā (b) a** by Sutta 12 . Then lengthen **(a) i** into "**ī**" **(b) u** into "**ū**" by this Sutta.
Then combine vowel-less front consonants **(a) dh (b) c** to the next vowels "**ī**" and "**ū**" respectively. It is thus done.

Kvacī'ti kasmā?
Why there is the word "Kvaci" in Sutta?
It is to show that the function of this rule is inapplicable in examples shown below as restricted by "kvaci".
* Pañcahu'pāli aṅgehi samannāgato. * Nattha'ññaṁ kiñci.

[CS] (a) * Pañcahu'pāli aṅgehi samannāgato.
(b) * Nattha'ññaṁ kiñci

[SS] (a) * Pañcah**i**+**u**pāli aṅgehi samannāgato.
Pañcahi-by five. **upāli**-Upāli! **aṅgehi**-factors. **samannāgato**-the one who has. **i.e.** Upāli! The one who has five factors.
(b) * Natth**i**+**a**ññaṁ kiñci
Natthi-there is no. **aññaṁ**-else, other. **kiñci**-something. **i.e.** There is nothing else.

[SM] For both examples (**a** & **b**), Elide the front vowels "**i**". It is done.

१६, १८. पुब्बो च

16, 18. **Pubbo ca.** [Pubbo+ca. 2 words]

[V] Pubbo ca saro parasaralope kate kvaci **dīghaṁ** pappoti.

When the next (rear) vowel has been elided, the one in the front is sometimes made into a Dīgha-Sara, **i.e.** lengthened.

[CS] (a) • Kiṁsū'dha vittaṁ purisassa seṭṭhaṁ.
Kiṁ su-what is. **idha**-in this world. **vittaṁ**-wealth. **purisassa**-for a person. **seṭṭhaṁ**-the best. [**su**-is expletive, meaningless] **i.e.** What is the best asset for a person in this world?

(b) • Sādhū'ti paṭissuṇitvā,
Sādhu-well. **iti**-thus. **paṭissuṇitvā**-having replied, **i.e.** Having replied thus (by saying the word) "well".

[SS] (a) • Kiṁs**u**+**i**dha
(b) • Sādh**u**+**i**ti.

[SM] Just elide or wipe out rear vowels **(a) i (b) i** by Sutta 12 . Then lengthen both front **(a) u (b) u** into "**ū**" by this Sutta. It's done!

Kvacī'ti kasmā?
Why there is the word "Kvaci" in Sutta?
It is to show that the function of this rule is inapplicable in some examples shown below as restricted by "kvaci".
* Iti'ssa muhuttam'pi.

[CS] * Iti'ssa muhuttam'pi (2 points of Sandhi)

[SS] * It**i**+**a**ssa muhutta**ṁ**+**a**pi.
Iti-therefore. **assa**-for that monk. **muhuttaṁ**-for a moment. **api**-even.

[SM] For the first point, elide the next vowel "**a**" by Sutta 13. For the second point, elide "**a**" behind "**ṁ**" by Sutta 40. Change "**ṁ**" into "**m**" by 31 and attach it to next "**p**". It is done.

१७, १९. यमेदन्तस्सादेसो

17, 19. **Ya'me'dantassā'deso.**

[Yaṁ+e-antassa+ādeso. 3 words]

[V] **E**-kārassa antabhūtassa sare pare kvaci **ya**-kārā'deso hoti.

When a vowel follows (**i.e.** Present behind), the front vowel "**e**" sometimes changes into consonant "**ya**".
[This Sutta changes "**e**" into "**y**". Usually, this "e" is part of "**me**-my, **te**-your, those, **kiṁ**-what, why" etc.,]
Note: First study SS below before you read the translation of examples.

[CS] (a) Adhigato kho • myā'yaṁ dhammo.
Adhigato-realized, known. **kho**-really. **me**-by me. **ayaṁ**-this. **dhammo**-Dhamma.
i.e. This Dhamma realized by me is, in fact, (very deep).

(b) • Tyā'haṁ evaṁ vadeyyaṁ.
Te-your. **ahaṁ**-I. **evaṁ**-thus. **vadeyyaṁ**-should say.
i.e. If I should say thus to you.

(c) • Tya'ssa pahīnā honti.

Te-those defilements. **assa**-by that person (genitive case in nominative sense). **pahīnā**-being removed. **honti**-are.
i.e. Those defilements are being removed by that person.

[SS] (a) • myā'yaṁ > • m**e**+**a**yaṁ,
(b) • Tyā'haṁ > • T**e**+**a**haṁ
(c) • Tya'ssa > • T**e**+**a**ssa

[SM] Just change all "**e**" of **(a) (b) (c)** by this Sutta into "**y**". Then lengthen all next "**a**" of **(a) (b)** into an "**ā**" by Sutta 15. Now, It becomes:
(a) •m**y**+**ā**yaṁ,
(b) • T**y**+**ā**haṁ
Now, attach all the front newly morphed consonant "**y**" to next "**ā**" and it is done.
For example (c), no dīgha (lengthening of a into ā) is necessary. Just attach "y" to next "a". It is done.

Kvacī'ti kasmā?
Why there is the word "Kvaci" in Sutta?
It is to show that the function of this rule is inapplicable in the examples shown below as restricted by "kvaci".
* Ne'nāgatā. * Iti ne'ttha.

[CS] (a) * Ne'nāgatā.
(b) * Iti ne'ttha

[SS] (a) * N**e**+**a**nāgatā.

Ne-those people. **anāgatā**-not coming.[na+āgatā]
i.e. Those people do not come.

(b) * Iti n**a**+**e**ttha.

iti-thus. **na**-not. **ettha**-here.

[SM] For (a), Just elide next vowel "**a**" by Sutta 13. It is done. No need to attach anything here!
For (b), elide front vowel "**a**" as per Sutta 12 and attach "**n**" to next "**e**". It is quite simple and easy.

१८, २०. वमोदुदन्तानं

18, 20. **Va'mo'du'dantānaṁ.**

[Vaṁ+o, u, antānaṁ. 2 words]

[V] **O**-kār**u**'kārānaṁ antabhūtānaṁ sare pare kvaci **va**-kārā'deso hoti.

When there is a vowel present behind, the front vowels "**o** or **u**" sometimes changes into the consonant "**Va**".
[This Sutta changes "**o**" or "**u**" into "**v**"]

[CS] (a) Atha • khva'ssa.
(b) • Sva'ssa hoti.
(c) • Bahvā'bādho.
(d) • Vatthve'ttha vihitaṁ niccaṁ.
Vatthu-location place. **ettha**-here. **vihitaṁ**-arranged. **niccaṁ**-always. **i.e.** A place is always arranged here.
(e) • Cakkhvā'pātha'māgacchati. (Here Sandhi is at two points. So one extra function is necessary)

[SS] (a) • Atha kh**o**+**a**ssa.
Atha kho-then. **assa**-of that person.
(b) • S**o**+**a**ssa hoti.
So-that. **assa**-of that person. **hoti**-is.
(c) • Bah**u**+**ā**bādho.
Bahu-much. **ābādho**-disease.
(d) • Vatth**u**+**e**ttha
(e) • Cakkh**u**+**ā**pātha**ṁ**+**ā**gacchati. (2 points of Sandhi in **e**)
Cakkhu+āpāthaṁ-clear vision of wisdom eye. **āgacchati**-comes. **i.e.** The clear vision of the wisdom eye comes. **i.e.** appears. [**Cakkhu**-the eye+**āpāthaṁ**-to a state of being vivid. **i.e.** clear vision]

[SM] Just change all **(a) o (b) o (c) u (d) u** by this Sutta into "**v**". Now by Sutta 11, attach all the newly morphed consonant "**v**" to next **(a) a (b) a (c) ā (d) e** and it is done.
For first point of **(e),** change "**u**" into "**v**" by this Sutta and attach it to next vowel. For the second point: Change "**ṁ**" into "**m**" by Sutta 34 and attach the morphed "**m**" to next "**ā**". It is done.

Kvacī'ti kasmā?
Why there is the word "Kvaci" in Sutta?
It is to show that the function of this rule is inapplicable in such instances of phrase examples as " * Cattāro'me bhikkhave dhammā. * Kinnumā'va samaṇiyo" etc.

[CS] (a) * Cattāro'me bhikkhave dhammā.
(b) * Kinnu'mā'va samaṇiyo.

[SS] (a) * Cattār**o**+**i**me bhikkhave dhammā.
(b) * Kinn**u**+**i**mā'va samaṇiyo.

[SM] These examples are already explained in Sutta 13.

१९. २२. सब्बो चं ति

19, 22. **Sabbo caṁ ti.** [Sabbo+caṁ+ti. 3 words]

[V] Sabbo icce'so **ti**saddo byañjano sare pare kvaci **ca**-kāraṁ pappoti.

The whole "**ti**"(which is part of **ati, pati, iti** Upasagga particles), sometimes changes into consonant "**c**".
(This "**c**" is reduplicated so that it becomes a conjunct consonant "**cc**" by Sutta 28)

[CS] (a) • Icce'taṁ kusalaṁ. (b) • Icca'ssa vacanīyaṁ.
(c) • Paccu'ttaritvā. (d) • Paccā'harati.

[SS] (a) • **Iti**+**e**taṁ kusalaṁ.
Iti+etaṁ-such this result. **kusalaṁ**-is good.
(b) • I**ti**+**a**ssa vacanīyaṁ.
Iti-thus. **assa**-should be. **vacanīyaṁ**-said. **i.e.** It should be said thus.
(c) • Pa**ti**+**u**ttaritvā.
Pati-uttaritvā-having crossed again. [**pati**-again+ **uttaritvā**-having crossed]
(d) • Pa**ti**+**ā**harati.
Patiāharati-(he) carries again. [**Pati**-again+**āharati**-carries]

[SM] Just change all "**ti**" of **(a) (b) (c) (d)** by this Sutta into "**c**". Then double one more "c" to that morphed "c" by rule of Sutta 28. Then attach duplicated "**cc**" to next vowels. It is all done.

Kvacī'ti kasmā?
Why there is the word "Kvaci" in Sutta?
It is to show that the function of this rule is inapplicable in examples shown below as restricted by "kvaci".
* Iti'ssa muhuttam'pi.

[CS] * Iti'ssa muhuttam'pi (Sandhi at two points)

[SS] * It**i**+**a**ssa muhutta**ṁ**+**a**pi

[SM] Explained in Sutta 16.

२०, २७. दो धस्स च

20, 27. **Do dhassa ca.** [Do+dhassa+ca. 3 words]

[V] **Dha**-icce'tassa sare pare kvaci **da**-kārā'deso hoti.

When a vowel follows, the front consonant "**Dha**" sometimes changes into a "**da**". (The main function of this Sutta is changing one form of syllable into another form).

[CS] • Ekami'dā'haṁ bhikkhave samayaṁ. (2 points of Sandhi)
Ekaṁ-one. **ida**-here. **ahaṁ**-I. **bhikkhave**-monks! **samayaṁ**-at a time. **i.e.** Monks! here, at one time (once).

[SS] • Eka**ṁ**+**idh**a+**a**haṁ

[SM] **(1st point** of Sandhi solution**)** Change "**ṁ**" into "**m**" by Sutta 34 and attach it to next "**i**".
(2nd point) Change "**dh**" into "**d**" by this Sutta. Then elide one front "**a**" by Sutta 12 and lengthen next "**a**" into "**ā**" by Sutta 15 and attach "**d**" to that lengthened "**ā**"**.** It's done.

Kvacī'ti kasmā?
Why there is the word "Kvaci" in Sutta?
It is to show that the function of this rule is inapplicable in some instances shown below as restricted by "kvaci".
* Idhe'va maraṇaṁ bhavissati.

[CS] * Idhe'va maraṇaṁ bhavissati.

[SS] * Idh**a**+**e**va maraṇaṁ bhavissati.
Idha-here. **eva**-only. **maraṇaṁ**-death. **bhavissati**-shall be**.**
i.e. My death shall be only here at this place! (I will not get up until you grant my wishes to become a monk, a request made by a son to his parents)

[SM] Just elide the front vowel "**a**" as per Sutta 12 and attach "**dh**" to next "**e**"**.** It is done.

Vaggahaṇena **dha-**kārassa **ha**-kārā'deso hoti
By means of the word "Vā" (which had followed to this Sutta from Sutta No. 13), the consonant "**dha**" sometimes changes into "**ha**".
[An additional sub-function applied by force of the word **'Vā'**]

[CS] • Sā'**h**u dassana'mariyānaṁ.

[SS] • Sā+**dh**u dassana**ṁ**+**a**riyānaṁ. (Sandhi at two points)
Sādhu-is good. **dassanaṁ**-even seeing or meeting. **ariyānaṁ**-the noble saints. **i.e.** Even meeting saintly persons is good.

[SM] Change "**dh**" into "**h**"**.** For 2nd point, apply the function of Sutta 34 & 11 as shown before and it is done!

Functions by "yogavibhāga" (the split-Sutta procedure)

Suttavibhāgena bahudhā siyā.

By means of splitting multiple partial Suttas such as "To dassa ca" etc., other forms of various morphological changes are made possible. (See examples below shown in bold-letters. This sign > means it becomes. All examples are quite easy to understand. **As a matter of fact, these examples are not Sandhi but a kind of word-form changes only**)

(1) **To da**ssa,

The consonant "**d**" is changed into "**t**".

yathā? for example,

• Sugato-well-gone or the Buddha who speaks only the wholesome, beneficial and truthful words. [**Su**-well+**gato**-gone, uttered or said]

• Suga**t**o>Suga**d**o.

[SM] Just change "**d**" to "**t**". Then morphological procedure for the word "Sugato" as prescribed by this split-Sutta function is done.
Note: No procedure of separation and combination of Sandhi is needed. The SM of subsequent examples are also the same. Just change into any syllable as required by the enjoined rules.

(2) Ṭo **ta**ssa.

The consonant "**t**" is changed into "**ṭ**".

yathā? • Dukkaṭaṁ-a badly done deed.

e.g., • Dukka**ṭ**aṁ> Dukka**t**aṁ. [**Du**-badly+**kaṭaṁ**-done, an improper act]

(3) **Dho ta**ssa.

The consonant "**t**" is changed into "**dh**".

yathā? •Gandhabbo-a would-be being who is going to be conceived into a would-be mother's womb.

e.g. • Gan**dh**abbo>Gan**t**abbo. [Gan-a derivative of **gamu**+**tabba**-a Kita affix]

(4) **Tro tta**ssa.

The conjunct-consonant "**tt**" is changed into "**tr**".

yathā? • Atrajo-self-generated, the child born of oneself, one's own child.

e.g., • At**r**ajo>A**tt**ajo. [**Atta-**self+**jo-**born of]

(5) **K**o **ga**ssa.

The consonant "**g**" is changed into "**k**".

yathā? • Kulūpako-the monk who always used to visit lay people's home.

e.g., • Kulūpa**k**o> Kulūpa**g**o. [**Kula-**family+**upago-**approacher]

(6) **L**o **ra**ssa.

The consonant "**r**" is changed into "**l**".

yathā? • Mahāsālo-the one who has great wealth.

e.g., • Mahāsā**l**o>Mahāsā**r**o. [**Mahā-**great+**sāro-**wealth]

(7) **J**o **ya**ssa.

The consonant "**y**" is changed into "**j**".

yathā? • Gavajo-a kind of cattle raised in hilly regions or anything that is a product of cattle such as milk, ghee etc.

e.g., • Gava**j**o>Gava**y**o. [**gava-**cattle+**jo-**born of, derived from].

(8) **Bb**o **vva**ssa.

The consonant "**vv**" is changed into "**bb**".

yathā? • Kubbato-of the one who has done, of doer.

e.g., • Ku'**bb**ato>Ku**vv**ato. [Ku<derivative of kara+bbato<anta. See Sutta 127 for "to"]

(9) **K**o **ya**ssa.

The consonant "**y**" is changed into "**k**".

yathā? • Sake-of one's own.

e.g., • Sa**k**e>Sa**y**e.

(10) Yo jassa.

The consonant "**j**" is changed into "**y**".

yathā? • Niyaṁputtaṁ-the child born of oneself.

e.g., • Ni**y**aṁputtaṁ>Ni**j**aṁputtaṁ

(11) **K**o **ta**ssa.

The consonant "**t**" is changed into "**k**".

yathā? • Niyako-permanent.
e.g., • Niya**k**o>Niya**t**o.

(12) **Cco tta**ssa.
The consonant "**tt**" is changed into "**cc**".
yathā? • bhacco-wage-earning worker, the servant.
e.g., • bha**cc**o>Ba**tt**o.

(13) **Pho pa**ssa.
The consonant "**p**" is changed into "**ph**".
yathā? • Nipphatti-accomplishment, the act of finishing.
e.g., • Ni**pph**atti>Ni**p**atti.

(14) **Kho ka**ssa.
The consonant "**k**" is changed into "**kh**".
yathā? • Nikkhamati-(He) goes out, leaves.
e.g., • Ni**kkh**amati>Ni**kk**amati.
Change the last "k" into "kh". It becomes Nikkhamati.

Icceva'mādī yojetabbā.
Other similar examples (like these shown here), should be applied as per these rules. [**The split-Sutta functions: 14**]

२१, २१. इवण्णो यं नवा

21, 21. **Ivaṇṇo yaṁ navā.** [Ivaṇṇo+yaṁ+navā. 3 words]

[V] Pubbo **ivaṇṇo**[12] sare pare **ya**-kāraṁ pappoti navā.

When a vowel is present behind, the vowels of front consonants "**i and ī**" called "**ivaṇṇa**" sometimes morph into consonant "**ya**". [This Sutta changes "**i** or **ī**" into "**y**"]

---

[12] There are other names of vowels (except **e** & **o**) named for the purpose of easy referencing in the matters of morphological procedures. They are:
(1) **avaṇṇa= a & ā** are called **avaṇṇa** (Homogenous vowels of "a")
(2) **ivaṇṇa= i & ī** are called **ivaṇṇa** (Homogenous vowels of "i")
(3) **uvaṇṇa= u & ū** are called **uvaṇṇa.** (Homogenous vowels of "u")
It is a common morphological pattern of change that **i & ī** used to change into "**y**", while **u & ū** change into "**v**". Please note this consistent pattern of change carefully.

[CS] (a) • Paṭisanthāravuttya'ssa.
(b) Sabbā • vittyā'nubhūyate.

[SS] (a) • Paṭisanthāravutti+assa.
Paṭisunthāravutti-diplomatically courteous. **assa**-(one) should be. **i.e.** (one) should be diplomatically courteous. (to avoid conflict and maintain harmony)
(b) • vitti+anubhūyate.
sabbā-all. **vitti**-wealth. **anubhūyate**-is enjoyed. **i.e.** all the wealth is enjoyed.

[SM] These examples will be explained in Sutta 41 later.

Navā'ti kasmā?
Pañcaha'ṅgehi samannāgato. Muttacāgī anu'ddhato.
Why is there the word "Navā" in Sutta?
It is to show that the function of this rule is inapplicable in such instances of phrase examples as "Pañcaha'ṅgehi samannāgato, Muttacāgī anu'ddhato" and so on as it is being restricted by the word "navā".

[CS] (a) * Pañcaha'ṅgehi samannāgato.
(b) * Muttacāgī anu'ddhato

[SS] (a) * Pañcahi+aṅgehi samannāgato.
(b) * Muttacāgī+anu'ddhato
Muttacāgī-the one who used to offer generously. **anu'ddhato**-is not restless, **i.e.** calm.
i.e. The one who used to offer generously is calm with joy, not being restless.

[SM] (a) Just elide the front vowel and attach "**h**" to next "**a**".
(b) Keep as pakati (**i.e.** as it is). No specific function needed.

२२, २८. एवादिस्स रि पुब्बो च रस्सो
22, 28. Evā'dissa ri pubbo ca rasso.

[Eva-ādissa+ri+pubbo+ca+rasso. 5 words]

[V] Saramhā parassa **eva**ssa **e**-kārassa ādissa **ri**kāro hoti.
Pubbo ca saro rasso hoti navā.

The component vowel "**e**" of the Nipāta particle "**eva**" after the front vowel, changes into "**ri**" while the front vowel is also made into a "rassa" (**i.e.** shortened) sometimes.

Summary: This Sutta changes "**e**" of "**eva**" into "**ri**" and also shortens the vowel in front of "**eva**". (2 Functions)

[CS] (a) • Yatha**'r**iva vasudhātalañ'ca sabbaṁ,
Yatha'riva-like, just as, **vasudhātalañ'ca**-the surface of the earth. **sabbaṁ**-all. [**vasudhā**-earth. **talaṁ**-surface+**ca**-also]
(b) • Tatha**'r**iva guṇavā supūjaniyo.
Tatha'riva-similarly in that manner. **guṇavā**-the virtuous one. **supūjaniyo**-is to be honored well. **i.e.** Just as all the surface of earth (is to be appreciated), so is the virtuous one to be honored.

[SS] (a) • Yath**ā**+**e**va (b) • Tath**ā**+**e**va

[SM] For both examples, just change "**e**" into "**ri**" and shorten the front "**ā**" into "**a**". It is done.

Navā'ti kasmā? *Yathā eva. *Tathā eva.
Why is there the word "Navā" in Sutta?
It is to show that the function of this Sutta's rule is inapplicable in such instances of phrase examples as "Yathā eva, Tathā eva" etc. (There is no Sandhi in the example. Hence, inapplicable. These words are already separate words)

Iti sandhikappe dutiyo kaṇḍo.

The Second Section of Sandhi ends.

Tatiya Kaṇḍa
The Third Section

२३, २६. सरा पकति ब्यञ्जने

23, 26. **Sarā pakati byañjane.** [Sarā+pakati+byañjane. 3 words]

[V] Sarā kho byañjane pare pakatirūpāni honti.

When a consonant follows, the front vowel is to be kept as a "Pakati"(without applying any morphological function).

Note: Withholding any specific function such as elision, changing into other word forms as prescribed in certain Suttas such as 12, 13, 14, 15, 17, is called a "**pakati sandhi**" process).
Why a "Pakati" procedure?
Because it is totally unnecessary to have any Sandhi process lest it may corrupt the structural pattern of words or phrases. Thus keeps the proper meaning of the words.
See examples carefully. Even though a next consonant is present in each examples shown by the side of a plus sign, there is no specific function of Sandhi applied on the front vowels.

[CS] (a) • Mano'pubbaṅgamā dhammā.
(b) • Pamādo'maccuno padaṁ,
(c) Tiṇṇo'pāraṅgato ahu.

[SS] (a) • Man**o**+**p**ubbaṅgamā dhammā.
Manopubbaṅgamā-are preceded by mind. **dhammā**-all mental states and physical actions. **i.e.** All mental states and physical phenomenon are preceded by the mind.
(b) • Pamādo+maccuno padaṁ,
Pamādo-the carelessness. maccuno-of death. padaṁ-is the cause. **i.e.** the carelessness is the cause of (repeated) death (in Samsāra).
(c) Tiṇṇ**o**+**p**āraṅgato ahu.
Tiṇṇo-the one who had crossed. **pāraṅgato**-the one who had gone to the other shore of safety and peace. **ahu**-was.
i.e. (The enlightened saint) had crossed the ocean of suffering and had gone to the shore of Nibbāna.

[SM] For all examples (a-b-c), keep the vowel "**o**" as a "**pakati, o**" without performing any morphological procedure.

२४, ३५. सरे क्वचि

24, 35. **Sare kvaci.** [Sare+kvaci. 2 words]

[V] Sarā kho sare pare kvaci pakatirūpāni honti.

When a vowel follows, the front vowel is sometimes kept as a pakati (as an un-altered one).

[CS] • Ko imaṁ pathaviṁ vicessati.
[SS] • K**o**+**i**maṁ pathaviṁ vicessati.

Ko-who. **imaṁ**-this. **pathaviṁ**-earthly body. **vicessati**-will analyze (with insight knowledge) ? **i.e.** Who is going to analyze this earthly body with insight knowledge?

[SM] Keep the front vowel "**o**" as a "**pakati, o**". No specific Sandhi procedure is applied on the front vowel "**o**" despite the presence of next vowel "**i**".

Kvacī'ti kasmā?
Why there is the word "Kvaci" in Sutta?
It is to show that the function of this rule is inapplicable in the examples shown below as restricted by the word "kvaci".

* Appassutā'yaṁ puriso.

[CS] * Appassutā'yaṁ puriso
[SS] * Appassut**o**+**a**yaṁ puriso

Appassuto-is of less knowledge. **ayaṁ puriso**-this person. **i.e.** This person is of less knowledge.

[SM] Just elide the front vowel "**o**" and lengthen next vowel "**a**" into "**ā**" by Sutta 15. Then attach the front consonant "**t**" to "**ā**".
Note: The relevant Sutta for each relevant function is an easy guess work for a keen student. So sometimes it will be intentionally left unexplained.

२५, ३७. दीघं

25, 37. **Dīghaṁ.** [Dīghaṁ. 1 word]

[V] Sarā kho byañjane pare kvaci dīghaṁ papponti.

When a consonant follow, the front vowel is sometimes made into "dīgha", **i.e.** lengthened.

[CS] (a) • Sammā dhammaṁ vipassato.

Sammā-well or rightly. **dhammaṁ**-the Dhamma. **vipassato**-to the one who sees.

(b) Evaṁ gāme • munī care.

Evaṁ-thus. **gāme**-in the village. **muni**-the wise monk**. care**-should conduct. **i.e.** The wise monk should thus conduct in the village (to the devotees without negatively affecting their faith or wealth)

(c) • Khantī paramaṁ tapo titikkhā.

Khantī-the practice of patience**. paramaṁ**-noble. **tapo**-is highest ethical virtue. **titikkhā-**a spiritual quality called "**titikhā**". **i.e.** A spiritual quality called "**titikhā**", the practice of patience is the highest noble ethical virtue.

[SS] (a) • Samm**a**+**d**hammaṁ

(b) • mun**i**+**c**are.

(c) • Khant**i**+**p**aramaṁ

[SM] Lengthen "**a**" of (a) into "**ā**" and "**i**" of both (b) and (c) into "**ī**" by this Sutta. It is done.

Kvacī'ti kasmā?

Why is there the word "Kvaci" in Sutta?

It is to show that the function of this rule is inapplicable in examples shown below as restricted by "kvaci".

* Idha modati * pecca modati.

Idha-Here in this life. **modati-**(he) rejoices.

pecca-there in next life. **modati**-(he) rejoices.

* patilīyati. * Paṭihaññati.

patilīyati-(he) hesitates. **Paṭihaññati**-(he) is stressed out or hurt.

Note: No Sandhi procedure in * examples. This function occurs:

(1) where a convenient and easy recitation of a verse is required,

(2) and where exact metrical measure of a Pāli verse (gāthā) is needed to be maintained for the smooth versification.

२६, ३८. रस्सं

26, 38. **Rassaṁ.** [Rassaṁ. 1 word]

[V] Sarā kho byañjane pare kvaci rassaṁ papponti.

When a consonant follows, the front vowel is sometimes made into "rassa", **i.e.** shortened.

Note: This function occurs:

(1) when preserving exact metrical measure in a Gathā (verse),

(2) where a new syllable is inserted,

(3) in the instances with conjunct-consonants.

[CS] (a) • Bhovād**i**'nāma so hoti.

Bhovādi'nāma-is called bhovādī. **so**-that person. **hoti**-is. **i.e.** That person is called **Bhovādi**-the one who used to say the term "bho".

(b) Yathābhāv**i'**guṇena so.

Yathābhāvī-is calledYathābhāvī. **guṇena**-by virtue. **so**-that person.

[SS] (a) • Bhovād**ī**+**n**āma

(b) • Yathābhāv**ī**+**gu**ṇena so.

[SM] Shorten "**ī**" of both (a) and (b) into "**i**" by this Sutta. It is done.

Kvacī'ti kasmā?

Why is there the word "Kvaci" in Sutta?

It is to show that the function of this rule is inapplicable in such instances of phrase examples shown below as it is being restricted by the word "kvaci".

* Sammā samādhi. * Sāvittī chandaso mukhaṁ.

* Upanīyati jīvita'mappa'māyu.

[CS] (a) * Sammāsamādhi.

(b) * Sāvittī chandaso mukhaṁ.

(c) * Upanīyati jīvita'mappa'māyu.

[SS] (a) * Sammā+samādhi-the right concentration.

(b) * Sāvittī+chandaso mukhaṁ.

Sāvittī-the verse addressed to "Sāvitri-the sun god". **chandaso**-of Vedic hymns. **mukhaṁ**-(is) the beginning. **i.e.** the verse addressed to "sāvitri" is the beginning of vedic hymns (Rig veda III, 62,10).

(c) * Upanīyati jīvita**ṁ**+appa**ṁ**+**ā**yu

Upanīyati-is brought nearer (to death). **jīvitaṁ-**life. **appaṁ-**short. **āyu-**age. **i.e.** Short life and age (of living beings) is brought nearer (to death day by day).

[SM] No rassa function for vowels **ā**, & **ī** in (a-b) before plus sign.

There is Sandhi in non-example words "jīvita**ṁ**+appa**ṁ**+**ā**yu".

[SM] Just change both "**ṁ**" into "**m**" by 34 and attach it to next vowels.

Note: This function of Sutta occurs:

(1) when preserving exact metrical measure in prosody,

(2) where a new syllable is being inserted,

(3) in the words with conjunct-consonants.

See the examples shown in order of point of occurrence. **Please see the underlined short vowels** which are made into a Rassa (shortened vowel).

(1) Bhovadi Nāma So Hoti (Here "i" is intentionally shortened to preserve the metrical measure of the verse)

(2) Samma'dakkhato [Sammā+akkhāto] (Here "a" is intentionally shortened due to an inserted syllable "d")

(3) Parakkamo [Parā+kamo] (Here "a" is intentionally shortened due to the conjunct-consonants "kk")

२७, ३९. लोपञ्च तत्राकारो

27, 39. **Lopañ'ca tatrā'kāro** [Lopaṁ+ca+tatra+a-kāro. 4 words]

[V] Sarā kho byañjane pare kvaci lopaṁ papponti.
Tatra ca lope kate **a**-kārā'gamo hoti.

When a consonant is present behind, the front vowel is sometimes elided. In place of the elided vowel, an "**a**" is inserted to replace it. [See SS before reading translations]

[CS] (a) • **Sa** sīlavā.

So-that person. **sīlavā-(**is) virtuous.

(b) • **Sa** paññavā.

So-that person. **paññavā-(**is) wise.

(c) • Es**a** dhammo sanantano.

Eso-this. **dhammo-**Dhamma. **sanantano-**is ancient. **i.e.** This is ancient Dhamma.

(d) • S**a** ve kasāva'marahati.

So-that person. **ve-**in fact. **kasāvaṁ-**the robe. **arahati-**deserves (to wear). **i.e.** That person indeed deserves to wear the robes.

(e) • S**a** mānakāmo'pi bhaveyya.

So-that person. **mānakāmo'pi-**desirous of admiration. **bhaveyya-**should be.

(f) • S**a** ve muni jātibhayaṁ adassi.

So. ve-indeed. **muni-**sage, monk. **jātibhayaṁ-**the danger of rebirth. **adassi-**saw. **i.e.** That sage saw the danger of rebirth.

[SS] (a) • S**o**+**s**īlavā. (b) • S**o**+**p**aññavā.
(c) • Es**o**+**d**hammo
(d) • S**o**+**v**e kasāva**ṁ**+**a**rahati.
(e) • S**o**+**m**ānakāmo'pi bhaveyya.
(f) • S**o**+**v**e muni jātibhayaṁ adassi.

[SM] Just elide "o" of all examples and insert "a" in its place. It is done. In **(d)** Sandhi is at two points. In 2nd point, just change "**ṁ**" into "**m**" by 34.

Kvacī'ti kasmā?

Why is there the word "Kvaci" in Sutta?

It is to show that the function of this rule is inapplicable in some examples shown below as implied by the word "kvaci".

* So muni-that monk.

* Eso dhammo padissati.

Eso dhammo-That Dhamma. **padissati-**is clearly seen (that Dhamma is seen clearly).

* Na so kāsāva'marahati.

Na-does not. **so-**that person. **kāsāvaṁ-**the robe. **arahati-**deserves (to wear). **i.e.** That person does not deserve (to wear) the robe.

Note: There is no Sandhi process occurred in the examples except in the non-example word "kāsāva'marahati".

[SS] Kāsāva**ṁ**+**a**rahati.

[SM] Just change "**ṁ**" into "**m**" and attach it to the next vowel "a" by 34.

२८, ४०. पर द्वेभावो ठाने

28, 40. **Para dvebhāvo ṭhāne.** [Para+dvebhāvo+ṭhāne. 3 words]

[V] Saramhā parassa byañjanassa dvebhāvo hoti ṭhāne.

The consonant after the front vowel is to be reduplicated by adding a similar consonant to it wherever appropriate and applicable.

[See the examples below carefully as said in the Vutti of Sutta. There is a vowel before the apostrophe and plus signs. The consonant behind it is to be reduplicated]

[CS] (a) • Idha'**pp**amādo purisassa jantuno.
(b) • Pa'**bb**ajjaṁ kittayissāmi.
(c) • Cātu'**dd**asiṁ.
(d) • Pañca'**dd**asiṁ.
(e) • Abhi'**kk**antataro cando.

[SS] (a) • Idh**a**+**p**amādo purisassa jantuno.
Idha-in this world. **pamādo**-lack of diligence, carelessness. **purisassa**-of a person. **jantuno**-of a being. **i.e.** In this world, the carelessness of a person, a living being.
(b) • P**a**+**b**ajjaṁ kittayissāmi.
Pabajjaṁ-the monkhood. **kittayissāmi**-(I) shall announce.
(c) • Cāt**u**+**d**asiṁ.
Cātudasiṁ-on the the fourteenth day.
(d) • Pañc**a**+**d**asiṁ.
Pañcadasiṁ-on the fifteenth day.
(e) • Abh**i**+**k**antataro cando.
Abhikantataro-is more beautiful. **cando**-the moon.
[**Abhi**-specially.+ **kanta**-beautiful+**taro**-more] **i.e.** The moon is more beautiful on the 14th and 15th days.
[Examples c, d, e are translated together in the same context.]

[SM] Just reduplicate similar consonants of each example shown in bold-faced letters. It is done.

Ṭhāne'ti kasmā?

Why is there the word "ṭhāne" in Sutta?

It is to show that the function of this rule is inapplicable in some instances as shown below as they are not the right point for reduplication procedure.

* Idha modati, * pecca modati. (Refer to Sutta 25)
Note: No Sandhi process in these examples.

Table of Reduplication with Similar Consonants.

The Consonants eligible for homogenous reduplication process by the rule of this Sutta No.28, are shown in order of their own grouping.

Vagga Groups	The first	The second	The third	The fourth	The fifth
Ka-group	k+k>**kk**	N/A	g+g>**gg**	N/A	N/A
Ca-group	c+c>**cc**	N/A	j+j>**jj**	N/A	ñ+ñ> **ññ**
Ṭa-group	ṭ+ṭ>**ṭṭ**	N/A	ḍ+ḍ>**ḍḍ**	N/A	ṇ+ ṇ>**ṇṇ**
Ta-group	t+t>**tt**	N/A	d+d>**dd**	N/A	n+n>**nn**
Pa-group	p+p>**pp**	N/A	b+b>**bb**	N/A	m+m>**mm**
Non-Vagga	y+y>**yy**	N/A	l+l>**ll**	v+v>vv>bb	s+s>**ss**
y, r, l, v, s, h, ḷ,	"**r, ḷ** and **h**" are inapplicable for reduplication. Though v+v are augmented as "**vv**", it usually further changes as "**bb**".				

२९, ४२. वग्गे घोसाघोसानं ततियपठमा

29, 42. Vagge ghosā'ghosānaṁ tatiya, paṭhamā.

[Vagge+ghosa, aghosānaṁ+tatiya, paṭhamā. 3 words]

[V] Vagge kho pubbesaṁ byañjanānaṁ ghosā'ghosabhūtānaṁ saramhā yathāsaṅkhyaṁ tatiya, paṭhama'kkharā dvebhāvaṁ gacchanti ṭhāne.

To vagga group consonants which may be either **ghosa** (**i.e.** the second) or **aghosa** (**i.e.** The fourth) followed by a vowel, a reduplication process is to be carried out by adding the dissimilar consonants of either the **first** (to the second) or the **third** (to the fourth) from the same vagga group respectively wherever applicable.

Note: Even though it is categorically said as "**ghosā'ghosabhūtānaṁ**" in Vutti, not all **ghosa** or **aghosa** are eligible to be the candidate (**i.e.** the base word) for reduplication. The eligible ghosa is only **the second** and the aghosa eligible to be reduplicated is **the fourth** one. **This Sutta enjoins** to reduplicate the second ghosa with the first of the same vagga group while the fourth is to be reduplicated with the third. Note that **non-vagga ghosa and aghosa are inapplicable**. Please refer to Sutta 7 & 9 regarding Vagga and ghosa or aghosa. Normally, the procedure of this Sutta is quite challenging to understand without a more simplified explanation and elucidation. The wording structure of the Sutta itself seems a bit misplaced. If Sutta is structured as "Vagge ghosā'ghosānaṁ paṭhama, tatiyā", it could be more simple to understand its meaning for the students.

Method:

(1) If the candidate base word is **the second** in Vagga group. Then, the **first** dissimilar letter from the same group is to be added to it.

(2) If **the fourth** is the candidate base word, then **the third** from the group is to be added to it. See all the examples and accompanying tables.

Table of Reduplication with Dissimilar Consonants

(Only the second and the fourth consonants are to be reduplicated)

Vagga Group	**Ghosa** (aspirated)		**Aghosa** (Unaspirated)		**The Fifth**
	The First	**The Second** Base syllable (shown in bold)	**The Third**	**The Fourth** Base syllable (shown in old)	
Ka-group	K>	K+**kha**=kkha	G>	G+**gha**=ggha	n/a
Ca-group	C>	C+**cha**=ccha	J>	J+**Jha**=jjha	n/a
Ṭa-group	Ṭ>	Ṭ+**ṭha**=ṭṭha	Ḍ>	Ḍ+**ḍha**=ḍḍha	n/a
Ta-group	T>	T+**tha**=ttha	D>	D+**dha**=ddha	n/a
Pa-group	P>	P+**pha**=ppha	B>	B+**bha**=bbha	n/a

Ghosa-group Reduplication Table

Vagga	**Ghosa**		**Examples** (Drawn from Pāli texts)
	The first	The second	
Ka-vagga	k>	+kh	Nakkhamati-(he) dislikes[ni+khamati]
Ca-group	c>	+ch	Ducchannaṁ-badly covered [du+channaṁ]
Ṭa-group	ṭ>	+ṭh	adhiṭṭhāti-(It) stands firmly.[adhi+ṭhāti]
Ta-group	t>	+th	Vitthāreti-(It) expands.[vi+thāreti]
Pa-group	p>	+ph	Nipphalaṁ-without result.[ni+phalaṁ]

Aghosa-group Reduplication Table

Vagga	**Aghosa**		**Examples** (Drawn from Pāli texts)
	The third	The fourth	
Ka-vagga	g>	+gh	paggharati-(It) drips.[pa+gharati]
Ca-group	j>	+jh	Ujjhāyanti-(they) complain. [u+jhāyanti]
Ṭa-group	ḍ>	+ḍh	*Vaḍḍheti-(It) grows.[vaḍheti] (The examples are rare in this group)
Ta-group	d>	+dh	Niddhāreti-(he) carries out.[ni+dhāreti]
Pa-group	b>	+bh	Vibbhamati-(It) totters.[vi+bhamati]

Note: The Sandhi applicable by the rule of this Sutta usually used to occur mostly in the individual words prefixed with upasagga particles though it also occurs occasionally in the union of two different words like those cited in the Sutta below.

The examples of Sutta (these examples are at the union of two words) :

[CS] (a) Eseva • ca**j'jh**ānapphalo.
(b) • Yatra**ṭ'ṭh**itaṁ nappasaheyya maccu.
(c) Sele yathā • pabbatamuddhani **ṭ'ṭh**ito.
(d) • Cattāri **ṭ'ṭh**ānāni naro pamatto.

[SS] (a) Eseva • ca+**jh**ānapphalo.
Ese'va ca-only this. **jhānapphalo**-is the result of Jhānas. **i.e.** Only this is the result of Jhānas (deep mental absorption states).
(b) • Yatra+**ṭh**itaṁ nappasaheyya maccu.
Yatra-where. **ṭhitaṁ**-to the one standing. **na'ppasaheyya**-would not overwhelm. **maccu**-death. **i.e.** A place where death cannot overwhelm.
(c) Sele yathā • pabbatamuddhani+**ṭh**ito.
Sele-rocky. **yathā**-like. **pabbatamuddhani**-on top of mountain. **ṭhito**-standing. **i.e.** Like the one standing on top of the rocky mountain (can see things below clearly)
(d) • Cattāri+**ṭh**ānāni naro pamatto.
Cattāri-the four. **ṭhānāni**-points. **naro**-man. **pamatto**-being ignorant of. **i.e.** The man who is ignorant of the four points.

[SM] For (a) add dissimilar "**j**" to "**jh**". [Here "**jha**" **is the fourth** in Vagga. Therefore, "**j**", **the third** becomes its reduplicate]
For (b) add "**ṭ**" to "**ṭh**" for (b) (c) and (d). [Here, "**ṭha**" **is the second** in Vagga. So "**ṭ**", **the first** is its reduplicate]
[See both the front and rear letters carefully as shown in bold-faced letters. Check what kind of dissimilar letter is to be reduplicated in each example.]

Ṭhāne'ti kasmā?
Why is there the word "ṭhāne" in Sutta?
It is to show that the function of this rule is inapplicable in the example shown below as it is not the due place for this rule.
* Idha cetaso daḷhaṁ gaṇhāti thāmasā.
Idha-in this noble teaching of Budda. **cetaso**-of the mind. **daḷhaṁ**-

firmly. **gaṇhāti**-holds or focuses. **thāmasā**-by power of. **i.e.** In this noble teaching of Buddha, (The disciple who is committed) firmly holds his (object of meditation) by power of the concentrated mind.

[CS] * Idha cetaso

[SM] The function of this Sutta is inapplicable as it is not the due point. ("**ṭhāna**-means due point")

Iti sandhikappe tatiyo kaṇḍo.

The Third Section of Sandhi ends.

Catuttha Kaṇḍa

The Fourth Section

३०, ५८. अं ब्यञ्जने निग्गहितं

30, 58. **Aṁ byañjane niggahitaṁ**

[Aṁ+byañjane+niggahitaṁ. 3]

[V] Niggahitaṁ[13] kho byañjane pare **aṁ**-iti hoti.

When a consonant follows, [**i.e.** Present behind] the "niggahita-**ṁ**" in the front changes into **aṁ.** [See the footnote.]

[CS] (a) • Evaṁ'vutte.

(b) • Taṁ'sādhū'ti paṭissuṇitvā. (Sandhi at 2 points in this example)

[SS] (a) • Evaṁ+**v**utte.

Evaṁ-thus. **vutte**-(when) said. **i.e.** When thus said.

(b) • Ta**ṁ**+**s**ādh**u**+**i**ti paṭissuṇitvā.

Taṁ-to that said word of Buddha. **sādhu iti**- "Well Sir!"(replying) thus. **paṭissuṇitvā**-having accepted and replied. **i.e.** Having replied to Buddha's call by saying "Well, Venerable Sir!".

[SM] For (a), By this Sutta, change "**ṁ**" into "**aṁ**"**.** Now, it will look like this: [• Eva+**aṁ**+vutte.] Elide the "**a**" of "**eva**"**.** Now, it will look like this: [• Ev+**aṁ**+vutte.]. It is done.

For (b) the first point of Sandhi, By this Sutta, change "**ṁ**" into "**aṁ**"**.** Now, it will look like this: [• Ta+**aṁ**+sādh**u**+**i**ti paṭissuṇitvā] Elide the front "**a**" of "**Ta**"**.** Now, it will look like this: [• T+**aṁ**+sādh**u**+**i**ti paṭissuṇitvā].

For the second point of Sandhi, elide the next vowel "**i**" by Sutta 13 and lengthen the front "**u**" into "**ū**" by Sutta 16.

---

[13] This Sutta keeps the niggahita represented by a dot as it is without changing it into any word-form. SM is actually not necessary but shown in view of "Rūpasiddhi" which said: *Saralopo'ti ādinā pubbasaralopo vā.*

Though the function of the Sutta seems redundant, it has to be assumed as a matter of the grammatical principle and necessity which prevents any kind of morphological alteration of an independent niggahita in singular, accusative case. In such cases, it usually plays either as an adverb or an object etc., in a sentence.

Now, it will be combined in Sandhi like this: [• Taṁ sādhūti paṭissuṇitvā]. It is done.

३१. ४९. वग्गन्तं वा वग्गे

31, 49. **Vagga'ntaṁ vā vagge**

[Vagga-antaṁ+vā+vagge. 3 words]

[V] Vaggabhūte byañjane pare niggahitaṁ kho vaggantaṁ vā pappoti.

When a consonant belonging to a specific vagga group follows (**i.e.** Is present behind), the "niggahita-**ṁ**" in front is to be sometimes changed into the last consonant of that vagga group accordingly.

Summary: This Sutta enjoins to change so-called Niggahita "**ṁ**" into "**ṅ, ñ, ṇ, n, m**" depending on the next letter of relevant Vagga-groups it precedes. The five consonants "**ṅ, ñ, ṇ, n, m**" are called "**Vagganta**-the end-consonants of the Vagga-group, or **nasal stops**". [Refer to Sutta 7 to clearly understand this function.]

Here is how the rule of this Sutta is to be applied:

(a) If "ṁ" precedes one of **k, kh, g, gh.** Then it will be changed into "**ṅ**".

(b) If "ṁ" precedes one of **c, ch, j, jh,**>it will be changed into "**ñ**".

(c) If "ṁ" precedes one of **ṭ, ṭh, ḍ, ḍh,**> it will be changed into "**ṇ**".

(d) If "ṁ" precedes one of **t, th, d, dh,*n,**>it will be changed into "**n**".

(e) If "ṁ" precedes one of **p, ph, b, bh, m**>it will be changed into "**m**".

Note: The **anomalous examples** where ***n** constitute as the last syllable of Vagga are also found in some Pāli texts such as "**tan'niccutaṁ, Kinnu**" etc. In this grammar text, in Sutta No. 573, Sā'disanta puccha, bhanja, hansā'dīhi ṭṭho, "**hansādīhi**" is an anomalous Sandhi-form where a non-vagga "**s**" is preceded by "**ṁ**". Without such Sandhi being applied, it should be "**haṁsādīhi**-from the root **haṁsa** etc,".

[CS] (a) • Ta**n'n**iccutaṁ. Here "**ṁ**" precedes "**n**".

(b) • Dhammañ'care sucaritaṁ. Here "ṁ" precedes "c", so it becomes "ñ".

(c) • Cirap'pavāsiṁ purisaṁ. Here "ṁ" precedes "p", so it becomes "m".

(d) • Santan'tassa manaṁ hoti. Here "ṁ" precedes "t", so it becomes "n".

(e) • Taṅ'kāruṇikaṁ. Here "ṁ" precedes "k", so it becomes "ṅ".

(f) • Evaṅ'kho bhikkhave sikkhitabbaṁ. Here "ṁ" precedes "kh", hence it becomes "ṅ".

Note: Though the Sutta enjoins to change "ṁ" into the end-syllables "**ṅ, ñ, ṇ, n, m**", **there are some anomalous examples** such as the example (c).

See the points of Sandhi in these examples **shown in bold-faced two letters.** Check which Vagga group the next letter belongs to. The solution as to which letter is to become the morpheme of the front niggahita will be quite easy to understand.

[SS] (a) • Taṁ+**n**iccutaṁ.

Taṁ-That Nibbāna. **niccutaṁ**-is without change [**Ni**-without+**cuta**-death or change]

(b) • Dhammaṁ+**c**are sucaritaṁ.

Dhammaṁ-the Dhamma. **care**-(one) should practice. **sucaritaṁ**-by being well-practiced. **i.e.** One should practice Dhamma well, (not half-heartedly nor sporadically but with consistent effort).

(c) • Ciraṁ+**p**avāsiṁ purisaṁ.

Ciraṁ-for long. **pavāsiṁ**-used to be living abroad. **purisaṁ**-to the person. **i.e.** To the person who used to live in other lands for long (when he safely returns, both family and friends warmly welcome him).

(d) • Santaṁ+**t**assa manaṁ hoti.

Santaṁ-calm. **tassa**-of that person. **manaṁ**-mind. **hoti**-is. **i.e.** The mind of that person (who progressed in meditation) is calm.

(e) • Taṁ+**k**āruṇikaṁ.

Taṁ-to that. **kāruṇikaṁ**-compassionate Buddha.

(f) • Evaṁ+**kh**o bhikkhave.

Evaṁ kho-thus. **bhikkhave**-monks!

[SM] For example (a), Change "**ṁ**" into "**n**", For (b) change into "**ñ**", For (c) change into "**m**", this "m" is to be changed into "p" by means of "Ca" in Sutta 35. If directly changes into "p" by this Sutta alone, it will contravene the injunction of this Sutta. For (d) change into "**n**",

For (e-f), change into "**ṅ**".

Vāggahaṇena niggahitaṁ kho la-kārādeso hoti.
By the word "**vā**" included in this Sutta, the niggahita changes into consonant "**l**".

[CS] • Puggalaṁ-to an individual. [SS] Pugga**ṁ**+aṁ
[SM] Change the front "**aṁ**" into "**l**" and attach it to next "**a**". It is done.

Vā'ti kasmā?
Why is there the word "vā" in Sutta?
It is to show that the function of this rule is inapplicable in the examples shown below as restricted by "vā".

[CS] * Na taṁ kammaṁ kataṁ sādhu.
Na-not. **taṁ**-that. **kammaṁ**-deed. **kataṁ**-which is done. **sādhu**-good. **i.e.** That (unwholesome) deed which has been done is not good.
[SS] * Na taṁ+kammaṁ kataṁ sādhu. [SM]No Sandhi function.

TABLE OF VAGGANTA-FUNCTION

This table explains how "**ṁ**" is to be systematically morphed into the respective end-consonants of vagga.

Vagga Group	The first	The second	The third	The fourth
Ka group	ṁ+ka>**ṅka** **Taṅkāruṇikaṁ**	ṁ+kha>**ṅkha** **taṅkhaṇaṁ**	ṁ+ga>**ṅga** **Saṅgaho**	ṁ+gha>**ṅgha** **Saṅghāto**
Ca group	ṁ+ca>**ñca** **tañca** [taṁ+ca]	ṁ+cha>**ñcha** **Sañchanno** [Saṁ+channo]	ṁ+ja>**ñja** **Sañjānāti** [Saṁ+jānāti]	ṁ+jha>**ñjha** * **Sañjhāyati** [Saṁ+jhāyati]
Ṭa group	ṁ+ṭa>ṇṭa No examples found in the texts though applicable by the rule.	ṁ+ṭha>**ṇṭha** **Saṇṭhāti** [Saṁ+ṭhāti]	ṁ+ḍa>**ṇḍa** * **Saṇḍahati** [Saṁ+ḍahāti]	ṁ+ḍha>ṇḍha No examples found though it is applicable.
Ta group	ṁ+ta>**nta** **Santussati** [Saṁ+tussati]	ṁ+tha>**ntha** **Santhāro** [Saṁ+thāro]	ṁ+da>**nda** **Sandiṭṭhiko** [Saṁ+diṭṭhiko]	ṁ+dha>**ndha** **Jutindharo** [Jutiṁ+dharo]
Pa group	ṁ+pa>**mpa** **Sampatto** [Saṁ+patto]	ṁ+pha>**mpha** **Tamphalaṁ** [Taṁ+phalaṁ]	ṁ+ba>**mba** **Sambodho** [Saṁ+bodho]	ṁ+bha>**mbha** **Sambhujjhati** [Saṁ+bhujjati]
Note: The example shown with * mark are not frequently found in the majority of Pāli texts.				

३२, ५०. एहे ञं

32, 50. **E,he ñaṁ** [E-he+ñaṁ. 2 words]

[V] **E**-kāra, **ha**-kāre pare niggahitaṁ kho **ña**-kāraṁ pappoti vā.

When either vowel "**e**" or consonant "**h**" are present behind, the "niggahita-**ṁ**" in front sometimes changes into "**ñ**". [See "e" is behind in the examples **a, b.** "h" is behind in **c, d**]

[CS] (a) • Paccattañ'ñeva parinibbāyissāmi.

Paccattañ'ñeva-by oneself. **parinibbāyissāmi**-(I) will enter into Nibbānic peace by oneself.

(b) • Tañ'ñeve'ttha paṭipucchissāmi.

Tañ'ñeva-only to you. **ettha**-here. **paṭipucchissāmi**-(I) will re-question. **i.e.** I will question you again in this matter.

(c) • Evañ'hi vo bhikkhave sikkhitabbaṁ.

Evañ'hi-only thus. **vo**-by you. **bhikkhave**-monks! **sikkhitabbaṁ**-should train. **i.e.** You should thus train (practice).

(d) • Tañ'hi tassa musā hoti.

Tañ'hi-that word. **tassa**-of that person. **musā**-wrong. **hoti**-is. **i.e.** His word is wrong.

[SS] (a) • Paccatta**ṁ**+**e**va.

(b) • Ta**ṁ**+**e**vettha. (**e** of a **Nipāta** word "**eva**" is present in these examples)

(c) • Eva**ṁ**+**h**i

(d) • Ta**ṁ**+**h**i. (**h** of a **Nipāta** word "**hi**" is present in these examples)

[SM] For (a) (b), change "**ṁ**" of all examples into one single "**ñ**" and redouble it by Sutta 28. Then attach the double "**ññ**" to next respective vowels.

For (c) (d), just change "**ṁ**" into "**ñ**" and attach it to next consonant "**h**". It is done.

Vā'ti kasmā?

Why is there the word "vā" in Sutta?

It is to show that the function of this rule is inapplicable in some instances shown below as restricted by the word "vā".

[CS] * Eva'metaṁ abhiññāya, *Evaṁ hoti subhāsitaṁ.

Evaṁ-thus. **etaṁ**-that Dhamma. **abhiññāya**-having known. **Evaṁ**-

thus. **hoti**-is. **subhāsitaṁ**-well-said. **i.e.** Having known that Dhamma thus, (the word thus said) is well-said.

[SS] *(a) Evaṁ+etaṁ (b) *Evaṁ hoti

[SM] (a) Change "**ṁ**" into "**m**" by 34 and attach it to the next vowel. It is done. (b) Same as in example "evaṁ vutte" at Sutta 30.

३३. ५०. स ये च

33, 50. **Sa ye ca** [Sa+ye+ca. 3 words]

[V] Niggahitaṁ kho **ya**-kāre pare saha ya-kārena **ñakā**raṁ pappoti vā.

When consonant "**ya**" follows, the "niggahita-**ṁ**" in front, along with "ya", sometimes changes into "**ñ**".

[CS] (a) • Sañ'ñogo-joined together. (b) • Sañ'ñuttaṁ-conjoined.

[SS] (a) • Sa**ṁ**+**y**ogo (b) • Sa**ṁ**+**y**uttaṁ.

[SM] Change "**ṁ**" together with "**y**" as prescribed by Sutta into one single "**ñ**". Reduplicate it by 28 and attach to respective vowels "**o** and **u**" of each example. It is done.

Vā'ti kasmā?

Why is there the word "vā" in Sutta?

It is to show that the function of this rule is inapplicable in some instances shown below as restricted by "vā".

* Saṁyogo. * Saṁyuttaṁ.

[SM] No Sandhi in these examples. That is why there is an "**ṁ**" still remaining intact without changing into any specific word-form.

३४, ५२. मदा सरे

34, 52. **Ma,dā sare** [Ma, dā+sare. 2 words]

[V] Niggahitassa kho sare pare **ma**-kāra, d**a**-kārā'desā honti vā.

When a vowel is present behind, the "niggahita-**ṁ**" in front is to be sometimes changed into consonants "**m** or **d**".

[CS] (a) • Ta'mahaṁ brūmi brahmaṇaṁ.
(b) • Eta'davoca satthā.

[SS] (a) • Ta**ṁ**+**a**haṁ brūmi brahmaṇaṁ.

Taṁ-to that person. **ahaṁ**-I. **brūmi**-declare. **brahmaṇaṁ**-as Brāhmaṇa. **i.e.** I say that person as Brahmaṇa (the one who have had removed sins. **i.e.** saint).

(b) • Eta**ṁ**+**a**voca satthā.

Etaṁ-this. **avoca**-said. **satthā**-Lord Buddha. **i.e.** Lord Buddha said this discourse.

[SM] (a) Change "**ṁ**" into "**m**" (b) into "**d**". Then attach those "**m**" and "**d**" to next vowels. Then they become perfectly combined words in the Sandhi.

Vā'ti kasmā?

Why is there the word "vā" in Sutta?

It is to show that the function of this rule is inapplicable in examples shown below as it is restricted by the word "vā".

*Akkocchi maṁ, *avadhi maṁ, *ajini maṁ, *ahāsi me. (Re: Sutta 11)

[SM] No Sandhi process occurred in these examples.

३५, ३४. य व म द न त र ळा चागमा

35, 34. **Ya, va, ma, da, na, ta, ra, lā cā'gamā**

[Ya, va, ma, da, na, ta, ra, lā+ca+āgamā. 3 words]

[V] Sare pare **ya**kāro **va**kāro **ma**kāro **da**kāro **na**kāro **ta**kāro **ra**kāro **la**kāro ime āgamā honti vā.

The consonants "**y, v, m, d, n, t, r, ḷ**" are sometimes to be inserted when a vowel is present behind(**i.e.** follows).

See the examples below where the consonants to be inserted are clearly shown in brackets. The points to be inserted are behind the + plus sign, right in front of the vowels in each example.

SM is quite simple for these examples except a few.

[y] • Na'yimassa vijjā.>[ss]Na+**i**massa vijjā

Na-not. **imassa**-of this person. **vijjā**-knowledge.

i.e. There is no knowledge in this person.

[SM] Insert "**y**" in front of "**i**" and it is done.

• Yatha'yidaṁ cittaṁ.>Yathā **i**daṁ cittaṁ.

Yathā-like. **idaṁ cittaṁ**-this mind.

[SM] Insert "**y**" in front of "**i**" and shorten the front "**ā**" into "**a**" by Sutta 26.

[**v**] Migī bhantā • vudikkhati>**u**dikkhati.

Migī bhantā • udikkhati.

Migī-female-deer. **bhantā**-being shaken. **udikkhati**-looks.
i.e. The female deer looks shaken.

[**m**] Sittā te • lahu'messati.>lahu+**e**ssati.

Sittā-the boat with water being thrown out or removed. **te**-your. **lahu**-quickly. **essati**-will move.
i.e. With the seeped water being taken out, your boat will move fast.

Asittā te • garu'messati>garu+**e**ssati

Asittā-the boat with water not being thrown out. **te**-your. **garu**-heavily. **essati**-will move. **i.e.** With the seeped water not taken out, your boat will move heavily.

Asso bhadro • kasā'miva> kasā'+**i**va

Asso-the horse. **bhadro**-good. **kasā iva**-(keeps off) from goading stick. **i.e**. A good horse keeps off the goading stick (It does not need to be hit with a whipping stick).

[**d**] • Samma'daññā vimuttānaṁ.>• Sammā+**a**ññā

Sammā-well. **aññā**-having known. **vimuttānaṁ**-of those liberated.

[SM] Shorten the front "**ā**" into "**a**" by Sutta 26 after "**d**" is inserted and attached to next vowel.

• Manasā'daññā vimuttānaṁ.> Manasā+**a**ññā

Manasā-by mind. **aññā**-having known. **vimuttānaṁ**-of those liberated. [SM same as before]

• Attad'attha'mabhiññāya.> • Atta+**a**ttha**ṁ**+**a**bhiññāya

(2 points of Sandhi)

Atta atthaṁ-the well-being of oneself. **abhiññāya**-having known.
i.e. knowing one's wellbeing, (one should care about one's own business).

[SM] Insert "d" at the first point and attach it to next vowel. Then at second point, change the front "**ṁ**" into "**m**" by 31 and attach it to the next vowel.

[**n**] • Ciraṁ'nāyati>ciraṁ āyati. • Ito'nāyati>ito āyati.

Ciraṁ-after a long time. **āyati-**(he) comes. **Ito**-from here. **āyati-**(he) comes.

• nāyati>**ā**yati. (Both are the same, insert "n" before ā)

[**t**] • Yasmā'tiha bhikkhave.> Yasmā'+**i**ha bhikkhave

Yasmā-for which reason. **iha**-in this world. **bhikkhave**-monks!

• Tasmā'tiha bhikkhave.>Tasmā'+**i**ha bhikkhave

(Both examples are the same)

Tasmā-for that reason. **iha**-in this world. **bhikkhave**-monks!

• Ajja'tagge pāṇupetaṁ.> Ajja+**agge**

Ajja-today. **agge**-starting from. **pāṇupetaṁ**-for life.
i.e. Starting today for life (I take refuge in Buddha).

[r] • Sabbhi'reva samāsetha.> Sabbhi+**e**va samāsetha.

Sabbhi-with saints. **eva**-only. **samāsetha**-(one) should associate.

• Āragge'riva>• Āragge+iva-Like on the edge of wood-chisel.

• Sāsapo'riva>Sāsapo'+**i**va-like a mustard seed. (both are the same in matters of function, just insert "r" before "i")

[l] • Cha'ḷabhiññā.> Cha+**a**bhiññā-Six psychic powers.
(Insert "ḷ", **Note** that both "**l**" and "**ḷ**" are the same)

• Sa'ḷāyatanaṁ.>Cha+**ā**yatanaṁ-six sense-bases.
(In this example, after "**ḷ**" is inserted, change "cha" into "sa" by Sutta 374.)

Vā'ti kasmā?
Why is there the word "vā" in Sutta?
It is to show that the function of this Sutta is inapplicable in some instances shown below as it is restricted by the word "vā".

* Evaṁ mahiddhiyā esā.

Evaṁ-thus. **mahiddhiyā**-is of great power. **esā**-This condition of having wholesome deeds.
i.e. This condition of having wholesome deeds is thus of great power.

* Akkocchi maṁ, avadhi maṁ, ajini maṁ, ahāsi me.
(Re: Sutta 11)

* ajeyyo anugāmiko.

ajeyyo-unconquered by enemies. **anugāmiko**-something which accompanies.

Caggahaṇena idhe'va **ma**-kārassa **pa**-kāro hoti.
By means of the word "ca" in Sutta, the consonant "**m**" is changed into "**p**".

[CS] • Cira**p'**pavāsiṁ purisaṁ
[SS] Cira**m+p**avāsiṁ purisaṁ (Re Sutta 31)
[SM] Change "**m**" into "**p**" by means of "ca" in this Sutta and attach it to the next "**p**".

Kakārassa ca **da**kāro hoti.

The consonant "**k**" is changed into "**d**". (These also are additional functions applicable through "ca")

[CS] • Sa**d'**atthapasuto siyā

[SS] Sa**k**atthapasuto siyā.

Sakatthapasuto-focused on one's own best interest. **siyā**-one should be. **i.e.** One should be focused on one's own wellbeing. [**Saka**-self+**attha**-interest or business+**pasuto**-involved or focused]

Dakārassa ca **ta**kāro hoti.

The consonant "**d**" changes into "**t**".

[Note that this function is similar to the function applied by means of "ca" in Sutta 20. Refer to "to dassa" the split-Sutta function]

• Suga**t**o>Suga**d**o-gone well, or the one who speaks good words.

३६, ४७. क्वचि ओ ब्यञ्जने

36, 47. **Kvaci o byañjane** [Kvaci+o+byañjane. 3 words]

[V] Byañjane pare kvaci **o**-kārā'gamo hoti.

When a consonant follows behind, the vowel "**o**" is sometimes inserted (in front of it).

[CS] (a) • Atippago' kho tāva sāvatthiyaṁ piṇḍāya carituṁ.

Atippago' kho-it is too early. **tāva**-first. **sāvatthiyaṁ**-in the city of sāvatthi. **piṇḍāya**-for alms. **carituṁ**-to go around.

i.e. It is still early to go for alms in the city of sāvatthi.

(b) • Paro'sahassaṁ-more than thousands.

[**para**-more than+**sahassaṁ**-thousand]

[SS] (a) • Atippa+**kh**o (b) • Para+**s**ahassaṁ.

[SM] For (a), Insert "**o**" in front of "**kh**" by this Sutta. [atippa+o+kho] Insert "**g**" by the preceding Sutta in front of "**o**" [atippa+g+o+kho] Attach "**g**" to "**o**". It is done.

For (b), Insert "**o**" by this Sutta in front of "**s**". At this stage, it will look like this: [• Para+o+**s**ahassaṁ]. Elide "**a**" as there is "**o**" present behind at the union of two vowels [Par+o+**s**ahassaṁ.]. Attach "**r**" to next "**o**" . It is done.

Kvacī'ki kasmā?
Why is there the word "kvaci" in Sutta?
It is to show that the function of this rule is inapplicable in some instances shown below as restricted by "kvaci".

[CS] (a) * Etha'passathi'maṁ lokaṁ.
(b) * andhībhūto ayaṁ'loko.

[CS] (a) * Etha+passatha+imaṁ lokaṁ. (2 points of Sandhi)
Etha-come! **passatha**-see! **imaṁ**-this. **lokaṁ**-world.
i.e. Come and see this world!
(b) * andhī bhūto ayaṁ loko.
andhī bhūto-is being blind. **ayaṁ**-this. **loko**-world. **i.e.** This world is being blind (as majority of beings lack wisdom).

[SM] For (a), no Sandhi function at the first point, inserting "o" in front of "p" is inapplicable. At the second point, the front vowel "**a**" of "**tha**" is elided and "**th**" is attached to the next "**i**".
For example (b), No specific Sandhi function is applied.

३७, ५७. निग्गहितञ्च

37, 57. **Niggahitañ'ca** [Niggahitaṁ+ca. 2 words]

[V] Niggahitañ'cā'gamo hoti sare vā byañjane vā pare kvaci.

When either a consonant or a vowel is present behind, "the niggahita-**ṁ**" is sometimes inserted (in front of that vowel or consonant).

[CS] (a) • Cakkhu**ṁ'u**dapādi.
(b) • Ava**ṁ's**iro.
(c) • Yāva'ñ**c'i**dha bhikkhave
(d) • purima**ṁ**'jātiṁ sarāmi.
(e) • Aṇu**ṁ'th**ūlāni sabbaso.
(f) • Manopubba**ṅ**gamā dhammā.

[SS] (a) • Cakkhu+**u**dapādi.
Cakkhu-the wisdom eye. **udapādi**-arises, appears.
(b) • Ava+**s**iro-with the head being downward.
(c) • Yāva+ca+**i**dha bhikkhave (2 points).
Yāva ca-very much. **idha**-here. **bhikkhave**-monks!

(d) • purima+**j**ātiṁ sarāmi.

purimajātiṁ-the previous life. **sarāmi**-(I) remember.

(e) • Aṇu+**th**ūlāni sabbaso.

Aṇuthūlāni-small and big unwholesome things. **sabbaso**-by all means.

(f) • Mano pubba+**g**amā dhammā. (Re Sutta 23)

[SM] For (a) (b) (d) (e), just insert "**ṁ**" in front of each "**u, s, j, th**". It is done quite easily.
For the first point of (c), insert "**ṁ**" in front of "**c**". Change that "**ṁ**" into "**ñ**" by Sutta 31 and attach it to next consonant "**c**". It will look like this [**• Yāva+ñca+idha**]. Now, at the second point, elide the front vowel "**a**" of "**ñca**" and attach the conjunct consonants "**ñc**" to next "**i**". Then, it will look like ["**• Yāva'ñc'idha**".] It is done now and becomes a perfectly combined Sandhi.
As for (f), insert "**ṁ**" in front of "**g**". Then, change it into "ṅ" by Sutta 31. Attach it to next "**ga**". It is done.

Kvacī'ti kasmā?

Why is there the word "kvaci" in Sutta?

It is to show that the function of this Sutta is inapplicable in some instances shown below as restricted by "kvaci".

* Idhe'va naṁ pasaṁsanti. * Pecca sagge pamodati.

Idha eva-even here in this world. **naṁ**-to that person. **pasaṁsanti**-(the wise) praise. **Pecca**-in the next life. **sagge**-in the heaven. **pamodati**-(he) rejoices. **i.e.** Even in this world, the wise praise him. In next life too, he rejoices in the heaven.

*Na hi etehi yānehi, gaccheyya agataṁ disaṁ.

Na-not. **hi**-in fact. **etehi**-by these. **yānehi**-vehicles, **gaccheyya**-(one) may go. **agataṁ**-never gone before. **disaṁ**-to the direction of Nibbāna. **i.e.** In fact, one would not reach the never-gone-before direction of Nibbāna by means of these physical vehicles.

In the stanza above, there are only two examples:

[CS] (a) * Idhe'va (b) * Pecca Sagge (c) * na hi etehi

[SS] (a) * Idha+eva (b) * Pecca+Sagge (c) * na hi etehi

[SM] For (a) Just elide the front vowel "**a**" and attach "**dh**" to next "**e**". It is done. This example is where a possible Sandhi is inapplicable between two vowels **a and e.**
For (b,c), There is no Sandhi at all.

Caggahaṇena **vi**-saddassa ca **pa**-kāro hoti.
By means of "ca" in the Sutta, "**vi**" sometimes becomes "**pa**".

[CS] • P'acessati. * Vicessati vā. (*means inapplicable example)

[SS] • Pa'cessati-will choose.>**Vi'**cessati-will choose.

[SM] A very simple procedure. Just change "**vi**" into "**pa**"**.** It is done. **Note** that both "**vi**" and "**pa**" are two **Upasagga** words which are interchangeable in terms of meaning. The Upasagga "**vi**" means specially or specifically and "**pa**" means "in various ways, or analytically" . Both are widely used as prefixes of the Pāli verbs which can impact the meaning of roots in various ways.

३८, ५३. क्वचि लोपं

38, 53. **Kvaci lopaṁ** [Kvaci+lopaṁ.2]

[V] Niggahitaṁ kho sare pare kvaci lopaṁ pappoti.

When a vowel follows behind, the front "the niggahita-**ṁ**" is sometimes elided.

[CS] (a) • Tāsā'haṁ santike. (b) • Vidūna'gga'miti.

[SS] (a) • Tās**aṁ**+**a**haṁ santike.

Tāsaṁ-of those women. **ahaṁ**-I. **santike**-at the proximity, near. **i.e.** I (am) at proximity of those women.

(b) • Vidūna**ṁ**+**a**gga**ṁ**+**i**ti (2 points of Sandhi).

Vidūnaṁ-among the wise. **aggaṁ iti-**as the most noble.

[SM] For (a), elide "**aṁ**" by this Sutta and lengthen next "**a**" into "**ā**" by 15. Then, attach "**s**" to next "**ā**". It is done.
For the first point of (b), elide "**aṁ**" and attach "**n**" to next "**a**"**.** For the second point, change "**ṁ**" into "**m**" by 34 and attach it to next "**i**"**.** It is done .

Kvacī'ti kasmā?
Why is there the word "kvaci" in Sutta?
It is to show that the function of this rule is inapplicable in some examples like the one shown below as restricted by the word "kvaci".
* Aha'meva nūna bālo. * Eta'matthaṁ viditvāna.

[CS] (a) * Aha'meva nūna bālo.
(b) "Eta'matthaṁ viditvāna.

[SS] (a) "Ahaṁ+eva nūna bālo.

Ahaṁ eva-I only. **nūna-**? **bālo-**(am) stupid? **i.e.** Am I only stupid?

[**nūna-**is a **nipāta** particle which signifies both question and doubt]

(b) "Etaṁ+atthaṁ viditvāna.

Etaṁ-this. **atthaṁ-**meaning or fact. **viditvāna-**having known. **i.e.** Having known this meaning or fact.

[SM] In both (a-b), change "**ṁ**" into "**m**" by 34 and attach it to next vowels. That is it.

३९, ५४. ब्यञ्जने च

39, 54. **Byañjane ca** [Byañjane+ca. 2 words]

[V] Niggahitaṁ kho byañjane pare kvaci lopaṁ pappoti.

When a consonant is present behind, the front "niggahita-**ṁ**" is sometimes elided.

[CS] (a) • Ariyasaccāna'dassanaṁ.

(b) Etaṁ • buddhāna'sāsanaṁ.

[SS] (a) • Ariyasaccānaṁ+dassanaṁ.

Ariyasaccānaṁ-of the noble truths. **dassanaṁ-**seeing or knowing.

i.e. Seeing of noble truths.

(b) Etaṁ • buddhānaṁ+sāsanaṁ.

Etaṁ-this. **buddhānaṁ-** of Buddhas. **sāsanaṁ-**is the teaching. **i.e.** This is the teaching of Buddhas.

[SM] For both examples, just elide the front "**ṁ**" by this Sutta and it is done. No further action required.

Kvacī'ti kasmā?

Why is there the word "kvaci" in Sutta?

It is to show that the function of this rule is inapplicable in some examples shown below as restricted by "kvaci".

(a) * Etaṁ maṅgala'muttamaṁ.

(b) * Taṁ vo vadāmi bhaddante.

[CS] (a) * Etaṁ maṅgalam'uttamaṁ.

[SS] (a) * Etaṁ maṅgalaṁ+uttamaṁ.

Etaṁ-this. **maṅgalaṁ**-is blessing. **uttamaṁ**-the noble.
i.e. This is the noble blessing.

(b) * Taṁ vo vadāmi bhaddante. [No sandhi]

Taṁ-that word. **vo**-to you. **vadāmi**-(I) say. **bhaddante**-your honorable. **i.e.** Your honorable! I say that to you.

[SM] Although "**ṁ**" should be elided in both examples, it is not elided. No Sandhi process except in (a) where it is shown by a plus sign. Just change "**ṁ**" into "**m**" by 34 and attach it to the next vowel "**u**" . It is done. There is no Sandhi in (b).

४०, ५५. परो वा सरो

40, 55. **Paro vā saro** [Paro+vā+saro. 3 words]

[V] Niggahitamhā paro saro lopaṁ pappoti vā.

The vowel after "the niggahita-**ṁ**" is sometimes elided.

[CS] (a) Bhāsitaṁ • abhinandu**n'ti**.
(b) • Uttattaṁ'va. (c) • Yathābījaṁ'va.
(d) • yathādhaññaṁ'va.

[SS] (a) Bhāsitaṁ • abhinandu**ṁ**+**i**ti.

Bhāsitaṁ-to what has been said (by Buddha). **abhinanduṁ**-(they) were rejoiced. **iti**-this is the end of discourse.

(b) • Uttatta**ṁ**+**i**va.

Uttattaṁ iva-like the refined and sufficiently heated gold.

(c) • Yathābīja**ṁ**+**i**va-like the seed.

(d) • yathādhañña**ṁ**+**i**va-like whatever kind of grain.

[SM] For (a), elide "**i**" behind "**ṁ**" by this Sutta**.** Then, change "**ṁ**" into "**n**" by Sutta 31. It is done.
For (b-c-d) Just elide all the vowels behind "**ṁ**" by this Sutta**.** It is done.

Vā'ti kasmā?
Why is there the word "vā" in Sutta?
It is to show that the function of this rule is inapplicable in some instances shown below as restricted by "vā".
* Aha'meva nūna bālo. * Eta'dahosi.

[CS] (a) "Aha'meva nūna bālo. (b) "Eta'dahosi.

[SS] (a) "Ahaṁ+**e**va nūna bālo. (Re: Sutta 38)
(b) "Etaṁ+**a**hosi.
Etaṁ-this thought. **ahosi**-happened, occurred.

[SM] For (a), Change "**ṁ**" into "**m**". For (b), Change "**ṁ**" into "**d**" by Sutta 34. Then, attach those "**m**" and "**d**" to the next vowel.

४१, ५६. ब्यञ्जनो च विसञ्ञोगो

41, 56. **Byañjano ca visaññogo.**

[Byañjano+ca+visaññogo.3 words]

[V] Niggahitamhā parasmiṁ sare lutte yadi byañjano sasaññogo, visaññogo hoti.

After the vowel behind "the niggahita-**ṁ**" had been elided, if that consonant right next to the elided vowel is a double conjunct-consonant, then it has to be made into a single consonant.

Summary: This Sutta changes conjunct-consonants located behind the deleted vowel after "niggahita-**ṁ**" into a single consonant. [See the examples and SM to clarify this function]

[CS] (a) • Evaṁ'**s**a te āsavā. (b) • Pupphaṁ'**s**ā uppajji.
See conjunct consonants shown below in bold, underlined.

[SS] (a) • Evaṁ+a<u>**ss**</u>a te āsavā.
Evaṁ-thus. **assa**-of that person. **te āsavā**-those mental taints.
(b) • Pupphaṁ+a<u>**ss**</u>ā uppajji.
Pupphaṁ-flower, **i.e.** menstruation (figurative expression). **assā**-of that woman. **uppajji**-occurs. **i.e.** The flower of that woman **i.e.** menses occurs.

[SM] For both (a-b), elide "**a**" behind "**ṁ**" by Sutta 40. Now, change conjunct "**ss**" into single "**s**" by eliding one "**s**" through this Sutta. It is done.

Lutte'ti kasmā?
Why is there the word "lutte" included in Sutta?
It is to show that in the examples below, there is no "Lutta-elision procedure" occurred. So, inapplicable for the rule of this Sutta to be applied on them.
* Evama'ssa. * Vidūna'gga'miti. (2 points)

[CS] * Eva'massa. * Vidūna'gga'miti (Re: Sutta 38)

[SS] (a) " Evaṁ+**a**ssa.

Evaṁ-thus. **assa**-should have been.

(b) " Vidūna**ṁ**+**a**gga**ṁ**+**i**ti.

[SM] For (a), Just change "**ṁ**" into "**m**" by Sutta 34 and attach it to next vowel "**a**". (For example (b) refer to Sutta 38.)

Caggahaṇena tiṇṇaṁ byañjanāna'mantare ye sarūpā, tesam'pi lopo hoti.

By means of "ca" included in Sutta, one of similar consonants conjoined in a cluster of three consonants, has to be elided. (See the examples and detailed explanation)

Note: Only "**gg,** and **tt**"**,** two similar consonants can be seen in the separation. It will become three when "**i**" changes into "**y**" in the morphological procedure as per Sutta 21. Then, one "**g**" and one "**t**" has to be elided as per the function of the word "ca" in this Sutta. **See SM to understand on how all the necessary procedures are done** to complete the word.

[CS] (a) • A**gyā**'gāraṁ-fire-hut (where sacrifices are performed or cooking etc., is done).

(b) • Paṭisanthāravu**ty**'assa. (Re: Sutta 21)

[SS] (a) • Ag**gi**+āgāraṁ.

(b) • Paṭisanthāravu**tt**i+assa.

[SM] For (a), Change "**i**" into "**y**" by Sutta 21. Now, it will look like: "(a) • A**ggy**+āgāraṁ". By means of applying the function of "**ca**" in this Sutta, elide one "**g**" of "**gg**" where three conjunct consonants "**ggy**" are clustered. It then looks like: "(a) • A**gy**+āgāraṁ". Now, attach "**gy**" to the next vowel "**ā**"**.** It is done.

For (b), Change "**i**" into "**y**" by Sutta 21. Now, it looks like: "(b) • Paṭisanthāravu**tty**+assa". By means of applying the function of "**ca**" in this Sutta, elide one "**t**" of "**tt**" where three conjunct consonants "**tty**" are clustered. Now, it looks like: "(b) • Paṭisanthāravu**ty**+assa". It will become a perfectly combined word in a Sandhi when conjunct consonants "**ty**" are attached to next vowel "**a**"**.**

Iti sandhikappe catuttho kaṇḍo.

The Fourth Section of Sandhi ends.

Pañcama Kaṇḍa

The Fifth Section

४२, ३२. गो सरे पुथस्सागमो क्वचि

42, 32. **Go sare puthassā'gamo kvaci.**

[Go+sare+puthassa+āgamo+kvaci. 5 words]

[V] **Putha**-icce'tassa ante sare pare kvaci **ga**-kārā'gamo hoti.

When a vowel is present behind, the consonant "**g**" is sometimes inserted at the end (back) of the word "**putha**". [This Sutta inserts a "g" after the word "putha"]

[CS] • Putha'geva-is separate (from the enlightened ones.)
i.e. (The unenlightened one) is separate from the enlightened ones.

[SS] • Putha+**e**va.

[SM] Just insert "**g**" in front of "**e**" by this Sutta and attach it to next vowel "**e**". It is done.

Kvacī'ti kasmā?
Why is there the word "kvaci" in Sutta?
It is to show that the function of this rule is inapplicable in examples shown below as restricted by "kvaci".
* Putha eva.

[CS] * Putha eva (No Sandhi. Already separated individual words)

४३, ३३. पास्स चन्तो रस्सो

43, 33. **Pāssa ca'nto rasso.** [Pāssa+ca+anto+rasso. 4 words]

[V] **Pā-**icce'tassa ante sare pare kvaci **ga-**kārā'gamo hoti.
anto ca saro rasso hoti.

When a vowel is present behind, the consonant "**g**" is sometimes inserted at the back of (**i.e.** after) the word "**pā**" while the component vowel "**ā**" is also shortened into "**a**".

[CS] • Pa'geva vutty'assa.

[SS] • P**ā**+**e**va vutty'assa.
Pā eva-is early. **vutti-**occurrence. **assa-**of that thing or person.
i.e. That person's or thing's occurrence is early.

[SM] Insert "**g**" after the Upasagga word "**pā**" and shorten "**ā**" into "**a**" by 26. Attach "**g**" to that shortened "**a**"**.** It is done.

Kvacī'ti kasmā?
Why is there the word "kvaci" in Sutta?
It is to show that the function of this rule is inapplicable in the examples shown below as restricted by "kvaci".
* Pā eva vutty'assa.

[CS] * Pā eva (No Sandhi) * Vutty'assa [SM explained in Sutta 41]

४४, २४ अब्भो अभि

44, 24. **Abbho abhi.** [Abbho+abhi. 2 words]

[V] **Abhi**-icce'tassa sare pare **abbhā**'deso hoti.

When a vowel follows behind, the upasagga particle "**abhi**" in front, is to be morphed into "**abbha**". [This Sutta enjoins to change Upasagga "**abhi**" into "**abbha**" when there is a vowel following next to it]

[CS] (a) • Abbhu'dīritaṁ.
(b) • Abbhu'ggacchati.

[SS] (a) • Abhi+**u**dīritaṁ-excessively said.
(b) • Abhi+**u**ggacchati-excessively rises up, spreads.

[SM] For both (a-b), change Upasagga particle "**abhi**" into "**abbha**". Elide the last vowel "**a**" of "**abbha**". Attach "**abbh**" to next "**u**"**.** It is done.

४५, २५. अज्झो अधि

45, 25. **Ajjho adhi.** [Ajjho+adhi. 2 words]

[V] **Adhi**-icce'tassa sare pare **ajjh**ā'deso hoti.

When a vowel is present behind, the upasagga particle "**adhi**" in front, is to be morphed into "**ajjha**"**.** [Function is easy to understand as it is to change "**adhi**" into "**ajjha**"**.**]

[CS] (a) • Ajjho'kāse-in the open space.
(b) • Ajjhā'gamā-(he) came or realized, attained.

[SS] (a) • Adhi+**o**kāse.
(b) • Adhi+**ā**gamā.

[SM] For both (a-b), change Upasagga "**adhi**" into "**ajjha**". Elide the last vowel "**a**" of "**ajjha**". Attach "**ajjh**" to next "**o**" **and** "**ā**"**.** It is done.

४६, २६. ते न वा इवण्णे

46, 26. **Te na vā ivaṇṇe.** [Te+na+vā+ivaṇṇe. 4 words]

[V] Te ca kho abhi,adhi-iccete ivaṇṇe pare abbho, ajjho-iti vuttarūpā na honti vā.

When "**i** or **ī**" vowels are present behind, changing the two upasagga particles "**abhi** and **adhi**" into "**abbha** and **ajjha**" are not to be carried out. (**i.e.** not applicable)

Summary: This Sutta debars changing of two Upasagga "**abhi** & **adhi**" into "**abbha, ajjha**" when an "**i** or **ī**" is present next to it.

What does it mean? It means that when "**i** or **ī**" is present in a word next to "**abhi or adhi**", the "abbha, ajjha" function does not usually occur. [It is a common language pattern found in the Pāli texts.]

[CS] (a) • Abhi'cchitaṁ-excessively wanted.
(b) • Adhī'ritaṁ-excessively said.

[SS] (a) • Abhi+**i**cchitaṁ. [Here, "**i**" is present]
(b) • Adhi+**ī**ritaṁ. [Here, "**ī**" is present]

[SM] For both (a-b), Elide the front vowels "**i**" of "**abhi** and **adhi**". Attach "**abh** and **adh**" to next "**i**" and "**ī**" respectively**.** It is done.

Vā'ti kasmā?

Why is there the word "vā" in Sutta?

It is to show that the function of this rule is inapplicable in some examples shown below.

(a) "Abbhī'ritaṁ"-(It is) excessively said.

(b) "Ajjhiṇamutto"-(He) is very much free from debts.

[CS] (a) "Abbhī'ritaṁ."
(b) "Ajjhiṇamutto"

[SS] (a) "Abbhi+**ī**ritaṁ."
(b) "Adhi+**i**ṇamutto"

[SM] For (a), Elide the vowel "**i**" of "**abhi**" Attach "**abbh**" to next "**ī**" **.** It is done.
For (b), Change "**adhi**" into "**ajjha**". Elide the last vowel "**a**" of it. Attach "**ajjh**" to next "**i**"**.** It is done.

४७, २३. अतिस्स चन्तस्स

47, 23. **Atissa ca'ntassa.** [Atissa+ca+antassa. 3 words]

[V] **Ati**-icce'tassa antabhūtassa **ti**-saddassa ivaṇṇe pare "sabbo caṁ tī"ti vuttarūpaṁ na hoti.

When "**i** or **ī**" vowels are present behind, changing the word "**ti**" into "**ca**" as prescribed in Sutta "sabbo caṁ tī", is not applicable. [This Sutta debars the rule of "sabbo caṁ ti" when an "i or ī" is after **ati, pati, iti.** This is also a statement about common language pattern where changing into "c" of "ti" is not always applicable in some word-structures.]

[CS] (a) • Atī'sigaṇo-many group of hermits.
(b) • Atī'ritaṁ-excessively said.

[SS] (a) • Ati+**i**sigaṇo.
(b) • Ati+**ī**ritaṁ.

[SM] For (a) Just elide the front vowel and lengthen next "i" into "ī". Attach vowel-less "**t**" to next vowel "ī". It is done.
For (b), just elide front vowel "i" and attach "t" to next vowel "ī". It is done.

Ivaṇṇe'ti kasmā?
Why is there the word " ivaṇṇe" in Sutta?
It is to show that the function of this rule is inapplicable in examples shown below as there is no "**i** or **ī**" after it.
* Acca'ntaṁ (In this example, "ti" of "ati" changes into "cca" as there is no "i or ī" behind it, only an "a")

[CS] * Acca'ntaṁ-beyond the end (limit), certainly (two meanings).

[SS] * Ati+**a**ntaṁ

[SM] Change "**ti**" of Upasagga "**ati**" into "**c**" by Sutta 19. Then, reduplicate it into "**cc**". Attach "**cc**" to next "**a**"**.** It is done.

४८, ४३. क्वचि पटि पतिस्स

48, 43. **Kvaci paṭi patissa.** [Kvaci+paṭi+patissa. 3 words]

[V] **Pati**-icce'tassa sare vā byañjane vā pare kvaci **paṭi-**ādeso hoti.

When either a vowel or a consonant follows, the upasagga particle "**pati**" in the front optionally changes into "**paṭi**". **Note:** Both "**pati** and **paṭi**" are Upasagga particles of the same meaning. Only "**t & ṭ**" are different but interchangeably used in the Pāli texts.

[CS] (a) • Paṭa'ggi dātabbo.

Paṭa'ggi-counter-fire. **dātabbo-**should be given. (When a forest-fire breaks out, one should start a small fire before it reaches one's place. This preventive fire is called "**Paṭa'ggi**")

(b) • Paṭi'haññati. (Re Sutta 25)

[SS] (a) • Pati+**a**ggi dātabbo.

(b) • Pati+**h**aññati.

[SM] For (a), Change the Upasagga word "**pati**" into "**paṭi**". Elide "**i**" of Pati. Attach "**paṭ**" to the next "**a**"**.** It is done.
For (b), Just change "**pati**" into "**paṭi**". It is done.

Kvacī'ti kasmā?

Why is there the word "kvaci" in Sutta?

It is to show that the function of this rule is inapplicable in some instances shown below as restricted by "kvaci".

* Paccantimesu janapadesu. * Patilīyati.

* Patirūpadesavāso ca.

[CS] (a) "Paccantimesu janapadesu."

Paccantimesu-at extremely distant, far-flung. **janapadesu-**districts.

(b) "Patilīyati." (Re Sutta 25)

(c) " Patirūpadesavāso ca."

Patirūpadesavāso ca-living at suitable place also (is good for general progress).

[SS] (a) * Pati+antimesu janapadesu.

(b) * Patilīyati.

(c) * Patirūpadesavāso ca.

[SM] For (a), change "**ti**" of "**pati**" into "**c**" and reduplicate it as "**cc**". Attach "**cc**" to next "**a**". It is done.
For (b-c), there is no Sandhi process. Hence, no SM required.

४९, ४४. पुथस्सु ब्यञ्जने

49, 44. **Puthass'u byañjane.** [Puthassa+u+byañjane. 3 words]

[V] **Putha**-icce'tassa anto saro byañjane pare **u**-kāro hoti.

When a consonant is present behind, the vowel "**a**" of the word "**putha**", changes into an "**u**". [present behind=follows]

[CS] (a) • Puthu'jjano-un-enlightened person, common worldling.
(b) • Puthu'bhūtaṁ-being multitude.
[SS] (a) • Putha+**j**ano.
(b) • Putha+**bh**ūtaṁ.
[SM] For (a), Change "**a**" of "**putha**" into "**u**" by this Sutta. Reduplicate "**j**" as "**jj**" by Sutta 28. It is done.
For (b), Change "**a**" of "**putha**" into "**u**" by this Sutta. It is done.

Antaggahaṇena aputhassā'pi sare pare antassa u-kāro hoti. By means of anta (included in Vutti, see the word "**anto**"), the component vowels of other words rather than the word "putha", also changes into "**u**".

[CS] • Manu'ññaṁ-the pleasing object (***n***) or being pleasant (***adj***).
[SS] • Man**o**+**a**ññaṁ.
[SM] Change the front vowel "**o**" into "**u**" by means of the word "**anta**" in the Sutta. Elide the next dissimilar vowel "**a**" by Sutta 13. It is done.

५०, ४५. ओ अवस्स

50, 45. **O avassa.** [O+avassa. 2 words]

[V] **Ava**-icce'tassa byañjane pare kvaci **o**-kāro hoti.

When a consonant is present behind, the upasagga "**ava**" sometimes changes into an "**o**".
Note: This Sutta changes "**ava**" into "**o**". So, keep in mind that "**ava**" and "**o**" are interchangeable.

[CS] Andhakārena • o'naddhā.

Andhakārena-by darkness of ignorance. **o'naddhā**-are entangled, blinded.

[SS] • a**va**+naddhā.

[SM] Change Upasagga word "**ava**" into "**o**". It is done.

Kvacī'ti kasmā?

Why is there the word "kvaci" in Sutta?

It is to show that the function of this rule is inapplicable in some instances shown below as being restricted by "kvaci".

[CS] * Ava'sussatu me sarīre maṁsalohitaṁ.

Ava'sussatu-let it dry up. **me**-my. **sarīre**-in the body. **maṁsa, lohitaṁ**-flesh and blood. **i.e.** "Let flesh and blood in my body dry up" (I will not cancel my sitting meditation until I attain enlightenment- a firm vow made by the Buddha-to-be).

[SM] * Avasussatu (Ava+susa+tu, ***āv***) No change of "**ava**" into "**o**" occurred. So, no Sandhi in this example.

५१, ५९. अनुपदिट्ठानं वुत्तयोगतो

51, 59. **Anu'padiṭṭhānaṁ vuttayogato.**

[na-upadiṭṭhānaṁ+vuttayogato.2]

[V] Anupadiṭṭhānaṁ upasagga, nipātānaṁ sarasandhīhi byañjanasandhīhi vuttasandhīhi ca yathāyogaṁ yojetabbaṁ.

The Sandhi procedures not previously shown regarding the vowel Sandhi or the consonant Sandhi or the niggahita Sandhi for any [14]*Upasagga* and *Nipāta*-prefixed words, can

---

[14]There are **twenty *Upasagga* particles** commonly used as prefixes in the beginnings of certain verbs and words. They are: **Pa, parā, ni, nī, u, du, saṁ, vi, ava, anu, pari, adhi, abhi, pati, su, ā, ati, api, apa, upa.**

There are many ***Nipāta*** particles.Some of the Nipāta particles found in this grammar text are: **Na, no, hi, ca, tu, pana, vā, navā, ve, vibhasā, atha, athavā, atha kho, iva, eva, viya, sammā.** See **Sutta 221** for a more detailed explanation.

be carried out ([15]either by any applicable means shown in the preceding Suttas or by this great Sutta *Mahāvutti*).

Examples: The word in squiggly brackets shows an *upasagga* or a *nipāta* as an initial part of the example word. See footnote below.

(1) {pa} •Pā'panaṁ>Pa+**ā**panaṁ-specifically arriving.

[SM]Elide the front "**a**" and attach "**p**" to the next "**ā**".

(2) {parā}• Parā'yaṇaṁ.>Para+**ā**yaṇaṁ-shelter, refuge.

(3) {upa}• Upā'yanaṁ.>Upa+**ā**yanaṁ-carrying closely.

• Upā'hanaṁ.>Upa+**ā**hanaṁ-slippers, such as shoes etc,.
(MS is the same as foregoing example)

(4) {ni} •Nyā'yogo.>Ni+**ā**'yogo-consistent effort.

[SM]Change "**i**" into "**y**" and attach it to next "**ā**".

• Ni'rupadhi.>Ni+**u**padhi-without Upadhi (base).

[SM]Insert "**r**" in front of "**u**" and attach it to next "**u**".

Note: Attaching the inserted consonant to the next vowel is quite a necessary process for Pāli words written in Asian Languages. But, **for Romanized Pāli, it is almost unnecessary as both vowel and consonants are written in tandem without being conjoined together. Even if it is unnecessary, it is shown in SM as a way of adhering to formal standard morphological procedures.**

(5) {anu}• Anu'bodho.>Anu'bodho-knowledge based on method or inference.

[SM]Keep as a "**Pakati**" without any alteration through Sandhi procedure. This is the only example of "**pakati Sandhi**".

(6) {Du}• Du'vūpasantaṁ.>Du+**u**pasantaṁ-bad calm.

[SM]Insert "**v**" in front of "**u**" and lengthen "**u**" by 25 attach it to "**ū**".

(7) {su} • Suv'ūpasantaṁ.>Su+**u**pasantaṁ-good calm.

[SM]Insert "**v**" in front of "**u**" and lengthen "**u**" by 25 attach it to "**ū**".

---

[15] Some grammarians view this Sutta as an ***atidesa*** Sutta without having any specific rule while some such as Bālāvatāra view it as a ***vidhi*** Sutta having broader specific functions. The latter is more relevant as there are some words in the Pāli texts whose Sandhi-procedures are not shown. The words added inside the parenthesis are reflective of those views of the grammarians.

(8) {du} • Dvā'layo.>Du+**ā**'layo-bad base or bad desire.
[SM]Change "**u**" into "**v**" and attach "**dv**" to "**ā**".

(9) {Su} • Svā'layo.>Su+**ā**'layo-good base, good desire.
[SM]Change "**u**" into "**v**" and attach "**dv**" to "**ā**".

(10) {du}• Du'rākhyātaṁ.>Du'+**ā**khyātaṁ-badly said.
[SM] Insert "**r**" in front of "**ā**" and attach it to "**ā**".

(11) {su}• Svā'khyāto.>Su+**ā**'khyāto-well said.
[SM]Change "**u**" into "**v**" and attach "sv" to "**ā**".
Note: In majority of Buddhist texts, the word "Svakhāto" is mostly found without consonant "y" after "kh". It is to be separated as Su+akkhāto. Just change "u" into "v".

(12) {u} • U'dīritaṁ.>U+**ī**ritaṁ-much said.
[SM]Insert "**d**" in front of "**ī**" and attach it to "**ī**".

(13) {Saṁ} • Sa'muddiṭṭhaṁ.>Saṁ+**u**ddiṭṭhaṁ-well expounded.
[SM]Change "**ṁ**" into "**m**" by 34 and attach it to next vowel "**u**".

(14) {vi}• Vi'yaggaṁ.>Vi+**a**ggaṁ-specially noble.
[SM]Insert "**y**" in front of "**a**" and it is done.

(15) {vi}• Vi'jjhaggaṁ.>Vi+**adhi**+**a**ggaṁ-especially more noble.
[SM]Change "**adhi**" into "**ajjha**" by 45 [Vi+ajjha+aggaṁ]. Elide the initial "**a**" of "**ajjha**" by Sutta 13[Vi+jjha+aggaṁ]. Also, elide the last "**a**" of "**jjha**" by Sutta 12 and attach triple consonant "**jjh**" to next "**a**". It is done [Vi+jjh+aggaṁ].

(16) {vi}• Bya'ggaṁ.>Vi+**a**ggaṁ-specially noble.
[SM]Change "**i**" into "**y**" by 21 and attach "**vy**" to next "**a**". It is done.

(17) {Ava}• Ava'yāgamanaṁ. Ava+**ā**gamanaṁ-badly coming.
[SM]Insert "**y**" in front of "**ā**" by 35. It is done.

(18) {anu}• Anve'ti.>Anu+**e**ti-subsequently follows.
[SM]Change "**u**" into "**v**" by 18 and attach "**nv**" to next vowel "**e**".
• Anu'paghāto.>Ana+**u'**paghāto-unharmed.
[SM]Elide front "**a**" by 12 and attach "**n**" to next "**u**".

(19) {ana or anu} • Ana'cchariyaṁ.>Ana+**a**cchariyaṁ-not surprising. **Also:** Anu+**a**cchariyaṁ-repeatedly surprising.

(**Please Note:** Two possible SS for this word as "**ana**" can be a morpheme of Nipāta particle "**na**-not" or Upasagga "**anu**-repeatedly"

[SM]In both SS, elide the front vowels and attach "**n**" to next vowels. It is quite a simple process.

(20) {pari} • Pari'yesanā.>Pari+**e**sanā-search.

[SM] Insert "**y**" in front of "**e**" by 35.

(21) {para} • Parā'māso.> Para+**ā**māso-repeatedly rubbing and touching something or wrongly holding a view or an idea.

[SM] Elide the front "**a**" and attach "**r**" to next "**ā**".

evaṁ sare ca honti.

Thus, (these shown above are examples of) Vowel-Sandhi.

(1) {pari} • Pari'ggaho.> Pari+**g**aho-taking possession.

(2) {pa} • Pa'ggaho.> Pa+**g**aho-supporting by means of encouragement etc.

• Pak**k**amo.>Pa+kamo-leaving away, departure.

• Prakkamo>Para+**k**amo-continuous effort.

(3) {ni}• Ni'kkamo.>Ni+**k**amo-departure.

• Ni'kkasāvo.> Ni+**k**asāvo-without taint of defilements.

• Ni'llayanaṁ.> Ni+**l**ayanaṁ-hiding.

(4) {du} • Du'llayanaṁ.>Du+**l**ayanaṁ-badly based.

[SM] For all these examples above, reduplicate a similar consonant in front of each relevant consonant and attach to it.

• Du'bbhikkhaṁ.>Du+**bh**ikkhaṁ-famine, scarcity of food.

[SM]Reduplicate a dissimilar consonant "**b**" in front of "**bh**" and attach to it.

(5) {du} • Du'bbbuttaṁ.>Du+**b**uttaṁ-badly said.

[SM] Reduplicate a similar consonant "b" and attach to it.

(6) {saṁ} • Sandi'ṭṭhaṁ >Saṁ+diṭhaṁ-well seen or to be seen by oneself.

[SM] Change "**ṁ**" into "**n**" by Sutta 31 and attach that "**n**" to "**di**".

(7) {du} • Du'ggaho.>Du+**g**aho-bad taking.

(8) {vi}• Vi'ggaho.>Vi+**g**aho-specially taking or dispute.

(9) {ni} • Ni'ggato.>Ni+**g**ato-leaving.

(10) {abhi}• Abhi'kkamo.>Abhi+**k**amo-advancing.

(11) {paṭi}• Paṭi'kkamo.>Paṭi+**k**amo-going backward.

[SM] For all these examples, just reduplicate similar consonants and attach it to next consonant to form conjuncts.

evaṁ byañjane ca.

Thus, (these shown above are examples of) Consonant-Sandhi.

Sesā sabbe yojetabbā.

All the rest (of other similar examples from various source of texts) should be similarly applied.

Note: Necessary morphological procedures for completing all the examples shown in the Sutta can be performed by means of this Sutta although most of examples are similar to those already shown in the previous Suttas. In addition, other various examples of Sandhi found in the wider areas of Pāli texts can also be completed.

Iti sandhikappe pañcamo kaṇḍo.

The Fifth Section of Sandhi ends.

Sandhikappo niṭṭhito.

Sandhi Chapter ends.

2. Nāma Kappa

Nouns Chapter

Paṭhama Kaṇḍa

The First Section

५२, ६०. जिनवचनयुत्तं हि

52, 60. Jinavacanayuttaṁ hi. [Jinavacanayuttaṁ+hi. 2 words]

[V] "Jinavacanayuttaṁ hi" icce'taṁ adhikāratthaṁ veditabbaṁ.

This "**Jinavacanayuttaṁ hi**" Sutta is to be known as an Adhikāra (Prevailing or governing rule) Sutta.

Summary: Jinavacanayuttaṁ hi means that "only what conforms to the words of Buddha," **i.e.** usage in the Buddhist texts, (shall be applied throughout this grammar.)

Note: This influences all the preceding and succeeding Suttas regarding the observation of important grammatical principle of conformity to the relevant and applicable usages in the Pāli Buddhist texts.

[**Adhikāra**=**Adhi**-By prevailing over, influencing+**kara**-to do+**ṇa**-act of.]

There are three kinds of adhikāra:

(1) sīha-gatika.This type affects all the preceding and succeeding Suttas. [**sīha**-the lion's+**gatika**-mode of motion all over]

(2) maṇḍūka-gatika. This only affects a certain few Suttas of relevant and related nature from here and there. [**maṇḍūka**-the frog's+**gatika**- mode of leaping]

(3) yathānupubbika. This kind of Sutta affects in orderly manner of sequences, especially succeeding Suttas [**yathā**-according to+**anu pubbika**-the order of sequence. This Sutta is the first type which is also very important grammatical principle for the whole text.

५३, ६१. लिङ्गञ्च निप्पज्जते

53, 61. Liṅgañ'ca nippajjate. [Liṅgaṁ+ca+nippajjate. 3 words]

[V] Yathā yathā jinavacanayuttaṁ hi liṅgaṁ, tathā tathā idha liṅgañ'ca nippajjate.

The genders of nouns will be laid out and explained here in this grammar only in ways that conform to the usage patterns of Buddha' words. **i.e.**, prevalent linguistic pattern and usage applicable in the Buddhist texts.

Taṁ yathā?
What is that? (**i.e.** for example)
• Eso no satthā. • Brahmā . • Attā. • Sakhā. • Rājā.
[Translation of Examples] Eso-that person, no-our, satthā-(is) teacher. **i.e.** That person is our teacher.
Brahmā-Holy Brahmā, God. Attā-soul, oneself (a reflexive pronoun, two meanings). Sakhā-friend. Rājā-King.

Liṅga, (Genders)

There are **three genders**: masculine, feminine and neuter genders.

(1) The outstanding feature of masculine gender nouns is "**o**". e.g. manusso (the man), Buddho (Buddha) etc.

(2) The outstanding feature of the feminine gender nouns are "**ā, ī** and **inī**". e.g., mālā (the flower), nadī (the river), rājinī (the princess).

(3) Major feature for the neuter gender nouns is "**aṁ**". e.g., Vanaṁ (the forest), phalaṁ (the fruit) etc.

Note: All features are for nouns in nominative singular. This is a traditionally taught basic for the beginners. Please note this fact clearly.

Gender and Nouns

These liṅga(genders) are to be assigned to each individual nouns such as masculine gender noun, feminine gender noun and neuter gender nouns. There are various kinds of nouns which students of grammar should understand as a basic knowledge. They are:

(1) **Nāma** nāma-**individual nouns** with specific gender.

(2) **Sabba** nāma-**common nouns** such as **ya**-which, **ta, eta**-that, **ima**-this, **kiṁ**-what, **amu**-so and so, which have variable three genders.

(The **pronouns** such as **tumha**-you, and **amha**-me, are included in this group though they have no specific gender)

(3) **Samāsa** nāma-**compound nouns** with specific gender.

(4) **Taddhita** nāma-**nouns in taddhita-affixes** with specific gender. **Numerical nouns** are also included in this group though some are of variable gender.

(5) **Kita** nāma-**nouns in kita-affixes** with specific gender (**Uṇādi**-affixed words included in this category).

Note: The term "Nāma" means noun.

५४, ६२. ततो च विभत्तियो

54, 62. Tato ca vibhattiyo. [Tato+ca+vibhattiyo. 3 words]

[V] Tato jinavacanayuttehi liṅgehi vibhattiyo parā honti.

The **Vibatti**, (**i.e.** prepositions or **case-endings of nouns**) are **to be applied after those nouns** of specific genders in line with the prevalent usage in the Buddhist texts.

Summary: This Sutta clearly sets out the rule that the vibattis are to be applied after nouns of clearly defined three genders in order to be changed into various word-forms and inflections in accordance with the prescribed morphological rules of Suttas in this grammar text.
Verb-terminations also similarly known as **vibatti** are to be applied after the roots in the case of Pāli Ākhyāta verbs. See **Vibattis for nouns** in the next Sutta. The other **Vibattis for verbs** will be shown in the first section of Ākhyāta.
Note: Even though it cannot be defined in terms of noun or gender, some certain upasagga and nipāta particles, which are used as an independent word in a sentence are applicable to this rule as an exception.

Vibatti means that which defines and distinguishes between what is one and what is more than one, **i.e.** singular and plural. (**vi**-specifically, **batti**-setting aside, to divide). **Vibatti** means preposition, but the translated English term is a misnomer as the vibattis are to be applied after nouns, a rather different linguistic norm most prevalent in the ancient Indian languages and one aspect different from the English grammar. **"14 Vibattis" will be shown in the next Sutta.** [**Vibatti**=**Vi**-specially+**baja**-to assign+**ti**-act of. A feminine gender Kita-noun word]

५५, ६३. सि यो, अं यो, ना हि, स नं, स्मा हि, स नं, स्मिं सु

55, 63. **Si yo, aṁ yo, nā hi, sa naṁ, smā hi, sa naṁ, smiṁ su.**

[Si yo, aṁ yo, nā hi, sa naṁ, smā hi, sa naṁ, smiṁ su.1 word]

[V] Kā ca pana tāyo vibhattiyo?

What are those Vibatti (noun case-endings) ?

Si, yo iti **paṭhamā.**
aṁ, yo iti **dutiyā.**
nā hi iti **tatiyā.**
sa, naṁ iti **catutthī.**
smā, hi iti **pañcamī.**
sa, naṁ iti **chaṭṭhī.**
smiṁ, su iti **sattamī.**

They are namely:

(1) **Si, yo,** these two are called **paṭhamā vibatti** (Nominative case, **si** is nominative singular, **yo** is nominative plural).

(2) **Si, yo,** these two are called **ālapana paṭhamā vibatti** (Vocative case). (**This is not in the original text**, added for the completeness's sake for vocative case.)

(3) **aṁ, yo,** these two are called **dutiyā vibatti** (Accusative case, **aṁ** is singular, **yo** is plural).

(4) **nā, hi,** these two are called **tatiyā vibatti** (Instrumental case, **nā** is singular, **hi** is plural).

(5) **sa, naṁ,** these two are called **catutthī vibatti** (Dative case, **sa** is singular, **naṁ** is plural).

(6) **smā, hi,** these two are called **pañcamī vibatti** (Ablative case, **smā** is singular, **hi** is plural).

(7) **sa, naṁ,** these two are called **chaṭṭhī vibatti** (Genitive case, **sa** is singular, **naṁ** is plural).

Note that Dative and Genitive case are similar except in the meaning.

(8) **smiṁ, su,** these two are called **sattamī vibatti** (Locative case, **smiṁ** is singular, **su** is plural).

Vibhatti-icca'nena kvattho?
By terming these vibattis, what is the benefit?
Amhassa mamaṁ savibhattissa se.
It has the benefit of making easy reference in Suttas such as "Amhassa mamaṁ savibhattissa se" etc.

Note: This Sutta shows all **14 vibattis**. It is very important as it explains all fourteen noun-vibattis or case-endings to be applied after every noun. All keen students need to try to familiarize with all fourteen of them. **See the two tables and study it repeatedly until one clearly understands the way they are used as well as the way they are transformed into finished words after due procedures as enjoined by the rules of respective Suttas .**

The first table explains everything related to noun vibatti (case-endings of nouns) to be applied after them.
The second table shows a sample of morphological stages of the word "**Purisa** (man) " which is an **a**-ending noun. By studying the table, the student will get an idea how each noun has to go through various stages of morphological change as enjoined by the rules of relevant Suttas (whose numbers are shown alongside in the table) until it becomes a complete word.
Although these tables are not a complete guide to all the grammatical nuances and aspects, it will surely acquaint the student with all essential elementary facts of grammar and the structural morphology of words. If the students understand this, all procedures explained in this grammatical text will be much easier and simple to study and understand clearly.

THE ENDING OF NOUNS

All nouns are simply grouped according to their base-endings. These endings are called "Kāranta". [**kāra**-syllable+**anta**-the end. **i.e.** the end-syllable]
This is the vowel-ending of a noun in its initial base stage before all the necessary morphological procedures are done. Altogether, there are eight "Kārantas" in Pāli Language. They are **a, ā, i, ī, u, ū, o** and **ṁ.** There is absolutely **no "e" nor any consonant-ending** as in the Sanskrit grammars.

NOUN-ENDINGS BASED ON GENDER

(a) Seven Kāra'ntas in the Masculine gender

There are **seven Kārantas** in the Masculine gender.
They are **a, ā, i, ī, u, ū and o.**

Examples in order of endings:
To clarify, please see the last ending-vowel in each of these nouns.
Purisa-man, **Sā**-dog, **Aggi**-fire, **Daṇḍī**-the one who has stick, **Setu**-bridge, **Kataññū**-the grateful person, **Go**-cow [Pronounce "go" as "gaw"]

(b) Six Kārantas in the Feminine gender

There are **six Kārantas** in Feminine gender. They are **ā, i, ī, u, ū and o.**

Examples in order of endings:
Mālā-flower, **Ratti**-night, **Nadī**-river, **Yāgu**-porridge, **Vadhū**-daughter-in-law, **Go**-cow [This word is dual gender word]

(c) Seven Kārantas in the Neuter gender

There are **seven Kārantas** in the Neuter gender.
They are **aṁ, ā, i, ī, u, ū and o.**

Examples in order of endings:
Cittaṁ-mind, **Asaddhā**-the family without faith. **Vāri**-water, **Sukhakārī**-the happiness-making good deed, **Āyu**-life. **Gotrabhū**-the mind which transcends unenlightened state, **Cittagu**-the cow with color-streaks.
Note: In the Rūpasiddhi, it is stated "akāranto napuṁsakaliṅgo Cittasaddo" which means "the neuter-gender word **Citta** ending in **a**". However, many teachers rather prefer as "**aṁ-ending**" because it is a very outstanding mark of the neuter gender nouns found in the Pāli canon. In the Sanskrit grammars, there are not only vowel-endings, but also consonant-endings. In Pāli, all nouns are grouped only in vowel-endings though there are some affix-based nouns which can be assumed as the consonant endings such as those **ntu**-affixed ones and those which ends in an **āra**-morpheme. However, it has been grouped based on their base-ending of vowels by the traditional teachers of Pāli grammar.

TEMPORARY TERMS FOR SOME ENDINGS

Some of the endings are given formal temporary terms such as "**gha, pa, jha** and **la**" in order to carry out some specific morphological procedures. Among such endings:

(1) The "**ā**" **of ā-ending nouns of feminine gender** are given a formal temporary name "**gha**". [Re: Sutta 60]
(2) The "**i, ī, u and ū**" **of feminine gender nouns** ending in **i, ī, u** and **ū** are given the formal name of "**pa**"**.** [Re: Sutta 59]

(3) The **i, ī, of masculine and neuter nouns** ending in **i** and **ī,** are given a formal name "**jha**" while **u, ū of masculine and neuter gender nouns** ending in **u** and **ū** are given a temporary formal name of "**la**". [Re: Sutta 58]

५६, ६४. तदनुपरोधेन

56, 64. **Ta'danu'parodhena.** [Taṁ-ana-uparodhena. 1 word]

[V] Yathā yathā tesaṁ jinavacanānaṁ anu'parodho.
Tathā tathā idha liṅgañ'ca nippajjate.

The gender and the word-forms are to be defined and completed (with due morphological procedures) in a way not going against the Buddha's words. (**i.e.** according to the prevalent usage in the canonical texts).

५७, ७१. आलपने सि गसञ्ञो

57, 71. **Ālapane si gasañño.** [Ālapane+si+gasañño. 3 words]

[V] Ālapana'tthe si **ga**sañño hoti.

When signifying vocative case, the paṭhamā singular vibatti "**si**" is to be termed "**ga**" (by means of this Sutta).

• Bhoti ayye. • Bhoti kaññe. • Bhoti kharādiye. (All three are examples of Vocative singular, addressed to female gender nouns)
Bhoti ayye-Oh madam! Bhoti kaññe-Oh Girl!
Bhoti kharādiye-Oh girl named kharādiya! (All examples are ***vs***.)

Ālapane'ti kimatthaṁ? What is the word "Ālapane " for? To show that this example " Sā ayyā" is not an "Ālapana, a vocative". But, it is an ordinary noun.
* Sā ayyā-that lady, ***ns***

Sī'ti kimatthaṁ? [sīti=**si**-the word "si"+**it**-this]
What is this word "**si**" for?
To show this example "Bhotiyo ayyāyo" is vocative noun in plural, not a singular "si". So, irrelevant to name as "ga" though it is a noun in vocative case.
* Bhotiyo ayyāyo.
* Bhotiyo ayyāyo-Oh Madams! ***vp***.

Ga-icca'nena kvattho? Ghate ca.
What is the benefit by this term "ga"?
(When setting out morphological rules), it has the benefit of making easy reference in Suttas such as "Ghate ca" and so on.

Note: There are two "**si**" vibattis:
(1) **paṭhamā** (Nominative) **singular** vibatti "si" and
(2) an **Ālapana** (vocative) **Singular** "si". The second is also called "**ga-termed si**" as it is named as "**ga**" by this Sutta.

The purpose of naming "ga" is to duly perform any necessary morphological procedure as prescribed by the relevant Suttas. **It also enables to easily distinguish between two "si" vibattis,** one being nominative and the other vocative.

५८, २९. इवण्णुवण्णा झला

58, 29. Ivaṇṇu'vaṇṇā jha, lā. [Ivaṇṇa, uvaṇṇā+jha, lā. 2 words]

[V] Ivaṇṇu'vaṇṇā-icce'te **jha, la**saññā honti yathāsaṅkhyaṁ.

The nouns (of masculine and neuter genders) ending in "**i-ī, u-ū**" are to be formally termed "**jha, la**" respectively (by means of this Sutta).

Note:(1) the **i, ī** of **i, ī**-ending **nouns of masculine and neuter gender** are to be termed "**jha**" and
(2) the **u, ū** of u , ū-ending **nouns of masculine and neuter gender** are to be termed "**la**" by this Sutta.

The purpose of giving this formal temporary term of "jha, la" is for easy referencing in the relevant Suttas and to facilitate necessary morphological procedures.

Examples:

Isi-hermit, (**i**-ending noun)
Daṇḍī-the one who has a stick, (**ī**-ending noun),
Setu-Bridge, (**u**-ending noun),
Sayambū-Self-enlightened Buddha, (**ū**-ending noun).
[Benefit of this formal procedure] By terming "jha, la", all necessary procedures such as changing the applied vibatti

after each of these nouns into "**no**" etc., can be duly carried out.

Examples of Sutta

[**i**-ending nouns] • Isino-of/for hermits. Aggino-of/for fire.
• Gahapatino-of/for householder.

[**ī**-ending noun] • Daṇḍino-of/for those who have stick.

[**u**-ending nouns] • Setuno-of/for bridge.
• Ketuno-of/for banner.
• Bhikkhuno-of/for monk.

[**ū**-ending nouns] • Sayambhuno-of/for self-enlightened ones (**i.e.** those Buddhas who attained Buddhahood themselves, without any help of outside agent).
• Abhibhuno-of/for the Buddhas who has over-powering capacities on defilements etc. All examples are of ***ds, gs***

Jha, la-icca'nena kvattho? Jhalato sassa no vā.
What is the benefit by this terming of "jha, la"?
It serves a purpose in duly referencing in Suttas such as "Jhalato sassa no vā" and so on.

५९, १८२. ते इत्थिख्या पो

59, 182. **Te itthikhyā po.** [Te+itthikhyā+po. 3 words]

[V] Te ivaṇṇu'vaṇṇā yadā itthikhyā, tadā **pa**saññā honti.

When those nouns ending in "**i ī, u ū**" signify feminine gender, they are to be formally termed "**pa**".

[**i**-ending noun] • Rattiyā-night.

[**ī**-ending noun] • itthiyā-woman.

[**u**-ending noun] • Dhenuyā-cow.

[**ū**-ending noun] • Vadhuyā-daughter-in-law. (All examples are in ***is, ds, abs, gs, ls***. Therefore, the meaning of each example can be translated accordingly)

Itthikhyā'ti kimatthaṁ?
What is the word "Itthikhyā" for? [**Itthi**-feminine gender, **khyā**-indicative of]
To show that the examples shown below are of masculine

gender, not of feminine gender. So, they are not to be named "pa" by this Sutta.
* Isinā-hermit *(is)*. * Bhikkhunā-monk *(is)*.

Pa-icca'nena kvattho? Pato yā.
What is the benefit by this term "pa"?
It serves a purpose in duly referencing regarding **pa**-termed nouns in Suttas such as "Pato yā" and so on.

६०, १७७. आ घो

60, 177. **Ā gho.** [Ā+gho. 2 words]

[V] Ā-kāro yadā itthikhyo, tadā **gha**sañño hoti.

When an "**ā**-ending noun" signifies feminine gender, it has to be formally termed "**gha**" by means of this Sutta. (All examples below are **ā**-ending feminine gender nouns. All are of ***Instrumental, singular cases.*** However, all these examples can also be in ***dative, ablative, genitive and locative*** **singular** as they share the same morphological procedure.)

• Saddhāya-faith. • Kaññāya-young girl. • Vīṇāya-harp.
• Gaṅgāya-the river Ganges. • Disāya-the direction.
• Sālāya-public rest house. • Mālāya-flower. • Tulāya-the scale.
• Dolāya-the cradle. • Pabhāya-the light. • Sobhāya-the beauty (In some books, it is found as **Sotāya**-flowing current of the river etc.).
• Paññāya-wisdom. • Karuṇāya-compassion. • Nāvāya-boat.
• Kapālikāya-small cup or a piece of broken clay pot.

Ā'ti kimatthaṁ?
What is the word "Ā" for?
To show that the following examples below are not **ā**-ending nouns. Hence, they are not to be named "gha".
* Rattiyā-the night. * Itthiyā-the woman (both examples are of ***is, ds, abs, gs, ls***).

Itthikhyo'ti kimatthaṁ?
What is the word "Itthikhyo" for?
To show the example word "Satthārā" shown below is of a masculine gender, not of feminine gender. So, it is

irrelevant to be named as "gha". (It means that despite the word Satthārā ends in an ā, it does not denote feminine gender. It is a only vibatti-morpheme "**ā**")

* Satthārā desito ayaṁ dhammo.

* Satthārā-by teacher, **i.e.** Lord Buddha ***is***. desito-was taught, ***kv***. ayaṁ-this ***as***. dhammo-Dhamma ***as***. **i.e.** This Dhamma was taught by Buddha. [The sentence is in passive voice construction, with the use of a *Kita* verb]

Gha-icca'nena kvattho? Ghato nādīnaṁ.
What is the benefit by terming "gha" ?
It serves a purpose in duly referencing in Suttas such as "Ghato nādīnaṁ" and so on.

६१, ८६. सागमो से

61, 86. **Sā'gamo se.** [Sa-āgamo+se. 2 words]

[V] Sa-kārā'gamo hoti se vibhattimhi.

An **"s"** is to be inserted and added (to the front of) **"sa"** when a Catutthi or Chaṭṭhi vibatti singular **"sa"** is applied after a noun. [s+sa>**ssa**]
See the **added** "**s**" in front of "**sa**" **shown in bold, underlined.**

• Purisassa-of man. • Aggissa-of fire. • Isissa-of hermit.
• Daṇḍissa-of the one who has stick. • Bhikkhussa-of monk.
• Sayambhussa-of self-enlightened Buddha. • Abhibhussa-of the Buddha who possess great dominating power. ***ds, gs.***

Se'ti kimattaṁ? What is the word "Se" for? To show that the example below is a noun in smiṁ vibatti, not of "sa". (So, the function of this Sutta is not applicable)

* Purisasmiṁ-in man (***ls***).

६२, २०६. संसास्वेकवचनेसु च
62, 206. **Saṁ, sā, sve'kavacanesu ca.**

[Saṁ, sā, su+ekavacanesu+ca. 3 words]

[V] Saṁ, sā, su ekavacanesu vibhattā'desesu sa-kārā'gamo hoti.

An "**s**" is to be similarly inserted to (the front of) "**saṁ** and **sā**" when Sattamī, Catutthī, Chaṭṭhī, singular vibattis have been transformed into "**saṁ** or **sā**".
[s+saṁ>**ssaṁ**, s+sā>**ssā**]

Summary: "**smiṁ**" vibatti applied after feminine gender noun words such as "**ya** (which), **ta, eta** (that), **ima** (this) and **amu** (so and so) ", change into "**saṁ**" while "**sa**" changes into "**sā**".

This Sutta enjoins an additional "**s**" to be added to that "**saṁ & sā**". The added "**s**" is shown in bold, underlined. Note that **Saṁ** is a derivative morpheme of **Smiṁ**. **Sā** is a morpheme of **sa.** Refer to Sutta 179.

(1) [eta-saṁ] • Etissaṁ-at that woman or that thing, ***ls.***
[eta-sā] • Etissā-of that woman or that thing, ***ds, gs.***
(2) [ima-saṁ] • Imissaṁ-at this woman or that thing, ***ls.***
[ima-sā] • Imissā-of this woman or that thing, ***ds, gs***.
(3) [ta-saṁ] • Tissaṁ- at that woman or that thing, ***ls***.
[ta-sā] • Tissā-of that woman or that thing, ***ds, gs***.
(4) [ta-saṁ] • Tassaṁ- at that woman or that thing, ***ls***.
[ta-sā] • Tassā-of that woman or that thing, ***ds, gs***.
(5) [ya-saṁ] • Yassaṁ- at which woman or that thing, ***ls.***
[ya-sā] • Yassā-of which woman or that thing, ***ds, gs***.
(6) [amu-saṁ] • Amussaṁ-at such and such a woman or that thing, ***ls.***
[amu-sā] • Amussā-of such and such a woman or thing, ***ds, gs***.

Saṁsāsvī'ti kimatthaṁ? [saṁsāsvīti=saṁsāsu+it]
What is this word "**Saṁsāsu**" for? To show that the examples shown below have no morpheme "**Saṁ, sā**" in them. So, they are inapplicable. (They have only a **nā** vibatti which is shown underlined)
* Agginā-by fire, from fire, ***is, abs***. * Pāṇinā-by hand, from hand, ***is, abs***.

Ekavacanesvī'ti kimatthaṁ? [ekavacanesvīti=ekavacanesu+it]
What is this word "Ekavacanesu" for? To show that the examples shown below are of plural vibattis. So, they are inapplicable.
* Tāsaṁ-those women or things.
* Sabbāsaṁ-all women or things. ***dp, gp.***

Vibhattādesesvī'ti kimatthaṁ?
[vibattādesesvīti=vibattādesesu+it]
What is this word "Vibhattādesesu" for?
To show that the examples shown below have no vibatti-morpheme in them, hence inapplicable.
* Manasā-mind. * Vacasā-speech.
* Thāmasā-energy or power. All ***is.***

Note: sā in the words is not a vibattādesa, which means vibatti-origin morpheme, so, inapplicable.
Vibattādesa=vibatti+ādesa=a Vibatti derivative, a morpheme of vibatti. It refers to **saṁ,** & **sā** which derives from vibattis, vibatti-derivative.

६३, २१७. एतिमास मि

63, 217. **Eti'māsa'mi.** [Etā, imāsaṁ+i. 2 words]
[V] Etā, imā-icce'tesa'manto saro i-kāro hoti saṁsāsu ekavacanesu vibhattā'desesu.

The last vowel "**ā**" of "et**ā** and im**ā**" changes into "**i**" when "**saṁ, sā**" functions have been carried out. [See the completed examples carefully. The applied "**i**" is shown in bold, underlined]

• Et**i**ssaṁ. ***ls*** • Et**i**ssā. ***ds, gs.***
• Im**i**ssaṁ. ***ls*** • Im**i**ssā. ***ds, gs.***
(The meaning shown in the preceding Sutta).

Saṁsāsvī'ti kimatthaṁ?
What is the word "Saṁ sāsu" for?
To show that examples below are inapplicable as they have no "**Saṁ, sā**" in them.
* Etāya-of that woman or thing. * Imāya-of this woman or thing (Both are in ***ds, gs.***)

Ekavacanesvī'ti kimatthaṁ?
What is the word "Ekavacanesu" for? To show that the examples shown below are of plural vibattis. So, they are inapplicable.
* Etāsaṁ-of those women. * Imāsaṁ-of these women. (Both are in ***dp, gp***).

६४, २१६. तस्सा वा

64, 216. **Tassā vā.** [Tassā+vā. 2 words]

[V] Tassā itthiyaṁ vattamānassa antassa ā-kārassa i-kāro hoti vā saṁsāsu ekavacanesu vibhattā'desesu.

The last vowel "**ā**" of "**tā**-that lady, that thing of feminine gender" changes into "**i**" when "**saṁ, sā**" functions have been carried out. [See the completed examples carefully. The applied "**i**" is shown in bold, underlined. The function of Both Sutta 63, 64 are the same except the nouns they change].

• T<u>**i**</u>ssaṁ-in that woman, ***ls***. • T<u>**i**</u>ssā-of that woman ***ds, gs***.
* Tassaṁ ***ls***. * Tassā ***ds, gs***. (These are Inapplicable examples. Refer to Sutta No. 62 for the meaning of examples)

६५, २१५. ततो सस्स स्साय

65, 215. **Tato sassa ssāya.** [Tato+sassa+ssāya. 3 words]

[V] Tato tā, etā, imā-to sassa vibhattissa ssāyā'deso hoti vā.

The vibatti "**sa**" applied after the feminine Sabbanāma gender noun "**tā, etā** (that woman) and **imā** (this woman) " sometimes changes into "**ssāya**".
[The function of Sutta is easy to understand. See the effect of function shown in bold, underlined]

• Ti<u>**ssāya**</u>-that woman. • Eti<u>**ssāya**</u>-that woman.
• Imi<u>**ssāya**</u>-this woman (All examples are of ***ds, gs***).

Vā'ti kimatthaṁ? [vāti=vā+it]
What is the word "**vā**" for?
* Tissā. * Etissā. * Imissā. ***ds, gs*** (meaning shown)

To show that in the above examples, there is no function of this Sutta as restricted by the word "vā".

६६, २०५. घो रस्सं

66, 205. **Gho rassaṁ.** [Gho+rassaṁ. 2 words]

[V] Gho rassa'māpajjate saṁsāsu ekavacanesu vibhattā'desesu.

The **gha**-termed vowel "**ā**" of feminine gender nouns such as "**tā, yā,** and **sabbā** (all things of feminine gender), is to be shortened when "**saṁ, sā**" function follows it (**i.e.** After that function had been done). [The shortened "**a**" is shown in bold, underlined]

- T**<u>a</u>**ssaṁ ***ls***. • T**<u>a</u>**ssā ***ds, gs***.
- Y**<u>a</u>**ssaṁ ***ls***. • Y**<u>a</u>**ssā ***ds, gs***.
- Sabb**<u>a</u>**ssaṁ-all woman or thing ***ls***.
- Sabb**<u>a</u>**ssā-all woman or thing ***ds, gs***.

Saṁsāsvī'ti kimatthaṁ?
What is the word "**Saṁ sāsu**" for?
To show these examples shown below have no morpheme "**Saṁ, sā**" in them. Hence, inapplicable.
* Tāya-that woman or thing. * Sabbāya-all woman or thing (Both are of ***ds, gs***).

Ekavacanesvī'ti kimatthaṁ?
What is the word "Ekavacanesu" for?
It shows that the examples shown below are of plural vibattis. So, they are inapplicable.
* Tāsaṁ-those women or things. * Sabbāsaṁ-all women or things (Both are of ***dp, gp***).

६७, २२९. नो च द्वादितो नंम्हि
67, 229. No ca dvā'dito naṁmhi.

[No+ca+dvi-ādito+naṁmhi. 4 words]

[V] **Dvi-**icce'vamā'dito saṅkhyāto **na-**kārā'gamo hoti **naṁ**mhi vibhattimhi.

An additional consonant "**n**" has to be added to dative and plural case-ending vibatti "**naṁ**" applied after numerical nouns such as "**dvi**-two" etc. **[n+naṁ>nnaṁ]**
[An added "**n**" before **naṁ** is clearly visible as it is shown in bold, underlined]

• Dvi**n**naṁ-two. • Ti**n**naṁ-three. • Catu**n**naṁ-four.
• Pañca**n**naṁ-five. • Cha**n**naṁ-six. • Satta**n**naṁ-seven.
• Aṭṭha**n**naṁ-eight. • Nava**n**naṁ-nine. • Dasa**n**naṁ-ten (All examples are of ***dp, gp***).

Dvādito'ti kimatthaṁ? [dvāditoti=dvādito+it]
What is the word "dvādito" for?
* Sahassānaṁ-thousands ***dp, gp***.
The example above is not the word "**dvi**-two". It is **Sahassa** (thousand). Hence, inapplicable.

Naṁmhī'ti kimatthaṁ? [naṁmhīti=naṁmhi+it]
What is the word "naṁmhi" for?
* Dvīsu-in two, * Tīsu-in three (Both are of ***lp***).
The examples shown are of vibatti "su", not of "naṁ". Hence, it is inapplicable.

Caggahaṇena **ssañ**'cā'gamo hoti.
[**ssañ'cā'gamo**=**ssaṁ**-ss+**ca**-also+**āgamo**-to come]
By means of the word "Ca" in Sutta, a double "**ssa**" is also to be inserted and attached to vibatti "**naṁ**"[after **catu**-four and **ti**-three. ssa+nnaṁ>**ssannaṁ**].
(See the examples carefully. "**ssa**" is shown in bold, underlined. An added "**n**" before "**naṁ**" is the function applied through main function of this Sutta)
• Cata**ssa**nnaṁ-four. itthīnaṁ-women, **i.e.** of four women.
• Ti**ssa**nnaṁ-three. vedanānaṁ-feelings. **i.e.** of three feelings.
(All examples are of ***dp, gp***).

६८, १८४. अमा पतो स्मिंस्मानं वा

68, 184. A'mā pato smiṁ, smānaṁ vā.

[Aṁ, ā+pato+smiṁ, smānaṁ+vā. 4 words]

[V] Pa-icce'tasmā **smiṁ, smā**-icce'tesaṁ **aṁ, ā,** ādesā honti vā yathāsaṅkhyaṁ.

The **smiṁ, smā** vibattis, applied after "**pa**-termed, **i, ī**-ending" nouns of feminine gender, change into **aṁ** and **ā** respectively.[**Smiṁ**>**aṁ, smā**>**ā**.]

See examples, **smiṁ** changed into **aṁ, smā** into **ā.** Both are shown in bold, underlined. Both **aṁ** and **ā** functions are shown in each pair of examples.

(1) [i-ending nouns, **aṁ** function of smiṁ]

• Maty**aṁ**. • Matiy**aṁ**-at wisdom ***ls***.

• Maty**ā**. • Matiy**ā**-from wisdom ***abs***. [**ā** function of smā]

(2) • Nikaty**aṁ**. • Nikatiy**aṁ** ***ls***.

• Nikaty**ā**. • Nikatiy**ā**-cunning ***abs***.

(3) • Vikaty**aṁ**. • Vikatiy**aṁ** ***ls***.

• Vikaty**ā**. • Vikatiy**ā**-change, transformation ***abs***.

(4) • Viraty**aṁ**. • Viratiy**aṁ** ***ls***.

• Viraty**ā**. • Viratiy**ā**-abstaining ***abs***.

(5) • Raty**aṁ**. • Rattiy**aṁ** ***ls***.

• Raty**ā**. • Rattiy**ā**-night ***abs***

(6) [ī-ending nouns]

• Puthavy**aṁ**. • Puthaviy**aṁ** ***ls***.

• Puthavy**ā**. • Puthaviy**ā**-earth ***abs***.

(7) [i-ending nouns]

• Pavaty**aṁ** ***ls***. • Pavaty**ā** ***abs***.

• Pavattiy**aṁ** ***ls***. • Pavattiy**ā**-event. ***abs***.

६९, १८६. आदितो ओ च

69, 186. **Ādito o ca.** [Ādito+o+ca. 3 words]

[V] **Ādi**-icce'tasmā **smiṁ**vacanassa **aṁ, o**-ādesā honti vā.

The vibatti "**smiṁ**" applied after the noun word "**ādi**", sometimes changes into "**aṁ** or **o**".
(**ādi** means beginning, so forth. Sometimes used as an equivalent of "etc." in this grammar. See examples. Both **ṁ** and **o** are shown in bold, underlined)

• Ādī**ṁ** [**aṁ**-function]. • Ād**o** [**o**-function]-in the beginning ***ls***.

Vā'ti kimatthaṁ?
What is the word "vā" for?
In the examples below, the function of Sutta is not applied as indicated by the word "vā". (That is why the vibatti smiṁ and its morpheme "mhi" are seen after "ādi". See below underlined)
* Ādismiṁ. * Ādimhi nāthaṁ namassitvāna.
* Ādismiṁ. * Ādimhi-in the beginning ***ls***. nāthaṁ-to the lord Buddha ***as***. namassitvāna-having bowed down***, kv, gerund***.
i.e. Having bowed down to the Lord Buddha in the beginning.

Caggahaṇena aññasmā'pi smiṁ-vacanassa **ā, o, aṁ**-ādesā honti.

By means of the word "Ca" in Sutta, the vibatti "**smiṁ**", applied after other words, can also be morphed into "**ā, o** and **aṁ**". (The changed letters are shown in bold, underlined)
• Div**ā** ca • ratt**o** ca haranti ye baliṁ.
• Div**ā**-in day time ***ls***, ca-also ***nip*** • ratt**o**-at night ***ls***. ca-also ***nip***. haranti-carry (offer) ***āv***. ye-those who ***np***. baliṁ-offering, sacrifice ***as***.
i.e. Those who carry (offer) sacrifice to (deities) day and night.
(In each of both examples one "**smiṁ**" changes into **ā** and the other "**smiṁ**" changes into "**o**")
• Vārāṇasi**ṁ** ahu rājā. (Here, the "**smiṁ**" changes into an "**aṁ**".)
• Vārāṇasi**ṁ**-in the city of Vārāṇasī ***ls***. ahu-there was. ***āv***. rājā-king ***ns***. **i.e.** there was a king in the city of Vārāṇasī.

Note: These examples are frequently found in the Pāli texts.

७०, ३०. झलान मियुवा सरे वा

70, 30. **Jha, lā, na'miyu'vā sare vā.**

[Jha, lā, naṁ+iya, uvā+sare+vā. 4 words]

[V] Jha, la, icce-tesaṁ **iya, uva**-icce'te ādesā honti vā sare pare yathāsaṅkhyaṁ.

Jha-termed "**i**" changes into "**iya**", while **la**-termed "**u**" changes into "**uva**" respectively when followed by a vowel (in a word structure).

[See the examples underlined to clarify the function]

• T**iy**antaṁ • pacch**iy**āgāre. • Agg**iy**āgāre.

In these examples, the consonant "y" after "i" is a morpheme which becomes **iya**.

• T**iy**antaṁ-Ti+antaṁ-three edge ***ns***. [Ti-three+antaṁ-edge]

• pacch**iy**āgāre- pacch**i**+āgāre-at basket house ***ls***. [pacch**i**-basket+āgāre-home]

• Agg**iy**āgāre- Agg**i**+āgāre-fire-house, where sacrifices are performed ***ls***. [Aggi-fire+āgāre-house]

• Bhikkh**uv**āsane nisīdati. • Puth**uv**āsane nisīdati.

(In these examples, the consonant "v" behind "u" is a morpheme which becomes **uva**)

• Bhikkh**uv**āsane-Bhikkh**u**+āsane-at the monk's place ***ls***. nisīdati-(he) sits. ***āv***. [Bhikkh**u**-monk's+āsane-place]

• Puth**uv**āsane- Puth**u**+āsane-at the wide place ***ls***. nisīdati-(he) sits. ***āv***. [Puth**u**-wide and big+āsane-place]

Sare'ti kimatthaṁ?

What is the word "sare" for?

It shows that in examples below, there is no Sara (vowel) behind **i** and **u.** So, the function of Sutta is not applied.

(There is no vowel behind each **i & u .** See all bold-faced letters shown in each example to make it understandable. All examples except the last one are ***Digu*** compound nouns preceded by numerals. The last example is a **Kammadhāraya** compound noun.)

* Ti**m**alaṁ-three stains [Ti-three+**mala**-stain, impurity].

* Ti**ph**alaṁ-three fruits [**phala**-fruit].

* Ti**c**atukkaṁ-three quadriads [**catukka**-a group of four, quadriad].

* Ti**d**aṇḍaṁ-three walking-stick [**daṇḍa**-stick].

* Ti**l**okaṁ-three worlds [**loka**-world].
* Ti**n**ayanaṁ-three eyes [**nayana**-eye].
* Ti**p**āsaṁ-three traps [**pāsa**-trap, snare].
* Ti**h**aṁsaṁ-three swans [**haṁsa**-swan].
* Ti**bh**avaṁ-three existences [**bhava**-life].
* Ti**kh**andhaṁ-three aggregates [**khanda**-aggregate].
* Ti**p**iṭakaṁ-three baskets (Canonical texts) [**piṭaka**-basket].
* Ti**v**edanaṁ-three feelings [**vedanā**-feeling].
* Catu**d**disaṁ-the four directions [**disā**-direction].
* Puthu**bh**ūtaṁ-the wide and big [**puthu**-big+**bhuta**-that which is].

Note: aṁ is derivative morpheme of **si,** an ***ns*** vibatti applied after all nouns of neuter gender.

Vā'ti kimatthaṁ?

What is the word "vā" for?

In the examples below, the function of Sutta is not applied as indicated by the word "vā"

* Pañcaha'ṅgehi. * Tīhā'kārehi. * Cakkhā'yatanaṁ. (These are in fact **Sandhi** examples. See the separation of Sandhi below)

[SS] * Pañcahi+aṅgehi. [Pañcahi-by five+aṅgehi-factors.]
* Tīhi+ākārehi [Tīhi-by three+ākārehi-manners].
* Cakkhu+āyatanaṁ [Cakkhu-eye+āyatanaṁ-base].

Vā'ti vikappana'tthaṁ, **i**-kārassa **ay**ā'deso hoti.

The word "vā" has a sense of vikappna (Speculative Grammatical Function). By means of it, the vowel "**i**" of the word "**ti**-three" changes into "**aya**".

(Of the word **Ti**, **i** becomes "**aya**">**taya**+aṁ=ttayaṁ, after having one "a" dropped, one "t" being reduplicated. See the applied function as shown in bold, underlined in the example below)

• Vatthutt**<u>aya</u>ṁ**-a group of three things ***ns***. [**Vatthu**-things+**ttya**-group of three] (Vatthu+ti=aya+aṁ)

७१, ५०५. यवकारा च

71, 505. **Ya, va, kārā ca.** [Ya, va, kārā+ca. 2 words]

[V] Jha, lā, naṁ ya-kāra, va-kārā'desā honti sare pare yathāsaṅkhyaṁ.

The vowels "**i** and **u**", formally termed as "**jha, la**", change into "**ya, va**" respectively when a vowel is present next to it. [**I>y and u>v**]

Note: This pattern of morphological change in the examples shown here is somewhat similar to the functions applied in Suttas 21 and 18 in Sandhi section. See **y** and **v** of each examples shown in bold to clearly understand the function of Sutta.

- Ag**y**ā'gāraṁ-fire-house ***ns***. • Cakkh**v**āyatanaṁ-eye-base ***ns***.
- S**v**ā'gataṁ te mahāvīra
- S**v**ā'gataṁ-good coming ***nv***. te-your ***gs***. mahāvīra-Oh great brave one! (a **vocative, singular**, being addressed to someone so-named. **i.e.** Mahāvīra, your coming is good. You are welcome Mahāvīra!

[SS] • Agg**i**+āgāraṁ. ("i" becomes "y" in this example)
- Cakkh**u**+āyatanaṁ.
- S**u**+āgataṁ. ("u" becomes "v" in these two examples)

Caggahaṇaṁ sam'piṇḍana'tthaṁ.
[sam'piṇḍanatthaṁ=**saṁ**+**piṇḍana**-merging+**atthaṁ**-for purpose of]
The "Ca" in Sutta is only for sampiṇḍana (merging the function of preceding Sutta and this Sutta as a whole because both Sutta somewhat resemble to each other in changing **i** into **iya, ya** and **u** into **uva, va**).
[sam'piṇḍana=**saṁ**-together+ **piṇḍana**-merging]

७२, १८५. पसञ्ञस्स च

72, 185. **Pa-saññassa ca.** [Pa-saññassa+ca. 2 words]

[V] Pasaññassa ca ivaṇṇassa vibhattā'dese sare pare ya-kārā'deso hoti.

The pa-termed front vowel "**i** or **ī**", sometimes changes into "**ya**" when followed by a morpheme vowel "**ā**" of the former vibatti "**smā**". (See applied function "y" shown underlined below)

• Puthavy̲ā-from earth. • Raty̲ā-from night. • Maty̲ā-from wisdom. (All three examples are of ***abs***)

Sare'ti kimatthaṁ? What is the word "sare" for?
To show that there is no vowel behind. So, the function of Sutta is inapplicable in the example shown below. (See consonant "y" behind "i" to clarify this).
* Puthavi**y**aṁ-on earth ***ls***.

७३, १७४. गाव से

73, 174. **G'āva se.** [Go+āva+se. 3 words]
[V] **Go**-icce'tassa **o**-kārassa **āvā**'deso hoti se vibhattimhi.

The vowel "**o**" of the word "go (cow) ", changes into "**āva**" when followed by a Catutthī and Chaṭṭhī singular vibatti "sa".(**i.e.** when "sa" has been applied after it)
Summary: "**o**" of "**go**" changes into "**āva**" in dative and genitive singular case-ending "**sa**".
[See the applied function "**āva**" shown underlined.]

• G<u>āva</u>ssa-of cow ***ds, gs***.

७४, १६९. योसु च

74, 169. **Yosu ca.** [Yosu+ca. 2 words]
[V] **Go**-icce'tassa **o**-kārassa **āvā**'deso hoti yo-icce'tesu paresu.

When a Pathamā, or an Ālapana, or a Dutiyā plural vibatti "yo" is applied behind, the component vowel "**o**" of the word "go", changes into "**āva**".

[Masculine] • Gāvo gacchanti. • Gāvo passanti.
• Gāvo-the cattle ***np***. gacchanti-go ***āv***.
• Gāvo-the cattle ***ap***. passanti-(they) see ***āv***.
[Feminine] • Gāvī gacchanti. • Gāvī passanti.
• Gāvī-the cows ***np***. gacchanti-go ***āv***.
• Gāvī-the cows ***ap***. passanti-(they) see ***āv***.

Caggahaṇaṁ kimatthaṁ?
Nā, smā, smiṁ-su vacanesu **āvā**'deso hoti.

What extra function can the word "Ca" in Sutta affect? By means of "ca", when "**Nā, smā, smiṁ, su**" vibattis are applied after the word "go", the component vowel "**o**" thereof also changes into an "**āva**".

• Gāvena-by cow ***is***. • Gāvā-from cow ***abs***. • Gāve-in cow ***ls***.
• Gāvesu-in cows ***lp***.

७५, १७०. अवम्हि च

75, 170. **Ava'mhi ca.** [Ava+amhi+ca. 3 words]

[V] **Go**-icce'tassa **o**-kārassa **āva, ava**-icce'te ādesā honti **aṁ**mhi vibhattimhi.

When a Dutiyā singular vibatti "**aṁ**" is applied behind, the vowel "**o**" of the word "go", changes into "**āva** and **ava**".

• Gāvaṁ [āva function],
• Gavaṁ-to the cow ***as*** [ava function].

Caggahaṇena sā'disesesu pubbu'ttavacanesu go-icce'tassa o-kārassa avā'deso hoti.

By means of the word "Ca" in Sutta, the component vowel "o" of the word "go" can also be changed into "**ava**" when all the remaining vibattis **except aṁ**, are applied after the word "go".

Note: This extra function is applicable when **eight** vibattis: two **yo,** two **sa** vibattis, **nā, sa, smiṁ, su,** are applied after the word "go".

• Gavassa ***ds, gs***. • Gavo ***np, ap***. • Gavena ***is***. • Gavā ***abs***.
• Gave ***ls***. • Gavesu ***lp***.

७६, १७१. आवस्सु वा

76, 171. **Āvass'u vā.** [Āvassa+u+vā. 3 words]

[V] **Āva**-icce'tassa gāvā'desassa antasarassa **u**-kārā'deso hoti vā **aṁ**mhi vibhattimhi.

The last "a" of āva, which in itself is a morpheme of "o" of the word "go", sometimes changes into "u" in Dutiyā singular vibatti "aṁ" case-ending.
[This Sutta changes the last vowel "**a**" of "**āva**" into "**u**" in accusative, singular case of "go". See "**u**" on first example shown in bold]

• Gāv**u**ṁ. * Gāvaṁ. ***as***.

Āvasse'ti kimatthaṁ?
What is the word "Āvassa" for?
To show that the example below is inapplicable as it has no "āva" function, only "ava" function.
* Gavaṁ ***as***.

Amhī'ti kimatthaṁ?
What is the word "Amhi" for?
To show that the example below is inapplicable as it is not of "aṁ", but of "yo".
* Gāvo tiṭṭhanti. * Gāvo-cows ***np***. tiṭṭhanti-stand ***āv***.

७७, १७५, ततो नमं पतिम्हालुत्ते च समासे

77, 175. **Tato na'maṁ patimhā'lutte ca samāse.**

[Tato+naṁ+aṁ+patimhi+alutte+ca+samāse. 7 words]

[V] Tato **go**-saddato **naṁ**vacanassa **aṁ**-ādeso hoti. **go**-icce'tassa **o**-kārassa **avā**'deso hoti patimhi pare alutte[16] ca samāse.

The component vowel "o" of "go" in Chaṭṭī plural "naṁ" changes into "**ava**". In addition, the Chaṭṭī plural vibatti "naṁ" also changes into an "**aṁ**" in an Alutta compound noun (which comprises the word "go" being combined with a rear word "pati"). [**go**-cow+**pati**-lord]

Note: This Sutta has two functions:(a) **ava** function and (b) **aṁ** function. See the example carefully to clarify it. **Alutta** compound means un-elided compound-noun whose trace of Vibatti applied during the Samāsa process is not disappeared nor elided. As a result, the visible trace of vibatti still remains in it. In the middle of this compound noun example **Gavaṁpati**, the trace of vibatti "**aṁ**" still remains. [**A**-not+**lutta**-elided]

• Gavaṁpati-the lord of cattle *cn*.

Alutte'ti kimatthaṁ? What is the word "alutte" for?
To show that the example below is inapplicable as it is a lutta-compound noun in which vibatti applied after "go" has been elided. Hence, inapplicable.
* Gopati-the lord of cattle *cn*.

Caggahaṇena asamāse'pi **naṁ**-vacanassa **aṁ**-ādeso hoti, **go**-icce'tassa **o**-kārassa **avā**'deso hoti.

[16] The word "**alutte**" means "unelided". It refers to a kind of compound noun named "**Alutta Samāsa**" where a vibatti applied after a front component noun remains intact without being elided. Most compound nouns are called "**Lutta Samāsa**" where vibattis applied after each component nouns of a completed compound noun are elided. In such compounds, **Lutta** means "having its vibatti elided".

By the word "Ca" in Sutta, the vibatti "**naṁ**" can also be changed into "**aṁ**" while the component vowel "**o**" of the word "go" can morph into "**ava**" in non-compound-noun (**i.e.** plain noun) words. [2 functions]

• Gavaṁ ***dp, gp***. [ava+aṁ, two functions]

७८, ३१. ओ सरे च

78, 3. **O sare ca.** [O+sare+ca. 3 words]

[V] Go-icce'tassa okārassa avā'deso hoti samāse ca sare pare.

The vowel "**o**" of the front word "go", usually changes into "**ava**" when followed by a vowel in a compound noun which consists of the word "go".

[See the examples carefully. the second component words in the examples, rather than "go", are vowel-initial words such as **assakaṁ**-horse, **eḷakaṁ**-sheep, **ajinaṁ**-leopard]

• Gavassakaṁ-cow and horse ***cn***. • Gaveḷakaṁ-cow and sheep ***cn***.

• Gavājinaṁ-cow and leopard ***cn***. (All examples are Dvanda, copulative compounds)

Caggahaṇena **uvaṇṇa**-icce'va'mantānaṁ liṅgānaṁ **uva, ava, urā**'desā honti **smiṁ, yo,** icce'tesu kvaci.

By means of "Ca" in Sutta, the component vowels "**u, ū**" of the certain nouns ending in "u, ū", can sometimes morph into "**uva, ava, ura**" when **smiṁ** and **yo** vibattis are applied after them. (See the examples carefully)

• Bhuvi-in the earth ***ls*** [**uva**-function examples].

• Pasavo-beasts ***np***, ***ap***. • Guravo-teachers ***np***, ***ap*** [Both are **ava**-function examples].

• Caturo-the fours ***np***, ***ap*** [**ura**-function].

Sare'ti kimatthaṁ?

What is the word "sare" for?

To show that despite being compound nouns, the examples shown below have no vowels. Instead, they have only consonants behind "o". Hence, inapplicable.

[See bold-faced consonants "**dh, v**" to clarify it]
* Go**dh**ano-the one having cows as an asset ***as, cn***. * Go**v**indo-the lord of cows ***as, cn***.

७९, ४६. तब्बिपरीतूपपदे ब्यञ्जने च
79, 46. Tabbiparītū'papade byañjane ca.

[Tabbiparīto+ūpapade+byañjane+ca. 4 words]

[V] Tassa **ava**-saddassa yadā upapade tiṭṭhamānassa tassa **o**kārassa viparīto hoti byañjane pare.

When a consonant is being present behind, the Upasagga word "**ava**" in the front, has to be conversely changed into "**u**" [as a way of grammatical morphology procedure known as "**tabbiparīta**] (**ta**-that, **viparīta**-reversal) ".
Summary: This Sutta changes **ava** into **u**. As a matter of morphological process, the "**ava**" is a base Upasagga particle which normally changes into "**o**" (Refer to Sutta 50). Here, instead, it changes into "**u**". This is called "**tabbiparita**". This process does not occur always. Sometimes, in some instances, the "**ava**" remains unchanged. See below regarding the function of "ca". "**U**" is shown in bold. Assume that it is a reversely changed form of the upasagga word "**ava**".

• Uggate-when arises, ***ls***. sūriye-the sun, ***ls***. **i.e.** when the sun arises, on sunrise.
• Uggacchati-(It) rises up ***āv***. • Uggahetvā-having learnt ***kv,*** (gerund).

Caggahaṇa'mavadhāraṇa'tthaṁ.
[**ca-gahaṇaṁ**-the word "ca"+**avadhāraṇa**-restrict+**atthaṁ**=purpose]
The word "Ca" in Sutta is meant for the purpose of "**avadhāraṇa**[17]", restricting the function of Sutta on the examples below. (So, there will be two kinds of words, one being

---

[17] **Avadhāraṇa** is of two kinds:(1) **Nivattāpanā'vadhāraṇa** and (2) **Sanniṭṭhānā'vadhāraṇa.** Of the two, N**ivattāpanā'vadhāraṇa** restricts the function of Sutta while the latter affirms the function. (**Nivattāpana**-by barring, **avadhāraṇa**-to limit. **Sanniṭṭhāna**-by affirming, **avadhāraṇa**-to limit).

changed into "u" and the other remaining in the original Upasagga form of "ava" in the Buddhist texts).
* Avasāne-in the end, finally ***ls***. * Avakiraṇe-in scattering ***ls***.
* Avakirati-(he) scatters ***āv***.

८०, १७३. गोण नंम्हि वा

80, 173. **Goṇa naṁmhi vā.** [Goṇa+naṁmhi+vā. 3 words]

[V] Sabbasse'va **go**-saddassa **goṇā**'deso hoti vā **naṁ**mhi vibhattimhi.

The entire "**go**" sometimes changes into the new word-form "**goṇa**" when a Catutthī, Chaṭṭī plural vibatti "**naṁ**" is applied after it. [See the changed form shown in bold]

- **Goṇ**ānaṁ-cows ***gp***. sattannaṁ-seven ***gp,*** numerical adjective. **i.e.** of seven cows.

Vā'ti kimatthaṁ?
What is the word "vā" for? To show that in the examples shown below, the function is not applied as indicated by it. [There is only one example in the stanza shown by a star mark]

Gāthā (stanza)

* Gonañ'ce taramānānaṁ, ujuṁ gacchati puṅgavo.
Sabbā gāvī ujuṁ yanti, nette ujuṁ gate sati.

taramānānaṁ-those moving, ***gp*** *adj*. [Gonañ'ce=Gonaṁ+ce]. Gonnaṁ-amongst cows, ***gp***, puṅgavo-(the leading) male-bull ***ns***, ujuṁ-straightly ***nip***, ***adv***. ce-if, ***nip***, conditional. gacchati-goes ***āv***. **i.e.** Among moving cows, if the male-bull (leading the herd) goes straight, (the first line of the verse)

nette-(the leading) bull ***cls***, ujuṁ-straightly ***nip, adv***, gate-(when) going ***cls***, sati-happens, ***cls***. Sabbā-all ***np*** *adj*
* gāvī-(the accompanying) cows ***np***. ujuṁ-straightly ***nip, adv***. yanti-go, follow. ***āv***.
i.e. When the male-bull (leading the herd) goes straight, all (the accompanying) cows will follow straightly. (This is an analogical statement which means that if a leader is in the straight moral

path, without being corrupt, then others will follow suit doing the same thing.)

Yogavibhāgena aññatrā'pi goṇā'deso hoti.

By means of Yogavibāga (split-Sutta function), the word "go" also morphs into "**goṇa**" in cases of other compound noun words. (In the example below, there is another word "bhūta" after the word "go".)

• Goṇabhūtānaṁ-(those which have been) cows. ***gp, cn***.

८१, १७२. सुहिनासु च

81, 172. **Su, hi, nā, su ca.** [Su, hi, nā, su+ca. 2 words]

[V] **Su, hi, nā,** icce'tesu sabbassa **go**-saddassa **goṇā**'deso hoti vā.

When one of "**su, hi, nā**" vibattis are being applied behind the word "go", the entire word "**go**" sometimes changes into another word-form "**goṇa**". (See the applied function shown in bold)

• **Goṇ**esu-cows. ***lp***. • **Goṇ**ehi ***ip***. • **Goṇ**ebhi ***ip***. • **Goṇ**ena ***is***.

Vā'ti kimatthaṁ? What is the word "vā" for?
To show that in the examples shown below, the function is not applied as restricted by it.
* Gosu ***lp*** * Gohi ***ip***. * Gobhi ***ip***. * Gavena ***is***.

Caggahaṇena syā'disesesu pubbu'ttaravacanesu'pi **goṇa, gu, gavayā**'desā honti.

By means of "Ca", the word "**go**" can change into "**goṇa, gu, gavaya**" when all the remaining vibattis such as "si" etc., are applied after it.

Note: (1) Changing into "**gu**" occurs only for **naṁ**-vibatti-applied "go".
(2) Changing into "**gavaya**" is only for **hi**-vibatti-applied "go". See the examples carefully to clarify this function.

[**goṇa**-function] • Goṇo ***ns***. • Goṇā ***np***. • Goṇaṁ ***as***.
• Goṇe ***ap***. • Goṇassa ***ds, gs***.
• Goṇamhā ***abs***. • Goṇamhi ***ls***.

[**gu**-function] • Gunnaṁ ***dp, gp***.
[**gavaya**-function] • Gavayehi ***ip***. • Gavayebhi ***ip***.

८२, १४९. अंमो निग्गहितं झलपेहि

82, 149. **Aṁ, mo niggahitaṁ jha, la, pehi.**

[Aṁmo+niggahitaṁ+jha, la, pehi. 3]

[V] **Aṁ**vacanassa **ma**-kārassa ca jha, la, pa, icce'tehi **niggahitaṁ** hoti.

Dutiyā(accusative) singular "**aṁ**", applied after "**jha, la, pa-**termed nouns" and the "**m**" of some compound nouns, changes into a "niggahita-**ṁ**".

Summary: This Sutta enjoins two functions:
(1) keeping **aṁ** of accusative, singular vibatti as an **aṁ**,
(2) changing an "**m**" of a component word "pu**m**a (male) " in a compound noun into a niggahita represented by a dot.

The purpose of first function is to show consistency of this "**ṁ**" pattern in accusative singular cases of those **jha, la, pa-termed, i, ī, u, ū-ending nouns** without any further morphological change being applied or occurred.

As for the second function, it is to further transform niggahita into "vagganta, **the end-letter** of vagga group" as prescribed in Sutta No. 31 of the Sandhi section.

Examples of "aṁ" function,
(the first function on **Masculine Gender Nouns**)

Note: All examples of both genders shown below are of ***as*** vibatti.

[**i**-ending, **jha**-termed nouns] • Aggiṁ-fire. • Isiṁ-hermit. • Gahapatiṁ-householder.
[**ī**-ending, **jha**-termed nouns] • Daṇḍiṁ-the one who has a stick. • Mahesiṁ-the holy Buddha.
[**u**-ending, **la**-termed nouns] • Bhikkhuṁ-monk. • Paṭuṁ-the skilled person.
[**ū**-ending, **la**-termed nouns] • Sayambhuṁ-the self-enlightened Buddha. • Abhibhuṁ-the Buddha of overpowering capacities.

(Feminine Gender Nouns)

[**i**-ending, **pa**-termed nouns] • Rattiṁ-night.

[**ī**-ending, **pa**-termed nouns] • Itthiṁ-woman.

[**ū**-ending, **pa**-termed nouns] • Vadhuṁ-daughter-in-law.

Note that only "**ṁ**" is visible behind such **i, ī, u, ū**-ending nouns in accusative, singular case.

Examples of niggahita function,
(the second function)

(Changed letters are shown underlined. All examples are compound nouns.)

• Pulliṅgaṁ-the male-gender, male manner. [Here, Niggahita changes into "**ṅ**" as it precedes "**g**"**.** Refer to Sutta 31]

• Pumbhāvo-manhood. [Here, Niggahita changes into "**m**" as it precedes "**bh**"]

• Puṅkokilo-male Koel bird. [Here, Niggahita changes into "**ṅ**" as it precedes "**k**"]

Aṁmo'ti kimatthaṁ?

What is the word "Aṁmo" for?

To show that in the examples shown below are neither "dutiyā singular **aṁ**" nor contain an "**m**" in them. Hence, inapplicable.

* Agginā. * Pāṇinā-hand. * Bhikkhunā.

* Rattiyā. * Itthiyā. * Vadhuyā

(All are of ***is*** . The Meaning of some words shown before are omitted).

Jha, la, pehī'ti kimatthaṁ?

What is the word "jha, la, pehi" for?

To show that the examples shown below are not of jha, la, pa-ending nouns. So, the function is not applied as indicated by that word. (Those examples end in "a". So, they are not named **jha, la, pa,** but ordinary **a-**ending nouns in accusative case. That is why "**aṁ**" can still be seen clearly in them).

* Sukhaṁ-happiness. * Dukkhaṁ-suffering ***as***.

Punā'rambhaggahaṇaṁ[18] vibhāsā-nivattana'tthaṁ.

Including the word "jhalapehi" again in the Sutta has a purpose of affirming the function of the Sutta as being consistent for such nouns as shown below.

• Aggiṁ. • Paṭuṁ. • Buddhiṁ-wisdom. • Vadhuṁ. (These words are already shown as examples of Sutta)

८३, ६७. सरलोपो मादेसपच्चयादिम्हि सरलोपे तु पकति

83, 67. Saralopo'mādesa paccayā'dimhi saralope tu pakati.

[Saralopo+ādesa, paccaya-ādimhi+saralope+tu+pakati. 5 words]

[V] **Saralopo** hoti am'ādesapaccayā'dimhi. saralope tu **pakati** hoti.

When various vibattis such as "**aṁ** etc." are applied and necessary morphological procedures are done, further process of eliding the vowel and keeping morphed forms of the word in a state of "pakati", (**i.e.** keeping as it is without further morphological modification) is to be carried out. (This Sutta's function is broadly applied to all words in all chapters)

This Sutta enjoins two functions:

(a) **the first** is eliding the vowels, morphemes and affixes etc., which need to be elided in the course of morphological change of words so that it becomes a complete word.

(b) **the second** is keeping a state of pakati as it is to prevent further action. In other words, it is like a stop-work order after the last major morphological procedure is done.

---

18 **Puna**-again+**ārambhaggahaṇaṁ**-taking the word "jalapehi" in the Sutta, **vibhāsā**-inconsistency, **nivattana**-restriction+**atthaṁ**-has a purpose. **i.e.** taking the word "jhalapehi" in the Sutta restricts the inconsistency of function. So, this means that the function of the Sutta in such words as those shown as main examples is a consistent procedure.

• Purisaṁ-man *as*. • Purise-men *ap*. • Pāpaṁ-sin *as*. • Pāpe-sins *ap*. • Pāpiyo-the one who is worse *ns / tn*. • Pāpiṭṭho-the worst *ns / tn*. (Taddhita-nouns)

Am'ādesapaccayā'dimhī'ti kimatthaṁ?
What is the word "am'ādesapaccayā'dimhi" for?
To show that in the example shown below, there is neither an "aṁ", nor any ādesa (morphological change), so it is inapplicable.
* Appamādo amataṁ padaṁ. (This is part of a verse)
* Appamādo-diligence. amataṁ-of deathlessness. padaṁ-is the reason. **i.e.** Being diligent is the reason of deathlessness (as it can lead to attainment of deathless Nibbāna).

Saralope'ti kimatthaṁ?
What is the word "saralope" for? To show that there is no procedure of eliding a vowel in the examples shown below. So, it is inapplicable.
* Purisassa *ds, gs*. * Daṇḍinaṁ-those who have sticks *dp, gp*.

Tuggahaṇa'mavadhāraṇa'tthaṁ.
The word "tu" in Sutta restricts the function of Sutta in the examples below. (It means that in the two examples below, there is no elision of preceding vowels)
* Bhikkhunī-female-monk *ns*. * Gahapatānī-housewife *ns*.

Pakatiggahaṇasāmatthena puna sandhibhāvo ca hoti.

By means of the word **"pakati"** in Sutta, further Sandhi-action is possible in the examples below.

• Seyyo-the noble one *ns*. • Seṭṭho-the noblest *ns*.
• Jeyyo-the senior one *ns*. • Jeṭṭho-the most senior *ns*.
(Sandhi procedure of changing "**i**" into "**e**" and doubling of "**y**" occurs in two examples of "Seyyo" and "Jeyyo". These four examples are Taddhita nouns, **tn**).

८४, १४४. अघो रस्समेकवचनयोस्वपि च

84, 144. **Agho rassa'mekavacanayosva'pi ca.**

[Agho+rassaṁ+ekavacanayosu+api+ca. 5 words]

[V] **Agho** saro **rassa'**māpajjate **ekavacana, yo**-icce'tesu.

The vowels " **ī, ū**" of **non-gha**-termed nouns ending in both singular and plural vibattis, are to be shortened and made into Rassa (short) vowels "**i** and **u**".

Note: The function of this Sutta is to shorten " **ī, ū**" into " **i, u**" for **ī, ū**-ending nouns in **yo, aṁ, nā, sa, smā, sa, smiṁ,** case-endings only.

Example words of Feminine gender nouns.

See all the shortened **i and u** in the examples shown in bold, underlined.

[ī-ending, **pa**-termed feminine gender nouns] • Itth<u>i</u>ṁ ***as***.

• Itth<u>i</u>yo ***np, vp, ap***. • Itth<u>i</u>yā ***is, ds, abs, gs, ls***.

[ū-ending, **pa**-termed feminine gender nouns] • Vadh<u>u</u>ṁ ***as***.

• Vadh<u>u</u>yo ***np, vp, ap***. • Vadh<u>u</u>yā ***is, ds, abs, gs, ls***.

Example words of Masculine gender nouns.

See all the shortened **i and u** in the examples shown in bold, underlined.

[ī-ending, **jha**-termed nouns] • Daṇḍ<u>i</u>ṁ ***as***. • Daṇḍ<u>i</u>no ***np, ap, ds, gs,***.

• Daṇḍ<u>i</u>nā ***is, abs***.

[ū-ending, **la**-termed nouns] • Sayambh<u>u</u>ṁ ***as***. • Sayambh<u>u</u>vo ***np, ap,***. • Sayambh<u>u</u>nā ***is, abs***.

Aghoti kimatthaṁ?

What is the word "agho" for? To show that examples below are inapplicable as they are **gha**-termed nouns.

* Kaññaṁ ***as***. " Kaññāyo ***np, vp, ap***. * Kaññāya-girl ***is, ds, abs, gs, ls***.

Ekavacanayosvī'ti kimatthaṁ?

What is the word "ekavacanayosu" for?

To show that the examples below are inapplicable as they are in plural "hi", which is excluded here.

* Itthīhi ***ip, abp***. * Sayambhūhi ***ip, abp***.

Caggahaṇa'mavadhāraṇa'tthaṁ.
The word "ca" in the Sutta has the purpose of affirming the function of this Sutta in such examples shown below. (It affirms the consistency of this morphological pattern in such nouns throughout Buddhist texts)

• Nadiṁ-river *as*. • Nadiyo ***np, vp, ap***. • Nadiyā ***is, ds, abs, gs, ls,***.

Apiggahaṇena na rassa'māpajjate.

By the word "api" in Sutta, it debars the "rassa" procedure in the examples shown below. (See the vowel "ī" in them remain unshortened. Note that they are in Nominative-case "**si**" vibatti. This pattern is a consistent one. Also see next Sutta to affirm this fact.)

* Itthī ***ns***. * Bhikkhunī-female monk ***ns***.

८५, १५०. न सिस्मिमनपुंसकानि

85, 150. **Na sismi'manapuṁsakāni.**

[Na+sismiṁ+anapuṁsakāni. 3 words]

[V] **Si**smiṁ anapuṁsakāni liṅgāni **na rassa'**māpajjante.

There is no procedure of shortening into "rassa vowel" for masculine, feminine gender, ī, ū-ending nouns in Pathamā singular vibatti "si" case. (**i.e.** They will retain their natural long vowels in the nominative singular case, without being shortened. See the examples carefully to clarify this. The unshortened vowels are shown in bold, underlined)

• Itth**ī** ***ns***. • Bhikkhun**ī** ***ns***. • Vadh**ū** ***ns***. • Daṇḍ**ī** ***ns***.
• Sayambh**ū** ***ns***.

Sismin'ti kimatthaṁ?
What is the word "sismiṁ" for?
To show that the examples shown below are not of vibatti "si", but of "ālapana-vocative case si". So, they are inapplicable. (So, they have their long-vowels shortened as a result of being in the ālapana case. See the examples carefully. The shortened vowels are shown in bold, underlined)

Bhoti * itth**i**-Oh woman! Bhoti * vadh**u**-Oh daughter-in-law!
Bho * Daṇḍ**i**-Oh the one with stick!
Bho * sayambh**u**-Oh self-enlightened Buddha! . ***vs***.

Anapuṁsakānī'ti kimatthaṁ?
What is the word "anapuṁsakāni" for?
To show that the examples below are of neuter gender. So, they are inapplicable here. (See shortened vowels shown in bold as these words are adjectives which modify their corresponding words such as "dānaṁ etc." which belong to neuter gender. As such, the rule of this Sutta can not affect these words of neuter gender.)

* Sukhakār**i**-happiness-maker, ***ns***, **adj**, dānaṁ-charitable deed ***ns***.
  i.e. The charitable deed which creates happiness.
* Sukhakār**i**-happiness-maker ***ns***, **adj**, sīlaṁ-morality ***ns***.
  i.e. The morality which creates happiness.
* Sīghayāy**i**-quickly-going, **i.e.** occurring ***ns***, **adj**, cittaṁ-mind ***ns***.
  i.e. The fast-going mind, quickly occurring mind .

८६, २२७. उभादितो नमिन्नं

86, 227. **Ubhā'dito na'minnaṁ.**

[Ubha-ādito+naṁ+innaṁ. 3 words]

[V] **Ubha**-icce'vamādito saṅkhyāto **naṁ**vacanassa **innaṁ** hoti.

The Catutthī-Chaṭṭī plural vibatti " **naṁ**" applied after the numerical word **ubha** etc, changes into "**innaṁ**"
[See the applied function shown underlined]

• Ubhinnaṁ-of two. ***dp, gp***. • Duvinnaṁ-of two ***dp, gp*** (both have the same meaning).

Ubhādito'ti kimatthaṁ?
What is the word "ubhādito" for? To show that the example below is "ubhaya", not "ubha". So, it is irrelevant for the function of this Sutta to be applied on it.

* Ubhayesaṁ-of two ***dp, gp***.

८७, २३१. इण्णमिण्णन्नं तीहि सङ्ख्याहि

87, 231. Iṇṇa'miṇṇannaṁ tīhi saṅkhyāhi.

[Iṇṇaṁ, iṇṇannaṁ+tīhi+saṅkhyāhi. 3 words]

[V] **Naṁ**vacanassa **iṇṇaṁ, iṇṇannaṁ,** icce'te ādesā honti tīhi saṅkhyāhi.

The Catutthī, Chaṭṭī plural vibatti " **naṁ**" which is applied after the numerical word "ti (three) ", changes into "**innaṁ, iṇṇannaṁ**". [See the applied function shown in bold]

• T**iṇṇaṁ**. • T**iṇṇannaṁ**-of three ***dp, gp***. (The "**i**" of "**ti**-three" is elided)

Tīhī'ti kimatthaṁ? What is the word "tīhi" for?
To show that the example below is "**dvi** (two) ", not "**ti** (three) ". So, it is irrelevant for the function of this Sutta to be applied.
* Dvinnaṁ-of two ***dp, gp***.

८८, १४७. योसु कतनिकारलोपेसु दीघं

88, 147. Yosu katanikāralopesu dīghaṁ.

[Yosu+kata, nikāra, lopesu+dīghaṁ. 3 words]

[V] Sabbe sarā **yo**su katanikāralopesu **dīgha**'māpajjante.

When Pathamā, Ālapana and Dutiyā plural vibatti "yo" had either been changed into "**ni**" or elided, the vowel in front of "yo", has to be made into a **dīgha,** i.e., to be lengthened.

The examples of **yo**-elided nouns

See the lengthened vowels shown in bold, underlined

[i-ending masculine noun] • Agg**ī**-fires. ***np, ap***.

[u-ending masculine noun] • Bhikkh**ū**-monks. ***np, ap***.

[i-ending feminine noun] • Ratt**ī**-nights. ***np, ap***.

[u-ending feminine noun] • Yāg**ū**-rice-porridges. ***np, ap***,

[i-ending neuter noun] • Aṭṭh**ī**-bones. ***np, ap***.

[u-ending neuter noun] • Āy**ū**-lives. ***np, ap***.

(In these examples above, **yo** is elided by undergoing a **lopa** process as per Sutta No.118. After elision procedure, short "**i**" "**u**" vowels are lengthened by this Sutta.)

The examples of **ni**-function-applied nouns of neuter gender
(The lengthened vowels are in front of "**ni**")

• Aṭṭh**ī**ni-bones. • Āy**ū**ni-lives.

• Sabb**ā**ni-all. • Y**ā**ni-whichever things. • T**ā**ni-those.

• K**ā**ni-whatever things. • Katam**ā**ni-whichever things.

• Et**ā**ni-those. • Am**ū**ni-so and so things. • Im**ā**ni-these.

[All examples are of ***np, ap.***]

Note: In these examples, "yo" is changed into "**ni**" as per Sutta No.217 after which there is a **dīgha procedure** by this Sutta. See the lengthened vowel **ī** & **ū** in each examples located in front of "ni", shown in bold. It is quite simple to understand the function of this Sutta.

Yosvī'ti kimatthaṁ? What is the word "yosu" for?
To show that the examples below are not of "yo". So, they are inapplicable here. (All are of "si" vibatti)

* Aggi-fire. * Bhikkhu-monk. * Ratti-night. * Yāgu-porridge ***ns,***. ["**si**" is elided in these examples. No other specific action is needed]

* Sabbo-all. * Yo-which. * So-that. * Ko-who or what.

* Amuko-such and such a thing or person ***ns***. ["**si**" is changed into "**o**" in these examples]

Katanikāralopesvī'ti kimatthaṁ?
What is the word "katanikāralopesu" for? To show that in the examples below, there is no "**ni** nor **lopa**" function. So, they are inapplicable here. (**yo** is still seen as it is neither elided nor changed into **ni**)

* Itthiyo-women. * Vadhuyo-daughters-in-law.

* Sayambhuvo-self-enlightened Buddhas ***np, vp, ap***.

Punā'rambhaggahaṇaṁ kimatthaṁ?
Why (such a Sutta with "dīgha" function) is repeated again?

Niccadīpana'tthaṁ.
To show that this procedure is a consistent process of morphological pattern for such words.

•Aggī. •Bhikkhū. •Rattī. •Yāni. •Tāni. •Katamāni. (This is just a repeated display of examples shown above to confirm the consistency of such morphological procedure)

८९, ८७. सुनंहिसु च

89, 87. **Su, naṁ, hi, su ca.** [Su, naṁ, hi, su+ca. 2 words]

[V] **Su, naṁ, hi,** iccetesu sabbe sarā **dīgha**'māpajjante.

When " **Su, naṁ, hi,** vibattis" are being applied after nouns, the front vowel before the applied vibattis is to be made into a "dīgha"(lengthened).
[To clarify this, see the long **ī, ū, ā,** vowels in front of **su, naṁ, hi,** vibattis of examples shown in bold, underlined.]

• Aggīsu *lp*. • Aggīnaṁ *dp, gp*. • Aggīhi-fire *ip, abp*.
• Rattīsu *lp*. • Rattīnaṁ *dp, gp*. • Rattīhi-night *ip, abp*.
• Bhikkhūsu *lp*. • Bhikkhūnaṁ *dp, gp*. • Bhikkhūhi-monk *ip, abp*. • Purisānaṁ-men *dp, gp*.

Etesvī'ti kimatthaṁ?
What is the word "etesu" for?
To indicate that in the examples below, inapplicable "nā" vibatti is applied. So, it is inapplicable.
* Agginā *ip*. * Pāṇinā-hand *ip*. * Daṇḍinā *ip*.

Caggahaṇa'mavadhāraṇa'tthaṁ.
The nipāta word "ca" in Sutta restricts the function of this Sutta on the examples shown below. (So, there is no dīgha process in front of "su, hi" vibattis)
Sukhettesu-(like) good soils, *lp*. adj * brahmacārisu-at those who practice the noble Dhamma *lp*.
dhamma'makkhāsi bhagavā

[SS] [dhamma'makkhāsi=dhammaṁ+akkhāsi, two words in Sandhi]
dhammaṁ-the noble Dhamma *as*. bhagavā-the lord Buddha *ns*. akkhāsi-taught *āv*. **i.e.** The lord Buddha taught the noble Dhamma.
* bhikkhunaṁ datvā sakehi * pāṇibhi.
* bhikkhunaṁ-to monks *dp*. sakehi-with one's own, *ip, adj*
* pāṇibhi-hands *ip*. datvā-having offered *kv,* gerund.
i.e. having offered to the monks by one's own hands.
Note: See that in the three examples shown with the mark *, there is no dīgha process. It is easily understandable.

९०, २५२. पञ्चादीनमत्तं

90, 252. **Pañcā’dīna’mattaṁ.** [Pañca-ādīnaṁ+attaṁ. 2 words]

[V] Pañcā’dīnaṁ saṅkhyānaṁ anto **a**tta’māpajjate
su, naṁ, hi-iccetesu.

When “ **Su, naṁ, hi,** vibattis” are being applied after numerical nouns such as Pañca etc., the component vowel thereof has to be remained in “a”.

Summary: This Sutta enjoins to keep the vowel “a” of **Pañca** etc as “a”. No other functions such as lengthening etc, are allowed.

This is a consistent pattern of such numerical nouns from **Pañca** to **dasa.** No specific change is applicable in these Vibattis. That is why the vibattis can be seen without any alteration to them or to any vowel before them. See the underlined vibattis. One “**n**” is augmented in “**naṁ**” vibatti. All these examples are simple and clear to understand.

- Pañcasu ***lp***. • Pañcannaṁ ***dp, gp***. • Pañcahi-fives ***ip, abp***.
- Chasu ***lp***. • Channaṁ ***dp, gp***. • Chahi-sixes ***ip, abp***.
- Sattasu ***lp***. • Sattannaṁ ***dp, gp***. • Sattahi-sevens. ***ip, abp***.
- Aṭṭhasu ***lp***. • Aṭṭhannaṁ ***dp, gp***. • Aṭṭhahi-eights ***ip, abp***.
- Navasu ***lp***. • Navannaṁ ***dp, gp***. • Navahi-nines ***ip, abp***.
- Dasasu ***lp***. • Dasannaṁ ***dp, gp***. • Dasahi-tens ***ip, abp***.

Pañcādīnamī’ti kimatthaṁ?

What is the word “Pañcādīnaṁ” for? To show the examples shown below are inapplicable.

* Dvīsu ***lp***. * Dvinnaṁ ***dp, gp***. * Dvīhi-two ***ip, abp***.

(Note that in these two numerical nouns, there is **a dīgha** in front of **Su, hi,** vibattis and an extra “n” is attached to **naṁ** vibatti though there is no dīgha in it.)

Atta-miti bhāvaniddeso ubhaya**ssā**’gamanatthaṁ.
anto **u**-kāro **a**tta’māpajjate.

By means of the bhāva taddhita-suffix word “atta (refer to the word **mattaṁ**) ” in Sutta, the double “**ssa**” is to be inserted (at the front of) **naṁ**-vibatti applied after some numeral nouns while the component vowel “**u**” of the word **catu** (four) also changes into "**a**". (2 Extra-functions. See "**ssa**" before **naṁ** in both examples and the "**u**" of **catu** becomes "**a**", which is shown in bold, underlined. The function of Sutta's rule is quite simple)

- Cat**assa**nnaṁ-four, ***dp, gp, adj.*** itthīnaṁ-women ***dp, gp***.
- Ti**ssa**nnaṁ-three ***dp, gp, adj.*** vedanānaṁ-feelings ***dp, gp***.

९१, १९४. पतिस्सिनीम्हि

91, 194. **Patissi'nīmhi.** [Patissa+inīmhi. 2 words]

[V] **Pati**ssa'nto **a**tta'māpajjate **inī**mhi paccaye pare.

The vowel "**i**" of the word "**pati**-lord" affixed with a feminine suffix "**inī**" after it, is to be changed into "a". [**pati+inī**=pata-inī. Other morphological procedures are yet required to become "patānī"]

- Gahapatānī-lord of the house, **i.e.** housewife ***ns***,.

Inīmhī'ti kimatthaṁ?
What is the word "inīmhi" for?
To show that in the example below, there is no "inī" affix.
So, it is inapplicable here.
* Gahapati-lord of the house, **i.e.** householder, a husband ***ns***.

९२, १००. न्तुस्सन्तो योसु च

92, 100. **Ntussa'nto yosu ca.** [Ntussa+anto+yosu+ca. 4 words]

[V] **Ntu**paccayassa[19] anto **a**ttamā'pajjate
su, naṁ, hi, yo-icce'tesu paresu.

When "**su, naṁ, hi, yo** vibattis" are applied after a **Ntu**-suffixed nouns, the component vowel "**u**" of **Ntu** is to be

[19] **Ntu** affix is in fact the last part of various suffixes ending in Ntu. They are **vantu, mantu, tavantu, āvantu, tāvantu.** See Sutta Nos. 368, 369, 555 for more details. Though the last two suffixes are not directly found in Kaccāyana grammar text, they are applied through Sutta No. 391 in Taddhita section. Examples of ntu-suffixed words are: **Gunavā, Satimā, Bhuttavā, Yāvatā, Kittāvatā** etc.

changed into an "**a**". (This function is to initiate other morphological procedures needed for the completion of **ntu**-suffixed words.)

[su] • Guṇavantesu-virtuous ***lp***.
[naṁ] • Guṇavantānaṁ ***dp, gp***.
[hi] • Guṇavantehi ***ip, abp***.
[paṭhmā-yo] • Guṇavantā ***np***. [dutiyā-yo] • Guṇavante ***ap***.

Ntusse'ti kimatthaṁ?
What is the word "ntussa" for?
To show that the example shown below has no "ntu" affix in it. So, it is inapplicable.
* Isīnaṁ-hermits ***dp, gp***.

Etesvī'ti kimatthaṁ? What is the word "etesu" for?
To show that the example below is of a "si" vibatti, not of "**su, naṁ, hi, yo**". So it is inapplicable.
* Guṇavā-the virtuous one ***ns***.

Caggahaṇena aññesu vacanesu attañ'ca hoti.

By means of "Ca", the same function of Sutta can also be applied on **smiṁ, nā**-vibatti applied, ntu-affixed words. (**i.e.** Change "**u**" of **ntu**-suffix into an "**a**" in these case-endings too)
[smiṁ] • Guṇavantasmiṁ ***ls***. [nā] • Guṇavantena ***is***.

Antaggahaṇena **ntu**paccayassa anto **a**tta'māpajjate,
Yonañ'ca **i**kāro hoti. (2 Functions by means of "**Anta**")

By the word "anto (refer to **anto** out of **ntuss'anto**) " in Sutta, the affix "**ntu**" changes into "**a**" while the applied "**yo**" after ntu-affixed noun changes into an "**i**". ["**a** and **i**" function]
Note that this function is limited only to "yo" applied after the word "gunavantu (virtuous) " in the neuter gender.
• Guṇavanti ***np***.

९३, १०६. सब्बस्स वा अंसेसु

93, 106. **Sabbassa vā aṁ, sesu.**

[Sabbassa+vā+aṁsesu. 3 words]

[V] Sabbasse'va **ntu**paccayassa **a**ttaṁ hoti vā **aṁ, sa**-icce'tesu.

When "**aṁ, sa,** vibattis" are applied after a **Ntu**-suffixed noun, the whole **Ntu** sometimes changes into an "**a**".

Note: The second in each set of examples is inapplicable example. To easily understand the function of Sutta, the difference between two examples regarding the function being applied or not applied are shown in bold-faced letters. The word "vā" means that there can also be some other form of the same word in Pāli texts. It also means "in other way of use" which implies inconsistency of the function of Sutta.

[aṁ] • Sati**maṁ**-the one who has Sati, ***as***, ***adj***. bhikkhuṁ-monk ***as***.

* Sati**mantaṁ** bhikkhuṁ vā. (the same meaning, function not applied)

[Explanation] • Sati**maṁ**=**sati**-alertness, or sati+**maṁ**=the one who has.

In second example, **mantaṁ** is of the same meaning, but function is not applied. [**mantaṁ**=mantu+aṁ]

[aṁ] • Bandhu**maṁ**-the one who has relatives ***as***, ***adj***. rājānaṁ-king ***as***.

* Bandhu**mantaṁ** rājānaṁ vā.

[sa] • Sati**massa** ***ds***, ***adj***. bhikkhuno ***ds***.

* Sati**mato** ***ds***, ***adj***. bhikkhuno vā ***ds***.

[sa] • Bandhu**massa** ***ds***, ***adj***. rañño ***ds*** suṅkaṁ-tax ***as***.

* Bandhu**mato** ***ds***, ***adj***. rañño ***ds***, vā suṅkaṁ ***as***, deti-(he) pays ***āv***,. **i.e.** (he) pays tax to the king who has relatives.

Etesvī'ti kimatthaṁ?

What is the word "etesu" for?

To show that the examples below are of "si" vibatti. So they are inapplicable.

* Satimā-the one who has Sati ***ns***, ***adj***, bhikkhu-monk ***ns***.

* Bandhumā-the one who has relatives ***ns***, ***adj***, rājā-king ***ns***.

९४, १०५. सिम्हि वा

94, 105. **Simhi vā.** [Simhi+vā. 2 words]

[V] **Ntu**paccayassa antassa **a**ttaṁ hoti vā **si**mhi vibhattimhi.

When a "**si**" is applied after a **Ntu**-suffixed noun, the component vowel "**u**" of **Ntu** is to be changed into vowel "**a**". (**i.e.** it becomes "**Nta**").

• Himavanto-the one which has snow ***ns, adj,*** pabbato-mountain ***ns***. **i.e.** the mountain which has snow (on it), the snowy mountain.

Vā'ti kimatthaṁ?
What is the word "vā" for?
To show that the function of this sutta is not applied in some instances even if it is of "si" vibatti and ntu-affixed as restricted by the word "vā".
* Himavā ***ns, adj,*** pabbato ***ns,***.
(the same meaning as in "himavanto pabbato".)

९५, १४५. अग्गिस्सिनि

95, 145. **Aggissi'ni.** [Aggissa+ini. 2 words]

[V] **Aggi**ss'antassa **ini**-hoti vā **si**mhi vibhattimhi.

When "si" is applied after the word "aggi", the component vowel "i" thereof, sometimes changes into "ini".

Purato-from/in front ***abs, ls, ind,*** • aggini-fire ***ns,***.
Pacchato-from/in behind ***abs, ls, ind,*** • aggini-fire ***ns,***.
Dakkhiṇato-from/at the right ***abs, ls, ind,*** • aggini-fire ***ns***.
Vāmato-from/at left ***abs, ls, ind,*** • aggini-fire ***ns***.

Vā'ti kimatthaṁ? What is the word "vā" for?
To show that the function of this sutta is not applied in some instances shown below as restricted by the word "vā".
(So, there will be two examples of nominative singular Aggi, one with "ini" function and one without it in the Pāli texts)
* Aggi ***ns***.

९६, १४८. योस्वकतरस्सो झो

96, 148. **Yosva'katarasso jho.** [Yosu+a'katarasso+jho. 3 words]

[V] **Yo**su akatarasso jho **a**tta'māpajjate.

When Pathamā, Ālapana and Dutiyā plural vibatti "**yo**" are applied after **jha**-termed, **i**-ending nouns, the component vowel "**i**" thereof, which is also an "akatarassa, **i.e.** natural short vowel, changes into an "**a**".

(This Sutta changes "**i**" into "**a**" for those "**i**-ending **jha**-termed nouns in "**yo**" vibatti. See "**a**" in examples shown in bold, underlined, to clarify it.)

• Agg**a**yo-fires. • Mun**a**yo-sages. • Is**a**yo-hermits.
• Gahapat**a**yo-householders ***np, vp, ap***.

Yosvī'ti kimatthaṁ?
What is the word "yosu" for?
To show that the example below is inapplicable as it is of "su" vibatti.
* Aggīsu-fire ***lp***.

Akatarasso'ti kimatthaṁ?
What is the word "akatarasso" for?
To show that the example below is inapplicable as the vowel "i" in it is a "katarassa, **i.e.** not a natural rassa, but morphologically shortened rassa".
* Daṇḍino-those who have sticks ***np, vp, ap***.

Jho'ti kimatthaṁ?
What is the word "jho" for?
To show that the example below is inapplicable as the vowel "i" in it is not a "**jha**-termed one". (the vowel "i" in it is a "**pa**-termed one")
* Rattiyo-the nights ***np, vp, ap***.

Note: **kata**-done, made morphologically+**rassa**-short vowel. **i.e.** intentionally changed short vowel.
Akatarassa=**na**-not+**kata**-done+**rassa**-short vowel. **i.e.** natural short vowel.

९७, १५६. वेवोसु लो च

97, 156. **Ve, vo, su lo ca.** [Ve, vo, su+lo+ca. 3 words]

[V] **Ve, vo,** icce'tesu akatarasso lo **a**tta'māpajjate.

When "morphed form **ve, vo**" is present after a natural rassa "**u**-ending noun", that vowel "u" changes into "**a**". (The function of this Sutta changes "**u**" into "**a**" for those **u**-ending, **la**-termed nouns. See "**a**" shown in bold, underlined)

• Bhikkh**a**ve- Oh monks ! ***vp***. • Bhikkh**a**vo-monks ***vp, np, ap***.

• Het**a**ve-Oh reasons! ***vp***. • Het**a**vo-reasons ***vp, np, ap***.

Akatarasso'ti kimatthaṁ?
What is the word "akatarasso" for?
To show that the examples below are inapplicable as the vowel "u" in them is a "katarassa, **i.e.** not a natural rassa, but morphologically shortened rassa".

* Sayambhuvo-Self-enlightened Buddhas ***np***.
* Vessabhuvo-Buddhas named Vessabu ***np***.
* Parābhibhuvo-those who can overwhelm others ***np***.

Vevosvī'ti kimatthaṁ?
What is the word "vevosu" for?
To show that the examples below are inapplicable as they have no "ve, vo" function in them.
* Hetunā-reason ***is***. * Ketunā-banner ***is***. * Setunā-bridge ***is***.

Caggahaṇa'manukaḍḍhana'tthaṁ.
[ca-gahaṇaṁ+**anukaḍḍana**=pulling+**atthaṁ**=purpose]
The word "ca" in Sutta has a purpose of pulling, **i.e.** taking "a-changing function" of preceding Sutta toward this Sutta. (That is why this Sutta is a bit similar in changing "**u**" into an "**a**". The preceding Sutta changes "**i**" into an "**a**" though).

९८, १८९. मातुलादीनमानत्तमीकारे

98, 189. Mātulā'dīna'mānatta'mīkāre.

[Mātula-ādīnaṁ+ānattaṁ+īkāre. 3 words]

[V] **Mātula**-icce'vamādīnaṁ anto **āna**tta'māpajjate **ī**-kāre paccaye pare.

The last component vowel "a" of **ī**-affixed feminine gender nouns such as **Mātula** and so forth, changes into "āna".
[āna+ī= ānī,]
Summary: This Sutta changes the last "**a**" into "**āna**" for **ī**-affixed feminine gender nouns such as **mātula**=mātulāna+ī >**mātulānī.**)
See this function shown in bold, underlined.

• Mātul**ānī**-aunt ***ns***. • Ayyak**ānī**-madam, or an honorable lady . ***ns***.
• Varuṇ**ānī**-a medium woman or wife of a deity named Varuṇa, ***ns***.

Īkāre'ti kimatthaṁ? What is the word "īkāre" for?
To show that the examples below are inapplicable as they have no " ī " in them. (They have only an "inī" affix)
* Bhikkhunī-female monk ***ns***. * Rājinī-princess or a lady of royal blood ***ns***. * Jālinī-a divine being so-named ***ns***.
* Gahapatānī-housewife ***ns***.

Ānattaggahaṇena **nadī**-icce'tassa **dī**-saddassa **jjo, jjā**-ādesā honti saha vibhattiyā **yo, nā, sa**-icce'tesu.

By means of the word "**Ānatta**" in Sutta, the component word "**dī**" of the word "**nadī** (river) " changes into "**jjo, jjā**" together with vibattis "**yo, nā, sa**", which are applied after "**nadī**". **[Yo>jjo, nā, sa>jjā.]**
See the effect of function shown in bold.

[yo] • Na**jjo** sandanti. [Na**jjo**-the rivers ***np***. sandanti-flow ***āv*, i.e.** The rivers flow]

[nā] • Na**jjā** kataṁ taraṅgaṁ.
[Najjā-by the river ***is***. kataṁ-done ***kv***. taraṅgaṁ-wave ***ns***.
i.e. The river caused waves. (Kita verb in Passive voice)

[sa] • Na**jjā** nerañjarāya tīre.
[Najjā-of river ***gs***. nerañjarāya-named nerañjarā ***gs, adj***. tīre-on the banks ***ls*** . **i.e.** on the bank of the river named Nerañjarā]

९९, ८१. स्माहिस्मिंनं म्हाभिम्हि वा

99, 81. **Smā, hi, smiṁ, naṁ mhā, bhi, mhi vā.**

[Smā, hi, smiṁ, naṁ+mhā, bhi, mhi+vā. 3]

[V] Sabbato liṅgato **smā, hi, smiṁ** iccetesaṁ **mhā, bhi, mhi** icce'te ādesā honti vā yathāsaṅkhyaṁ.

The "**smā, hi, smiṁ** vibattis" which are applied after all masculine and neuter gender nouns, sometimes changes into "**mhā, bhi, mhi**" respectively. [**smā**>**mhā, hi**>**bhi, smiṁ**>**mhi**]

Note: The functions are shown in bold. The second example in each pair is inapplicable. Hence, the applied vibattis remain unchanged in them. See those unchanged vibattis shown underlined.

[smā] • Purisa**mhā**. * Purisa<u>smā</u>-from man ***abs***.

[hi] • Purise**bhi**. * Purise<u>hi</u>-by/with men ***ip, abp***.

[smiṁ] • Purisa**mhi**. * Purisa<u>smiṁ</u>-in men ***ls***.

Smā, hi, smiṁnam'ti kimatthaṁ?

What is the word "smā, hi, smiṁnaṁ" in Sutta for?

To show that the examples below are inapplicable as they are not of "**smā, hi, smiṁ** "vibattis.

* Vaṇṇavantaṁ-that which has beautiful look ***as, adj***

* agandhakaṁ-that which has no fragrance ***as, adj***

* viruḷhapupphaṁ-a fully-blooming flower ***as, cn***.

i.e. Beautiful, non-fragrant, fully blooming flower.

[Mahantaṁ-big ***as, adj***. chattaṁ-umbrella ***as***] * mahāchattaṁ big umbrella ***as, cn***.

[Mahantaṁ-big ***as, adj***. dhajaṁ-bannar ***as***.] * mahādhajaṁ-big banner ***as, cn***.

Note: The words within brackets are called ED or viggaha, not examples. Such EDs will be found in Samāsa, Taddhita, Kita and Uṇādi chapters frequently.

१००, २१४. न तिमेहि कताकारेहि

100, 214. **Na ti'mehi katā'kārehi.**

[Na+ta, imehi+kata-akārehi. 3 words]

[V] **Ta, ima,** icce'tehi katākārehi **smā, smiṁ,** naṁ **mhā, mhi,** icce'te ādesā ne'va honti.

After Sabbanāma nouns such as "**ta** (that) and **ima** (this) " are being changed into "**a**", the **smā, smiṁ** vibattis applied after them, are never to be changed into "**mhā, mhi**".
[See Sutta No.176-177 to understand changing into "a"]
The function of Sutta keeps those **smā, smiṁ** vibattis as it is. Hence, there are no "**amhā, amhi**" word-forms applicable in the ablative and locative singular cases. In the examples shown below, "**smā, smiṁ**" vibattis are shown in unaltered states in bold, underlined.

• A**smā**-from that ***abs***. ṭhānā-place ***abs***. bhayaṁ-fear ***ns***. uppajjati-arises ***āv***. **i.e.** fear arises from that place.
• A**smiṁ** ***ls*** ṭhāne-at that place ***ls***. bhayaṁ-fear ***ns***. tiṭṭhati-exists ***āv***. **i.e.** fear stands/exists at that place.
• A**smā**-from that, from this ***abs***. • A**smiṁ**-at that, at this ***ls***. (These are plain examples without any contextual word)

Katākārehī'ti kimatthaṁ?
What is the word "katākārehi" for?
To show that the examples below are inapplicable as they do not have any morpheme "a" derived from "ta, ima". So, "**mhā, mhi**" functions are seen in them being applied.
[See "**mhā, mhi**" in examples shown underlined.]
* Tamhā-from that ***abs***. * Tamhi-at/in that ***ls***.
* Imamhā-from this ***abs***. * Imamhi-at/in this ***ls***.

१०१, ८०. सुहिस्वकारो ए

101, 80. **Su, hi, sva'kāro e.** [Su, hi, su+a'kāro+e. 3 words]

[V] **Su, hi,** icce'tesu **a**kāro **e**tta'māpajjate.

The component vowel "**a**" of nouns changes into an "**e**" when "**su, hi**" vibattis are applied after nouns. [See the examples. The "**e**" in front of Vibatti "**su, hi**" is shown in bold, underlined. This function is quite a consistent morphological pattern usually found in all **a-ending nouns** of masculine and neuter genders.]

[su] • Sabbesu-all *lp*. • Yesu-in which *lp*. • Tesu-in that *lp*.
• Kesu-at what *lp*. • Purisesu-in men *lp*. • Imesu-in this *lp*.
• Kusalesu-in wholesome deeds *lp*. • Tumhesu-in you *lp*.
• Amhesu-in us *lp*.

[hi] • Sabbehi *ip, abp*. • Yehi *ip*. • Tehi *ip, abp*. • Kehi *ip, abp*.
• Purisehi *ip, abp*. • Imehi *ip, abp*. • Kusalehi *ip, abp*.
• Tumhehi *ip, abp*. • Amhehi *ip, abp*.

१०२, २०२. सब्बनामानं नंम्हि च

102, 202. **Sabbanāmānaṁ naṁmhi ca.**

[Sabbanāmānaṁ+naṁmhi+ca. 3 words]

[V] Sabbesaṁ sabbanāmānaṁ anto **a**kāro **e**tta'māpajjate **naṁ**mhi vibhattimhi.

The last component vowel "**a**" of Sabbanāma nouns before the applied vibatti "**naṁ**", changes into "**e**".

[Sabbanāma nouns are **sabba**, **ya, ta, ka** and so on. See the examples carefully. "**e**" is shown in bold, underlined. The "**Saṁ, sānaṁ**" after "e" are morphed forms derived from the "**naṁ**" vibatti. Hence, it is invisible]

[**sabba**-all] • Sabbesaṁ. • Sabbesānaṁ.

[**ya**-which] • Yesaṁ. • Yesānaṁ.

[**ta**-that] • Tesaṁ. • Tesānaṁ.

[**ima**-this] • Imesaṁ. • Imesānaṁ. • Kesaṁ. • Kesānaṁ.

[**itara**-other] • Itaresaṁ-others. • Itaresānaṁ-others,

[**katama**-what] • Katamesaṁ-of which ones. • Katamesānaṁ-of which ones. All examples are ***dp, gp***

Sabbanāmānami'ti kimatthaṁ?

What is the word "sabbanāmānaṁ" for?

To show that examples below are inapplicable as they are not sabbanāma nouns.

* Buddhānaṁ * bhagavantānaṁ āciṇṇasam'āciṇṇo.

* Buddhānaṁ-Buddhas ***gp*** * bhagavantānaṁ-those having six

glories called "bhaga", ***gp, adj***, āciṇṇasamāciṇṇo-(is) habitually done sacred custom ***nv***.
i.e. (It) is a habitually done sacred custom of Buddhas who have six glories called as "bhaga".

Akāro'ti kimatthaṁ?
What is the word "akāro" for?
To show that examples below are inapplicable as they have no "akāra-the letter-**a**" in them, but "**ū**" instead.
* Amūsaṁ . * Amūsānaṁ- of so and so people or things ***dp, gp***.

Naṁmhī'ti kimatthaṁ?
What is the word "naṁmhi" for?
To show that examples below are inapplicable as they are of "yo", not of "naṁ".
* Sabbe-all ***np, ap***. * Ime-these ***np, ap***.

Caggahaṇa'manukaḍḍhana'tthaṁ.
The word "ca" in Sutta has a purpose of pulling in "e-changing function" from the preceding Sutta No.101 (to this Sutta).

१०३, ७९. अतो नेन

103, 79. Ato ne'na. [Ato+nā+ena. 3 words]

[V] Tasmā **a**kārato **nā**vacanassa **enā**'deso hoti.

The vibatti "**nā**" applied after **a**-ending nouns (masculine & neuter gender), changes into "ena". [See examples in their original form of a-endings shown in bracket. The "**ena**" is shown in bold, underlined]

[sabba] • Sabb**<u>ena</u>**-with all. [ya] • Y**<u>ena</u>**-with which.
[ta] • T**<u>ena</u>**-with that. [ka] • K**<u>ena</u>**-with what.
[ima] • An**<u>ena</u>**-with this. [ima-changes into "ana" by Sutta No.171 word]
[purisa] • Puris**<u>ena</u>**-with man.
[rūpa] • Rūp**<u>ena</u>**-with form, or any physical matter.
(All are **a**-ending nouns in ***is***)

Ato'ti kimatthaṁ?
What is the word "ato" for?

To show that examples below are inapplicable as they end in "i-u". So, the vibatti is kept as it is without being changed into "ena". [See Vibatti "nā" in the examples below which is shown underlined]

[muni] * Muninā-sage *is*. (This is an **i**-ending noun)

[amu] * Amunā-so and so person or thing *is*.

[Bhikkhu] * Bhikkhunā-monk *is*. (These are **u**-ending nouns. So they are inapplicable)

Nā'ti kimatthaṁ? What is the word "nā" for?
To show that example below is inapplicable as it is of "smā", not of "nā".
* Tasmā-from that *abs*.

१०४, ६६. सो

104, 66. **So'.** [Si+o. 2 words]

[V] Tasmā **a**kārato **si**vacanassa **o**kārā'deso hoti.

The Paṭhamā singular vibatti "**si**" applied after a-ending nouns of masculine gender, is to be changed into "**o**". [See examples, The applied function "**o**" is shown in bold-face]

• Sabb**o**-all *ns*. • Y**o**-which *ns*. • S**o**-that *ns*. • K**o**-who or what *ns*.
• Amuk**o**-such and such a person, thing etc. *ns*. • Puris**o**-man *ns*.

Sī'ti kimatthaṁ?
What is the word "si" for? To show that the example below is inapplicable as it is of "naṁ", not of "si".
* Purisānaṁ- of men *dp, gp*.

Ato'ti kimatthaṁ?
What is the word "ato" for?
To show that the example below is inapplicable as it does not end in an "a", but ends in "ū".
* Sayambhū *ns*.

१०५, ०. सो वा

105,...**So vā.** [So+vā. 2 words]

[V] Tasmā **a**-kārato **nā**vacanassa **so**-ādeso hoti vā.

The vibatti "**nā**" applied after a-ending nouns, changes into "**so**". [This Sutta changes "**nā**" into "**so**". Such examples are widely found in the Buddhist texts **used as either adjective or adverb**. See the applied function shown in bold, underlined]

• Attha**<u>so</u>** dhammaṁ jānāti.

[Trans] • Attha**so**-by means of meaning ***is.*** dhammaṁ-the Dhamma or Pāli ***as.*** jānāti-(he) knows ***āv.*** **i.e.** He knows the Dhamma by means of understanding the meaning.

• Byañjana**<u>so</u>** atthaṁ jānāti.

[Trans] • Byañjana**so**-by means of words ***is***...atthaṁ-the meaning ***as***...jānāti-(he) knows ***āv***. **i.e.** He knows the meaning by means of understanding the words.

• Akkhara**<u>so</u>**-by letter. • Sutta**<u>so</u>**-by Sutta (discourse). • Pada**<u>so</u>**-by word. • Yasa**<u>so</u>**-by fame. • Upāya**<u>so</u>**-by logic or method.

• Sabba**<u>so</u>**-by all means. • Thāma**<u>so</u>**-by capacity.

• Ṭhāna**<u>so</u>**-by the right reason. (All are of ***is***)

Vā'ti kimatthaṁ?

What is the word "vā" for?

To show that in examples below, the function of Sutta is inapplicable as implied by that word "vā". (That is why there is no "**so**" in three examples. Instead, the applied "**nā**" becomes "**ena**" as per Sutta 103)

* Pād**ena** vā * pādārah**ena** vā * atirekapād**ena** vā
yo bhikkhu * theyyacitt**ena** parassa bhaṇḍaṁ gaṇhāti,
so bhikkhu pārājiko hoti asaṁvāso.

* Pād**ena** vā-either by a quarter * pādārah**ena** vā-or by a quarter's worth. * atirekapād**ena** vā-or in excess of a quarter's worth.
yo bhikkhu-whoever monk. " theyyacitt**ena**-with an intent to steal. parassa-of other. bhaṇḍaṁ-belonging. gaṇhāti-(if) takes,
so bhikkhu-that monk. pārājiko-the one who is defeated, fallen from monk's sacred life, hoti-is. asaṁvāso-the one who doesn't have any more monastic communion.

i.e. Whoever a monk, with the intent of stealing, takes other's belonging (which is) either mere a quarter (in terms of cash) or a quarter's worth or in excess of it, he is defeated from monkhood and has no more shared monastic conduct (communion) with other good monks. (**i.e.** defrocked)

१०६, ३१३. दीघोरेहि

106, 313. **Dīgho'rehi.** [Dīgha, orehi. 1 word]

[V] **Dīgha, ora,** icce'tehi **smā**vacanassa **so-**ādeso hoti vā.

The vibatti "**smā**" applied after the words "**dīgha** and **ora**" sometimes changes into "**so**". [Function shown in bold]

• Dīgha**so**-by terms of length ***abs***. • Ora**so**-by this side ***abs***.
* Dīghamhā-from length ***abs***. * Oramhā-from this side ***abs***.
(Both are inapplicable examples)

Dīghorehi'ti kimatthaṁ?
What is the word "dīghorehi" for? To show that in the examples below, the function of Sutta is inapplicable as they are not "dīgha, and ora".
* Saramhā-from vowel/ or from sound, ***abs***.
* Vacanamhā-from speech, ***abs***.

१०७, ६९. सब्बयोनीनमाए

107, 69. **Sabbayonīna'mā-e.** [Sabba-yonīnaṁ+ā-e. 2 words]

[V] Tasmā **a**kārato sabbesaṁ **yo,nī**naṁ **ā-e**-ādesā honti vā yathāsaṅkhyaṁ.

The vibatti "**yo**" and a morpheme "**ni**" applied after all a-ending nouns are to be changed into "**ā** and **e**" respectively. [This Sutta changes **yo and ni** into **ā and e,** which is shown underlined]

Masculine Gender, a-ending noun Examples

• Puris<u>ā</u>-men ***np***. • Puris<u>e</u> ***ap***. (In these examples of masculine gender nouns, nominative, vocative plural "yo" changes into **ā** and accusative plural "yo" changes into **e**)

Neuter Gender, a-ending noun Examples

• Rūpā-form or matters ***np***. • Rūpe ***ap***. (In these examples of neuter gender nouns, all "**yo**" is to be first changed into "**ni**" and that "**ni**" changes into "**ā**" for nominative and vocative cases and into "**e**" for accusative plural case. Please **note this specific fact** carefully)

Vā'ti kimatthaṁ? What is the word "vā" for?
To show that in the examples below, the function of Sutta is inapplicable as implied by that word "vā".
* Aggayo. * Munayo. * Isayo. (See Sutta 96 for these examples.)

Yonīnan'ti kimatthaṁ? What is the word "yonīnaṁ" for?
To show that in examples below, there is no "**yo** or **ni**" as required by this Sutta. Hence, inapplicable.
* Purisassa-of man ***ds, gs***. * Rūpassa-of matter ***ds, gs***.

Akārato'ti kimatthaṁ?
What is the word "akārato" for? To show that the examples below do not end in "a", **i.e.** not a-ending nouns. So, inapplicable. (They end in " ī & i")
* Daṇḍino-those having sticks ***np***. [**Daṇḍī**-this noun ends in **ī**]
* Aṭṭhīni-bones ***np***. * Aggī-fire (s) ***np***. pajjalanti-shine ***āv***. **i.e.** The fires shine (are aflame). * Munī-sages ***np***. caranti-move ***āv***. **i.e.** The sages move. [**aṭṭhi, aggi, muni**, these three nouns end in **i**.]

१०८, ९०. स्मास्मिंनं वा

108, 90. **Smā, smiṁnaṁ vā.** [Smā, smiṁnaṁ+vā. 2 words]

[V] Tasmā **akārato** sabbesaṁ **smā, smiṁ**icce'tesaṁ **ā, e**-ādesā honti vā yathāsaṅkhyaṁ.

The two "**smā, smiṁ** vibattis" applied after a-ending nouns of masculine and neuter gender, sometimes changes into "**ā** and **e**" respectively. [**smā>ā, smiṁ>e**]
See **ā** & **e** shown in bold, underlined. The second in each pair is inapplicable. That is why there are the applied vibattis still visible in them.

• Purisā. * Purisasmā-from man ***abs***.
• purise. * Purisasmiṁ-in man ***ls***.

Akārato'ti kimatthaṁ?
What is the word "akārato" for? To show that in examples below, the function of Sutta is inapplicable as they do not end in "a". (They end in " ī & u")
* Daṇḍinā ***is, abs***. " Daṇḍismiṁ ***ls***. [Daṇḍī, this noun ends in **ī**]
* Bhikkhunā ***is, abs***. * Bhikkhusmiṁ ***ls***. [Bhikkhu, this noun ends in **u**]

१०९, ३०४. आय चतुत्थेकवचनस्स तु
109, 304. Āya catutthe'kavacanassa tu.

[Āya+catutthī-ekavacanassa+tu. 3 words]

[V] Tasmā **a**kārato catutthe'kavacanassa **āy**ā'deso hoti vā.

(To express a **purpose** or a **benefit** or a **result** of an action) the Catutthī singular vibatti "**sa**" (which is applied after **a**-ending nouns of masculine and neuter genders), is to be changed into an "**āya**" sometimes. **[sa>āya]**

Note: This Sutta changes Dative singular "sa" applied after a-ending masculine and neuter gender nouns into "āya. Such word forms in "āya" express purpose, benefit or result.
It is widely used in the canonical texts. See the examples carefully. The function **āya** is shown in bold, underlined to make it easily noticeable and understandable.

• Atth**āya**-for benefit, ***ds***. • hit**āya**-for wellbeing, ***ds***. • sukh**āya**-for happiness. ***ds***. devamanussānaṁ-of deities and men. ***gp***. Buddho-Buddha, ***ns***. loke-in the world. ***ls***. uppajjati-arises, emerges. ***āv***. [**attha**-benefit, **hita**-wellbeing, **sukha**-happiness. All are a-ending nouns] **i.e.** The Buddha appears in the world for benefit, for the wellbeing and for the happiness of deities and men.

Ato'ti kimatthaṁ?
What is the word "ato" for? To show that in the examples below, the function of Sutta is inapplicable as it does not end in "a". (It ends in "i")
* Isissa-of hermit ***ds, gs***. [Isi-this noun ends in **i**]

Catutthī'ti kimatthaṁ?
What is the word " catutthī " for? To show that the example

below is of a "chaṭṭī vibatti". So, it is inapplicable.
* Purisassa-of man ***gs***. mukhaṁ-face ***ns***. **i.e.** man's face.

Ekavacanasse'ti kimatthaṁ?
What is the word "ekavacanesu" for?
To show that example below is of plural "naṁ" vibatti, not of ekavacana (singular). So, it is inapplicable.
* Purisānaṁ ***dp.*** dadāti-(he) gives ***āv***. **i.e.** He gives men.

Vā'ti kimatthaṁ?
What is the word "vā" for? To show that in the examples below, the function of Sutta is inapplicable as being restricted by it.
Dātā hoti * samaṇassa vā * brāhmaṇassa vā.
* samaṇassa ***ds*** vā ***nip***-either to the monk * brāhmaṇassa ***ds*** vā ***nip***-or to a Brahmin. Dātā-giver ***ns***, ***kn***. hoti-is ***āv***. (Here, double use of nipāta word "vā" is equal to "either or".)
i.e. (He) is the donor either to monk or Brāhmin.

Tuggahaṇena **thañ**'ca hoti. [tthañ'ca=tthaṁ+ca]

By means of the word "tu" in Sutta, the Catutthī singular vibatti "**sa**" also changes into "**tthaṁ**".
Note: See "**tthaṁ**" shown in bold, underlined. **This word form too is widely used in scriptures** including in this Pāli grammar text. See, for example, "Vāti kimatthaṁ?".
Kimatthaṁ=kiṁ+atthaṁ, **kiṁ**-what+**atthaṁ**-for purpose, benefit?
• Attha**tthaṁ-**for benefit. • Hita**tthaṁ-**for the wellbeing.
• Sukha**tthaṁ-**for happiness. All ***ds***.

११०, २०१. तयो नेव च सब्बनामेहि

110, 201. **Tayo ne'va ca sabbanāmehi.**

[Tayo+na+eva+ca+sabbanāmehi. 5 words]

[V] Tehi sabbanāmehi **a**kāra'ntehi **smā, smiṁ, sa**-icce'tesaṁ tayo **ā, e, āyā**'desā ne'va honti.

Three functions of changing "**smā, smiṁ, sa** vibattis" into " **ā, e, āya**" are inapplicable for a-ending Sabbanāma nouns.

Note: This Sutta debars three functions: changing **smā** into "**ā**", **smiṁ** into "**e**", **sa** into "**āya**" in a-ending Sabbanāma nouns. See the examples carefully to clarify this injunction. Practically, this Sutta restricts the function of Sutta No.108, and 109 in Sabbanāma nouns. In other words, the most Venerable Great Grammarian states that in **a**-ending masculine and neuter gender Sabbanāma nouns, **there are no word-forms** in **smā, smiṁ, sa** vibatti cases which have "**ā, e. āya**" **functions.** [See all examples with unaltered vibattis shown underlined.]

• Sabbasmā-from all ***abs***. • Sabbasmiṁ-in all ***ls***.
• Sabbassa-of all ***ds, gs***.
• Yasmā-from which. ***abs***. • Yasmiṁ.***ls*** • Yassa. ***ds,gs***
• Tasmā-from that. ***abs***. • Tasmiṁ.***ls*** • Tassa.***ds,gs***
• Kasmā-from what. ***abs***. • Kasmiṁ.***ls*** • Kassa. ***ds, gs***
• Imasmā-from this. ***abs***. • Imasmiṁ. ***ls*** • Imassa. ***ds, gs***
(The meaning of examples are easily understandable as shown in the first example)

Sabbanāmehī'ti kimatthaṁ?
What is the word "sabbanāmehi" for?
To show that in examples below, the restriction of this Sutta is inapplicable as they are not Sabbanāma nouns. (That is why they are seen in "**ā, e, āya**" procedures.)
* Pāpā-from sin or evil ***abs***. * Pāpe-in sin or evil ***ls***.
* Pāpāya-for accruing sin or evil ***ds***.

Caggahaṇa'manukaḍḍhana'tthaṁ.
The word "ca" in the Sutta has a purpose of pulling in the word "ato" which comes from Suttas 103 all the way up to 104, 105,107, 108, 109 and 110 and withholding it here in this Sutta. What does it mean? It means that in the forthcoming Suttas, the function is generally focused on other nouns rather than a-ending nouns.

१११, १७९. घतो नादीनं

111, 179. **Ghato nādīnaṁ.** [Ghato+nā-ādīnaṁ. 2 words]

[V] Tasmā ghato **nā**'dīna'mekavacanānaṁ vibhattigaṇānaṁ **āyā**'deso hoti.

All five singular "**nā, sa. smā, sa, smiṁ** vibattis" applied after **ā**-ending feminine gender nouns, change into "**āya**".

Note: This means that in all **nā, sa. smā, sa, smiṁ** vibatti-applied cases of **ā-ending feminine nouns,** there will be the same word form marked by an "**āya**". See the examples carefully to familiarize with word-forms of ā-ending nouns of feminine gender. Also note that only those • marked are examples, the rest are predicates which complements the sentence. [See "**āya**" function shown underlined in the examples below.]

[nā] • Kaññāya-by girl *is*. kataṁ-done ***kv***. kammaṁ-deed ***as***. **i.e.** The deed done by girl. (Passive voice)

[sa] • **Kaññāya**-to the girl ***ds***. dīyate-is given ***āv***. **i.e.** the girl is given (something by somebody)

[smā] • **Kaññāya**-from girl ***abs***. nissaṭaṁ-came off, dropped ***kv***. vatthaṁ-the dress ***ns***. **i.e.** the cloth which comes off (slipped off) from the (body of) girl.

[sa] • **Kaññāya**-of girl ***gs***. pariggaho-possession ***ns, nv***. **i.e.** the girl's possession.

[smiṁ] • **Kaññāya**-in girl ***ls***. patiṭṭhitaṁ-stood, ***kv***. sīlaṁ-virtue ***ns***. **i.e.** The virtue exists in girl.

Ghato'ti kimatthaṁ?

What is the word "ghato" for? To show that in the examples below, the function of Sutta is inapplicable as they are not "gha-termed" ā-ending nouns. (They are nouns ending in i, ī, u, ū. Ratti, Itthī, Dhenu, Vadhū)

* Rattiyā. * Itthiyā. * Dhenuyā. " Vadhuyā. (All are ***is, ds, abs, gs, ls.*** The Meaning of examples shown before)

Nādīnam'ti kimatthaṁ?

What is the word "nādīnaṁ" for? To show that in examples below, the function of Sutta is inapplicable as they are not of applicable vibatti. (They are of **aṁ** vibatti)
* Kaññaṁ-the girl, ***as***. passati (he) sees ***āv***. **i.e.** (he) sees the girl.
* Vijjaṁ-knowledge. * Vīṇaṁ-the harp. * Gaṅgaṁ-the river Ganges. (All are ***as***)

Ekavacanānami'ti kimatthaṁ?
What is the word "ekavacanānaṁ" for? To show that in examples below, the function of Sutta is inapplicable as they are in plural "**su**" vibattis.
* Sabbāsu. * Yāsu. * Tāsu. * Kāsu-at what. * Imāsu.
* Pabhāsu-lights. (All are ***lp***, ā-ending sabbanāma nouns of feminine gender)

११२, १८३. पतो या

112, 183. **Pato yā.** [Pato+yā. 2 words]

[V] Tasmā pato **nā**dīna'mekavacanānaṁ vibhattigaṇānaṁ **yā**-ādeso hoti.

All five singular "**nā, sa. smā, sa, smiṁ** vibattis" applied after "**i, ī, u, ū-ending**" feminine gender nouns, are to be changed into "**yā**".

Note: This means that in all **nā, sa. smā, sa, smiṁ** vibatti-applied cases of **i, ī, u, ū**-ending feminine gender nouns, there will be the same word-form marked by a "**yā**". See the examples. "**yā**" is shown underlined.

• Rattiyā. • Itthiyā. • Deviyā-queen or female divine being.
• Dhenuyā. • Yāguyā-porridge. • Vadhuyā.
(All examples are ***is, ds, abs, gs, ls***)

Nādīnami'ti kimatthaṁ?
What is the word "nādīnaṁ" for? To show that in examples below, the function of Sutta is inapplicable as they are not of "**nā** etc. " vibatti.
* Rattī ***ns***. * Rattiṁ ***as***. * Itthī ***ns***. * Itthiṁ ***as***.

Pato'ti kimatthaṁ?
What is the word "pato" for? To show that in the examples below, the function of Sutta is inapplicable as they are not "**pa**-termed" nouns, but are **gha**-termed nouns.
* Kaññāya. * Vīṇāya. * Gaṅgāya. * Pabhāya-light.
* Sobhāya-beauty or allure. (All examples are **ā**-ending nouns in ***is, ds, abs, gs, ls***)

Ekavacanānami'ti kimatthaṁ?
What is the word "ekavacanānaṁ" for? To show that in the examples below, the function of Sutta is inapplicable as they are not singulars (ekavacana), but plurals (dative and genitive plurals).
* Rattīnaṁ ***dp, gp***. * Itthīnaṁ ***dp, gp***.

११३, १३२. सखतो गस्से वा

113, 132. **Sakhato gasse' vā.**

[Sakhato+gassa+e+vā. 4 words]

[V] Tasmā **sakha**to **ga**ssa **a**kāra, **ā**kāra, **i**kāra, **ī**kāra, **e**kārā'desā honti vā.

An Ālapana (vocative) "**si** vibatti" formally termed "ga" and applied after the word **sakha** (friend), changes into "**a, ā, i, ī, e**". (This Sutta changes "**si**" applied after a-ending, masculine, vocative-case word "**sakha**-friend" into "**a, ā, i, ī, e**". See examples carefully. The function-applied vowels are shown underlined).

Bho • sakha. Bho • sakhā. Bho • sakhi. Bho • sakhī.
Bho • sakhe-Oh friend! ***vs***.
(All examples are of the same meaning, ***vs*** . "**Bho**" is a vocative prefix used before male gender nouns when addressing the male. "Bho" is a derivative morpheme of the word **Bhavanta** which means "your honorable".)

११४, १७८. घते च

114, 178. **Ghate' ca.** [Ghato+e+ca. 3 words]

[V] Tasmā **gha**to **ga**ssa **e**kārā'deso hoti.

The Ālapana (vocative) "**si** vibatti" formally termed "**ga**" and applied after **ā**-ending feminine gender nouns, changes into "**e**". (This Sutta changes "vocative case-**si**" applied after feminine gender, vocative-case, **gha**-termed, ā-ending nouns such as "**ayyā**-madam" into an "**e**". See the examples. "**e**" is shown underlined).

Bhoti • ayy<u>e</u>. Bhoti • kaññ<u>e</u>. Bhoti • kharādiy<u>e</u> *vs*.
(Refer to Sutta No. 57 for these examples)

Caggahaṇa'mavadhāraṇa'tthaṁ sanniṭṭhānaṁ.
The word "ca" in Sutta has a purpose of re-affirming the function of Sutta as a consistent morphological pattern.

११५, १८१. न अम्मादितो

115, 181. **Na ammā'dito.** [Na+amma-ādito. 2 words]

[V] Tato ammā'dito **ga**ssa **e**kārattaṁ na hoti.

The Ālapana (vocative-case) "**si**" formally termed "ga" and applied after the word "amma (mother) " etc., is not to be changed into "**e**". (This Sutta debars function of "**e**," in vocative noun word "amma" etc. Therefore, there is an "ā" in the examples below shown in bold, underlined.)

Bhoti • amm<u>**ā**</u>. Bhoti • ann<u>**ā**</u>. Bhoti • amb<u>**ā**</u>. Bhoti • tāt<u>**ā**</u>-Oh mother! *vs* (All are of the same meaning).

Ammādito'ti kimatthaṁ?
What is the word "ammādito" for? To show that in example below, the function of Sutta is inapplicable as it is not the word "amma" etc.
Bhoti * kaññe-Oh girl. *vs*.

११६, १५७. अकतरस्सा लतो य्वालपनस्स वेवो

116, 157. **Akatarassā lato yvā'lapanassa ve, vo.**

[Akatarassā+lato+yo-ālapanassa+ve, vo. 4 words]

[V] Tasmā akatarassā lato yvā'lapanassa **ve, vo**-ādesā honti.

The Ālapana (vocative) plural "**yo**" applied after "**natural u-ending nouns**", changes into "**ve, vo**". (Natural "u" means not morphologically shortened "u".)
This Sutta changes vocative, plural "**yo**" applied after natural short vowel **u**-ending masculine gender nouns into "**ve** and **vo**" which is shown underlined below.

• Bhikkhave. • Bhikkhavo. • Hetave. • Hetavo ***vp***. (Refer to Sutta No.97 for other necessary function)

Akatarassā'ti kimatthaṁ?
What is the word "akatarassā" for? To show that in the example below, the function of Sutta is inapplicable as it is not "akata-rassa, **i.e.** natural rassa", but is a "katarassa-**i.e.** morphologically altered rassa".
* Sayambhuvo ***np, ap***. (Refer to Sutta 119).

Lato'ti kimatthaṁ?
What is the word "lato" for? To show that in the examples below, the function of Sutta is inapplicable as they are not **la**-termed nouns. (They are **pa**-termed feminine gender nouns, hence irrelevant and inapplicable)
* Nāgiyo-female-dragons ***np, vp, ap***. * Dhenuyo-cows. ***np, vp, ap***.
* Yāguyo-porridges ***np, vp, ap***.

Alapanasse'ti kimatthaṁ?
What is the word "ālapanassa" for? To show that in the examples below, the function of Sutta is inapplicable as they are not ālapana (vocative). (The examples are statement in nominative plural "yo")
Te-those ***np, ap, adj*** * hetavo-reasons, ***np, ap***. **i.e.** Those reasons.
Te-those ***np, ap, adj*** * bhikkhavo-monks, ***np, ap***. **i.e.** Those monks.

११७, १२४. झलतो सस्स नो वा

117, 124. **Jhalato sassa no vā.** [Jhalato+sassa+no+vā. 4 words]

[V] Tasmā jhalato **sa**ssa vibhattissa **no**-ādeso hoti vā.

The Catutthī and Chaṭṭī singular (Dative and genitive) "**sa** vibatti" applied after "**i, ī, u, ū-ending nouns**", sometimes changes into "**no**". [This Sutta changes "**sa**" into "**no**". See "no" shown underlined below. The second one in each pair is inapplicable example.]

[i] • Aggino. * Aggissa ***ds, gs***.
[i] • Sakhino. * Sakhissa ***ds, gs***.
[ī] • Daṇḍino. * Daṇḍissa ***ds, gs***.
[u] • Bhikkhuno. * Bhikkhussa ***ds, gs***.
[ū] • Sayambhuno. * Sayambhussa ***ds, gs***. (The meaning of examples shown before)

Sasse'ti kimatthaṁ?
What is the word "sassa" for? To show that in the examples below, the function of Sutta is inapplicable as they are not of "sa", but of "nā" vibatti. (See "**nā**" vibatti shown underlined below)
* Isinā ***is***. * Bhikkhunā ***is***.

Jhalato'ti kimatthaṁ?
What is the word "jhalato" for? To show that in the example below, the function of Sutta is inapplicable as it is not **jha, la**-termed noun. (It is only an ordinary a-ending noun in "sa" vibatti)
* Purisassa ***ds, gs***.

११८, १४६. घपतो च योनं लोपो

118, 146. **Gha, pa, to ca yonaṁ lopo.**

[Gha, pa, to+ca+yonaṁ+lopo. 4 words]

[V] Tehi gha, pa, jha, la, icce'tehi yonaṁ lopo hoti vā.

All Pathamā, Ālapana and Dutiyā plural "**yo** vibattis" being applied after nouns ending in "**ā, i, ī, u, ū**", are sometimes elided.

[This Sutta deletes all Nominative, Vocative and Accusative plural "**yo** vibattis" applied after gha, pa, jha, la-termed "**ā, i, ī, u, ū-ending**" nouns.]

See the examples below where "yo" is elided in the first examples. The second one is inapplicable. That is why there is still a "yo" visible in it.

Examples of Feminine gender:
[ā, gha-termed] • Kaññā. * Kaññāyo.
[i, pa-termed] • Rattī. * Rattiyo.
[ī, pa-termed] • Itthī. * Itthiyo.
[u, pa-termed] • Yāgū. * Yāguyo.
[ū, pa-termed] • Vadhū. * Vadhuyo.

Examples of Masculine gender:
[i, Jha-termed] • Aggī. * Aggayo.
[u, La-termed] • Bhikkhū. * Bhikkhavo.
[ū, La-termed] • Sayambhū. * Sayambhuvo.

Examples of Neuter gender:
[i, Jha-termed] • Aṭṭhī. * Aṭṭhīni.
[u, La-termed] • Āyū. * Āyūni-life or ages. (The meanings are shown before. All examples are ***np, vp, ap***)

Caggahaṇa'manukaḍḍhana'tthaṁ.
The word "ca" in Sutta has a purpose of pulling (taking in) the word "jhalato" from previous Sutta No.117 to this Sutta. (That is why jha, la-termed nouns are additionally included for the application of the function as prescribed in this Sutta).

११९, १५५. लतो वोकारो च

119, 155. **Lato vokāro ca.** [Lato+vokāro+ca. 3 words]

[V] Tasmā lato **yo**naṁ **vo**kāro hoti vā.

The Pathamā and Dutiyā plural "**yo** vibattis" applied after "**u, ū-ending nouns**" sometimes change into "**vo**".
[This Sutta changes Nominative and Accusative plural "yo" applied after **u, ū**-ending nouns into "vo". See the examples. The applied "vo" is shown underlined. The second is inapplicable one.]

[u, la-termed] • Bhikkha<u>vo</u>. * Bhikkhū, ***np, ap***.
[ū, la-termed] • Sayambhu<u>vo</u>. * Sayambhū, ***np, ap***.

Kāraggahaṇaṁ kimatthaṁ?
What benefit is there by the word "kāra"? (Refer to the word "vokāro" included in Sutta)

Yonaṁ no ca hoti.

By means of it, the vibatti "**yo**" becomes "**no**" in some words. (See "**no**" shown in bold)

• Jantu**no**-creatures, ***np, ap.***

Caggahaṇa'mavadhāraṇa'tthaṁ.
The word "ca" in the Sutta has a purpose of restricting the function of Sutta in the examples shown below.

What does it mean? It means that there can be no such words like "**Amuvo**" in the canonical texts as such nouns are excluded from the function of Sutta.

* Amū-so and so ***np, adj***. purisā-men ***np***. tiṭṭhanti-stand ***āv***.
i.e. So and so men stand.

* Amū ***ap, adj*** purise-so and so men ***ap***. passatha-(you) see ***āv***.
i.e. See so and so men!

Iti nāmakappe paṭhamo kaṇḍo.
The first Section of Noun ends.

Dutiya Kaṇḍa
The Second Section

१२०, २४३. अम्हस्स ममं सविभत्तिस्स से

120, 243. **Amhassa mamaṁ savibhattissa se.|**

[Amhassa+mamaṁ+savibhattissa+se. 4 words]

[V] Sabbasse'va **amha**saddassa savibhattissa **mamaṁ-**ādeso hoti se vibhattimhi.

The whole of "amha-I" together with the applied vibatti "sa" changes into "**mamaṁ**" when a Catutthī, Chaṭṭhī singular "**sa**" vibatti is applied after it. [amha+sa>mamaṁ] This function is quite simple and easy to understand.

- Mamaṁ-my (for me). ***ds***. dīyate-given, ***āv***. purisena-by man, ***is***. **i.e.** I am given (something) by man. (Passive voice sentence)
- Mamaṁ-my. ***gs***. pariggaho-possession, ***nv***. **i.e.** my possession.

१२१, २३३. मयं योम्हि पठमे

121, 233. **Mayaṁ yomhi paṭhame.**

[Mayaṁ+yomhi+paṭhame. 3 words]

[V] Sabbasse'va **amha**saddassa savibhattissa **mayaṁ-**ādeso hoti **yo**mhi paṭhame.

The whole of "amha" together with vibatti "**yo**" changes into "**mayaṁ**" when a Paṭhamā plural "**yo**" follows after it.

- Mayaṁ-we. ***np***. gacchāma-go. ***āv***. **i.e.** We go.
- Mayaṁ-we. ***np***. dema-give. ***āv***. **i.e.** We give.

Amhasse'ti kimatthaṁ?
What is the word "amhassa" for? To show that in example below, the function of Sutta is inapplicable as it is not the word "amha".
* Purisā-men. ***np***. tiṭṭhanti-stand. ***āv***. **i.e.** Men stand.

Yomhī'ti kimatthaṁ?
What is the word "yomhi" for?
To show that in example below, the function of Sutta is

inapplicable as it is not of "yo" vibatti.
* Ahaṁ-I. ***ns***. gacchāmi-go. ***āv***. **i.e.** I go.

Paṭhame'ti kimatthaṁ?
What is the word "paṭhame" for? To show that in example below, the function of Sutta is inapplicable as it is not of a "paṭhamā yo" vibatti. (It is of dutiyā "yo", accusative plural. Hence, inapplicable)
* Amhākaṁ-us. ***ap***. passasi-see. ***āv***. tvaṁ-you. ***ns***. **i.e.** You see us.

१२२, ९९. न्तुस्स न्तो

122, 99. **Ntussa nto.** [Ntussa+nto. 2 words]

[V] Sabbasse'va **ntu**paccayassa savibhattissa **nto-**ādeso hoti **yo**mhi paṭhame.

When a Paṭhamā plural "**yo**" vibatti is applied after the "**ntu-**suffixed nouns", the entire "**ntu**" together with vibatti "**yo**", changes into "**nto**". (See the example word clearly. **nto** is shown in bold, underlined)

- Guṇava**<u>nto</u>**-those who have virtue. ***np***. tiṭṭhanti-stand, ***āv***. **i.e.** The virtuous stand.

Ntusse'ti kimatthaṁ?
What is the word "ntussa" for? To show that in the examples below, the function of Sutta is inapplicable as they are not ntu-affixed nouns.
* Sabbe-all. ***np***. sattā-creatures. ***np***. gacchanti-go. ***āv***. **i.e.** All creatures go.

Paṭhame'ti kimatthaṁ?
What is the word "paṭhame" for? To show that in the example below, the function of Sutta is inapplicable as it is not of "paṭhamā yo" vibatti. (It is of dutiyā yo, accusative plural)
* Guṇavante-the virtuous or those having dignity. ***ap***. passanti-see. ***āv***. janā-people. ***np***. **i.e.** People see virtuous ones or people are impressed with those having worldly dignity.

१२३, १०३. न्तस्स से वा

123, 103. **Ntassa se vā.** [Ntassa+se+vā. 3 words]

[V] Sabbasse'va **ntu**paccayassa savibhattissa **ntassā**'deso hoti vā se vibhattimhi.

When a Catutthī, Chaṭṭhī singular "**sa**" vibatti is applied after a "**ntu-**suffixed noun", the whole of "**ntu**" together with vibatti "**sa**" sometimes changes into "**ntassa**". (See the example below. Function is shown in bold, underlined)

• Sīlava**<u>ntassa</u>**-the one having "sila-morality". ***ds* (adj).** jhāyino-who used to have jhānas. ***ds*.** **i.e.** Of the one having morality and jhānas.
* Sīlavato jhāyino vā. (This example is inapplicable, of the same meaning)

Se'ti kimatthaṁ?
What is the word "se" for? To show that in example below, the function of Sutta is inapplicable as it is not of "sa" vibatti. (It is of "si", a nominative singular. See next Sutta for morphological function of this example)
* Sīlavā-the one who has "sila". ***ns*.** tiṭṭhati-stands. ***āv*.**
i.e. The one who has Sīla (moral virtue) stands.

१२४, ९८. आ सिम्हि

124, 98. **Ā simhi.** [Ā+simhi. 2 words]

[V] Sabbasse'va **ntu**paccayassa savibhattissa **ā-**ādeso hoti **si**mhi vibhattimhi.

When a Paṭhamā singular "**si**" vibatti is applied after "**ntu-**affixed nouns, the whole of "**ntu**" together with vibatti "**si**" changes into an "**ā**". (See "**ā**" shown underlined in bold. The "**v**" in front is that "**v**" of "**vantu**". Please refer to Sutta 368. The "**m**" in front is that "**m**" of affix "**mantu**". Please refer to Sutta 369)

• Guṇav**<u>ā</u>**-the one who has "**guna**-virtue or dignity", the virtuous.
• Paññav**<u>ā</u>**-the one who has "**Pañña**-wisdom", the wise.
• Sīlav**<u>ā</u>**-the one who has "**sīla**-moral virtue".
• Balav**<u>ā</u>**-the one who has "**bala**-energy", the strong.
• Dhanav**<u>ā</u>**-the one who has **dhana**-wealth, the wealthy.

• Matim<u>ā</u>-the one who has **mati**-intellect, the intelligent.
• Satim<u>ā</u>-the one who has "**sati**-attention, alertness,", alert.
• Dhitim<u>ā</u>-the one who has "**dhiti**-knowledge", the wise.(all ***ns***.)

Ntusse'ti kimatthaṁ?
What is the word "ntussa" for? To show that in the example below, the function of Sutta is inapplicable as it is not a ntu-affixed word, but an ordinary word.
* Puriso-man. ***ns***. tiṭṭhati-stands. ***āv***.

Simhī'ti kimatthaṁ?
What is the word "simhi" for? To show that in the example below, the function of Sutta is inapplicable as it is not of "si" vibatti. (It is of "yo" vibatti.)
* Sīlavanto-those who have "sila-morality". ***np***. tiṭṭhanti-stand. ***āv***. **i.e.** Those having moral virtue stand.

१२५, १९८. अं नपुंसके

125, 198. **Aṁ napuṁsake.** [Aṁ+napuṁsake. 2 words]

[V] Sabbasse'va **ntu**paccayassa savibhattissa **aṁ-**ādeso hoti **si**mhi vibhattimhi napuṁsake vattamānassa.

When a Paṭhamā singular "**si**" vibatti is applied after a **ntu**-affixed neuter gender noun, the entire "**ntu**" together with "**si**" changes into "**aṁ**". (See the function shown underlined)

(1) • Guṇav<u>aṁ</u>-the virtuous. ***ns*** *(*adj). cittaṁ-mind. ***ns***. tiṭṭhati-exists. ***āv***. **i.e.** The virtuous mind exists.
(2) • Rucim<u>aṁ</u>-the bright. ***ns*** *(*adj). pupphaṁ-flower. ***ns***. virocati-looks beautiful. ***āv***. **i.e.** The bright flower looks beautiful.

Simhī'ti kimatthaṁ?
What is the word "simhi" for? To show that in the example below, the function of Sutta is inapplicable as it is not of "si" vibatti. (It of dutiyā "aṁ" vibatti.)
* Vaṇṇavantaṁ-that which has beauty. ***as*** *(*adj). agandhakaṁ-that which does not have fragrance. ***as*** (adj). virūḷhapupphaṁ-fully blooming flower. ***as***. passasi-see. ***āv***. tvaṁ-you. ***ns***.

i.e. You see fully blooming, beautiful flower without any fragrant smell.

१२६, १०१. अवण्णा च गे

126, 101. **Avaṇṇā ca ge.** [Avaṇṇā+ca+ge. 3 words]

[V] Sabbasse'va **ntu**paccayassa savibhattissa **aṁ, a**vaṇṇā ca honti ge pare.

When an Ālapana (vocative) singular "**si**" vibatti is applied after "**ntu**" suffixed noun, the entire "**ntu**" together with vibatti "**si**" changes into "**aṁ, a, ā**". [All three functions are shown underlined]

Bho • guṇavaṁ. Bho • guṇava.
Bho • guṇavā-Oh virtuous one! (All the same meaning, ***vs***)

Caggahaṇa'manukaḍḍhanatthaṁ.
The word "ca" has a purpose of pulling in the word "aṁ" from preceding Sutta (to this Sutta).
What does it mean? It means that the function of changing into **aṁ** is also included here in addition to **a, ā** functions.

१२७, १०२. तो तिता सस्मिंनासु

127, 102. **To, ti, tā sa, smiṁ, nā, su.**

[To, ti, tā+sa, smiṁ, nā, su. 2 words]

[V] Sabbasse'va **ntu**paccayassa savibhattissa **to, ti, tā,** ādesā honti vā **sa, smiṁ, nā**-icce'tesu yathāsaṅkhyaṁ.

When singular "**sa, smiṁ, nā**" vibattis are applied after **ntu**-affixed nouns, the entire "**ntu**" together with vibattis "**sa, smiṁ, nā**" sometimes changes into "**to, ti, tā**" respectively. [ntu+**sa**>to, ntu+**smiṁ**>ti, ntu+**nā**>tā,]
See all examples of three functions shown in pairs. The second one in each set is inapplicable example. The applied functions are shown underlined.

[sa] • Guṇavato. * Guṇavantassa. ***ds, gs.***
[smiṁ] • Guṇavati. * Guṇavantasmiṁ. ***ls,***
[nā] • Guṇavatā. * Guṇavantena. ***is,***

[sa] • Satimato. * Satimantassa. ***ds, gs***
[smiṁ] • Satimati. * Satimantasmiṁ. ***Ls***
[nā] • Satimatā. * Satimantena. ***is***

Etesvī'ti kimatthaṁ?
What is the word "etesu" for? To show that in the examples below, the function of Sutta is inapplicable as they are not of "**sa, smiṁ, nā**" vibatti. (They are of "si" vibatti.)
* Guṇavā. * Satimā. ***ns.***

१२८, १०४. नंम्हि तं वा
128, 104. **Naṁmhi taṁ vā.** [Naṁmhi+taṁ+vā. 3 words]

[V] Sabbasse'va **ntu**paccayassa savibhattissa **taṁ-**ādeso hoti vā **naṁ**mhi vibhattimhi.

When a Catutthī, or Chaṭṭhī plural "**naṁ**" vibatti is applied after **ntu**-suffixed nouns, the entire "**ntu**" together with vibatti "**naṁ**" sometimes changes into "**taṁ**".
(The function is shown underlined. The second is inapplicable example)

• Guṇavataṁ. * Guṇavantānaṁ.
• Satimataṁ. * Satimantānaṁ. (all are ***dp, gp***).

Naṁmhī'ti kimatthaṁ?
What is the word "naṁmhi" for? To show that in examples below, the function of Sutta is inapplicable as they are not of "**naṁ**" vibatti. (They are of "yo" vibatti)
* Guṇavanto, ***np***. tiṭṭhanti. ***āv***.
* Satimanto-those who have "sati". ***np***. tiṭṭhanti-stand. ***āv***.

१२९, २२२. इमस्सिदमंसिसु नपुंसके

129, 222. **Imassi'da'maṁsisu napuṁsake.**

[Imassa+idaṁ+aṁ, sisu+napuṁsake. 4 words]

[V] Sabbasse'va **ima**saddassa savibhattissa **idaṁ-**ādeso hoti vā **aṁ, si,** su napuṁsake vattamānassa.

When singular "**aṁ, si,**" vibattis are applied after **ima** (this) in neuter gender, the whole "**ima**" together with "**aṁ, si** vibattis" optionally changes into "**idaṁ**".

[aṁ] • Idaṁ cittaṁ-this mind. ***as***. passasi-(you) see. ***āv***.
i.e. You see this mind.

[si] • Idaṁ cittaṁ-this mind. ***ns***. tiṭṭhati-exists. ***āv***.
i.e. This mind exists.

Inapplicable examples:

[aṁ] * Imaṁ cittaṁ passasi.

[si] * Imaṁ cittaṁ tiṭṭhati. (The same meaning)

Napuṁsake'ti kimatthaṁ?
What is the word "napuṁsake" for?
To show that in examples below, the function of Sutta is inapplicable as they are of masculine gender.

* Imaṁ purisaṁ-this man. ***as***. passasi-(you) see. ***āv***.
i.e. You see this man.

* Ayaṁ puriso-this man. ***ns***. tiṭṭhati-stands. ***āv***.
i.e. This man stands.

१३०, २२५. अमुस्सादुं

130, 225. **Amussā'duṁ.** [Amussa+aduṁ. 2 words]

[V] Sabbasse'va **amu**saddassa savibhattissa **aduṁ**-ādeso hoti **aṁ, si**, su napuṁsake vattamānassa.

When singular "**aṁ, si,** " vibattis are applied after neuter gender noun word "amu-so and so", the whole of "**amu**" along with "**aṁ, si**" changes into "**aduṁ**".

• Aduṁ pupphaṁ-so and so flower. ***as***. passasi-(you) see. ***āv***.
i.e. You see so and so flower.

• Aduṁ pupphaṁ-so and so flower. ***ns***. virocati-looks beautiful.
i.e. Such and such a flower looks beautiful.

Napuṁsake'ti kimatthaṁ?
What is the word "napuṁsake" for?
To show that in examples below, the function of Sutta is inapplicable as they are of masculine gender.

* Amuṁ rājānaṁ-so and so king. ***as***. passasi-(you) see. ***āv***.
i.e. You see so and so a king.
* Asu rājā-so and so king. ***ns***. tiṭṭhati-stands. ***āv***.

१३१, ०. इत्थिपुमनपुंसकसङ्ख्यं

131,...**Itthi, puma, napuṁsaka, saṅkhyaṁ.**

[Itthi, puma, napuṁsaka, saṅkhyaṁ. 1 word]

[V] "Itthipumanapuṁsakasaṅkhyaṁ" icce'taṁ adhikāra'tthaṁ veditabbaṁ.

This Sutta is to be regarded as an "Adhikāra" Sutta effecting succeeding three Suttas (with regard to numerical nouns by implying that all numerical nouns are related to three genders).

Note: The Sutta itself means that "numerical nouns of feminine, masculine and neuter gender". So, it influences next three Suttas 132,133 and 134 by highlighting the relationship of numerical nouns with all genders.

१३२, २२८. योसु द्विन्नं द्वे च

132, 228. **Yosu dvinnaṁ dve ca.**

[Yosu+dvinnaṁ+dve+ca. 4 words]

[V] **Dvi**nnaṁ saṅkhyānaṁ itthipumanapuṁsake vattamānānaṁ savibhattīnaṁ **dve** hoti **yo**-icce'tesu.

The numerical word "**dvi** (two) " which belongs to all three genders, changes into "**dve**" along with vibatti "**yo**" applied after it. (See the examples carefully with its corresponding words in different genders)

• D<u>ve</u> itthiyo-two women (Feminine).
• D<u>ve</u> dhammā-two Dhammas (Masculine).
• D<u>ve</u> rūpāni-two forms (Neuter). (all ***np, ap***.)

Yosvī'ti kimatthaṁ?
What is the word "yosu" for?
To show that in the example below, the function of Sutta is inapplicable as it is not of "yo", but of "su".
* Dvīsu-at two.

Caggahaṇena duve, dvaya, ubha, ubhaya, duvi ca honti **yo, nā, naṁ** icce'tesu.

By means of "Ca" in Sutta, "**yo, nā, naṁ**" vibattis applied after "dvi" change into "**duve, dvaya, ubha, ubhaya, duvi**".

• D<u>uve</u> samaṇā-two monks. • D<u>uve</u> brahmaṇā-two Brāhmins.
• D<u>uve</u> janā-two persons. ***np. ap.***
• D<u>vay</u>ena-with two. ***is.*** • D<u>vay</u>aṁ-to two, **i.e.** two by two, mutually. ***as.***
• U<u>bh</u>innaṁ. • U<u>bhay</u>esaṁ. • D<u>uvi</u>nnaṁ-of two (All three are of the same meaning). ***dp, gp***.

१३३, २३०. तिचतुन्नं तिस्सो, चतस्सो, तयो, चत्तारो, तीणि, चत्तारि

133, 230. Ti catunnaṁ tisso, catasso, tayo, cattāro, tīṇi, cattāri. [Ti, catunnaṁ+tisso, catasso, tayo, cattāro, tīṇi, cattāri. 2 words]

[V] **Ti, catu**nnaṁ saṅkhyānaṁ itthipumanapuṁsake vattamānanaṁ savibhattīnaṁ **tisso, catasso, tayo, cattāro, tīṇi, cattāri** icce'te ādesā honti yathāsaṅkhyaṁ **yo**-icce'tesu.

The numerical words "**ti** (three), **catu** (four) " which belongs to all three genders, changes into "**tisso, catasso, tayo, cattāro, tīṇi, cattāri,**" respectively along with vibatti "**yo**" applied after them.

tisso (three), **catasso** (four) = [To be used with corresponding Feminine gender words only]

tayo, cattāro=[Masculine]
tīṇi, cattāri=[Neuter]
See the examples shown below with words of corresponding gender. The numerical nouns serve as adjective words.

[Feminine] • Tisso vedanā-three feelings.
• Catasso disā-four directions.
[Masculine] • Tayo janā, jane-three persons.
• Cattāro purisā, purise-four men.
[Neuter] • Tīṇi āyatanāni-three bases.
• Cattāri ariyasaccāni-four noble truths. ***All np. ap.***

Yosvī'ti kimatthaṁ? What is the word "yosu" for? To show that in examples below, the function of Sutta is inapplicable as they are not of "yo", but of "su" vibatti.
* Tīsu-at threes. * Catūsu-at fours. ***lp.***

१३४, २५१. पञ्चादीनमकारो

134, 251. **Pañcā'dīna'makāro.** [Pañca-ādīnaṁ+akāro. 2 words]

[V] **Pañcā**'dīnaṁ saṅkhyānaṁ itthipumanapuṁsake vattamānānaṁ savibhattissa antassa sarassa **a**kāro hoti **yo**-icce'tesu.

In numerical noun words such as "Pañca (five), etc.," which belongs to all three genders, the last component vowel thereof changes into an "**a**" along with vibatti "**yo**" applied after them.

Note: Only the last vowel changes into "**a**". Changing "**a**" back to "**a**" is a redundant function, which is stipulated so as to prevent any further morphological modification. Compare with the function of Sutta number 90.

• Pañca-five, • pañca-five.
• Cha, • cha-six.
• Satta, • satta-seven.
• Aṭṭha, • aṭṭha-eight.
• Nava, • nava-nine.
• Dasa, • dasa-ten. ***np, ap.***

Note: The same word shown two times, **the first** being **nominative plural** and **the second accusative plural**.

Pañcādīnami'ti kimatthaṁ?
What is the word "Pañcādīnaṁ" for?
To show that in the examples below, the function of Sutta is inapplicable as they are not Pañca etc.(They are **dvi** and **ti**. Hence, unlike Pañca etc., they undergo different morphological changes).
* Dve-two. * Tayo-three. ***np. ap.***

१३५, ११८. राजस्स रञ्ञो, राजिनो से

135, 118. **Rājassa rañño,rājino se.**

[Rājassa+rañño, rājino+se. 3 words]

[V] Sabbasse'va **rāja**saddassa savibhattissa **rañño, rājino-**icce'te ādesā honti se vibhattimhi.

The whole word "**Rāja** (king) " changes into "**rañño, rājino**" along with vibatti "**sa**" applied after it.
• Rañño. • Rājino-of the king. ***ds, gs.***

Se'ti kimatthaṁ? What is the word "se" for?
To show that in the example below, the function of Sutta is inapplicable as it is not of "sa", but of "nā".
* Raññā-by the king. ***is.***

१३६, ११९. रञ्ञं नंम्हि वा

136, 119. **Raññaṁ naṁmhi vā.**

[Raññaṁ+naṁmhi+vā. 3 words]

[V] Sabbasse'va **rāja**saddassa savibhattissa **raññaṁ-**ādeso hoti vā **naṁ**mhi vibhattimhi.

The entire word "**Rāja** (king) " sometimes changes into "**raññaṁ**" along with vibatti "**naṁ**" applied after it.
[The second is inapplicable example]

• Raññaṁ, * Rājūnaṁ-kings', ***gp***. idaṁ raṭṭhaṁ-this country (is) ***ns***...**i.e.** This country is of the kings.

१३७, ११६. नाम्हि रञ्ञा वा

137, 116. **Nāmhi raññā vā.** [Nāmhi+raññā+vā. 3 words]

[V] Sabbasse'va **rāja**saddassa savibhattissa **raññā**-ādeso hoti vā **nā**mhi vibhattimhi.

The entire word "**Rāja** (king) " sometimes changes into "**raññā**" along with the vibatti "**nā**" applied after it.

Tena • raññā-by that king. ***is***. kataṁ-done. ***kv***.
i.e. Done by that king.
* Rājena-by king. vā-in other way of usage of the same word. kataṁ-done. (This is inapplicable example, of the same meaning)

Nāmhī'ti kimatthaṁ?
What is the word "naṁ" for?
To show that in the example below, the function of Sutta is inapplicable as it is not of "naṁ", but of "sa".
* Rañño-king's. ***gs***. santakaṁ-belonging. ***nv-ns***.

१३८, १२१. स्मिम्हि रञ्ञे राजिनि

138, 121. **Smiṁmhi raññe, rājini.**
[Smiṁmhi+raññe, rājini. 2 words]

[V] Sabbasse'va **rāja**saddassa savibhattissa **raññe, rājini**-icce'te ādesā honti **smiṁ**mhi vibhattimhi.

The whole word "**Rāja** (king) " sometimes changes into "**raññe, rājini**" along with vibatti "**smiṁ**" applied after it.

• Raññe, • Rājini-in king. ***ls***. sīlaṁ-morality. ***ns***. tiṭṭhati-exists. ***āv***.

१३९, २४५. तुम्हम्हाकं तयि मयि

139, 245. **Tumha'mhākaṁ tayi, mayi.**

[Tumha, amhākaṁ+tayi, mayi. 2 words]

[V] Sabbesaṁ **tumha, amha**-saddānaṁ savibhattīnaṁ **tayi, mayi,** icce'te ādesā honti yathāsaṅkhyaṁ **smiṁ**mhi vibhattimhi.

The entire word "**tumha** (you), **amha** (I) " changes into "**tayi, mayi**" respectively along with vibatti "**smiṁ**" applied after them. (Tumha+smiṁ>**tayi** / Amha+smiṁ>**mayi**)

• Tayi-in you. • Mayi-in me. ***ls***.

Smiṁmhī'ti kimatthaṁ?
What is the word "smiṁmhi" for?
To show that in the examples below, the function of Sutta is inapplicable as they are not of "smiṁ", but of "si".
* Tvaṁ-you. ***ns***. bhavasi-are. ***āv***. **i.e.** You are.
* Ahaṁ-I. ***ns***. bhavāmi-am. ***āv***. **i.e.** I am.

१४०, २३२. त्वमहं सिम्हि च

140, 232. **Tva'mahaṁ simhi ca.**

[Tvaṁ, ahaṁ+simhi+ca. 3 words]

[V] Sabbesaṁ **tumha, amha**saddānaṁ savibhattīnaṁ **tvaṁ, ahaṁ,** icce'te ādesā honti yathāsaṅkhyaṁ **si**mhi vibhattimhi.

The whole words "**tumha** and **amha**" changes into " **tvaṁ, ahaṁ**" respectively along with vibatti "**si**" applied after them. [Tumha+si>**tvaṁ,** Amha+si>**ahaṁ**]

• Tvaṁ-you. • Ahaṁ-I. ***ns***.

Simhī'ti kimatthaṁ?
What is the word "simhi" for?
To show that in the examples below, the function of Sutta is inapplicable as they are not of "si", but of "smiṁ".
* Tayi. * Mayi. (Refer to Sutta 139)

Caggahaṇena **tuvaṁ** ca hoti.
By means of "Ca" in the Sutta, "tumha" also changes into "**tuvaṁ**" (together with vibatti) when "si" is applied after it.
• Tuvaṁ-you. ***ns***. satthā-(are) teacher. ***nv***. **i.e.** You are teacher.

१४१, २४१. तव मम से

141, 241. **Tava, mama se.** [Tava, mama+se. 2 words]

[V] Sabbesaṁ **tumha, amha**saddānaṁ savibhattīnaṁ **tava, mama**-icce'te ādesā honti yathāsaṅkhyaṁ **se** vibhattimhi.

The entire "**tumha,** and **amha**" changes into "**tava, mama**" respectively along with vibatti "**sa**" applied after them. [Tumha+sa>**tava,** Amha+sa>**mama**]

• Tava-yours. • Mama-my.

Se'ti kimatthaṁ?
What is the word "se" for?
To show that in the examples below, the function of Sutta is inapplicable as they are not of "sa", but of "smiṁ".
* Tayi. * Mayi. (Refer to Sutta 139)

१४२, २४२. तुय्हं मय्हञ्च

142, 242. **Tuyhaṁ, mayhañ'ca.**

[Tuyhaṁ, mayhaṁ+ca. 2 words]

[V] Sabbesaṁ **tumha, amha**saddānaṁ savibhattīnaṁ **tuyhaṁ, mayhaṁ**icce'te ādesā honti yathāsaṅkhyaṁ se vibhattimhi.

The whole "**tumha** and **amha**" changes into "**tuyhaṁ, mayhaṁ**" respectively along with vibatti "**sa**".
[Tumha+sa>**tuyhaṁ,** Amha+sa>**mayhaṁ**]

• Tuyhaṁ-your. • Mayhaṁ-my. ***ds***. dhanaṁ-wealth. ***as***. dīyate-(is) given (by someone) ***āv***.

Se'ti kimatthaṁ?
What is the word "se" for?

To show that in the examples below, the function of Sutta is inapplicable as they are not of "sa", but of "nā".
* Tayā-with/ by you. * Mayā-with/ by me. ***is***.

१४३, २३५. तंममंम्हि

143, 235. **Taṁ, mamaṁ'mhi.** [Taṁ, maṁ+amhi. 2 words]

[V] Sabbesaṁ **tumha, amha**saddānaṁ savibhattīnaṁ **taṁ, maṁ**icce'te ādesā honti yathāsaṅkhyaṁ **aṁ**mhi vibhattimhi.

The whole words "**tumha,** and **amha**" changes into "**taṁ, maṁ,**" respectively along with vibatti "**aṁ,**" applied after them. [Tumha+aṁ>**taṁ,** Amha+aṁ>**maṁ,**]

• Taṁ-to you. • Maṁ-to me. ***as***.

Aṁmhī'ti kimatthaṁ?
What is the word "aṁmhi" for?
To show that in the examples below, the function of Sutta is inapplicable as they are not of "aṁ", but of "nā".
* Tayā. * Mayā. (Refer to Sutta 145)

१४४, २३४. तवंममञ्च नवा

144, 234. **Tavaṁ mamañ'ca navā.**

[Tavaṁ, mamaṁ+ca+navā. 3 words]

[V] Sabbesaṁ **tumha, amha**saddānaṁ savibhattīnaṁ **tavaṁ, mamaṁ**icce'te ādesā honti navā yathāsaṅkhyaṁ **aṁ**mhi vibhattimhi

The entire "**tumha** and **amha**" sometimes changes into "**tavaṁ, mamaṁ,**" respectively along with vibatti "**aṁ,**" applied after them. [Tumha+aṁ>**taṁ,** Amha+aṁ>**maṁ,**]

• Tavaṁ-to you, • Mamaṁ-to me. ***as***. passati-(he) sees. ***āv***.
i.e. (he) sees you and me.

Navā'ti kimatthaṁ?
What is the word "navā" for?
To show that in the examples below, despite being in "aṁ"

vibatti, the function of Sutta is inapplicable as implied by the word "navā".
* Taṁ-to you. * Maṁ-me. passati-(he) sees (The same meaning like preceding ones, but different word forms).

Caggahaṇa'manukaḍḍhana'tthaṁ.
The word "ca" in Sutta has a purpose of pulling in the word "aṁmhi" from previous Sutta to this Sutta.

१४५, २३८. नाम्हि तया मया

145, 238. **Nāmhī tayā, mayā.** [Nāmhī+tayā, mayā. 2 words]

[V] Sabbesaṁ **tumha, amha**saddānaṁ savibhattīnaṁ **tayā, mayā**icce'te ādesā honti yathāsaṅkhyaṁ **nā**mhi vibhattimhi.

The whole words "**tumha** and **amha**" changes into "**tayā, mayā**" respectively along with vibatti "**nā**" applied after them. [Tumha+nā>**tayā,** Amha+nā>**mayā**]

• Tayā-by you, • Mayā-by me. ***is***. kataṁ-done. ***kv***.

Nāmhi'ti kimatthaṁ? What is the word "nāmhi" for?
To show that in the examples below, the function of Sutta is inapplicable as they are not of "nā", but of "hi".
* Tumhehi-by/from you, * Amhehi-by/from us. ***ip, abp***.

१४६, २३६. तुम्हस्स तुवंत्वमम्हि

146, 236. **Tumhassa tuvaṁ, tva'maṁ'mhi.**

[Tumhassa+tuvaṁ, tvaṁ+aṁmhi. 3 words]

[V] Sabbassa **tumha**saddassa savibhattissa **tuvaṁ, tvaṁ,** icce'te ādesā honti **aṁ**mhi vibhattimhi.

The whole word "**tumha** (you) " changes into "**tuvaṁ, tvaṁ**" along with vibatti "**aṁ**" applied after them.
[tumha+aṁ>tuvaṁ, tvaṁ]

(1) Kaliṅgarassa-(as if it were) worthless chaff . ***ds***. • tuvaṁ-to you. ***as***. maññe-(I) think. ***āv***. **i.e.** I think you as if worthless chaff.

(2) Kaṭṭhassa-(as if it were a) piece of wood. ***ds***. • tvaṁ-to you. ***as***. maññe-(I) assume. ***āv***. **i.e.** I regard you as if a piece of wood.

१४७, २४६. पदतो दुतियाचतुत्थीछट्ठीसु वो नो
147, 246. **Padato dutiyā, catutthī, chaṭṭhīsu vo, no.**

[Padato+dutiyā, catutthī, chaṭṭhīsu+vo, no. 3 words]

[V] Sabbesaṁ **tumha-amha**saddānaṁ savibhattīnaṁ yadā padasmā paresaṁ **vo, no-**ādesā honti navā yathāsaṅkhyaṁ dutiyā, catutthī, chaṭṭhī, iccetesu bahuvacanesu.

The whole words "**tumha** and **amha**", when used after a contextual word in a sentence, sometimes changes into "**vo, no**" respectively along with dutiyā plural "**yo**", catutthī, chaṭṭhī plural "**naṁ**" vibattis applied after them.
[Tumha+yo & naṁ>**vo,** Amha+yo & naṁ>**no**]

(1) Pahāya-leaving. ***kv***. • **vo**-you. ***ap***. bhikkhave-Oh monks! ***vp***. gamissāmi-(I) will go. ***āv***. **i.e.** I will go leaving you.

(2) Mā-do not. ***nip***. • **no**-us. ***ap***. ajja-today. ***ind***. vikantiṁsu-cut into pieces. ***āv***. rañño-king's, ***gs***. sūdā-royal cook. ***ns***. mahānase-at great kitchen. ***ls***. **i.e.** Today, do not cut us into pieces by the royal cook in the great kitchen.

evaṁ **dutiya'tthe.**
Thus, (these examples are) in the sense of accusative case.

(1) Dhammaṁ-Dhamma. ***as***. • **vo**-you. ***dp***. bhikkhave-Oh monks! ***vp***. desessāmi-(I) will teach. ***āv***.
i.e. I will teach you Dhamma, Oh monks!

(2) Saṁvibhajetha-distribute formally well, ***āv***. • **no**-us. ***dp***. rajjena-with (matters of ruling authority over) kingdom. ***is***.
i.e. Assign (distribute power) us well with kingdom!

evaṁ **catutthya'tthe.**
Thus, (these examples are) in the sense of dative case.

(1) Tuṭṭho'smi [Tuṭṭho+asmi] • **vo** bhikkhave pakatiyā.
Tuṭṭho-pleased. ***kn***. asmi-(I) am. ***āv***. • vo-you. ***gp***. bhikkhave-Oh monks! pakatiyā-by nature, naturally. ***is***.
i.e. I am naturally pleased with you, Oh monks!

(2) Satthā-teacher. ***ns***. • **<u>no</u>**-our. ***gp***. bhagavā-great honorable. ***ns***. anuppatto-has come, arrived. ***kv***.
i.e. Our great honorable teacher has arrived.

evaṁ **chaṭṭhya'tthe.**
Thus, (these examples are) in the sense of genitive case.

Navā'ti kimatthaṁ?
What is the word "navā" for?
To show that in the example below, despite being in "naṁ" vibatti, the function of Sutta is inapplicable as implied by the word "navā". ["Navā" restricts the function]
Eso-this. ***ns***. * amhākaṁ-our. ***gp***. satthā-(is) teacher. ***nv*** in ***ns***.
i.e. This is our teacher.

Tumha'mhākami'ti kimatthaṁ?
[tumha'mhākaṁ-tumha+amhākaṁ]
What is the word "tumhamhākaṁ" for?
To show that in the examples below, the function of Sutta is inapplicable as they are not "tumha, amha".
* Ete-these. ***ap***. * isayo-hermits. ***ap***. passasi-(you) see. ***āv***.
i.e. You see these hermits.

Padato'ti kimatthaṁ?
What is the word "padato" for?
To show that in the example below, the function of Sutta is inapplicable as it is not behind a word in the context of a sentence. It is an independent word not contextually related to any word in front of it. So, it is inapplicable.
* Tumhākaṁ-your. ***gp***. saṭthā-teacher. ***nv*** in ***ns***.

Etesvī'ti kimatthaṁ? What is the word "etesu" for?
To show that in the example below, the function of Sutta is inapplicable as it is of " paṭhmā yo".
Gacchatha-go. ***āv***. * tumhe-you. ***np***. **i.e.** You go!

१४८, २४७. तेमेकवचनेसु च

148, 247. **Te, me'kavacanesu ca.**

[Te, me+ekavacanesu+ca. 3 words]

[V] Sabbesaṁ **tumha, amha**-saddānaṁ savibhattīnaṁ yadā padasmā paresaṁ **te, me**-ādesā honti yathāsaṅkhyaṁ **catutthī, chaṭṭhī,** icce'tesu ekavacanesu.

The whole words "**tumha** and **amha**" positioned after a contextual word, changes into "**te, me,**" respectively along with catutthī, chaṭṭhī singular vibatti "**sa**" applied after them. [Tumha+sa>**te,** Amha+sa>**me**]

(1) Dadāmi-(I) give. ***āv***. • **te**-you. ***ds***. gāmavarāni-reward villages. ***ap***. pañca-five. ***ap*** (Numerical Adj).
i.e. I give you five villages as a reward.

(2) Dadāhi-give. ***āv***. • **me**-me. ***ds***. gāmavaraṁ-gift village(request). ***as***. **i.e.** Give me village as a reward! (Said to kings in ancient times)

(3) Idaṁ-this. ***ns***. • **te**-your. ***gs***. raṭṭhaṁ-(is) country. ***nv***.
i.e. This (is) your country.

(4) Ayaṁ-this. ***ns***. • **me**-my. ***gs***. putto-(is) son. ***nv***.
i.e. This (is) my son.

Padato'ti kimatthaṁ?
What is the word "padato" for?
To show that in the examples below, the function of Sutta is inapplicable as it is not after another word in the context of a sentence. (There is not a context-word before it)

* Tava-your. ***gs***. ñāti-relative. ***nv***.

* Mama-my. ***gs***. ñāti-relative. ***nv***.

१४९, २४८. न अंम्हि

149, 248. **Na aṁmhi.** [Na+aṁmhi. 2 words]

[V] Sabbesaṁ **tumha, amha**saddānaṁ savibhattīnaṁ yadā padasmā paresaṁ **te, me**-ādesā **na** honti **aṁ**mhi vibhattimhi.

The whole words "**tumha,** and **amha**" are not to be changed into "**te, me,**" when followed by dutiyā singular vibatti "aṁ". (There is no "te, me" function in accusative singular case. Instead, only ordinary vibatti "**aṁ**" applied after them. See the examples carefully)

(1) Passeyya-would like to see. ***āv***. • tam̲-you. ***as***. vassasataṁ-till hundred years. ***as*** (adv). arogaṁ-being healthy. ***cn*** in ***as*** (also adv).

(2) So-that person. ***ns***. • maṁ-to me. ***as***. bravīti-says. ***āv***.
i.e. He says to me (that he) would like to see you being healthy for a hundred years.

१५०, २४९. वा ततिये च

150, 249. **Vā tatiye ca.** [Vā+tatiye+ca. 3 words]

[V] Sabbesaṁ **tumha-amha**saddānaṁ savibhattīnaṁ yadā padasmā paresaṁ **te, me**-ādesā honti vā yathāsaṅkhyaṁ tatiye'kavacane pare.

The entire "**tumha,** and **amha**" which are after a contextual word, sometimes change into "**te, me,**" respectively along with tatiyā singular vibatti "**nā**" applied after them.
[Tumha+nā>**te,** Amha+nā>**me,**]

(1) Kataṁ-done. ***kv***. • te-by you. ***is***. pāpaṁ-unwholesome deed, evil,
sin. ***as***. **i.e.** unwholesome deed was done by you.

(2) Kataṁ, ***kv***. • me-by me. ***is***. pāpaṁ. ***as***.
i.e. unwholesome deed was done by me.
The following examples are inapplicable ones as restricted by "Vā". The meaning is very much the same though.

(1) Kataṁ * tayā-by you. ***is***. pāpaṁ.

(2) Kataṁ * mayā-by me. ***is***. pāpaṁ.

Padato'ti kimatthaṁ? What is the word "padato" for?
To show that in the example below, the function of Sutta is inapplicable as it is not after a contextual word.
* Tayā-by you. ***is***. kataṁ-done. * Mayā-by me. ***is***. kataṁ-done.

१५१, २५०. बहुवचनेसु वो नो
151, 250. **Bahuvacanesu vo, no.**

[Bahuvacanesu+vo, no. 2 words]

[V] Sabbesaṁ **tumha-amha**saddānaṁ savibhattīnaṁ yadā padasmā paresaṁ **vo, no**-ādesā honti yathāsaṅkhyaṁ tatiyā-bahuvacanesu paresu.

The whole words "**tumha** and **amha**", when used after the contextual words, sometimes changes into "**vo** and **no**" respectively along with tatiyā plural "**hi**" vibatti applied after them.

(1) Kataṁ-done. • **vo**-by you. ***ip***. kammaṁ-deed, action. ***as***.
i.e. The deed was done by you.

(2) Kataṁ • **no**-by us. ***ip***. kammaṁ. ***as***.
i.e. The deed was done by us.

Padato'ti kimatthaṁ?
What is the word "padato" for?
To show that in the examples below, the function of Sutta is inapplicable as they are not after a word in the context of a sentence.
* Tumhehi-by you. ***ip***. kataṁ. **i.e.** done by you.
* Amhehi-by us. ***ip***. kataṁ. **i.e.** done by us.

Bahuvacanaggahaṇena **yo**mhi **paṭhame vo, no**-ādesā honti.

By use of Bahuvacana (Refer to the word "**Bahuvacanesu**") in the Sutta, "tumha, and amha" of paṭhamā "yo-nominative plural" can also be changed into "**vo** and **no**" along with vibatti "yo".

(1) Gāmaṁ-to the village. ***as***. • **vo**-you. ***np***. gaccheyyātha-should go. ***āv***. **i.e.** You should go to village.

(2) Gāmaṁ, ***as***. • **no**-we. ***np***. gaccheyyāma-should go. ***āv***.
i.e. We should go to the village.

१५२, १३६. पुमन्तस्सा सिम्हि

152, 236. Puma'ntassā' simhi.

[Puma-antassa+ā+simhi. 3 words]

[V] **Puma**-icce'vamantassa savibhattissa **ā**-ādeso hoti **si**mhi vibhattimhi.

The last component vowel of the word "**puma** (man) ", changes into "**ā**" along with paṭhmā singular "**si**" vibatti applied after it. (See example. The function is shown underlined)

• Pumā-man. ***ns***. tiṭṭhati-stands. ***āv***. **i.e.** The man stands.

Simhī'ti kimatthaṁ?
What is the word "simhi" for?
To show that in the example below, the function of Sutta is inapplicable as it is not of "si". It is of "yo" vibatti.
* Pumāno-men. ***np***. tiṭṭhanti-stand. ***āv***. **i.e.** The men stand.

Antaggahaṇena **maghava, yuva**-icce'va'mādīna'mantassa savibhattissa **ā**-ādeso hoti.

By the word "anta", the last component vowel "**a**" of **maghava, yuva** etc, can also be changed into "**ā**" together with the applied vibattis.

• Maghavā-the king of heaven named Maghavā. ***ns***. • Yuvā-young man. ***ns***.

१५३, १३८. अमालपनेकवचने

153, 138. **A'mālapane'kavacane.**

[Aṁ+ālapana-ekavacane. 2 words]

[V] **Puma-**icce'vama'ntassa savibhattissa **aṁ-**ādeso hoti ālapane'kavacane pare.

The last component vowel "a" of the word "**puma** (man) ", changes into "**aṁ**" along with an Ālapana (vocative) singular "**si**" vibatti applied behind it. (See function shown underlined)

He • pum<u>aṁ</u>-Oh man! ***vs***. ["He" is a vocative particle similar to "hey" in English. "**He**" is to be pronounced as in "Hay"]

Ālapane'ti kimatthaṁ?
What is the word "ālapane" for?
To show that in the example below, the function of Sutta is not applied as it is not "ālapana (vocative) si" as stipulated by Sutta. It is an ordinary nominative singular "si".
* Pumā-man. ***ns***.

Ekavacane'ti kimatthaṁ?
What is the word "ekavacane" for?
To show that in the example below, the function of Sutta is not applied as it is not an ekavacana (vocative singular), but a plural "yo".
He * pumāno-Oh men! ***vp***.

१५४, ०. समासे च विभासा

154,...**Samāse ca vibhāsā.** [Samāse+ca+vibhāsā. 3 words]

[V] **Puma-**icce'vamantassa samāse ca **aṁ**-ādeso hoti vibhāsā samāse kate.

The last component vowel "**a**" of the word "**puma**", when used in compound nouns, sometimes changes into "**aṁ**" after a Samāsa (compound process) is complete.

See the example where bold-faced, double **nn** is shown. The first **n** is a morpheme derived from **aṁ** function applied as per this Sutta. The last component vowel "**a**" of **puma** changes into **aṁ>pumaṁ**. That "**ṁ**" is

further changed into "**n**" by means of Sutta No.31>**puman.** After this process, it thus becomes a complete word: "•Itthipuma**nn**apuṁsakānāni".
Note: This example is a Dvanda (Copulative) compound noun. The words inside bracket are called ED (etymological definition) also called viggaha. **There will be a lot of Viggaha (EDs) in Samāsa, Taddhita, Kita and Uṇādi sections as the example words are explained through the use of EDs.**

[Itthī ca-feminine also. pumā ca-masculine also. napuṁsako ca-neuter also] • Itthipuma**nn**apuṁsakānāni-feminine, masculine and neuter natures. [Dvanda compound]
[Itthipumanapuṁsakānaṁ-of feminine, masculine and neuter genders. samūho-group] • itthipuma**nn**apuṁsakasamūho-The group of feminine, masculine and neuter genders.
[This is a Chaṭṭhī-tatpurisa, determinative compound noun]

Vibhāsā'ti kimatthaṁ?
What is the word "Vibhāsā" for?
To show that the function of Sutta is inapplicable in the example below. (See the word "**puma**" in bold-face. There is no function of this Sutta applied)
* Itthi**puma**napuṁsakāni- feminine, masculine and neuter natures.

Note: Vibhāsā-means "sometimes" or "in some instances" which is similar to "vā, navā" etc.

१५५, १३७. योस्वानो

155, 137. **Yosvā'no.** [Yosu+āno. 2 words]

[V] **Puma**-icce'va'mantassa savibhattissa **āno**-ādeso hoti **yo**su vibhattīsu.

The last component vowel "a" of word "**puma**", changes into "**āno**" along with plural "**yo**" vibatti applied after it. [See "**āno**" shown in bold, underlined]

• Pum**āno**-men. ***np, ap***. • He • pum**āno**-Oh men! . ***vp***.

Yosvī'ti kimatthaṁ?
What is the word "yosu" for? To show that in the example below, the function of Sutta is inapplicable as it is not of

"yo". It is a singular "si" vibatti.
* Pumā-man.

१५६, १४२. आने स्मिंम्हि वा

156, 142. **Āne smiṁmhi vā.** [Āne+smiṁmhi+vā. 3 words]

[V] **Puma**-icce'va'mantassa savibhattissa **āne**-ādeso hoti vā **smiṁ**mhi vibhattimhi.

The last component vowel "a" of the word "**puma**", sometimes changes into "**āne**" along with sattmī singular "**smiṁ**" vibatti applied after it. [See "**āne**" in first example shown in bold, underlined. The second is inapplicable example.

• Pum**āne**-in man. * pume vā-in man. ***ls***.

१५७, १४०. हिविभत्तिम्हि च

157, 140. **Hivibhattimhi ca.** [Hivibhattimhi+ca. 2 words]

[V] **Puma**iccevamantassa **hi**vibhattimhi ca **āne**ādeso hoti.

The last component vowel "a" of the word "**puma**", sometimes changes into "**āne**" when tatiyā, pañcamī plural "**hi**" vibattis are applied after it. (See "āne" shown in bold, underlined below)

• Pum**āne**hi. • Pum**āne**bhi-with/from men (Both are of ***ip, abp,*** and of the same meaning).

Puna **vibhatti**ggahaṇaṁ kimatthaṁ?
Savibhattiggahaṇanivattana'tthaṁ.

Why is there the word "vibatti" included in Sutta again? (Please refer to Hi**vibhattimhi** in Sutta)
To prevent the word "**Savibhatti**" from being used in the Sutta and its function. (This means that the function of Sutta in the example below is carried out excluding "hi" vibatti, without making any morphological change to it, leaving the vibatti as it is. That is why there is "**hi**" still visible in the example)

• Pumāne**hi**.

Caggahaṇena **maghava, yuva**-icce'va'mādīna'mantassa **āna**-ādeso hoti **si, yo, aṁ, yo,** icce'tesu vibhattīsu. **Puma, kamma, thāma**'ntassa cu'kāro hoti **sa, smā, su** vibhattīsu.

By means of the word "Ca" in Sutta, the last component vowel "**a**" of **maghava, yuva** changes into "**āna**" when "**si, yo, aṁ, yo,**" vibattis are applied after them. Also, the last component vowel "**a**" of the words "**puma, kamma, thāma**" changes into "**u**" when "**sa, smā**" vibattis are applied after them. [2 functions by "ca"]

See the **āna**-function underlined in the examples below carefully.

• Maghavāno, ***ns***. • maghavānā. ***np***. • Maghavānaṁ, ***as***.

• maghavāne. ***ap***. a youth named "magha".

• Yuvāno-young man. ***ns***. • yuvānā, ***np***. • Yuvānaṁ, ***as***.

• yuvāne. ***ap***. (All **āna**-function examples)

Below are **u**-function examples. "**u**" is shown in bold, underlined before morpheme **no** and **nā** vibattis.

• Pum**u**no-of man, ***ds, gs***. • pum**u**nā-from man. ***abs***.

• Kamm**u**no, ***ds, gs***. • kamm**u**nā-with/by Kamma, ***abs.***

• Thām**u**no. ***ds, gs***. • thām**u**nā-with/by capacity or strength. ***abs.***

१५१, १४३. सुस्मि मा वा

158, 143. **Susmi'mā vā.** [Susmiṁ+ā+vā. 3 words]

[V] **Puma**-icce'va'mantassa **su**-icce'tasmiṁ vibhattimhi **ā**-ādeso hoti vā.

The last component vowel of the word "**puma**", sometimes changes into "**ā**" when sattamī plural vibatti "**su**" is applied after it. (See "**ā**" in front of "**su**" shown in bold, underlined. The second is inapplicable)

• Pum**ā**su-in men. * Pumesu vā ***lp***. (same meaning)

१५९, १३९. उ नाम्हि च

159, 139. **U nāmhi ca.** [U+nāmhi+ca. 3 words]

[V] **Puma-**icce'va'mantassa **ā, u-**ādesā honti vā **nā**mhi vibhattimhi.

The last component vowel of the word "**puma**", sometimes changes into "**ā** & **u**" when a tatiyā singular "**nā**" vibatti is applied after it. (See the first two examples carefully. Both **ā** and **u** are shown in bold, underlined)

• Pum**ā**nā, • Pum**u**nā-with man,
* Pumena vā (all *is*., This is inapplicable but of the same meaning).

Caggahaṇa'manukaḍḍhana'tthaṁ.
The word "ca" in Sutta has a purpose of pulling in "ā-function" from the preceding Sutta to this Sutta.

१६०, १९७. अ कम्मन्तस्स च

160, 197. **A kamma'ntassa ca.**

[A+kamma-antassa+ca. 3 words]

[V] **Kamma-**icce'vamantassa ca **u, a-**ādesā honti vā **nā**mhi vibhattimhi.

The last component vowel "**a**" of the word "**kamma** (action, volitional Kammic energy) ", sometimes changes into "**u** & **a**" when a Tatiyā singular "**nā**" vibatti is applied after it.

Note: Although the word "a" only is included in Sutta, "u" from the preceding Sutta is carried over to this Sutta. Therefore "u" function is also enjoined in this Sutta in addition to "a" function. See **u** and **a** shown in bold, underlined in the examples.

• Kamm**u**nā. • Kamm**a**nā-with/by Kamma.
* Kammena vā (All *is*, This is inapplicable example of the same meaning).

Caggahaṇena **maghava, yuva-**icce'va'mantassa **ā-**ādeso hoti kvaci **nā, su-**icce'tesu vibhattīsu.

By means of the word "Ca" in the Sutta, the last component vowel "**a**" of **maghava, yuva,** sometimes changes into "**ā**" when "**nā, su,** " vibattis are applied behind them. [See two pairs of examples in each group carefully. The " **ā**" is shown in bold, underlined. The second pair is inapplicable ones]

(1) • Maghav**ā**nā. ***is***. • Maghav**ā**su-with/by king of heaven named Magha. ***lp***.
 * Maghavesu. ***lp***. * Maghavena vā. ***is***. (Inapplicable words)
(2) • Yuv**ā**nā-with/by youth. ***is***. • Yuv**ā**su-in youths, ***lp***.
 * Yuvesu, ***lp***. * Yuvena vā. ***is***. (Inapplicable examples)

Iti nāmakappe dutiyo kaṇḍo.

The Second Section of Noun ends.

Tatiya Kaṇḍa

The Third Section

१६१, २४४. तुम्हम्हेहि नमाकं

161, 244. **Tumha'mhehi na'mākaṁ.**

[Tumha, amhehi+naṁ+ākaṁ. 3 words]

[V] Tehi **tumha, amhe**hi **naṁ**vacanassa **ākaṁ** hoti.

The Catutthī, Chaṭṭī plural vibatti "**naṁ**" which is applied after the words "**tumha** and **amha**" changes into "**ākaṁ**". [See "**ākaṁ**" shown in bold, underlined]

• Tumh**ākaṁ**-your. • amh**ākaṁ**-our. ***dp, gp.***

Nami'ti kimatthaṁ?
What is the word "naṁ" for? To show that the examples below are inapplicable as they are not of "naṁ" vibatti. (They are of "hi" vibatti)
* Tumhehi. * amhehi. ***ip, abp.***

१६२, २३७. वा य्वप्पठमो

162, 237. **Vā yva'ppaṭhamo.** [Vā+yo+a-ppaṭhamo. 3 words]

[V] Tehi **tumha, amhe**hi **yo** appaṭhamo **ākaṁ** hoti vā.

The dutiyā plural vibatti "**yo**", applied after "**tumha,** and **amha**" sometimes changes into "**ākaṁ**".
Note: dutiyā plural vibatti "yo" is also called appaṭhamā (non-paṭhamā) "yo". The second examples are inapplicable.

• Tumh**ākaṁ**-you. ***ap***. passāmi-(I) see. ***āv***. **i.e.** (I) see you.
* Tumhe, ***ap***. passāmi vā. **i.e.** (I) see you.
• Amh**ākaṁ**-us. ***ap***. passasi-(you) see, ***āv***. **i.e.** (You) see us.
* Amhe passasi vā. **i.e.** (You) see us.

Yo'ti kimatthaṁ?
What is the word "yo" for?
To show that the examples below are inapplicable as they are not of "yo" vibatti, but of "hi" vibatti.
* Tumhehi-with/by you. * Amhehi-with/by us.

Appaṭhamo'ti kimatthaṁ?
What is the word "apaṭhamo" for?
To show that the examples below are inapplicable as they are not of appaṭhama (non-paṭhamā) "yo" vibatti. (They are paṭhamā, nominative, plural "yo")
Gacchatha-go. ***āv***. * tumhe-you. ***np***. **i.e.** You go!
Gacchāma-go. ***āv***. * mayaṁ-we. ***np***. **i.e.** We go.

Vā'ti vikappanatthena **yo**naṁ **aṁ, ānaṁ** honti.

By the word "vā" which has a specific "vikappana" meaning, the vibatti "yo" (applied after **tumha** and **amha**), can change into "**aṁ, ānaṁ**". (accusative plural "yo" is applied. See both "**aṁ, ānaṁ-functions**" shown underlined below)
• Tumhaṁ. • Tumhānaṁ-you.
• Amhaṁ. • Amhānaṁ-we, us. ***ap***.

१६३, २४०. सस्सं

163, 240. **Sassaṁ'.** [Sassa+aṁ. 2 words]
[V] Tehi **tumha-amhe**hi **sa**ssa vibhattissa **aṁ**-ādeso hoti vā.

The Catutthi and Chaṭṭi singular vibatti "**sa**", which is applied after "**tumha** and **amha**" sometimes changes into "**aṁ**". [See function shown underlined. The second is inapplicable.]

[Catutthī] • Tumhaṁ-for you. ***ds***. dīyate-given. ***āv***.
* Tava dīyate. (inapplicable, but the same meaning)
[Chaṭṭī] • Tumhaṁ-your. ***gs***. pariggaho-possession. ***nv***.
* Tava pariggaho.(The same meaning)
[Catutthī] • Amhaṁ-for me. dīyate-given. * Mama dīyate.
[Chaṭṭī] • Amhaṁ-my. pariggaho. * Mama pariggaho.

Sasse'ti kimatthaṁ?
What is the word "sassa" for? To show that the examples below are inapplicable as they are not of "sa", but of "su".
* Tumhesu-in you. * Amhesu-in us. ***lp***.

१६४, २००. सब्बनामकारते पठमो
164, 200. **Sabbanāma'kārate' paṭhamo.**

[Sabbanāmakārato+e+paṭhamo. 3 words]

[V] Sabbesaṁ sabbanāmānaṁ **a**kārato **yo** paṭhamo **e**tta'māpajjate.

The paṭhamā plural vibatti "**yo**" which is applied after a-ending Sabbanāma nouns, changes into "**e**".
[a-ending Sabbanāma nouns are **ya, ta, eta, ima** and **sabba** etc. of masculine and neuter genders except **amu** and Sabbanāma nouns of feminine gender. The function "e" is shown in bold, underlined below]

• Sabb**e**-all. • Y**e**-which. • T**e**-those. • K**e**-who/what.
• Tumh**e**-you. • Amh**e**-we. • Im**e**-these. ***np***.

Sabbanāmā'ti kimatthaṁ?
What is the word "sabbanāma" for?
To show that the examples below are inapplicable as they are not Sabbanāma nouns.
* Devā-deities. * Asurā-demons. * Nāgā-dragons.
* Gandhabbā-celestial musician deities. * Manussā-humans. (all ***np***.)

Akārato'ti kimatthaṁ?
What is the word "akārato" for?
To show that the example below is inapplicable as it does not end in "a", but ends in "ū".
* Amū purisā-so and so men. ***np***. tiṭṭhanti-stand. ***āv***.

Yo'ti kimatthaṁ?
What is the word "yo" for? To show that the examples below are inapplicable as they are not of "yo", but of "si" vibatti.
* Sabbo-all. * Yo-which. * So-that. * Ko-who/what. * Ayaṁ-this. (all ***ns***.)

Paṭhamaggahaṇaṁ uttarasutta'tthaṁ.
[**uttara**-the next+**sutta**-Sutta+**atthaṁ**-for]
The word "paṭhama" in Sutta is meant to follow to the next Sutta. [See it in next Sutta]

१६५, २०८. द्वन्दट्ठा वा

165, 208. **Dvandaṭṭhā vā.** [Dvandaṭṭhā+vā. 2 words]

[V] Tasmā sabbanāma'kārato dvandaṭṭhā **yo** paṭhamo **e**tta'māpajjate vā.

The paṭhamā plural vibatti "**yo**" which is applied after Sabbanāma nouns in a Dvanda-samāsa compound, sometimes changes into "**e**".
[See "**e**" shown in bold, underlined in the example below. The second is inapplicable example, but the same meaning]

• Katara, katam**e**-what and which. * Katara, katamā vā.

Sabbanāmā'ti kimatthaṁ?
What is the word "sabbanāma" for?
To show that in the example below, there is no sabbanāma word in it despite being a dvanda compound. So, it is inapplicable.
* Devā'sura,nāga,gandhabba,manussā-deities, demons, dragons, musician deities and humans.

Dvandaṭṭhā'ti kimatthaṁ?
What is the word "dvandaṭṭhā" for? To show that the example below is not a dvanda compound. So, it is inapplicable. (They are only ordinary Sabbanāma nouns)
* Te-those. * Sabbe-all. (all ***np, ap***)

१६६, २०९. नाञ्ञं सब्बनामिकं

166, 209. **Nā'ññaṁ sabbanāmikaṁ.**

[Na+aññaṁ+sabbanāmikaṁ. 3 words]

[V] Sabbanāmikānaṁ dvandaṭṭhe nā'ññaṁ kāriyaṁ hoti.

The morphological functions such as "**ssaṁ, ssānaṁ**" and so forth, are not to be carried out for Sabbanāma nouns in a Dvanda-samāsa compound except some function of changing nominative plural "yo" into "e".
[This Sutta debars morphological functions such as "**ssaṁ, ssānaṁ**" and so forth, for Sabbanāma nouns in a Dvanda-samāsa.]

- Pubbā'parānaṁ-the east and west or the front and rear.
- Pubbu'ttarānaṁ-east and north.
- Adharu'ttarānaṁ-down and north. ***dp, gp.***

१६७, २१०. बहुब्बीहिम्हि च

167, 210. **Bahubbīhimhi ca.** [Bahubbīhimhi+ca. 2 words]

[V] Bahubbīhimhi ca samāse sabbanāmavidhānañ'ca nā'ññaṁ kāriyaṁ hoti.

In a Bahubbīhi samāsa (Attributive compound), no other morphological procedures (except "e" function of "yo"), are to be carried out for Sabbanāma nouns. [similar debarring function]

- Piyapubbāya-of the woman who have had ex-husband or ex-lover before. ***ds, gs.***
- Piyapubbānaṁ-of those who have had ex-spouse or ex-lover before. ***dp, gp***.
- Piyapubbe. ***ls***. • Piyapubbassa. ***ds, gs***. (Same meaning but in different case-ending)

Ce'ti kimatthaṁ?
What is the word "Ca" for?
Sabbanāmavidhānaṁ hoti. [sabbanāma+**vidhānaṁm**-function]
To show that some morphological functions of "**ssaṁ, ssā**" are allowed (as an exception) in some examples below for those compound nouns in "smiṁ, sa" vibattis. (See allowed functions of "ssaṁ and ssā" shown underlined).

- Dakkhiṇapubbassaṁ-South-east. ***ls***.
- Dakkhiṇapubbassā-South-east. ***ds, gs***.
- Uttarapubbassaṁ-North-east. ***ls***.
- Uttarapubbassā-North-east. ***ds, gs***.

१६८, २०३. सब्बतो नं संसानं

168, 203. **Sabbato naṁ saṁ, sānaṁ.**

[Sabbato+naṁ+saṁ, sānaṁ. 3 words]

[V] Sabbato sabbanāmato **naṁ**vacanassa **saṁ, sānaṁ**-icce'te ādesā honti.

The Catutthī, Chaṭṭī plural vibatti " **naṁ**" which is applied after the Sabbanāma nouns changes into "**saṁ, sānaṁ**". [See both functions in the examples below shown underlined]

[Masculine & Neuter] • Sabbesaṁ. • Sabbesānaṁ.
[Feminine] • Sabbāsaṁ. • Sabbāsānaṁ-all.
[M & N] • Yesaṁ. • Yesānaṁ.
[F] • Yāsaṁ. • Yāsānaṁ.
[M & N] • Tesaṁ. • Tesānaṁ.
[F] • Tāsaṁ. • Tāsānaṁ.
[M & N] • Kesaṁ. • Kesānaṁ.
[F] • Kāsaṁ. • Kāsānaṁ.
[M & N] • Imesaṁ. • Imesānaṁ.
[F] • Imāsaṁ. • Imāsānaṁ.
[M, N & F] • Amūsaṁ. • Amūsānaṁ-so and so. (all ***dp, gp***)

Nami'ti kimatthaṁ?
What is the word "naṁ" for? To show that examples below are inapplicable as they are not of "naṁ", but of "sa".
* Sabbassa, * Yassa, * Tassa, * Kassa. (all ***ds, gs***)
Evaṁ sabbattha.
Evaṁ-(Should note) in this way or thus. sabbattha-at all examples of Sabbanāma nouns.

१६९, ११७. राजस्स राजु सुनंहिसु च

169, 117. **Rājassa rāju su, naṁ, hi, su ca.**

[Rājassa+rāju+su, naṁ, hi, su+ca. 4 words]

[V] Sabbasse'va **rāja**saddassa **rāju**-ādeso hoti **su, naṁ, hi**-iccetesu.

The whole word "**rāja** (king) " changes into "**rāju**" when "**su, naṁ, hi**" vibattis are applied after it.

• Rājūsu-in kings, • rājūnaṁ-of kings, • rājūhi, • rājūbhi-with/by kings. ["**u**" is lengthened by 89]

Sunaṁhisū'ti kimatthaṁ?
What is the word "sunaṁhisu" for? To show that the example below is inapplicable as it is not of "su, naṁ, hi" vibattis, but of "si".
* Rājā-king.

Caggahaṇa'mavadhāraṇa'tthaṁ.
The word "ca" has a purpose of restricting the function of Sutta in the examples below.
* Rājesu,* Rājānaṁ,* Rājehi,* Rājebhi. (the same meaning as those of Sutta)

१७०, २२०. सब्बस्सिमस्से वा

170, 220. **Sabbassi'masse' vā.**

[Sabbassa+imassa+e+vā. 4 words]

[V] Sabbasse'va **ima**saddassa **e**kāro hoti vā
su, naṁ, hi-icce'tesu.

The entire word "**ima** (this) " sometimes changes into "**e**" when "**su, naṁ, hi**" vibattis are applied after it. (See "e" shown in bold, in the examples below. Second is inapplicable one.)

[M & N] • **E**su, * Imesu-in these, ***lp,***
[M & N] • **E**saṁ, * Imesaṁ-of these, ***dp, gp,***
[M & N] • **E**hi, • **E**bhi, * Imehi, * Imebhi-with/by these. ***ip, abp,***

Imasse'ti kimatthaṁ?
What is the word "imassa" for? To show that examples below are inapplicable as they are not "ima, but "eta-that".
[M & N] * Etesu, * Etesaṁ, * Etehi, * Etebhi-with/by those.
Note: The function of Sutta is applicable only to "ima" Sabbanāma noun of Masculine and neuter gender.

१७१, २१९. अनिमि नाम्हि च

171, 219. **Ani'mi nāmhi ca.** [Ana, imi+nāmhi+ca. 3 words]

[V] **Ima**saddassa sabbasse'va **ana, imi**-iccete ādesā honti **nā**mhi vibhattimhi.

The whole word "**ima** (this) " changes into "**ana, imi**" when tatiyā singular "**nā**" vibatti is applied after it.
[The functions are shown in bold, underlined]

• **<u>An</u>**ena dhammadānena, sukhitā hotu sā pajā.

[Trans] • Anena-by this. ***is,*** dhammadānena-gift of Dhamma, ***is,*** sukhitā-happy. ***ns*** (adj), hotu-may be. ***āv,*** sā pajā-that (community of living) beings. ***ns,***
i.e. By this gift of Dhamma, may that community of beings be happy!

• **<u>Imi</u>**nā Buddhapūjena, patvāna amataṁ padaṁ.

[Trans] • Iminā-by this. ***is,*** Buddhapūjena-act of worshipping of lord Buddha, ***is,*** patvāna-having reached, ***kv.*** amataṁ padaṁ-to the death-less Nibbāna. ***as,***
i.e. Having attained the deathless state of Nibbāna by this act of honoring of the Lord Buddha. (Both are Pāli stanzas)

Nāmhī'ti kimatthaṁ?
What is the word "nāmhi" for? To show that examples below are inapplicable as they are not of "nā" vibatti, but of "su, naṁ, hi".
* Imesu, ***lp,*** * Imesaṁ, ***dp, gp,*** * Imehi, * Imebhi. ***ip, abp,***

१७२, २१८. अनपुंसकस्सा यं स्मिम्हि

172, 218. **Anapuṁsakassā'yaṁ**[20] **simhi.**

[Anapuṁsakassā+ayaṁ+simhi. 3 words]

[V] **Ima**saddassa sabbasse'va anapuṁsakassa **ayaṁ**-ādeso hoti **si**mhi vibhattimhi.

The whole word "**ima**" belonging to non-neuter gender, changes into "**ayaṁ**" when paṭhamā singular "**si**" vibatti is applied after it. (Non-neuter means masculine and feminine gender. The function is shown underlined.)

[Masculine gender example] • <u>Ayaṁ</u> puriso-this man, ***ns,***
[Feminine gender example] • <u>Ayaṁ</u> itthī-this woman. ***ns,***

Anapuṁsakasse'ti kimatthaṁ?
What is the word "anapuṁskassa" for?
To show that example below is inapplicable as it is a neuter gender word.
* Idaṁ cittaṁ-this mind. tiṭṭhati-exists.

Simhī'ti kimatthaṁ?
What is the word "simhi" for?
To show that example below is inapplicable as it is not of "si" vibatti, but of "aṁ".
* Imaṁ purisaṁ-this man. ***as,*** passasi-See. ***āv,*** tvaṁ-(Do) you. ***ns,*** **i.e.** Do you see this man?

---

[20] Please note that all **Sabbanāma** nouns such as **ya, ta, eta, ima, amu, kiṁ** etc., are of three genders. Depending on gender, their word-forms too change. For example, the word "ima" of neuter gender in nominative singular case will be differently formed and declined from "ima" of masculine and feminine genders in the same case-ending. The same is similarly applicable to other Sabbanāma nouns. That is why there are different Suttas prescribing different morphological rules and procedures.

१७३, २२३. अमुस्स मो सं

173, 223. **Amussa mo saṁ.** [Amussa+mo+saṁ. 3 words]

[V] **Amu**saddassa anapuṁsakassa **ma**kāro **sa**kāra'māpajjate vā **si**mhi vibhattimhi.

The consonant "**m**" of the word "**amu** (so and so) " changes into "**s**" when paṭhamā singular "**si**" vibatti is behind it. [See the function shown in bold, underlined]

• A<u>s</u>u rājā-so and so king, ***ns,*** • A<u>s</u>u itthī-so and so woman, ***ns,***
* Amuko rājā, * Amukā itthī. ***ns,*** (Inapplicable examples with an extra "k" added behind, meaning the same though)

Anapuṁsakasse'ti kimatthaṁ?
What is the word "anapuṁsakassa" for? To show that the example below is inapplicable as it is a neuter gender word. (The function of Sutta is meant for non-neuter gender word "amu" only)
* Aduṁ-so and so. pupphaṁ-flower. ***ns,*** virocati-looks beautiful. ***āv,***

Amusse'ti kimatthaṁ?
What is the word "amussa" for?
To show that the example shown is inapplicable as it is not "amu", but of "ima (This) ".
* Ayaṁ puriso-this man. ***ns,*** tiṭṭhati-stands. ***āv.***

Simhī'ti kimatthaṁ?
What is the word "simhi" for? To show that example below is inapplicable as it is not of "si".
* Amuṁ purisaṁ-so and so man. ***as,*** passasi-(Do you) see. ***āv,*** **i.e.** (Do you) see so and so man?

१७४, २११. एततेसं सो

174, 211. **Eta, tesaṁ So.** [Eta, tesaṁ+So. 2 words]

[V] **Eta, ta**-icce'tesaṁ anapuṁsakānaṁ **ta**kāro **sa**kāramā'pajjate **si**mhi vibhattimhi.

The consonant "**t**" of the non-neuter-gender Sabbanāma word "**eta, ta** (that) " changes into "**s**" when a paṭhamā singular "**si**" vibatti is applied after it.[See changed "**s**" shown in bold, underlined]

Note: In majority of texts, it is found as "Etatesaṁ to". As the main function of the Sutta is to change **"t"** of **eta** and **ta** into **"s"**, "so" is more relevant and aptly reflective of the function.

In Moggalāna Pāli grammar text, Syādi chapter, there is a Sutta (number 128) with the same function titled **"tyate'tānaṁ tassa so"**. In Paṇinī, there is also a Sutta with similar function. It is **"tado: sa: sāvanantyayo"** (तदोः सः सावनन्त्ययो 7-2-106). In view of those two Suttas which use the word **"so "** and **"सः"** , **"so"** is a more likely relevant and correct text.

[Examples of "**eta**", Masculine] • E**s**o puriso-that man,

[Feminine] • E**s**ā itthī-that woman,

[Examples of "**ta**", Masculine] • **S**o puriso-that man.

[Feminine] • **S**ā itthī-that woman (all ***ns,***)

Etatesami'ti kimatthaṁ?

What is the word "etesaṁ" for?

To show that the examples below are inapplicable as they are not "eta, ta", but "itara-other".

[Masculine] * Itaro-the other. puriso-man, ***ns,***

[Feminine] * Itarā itthī-the other woman. ***ns,***

Anapuṁsakānami'ti kimatthaṁ?

What is the word "anapuṁsakānaṁ" for?

[See this word in the Vutti of Sutta]

To show that the examples below are inapplicable as they are not non-neuter gender words, but of neuter genders.

[Examples of "eta" Neuter] * Etaṁ cittaṁ-that mind,

* Etaṁ rūpaṁ-that matter.

[Examples of "ta" Neuter] * Taṁ cittaṁ,* Taṁ rūpaṁ. ***ns, as,*** (same meaning)

१७५, २१२. तस्स वा नत्तं सब्बत्थ

175, 212. **Tassa vā nattaṁ sabbattha.**

[Tassa+vā+nattaṁ+sabbattha. 4 words]

[V] **Ta**ssa sabbanāmassa **ta**kārassa **na**ttaṁ hoti vā sabbattha liṅgesu.

The consonant "**t**" of the word "**ta** (that) " sometimes changes into "**n**" for "**ta**" of all gender and in all cases. [See the function in the first word of each set of examples shown in bold, underlined. The second is inapplicable one.]

[Feminine] • **N**āya, * tāya, ***is,***

[M & N] • **n**aṁ, * taṁ, ***as,***

[M & N] • **n**e, * te, ***np, ap,***

[M & N] • **n**esu, * tesu, ***lp,***

[M & N] • **n**amhi, * tamhi, ***ls,***

[Feminine] • **n**āhi, * tāhi, ***ip, abp,***

[Feminine] • **n**ābhi, * tābhi. ***ip, abp,***

१७६, २१३. सस्मास्मिंसंसास्वत्तं

176, 213. **Sa, smā, smiṁ, saṁ, sā sva'ttaṁ.**

[Sa, smā, smiṁ, saṁ, sāsu+attaṁ. 2 words]

[V] Tassa sabbanāmassa **ta**kārassa sabbasse'va **a**ttaṁ hoti vā **sa, smā, smiṁ, saṁ, sā**-icce'tesu sabbattha liṅgesu.

The whole sabbanāma word "**ta** (that) " sometimes changes into "**a**" in all gender and in **sa, smā, smiṁ, vibatti** cases, as well as when **saṁ, sā** morphemes are already applied after it.
Note: This Sutta sometimes changes the whole "ta" into "a" in three **sa, smā, smiṁ** cases and those with **saṁ, sā,** function already applied. [See the applied function "**a**" in the first example of each set shown in bold, underlined]

[**sa**, in m & n] • **A**ssa, * tassa,

[**smā** in m & n] • **a**smā, * tasmā,

[**smiṁ** in m & n] • **a**smiṁ, * tasmiṁ,

[**smiṁ,** feminine with **saṁ**] • **a**ssaṁ, * tassaṁ,
[**sa,** feminine with **sā**] • **a**ssā, * tassā.

Takārasse'ti kimatthaṁ?
What is the word "takārassa" for?
To show that example below is inapplicable as it is not a "ta", but "amu".
[Feminine] * Amussaṁ, ***ls.*** * amussā. ***ds, gs.***

Etesvī'ti kimatthaṁ? What is the word "etesu" for?
To show that examples below are inapplicable as they are not of "**sa, smā, smiṁ**" vibattis, but of "su".
[m & n] * Nesu, * tesu-in those. ***lp.*** [See Sutta 175]

१७७, २२१. इमसद्दस्स च

177, 221. **Imasaddassa ca.** [Imasaddassa+ca. 2 words]

[V] **Ima**saddassa ca sabbasse'va **a**ttaṁ hoti vā
sa, smā, smiṁ, saṁ, sā-icce'tesu sabbattha liṅgesu.

The whole "**ima**" sometimes changes into "**a**" for all gender and in **sa, smā, smiṁ** vibattis, also when **saṁ, sā** functions have already been applied after it.
Note: This Sutta sometimes changes "**ima**" of all genders into "a" in "**sa, smā, smiṁ**" vibatti-cases or "**Saṁ or Sā**" functions already applied. The function "**a**" is shown in bold, underlined. Out of a pair of each examples, the second * marked is inapplicable. The unchanged "ima" is shown in bold, underlined. It is quite simple to understand.

[sa, m & n] • **A**ssa, * imassa-of this,
[smā, m & n] • **a**smā, * imasmā,
[smiṁ, m & n] • **a**smiṁ, * imasmiṁ,
[smiṁ, feminine with Saṁ] • **a**ssaṁ, * imissaṁ,
[sa, feminine with sā] • **a**ssā, * imissā.

Imasaddasse'ti kimatthaṁ?
What is the word "ima-saddassa" for?
To show that examples below are inapplicable as they are not "ima", but of "eta".
[Feminine] * Etissaṁ, ***ls.*** * etissā. ***ds, gs.***

Note: In view of the function of these two Suttas 176-177, it is clear that "**a**" is to be regarded as a derivative morpheme of either "**ta**" or "**ima**".
So, whenever one comes across such words as "assa" or "asmiṁ" and so on, correct interpretation should be made in accordance with context of the sentence.

१७८, २२४. सब्बतो को
178, 224. Sabbato ko. [Sabbato+ko. 2 words]
[V] Sabbato sabbanāmato **ka**-kārā'gamo hoti vā **si**mhi vibhattimhi.

Sometimes, there should be a consonant "**k**" affixed after all sabbanāma nouns in a paṭṭhmā singular **si**-vibatti.
(See "k" shown in bold, underlined. This "k" is meaningless though **it carries some meanings** in some other words depending on context)

• Sabba<u>k</u>o-all, • ya<u>k</u>o-which, • sa<u>k</u>o-that or one's own (Two meanings. The second meaning is widely used).
• amu<u>k</u>o, • asu<u>k</u>o-so and so. *ns* (both the same meaning).

Vā'ti kimatthaṁ? What is the word "vā" for?
To show that examples below are inapplicable as indicated by the word "vā".
* Sabbo-all, * yo-which, * so-that, * ko-who/what. *ns.*

Sabbanāmato'ti kimatthaṁ?
What is the word "sabbanāmato" for?
To show that example below is inapplicable as it is not a sabbanāma noun. (It is an ordinary noun). Hence, inapplicable.
* Puriso-man. *ns.*

Puna sabbatoggahaṇena aññasmā'pi **ka**-kārā'gamo hoti.

By including the word "sabbato" in the Sutta again, the affix "ka" can also be affixed after other common nouns rather than sabbanāma nouns.
[See "k" shown underlined below. **Sabbato**-means after all words]
• hīna<u>k</u>o-lowly and mean person, • pota<u>k</u>o-the young one. *ns.*

१७९, २०४. घपतो स्मिं सानं संसा

179, 204. **Ghapato smiṁ, sānaṁ saṁ, sā.**

[Ghapato+smiṁ, sānaṁ+saṁ, sā. 3 words]

[V] Sabbato sabbanāmato **gha, pa,** saññato **smiṁ, sa**-icce'tesaṁ **saṁ, sā-**ādesā honti vā yathāsaṅkhyaṁ.

The **smiṁ** vibatti applied after all **Gha, pa**-termed, **ā** , **u**-ending feminine gender sabbanāma nouns sometimes changes into "**saṁ**". Also, the **sa** vibatti which is applied after such nouns changes into "**sā**" respectively.

[smiṁ>saṁ / sa>sā]

Note that out of a pair of each examples, the **saṁ** is in the first example, the **sā** function is in the second examples which are shown underlined. Each is reduplicated with an additional "**s**".

sabbā-all, **feminine gender,**
gha-termed, ā-ending sabbanāma noun.

[sabbā+smiṁ. saṁ function] • Sabbas<u>saṁ</u>-in all,

[sabbā+sa, sā function] • sabbas<u>sā</u>-of all,

[sabba+smiṁ] * sabbāyaṁ,

[sabba+sa] * sabbāya, (Same meaning as the first set)

imā-this, **feminine gender**
gha-termed, ā-ending sabbanāma noun.

[imā+smiṁ] • imis<u>saṁ</u>-in this, [ima+sa] • imis<u>sā</u>-of this,

[ima+smiṁ] * imāyaṁ, [ima+sa] * imāya, (Same as the preceding set of examples)

Amu-so and so, **feminine gender,**
pa-termed, u-ending sabbanāma noun.

[amu+smiṁ] • amus<u>saṁ</u>-in so and so,

[amu+sa] • amus<u>sā</u>-of so and so,

[amu+smiṁ] * amuyaṁ,

[amu+sa] * amuyā. (Same as the preceding set of examples)

Note: Those shown inside the bracket are the original forms based on gender and case before any morphological process is being carried out.

Sabbanāmato'ti kimatthaṁ?
What is the word "sabbanāmato" for?

To show that examples below are inapplicable as they are not sabbanāma nouns.
* Itthiyaṁ-in woman, ***ls.*** * itthiyā-of woman. ***ds, gs.***

Smiṁ, sānami'ti kimatthaṁ?
What is the word "smiṁ, sānaṁ" for?
To show that example below is inapplicable as it is not of "smiṁ, sa" vibatti. (It is of "yo".)
* Amuyo-so and so women/those women. ***np, ap.***

१८०, २०७. नेताहि स्मिमायया
180, 207. **Ne'tāhi smi'māya yā.**

[Na+etāhi+smiṁ+āya, yā. 4 words]

[V] Etehi sabbanāmehi **gha, pa**saññehi **smiṁ**vacanassa ne'va **āya, yā-**ādesā honti.

No "**āya, yā**" functions are to be performed for all those "ā, u-ending, **gha, pa**-termed sabbanāma nouns in **smiṁ** vibatti (locative case). [This Sutta debars "**āya, yā**" function in ā, u-ending Sabbanāma nouns of feminine gender in **smiṁ** vibatti locative-case.]

[gha-termed, ā-ending "etā"] • Etissaṁ, • etāyaṁ-in that woman,
[gha-termed, ā-ending "imā"] • imissaṁ, • imāyaṁ-in this woman,
[pa-termed, u-ending "amu"] • amussaṁ, • amuyaṁ-in so and so woman. (all ***ls***)

Smin'ti kimatthaṁ?
What is the word "smiṁ" for?
To show that examples below are inapplicable as they are not of "smiṁ" vibatti, but of "chaṭṭhī **sa**". So, there is an "āya, yā" function applied.
* Tāya * itthiyā-of that woman ***gs.*** mukhaṁ-face. ***nv.***
i.e. That woman's face.

Etāhī'ti kimatthaṁ?
What is the word "etāhi" for?
To show that examples below are inapplicable as they are not of "smiṁ" vibatti. (they are of "catutthī & chaṭṭhī **sa**". So, there is an "āya" procedure applied. The restriction of this Sutta is void)

* Kaññāya, * vīṇāya, * gaṅgāya, (Refer to Sutta No. 111, 112)
* kapālikāya-piece of broken earthen jar. ***ds, gs.***

१८१, ९५. मनोगणादितो स्मिंनानमिआ

181, 95. Manogaṇā'dito smiṁ, nā, na'mi, ā.

[Manogaṇa-ādito+smiṁ, nā, naṁ+i, ā. 3 words]

[V] Tasmā manogaṇā'dito **smiṁ, nā**-icce'tesaṁ **i**kāra, **ā**kārādesā honti vā yathāsaṅkhyaṁ.

The **smiṁ, nā** vibattis applied after "mano (mind) etc., sometimes change into "**i, ā**" respectively.
[**smiṁ**>i, **nā** >ā. After changing into i & ā, an "**s**" is attached to them as per Sutta No.184>**si, sā**. See both functions shown underlined. The second example is inapplicable.]

- Manasi, * manasmiṁ-in the mind. ***ls.*** [**Mana**-mind]
- Sirasi, * sirasmiṁ-in the head. ***ls.*** [**Sira**-head]
- Manasā, * manena-with/by mind. ***is.***
- vacasā, * vacena-with/by speech, ***is.*** [**Vaca**-speech]
- sirasā, * sirena-with/by head, ***is.***
- sarasā,* sarena-with/by arrow, sound or pond, ***is.*** [**Sara**-arrow, sound, pond]
- tapasā,* tapena-with/by act of austerity, heat, ***is.*** [**Tapa**-Austerity, heat]
- vayasā, * vayena-with/by age, ***is.*** [**Vaya**-phase of life, age]
- yasasā, * yasena-with/by fame or following, ***is.*** [**Yasa**-fame or retinue]
- tejasā, * tejena-with/by power, ***is.*** [**Teja**-power]
- urasā, * urena-with/by chest, ***is.*** [**Ura**-bosom, chest]
- thāmasā, * thāmena-with/by strength. ***is.*** [**Thāma**-power, strength]

Smiṁ, nānami'ti kimatthaṁ?
What is the word "smiṁsānaṁ" for?
To show that examples below are inapplicable as they are not of "smiṁ, sa" vibatti. (They are of "si".)
* Mano-mind, * siro-head, * tamo-darkness,
* tapo-austerity practice, * tejo-power. all ***ns.***

Ādiggahaṇena aññāsmā'pi **smiṁ, nā**naṁ **i**kāra, **ā**kārā'desā honti.

By means of the word "**ādi**" comprised in the Sutta, the vibattis "**smiṁ, nā**" applied after other nouns rather than "mana" can also change into "**i** and **ā**" respectively.

- Bila<u>si</u>-at hole or den, ***ls.*** • bila<u>sā</u>-with/by hole, ***is.*** [**Bila**-hole]
- pada<u>si</u>-in word or foot, ***ls.*** • pada<u>sā</u>-with/by word or foot. ***is.*** [**pada**-word, foot]

१८२, ९७. सस्स चो

182, 97. **Sassa co'.** [Sassa+ca+o. 3 words]

[V] Tasmā manogaṇā'dito **sa**ssa ca **o**kāro hoti.

The "**sa**" vibatti, applied after that noun word **mano** and so on, changes into "o".

Note: After changing into an "o", an "**s**" is attached before it as per Sutta 184. See the function shown underlined in the examples.

- Mana<u>so</u>-of mind, • thāma<u>so</u>- of strength,
- tapa<u>so</u>- of austerity practice. ***ds, gs.***

१८३, ४८. एतेसमो लोपे

183, 48. **Etesa'mo lope.** [Etesaṁ+o+lope. 3 words]

[V] Etesaṁ manogaṇā'dīnaṁ anto **o**tta'māpajjate vibhattilope kate.

After eliding the applied-vibattis, the last component vowel "**a**" of those mano-group nouns, changes into "**o**".

Summary: This Sutta changes the last vowel of mano-group nouns such as **aya-**iron**, teja-**power and so on, which are joined in a compound noun into "**o**"**.** This must be done after the applied vibatti(case-endings) are deleted.
Note: The examples shown are compound nouns where the **mano**-group nouns such as **aya, teja, tapa,** constitute the first component. Normally, most component words comprised in a compound process lost their distinctive genders, vibattis (case-endings) as they have to be elided. But **these groups can retain their salient characteristic "o"** as

per this Sutta even after it becomes a complete compound.(See the changed "o" shown underlined)

• Man<u>o</u>mayaṁ-mind-made (mind-generated), • ay<u>o</u>mayaṁ-iron-made. (made of iron), ***ns.*** • tej<u>o</u>samena-with/by flame-like, • tap<u>o</u>guṇena-with/by virtue of austerity, • sir<u>o</u>ruhena-with/by head-grown hair. ***is.***

Ādiggahaṇaṁ kima'tthaṁ?
For what purpose the word "ādi" is included in the Vutti of Sutta? (refer to the word "manogaṇādīnaṁ")

Aññesa'manto **o**tta'mā'pajjate.

To show that changing into "o" can occur in other nouns too.

Note: This function enjoined by component part word "ādi" is very much the same as the main function of Sutta.

• Āp<u>o</u>samena-with/by water-like, • vāy<u>o</u>samena with/by air-like. ***is.***

Lope'ti kimatthaṁ? What is the word "lope" for?
To show that examples below are inapplicable as they have no "lopa-elision procedure".

* Padasā-with/by word or foot. * tapasā- with/by austerity.

* yasasā-with/by fame. * vacasā-with/by speech.

* manasā-with/by mind, ***is.***

eva'maññe'pi yojetabbā.
Thus, other examples too should be applied.

१८४, ९६. स सरे वागमो

184, 96. **Sa sare vā'gamo.** [Sa+sare+vā+āgamo. 4 words]

[V] Etehe'va manogaṇā'dīhi vibhattādese sare pare **sa**kārā'gamo hoti vā.

After changing of the **smiṁ, nā** vibattis into "**i** & **ā**" (as per Sutta No.181), an "**s**" should be inserted in front of those vowels and be combined to those vowels "**i** and **ā**".

Summary: This Sutta enjoins to insert an "**s**" in front of "**i** and **ā**" after which it becomes **Si** & **sā,** See the function below shown underlined.

[sā] • Manasā-with/by mind. • vacasā-with/by speech. ***is.***

[si] • manasi-in mind, • vacasi-in speech. ***ls.***

Vā'ti kimatthaṁ?
What is the word "vā" for?
To show that examples below are inapplicable as restricted by the word "vā"

* Manena-with/by mind, * tejena-with/by power, * yasena--with/by fame. ***is.***

Sare'ti kimatthaṁ?
What is the word "sare" for?
To show that examples below are inapplicable as they have no "vibatti-derivative morpheme vowel **i or ā**".

* Mano-mind. * tejo-power. * yaso-fame. ***ns.***

Puna **ādi**ggahaṇena aññasmim'pi paccaye pare **sa**kārāgamo hoti.

By including the word "ādi" in the Vutti again, the inserting of "sa" can also be applied in other nouns with "taddhita-affix".

[See the applied "**s**" shown underlined in the examples carefully. They are affixed with a **Taddhita affix** "**ika**"**.** The "**aṁ**" is case-ending]

• Mānasikaṁ-mind-related. • vācasikaṁ-speech-related. ***ns.***

१८५, ११२. सन्तसद्दस्स सो भे बो चन्ते

185, 112. **Santasaddassa so bhe bo ca'nte.**

[Santasaddassa+so+bhe+bo+ca+ante. 6]

[V] Sabbassa **santa**saddassa **sa**kārādeso hoti bhakāre pare, ante ca **ba**kārāgamo hoti.

The entire word "**santa** (saint) ", changes into "**sa**" when a morpheme "**bhi**" is present behind. Additionally, an extra "**b**" has to be added to "**bhi**". [Santa>**s**+b+bhi>**Sabbhi**]. (See the function-applied examples shown in bold, underlined.)

Note: There are two kinds of "**bha**":
(1) one is a vibatti-derivative morpheme **bha** from "**bhi**" as per Sutta No.99,
(2) the other is just an ordinary **bha** of the root word **bhu** etc.

The First Stanza

Examples in the stanza are shown in bold. Word-for-word detailed translation is provided for more detailed in-depth understanding of each word and the whole stanza.

• Sa**bbhi'**reva samāsetha,
• Sa**bbhi** kubbetha santhavaṁ.
Sataṁ saddhamma'maññāya,
Seyyo hoti na pāpiyo.

(Sandhi) Sabbhi'reva= **Sabbhi**+eva.
saddhamma'maññāya= saddhammamaṁ+aññāya.

[Trans] **Sabbhi**-with good people, or saints. ***ip.*** eva-only, ***ind.*** samāsetha-should congregate, or associate. ***āv.*** **Sabbhi**-with good people, or saints. ***ip.*** kubbetha-should be done. ***āv.*** santhavaṁ-friendship. ***as.*** Sataṁ-of saints. ***gp.*** saddhammaṁ-noble teaching or noble way of saints. ***as.*** aññāya-having known, ***kv.*** Seyyo-more noble. ***tn, ns.*** hoti-is. ***āv.*** na-not. ***ind.*** pāpiyo-evil or bad. ***tn, ns.***

The First Stanza in English

(One) should associate only with the saints.
The friendship should be done with the saints.
Knowing the noble way of saints,
Is more noble and is not evil.

The Second Stanza

Jīranti ve rājarathā sucittā,
Atho sarīram'pi jaraṁ upeti.
Satañ'ca dhammo na jaraṁ upeti,
Santo have • sa**bbhi** pavedayanti.

(Sandhi) Sarīram'pi=sarīraṁ+api/ Satañ'ca=sataṁ+ca

[Trans] Jīranti-gets old, dilapidated, ***āv***. ve-really, ***ind.*** rājarathā-the king's chariots. ***cn, np.*** sucittā-wonderful. ***cn, np, adj.*** Atho-besides, ***ind.*** sarīraṁ-the body. ***ns.*** api-also. ***ind.*** jaraṁ-to the (state of being) old. ***as.*** upeti-approaches. ***āv.*** Sataṁ-of the saint's. ***gp.*** Ca-however, ***ind***. dhammo-(the noble) Dhamma. ***ns.*** na-not. ***ind.*** jaraṁ-to getting old. ***as.*** upeti- approaches. ***āv.*** [**upeti**=**upa**-near+**eti**-gets, **i.e.** approaches.] Santo-saints. ***np.*** have-in fact. ***ind.*** • sa**bbhi**-with saints. ***ip.*** pavedayanti-made known, praise. ***āv.***

The Second Stanza in English

Really, the wonderful royal chariots of the king
fall into decay. Besides, the body too gets old.
But, the way of saints does not get old (by being out of fashion).
The saints, in fact, are to be known by saints (only).

The two examples below are compound nouns with an ordinary **bha** where the function of this Sutta is applied.

- **Sa**bbhūto-being a saint**,** ***cn, ns.*** [**Santa**-saints+**bhūta**-being]
- **sa**bbhāvo-being in a state of saint. ***cn, ns.*** [**Santa**-saints+**bhāva**-being in a state of. One more "b" is reduplicated]

Bhe'ti kimatthaṁ?
What is the word "bhe" for?
To show that example below is inapplicable as it does not have a vibatti-morpheme "**bh**" of "**bhi**" in it. (Example shown below has only a "**hi**", not a "bhi")

* Santehi-by saints. ***ip.*** pūjito-is honored. ***kv.*** bhagavā-the Lord Buddha. (***ns*** in accusative sense, passive voice sentence).
i.e. Buddha is honored by saints.

Caggahaṇaṁ kvaci **sa**kārasse'va pasiddhatthaṁ.

The word "Ca" in the Sutta has a purpose of affecting to change "**santa**" into "**sa**" in certain words as shown below. (See changed "**sa**" in both examples shown below. They are in Kita-affixes)

• Sakkāro-the saint's act, ***kn.*** **i.e.** devotion, practice of Dhamma etc. [**Santa**-saints+**kāro**-act]

• Sakkato-by saints+done. ***kv.*** **i.e.** an act done by saints. [**Santa**-saints+**kato**-done. One more "**K**" is reduplicated in both examples]

Note: In both examples, **sa** is assumed to be derived from **Santa**. However, it can also be derivative of an upasagga "**saṁ**-well, respectfully". In such case, sakkāro-means **act of devotion**. Sakkato-means **done well, respectfully**. This is widely found in the canonical texts.

The words can be brought to completion by eliding the niggahita "**ṁ**" of upasagga and augmenting with one more "k".

१८६, १०७. सिम्हि गच्छन्तादीनं न्तसद्दो अं

186, 107. **Simhi gacchantā'dīnaṁ ntasaddo[21] aṁ.**

[Simhi+gacchanta-ādīnaṁ+nta-saddo+aṁ. 4 words]

[V] **Si**mhi gacchantā'dīnaṁ **nta**-saddo **aṁ**-āpajjate vā.

The affix "**nta**" of the word gaccha**nta** etc. sometimes changes into "**aṁ**" when a " **si** " Vibatti is applied after them.

See each pairs of examples, Both "**aṁ** and **anto**" are shown in bold so that student can easily distinguish between the applied example and inapplicable examples. The second one *marked is inapplicable example.

[21] Ntasaddo=refers to those nouns affixed with "**nta**" affix. This **nta** is the last component part of "**anta**" affix applied by Sutta No. 565 which is widely used as a present participle affix for many Kita nouns. **Ntasaddo** means any noun affixed with "anta" but note that the letter "a" is left out in this expression and simply stated as "**ntasaddo**". [**nta**=nta, **saddo**=word]

- Gacch**aṁ**, * gacch**anto**-the one who goes, while going,
- mah**aṁ**, * mah**anto**-the one who is great or honorable,
- car**aṁ**, * car**anto**-the one who goes, while going,
- khād**aṁ**, * khād**anto**-the one who munches, while munching. ***ns.***

Gacchantādīnami'ti kimatthaṁ?
What is the word "gacchantādīnaṁ" for?
To show that examples below are inapplicable as they do not belong to "nta-affixed, gacchantādi-noun group" though they may seem like nta-affixed nouns. (They are in fact *Kita* **ta**-affixed verbal nouns)
* Anto-afflicted, * danto-tamed, * vanto-vomitted, * santo-peaceful. (Refer to Sutta 584 for details and relevant function of these examples)

१८७, १०८. सेसेसु न्तुव

187, 108. **Sesesu ntu'va.** [Sesesu+ntu+iva. 3 words]

[V] Gacchantā'dīnaṁ **nta**saddo **ntu**ppaccayo'va daṭṭhabbo sesesu vibhattipaccayesu.

The affix **nta** has to be recognized as an equal to **ntu**-affix except for nta-affixed nouns in **Si**-vibatti.

Q: Why "**nta**" has to be recognized like "**ntu**"?
A: The purpose of equating **nta** with **ntu** is to enable to perform necessary morphological procedures in the same way as ntu-affixed nouns, such as changing **nta**-affixed nouns into "**to, ti, tā**" and so forth.
[**to, ti, tā**" functions are shown underlined in the examples. Refer to Sutta 127 for this function.]

(1) • Gaccha<u>to</u>-of goer, • maha<u>to</u>-of great person, ***ds, gs.***
(2) • gaccha<u>ti</u>-in goer, • maha<u>ti</u>-in great person, ***ls.***
Note: This **second type of word form** is **easily confusable with an Ākhyāta verb** with "**ti**" termination.
(3) • gaccha<u>tā</u>-with/by goer, • maha<u>tā</u>- with/by great person. ***is.***

Sesesū'ti kimatthaṁ?
What is the word "sesesu" for?

To show that the examples below are inapplicable as they are of "si" vibatti. (The function for si-vibatti-applied, ntu-affixed nouns is already mentioned in Sutta No.186. So, it has to be excluded.)
* Gacchaṁ, * mahaṁ, * caraṁ, * khādaṁ. (Refer to preceding Sutta 186)

१८८, ११५. ब्रह्मत्त सख राजादितो अमानं
188,115. Brahma'tta, sakha, rājā'dito a'mānaṁ.
[Brahma, atta, sakha, rāja-ādito+aṁ+ānaṁ. 3 words]

[V] **Brahma, atta, sakha, rāja**-icceva'mādito **aṁ**-vacanassa **ānaṁ** hoti vā.

The "**aṁ**" vibatti applied after the noun words "**brahma, atta, sakha, rāja**" etc., sometimes changes into "**ānaṁ**". (The applied function of "**ānaṁ**" is shown underlined in the first. The second is inapplicable example)

• Brahm<u>ānaṁ</u>, * brahmaṁ-to the holy Brahmā, God.
• att<u>ānaṁ</u>, * attaṁ- to oneself (reflexive pronoun), soul.
• sakh<u>ānaṁ</u>, * sakhaṁ- to friend,
• rāj<u>ānaṁ</u>, * rājaṁ- to king. *as.*

Ami'ti kimatthaṁ?
What is the word "aṁ" for?
To show that example below is inapplicable as it is not of an "aṁ" vibatti. (It is of "si".)
* Rājā-king. *ns.*

१८९, ११३. स्या च
189, 113. Syā' ca. [Si+ā+ca. 3 words]

[V] **Brahma, atta, sakha, rāja**-icceva'mādito **si**-vacanassa **ā**-ca hoti.

The "**si**" vibatti applied after the noun words **brahma, atta, sakha, rāja** etc., changes into "**ā**".
[See the applied function of "ā" shown underlined below.]

• Brahm<u>ā</u>, • att<u>ā</u>, • sakh<u>ā</u>, • rāj<u>ā</u>, • ātum<u>ā</u>-body. *ns.*

१९०, ११४. योनमानो

190, 114. **Yona'māno.** [Yonaṁ+āno. 2 words]

[V] **Brahma, atta, sakha, rāja**-icce'va'mādito **yo**naṁ **āno**-ādeso hoti.

The "**yo**" vibatti applied after the noun words **brahma, atta, sakha, rāja** etc., changes into "**āno**".
[See the applied function "**āno**" shown underlined]

• Brahmāno-the Brahmās, holy Gods, • attāno, • sakhāno, • rājāno, • ātumāno. ***np, ap.***

१९१, १३०. सखतो चायो नो

191, 130. **Sakhato cā'yo no.** [Sakhato+ca+āyo, no. 3 words]

[V] Tasmā **sakha**to ca **yo**naṁ **āyo, no**-ādesā honti.

The "**yo**" vibatti applied after the noun word **sakha** changes into "**āyo, no**".
[See the applied function of "**āyo and no**" shown underlined. The first is **āyo**-function, the second example is **no**-function]

• Sakhāyo, • sakhino-friends. ***np, ap.***

Yonami'ti kimatthaṁ?
What is the word "yonaṁ" for? To show that example below is inapplicable as it is not of "yo" vibatti. (It is of "si".)
* Sakhā-friend. ***ns.***

१९२, १३५. स्मिमे

192, 135. **Smi'me.** [Smiṁ+e. 2 words]

[V] Tasmā **sakha**to **smiṁ**vacanassa **e**-kāro hoti.

The "**smiṁ**" vibatti applied after the noun word **sakha** changes into "**e**". [See the applied function "**e**" shown underlined]

• Sakhe-in friend. ***ls.***

१९३, १२२. ब्रह्मतो गस्स च

193, 122. **Brahmato gassa ca.** [Brahmato+gassa+ca. 3 words]

[V] Tasmā **brahma**to gassa ca **e**kāro hoti.

The vocative singular "**si**" vibatti formally termed as "ga" and applied after the noun word **brahma,** changes into "**e**". [See the applied function "**e**" shown underlined]

He • brahme-Oh Brahmā, Oh holy God! ***vs.***

१९४, १३१. सखन्तस्सि नोनानंसेसु

194, 131. **Sakha'ntassi' no, nā, naṁ, sesu.**

[Sakha-antassa+i+no, nā, naṁ, sesu. 3 words]

[V] Tassa **sakha**'ntassa **i**kāro hoti **no, nā, naṁ, sa**-icce'tesu.

When "**nā, naṁ, sa**" vibattis and a morpheme "**no**"(Re: Sutta No.191) is being present behind, the last component vowel "a" of the word "**sakha**" changes into "**i**". [See the applied function "**i**" shown in bold and underlined]

[sa, no-function] • Sakhino-of friend, [nā] • sakhinā-with/by friend, [naṁ] • sakhīnaṁ-of friends, [sa] • sakhissa-of friend.

Etesvī'ti kimatthaṁ?

What is the word "etesu" for?

To show that example below is inapplicable as it is not of "nā, naṁ, sa" vibatti. (It is of "hī".)

* Sakhārehi-with/by friends. ***ip, abp.*** (See morphological function of this word in the next Sutta)

१९५, १३४. आरो हिम्हि वा

195, 134. **Āro himhi vā.** [Āro+himhi+vā. 3 words]

[V] Tassa **sakha**'ntassa **āro** hoti vā **hi**mhi vibhattimhi.

The last component vowel "**a**" of "**sakha**" sometimes changes into "**āra**" when followed by vibatti "**hi**". [See the applied "**āra**" function shown underlined.]

• Sakhārehi, * sakhehi-with/by friends. ***ip, abp.***

१९६, १३३. सुनमंसु वा

196, 133. **Suna'maṁ, su vā.** [Su, naṁ, aṁsu+vā. 2 words]

[V] Tassa **sakha**'ntassa **āro** hoti vā **su, naṁ, aṁ**-icce'tesu.

The last component vowel "**a**" of "**sakha**" sometimes changes into "**āra**" when "**su, naṁ, aṁ**" vibattis are applied after it. [See the applied function of "**āra**" shown underlined in the first examples of each. The second is inapplicable.]

[su] • Sakh<u>ār</u>esu, * sakhesu-in friends,
[naṁ] • sakh<u>ār</u>ānaṁ, * sakhīnaṁ-of friends,
[aṁ] • sakh<u>ār</u>aṁ, * sakhaṁ-to friend.

१९७, १२५. ब्रह्मतो तु स्मिंनि

197, 125. **Brahmato tu smiṁ ni.**

[Brahmato+tu+smiṁ+ni. 4 words]

[V] Tasmā **brahma**to **smiṁ**-vacanassa **ni**-ādeso hoti.

The locative singular vibatti "**smiṁ**" which is applied after the noun word **brahma,** changes into "**ni**".
[See the applied function "ni" shown underlined]

• Brahma<u>ni</u>-in Brahmā. ***ls.***

Tuggahaṇena abrahmato'pi smiṁ-vacanassa **ni** hoti.

By means of the nipāta "tu" in Sutta, the vibatti "**smiṁ**" applied after other nouns rather than "brahma" can also be changed into "**ni**". [See the applied function "**ni**" shown underlined in the examples.]
• Kamma<u>ni</u>-in Kamma, • camma<u>ni</u>-in skin, • muddha<u>ni</u>-in the head. ***ls.***

१९८, १२३. उत्तं सनासु

198, 123. **Uttaṁ sa, nā, su.** [Uttaṁ+sanāsu. 2 words]

[V] Tassa **brahma**saddassa anto **u**tta'māpajjate
sa, nā-icce'tesu.

The last component vowel "**a**" of "**brahma**" changes into "**u**" when "**sa, nā**" vibattis are applied after it.
[See the applied function "**u**" shown in bold, underlined.]

[sa] • Brahm**u**no-of Brahmā. [nā] • brahm**u**nā-with/by Brahmā

Sanāsū'ti kimatthaṁ? What is the word "sanāsu" for?
To show that the example below is inapplicable as it is not of "sa, nā" vibatti. (It is of "si".)
* Brahmā-Brahmā. ***ns.***

१९९, १५८. सत्थुपितादीनमा सिस्मिं सिलोपो च

199, 158. **Satthupitā'dīna'mā sismiṁ silopo ca.**

[Satthupitu-ādīnaṁ+ā+sismiṁ+silopo+ca. 5 words]

[V] **Satthu, pitu**-ādīna'manto **a**tta'māpajjate **si**smiṁ.
silopo ca hoti.

When a nominative singular "**si**" vibatti follows, the last component vowel "**u**" of the word **Satthu** (teacher) and **pitu** (father) etc, changes into "**ā**". Besides, the "**si**" vibatti which is applied after it, is to be elided.
Summary: This Sutta changes "**u**" of satthu, pitu etc, into "**ā**" and deletes "**si**" applied after them. See the applied function "**ā**" shown underlined in the examples.

• Satthā-teacher, • pitā-father, • mātā-mother,
• bhātā-brother, • kattā-doer. ***ns.***

Sismin'ti kimatthaṁ?
What is the word "sismiṁ" for?
To show that the examples below are inapplicable as they are not of "si" vibatti. (They are of "catutthī, chaṭṭhī, sa").
* Satthussa-of teacher, * pitussa, * mātussa, * bhātussa,
* kattussa-of doer. ***ds, gs.***

२००, १५९. अञ्ञेस्वारत्तं

200, 159. **Aññesvā'rattaṁ.** [Aññesu+ārattaṁ. 2 words]

[V] **Satthu, pitu-**ādīna'manto aññesu vacanesu **āra**tta'māpajjate.

The last component vowel "**u**" of noun word **Satthu, pitu** etc; changes into "**āra**" when all the vibattis except "**si**", are applied after them. [See the applied function "**āra**" shown underlined in the examples. Also note that "**ā**" is shortened in some words.]

[aṁ] • Satthāraṁ-to teacher, • pitaraṁ-to father,
• mātaraṁ-to mother, • bhātaraṁ-to brother.
• kattāraṁ-to doer,
[hi] • satthārehi-with/by teachers, • pitarehi, • mātarehi,
• bhātarehi. • kattārehi.

Aññesvī'ti kimatthaṁ?
What is the word "**Aññesu**" for?
To show that the examples below are inapplicable as they are of "si" vibatti, which is excluded by the word "aññesu". (Note the function for those nouns of **si**-vibatti case-endings are already prescribed in Sutta No.199. Hence, excluded. See examples below)
* Satthā-teacher, * pitā, * mātā, * bhātā, * kattā. ***ns.***

२०१, १६३. वा नंम्हि

201, 163. **Vā naṁmhi.** [Vā+naṁmhi. 2 words]

[V] **Satthu, pitu-**ādīna'manto **āra**tta'māpajjate vā **naṁ**mhi vibhattimhi.

The last component vowel "**u**" of noun word **Satthu, pitu** etc., sometimes changes into "**āra**" when dative, genitive plural "**naṁ**" vibatti follows. [See the applied function "**āra**" shown underlined in the examples.]

• Satthārānaṁ-of teachers, • pitarānaṁ, • mātarānaṁ, • bhātarānaṁ. ***dp, gp.***

Vā'ti kimatthaṁ?
What is the word "vā" for?
To show that examples below are inapplicable as stipulated by the word "vā"
* Satthānaṁ-of teachers, * pitūnaṁ, * mātūnaṁ, * bhātūnaṁ. ***dp, gp.***

२०२. १६४. सत्थुनत्तञ्च

202, 164. **Satthun'attañ'ca.** [Satthunaṁ+attaṁ+ca. 3 words]

[V] Tassa **satthu**saddassa anto **a**tta'māpajjate vā **naṁ**mhi vibhattimhi.

The last component vowel "**u**" of that noun word **Satthu**, sometimes changes into "**a**" when dative, genitive plural "**naṁ**" vibattis is applied after it.
[See the applied function "**a**" shown underlined. This "**a**" is lengthened as "**ā**" due to presence of "**naṁ**" vibatti] (Refer to the rule of Sutta 89).

• Satthānaṁ-of teachers, • pitānaṁ, • mātānaṁ,
• bhātānaṁ, • kattānaṁ. ***dp, gp.***

Vā'ti kimatthaṁ?
What is the word "vā" for?
To show that the examples below are inapplicable as restricted by the word "vā"
* Satthārānaṁ, * pitarānaṁ, * mātarānaṁ,
* bhātarānaṁ, * dhītarānaṁ-of daughters.

Caggahaṇaṁ aññesam'pi saṅgahaṇatthaṁ.
The word "ca" has a purpose of taking in other nouns such as "**dhitu**-daughter" for the application of this Sutta. (example already shown).

२०३, १६२. उ सस्मिं सलोपो च

203, 162. **U sasmiṁ salopo ca.**[U+sasmiṁ+salopo+ca. 4 words]

[V] **Satthu, pitu**-icce'va'mādīna'mantassa **u**ttaṁ hoti vā **sa**smiṁ, salopo ca.

The last component vowel "**u**" of the words **Satthu, pitu** etc., remains unchanged when a dative and genitive singular "**sa**" is applied after them. The applied vibatti "sa" is sometimes elided in such instances.
[The rule of Sutta is to keep "u" as "u". See that in the first example "**Satthu**", "sa" is elided. In the second example "**satthussa**", the eliding of "sa" is not carried out sometimes but reduplicated with another "s". For the word "**Satthuno**", please refer to Sutta 117 for its "**no**" function. There are three forms of word possible in this "**sa-vibatti**" case. The contextual verb "**dīyate**" implies the dative case while the word "**priggaho**" signifies genitive of the examples.]

- Satthu, • satthussa, • satthuno-to/of teacher. ***ds, gs.*** dīyate-(it is) given, ***āv.*** pariggaho-possession. ***nv.*** vā.
- Pitu, • pitussa, • pituno-to/ of father. dīyate, pariggaho vā.
- Bhātu, • bhātussa, • bhātuno-to/of brother. dīyate, pariggahovā.

Caggahaṇaṁ dutiyasampiṇḍana'tthaṁ.
[dutiyasampiṇḍana'tthaṁ=dutiya-the second function+sampiṇḍana+atthaṁ]
The word "ca" in the Sutta has a purpose of bringing in the second function of "eliding **sa**" to this Sutta.

२०४, १६७. सक्कमन्धातादीनञ्च

204, 167. **Sakkamandhātā'dīnañ'ca.**
[Sakkamandhātu-ādīnaṁ+ca. 2 words]

[V] **Sakkamandhātu**-icce'va'mādīna'manto **u**tta'māpajjate **sa**smiṁ **sa**lopo ca hoti.

The last component vowel "**u**" of the word **Sakkaman dhātu,** (a king so-named), remains unchanged when dative or genitive singular "**sa**" vibatti is after it.

- Sakkamandhātu-that of king Sakkamandhātu. ***gs.*** iva-like. ***ind.***

assa-of that. ***gs.*** rājino-king. ***gs.*** vibhavo-wealth. ***ns.***
i.e. That king's wealth is like that of the Universal monarch named "Sakkamandhātu".

Evaṁ

• kattu-of doer, • gantu-of goer, • dātu-of donor. ***ds, gs.***
icce'va'mādī-and so on.

Punā'rambhaggahaṇaṁ kimatthaṁ?
Why this Sutta enjoins this redundant function of keeping "u" as "u"?

Niccadīpana'tthaṁ. [**Nicca**-as permanent function +**dīpana**-showing+**atthaṁ**-for the purpose of.]
The purpose of the function of keeping "u" as an "u" again, is to show the consistency of this pattern of the word "sakkamandhātu".

• Sakkamandhātu-of king Sakkamandhātu.

Caggahaṇaṁ dutiyasampiṇḍana'tthaṁ.
The word "ca" in the Sutta also has a purpose of bringing the second function of eliding "sa" from Sutta 203 to this Sutta.

२०५, १६०. ततो योन मो तु

205, 160. **Tato yona'mo tu.** [Tato+yonaṁ+o+tu. 4 words]

[V] Tato **ārā**'desato sabbesaṁ **yo**naṁ **o**kārā'deso hoti.

The vibatti "**yo**" applied after nouns like **satthu, pitu,** whose component vowels have already been morphed into "**āra**", changes into "**o**".
[This Sutta changes "**yo**" into "**o**" after "āra" function has been applied. The function is shown underlined below. Re:200, 201 for "āra" process]

• Satthāro-teachers, • pitaro, • mātaro, • bhātaro, • kattāro,
• vattāro-speakers. ***np, vp, ap.***

Tuggahaṇena aññasmā'pi **yo**naṁ **o**kāro hoti.
By the word "tu" in Sutta, the vibatti "yo" applied after other nouns can also change into "o".
[See "o" shown underlined in the examples]

• Caturo-four. janā-people, • gāvo-cows, • ubho-two. purisā-men. ***np.***

२०६, १६५. ततो स्मिमि

206, 165. Tato smi'mi. [Tato+smiṁ+i. 3 words]

[V] Tato **ārā**'desato **smiṁ**-vacanassa **i**-kārā'deso hoti.

The vibatti "**smiṁ**" applied after nouns like **satthu, pitu** whose component vowels had been changed into "**āra**", morphs into an "**i**". [This Sutta changes "**smiṁ**" into "**i**" after "āra" function is done. See the function shown in bold, underlined]

• Satthari, • pitari, • mātari, • dhītari-in daughter, • bhātari, • kattari, • vattari-in speaker. ***ls.***

Puna **tato**gahaṇena aññasmā'pi **smiṁ**vacanassa **i**kāro hoti.

By using the word "tato" again in Sutta, the vibatti "**smiṁ**" applied after other nouns can also change into "**i**". [See the example. "i" is shown in bold, underlined]

• Bhuvi-in the earth. ***ls.***

२०७, १६१. ना आ

207, 161. Nā ā. [Nā+ā. 2 words]

[V] Tato **ārā**'desato **nā**vacanassa **ā**-ādeso hoti.

The vibatti "**nā**" applied after nouns like **satthu, pitu** whose component vowels have become" **āra**", changes into "**ā**". [This Sutta changes "**nā**" into "**ā**" after "āra" function is done, see applied function "**ā**" shown in bold, underlined in the examples]

• Satthārā-with/by teacher, • pitarā, • mātarā, • bhātarā, • dhītarā, • kattārā, • vattārā. ***is.***

२०७, १६६. आरो रस्समिकारे

208, 166. **Āro rassa'mikāre.** [Āro+rassaṁ+ikāre. 3 words]

[V] **Ārā**'deso rassa'māpajjate **i**kāre pare.

The vowel "**ā**" of "**āra**" has be shortened into "**a**" when followed by an "**i**" which is a morpheme of vibatti "**smiṁ**". (Refer to Sutta No. 206 for "**i**" function. The shortened "**a**" is shown underlined).

• Satthari-in teacher, • pitari, • mātari, • dhītari,
• kattari-in doer, • vattari-in speaker. ***ls.***

२०९, १६८. पितादीन मसिम्हि

209, 168. **Pitā'dīna'masimhi.** [Pitu-ādīnaṁ+asimhi. 2 words]

[V] Pitā'dīna'mārādeso rassa'māpajjate **asi**mhi vibhattimhi.

The vowel "**ā**" of "**āra**-function", applied in the words **pitu** etc., have to be similarly shortened into "**a**" in all cases (vibatti) except "si". (Also **smiṁ,** is to be excluded as the function of rassa had been done as per Sutta No.208. The Shortened "a" is shown underlined)

Note: This procedure is applicable only for all **yo, aṁ, nā, hi, naṁ, smā, su,** vibattis applied after **pitu, mātu** (mother), **bhātu** (brother), **dhītu** (daughter).

• Pitarā-with/by father, • mātarā, • bhātarā, • dhītarā-. (These examples are in **nā** vibatti case-ending)

• pitaro-fathers, • mātaro, • bhātaro, • dhītaro. (These examples are in **yo** vibatti case-ending)

Asimhiggahaṇaṁ **to**mhi pare **i**kārā'desañāpana'tthaṁ.
The word "asimhi" in Sutta, has a purpose of changing the last component vowel of other nouns affixed with a "to" suffix into an "**i**". [asimhi=**na**-not+**si**-vibatti "si"+**mhi**-derived from **smiṁ**, which means "due to, when". See an "**i**" before "**to-affix**" on the examples shown in bold, underlined. "**To**" is an indeclinable affix. See Sutta No.248. It is not a Vibatti per se.]

• Mātito-from mother, • pitito-from father,
• bhātito-from brother, • duhitito-from daughter.

२१०, २३९. तयातयीनं तकारो त्वत्तं वा

210, 239. **Tayā, tayīnaṁ takāro tvattaṁ vā.**

[Tayā, tayīnaṁ+takāro+tvattaṁ+vā. 4 words]

[V] **Tayā, tayi**-icce'tesaṁ **ta**kāro **tva**tta'māpajjate vā.

The "**ta**" of "**Tayā, tayi**" morphemes (See Suttas.139,145), sometimes changes into "**tva**".
[See the applied function "tva" shown underlined in the examples.]

- Tvayā, * tayā-with/by you, ***is.***
- tvayi, * tayi-in you. ***ls.***

Etesami'ti kimatthaṁ?
What is the word "etesaṁ" for?
To show that examples below are inapplicable as the word "etesu" refers only to "tayā & tayi".
* Tuvaṁ. * tavaṁ-to you. ***as.***

Iti nāmakappe tatiyo kaṇḍo.
The Third Section of Noun ends.

Catuttha Kaṇḍa

The Fourth Section

२११, १२६. अत्तन्तो हिस्मिमनत्तं

211, 126. **Atta'nto hismi'manattaṁ.**

[Atta-anto+hismiṁ+anattaṁ. 3 words]

[V] Tassa **atta**no anto **ana**tta'māpajjate **hi**mhi vibhattimhi.

The last component vowel of that noun word "**atta** (self) " when followed by the Vibatti "**hi**", changes into "**ana**". [This Sutta changes the last "a" of "atta" into "ana". The applied function "**an**" is shown underlined. "**e**" is the function applied by Sutta 101.

• Att<u>an</u>ehi, • att<u>an</u>ebhi-with/by/from oneself, ourselves. ***ip. abp.***

Attanto'ti kimatthaṁ?
What is the word "attanto" for?
To show that examples below are inapplicable as they are not the word "atta".
* Rājehi, * rājebhi-with/by/from kings. ***ip. abp.***

Hismi'nti kimatthaṁ? [hismiṁ+iti]
What is the word "hismiṁ" for?
To show that example below is inapplicable as it is not of "hi", but of "sa". (See the function of the example in Sutta 213)
* Attano-of oneself. ***ds, gs.***

Anatta'miti bhāvaniddesena attasaddassa **sakā'**deso hoti sabbāsu vibhattīsu.

By using the word "anatta" in a Bhāva taddhita expression as "anattaṁ" (See Sutta), the word "atta (self) " changes into another word-form "saka-one's own" in all vibattis. [See "**saka**" shown underlined below.]
• S<u>ak</u>o-oneself, one's own, ***ns.*** • s<u>ak</u>ā, ***np.*** • s<u>ak</u>aṁ, ***as.*** • s<u>ak</u>e. ***ap.***
Note: The ending vowels "o" "ā" etc. in the examples are Vibatti-derivative morphemes of the relevant vibattis.

२१२, १२९. ततो स्मिं नि

212, 329. **Tato smiṁ ni.** [Tato+smiṁ+ni. 3 words]

[V] Tato **atta**to **smiṁ**vacanassa **ni** hoti.

The vibatti "**smiṁ**" applied after that noun word "**atta**", changes into "**ni**". [See "**ni**" shown underlined in the example.]

- Atta<u>ni</u>-in onself. ***ls.***

२१३, १२७. सस्स नो

213, 127. **Sassa no.** [Sassa+no. 2 words]

[V] Tato **atta**to **sa**ssa vibhattissa **no** hoti.

The vibatti "**sa**" applied after "**atta**", changes into "**no**". [See "**no**" shown underlined in the example.]

- Atta<u>no</u>-of oneself. ***ds, gs.***

२१४, १२८. स्मा ना

214, 128. **Smā nā.** [Smā+nā. 2 words]

[V] Tato **atta**to **smā**-vacanassa **nā** hoti.

The vibatti "**smā**" applied after that noun word "**atta**", changes into "**nā**". [See "**nā**" shown underlined in the example.]

- Atta<u>nā</u>-from oneself. ***abs.***

Note: Sometimes, this type of word may be in instrumental singular case "nā". [atta+nā]. In this case, no specific function is required as the word itself is complete to convey the necessary meaning "by oneself, or by itself ". It is a reflexive pronoun in case of the second meaning.

Puna **tato**gahaṇena tassa **atta**no **ta**kārasse'va **ra**kāro hoti sabbesu vacanesu.

By using the word "tato" again in the Vutti of Sutta, the last component word "ta" of "atta" changes into "ra" in all vibatti cases. (**i.e.** last "t" of "tta" becomes "r". See it below shown underlined)

- At<u>**ra**</u>jo-son born of oneself, one's own child, ***ns***
- at<u>**ra**</u>jaṁ-to son born of oneself, to one's own child. ***as.***

२१५, १४१. झलतो च

215, 141. **Jhalato ca.** [Jhalato+ca. 2 words]

[V] **Jha, la**-icce'tehi **smā**vacanassa **nā** hoti.

The vibatti "**smā**" applied after "**i, ī, u, ū**-ending, **jha, la**-termed nouns of masculine gender, changes into "**nā**".
[This Sutta changes "smā" applied after **i, ī, u, ū**-ending, **jha, la**-termed nouns of masculine gender into "**nā**". See "**nā**" shown underlined]

[jha-termed, i-ending noun] • Agginā-from fire,
[jha-termed, ī-ending noun] • daṇḍinā-from the one who has a stick,
[la-termed, u-ending noun] • bhikkhunā-from monk,
[la-termed, ū-ending noun] • sayambhunā-from self-enlightened Buddha. **All examples *abs.***

Smā'ti kimatthaṁ?
What is the word "smā" for?
To show that examples below are inapplicable as they are not of "smā". (They are of "yo")
* Aggayo, * munayo, * isayo. ***np, ap.*** [The meaning shown before]

२१६, १८०. घपतो स्मिं यं वा

216, 180. **Gha, pato smiṁ yaṁ vā.**

[Gha, pato+smiṁ+yaṁ+vā. 4 words]

[V] Tasmā **gha, pa**to **smiṁ**vacanassa **yaṁ** hoti vā.

The vibatti "**smiṁ**" applied after **gha, pa**-named, "**ā, i, ī, u, ū**-ending nouns of feminine gender sometimes changes into "**yaṁ**". ["Smiṁ" becomes "yam". See it shown underlined]

[gha-termed, ā-ending noun] • Kaññāyaṁ, * kaññāya-in girl.
[pa-termed, i-ending noun] • Rattiyaṁ, * rattiyā- in night.
[pa-termed, ī-ending noun] • Itthiyaṁ, * itthiyā- in woman.
[pa-termed, u-ending noun] • Yāguyaṁ, * yāguyā- in rice-porridge.
[pa-termed, ū-ending noun] • Vadhuyaṁ, * vadhuyā-in daughter-in-law. ***ls.***
Note: All examples are of feminine gender. The second example in each pair is inapplicable.

२१७, १९९. योनं नि नपुंसकेहि

217, 199. **Yonaṁ ni napuṁsakehi.**

[Yonaṁ+ni+napuṁsakehi. 3 words]

[V] Sabbesaṁ **yo**naṁ **ni** hoti vā napuṁsakehi liṅgehi.

The vibatti "**yo**" applied after all neuter gender nouns changes into "**ni**" sometimes.

[This Sutta changes "yo" applied only after **i, ī, u, ū**-ending neuter-gender nouns into "**ni**". See "**ni**" in the first example of each pair shown by being underlined. The second is inapplicable example.]

[i-ending noun] • Aṭṭhīni, * aṭṭhī-bones,

[la-termed, u-ending noun] • āyūni, * āyū-age, life. ***np, ap.***

Napuṁsakehī'ti kimatthaṁ?

What is the word "napuṁsakehi" for? To show that example below is inapplicable as it is not a "napuṁsaka-neuter gender word". (It is of feminine gender)

* Itthiyo-women. ***np, ap.***

Note: Next Sutta also changes "yo" applied after a-ending neuter gender nouns into "ni".

२१८, १९६. अतो निच्चं

218, 196. **Ato niccaṁ.** [Ato+niccaṁ. 2 words]

[V] **A**kārantehi napuṁsakaliṅgehi **yo**naṁ **ni** hoti niccaṁ.

The vibatti "**yo**" applied after neuter gender nouns ending in "**a**", always changes into "**ni**".

["**Ni**" is shown underlined. In each pair of examples, the first is nominative, vocative plural and the second is accusative plural though both may look the same in the physical structure.]

• Yāni. • yāni-which.

• Tāni. • tāni-those.

• Kāni. • kāni- which/what.

• Bhayāni. • bhayāni-dangers.

• Rūpāni. • rūpāni-forms/physical matters. ***np, ap.***

२१९, १९५. सिं

219, 195. **Siṁ’.** [Si+aṁ. 2 words]

[V] **A**kāra’ntehi napuṁsakaliṅgehi **si**vacanassa **aṁ** hoti niccaṁ.

The vibatti “**si**” applied after **a**-ending neuter gender nouns, always changes into “**aṁ**”. [The applied function “**aṁ**” is shown underlined.]

• Sabbaṁ-all, • yaṁ-which, • taṁ-that, • kaṁ-what,
• rūpaṁ-form. ***ns.***

२२०, ७४. सेसतो लोपं गसिपि

220, 74. **Sesato lopaṁ gasi’pi.**

[Sesato+lopaṁ+gasi+api. 4 words]

[V] Tato niddiṭṭhehi liṅgehi sesato **ga, si**-icce’te lopa’māpajjante.

The pathamā (Nominative) and **ga**-named vocative singular vibatti “**si**”, are to be elided.

Note: The first example **is vocative** “**si**”, **the second one is** an ordinary **nominative** “**si**”. both “si” are elided by this Sutta.
Bhoti is a vocative particle to be used before feminine gender nouns.
Bho is used in front of masculine gender nouns.

Bhoti • itthi-Oh woman! ***vs.*** sā • itthī-that woman. ***ns.***
Bho • daṇḍi-Oh stick-holding person! ***vs.***
so • daṇḍī-that person having stick. ***ns.***
Bho • sattha-Oh teacher! ***vs.*** so • satthā-that teacher. ***ns.***
Bho • rāja-Oh king! ***vs.*** so • rājā-that king. ***ns.***

Sesato’ti kimatthaṁ?
What is the word “sesato” for?
To show that example below is inapplicable as it is of “paṭhmā si”, not ga-termed “si”. (So, that “si” is not elided. Instead, it changed into “o” by Sutta No.104)
* Puriso-man. ***ns.*** gacchati-goes. ***āv.***

Gasī’ti kimatthaṁ?
What is the word “gasi” for? To show that examples below

are inapplicable as they are not "ga-termed si", but "sa-vibatti".

* Itthiyā-of woman, * satthussa-of teacher. ***ds, gs.***

Note:

(1) The nominative "**si**" applied after a-ending nouns in **masculine gender** usually changes into "**o**" (see Sutta 104),

(2) "**si**" applied after a-ending nouns in **neuter gender** usually changes into "**aṁ**" (See Sutta 219).

(3) "**si**" applied after the word "Satthu-teacher, rajā etc," changes into an "**ā**" (Refer to Sutta 199,189).

The function of this Sutta is applicable only for nominative and vocative "si" vibattis applied after some **i, ī, u, ū,** ending nouns. It is inapplicable for nouns which are applicable by the function of Suttas 104,113,114, 124, 125, 126, 152,189,193 and 219. In view of this procedure, it should be noted that **both nominative, vocative singular vibatti "si" is usually invisible in majority of nouns of all genders and declensions** though traces of vibatti-forms of other 13 vibatti-applied nouns are still visible even after various kinds of morphological procedures have been applied.

Traces of vibatti-forms

Shown below are traces of various Vibattis (case-endings) except for nouns in "si" Vibatti. Traces of unchanged vibatti-forms are shown in bold.

Kaññā**yo** (Nominative plural "**yo**")
Puris**aṁ** (Accusative singular "**aṁ**")
Muna**yo** (Accusative plural "**yo**")
Kammu**nā** (Instrumental singular "**Nā**")
Purise**hi**, (Instrumental plural "**hi**")
purisas**sa**, (Dative & Genitive singular "**sa**")
Purisā**naṁ**,(Dative & Genitive plural "**naṁ**")
Purisa**smā**, (Ablative singular "**smā**")
Purise**hi**, (Ablative plural "**hi**")
Purisa**smiṁ**, (Locative singular "**smiṁ**")
Purise**su** (Locative plural "**su**")

२२१, २८२. सब्बास मावुसोपसग्गनिपातादीहि च

221, 282. **Sabbāsa'māvuso'pasagga, nipātā'dīhi ca.**

[Sabbāsaṁ+āvuso, upasagga, nipāta-ādīhi+ca. 3 words]

[V] Sabbāsaṁ vibhattīnaṁ ekavacana, bahuvacanānaṁ paṭhamā, dutiyā, tatiyā, catutthī, pañcamī, chaṭṭhī, sattamīnaṁ lopo hoti.
āvuso, upasagga, nipāta-icceva'mādīhi ca.

All (the singular and plural of "paṭhamā, dutiyā, tatiyā, catutthī, pañcamī, chaṭṭhī, sattamī") vibattis, applied after ***Upasagga*** and ***Nipāta*** words, including vocative particle "**āvuso**", are to be elided.

Summary: This Sutta enjoins to delete any Vibatti (case-endings) applied after *Upasagga* and *Nipāta* particles including the vocative particle "**āvuso**-my friend,".

Q: Why **vibattis** (case-ending of nouns) applied after ***Upasagga*** and ***Nipāta*** particles have to be elided?

A: Because it is not necessary to apply any morphological function of structural and physical change to them.

Q: If to be elided, why then the vibattis are applied after them?

A: It is applied as a rule of the grammatical necessity. A complete word in a meaningful sentence has to end in a certain vibatti so that it can convey and signify its meaning according to the relevant vibatti being applied even though it might had been either elided or changed into other newly-morphed forms.

Q: Do all *Upasagga* and *Nipāta* particles require to be applied with Vibattis?

A: Only those certain *Upasagga* and *Nipāta* words (which are used independently in a sentence as an individual word) are necessary to be applied with a Vibatti. However, most of *Upasagga* words used as prefixes of the verbs and verbal nouns are not required to be applied with Vibattis.

Q: What kind of Vibattis are generally applied then?

A: Most are found to be applied with a nominative singular or plural. In cases of vocative words, vocative is applied. Some scholars state that nominative is usually applied after independent *Upasagga* words and all seven vibattis can be applied after independent *Nipāta* words. However, it should be noted that **any relevant vibatti can be applied**

after them depending on the contextual position and the role each word plays such as adjective, adverb or disjunctive and so forth.

Examples cited in Sutta

Tvaṁ • panā'**vuso**, (tvaṁ-you, • panā'**vuso=pana+āvuso,** pana-no meaning, āvuso-my friend? **i.e.** how about you, my friend? Singular)
tumhe panā'**vuso,** (tumhe • panā'**vuso=pana+āvuso, i.e.** How about you? in plural sense here.)
• padaso dhammaṁ vāceyya, (He) should teach and say Dhamma word by word, **i.e.** in detail. **padaso**-by word, ***is.*** **dhammaṁ**-the dhamma, ***as.*** **vāceyya**-(one) should cause to say students, ***āv.*** **i.e.** teach. (a causative verb)
vihāraṁ • sve upagaccheyya.
vihāraṁ-to the temple, ***as.*** **sve**-tomorrow, ***nip.*** **upagaccheyya**-(one) should approach. ***āv.*** **i.e.** (He) should come to the temple tomorrow.

(**Pana**, **āvuso,** and **sve** are ***Nipātas.*** The rest are **non-*Nipāta*** words. Both numbers of "**si**" **and** "**yo**" in vocative case can be applied to **āvuso** and must be elided. The word **āvuso** means "my friend", a peer-language used to address among equals of both by monks and lay people alike. The nipāta "**pana**" has no meaning here though it has some distinctive meanings occasionally based on context of where it is positioned in a sentence. **Padaso** is a **nā**-vibatti-ending word with indeclinable affix "**so**"**. Sve** is a plain nipāta without an affix in the locative sense)

20 *Upasagga* Words

(Important to be memorized by serious students)

• Pa, • parā, • ni, • nī, • u, • du, • saṁ, vi, ava, anu, pari, adhi, abhi, pati, su, ā, ati, api, apa, upa, (These are called 20 *Upasagga* words, with no vibatti. However, ***upasagga*** **words can affect various meanings and usages when they are prefixed to the roots of verbs**.

Upasagga particles prefixed in front of Roots

Below is only a sample of *Upasagga* words prefixed to the roots "**hara**-to carry and **Bhu**-to be" shown in the Sutta, thus forming various Kita-nouns. **The *Upasagga* (prefix) words are shown underlined.**

• <u>pa</u>hāro, • <u>parā</u>bhavo, • <u>ni</u>hāro, • <u>nī</u>hāro, • <u>u</u>hāro, • <u>du</u>hāro, • <u>saṁ</u>hāro, • <u>vi</u>hāro, • <u>ava</u>hāro, • <u>anu</u>hāro, • <u>pari</u>hāro, • <u>adhi</u>hāro, • <u>abhi</u>hāro, • <u>pati</u>hāro, • <u>su</u>hāro, • <u>ā</u>hāro, • <u>ati</u>hāro, • <u>api</u>hāro,

• apahāro, • upahāro, [These will be translated later. all *ns.*] **evaṁ vīsati upasaggehi ca.** Thus, (vibatti are applied) after twenty *Upasagga* words. [This is only a generalized statement only. Except after some independently used *Upassagga* words, other *Upasagga* words used as prefix such as these, do not require to have any vibatti case-endings]

Note: Vibattis are not elided in these examples shown above as they have become nouns. That is why there is an "**o**-ending" in these words. See each *Upasagga* is prefixed to the front of the root "**hara** or **Bhu**" and becomes a complete word "**pahāro**" etc, after going through necessary morphological procedures. Note that the only example where the root "bhu" contains is "**parābavo**"**.** The rest are made up of one single root "hara".

The Use of *Upasagga* Particles

The meaning of each *Upasagga* words in examples will be explained in some detail so that the students will be able to figure out some possible meaning of *Upasagga* words they may encounter and develop some basic knowledge of them.

Usage: *Upasagga* words are generally used as prefixes placed before the roots of **Ākhyāta verbs** and Kita-affixed **Kita-nouns. There are quite a few *Upasagga* words which can be independently used.** *Nipāta* words are used in various places of sentences and words. **When an *Upasagga*** word **or a *Nipāta* word is used as an independent word** in a sentence, some **certain vibattis, especially nominative, can be applied.** After application, the Vibattis are to be elided by this Sutta as a general rule of grammar.

Three kinds of *Upasagga* particles

There are **three kinds of *Upasaggas***. They are:

(1) Those that follow the meaning of the root, without affecting its original meaning. This kind of *Upasagga* is called "Dhātva'tthā'nuvattaka".
[**Dhātu**-root+**attha**-meaning+**anu**-following+**vattaka**-that which happens]

(2) Those that absolutely mean opposite of the root. These categorically change the original meaning of the root. This is called "Dhātva'tthabādhaka". [**Dhātu**+**attha**+**bādhaka**-that which debars, is opposite of the meaning of the root.]

(3) Those that enhance the original meaning of the root by adding more specific meaning and flavor to it. This kind of

Upasagga is called "Dhātva'tthavisesaka".
[**Dhātu+attha+visesaka**-modifier or enhancer]

Detailed Meanings of *Upasagga* Particles

Note: Sometimes, certain *Upasagga* words shown by the ◊ mark can also be used independently in sentences in addition to being used as prefixes.

• Pa

(a) specifically, specially, in various ways,
e.g. pajānāti-(He) knows specifically, in various ways. [Pa+jānāti],
Paññā- knowing specifically, in various ways, **i.e.** wisdom, knowledge [Pa+ñā].

(b) Up,
e.g. Paggaṇhāti-(He) takes up, lifts up by praise and support etc. [Pa+gaṇhāti]
Paggāho-such an act. [Pa+gāho]

(c) away, abroad, far away,
e.g. Pakkamati-(He) goes away [Pa+kamati]
Pakkanto-gone away [Pa+kanto]
Pavāsaṁ-living abroad, the distant place [Pa+vāsaṁ]
Pavāsī-Resident abroad, one who lives at a distant region or country [Pa+vāsī]

(d) the source.
e.g. Pabhavati-(It) originates, **i.e.** It starts to happen [Pa+bhavati].
Pabhavo-origin [Pa+bhavo].

(e) Successively.
e.g. Papitāmaho-great-grandfather [Pa+pitāmaho].
Panattā-great-grandchildren [Pa+nattā]
Pācariyā-successive generation of preceding teachers. [Pa+ācariyā]

(f) chief, noble.
e.g. Padhānaṁ-chief, principal. [Pa+dhānaṁ].

Pāvacanaṁ-the noble words of Buddha, **i.e.** canonical texts. [Pa+vacanaṁ, "a" is lengthened].
Paṇītaṁ-noble, the best, [Pa+nītaṁ].

(g) being clear and clean,
e.g. Pasīdati-(It) settles clear (as the mind being clear with joy and faith) [Pa+sīdati].
Pasanno-being joyous or pleased with joy etc. [Pa+sanno].

(h) Inside,
Pakkhipati-(He) puts inside [Pa+khipati].
Pakkhitto-having put inside [Pa+khitto].
Pasassati-(He) breathes in [Pa+sassati].
Passāso-inhalation [Pa+ssāso].

(i) Intensifier,
Padahati-(he) firmly exerts effort [Pa+dahati].
Padhānaṁ-Effort in meditation practice or in any pursuit [Pa+dhānaṁ].
Pavassati-(It) rains heavily [pa+vassati]
Pavanaṁ-thick forest. [pa+vanaṁ]

• parā

(a) opposite of,
e.g. Parājayati-(He) fails or is defeated [Parā+jayati],
Parājayo-defeat, failure [Parā+jayo]. Compare with>Jayati-conquers.
Parābhavati-(He) loses [Parā+bhavati].
Parābhavo-loss, ruin [Parā+bhavo], compare with>Bhavati-happens, arises.

(b) again and again, continuously
e.g. Parakkamati-(He) makes effort again and again [Para+kamati],
Parakkamo-continuous, successive effort [Para+kamo].

(c) wrongly,
e.g. Parāmasati-(He) touches it wrongly, takes it in wrong way [Para+āmasati].
Parāmāso-touching wrongly, wrong view [Para+āmāso]

• **ni**

(a) out, away,

e.g. Nikkhamati-(He) comes out [Ni+kamati], Niggato-gone out, left [Ni+gato].

(b) down, into

e.g. Nidahati-(He) keeps underneath, stores (as of precious things by burying) or takes it deeply [Ni+dahati].
Nidhānaṁ-such an act [Ni+dhānaṁ].
Nihito-having kept down [Ni+hito].
Nikkhipati-(He) drops down [Ni+khipati].
Nikkhitto-having dropped [Ni+khitto].
Nisīdati-(He) settles down. **i.e.** sits [Ni+sīdati].
Nisinno- having sat [Ni+sinno]
Niggaṇhāti-(he) takes down, **i.e.**censures. [Ni+gaṇhāti] Compare>Paggaṇhāti-lifts up by praise etc. [Pa+gaṇhāti]
Niggaha-censure [Ni+gaha]
Compare>Paggaha-encouragement and support [Pa+gaha]

(c) Back down, as in going or in an action, opposite of,

e.g. Nivattati-backs down or gives up [Ni+vattati]. Nivattanaṁ-returning or act of giving up.

(d) without, lack of,

e.g. Nidukkho-without suffering, [Ni+dukkho].
Nirogo-without disease, healthy [Ni+rogo].
Nillajjo-without shame, shameless, [Ni+lajjo].

• **nī**

out, off, to remove

e.g. Nīharati-(He) takes out, removes [Nī+harati],
Nīharaṇaṁ-act of taking out, removal [Nī+haraṇaṁ].

Note: Both **Ni** and **Nī** are not different from each other except the fact that one is a lengthened-form of *Upasagga.*

• u

(a) up, upward

e.g. Uggacchati-(It) goes upward [U+gacchati], Uggamanaṁ-act of going up [U+gamanaṁ], Unnamati-(It) leans up (as a young shoot of tree or like a person growing arrogant) [U+namati], Unnamanaṁ-act of leaning up, arrogance, pride. [U+namanaṁ]. Uggaṇhāti-takes upward **i.e.** Learns [U+gaṇhāti]

(b) wrong, opposite of,

e.g. Ummaggo-the wrong path [U+maggo]. Uddhammaṁ-wrong Dhamma [U+dhammaṁ]. Ubbinayaṁ-wrong Vinaya (discipline) [U+vinayaṁ].

(c) Intensifier

Uyyuñjanti-to make intensive effort. [U+yuñjanti] Ubbādhati-(It) stresses out intensely, exhausts [U+bādhati]. Ubbādhanaṁ-such a condition [U+bādhanaṁ].

• du

(a) bad, unwholesome, poor in nature,

e.g. Duccarati-(He) acts badly or unethically [Du+carati], Dukkaṭaṁ-bad deed [Du+kataṁ]. Duggati-bad rebirth, bad destiny [Du+gati],

(b) ill, inauspicious,

Dumaṅgalaṁ-inauspiciousness, [Du+maṅgalaṁ] Dunnimittaṁ-bad omen [Du+nimittaṁ]

(c) without, lack of,

e.g. Dubikkaṁ-without food, famine [Du+Bhikkaṁ], Dussīlo-without morality [Du+sīlo]. Duppañño-without wisdom, ignorant [Du+pañño]. Dusassaṁ-lack of paddy, having poor crops of rice due to draught or pests etc. [Du+sassaṁ].

(d) being difficult of,

e.g. Dukkaraṁ-hard to do [Du+karaṁ], Dullabhaṁ-hard to get [Du+labaṁ],

Dujjānaṁ-hard to know [Du+jānaṁ].

- **saṁ**

(a) together, in union,

e.g. Saṁvasati-(He) lives together [Saṁ+vasati]
Saṁvāso-act of being together, co-hbitation [Saṁ+vāso].
Saṁyujjati-(It) joins together [Saṁ+yujjati]
Saṁyogo-act of joining together [Saṁ+yogo].

(b) well, unitedly,

e.g. Siṅgāyati-(He) sings or chants together [Saṁ+gāyati]
Siṅgiti-act of singing together [Saṁ+gīti]
Saṅkharoti-(It) acts together [Saṁ+karoti]
Saṅkhāro-such an act or state, **i.e.** conditioned things [Saṁ+karo].
Saṅgahṇāti-(He) takes well, such as by means of praise, support etc. [Saṁ+gaṇhāti]
Saṅgaho-such an act. [Saṁ+gaho]
Note: "ṁ" becomes "ṅ" as it precedes "kh" or "g" in the words above.

(c) self, oneself

e.g. Sambhujjati-(He) knows by himself (without any outside help) [Saṁ+bhujjati],
Sambuddho-the one who knows by himself, **i.e.** a Buddha [Saṁ+bhuddho].
Note: "ṁ" becomes "m" as it precedes "bh" here.
Sandiṭṭhiko-seen by oneself. [Saṁ+diṭṭhiko]
Note: "ṁ" becomes "n" as it precedes "d" here.

(d) again and again.

e.g. Sandhāvati-(It) runs again and again (from one life to another) [Saṁ+dhāvati],
Note: "ṁ" becomes "n" as it precedes "dh" here.
Saṁsarati-(It) happens again and again [Saṁ+sarati].

(e) Intense, intensifier,

e.g. Sāratto-attached with strong lust or attachment [Saṁ+ratto] **Note:** "saṁ" becomes "sā" here.

• vi

(a) specially,

e.g. Vipassati-(He) sees specially [Vi+passati],
Vipassanā-act of seeing in a special way. **i.e.** Insight meditation [Vi+passanā].

(b) Transformed,

e.g. Vikaroti-(He) makes so that it becomes something else. [Vi+karoti],
Vikati-such an act, a non-natural state [Vi+kati].
Compare >Pakati-natural<vikati-non-natural.
Vimukho-face being changed, the changed face due to unhappiness or anger etc.[Vi+mukho]
Vipatisāro-thinking with guilt, regret [Vi+patisāro]

(c) Variously, in different ways,

e.g. Vimati-various thought, different view, doubt. [Vi+mati]

(d) opposite of, against,

e.g. Vivadati-(He) speaks against, disputes or quarrels [Vi+vadati].
Vivādo-dispute, bickering, conflicting talk [Vi+vādo].
Vya'sanaṁ-ruin, loss [Vi+asanaṁ]

(e) without, out,

e.g. Virajjati-(He) does not crave, detaches [Vi+rajjati].
Virāgo-such an act, detachment [Vi+rāgo].

(f) being off, separated, being apart,

e.g. Viyujjati-(It) does not join, disjoin [Vi+yujjati],
Viyogo-such an act [Vi+yogo],
Vippayutto-disjoined [Vi+pa+yutto]
Vigacchati-goes off, disappears [Vi+gacchati].
Vigamo-such an act [Vi+gamo].

• ava

(a) down, inside,

e.g. Avagacchati-(It) goes down [Ava+gacchati],
Avagamanaṁ-such an act [Ava+gamanaṁ],
Oggacchati, Oggamanaṁ (Same meaning as in previous examples, except that "Ava" changes into "O")
Avagaṇhāti>Oggaṇhāti-(It) submerges, goes down into water etc. or looks into the problem, ponders upon (figuratively used) [Ava+gaṇhāti].
Avagāho-such an act [Ava+gāho].
Osarati>-(He) goes down into water etc. [ava+sarati]

(b) Contemptuously, mean,

e.g. Avajānāti-(He) knows contemptuously, Looks down [Ava+jānāti].
Avamāno-such an act, disdain [Ava+māno].
Avaharati-(He) takes it in a mean manner, steals [Ava+harati].
Avahāro-such an act, stealing [Ava+hāro].

Note: "**Ava**" and "**O**" are two interchangeable *upasagga* words.

◊ anu

(a) At every frequency of time, occurring at certain times, repeatedly (followed by descriptive word of time such as māsa-month, Addhamāsa-half month, dina-day or saṁvacchara-year etc.)

e.g. Anumāsaṁ-every month [Anu+māsaṁ],
Anvaddhamāsaṁ-every half month [Anu+addhamāsaṁ],
Anudinaṁ-every day [Anu+dinaṁ],
Anusaṁvaccharaṁ-every year [Anu+saṁvaccharaṁ].

(b) following, after,

e.g. Anugacchati-(He) goes following, accompanies. [Anu+gacchati],
Anve'ti [Anu+eti] (Same meaning).
Anugati-such an act [Anu+gati].

Anujānāti-(He) knows accordingly as requested, **i.e.** permits [Anu+jānāti].
Anuññā-permission [Anu+ñā],
Anuññāto-allowed, permitted [Anu+ñāto],
Anukūlaṁ-suitable, appropriate, following the course of a person's action [Anu+kūlaṁ].

(c) again and again, repeatedly,
e.g. Anuyuñjati-(He) engages again and again, **i.e.** makes repeated effort, interrogates. [Anu+yuñjati].
Anuyogo-such an act, questioning repeatedly, sustained effort [Anu+yogo].
Anussarati-(He) remembers repeatedly [Anu+sarati].
Anussati-such an act [Anu+sati].
Anumodati-(He) rejoices repeatedly,
Anumodanaṁ, Anumodo-such an act [Anu+modati].
Anusaṁvaṇṇeti-explains again and again, re-explains [Anu+saṁ+vaṇṇeti],
Anusaṁvaṇṇanā-re-explanation, sub-commentary. [Anu+saṁ+vaṇṇanā]

(d) Behind,
e.g. Anurathaṁ-behind chariot or vehicle [Anu+rathaṁ].

(e) alongside, in imitation of.
e.g. Soto nadiṁ anusandati-the current flows along the river [anu+sandati].
Bhagavantaṁ anupavajjiṁsu-(Young Sakyan princes too) ordained in imitating the Buddha [anu+pavajjiṁsu].
Sisso ācariyaṁ anugcchati ca anuvattati ca. The pupil follows teacher and imitates too. [Anu+gacchati] [anu+vattati].

(f) inferior or lower in rank, sub-standard.
e.g. Anutherā-those below senior monks, **i.e.** less-senior monks [Anu+therā].
Anunāyakā-those below senior leaders, **i.e.** less-senior leaders [Anu+nāyakā].

(g) In compliance with, Suitable, being appropriate, favorable, agreeable, according to,
e.g. Anurūpaṁ-suitable, appropriate [Anu+rūpaṁ],
compare>Patirūpaṁ-* suitable [Pati+rūpaṁ],
Anukūlaṁ-suitable, agreeable. following [Anu+kūlaṁ-the bank of a river etc. a figurative expression.],
Compare>Paṭikūlaṁ-disagreeable, unlikable [Paṭi+kūlaṁ. This is also a figurative expression]
Anulomaṁ-in sequential order. [Anu-following+lomaṁ-the hair, a figurative expression.], Compare>Paṭilomaṁ-in reverse order, [Paṭi-against+lomaṁ. This is also a figurative expression]
Anurujjhati-favors, likes [Anu+rujjhati].
Anurodho-favour, agreement [Anu+rodho]
Compare> Virodho-disfavor, dislike

(h) small, in detail
Anubyañjanaṁ-small bodily marks or parts and figure. [Anu+byañjanaṁ]
Anusaṁvaṇṇeti-explains in detail. [Anu+saṁ+vaṇṇeti]

• pari

(a) from all around, round and round, being surrounded.
e.g. Parikkharitvā-having surrounded [Pari+karitvā],
parikkhāro-accessory [Pari+karo],
Paribhāsati-(He) says condescendingly (as in giving instructions or yelling abusive language) [Pari+bhāsati].
Paribhāsā-such an act as a directive or a revilement [Pari+bhāsā],
paricchedati-(He) cuts from all around, sets the limits,
Paricchedo-such an act, limitation, section, chapter [pari+chedati].
Parikhā-moat, dug around the palace premises in ancient times [pari+khā]

(b) overall,
e.g. Parijānāti-(He) knows overall [Pari+jānāti],
Pariññā-overall knowledge [Pari+ñā],

(c) Being dominant,

e.g. Paribhavati-(He) is from all around, dominates, bullies. [Pari+bhavati]

Paribhavo-such an act [Pari+bhavo]

◊ adhi

(a) Up, above, over,

e.g. adhivāseti-(He) let it on him, **i.e.** accepts or enjoys without resisting [adhi+vāseti].

Adhivāsanā-such an act, acceptance of a request or desire etc. [Adhi+vāsanā].

adhiṭhāti-(It) firmly stands, **i.e.** firmly resolves in mind [adhi+ṭhāti].

adhiṭhānaṁ-firm mental resolve, strong decision,

(b) specially, superior, supreme,

e.g. Adhisīlaṁ-superior Sīla [Adhi+sīlaṁ],

Adhirājā-supreme king [Adhi+rājā].

Adhidevatā-supreme deity [Adhi+devatā].

(c) being dominant of, the lord over (usually followed by a noun in locative case when it means being "the lord over" as an independently used word),

E.g. *Adhi* devesu Buddho. The Buddha is supreme lord of deities.

As a prefix to a verb: **e.g.** Adhigahṇāti-(It) takes up all, **i.e.** exceeds [Adhi+gahṇāti].

Adhipati-lord [Adhi+pati],

Ajjhāvasati-(He) lives as a lord or being dominant, reigns. (as a king or chief authority of a location) [Adhi+ā+vasati]

Ajjhāvāso-such an act [Adhi+ā+vāso].

(d) Attain, reach

e.g. adhigacchati-realizes, knows, attains [Adhi+gacchati],

adhigamo-such an act [Adhi+gamo].

(e) deeply,

e.g. adhimuccati-(One) keeps in depth (such as tendencies, thoughts etc.) [adhi+muccati].

adhimutti-such a mental condition, inner tendency or preferences [adhi+mutti].

(f) Excessively, very much

Adhimaññati-(He) thinks highly [Adhi+maññati].
Adhimāno-viewing oneself highly. Extreme self-pride, such as thinking oneself that one has attained a higher state of spiritual progress which is not true. [Adhi+māno].

(g) with regard to, relating to, in connection with,

Adhikicca-concerning. in respect of [adhi+kicca].

• abhi

(a) specially, being special, distinctive,

e.g. Abhijānāti-(One) knows in a special manner. [Abhi+jānāti],
Abhiññā-special knowledge, Psychic powers etc. [Abhi+ñā].
abhidhammo-special Dhamma [abhi+dhamma].

(b) beyond,

e.g. abhikkamati-(It) goes beyond, proceeds, pleased. [abhi+kamati],
Abhikkanto-gone ahead, pleased [abhi+kanto].

(c) Very much, predominantly.

e.g. Abhicchati-(He) wants it very much [Abhi+icchati],
Abhibhavati-(It) dominates [Abhi+bhavati].
Abhibhūto-being overwhelmed [Abhi+bhūto].
Abhirūpo-very beautiful [Abhi+rūpo].
Abhinandati-(He) enjoys or likes very much[Abhi+nandati]
Abhiniggaṇhāti-(It) represses very much, restrains. [Abhi+ni+ggaṇhāti]
Abhijjā-looking beyond, **i.e.** covetousness [Abhi+jā].

(d) towards,

e.g. Abhimukhaṁ-face-ward, toward oneself. [Abhi+mukaṁ].

(e) opposite, recklessly, wrongly.

e.g. Abbhācikkhati-(he) wrongly accuses, says the opposite. [Abhi+ācikkhati].

(f) up, above, upward.

e.g. Abhiruhati-(It) climbs up, grows up (as a tree). [Abhi+ruhati]

Abhisiñjati-(It) pours on, sprinkles on (as on a tree or on the hand or head) [Abhi+siñjati].

Abhiseko-such an act of sprinkling, in times of coronation of kings in ancient times, coronation itself is called "Abhiseka" [Abhi+seko].

◊ pati

(a) again,

e.g. Paccāgacchati-(He) comes back, returns. [Pati+ā+gacchati],

Paccāgamanaṁ-such an act, coming back. [Pati+ā+gamanaṁ].

Note: Refer to Sutta 19 for **Pacca**-function.

Patikaroti-(It) acts back, reacts, cures as with medicine [Pati+karoti]

(b) in response to,

e.g. Patijānāti-(He) knows back, admits [Pati+jānāti].

paṭiññā-such an act, confession, promise. [pati+ñā].

Pativadati-replies or responds. [Pati+vadati]

Patikaroti-reacts, heals (an offence or a disease), repays a gratitude. [Pati+karoti]

Patisuṇāti-listens or responds. [Pati+suṇāti]

pativacanaṁ-reply word, response. [pati+vacanaṁ].

(c) instead of, in exchange for, (usually preceded by the word denoting to be replaced in ablative case)

e.g. Telasmā *pati* ghataṁ dadāti. (Instead of sesame oil, (he) gives ghee). Tilehi *pati* māse dadāti. (Instead of sesame, (he) gives beans)

(d) opposite of, against, contrary to.

e.g. Pativirujjhati-(It) counteracts. opposes [Pati+virujjhati].
Pativirodho-opposition, disfavor [Pati+virodho].
Patipakkho-opposite party [Pati+pakkho],
Patimukhaṁ-facing against, face to face, [Pati+mukhaṁ].
Patisotaṁ-against current, upstream [Pati+sotaṁ].
Pativātaṁ-against the direction of the wind [Pati+vātaṁ].
Patikūlaṁ-disagreeable, unfavorable [Pati+kūlaṁ].

(e) back, Backward,
e.g. Patikkamati-(He) moves back, returns [Pati+kamati],
patikkante-when returned [pati+kante].
patilomaṁ-backward order, reversely [pati+lomaṁ-hair].
Patikkhipati-(He) throws back, rejects [Pati+khipati].
patikkhitto-having thrown back, being rejected, given up on. [Pati+khitto].

(f) Representing, on behalf of, (usually preceded by a word to be represented in ablative case, used as independent word).
e.g. Buddhasmā *pati* Sāriputto Dhammaṁ deseti. **i.e.** Representing Lord Buddha, Venerable Sāriputta teaches Dhamma.

(g) similar to, an imitation of (a fake), being suitable.
e.g. patirūpaṁ-image, suitable [pati+rūpaṁ].

(h) minor parts or limbs of the body such as fingers etc.
e.g. paccaṅgāni-minor parts of the body [pati+aṅgāni].

(i) intensifier,
e.g. Patihaññati-(he) feels hurt, stresses out. [pati+haññati].
Patigho-anger, stress [Pati+gho]
Pativijjhati-knows penetratingly, enlightened [Pati+vijjhati]

• su

(a) well, good,
e.g. Sucaritaṁ-good conduct or action [Su+caritaṁ].
Sugandho-good smell [Su+gandho],
Sujano-good person [Su+jano].
Sugati-good rebirth [Su+gati].

(b) auspicious,
e.g. Sukhaṇo-auspicious moment [Su+khaṇo],

Svāgataṁ-auspicious coming, good coming. **i.e.** Welcome! [Su+ā+gataṁ]

(c) being easy of,

e.g. Sukaraṁ-easy to do [Su+karaṁ],
Sulabaṁ-easy to obtain [Su+labaṁ],
Sujjānaṁ-easy to know [Su+jānaṁ].

(d) abundance,

e.g. Subikkhaṁ-abundance of food. [Su+bikkhaṁ]

◊ ā

(a) till, up to, (Used as an independent word in a sentence)

e.g. *ā* bavaggā-till the uppermost heaven. *ā* Brahmalokā-till the world of Gods.

(b) Modifier affecting opposite meaning of the root it prefixed. in reverse of,

e.g. Gacchati (he) goes>Āgacchati-(He) comes [Ā+gacchati],
Gamanaṁ-going>Āgamanaṁ-coming [Ā+gamanaṁ].
Yāti (he) goes>Āyāti-(He) comes [Ā+yāti],
Dāti-(he) gives. Ādāti-(he) takes.
Dānaṁ- giving>Ādānaṁ-taking.
Neti-(He) carries>Āneti-(He) brings [Ā+neti].

(c) Upward,

e.g. Āruhati-(He) climbs up, [Ā+ruhati]

(d) intensely, firmly, Intensifier.

e.g. Ādānaṁ-Intensely grabbing, clinging. [Ā+dānaṁ]
Āhaññati-(It) hurts intensely. [Ā+haññati]
Āghāto-hurt feelings, grudge. [Ā+ghāto]

• ati

(a) over, very much, excessively.

e.g. Aticchati-(He) wants it very much [Ati+icchati],
Aticchā-such an act [Ati+icchā],
Atirocati-(It) looks very much beautiful, [Ati+rocati].
Atipaṇītaṁ-Very noble, the best. [Ati+Paṇītaṁ]

(b) beyond, transgress, across,

e.g. Atikkamati-(He) moves beyond, transgress [Ati+kamati].
Atikkanto-gone beyond [Ati+kanto].
accayo-act of going beyond, **i.e.** offense, fault. [Accayo=ati+ayo].

◊ **api**

(a) also, too.

e.g. Dhammaṁ api-to the Dhamma also.

(b) even though, although, even if, despite,

e.g. Api Dibbesu Kāmesu-even in divine pleasures (he does not enjoy)

(c) Introducing a Question,

e.g. Api bhante Bhikkam Labittha? Have you got food Venerable Sir?

(d) above, cover up, close on (used as prefix),

Pidahati-(He) closes, covers [Pidahati=api+dahati] (Here, "a" is to be elided always).
Apidhānaṁ-cover of a pot etc. [Api+dhānaṁ].

◊ **apa**

(a) away from, off,

e.g. Apakkamati-(He) moves away [Apa+kamati],
Apagacchati-(It) moves away, disappears [Apa+gacchati].
Apeti (Same) [Apeti=apa+i+ti].
Apaneti-(It) carries off, removes [Apa+neti].
Apanayanaṁ-removal [Apa+nayanam].

(b) do away with, negatively, wrongly.

e.g. Apavadati-(he) negatively says, rejects [Apa+vadati]
Apavādo-verbal rejection of something [Apa+vādo].
Apakaroti-(He) does ungratefully or does away with other's good deed, ignores good-deed received from friends. [Apa+karoti].

Apakāro-improper deed, wrong action, act of ingratitude, [Apa+karo]
Aparajjhati-(He) offends, or sometimes (It) fails to hit the target [Apa+rajjhati].
Aparādho-Fault, offense, failure [Apa+rādho].

• upa

(a) near to, close by, towards.
e.g. Upanisīdati-(He) sits near [Upa+ni+sīdati],
Upanisinno- having sat closely [Upa+ni+sinno].
Upanagaraṁ-Near the city [Upa+nagaraṁ].
Upagacchati-approaches, **i.e.** goes near, toward. [Upa+gacchati].
Upapajjati-closely happens, **i.e.** conceives or born. [Upa+pajjati].
Upapatti-conception or birth [Upa+patti].
(b) Firmly. Intensifier
e.g. Upādānaṁ-clinging [Upa+ā+dānaṁ].
(c) Up, high (as in good-willed act, attaining a high condition etc.),
e.g. Upakaroti-highly acts, **i.e.** helps [Upa+karoti].
Upakāro-such an act, a good-willed help (done usually by parents, good friends etc. [Upa+karo].
Upasampajjati-attains higher state [Upa+saṁ+pajjati].
Upasampanno-having attained a higher state [Upa+saṁ+panno].
Note: "ṁ" becomes "m" as it precedes "p".
(d) Allegation
e.g. Upavadati-(He) speaks closely, **i.e.** accuses. [Upa+vadati].
Upavādo-accusation [Upa+vado].
(e) deputy or assistant or the second in rank. subordinate,
e.g. Uparājā-the crown prince [Upa+rājā].
Upaukkaṭho-vice-chairman [Upa+ukkaṭho]

(f) over, exceeds (usually followed by a locative word in its context denoting the lesser amount or value)
e.g. *Upa* khāriyaṁ doṇo. A measure of "doṇa" is in excess of a "khāri".

Translation of the Examples

Having explained the meanings of *Upasagga* particles in some detail, it is now more simple and easy for the students to figure out and understand the meaning of ***Upasagga*-prefixed nouns in Kita-affixes shown as examples** in this Sutta. The following is a translation of the example words of Sutta:

- pahāro-carrying (instruments of harm) specially, **i.e.** beating, striking [**pa**-specially+hara-carrying]
- parābhavo-loss, ruin. [**parā**-opposite+bhava-to be, being=ruin, loss]
- nihāro, • nīhāro-taking out, evicting, [**ni**-out+hara-carrying] (Both **ni** and **nī** are the same)
- uhāro-carrying up, [**u**-up+hara-carrying]
- duhāro-carrying badly, [**du**-bad+hara-carrying]
- saṁhāro-carrying well, [**saṁ**-well+hara-carrying]
- vihāro-carrying one's body specially, staying, [**vi**-specially+hara-carrying. **i.e.** act of staying at a place using alternating bodily modes]
- avahāro-carrying in a mean manner, **i.e.** stealing, [**ava**-lowly, contemptuous, mean+hara-carrying]
- anuhāro-carrying accordingly, [**anu**-following, subsequent+hara-carrying]
- parihāro-carrying from all around, [**pari**-all around+hara-carrying]
- adhihāro-carrying nicely, [**adhi**-specially, nicely+hara-carrying]
- abhihāro-carrying toward, [**abhi**-toward+hara-carrying]
- patihāro-carrying again, [**pati**-again+hara-carrying]
- suhāro-carrying well, [**su**-well+hara-carrying]
- āhāro-carrying toward, food or meal, [**ā**-toward+hara-carrying]
- atihāro-carrying beyond or excessively, [**ati**-beyond, excessive+hara-carrying]
- apihāro-carrying down, [**api**-downward+hara-carrying]

• apahāro-carrying outward, **i.e.** removing, [**apa**-out, away+hara-carrying]

• upahāro-carrying toward proximity, bringing up closer, [**upa**-near, close to+hara-carrying. Complementary gift etc.]

THE *NIPĀTA* PARTICLES

The ***Nipāta*** words or particles are many and varied throughout Pāli literature. They are so called as they can be found placed in the beginning, in the middle or at the end of sentences and words, but not as the prefixes of the roots. [**Ni√pata**-to fall. **i.e.** to be placed anywhere]. However, there are quite a few Nipāta particles which are placed before some verbs or Kita-affixed nouns and similarly used like prefixes. Here are a few of them:
Antra-between, **Āvi, Pātu**-vividly, clearly. **Sacchi**-being a witness to, together. **Vinā**-without, being apart. **Saha**-together. **Puna**-again.

Examples in front of the roots and verbs:
(1) **Antra**dhāyati-(he) disappears. [Antra+dhāyati]
(2) **Āvi**karoti-(he) makes it openly, displays clearly. [Āvi+karoti]
(3) **Pātu**bhavati-(It) arises visibly, **i.e.** appears. [Pātu+bhavati]
(4) **Sacchi**karoti-(he) realizes, **i.e.** attains. All are ***āv*** [Sacchi+karoti]
Examples in front of various nouns:
(5) **Vinā**bhāvo-separation, being apart. ***kn*** [Vinā+bhāvo]
(6) **Saha**cārī-the one who used be together, a friend. ***kn*** [Saha+cārī]
(7) **Puna**bbhavo-being born again, rebirth. ***kn*** [Puna+bhavo]

The following is a brief descriptive list of some *Nipāta* words shown in this Sutta. **Some are plain** *Nipātas* without any affix, **while some are with indeclinable affixes. Some may even have a sort of vibatti-ending** in them. Any vibatti applied after most of the *Nipāta* words are generally elided. As a rare exception, some may still have traces of vibattis. Please note that the implied meaning of elided vibatti still remain in effect for some *Nipāta* words such as **yathā, tathā and evaṁ** etc. To gain mastery of the language, the students should also study the meanings and usage of both *Upasagga* and *nipāta* words in addition to the general aspects of grammar.

• Yathā, • tathā-in a manner that, in such a way as [A combination of Sabbanāma noun "**ya**" "**ta**" with indeclinable affix "**thā**"**.** The affix itself is expressive of manner or mood.]

• evaṁ-thus, in this way, True as it is said, Yes. (Many meanings) [This *Nipāta* is used in accusative-case ending "**aṁ**", very frequently used in Pāli texts.]

- khalu-Used mostly in a reported narrative.
- kho, a plain *Nipāta*, mostly meaningless, but found often in main Buddhist texts. Used together with "**atha**" "**evaṁ**" "**taṁ**" etc. Sometimes it may mean "only, really".
- tatra-there, [A combination of Sabbanāma noun "**ta**" with indeclinable affix "**tra**".]
- atho-in addition, besides,
- atha-now, then, later on, if. [Sometimes used in the beginning of a chapter or an episode, as an introductory or initiating word]
- hi-really, for, only. [Sometimes a meaningless particle.]
- tu-In addition, only. [Also an expletive without meaning, sometimes added to be more emphatic in a statement.]
- ca-also, too,[It is used to express some additional meaning in grammatical texts. Sometimes meaningless. Sometimes it has a lot of meanings when used after other *nipāta* particles]
- vā-Similar to either or, in other ways. [In grammatical texts, sometimes it is used to express other option or method or inconsistency of a function. Sometimes with no particular meaning.]
- vo-you, [It is sometimes a meaningless expletive.]
- haṁ, • ahaṁ, the use of these two *nipāta* are seldom found in texts unless it means "I".
- alaṁ-is widely used to express:
  (a) enough, **(b)** suitable, **(c)** worthiness, **(d)** appropriateness, **(e)** ability. Also, **(f)** sometimes used as a prohibition or rejection, usually used in combination with (1) **noun in instrumental case**, or (2) **tuṁ-infinitive *Kita* verbs** or (3) an **āya-infinitive in Dative case** nouns.
- eva, equal to "only", used next to the word it want to modify or restrict or confirm in its implied meaning. [A plain *Nipāta*.]
- ho, • aho, these are expression of interjection or surprise. No vibatti.
- he, • ahe, • re, • are. Vocative *Nipāta* particles, similar to "**hey**" in English. Usually vocative case Vibatti is applicable, but to be elided.

Eva'mādīhi nipātehi ca yojetabbāni.
Thus, after such and other *nipāta* words too, the function of this Sutta (**i.e.** elision of the applied vibattis) should be applied.

Caggahaṇa'mavadhāraṇa'tthaṁ.
The word "ca" in Sutta has a purpose of affirming the function of the Sutta.

२२२, ३४२. पुमस्स लिङ्गादीसु समासेसु
222, 342. **Pumassa liṅgā'dīsu samāsesu.**

[Pumassa+liṅga-ādīsu+samāsesu. 3 words]

[V] **Puma**-iccetassa anto lopa'māpajjate liṅgā'dīsu parapadesu samāsesu.

When the word "puma (male) " is joined in a compound process with other words (such as **liṅga, bhāva, kokila,**) in a samāsa, the last component vowel **"a"** of **"ma"** in the word **"puma"** is to be elided. [After elision, only "pum" will remain.]

(See example words shown below. See that after "a" is elided, "m" also changed into either **ṅ** or **m.** See the underlined words in the examples which derives from it. This function is almost similar to Sutta 31. If "**k** or **g**" is next, then change "**m**" into "**ṅ**". If "**bh**", then change it into "**m**". It is quite simple and easy to understand. The function is shown underlined)

• Pulliṅgaṁ-male manner, • pumbhāvo-malehood, • puṅkokilo-male Koel bird, also called black cuckoo. ***Cn, ns.***

Pumasse'ti kimatthaṁ?

What is the word "pumassa" for? To show that examples below are inapplicable as they do not have the word "puma" in them.

* Itthiliṅgaṁ-feminine manner/gender, * napuṁsakaliṅgaṁ-neuter manner/neuter gender. ***Cn, ns.***

Liṅgādīsū'ti kimatthaṁ?

What is the word "liṅgādisu" for? To show that example below is inapplicable as it does not have the word "liṅga".

* Pumitthī-male, female. ***Cn, ns.***

Samāsesū'ti kimatthaṁ?

What is the word "samāsesu" for? To show that example below is inapplicable as it is not a compound noun word (samāsa). (It is only an incomplete sentence)

* Pumassa-of male. ***gs.*** liṅgaṁ-appearance. ***ns.***

२२३, १८८. अं यमीतो पसञ्ञतो
223, 188. **Aṁ ya'mīto pasaññato.**

[Aṁ+yaṁ+īto+pasaññato. 4 words]

[V] **Aṁ**vacanassa **yaṁ** hoti vā **ī**to **pa**saññato.

The dutiyā singular vibatti "**aṁ**", applied after **pa**-named, "**ī**-ending nouns of feminine gender, sometimes changes into "**yaṁ**". [This Sutta changes accusative, singular "**aṁ**" into "**yaṁ**". See "**yaṁ**" shown underlined in the example. The second is inapplicable.]

• Itthi<u>yaṁ</u>, * itthiṁ-to the woman. ***as.***

Pasaññato'ti kimatthaṁ?
What is the word "pasaññato" for? To show that examples below are inapplicable as they are not pa-termed nouns. (The ending "ī" of these nouns is a "jha", not "pa". Hence, inapplicable)
* Daṇḍinaṁ-to the one having stick.
* Bhoginaṁ-to the one having wealth. ***tn*** in ***as.***

Ami'ti kimatthaṁ? What is the word "aṁ" for? To show that example below is inapplicable as it is not of "aṁ-vibatti".
* Itthīhi-with/by/from women. ***ip, abp.***

२२४, १५३. नं झतो कतरस्सा
224, 153. **Naṁ jhato katarassā.**

[Naṁ+jhato+katarassā. 3 words]

[V] Tasmā **jha**to katarassā **aṁ**vacanassa **naṁ** hoti.

The vibatti "**aṁ**" applied after nouns ending in jha-named "**ī**" but later shortened into an "i", sometimes changes into a "**naṁ**". [This Sutta changes accusative singular **aṁ** into **naṁ** after "**ī**" is shortened by Sutta 84. The applied function "**naṁ**" is shown underlined below]

• Daṇḍi<u>naṁ</u>, • bhogi<u>naṁ</u>. (Refer Sutta 223 for meaning)

Jhato'ti kimatthaṁ?
What is the word "jhato" for? To show that example below

is inapplicable as it does not have a jha-termed " ī ". (It has only a "la-termed ū".)
* Vessabhuṁ-to the Buddha named "Vessabū". ***as.***

Katarassā'ti kimatthaṁ?
What is the word "katarassā" for?
To show that the example below is inapplicable as it has a natural rassa (akatarassa). (This Sutta's function is applicable for only those nouns with morphologically altered rassa).
* Kucchiṁ-to the stomach. ***as.***

२२५, १५१. योनं नो

225, 151. **Yonaṁ no.** [Yonaṁ+no. 2 words]

[V] Sabbesaṁ **yo**naṁ **jha**to katarassā **no** hoti.

The vibatti "**yo**" applied after **jha**-named "**ī-**ending" nouns and later shortened into "i", changes into "**no**".
[This Sutta changes "**yo**" into "**no**" after Rassa process by Sutta No. 84. See "**no**" function shown underlined below]

[Nominative "yo"] • Daṇḍino-those having sticks
• bhogino-those having wealth, Wealthy, ***np, ap.***
[Vocative "yo"] He • daṇḍino-Oh those having sticks!,
He • bhogino-Oh wealthy! ***vp.***

Katarassā'ti kimatthaṁ?
What is the word "katarassā" for? To show that examples below are inapplicable as they have a natural rassa(akatarassa).
* Aggayo, * munayo, * isayo.

Jhato'ti kimatthaṁ?
What is the word "jhato" for? To show that example below is inapplicable as it does not have a jha-termed " ī ". (The example has only a "la-termed ū".)
* Sayambhuno ***np, ap.***

Yonan'ti kimatthaṁ?
What is the word "yonaṁ" for? To show that examples

below are inapplicable as they are not of "yo". (It is only a "nā" vibatti in both examples)
* Daṇḍinā-with the one who has stick,
* bhoginā-with wealthy one. ***is.***

२२६, १५४. स्मिं नि

226, 154. **Smiṁ ni.** [Smiṁ+ni. 2 words]

[V] Tasmā **jha**to katarassā **smiṁ**vacanassa **ni**-ādeso hoti.

The vibatti "**smiṁ**" applied after **jha**-named "**ī-**ending" nouns and later shortened into "i", changes into "**ni**". [This Sutta changes "**smiṁ**" into "**ni**" which is applied after **jha**-termed, **ī**-ending nouns, after ī has been shortened by Sutta No.84]

• Daṇḍini-in the one having stick, • Bhogini-in wealthy one. ***ls.***

Katarassā'ti kimatthaṁ?
What is the word "katarassā" for? To show that example below is inapplicable as it has a natural rassa (akatarassa).
* Vyādhimhi-at disease/sickness. ***ls.***

२२७, २७०. किस्स क वे च

227, 270. **Kissa ka ve ca.** [Kissa+ka+ve+ca. 4 words]

[V] **Ki'm**icce'tassa **ko** ca hoti **va-**paccaye pare.

The interrogative sabbanāma noun "**kiṁ** (what) " changes into "**ka**" when a "**va**" affix is applied after it.
[See changed "k" shown underlined below.]

• Kva-where. ***ind.*** gato'si [gato'si=gato+asi] Gato-gone. ***kn.*** Asi-is. ***āv.*** tvaṁ-you. devānaṁ piyatissa-King devānaṁ piya tissa! **i.e.** Where did you go King Devānaṁ Piyatissa?

Caggahaṇena **a-va**paccaye pare'pi **ko** ca hoti.

By the word "Ca" in Sutta, "kiṁ" can also be changed into "ka" when **non-va** affixes such as "**htaṁ**" and other ordinary vibattis are applied after "kiṁ". [See changed "k" of "kiṁ" shown underlined below.]

[Kiṁ in "**Si**" Vibatti Example] • Ko-who. ***ns.*** taṁ-to that person. ***as.***

ninditu'marahati. [ninditu'marahati= nindituṁ+arahati] nindituṁ-for blaming, censuring. ***kv.*** arahati-deserves. ***āv.*** **i.e.** Who deserves to blame that person?

[kiṁ in **thaṁ**-affix] • Kathaṁ-how. ***ind.*** bodhayituṁ-to enlighten or to made known. ***kv.*** dhammaṁ-Dhamma. ***as.*** **i.e.** How one should make Dhamma known?

Ve'ti kimatthaṁ?

What is the word "ve" for? To show that example below is inapplicable as it does not have a "va" affix in it. [It means that there is no function in case of **to**-affixed words such as "kato" etc. Instead, another function of changing into "ku" etc. is applicable]

* Kuto-Whence, from where. ***ind.*** āgato'si [āgatosi=āgato+asi] āgato=come. ***kn*** in ***ns.*** asi-is?. ***āv.*** tvaṁ-you. ***ns.*** **i.e.** Where did you come from?.

२२८, २७२. कु हिंहंसु च

228, 272. **Ku hiṁ, haṁ, su ca.** [Ku+hiṁ, haṁ, su+ca. 3 words]

[V] **Kiṁ**'icce'tassa **ku** hoti **hiṁ, haṁ,** icce'tesu ca.

The interrogative sabbanāma noun "**kiṁ**" changes into "**ku**" when "**hiṁ, haṁ**" affixes follow after it (**i.e.** applied after it). [See changed "ku" of "kiṁ" shown underlined below.]

- Kuhiṁ-Where. ***ind.*** gacchasi-(do you) go?. ***āv.*** **i.e.** Where do you go?
- Kuhaṁ, ***ind.*** gacchasi. ***āv.*** (The same meaning)

Caggahaṇena **hiñcanaṁ, dācanaṁ**-paccayesu paresu aññatthā'pi **ku** hoti.

By means of "Ca", "kim" can also change into into "ku" when affixed with "**hiñcanaṁ, dācanaṁ**".

[See changed "ku" of "kiṁ" shown underlined]

• Kuhiñcanaṁ. • Kudācanaṁ-occasionally, in no time. ***ind.***

२२९, २२६. सेसेसु च

229, 226. **Sesesu ca.** [Sesesu+ca. 2 words]

[V] **Kiṁ**'icce'tassa **k**o hoti sesesu vibhattipaccayesu paresu.

The interrogative sabbanāma noun "**kiṁ**" changes into "**ka**" when followed by the remaining vibatti and affixes.

[Ko-what. pakāro-manner?.] • kathaṁ-how, what manner?, [kaṁ-to what. pakāraṁ-manner?] • kathaṁ-how, to what manner?. ***ind.***

Note: The words shown within bracket are called "**Viggaha**" or etymological definition or expansion of the example word in the grammatical analysis known as "Viggaha". Here, **Ka** is expanded by "**Ko**" a nominative singular while "**thaṁ**" is expanded by the word "**pakāro**" which means that the indeclinable affix **thaṁ** here signifies manner. In the second Viggaha, the expansion is shown by using accusative singular for both components with the same meaning. Finally, when these two words are combined, it becomes **Kathaṁ** which means "which manner" "how".

Caggahaṇa'manukaḍḍhana'tthaṁ.
The word "ca" in Sutta has a purpose of pulling in "the **ka**-changing function" from Sutta 227 to this Sutta.

२३०, २६२. त्र तो थेसु च

230, 262. **Tra, to, the, su ca.** [Tra, to, the, su+ca. 2 words]

[V] **Kim**icce'tassa **ku** hoti **tra, to, tha,** icce'tesu ca.

The interrogative sabbanāma noun "**kim**" changes into "**ku**" when affixed with "**tra, to, tha** affixes".
[See changed "ku" of "kiṁ" shown underlined below.]

• <u>Ku</u>tra-where, • <u>Ku</u>to-from where, for what reason, why [2 meanings] • <u>Ku</u>ttha-where. ***ind.***

Caggahaṇa'manukaḍḍhana'tthaṁ.
The word "ca" in Sutta has a purpose of pulling in the word "Kissa" from Sutta No.227, and "ku-changing function" from Sutta No.228 to this Sutta. ["Ca" thus pulls two things from the preceding Suttas to this Sutta]

२३१, २६३. सब्बस्सेतस्साकारो वा

231, 263. **Sabbasse'tassa'kāro vā.**

[Sabbassa+etassa+akāro+vā. 4 words]

[V] Sabbassa **eta**saddassa **a**kāro hoti vā **to, tha**-icce'tesu.

The entire sabbanāma noun "**eta** (that) " sometimes changes into "**a**" when affixed with "**to, tha**". [See changed "a" of "eta" shown underlined below]

• A̲to-thence, for that reason, • A̲ttha-there, at that place,
* Etto, * Ettha. ***ind.*** (Inapplicable examples of the same meaning)

२३२, २६७. त्रे निच्चं

232, 267. **Tre niccaṁ.** [Tre+niccaṁ. 2 words]

[V] Sabbassa **eta**saddassa **a**kāro hoti niccaṁ **tra**-paccaye pare.

The entire sabbanāma noun word "**eta**" always changes into "**a**" when affixed with "**tra**". [This means that "atra" not "etra" is a consistent pattern. See changed "a" of "eta" shown underlined]

• A̲tra-there, at that place or position. ***ind.***

२३३, २६४. ए तोथेसु च

233, 264. **E to, the, su ca.** [E+to, the, su+ca. 3 words]

[V] Sabbassa **eta**saddassa **e**kāro hoti vā **to, tha**-icce'tesu.

The whole sabbanāma word "**eta**" sometimes changes into "**e**" when affixed with "**to, tha**".
[See changed "e" of "eta" shown underlined]

• Etto, * ato-from therc, • e̲ttha, * attha-at that place, there. ***ind.***

२३४, २६५. इमस्सि थं दानि ह तो धेसु च

234, 265. **Imassi'thaṁ, dāni, ha, to, dhe, su ca.** [Imassa+i+thaṁ, dāni, ha, to, dhe, su+ca. 4 words]

[V] **Ima**saddassa sabbasse'va **i**kāro hoti
thaṁ, dāni, ha, to, dha-icce'tesu.

The whole sabbanāma word "**ima** (this) " changes into "**i**" when affixed with "**thaṁ, dāni, ha, to, dha**". [This Sutta changes "**ima**" which is suffixed with "**thaṁ, dāni, ha, to, dha**" affixes into "**i**". See changed "i" of "ima" shown in bold, underlined below.]

- **I**tthaṁ-in this manner, thus [one dissimilar "t" reduplicated].
- **i**dāni-now, at this moment. • **i**ha-here, at this place.
- **i**to-from here. • **i**dha-here, at this place, in this world. ***ind.***

२३५, २८१. अ धुनाम्हि च

235, 281. **A dhunāmhi ca.** [A+dhunāmhi+ca. 3 words]

[V] **Ima**saddassa sabbasse'va **a**kāro hoti **dhunā**mhi paccaye pare.

The entire sabbanāma word "**ima**" changes into "**a**" when affixed with "**dhunā**".
[See changed "a" of "ima" shown underlined below]

- Adhunā-now, at this moment, nowadays. ***ind.***

Caggahaṇa'mavadhāraṇa'tthaṁ.
The word "ca" has a purpose of affirming the function of the Sutta as being consistent.

२३६, २८०. एत रहिम्हि

236, 280. **Eta rahimhi.** [Eta+rahimhi. 2 words]

[V] Sabbasse'va **ima**saddassa **etā**'deso hoti **rahi**mhi paccaye pare.
The whole sabbanāma word "**ima**" changes into "**eta**" when affixed with "**rahi**".
[See changed "eta" of "ima" shown underlined below.]

- Etarahi-now, at this time, in this moment, nowadays. ***ind.***

२३७, १७६. इत्थिय मतो आपच्चयो

237, 176. **Itthiya'mato āpaccayo.**

[Itthiyaṁ+ato+āpaccayo. 3 words]

[V] Itthiyaṁ vattamānāya **a**kārato **ā**paccayo hoti.

An "**ā**" affix has to be added to all a-ending nouns when signifying the feminine gender. (See the affix "**ā**" shown underlined below)

• Sabbā-all. • yā-which. • sā-that. • kā-what/what woman.
• Katarā-which. ***ns.***

Note: This affix "**ā**" and "**ī**" "**inī**" affixes signify feminine gender. The affix "**ī**" is applied by next two Suttas 238-239 while "**inī**" is applied by Sutta 240.

२३८, १८७. नदादितो वा ई

238, 187. **Nadā'dito vā ī.** [Nada-ādito+vā+ī. 3 words]

[V] Nadā'dito vā anadā'dito vā itthiyaṁ vattamānāya **ī**-paccayo hoti.

To signify feminine gender, an "**ī**" affix should be applied after "**nadī** (river) " and other words.
(See the affix "**ī**" shown in bold, underlined below)

• Nad**ī**-river. • mah**ī**-earth. • kumār**ī**-unmarried girl. • taruṇ**ī**-young female. • sakh**ī**-female friend. • itth**ī**-woman. ***ns.***

२३९, १९०. णव णिक णेय्य णन्तुहि

239, 190. **Ṇava, ṇika, ṇeyya, ṇa, ntu, hi.**

[Ṇava, ṇika, ṇeyya, ṇa, ntu, hi. 1 word]

[V] **Ṇava, ṇika, ṇeyya, ṇa, ntu,** icce'tehi itthiyaṁ vattamānehi **ī**-paccayo hoti.

To signify feminine gender of the nouns already affixed with **Ṇava, ṇika, ṇeyya, ṇa, ntu,** affixes, one more vowel "**i**" is to be added after them. (See the affix "**ī**" shown in bold, underlined below)

[Ṇava-affixed example] • Māṇav**ī**-the daughter of Manu,
• paṇḍav**ī**- the daughter of Paṇḍu.
[Ṇika-affixed] • nāvik**ī**-boatman's wife.
[Ṇeyya-affixed] • venateyy**ī**- the daughter of Vinatā.
• kunteyy**ī**- the daughter of Kunti.
[Ṇa-affixed] • gotam**ī**- the daughter of Gotama.
[ntu-affixed] • guṇavat**ī**-the virtuous lady [**guṇa**-virtue+**vatī**-the woman who has].
• sāmāvat**ī**-the woman who has golden color of skin, [**sāmā**-golden complexion+**vatī**-the woman who has] (all ***ns.***)

२४०, १९३. पतिभिक्खुराजीकारन्तेहि इनी

240, 193. Pati, bhikkhu, rājī'kārantehi inī.

[Pati, bhikkhu, rājī'kārantehi+inī. 2 words]

[V] **Pati, bhikkhu, rājī'**kāra'ntehi itthiyaṁ vattamānehi **inī**paccayo hoti.

To signify feminine gender, an " **inī**" affix is to be added after **Pati, bhikkhu, rāja** and other **ī**-ending nouns. (See the affix "**inī**" shown in bold, underlined below. There is some morphological change in the first two examples)

• Gahapatā**nī**-the female lord of the house, housewife.
• bhikkhu**nī**-female monk. • rāj**inī**-wife of someone of royal blood.
• hatth**inī**-she-elephant. • daṇḍ**inī**-the woman who has a stick.
• medhāv**inī**-woman-scholar. • tapass**inī**-female-ascetic.
(all examples are ***ns.***)

२४१, १९१. न्तुस्स त मीकारे

241, 191. Ntussa ta'mīkāre. [Ntussa+taṁ+īkāre. 3 words]

[V] Sabbasse'va **ntu**paccayassa **t**-kāro hoti vā **ī**kāre pare.

When an "**ī**" affix is applied after a **ntu**-suffixed feminine gender noun, that whole "**ntu**" shall change to become a single "**t**". (Later, that "**t**" has to be attached to "**ī**"). [See each pair shown below. The second is inapplicable. "**tī** & **ntī**" are shown in bold to make it easily understandable]

- Guṇavatī, * guṇavantī-the virtuous woman.(all examples are ***ns.***)
- kulavatī, * kulavantī-a lady of prestigious family.
- satimatī. * Satimantī-the woman who has "**sati**-alertness".
- mahatī, * mahantī-the noble or great woman.
- gottamatī, * gottamantī-the woman who has high caste, woman of high caste (by being born into it).

२४२, १९२. भवतो भोतो

242, 192. **Bhavato bhoto.** [Bhavato+bhoto. 2 words]

[V] Sabbasse'va **bhavanta**saddassa **bhotā'**deso hoti īkāre itthigate pare.

The whole word **bhavanta-**(your honorable), changes to "**bhota**" when a feminine-gender "**ī**" affix follows it. (See Sutta No.238 for affix "**ī**". The example is only the word "Bhoti", not accompanying words. The affix "**ī**" is shortened which later becomes "Bhoti".)

- Bhoti ayye, • bhoti kaññe, • bhoti kharādiye. ***vs.***

(Refer to Sutta No.57 for the meaning of examples.)
Note: The word "Bhoti" is a polite form of address to a female.

२४३, ११०. भो गे तु

243, 110. **Bho ge tu.** [Bho+ge+tu. 3 words]

[V] Sabbasse'va **bhavanta**saddassa **bho-**ādeso hoti ge pare.

When vocative singular "**si**" vibatti follows, the whole of the word **bhavanta** changes to "**bho**". (The example is only the word "Bho", not accompanying words in vocative case.)

- Bho purisa-Oh man! • bho aggi-Oh fire! • bho rāja-Oh king!
- bho sattha-Oh teacher! • bho daṇḍi-Oh the one who has stick!
- bho sayambhu-Oh self-enlightened Buddha! ***vs.***

Note: "**Bho**" is a vocative particle used before nouns of masculine gender, while "**Bhoti**" is used for the nouns of feminine gender.

Ge'ti kimatthaṁ?
What is the word "ge" for?
To show that examples below are inapplicable as they are

not "ga-termed si". They are of "nā" and ordinary "si" vibattis.

* Bhavatā-by your honor, ***is.*** * bhavaṁ-your honor. ***ns.***

[22]**Tu**ggahaṇena aññasmim'pi vacane sabbassa **bhavanta**saddassa **bhonta, bhante, bhonto, bhadde, bhotā, bhoto,** icce'te ādesā honti.

---

१०९. ओभावो क्वचि योसु वकारस्स.

[22] 109. **Obhāvo kvaci yosu vakārassa.**

[Obhāvo+kvaci+yosu+vakārassa. 4 words]

[V] **Bhavanta-**iccetassa **va**karassa **o**-bhavo hoti kvaci yo-iccetesu.

The "va" of "bhavanta" optionally changes into "**o**" when "yo" is applied after the bhavanta.

[Function is shown in bold, underlined. It is easily understandable]

Imam-this stuff. ***as***. • Bh**o**nto-your venerable. ***np***. nisāmetha-keep it back or keep in mind. **i.e.** restore this stuff (in its original place in an orderly manner) or keep in mind (by listening attentively. Two possible meanings)

* Bhavanto-your honorable. ***np. ap.*** [This is inapplicable example]

१११. भदन्तस्स भद्दन्त,भन्ते.

111. **Bhadantassa Bhaddanta, bhante.**

[Bhadantassa+Bhaddanta, bhante. 2 words]

[V] Sabbasse'va **bhadanta-**saddassa **bhaddanta, bhante**-iccete ādesā honti kvaci ge pare yosu ca.

The whole word "**bhadanta**-your honorable" optionally changes into either **Bhaddanta** or **Bhante** when "a vocative singular ga-termed si' or "yo" is applied after it.

He • Bhaddanta! ***vs. vp.*** • Bhante-Oh, Your honorable, or venerables! ***vs. vp.***

* Bhaddantā-Your honorables or venerables. ***np, ap.*** vā-also in noun word "bhadanta" of "yo". (Inapplicable example)

By the word "tu" in Sutta, the word "**Bhavanta**" can also change into " **bhonta, bhante, bhonto, bhadde, bhotā, bhoto**" in cases of other vibattis.

- Bhonta, ***vs.*** • bhante, ***vs. vp.*** • bhonto-honorable sir!, ***vs. vp. np, ap.***
- bhadde-Oh honorable lady, madam!, ***vs.***
- bhotā-by honorable. ***is.*** • bhoto-of honorable person. ***ds, gs.***

Note: Some of the functions applicable by means of **"tu"** are quite similar to the two Suttas mentioned in Rūpasiddhi and in earlier version of the text though not found in Myanmar and Sri Lanka versions. **See those two Suttas together with complete translation shown in the footnote.**

The Different Usages

of Vocative Form "Bhavanta".

(1) **Bhante** is generally used when addressing monks and ascetics.

(2) **Bhonta, Bhonto** are forms of both vocative particle and nominative plural used to address general class of people as a polite form of address.

(3) **Bhadde** is specifically used for addressing women of respect and to politely address one's wife or any woman.

२४४, ७२. अकारपिताद्यन्तान मा

244, 72. **Akārapitādya'ntāna'mā.**

[Akāra, pitu-ādi-antānaṁ+ā. 2 words]

[V] Akāro ca pitādīna'manto ca **a**tta'māpajjate ge pare.

The component vowels "**a, u**" of words like Purisa (man), pitu (father) etc., changes to "**ā**" when a vocative singular ga-named "**si**" vibatti is applied after it. (See the applied "**ā**" shown in bold, underlined below)

Bho • puris**ā**-Oh man! Bho • rāj**ā**-Oh king! Bho • pit**ā**-Oh father! Bho • māt**ā**-Oh mother! Bho • satth**ā**-Oh teacher! ***vs.***

२४५, १५२. झलपा रस्सं

245, 152. **Jha, la, pā rassaṁ.** [Jha, la, pā+rassaṁ. 2 words]

[V] **Jha, la, pa,** icce'te rassa'māpajjante ge pare.

The "**ī, ū**" of **jha, la, pa**-named, "ī, ū-ending nouns are to be shortened when a vocative singular "**si**" vibatti is applied after them.

(See the shortened "**i-u**" shown in bold, underlined)

Bho • daṇḍ**i**-Oh the one who has stick!

Bho • sayambh**u**-Oh self-enlightened Buddha!

Bhoti • itth**i**-Oh woman! Bhoti • vadh**u**-Oh daughter-in-law! ***vs.***

२४६, ७३. आकारो वा

246, 73. **Ākāro vā.** **[Ākāro+vā. 2 words]**

[V] Ākāro rassa'māpajjate vā ge pare.

The morpheme vowel "**ā**" of nouns (prescribed in Sutta No.244) is shortened into "**a**" sometimes when a vocative singular "**si**" vibatti is applied after it.

(Both examples in each pair are in vocative, one with a shortened "**a**", shown in bold, underlined and the other not shortened, inapplicable example)

Bho • rāj**a**, * Bho rājā-Oh king!

Bho • att**a**, * Bho attā-Oh body or soul!

Bho • sakh**a**, * Bho sakhā-Oh friend!

Bho • satth**a**, * Bho satthā-Oh teacher! ***vs.***

Iti nāmakappe catuttho kaṇḍo.

The Fourth Section of Noun ends.

Pañcama Kaṇḍa
The Fifth Section

२४७, २६१. त्वादयो विभत्तिसञ्ञायो
247, 261. **Tvā'dayo vibhattisaññāyo.**
[To-ādayo+vibhattisaññāyo. 2 words]

[V] **To-**ādi yesaṁ paccayānaṁ, te honti **tvā'dayo**.
[This is a Bahubbīhi Samāsa ED of the word "tvā'dayo"]
Te paccayā tvā'dayo vibhattisaññā'va daṭṭhabbā.

All the indeclinable affixes such as "**to**"(pronounce as "taw") etc, are to be regarded as equals to the ordinary vibattis applied after ordinary nouns.
[This means that those affixes have the same grammatical role of providing various meanings such as locative, ablative and so on in the same way just as the ordinary **vibattis** do although they may assume morphologically unchanged forms. See the examples below to clarify this. See "**to, dā, dha**" **and** "**dāni**" affixes shown underlined in the examples.]

[**to**-affixed] • Sabbato-from all, • yato-from which, • tato-from that, • kuto-from where?, • ato-from that, • ito-from here,
[**dhā**-affixed] • sabbadā-at all times, always, • yadā- at which time, • tadā-at that time, then, • kadā-which time, when?
[**dha**-affixed] • idha-here, at this place, at this point,
[**dāni**-affixed] • idāni-now, at this time, at this moment. ***ind.***

२४८, २६०. क्वचि तो पञ्चम्यत्थे
248, 260. **Kvaci to pañcamya'tthe.**
[Kvaci+to+pañcamī-atthe. 3 words]

[V] Kvaci **to-**paccayo hoti pañcamya'tthe.

The "**to**" affix is sometimes to be affixed after various nouns in the sense of pañcamī vibatti (ablative case).

• Sabbato, • yato, • tato, • kuto, • ato, • ito. ***ind.***

Kvacī'ti kimatthaṁ?
What is the word "kvaci" for?

To show that the examples below are inapplicable as the word "kvaci" restricts the function of this Sutta on some words like those shown.
It means that in addition to indeclinable affixes, ordinary vibattis are also applicable after Sabbanāma nouns. See "smā" applied after them.
* Sabbasmā-from all, * imasmā-from this. ***abs.***

२४९, २६६. त्र थ सत्तमिया सब्बनामेहि

249, 266. **Tra, tha, sattamiyā sabbanāmehi.**
[Tra, tha+sattamiyā+sabbanāmehi. 3 words]

[V] **Tra, tha,** icce'te paccayā honti sattamya'tthe sabbanāmehi.

The "**tra, tha**" affix are applied after various sabbanāma nouns in the sense of locative (Sattamī vibatti).
[See "**tra, tha**" affixes in the examples shown underlined. In "**tha**" affix, one dissimilar "**t**" is reduplicated.]

• Sabbatra, • sabbattha-at all places, everywhere,
• yatra, • yattha-at which place, where,
• tatra, • tattha-at that place, there. ***ind.***

२५०, २६८. सब्बतो धि

250, 268. **Sabbato dhi.** [Sabbato+dhi. 2 words]

[V] **Sabba,** icce'tasmā **dhi**paccayo hoti kvaci sattamya'tthe.

The "**dhi**" affix is sometimes applied after the word "**sabba**-all" in the sense of locative(Sattamī vibatti).
[See "**dhi**" affix in the example shown underlined.]

• Sabbadhi, ***ind.***
* sabbasmiṁ-at all places, everywhere. ***ls.*** (Only ordinary vibatti "smiṁ" is applied in this example as implied by "kvaci").

२५१, २६९. किंस्मा वो

251, 269. **Kiṁsmā vo.** [Kiṁsmā+vo. 2 words]

[V] **Kim**icce'tasmā **va**paccayo hoti sattamya'tthe.

The "**va**" affix is applied after interrogative sabbanāma noun "kiṁ" in the sense of locative (Sattamī vibatti).
[See "**va**" affix in the example shown underlined.]

• Kva gato'si tvaṁ devānaṁ piyatissa. ***ind.*** (Re: Sutta 227)

२५२, २७१. हिंहंहिञ्चनं

252, 271. **Hiṁ, haṁ, hiñcanaṁ.**

[Hiṁ, haṁ, hiñcanaṁ. 1 word]

[V] **Kim**icce'tasmā **hiṁ, haṁ, hiñcanaṁ,** icce'te paccayā honti sattamya'tthe.

The "**hiṁ, haṁ, hiñcanaṁ**" affixes are affixed after interrogative noun "kiṁ" in the sense of locative (Sattamī vibatti).
[See "**hiṁ, haṁ, hiñcanaṁ**" affixes in the examples shown underlined.]

• Kuhiṁ, • kuhaṁ, • kuhiñcanaṁ-where? ***ind.***

२५३, २७३. तम्हा च

253, 273. **Tamhā ca.** [Tamhā+ca. 2 words]

[V] **Ta**mhā ca **hiṁ, haṁ,** icce'te paccayā honti sattamya'tthe.

The "**hiṁ, haṁ**" affixes are to be affixed after sabbanāma noun "ta" in the sense of locative (Sattamī vibatti).
[See "**hiṁ, haṁ**" affixes in the examples shown underlined.]
• Tahiṁ, • tahaṁ-at that place, there. ***ind.***

Caggahaṇaṁ **hiñcana**ggahaṇanivattana'tthaṁ.

The word "ca" in the Sutta has a purpose of debarring the use of affix "hiñcanaṁ" in the application of this Sutta's function.
(This means that there can be no such usage of words as **tahiñcanaṁ** in the Buddhist texts).

२५४, २७४. इमस्मा हधा च

254, 274. **Imasmā ha, dhā ca.** [Imasmā+ha, dhā+ca. 3 words]

[V] **Ima**smā **ha, dha,** icce'te paccayā honti sattamya'tthe.

The "**ha, dha**" affixes are applied after "ima" in the sense of locative (Sattamī vibatti).
[See "**ha, dhā**" affixes in the examples shown underlined.]

• Iha, • idha-at this place, at this point, here. ***ind.***

Caggahaṇa'mavadhāraṇa'tthaṁ.
The word "ca" in the Sutta has a purpose of affirming the function of Sutta.

२५५, २७५. यतो हिं

255, 275. **Yato hiṁ.** [Yato+hiṁ. 2 words]

[V] Tasmā **ya**to **hiṁ**-paccayo hoti sattamya'tthe.

The "**hiṁ**" affix is applied after "ya" in the sense of locative (Sattamī vibatti). [See "**hiṁ**" affix shown underlined.]

• Yahiṁ-at which place. ***ind.***

२५६, ०. काले

256...**Kāle.** [Kāle. 1 word]

[V] "Kāle" icce'taṁ adhikāra'tthaṁ veditabbaṁ.

This "Kāle" Sutta is to be regarded as an adhikāra Sutta.
[This influences next three Suttas from 257 to 259, stating to the effect that the affixes to be applied through those four Suttas are meant for the expression of time. See the examples in those Suttas carefully to clarify this. In accordance with the term "adhikāra", the word "Kāle" will follow to next three Suttas 257, 258, 259 which can be found in the Vutti of each Sutta.]

२५७, २७६. किंसब्बञ्ञेकयकुहि दादाचनं

257, 276. **Kiṁ, sabba'ññe'ka, ya, kuhi dā, dācanaṁ.**

[Kiṁ, sabba, añña, eka, ya, ku, hi+dā, dācanaṁ. 2 words]

[V] **Kiṁ, sabba, añña, eka, ya, ku,** icce'tehi **dā, dācanaṁ,** icce'te paccayā honti kāle sattam'yatthe.

The "**dā, dācanaṁ**" affixes are to be affixed after sabbanāma nouns "**Kiṁ, sabba, añña, eka, ya, ku,**" when expressing time in the sense of locative (Sattamī vibatti). [See "**dā, dācanaṁ**" affixes in the examples shown underlined.]

- Kadā-when, at what time, • sabbadā-at all times, always,
- aññadā-at other time, • ekadā-at one time, once.
- yadā-at what time, when, • kudācanaṁ-occasionally, never. ***ind.***

२५८, २७८. तम्हा दानि च

258, 278. **Tamhā dāni ca.** [Tamhā+dāni+ca. 3 words]

[V] **Ta**-icce'tasmā **dāni, dā**-iccete paccayā honti, kāle sattamya'tthe.

The "**dāni, dā**" affixes are to be affixed after sabbanāma noun "**ta**" to express time in the sense of locative (Sattamī vibatti). [See "**dāni, dā**" affixes in the examples shown underlined.]

- Tadāni, • tadā-at that time, then. ***ind.***

Caggahaṇa'manukaḍḍhana'tthaṁ.
The word "ca" in Sutta has a purpose of taking in (pulling) "dā" from the preceding Sutta.
This means that although "**dāni** affix" only is shown in Sutta, the "**dā**" affix is also included in the application of this Sutta's function. Note that the word "**tadā**" is more frequently found in Pāli texts than "**tadāni**".

२५९, २७९. इमस्मा रहिधुनादानि च

259, 279. **Imasmā rahi, dhunā, dāni ca.**

[Imasmā+rahi, dhunā, dāni+ca. 3 words]

[V] **Ima**smā **rahi, dhunā, dāni** icce'te paccayā honti kāle sattamya'tthe.

The "**rahi, dunā, dāni**" affixes are to be affixed after the sabbanāma noun "**ima**" in expression of time, in the sense of locative (Sattamī vibatti).
[See "**rahi, dhunā, dāni**" affixes in the examples shown underlined.]

• Eta<u>rahi</u>, • a<u>dhunā</u>, • i<u>dāni</u>-now, at this time, at this moment. ***ind.***

Caggahaṇa'manukaḍḍhana'tthaṁ.
The word "ca" in Sutta has a purpose of taking in (pulling) the words "kāle sattam'yatthe" from the preceding Suttas.
(This means that the affixes shown in this Sutta signify "time in the locative sense")

२६०, २७७. सब्बस्स सो दाम्हि वा

260, 277. **Sabbassa so dāmhi vā.**

[Sabbassa+so+dāmhi+vā. 4 words]

[V] **Sabba**-icce'tassa **sa**kārādeso hoti vā **dā**mhi paccaye pare.

The whole of **sabba** changes into "**sa**" when a "**dā**" affix is applied after it. [See changed "**sa**" shown underlined. The second example is inapplicable]

• <u>Sa</u>dā, * sabbadā-at all times, always. ***ind.***

२६१, ३६९. अवण्णो ये लोपञ्च

261, 369. **Avaṇṇo ye lopañ'ca.**

[Avaṇṇo+ye+lopaṁ+ca. 4 words]

[V] Avaṇṇo ye paccaye pare lopa'māpajjate.

The component vowel of last consonant in a "**ṇya**-affixed" taddhita noun, is to be elided when "ya" of that "**ṇya**-affix is after the word. (See Sutta No.360 regarding "**ṇya**" affix and how the "**ṇ**" is elided).

Note: This Sutta elides the component vowel of the last consonant of a Taddhita-noun applied with a **ṇya** affix. The vowel is located right before "ya". Later, that vowel-less consonant is attached to "ya" for further morphological procedures. See more detailed explanation in Sutta 269 to clearly understand this complex procedure. **All examples are Taddhita-nouns from Taddhita section.**

- Bāhussaccaṁ-a state of having much knowledge, knowledgeability.
- paṇḍiccaṁ-a state of being wise, eruditeness.
- vepullaṁ-a state of being abundant, abundance.
- kāruññaṁ-a state of being kind, compassion.
- kosallaṁ-a state of being skilled, skillful.
- sāmaññaṁ-(a) a state of being a monk, monkhood, the goal of monkhood. Also, (b) a state of being similar, commonality, the ordinary. [Two possible meanings. Base word structure is also different depending on each different meaning]
- sohajjaṁ-a state of having good heart, the good-willed. ***tn*** in ***ns.***

२६२, ३९१. वुड्ढस्स जो इयिट्ठेसु
262, 391. Vuḍḍhassa jo iyi'ṭṭhesu.

[Vuḍḍhassa+jo+iya, iṭṭhesu. 3 words]

[V] Sabbasse'va **vuḍḍha**saddassa **j**o-ādeso hoti **iya, iṭṭha,** icce'tesu paccayesu.

The entire word "**vuḍḍha**" changes into "**j**" when "**iya, iṭṭha**" affixes are applied after the word Vuddha.
[Refer to Sutta 363 regarding affixes. See changed "**j**" shown in bold, underlined.]

- **J**eyyo-more senior. • **J**eṭṭho-the most senior. ***tn*** in ***ns.***

२६३, ३९२. पसत्थस्स सो च

263, 392. **Pasatthassa so ca.**

[Pasatthassa+so+ca. 3 words]

[V] Sabbasse'va **pasattha**saddassa **s**o-ādeso hoti. **j**ā-deso ca **iya, iṭṭha,** icce'tesu paccayesu.

The whole word "**pasattha**" changes into "**s** and **j**" when "**iya, iṭṭha**" affixes are applied after the word pasattha. [See changed "**S** and **J**" shown in bold, underlined.]

- Seyyo-more praised. • seṭṭho-the most praised, the best. ***tn*** in ***ns.*** (**S**-function applied in these examples)
- Jeyyo, • Jeṭṭho-the best, the most senior. ***tn*** in ***ns.*** (These two are examples of **J**-function).

२६४, ३९३. अन्तिकस्स नेदो

264, 393. **Antikassa nedo.** [Antikassa+nedo. 2 words]

[V] Sabbassa **antika**saddassa **nedā**'deso hoti
iya, iṭṭha, icce, tesu paccayesu.

The entire word "**antika**" changes into "**neda**" when followed by "**iya, iṭṭha**" affixes. [See changed "**ned**" shown underlined.]

- Nediyo-more near. • nediṭṭho-the nearest. ***tn*** in ***ns.***

२६५, ३९४. बाळ्हस्स साधो

265, 394. **Bāḷhassa sādho.** [Bāḷhassa+sādho. 2 words]

[V] Sabbassa **bāḷha**saddassa **sādhā**'deso hoti
iya, iṭṭha, icce'tesu paccayesu.

The whole word "**bāḷha**" changes into "**sādha**" when "**iya, iṭṭha**" affixes follows after it. [See changed "**sādha**" shown underlined.]

- Sādhiyo-more strong. • sādhiṭṭho-the strongest. ***tn*** in ***ns.***

२६६, ३९५. अप्पस्स कण

266, 395. **Appassa kaṇ.** [Appassa+kaṇ. 2 words]

[V] Sabbassa **appa**saddassa **kaṇ-**ādeso hoti **iya, iṭṭha,** icce'tesu paccayesu.

The whole word "**appa**" changes into "**kaṇ**" when followed by "**iya, iṭṭha**" affixes. [See changed "**kaṇ**" shown in bold.]

• **Kaṇ**iyo-the lesser. • **kaṇ**iṭṭho-the least. ***tn*** in ***ns.***

२६७, ३९६. युवानञ्च

267, 396. **Yuvānañ'ca.** [Yuvānaṁ+ca. 2 words]

[V] Sabbassa **yuva**saddassa **kan-**ādeso hoti **iya, iṭṭha,** icce'tesu paccayesu.

The whole word "**yuva**" changes into "**kan**" when "**iya, iṭṭha**" affixes are applied after it. [See changed "**kan**" shown in bold.]

• **Kan**iyo-the younger. • **kan**iṭṭho-the youngest. ***tn*** in ***ns.***
[The second word form is found to be in widespread usage in the texts]

Caggahaṇa'manukaḍḍhana'tthaṁ.
The word "ca" in Sutta has a purpose of pulling in the function of "kan" from preceding Sutta to this Sutta.

२६८, ३९७. वन्तुमन्तुवीनञ्च लोपो

268, 397. **Vantu, mantu, vī, nañ'ca lopo.**
[Vantu, mantu, vī, naṁ+ca+lopo. 3 words]

[V] **Vantu, mantu, vī,** icce'tesaṁ paccayānaṁ lopo hoti **iya, iṭṭha,** icce'tesu paccayesu.

The entire suffixes "**Vantu, mantu** and **vī,**" are elided when the additional "**iya, iṭṭha**" affixes are to be applied after a noun which have already been suffixed with those "**Vantu, mantu** and **vī,**" affixes.
Note: This Sutta elides the pre-existing affixes such as "**vantu, mantu, vī**" if other secondary form of affixes like " **iya,** or **iṭṭha**" are necessary

to be added. (Refer to Suttas **368, 369, 364** regarding affixes "**vantu, mantu, vī**")

- Guṇiyo-more virtuous. • guṇiṭṭho-the most virtuous.
- satiyo-more attentive. • satiṭṭho-the most attentive.
- medhiyo-the wiser. • medhiṭṭho-the wisest. ***tn*** in ***ns.***

२६९, ४१. यवतं तलणदकारानं ब्यञ्जनानि चलञजकारत्तं

269, 41. **Yavataṁ ta, la, ṇa, da, kārānaṁ byañjanāni ca, la, ña, ja, kārattaṁ.**

[Yavataṁ+ta, la, ṇa, da, kārānaṁ+byañjanāni+ca, la, ña, ja, kārattaṁ. 4 words]

[V] **Y**akāravantānaṁ **ta, la, ṇa, da, k**ārānaṁ byañjanāni **ca, la, ña, ja,** kāratta'māpajjante yathāsaṅkhyaṁ.

Those **ta, la, ṇa, da,** consonants of Taddhita nouns having a residual trace "ya" of **ṇya**-affix after them, respectively change into "**ca, la, ña, ja**".

Note: "ya" affix in this Sutta refers to "**ṇya**" taddhita affix whose "ṇ" has been elided and only "ya" remained after elision (See Sutta No. 360, 396). Those morphed consonants "**ca, la, ña, ja**" are reduplicated afterwards to become complete words. Sutta 261 & 269 are related to each other in performance of necessary morphological procedure on these words. All the complex morphological procedures are explained below in a very simple, understandable way.

Explanation

Now, Let's take a closer look at morphological solution by taking four example words because each of them consists of **ta, la, ṇa, da,** in them. (See those **ta, la, ṇa, da,** letters shown in bold) Here they are:

(a) paṇḍi**ta**-wise. (b) Kusa**la**-skill. (c) karu**ṇā**-kindness.

(d) Suha**da**-good-heart. [**su**-good+**hada**-heart, **i.e.** goodwill]

Step (a)

Because we want all these words to express "being in a state of" **i.e.** the abstract expression, an affix "**ṇya**" has to be applied after each word by **Sutta 360.** So, t**he basic structural pattern of**

each example becomes as follows:
(a) • paṇḍita+ṇya. (b) • Kusala+ṇya. (c) • Karuṇa+ṇya.
(d) • suhada+ṇya.

Step (b)
Here are necessary **morphological procedures** to be carried out further.

(1) First, Let's elide "**ṇ**" of "**ṇya**-affix" in each example by Sutta **No. 396** in Taddhita section. It will now look like this:
 (a) • paṇḍita+ya.
 (b) • Kusala+ya.
 (c) • Karuṇa+ya.
 (d) • Suhada+ya.

(2) Second, by **Sutta 261**, all the vowel "**a**" of **ta, la, ṇa, da** are to be elided. It becomes like this: **t, l, ṇ, d.** No more "a" is left. See below how it may looks like now:
 (a) • paṇḍi**t**+ya.
 (b) • Kusa**l**+ya.
 (c) • Karu**ṇ**+ya.
 (d) • Suha**d**+ya.

(3) Now, combine these "**t, l, ṇ, d,**" vowel-less plain consonants to **ya** (a residual trace of a ṇya-taddhita affix). Now, it will look like this: **tya, lya, ṇya, dya.**

See the examples carefully as shown. Remember what is said in the translation of Sutta which states: "Those **ta, la, ṇa, da** consonants of taddhita nouns having a residual trace 'ya' of ṇya-affix".
Also please refer to Pāli words in Vutti of Sutta which said:
"**Yavataṁ ta, la, ṇa, da, kārānaṁ** (**yavataṁ-**having a ya, **talaṇada kārānaṁ-**of those ta, la, ṇa, da, letters) ".
This is what it becomes of now as shown here. The practical morphological solution and the explained rule of the Sutta are perfectly matched. See below how it all looks now:
(a) • paṇḍi**tya**. (b) • Kusa**lya**. (c) • Karu**ṇya**. (d) • Suha**dya**.

Step (c)

(1) Now, let's perform next morphological procedure again. This time, by this Sutta. We will change those ya-conjoined **t, l, ṇ, d,** consonants into **c, l, ñ, j** consonants respectively.

(2) Now, here is the result:

(a) **ty>c>**Augment it as per **Sutta 28** with another similar **c> cca>** • paṇḍicca.

(b) **ly>l** >Augment it with a similar **l>lla>** • Kusalla.

(c) **ṇy>ñ>**Augment it with a similar **ñ> ñña>** • Karuñña.

(d) **dy> j** >Augment it with a similar **j>jja>** • Suhajja.

(3) Now, we need to do a **Vuddhi** procedure by **Sutta No.400** on **b, d** and **c** . This means that vowel "**u**" of both **b** and **d** has to be changed into an "**o**" while "**a**" of "ka" in **c** is to be length-ened. Suppose it has been carried out now and finished. It will look like this:

(b) • K**o**salla.

(c) • K**ā**ruñña.

(d) • S**o**hajja. (Now, it is almost done, but, not over yet).

(4) To finalize all this, let's do a formal recognition procedure of all this almost-finished words as noun by **Sutta 601** as these words are not actual nouns yet, but words in taddhita-affix ṇya, in a state of morphological transit pending completion. After this formal recognition as "nouns", a nominative singular "**si**" is to be applied after each word.

(5) Let's assume that all this is done and the words have been applied with "**si**" and will look like this:

• paṇḍicca+si • Kosalla+si • Kāruñña+si • Sohajja+si

(6) Next, that "**si**" is to be further changed into an "**aṁ**" by **Sutta 219.** (Know that any noun affixed with a Taddhita affix "**ṇya**" belongs to neuter gender group. As such, the "si" has to be changed into an "aṁ") Now, It will look like this:

• paṇḍicca+aṁ • Kosalla+aṁ • Kāruñña+aṁ • Sohajja+aṁ

(7) Then, all vowel "a" after each duplicated words (Refer to **cca** etc.) before the plus sign+ are to be elided and keep as a

"pakati" by **Sutta 83** (Keeping **pakati** means putting a stop to all further procedures. It also means that morphological procedures for these words are almost complete. **So, no more action!**).

(8) Then, vowel-less conjuncts are attached to next "**aṁ**" by means of **Sutta 11.** (A consonant can not be combined to two vowels at the same time. Hence, one must be elided.) Now, all the words become perfectly complete words with a distinctive gender and case-endings, ready to play any important role in the structure of a sentence and convey their relevant meanings. See the examples of Sutta as completed words shown below.

- Bāhussa**cc**aṁ, (a state of having much knowledge) [**Bahu**-much+**suta**-knowledge+ṇya]
- paṇḍi**cc**aṁ (a state of being wise),
- vepu**ll**aṁ,(a state of abundance)
- kāru**ññ**aṁ (a state of being kind),
- kosa**ll**aṁ (a state of being skilled),
- nepu**ññ**aṁ, (a state of having deep wisdom) [**nipuṇa**-deep wisdom+ṇya]
- sāma**ññ**aṁ, (a state of being a monk, monkhood. or commonality, sameness) [**samaṇa**-monk, or **samāna**-same, common+ṇya]
- soha**jj**aṁ (a state of being good-hearted). ***tn*** in ***ns.***

Yavatami'ti kimatthaṁ?

What is the word "yavataṁ" for?

To show that example below is inapplicable as it does not have a "ya" in it.

* Tiṇadalaṁ-grass and leaves(A Dvanda, Copulative compound noun).

Talaṇadakārānami'ti kimatthaṁ?

What is the word "talaṇadakārānaṁ" for?

To show that the examples below are inapplicable as there is no "ta, la, ṇa, da", although they may have a "ya" in them.

* Ālasyaṁ-a state of being idle, **i.e.** laziness, [**Alasa**-being lazy+**ṇya**-state]

* ārogyaṁ-a state of being without disease, or being healthy. **i.e.** healthiness. [**Aroga**-being healthy+**ṇya**]

Byañjanānami'ti kimatthaṁ?
What is the word "byañjanānaṁ" for?
To show that the example below is inapplicable as there is no "byañjana-consonant", but an "ā" of Vibatti "nā" in the instrumental case.
* Maccunā-by death (A plain noun).

Kāraggahaṇaṁ kimatthaṁ?
Yakārassa **ma**kārā'desañāpana'tthaṁ.
The word "**kāra** (Refer to kāranaṁ) " in the Sutta, shows that the "**y**"(affix "**y**" of "**ṇya**") can change into an "**m**". (It has to be reduplicated later on. See the example below to clarify this. "m" is shown in bold.)
• Opa**mm**aṁ-similitude. [**Upamā**-being similar+**ṇya**.]
"**U**" becomes "**o**". Then, "**ā** & **ṇ**" are elided. "**my**" then becomes "**m**" and augmented as [Opamma] . Afterwards, a nominative singular "**si**" is applied [Opamma+si] and changed into "**aṁ**". [Opamma+aṁ] . One "a" is to be elided. This is how the word is brought to completion by means of due morphological process.

२७०, १२०. अम्ह तुम्ह न्तु राज ब्रह्मत्त सख सत्थु पितादीहि स्मा नाव

270, 120. **Amha, tumha, ntu, rāja, brahma'tta, sakha, satthu, pitā'dīhi smā nā'va.**
[Amha, tumha, ntu, rāja, brahma, atta, sakha, satthu, pitu-ādīhi+smā+nā+iva. 4 words]

[V] **Amha, tumha, ntu, rāja, brahma, atta, sakha, satthu, pitu**-icceva'mādīhi **smā**vacanaṁ **nā**'va daṭṭhabbaṁ.

A "**smā**" vibatti applied after nouns such as **Amha, tumha, ntu-affxed nouns, rāja, brahma, atta, sakha, satthu, pitu** etc. is to be regarded as an equal to ordinary "**nā** vibatti". (so that any necessary morphological procedure applicable to an ordinary **nā**-vibatti-applied nouns of instrumental case can be done in the same way as in an original **nā**-vibatti-applied nouns.)
Summary: This Sutta enjoins to recognize ablative singular "**smā**" as an equal of instrumental singular "**nā**".

[amha] • Mayā-from me. [all examples are ***abs.***]
[tumha] • tayā-from you.
[ntu-affixed nouns] • guṇavatā-from virtuous one.
[rāja] • raññā-from king,
[Brahma] • brahmunā-from Brahmā, God.
[atta] • attanā-from oneself.
[sakha] • sakhinā-from friend.
[satthu] • satthārā-from teacher.
[Pitu etc.] • pitarā-from father. • mātarā-from mother.
• bhātarā-from brother. • dhītarā-from daughter.
• kattārā-from doer. • vattārā-from speaker.

Etehī'ti kimatthaṁ?
What is the word "etehi" for?
To show that example below is inapplicable as the word is not relevant to those shown in Sutta such as "amha, tumha, etc.".
(There is no need to recognize the vibatti in it as a "nā". Actually, the vibatti itself is an original "smā-vibatti". Besides, there are no further morphological procedures needed for that word to be recognized as a "nā", except changing that smā-vibatti directly into an **ā**).
* Purisā-from man. ***abs.***

Note: The purpose of recognition by this Sutta is only to facilitate the necessary morphological procedures applicable for the ordinary instrumental singular "nā" to be similarly applied on the ablative singular case smā-applied nouns too. However, the meaning of completed word will remain unchanged though. It has to be interpreted the same meaning of ablative, singular case "smā" such as "from, due to" etc., not "with, by".

Iti nāmakappe pañcamo kaṇḍo.
The Fifth Section of Noun ends.

Nāmakappo niṭṭhito.
Nouns Chapter ends.

3. Kāraka Kappa

Kāraka[23] Chapter

Various meanings and usage-rules of the Vibatti (Noun case-endings) applied after parts of the sentences are explained in detail. Those parts, with the exception of *Ākhyāta*-verbs, *upasagga* & *nipāta* particles, are formally known as "Kāraka or non-kāraka".

Chaṭṭha Kaṇḍa

The Sixth Section of Noun

२७१, ८८, ३०८. यस्मा दपेति भयमादत्ते वा तदपादानं

271, 88, 308. **Yasmā'dapeti bhaya'mādatte vā ta'dapādānaṁ.**

[Yasmā+apeti+bhayaṁ+ādatte+vā+taṁ+apādānaṁ. 7 words]

[V] Yasmā vā apeti, yasmā vā bhayaṁ jāyate, yasmā vā ādatte, taṁ kārakaṁ apādānasaññaṁ hoti.

The place or source from which someone left or something originated, the source from which fear arises, the one from which one learns, such a source is named an "**apādāna**".

---

[23] There are six **Kārakas.** Viz. Kattu, Kamma, Karaṇa, Sampadāna, Apādāna and Okāsa (also called Adhikaraṇa) which are explained in this chapter. "Kāraka" literally means the doer [kara+ṇvu]. Here, it means facilitator of an action. All necessary components of a sentence such as subject (Kattā), object (Kamma) and so on, which helps in expressing a specific action and syntactically related to the verb (**i.e.** action) are called "kāraka" as they play their respective roles in the expression of an action (**i.e.** verb) to be complete. Hence, each word named as a specific Kāraka always has to have a specific vibatti (noun case-ending) as prescribed in the relevant Suttas of the Kāraka chapter. See the table on the next page.

[Reference] (1) *Tattha Kārakaṁ sādhakaṁ kriyānipphattiyā kāraṇa' muccate. Taṁ pana kārakaṁ chabbidhaṁ: kammaṁ, kattā, karaṇaṁ, sampadāna'ma pādana'mokāso cā'ti.* (Rūpasiddhi Pāli Grammar, Sutta 285)

(2) *Yo karoti kriyaṁ katu-kammaṭṭhan'ti sa kārako.* (Saddha'ttha-bhedacintā, Verse No.53)

Taṁ yathā?

What is that? **i.e.** For example.

(1) • Gāmā-from village. apenti-come off, depart. munayo-the sages. **i.e.** The sages depart from village.

[Here, the sages left from village. So, the village has to be in ablative case to signify an apādāna]

(2) • nagarā-from city. niggato-(had) left. rājā-the king.
i.e. The king departed from city.
[Here, the king left from city. So, the city has to be in ablative case]

(3) • corā-from thief. bhayaṁ-fear. jāyate-arises.
i.e. The fear arises from thief.
[Here, fear arises from thief. So, the thief has to be in ablative case]

(4) • ācariyu'pajjhāyehi-from teachers and preceptors. sikkhaṁ-lesson. gaṇhāti-takes. sisso-the pupil. **i.e.** The pupil takes lesson from teacher and preceptors.

[Here, the pupil takes lessons from teachers and preceptors. So, they have to be in ablative, plural case to signify an apādāna]

Apādāna-micca'nena kva'ttho? Apādāne pañcamī.
What is the benefit by terming "apādāna" ?
It has the benefit of ease of reference in such Suttas as: "Apādāne pañcamī" etc.

The Six Kāraka and Applicable Vibattis

	Name of Kāraka	**Applicable Vibatti** (Case-ending)	**Applicable Sutta**
1	**Kattu**	Nominative	Liṅgatthe Paṭhmā
2	**Kamma**	Accusative	Kammatthe Dutiyā
3	**Karaṇa**	Instrumental	Karaṇe Tatiyā
4	**Sampadāna**	Genitive	Sampadāne Catutthī
5	**Apādāna**	Ablative	Apādāne Pañcamī
6	**Okāsa**	Locative	Okāse Sattamī

Note: This table shows only the general rules of applicable vibatti for each Kāraka. There are other applicable exceptions which will be explained in detail in later part of this chapter.

२७२, ३०९. धातुनामानमुपसग्गयोगादीस्वपि च
272, 309. **Dhātunāmāna'mupasaggayogādīsva'pi ca.**

[Dhātunāmānaṁ+upasaggayoga-ādīsu+api+ca. 4 words]

[V] Dhātunāmānaṁ payoge ca upasaggayogā'dīsva'pi ca taṁ kārakaṁ apādānasaññaṁ hoti.

An expression of "**apādāna**" can also occur when used in the context of verbs with certain roots, nouns and some Upasagga words and so on.

Dhātūnaṁ payoge tāva:
First, (here are) the example of apādāna expression in the context of (certain) roots of verbs.

ji-iccetassa dhātussa **parā**pubbassa payoge yo asaho. so apādānasañño hoti.

When the root "**ji**" (to conquer) prefixed with **parā** is used together, (the source from which) one is defeated, is named an **apādāna**. (Hence, it has to be in the ablative case to signify it). The root **Ji** prefixed with **parā** means "being defeated, to lose in a fight or the struggle".
Taṁ yathā? For example:
• Buddhasmā-from Buddha. parājenti-(are) defeated. aññatitthiyā-(those) holding other views, heretics.
i.e. The heretics are defeated from (**i.e.** by) the Buddha.

Bhū-icce'tassa dhātussa **pa**pubbassa payoge yato acchinnappabhavo. so apādānasañño hoti.

When the root "**bhu**", prefixed with "**pa**" is used together (as a verb in a sentence, which means an initial **originating source** of a continuous occurrence, that source is an apadana.
Taṁ yathā? For example,
(1) • Himavatā-from the mount Himavantā. pabhavanti-originate. pañca-five. mahānadiyo-great rivers. **i.e.** The five great rivers originate from the mount Himavantā (Himālaya mountains from where rivers flow continuously). [**pabhavanti=pa√bhū+anti**]
(2) • anavatattamhā-from lake anavatatta. pabhavanti-originate. mahāsarā-the great lakes.
i.e. The great lakes originate from lake Anavatatta.
(3) • aciravatiyā-from the river Aciravatī. pabhavanti-originate.

kunnadiyo-The small creeks.
i.e. The small creeks originate from the river Aciravatī.

Nāmappayoge'pi taṁ kārakaṁ apādānasaññaṁ hoti.

When used in contexts of certain nouns, that noun can also be named an apādāna. [This is the most common type of apādāna]

Taṁ yathā?

(1) • Urasmā-from chest (womb). jāto-(was) born. putto-the son. **i.e.** The son was born from chest (**i.e.** womb).

(2) • bhūmito-from earth. niggato-came out. raso-the taste (of fruit etc.). **i.e.** The taste came out from the earth.

(3) • ubhato-from both sides. sujāto-well-bred, well-born. putto-son. • mātito-from mother. ca-also. • pitito ca-from father's side also. **i.e.** also from mother's side, also from father's side, from both sides, the son was well-bred, well-born.

Here are three example words:
• ubhato, • mātito • pitito which are affixed with an indeclinable affix "**to**". [See Sutta 248. This affix has an ablative sense.]

Upasaggayoge taṁ kārakaṁ apādānasaññaṁ hoti.

When a word is used in the context of some Upasagga words, that word can also be an apādāna.

Taṁ yathā?

(1) **Apa-**by skirting. • sālāya-from the rest house. āyanti-come. vāṇijā-the traders. **i.e.** The traders come by skirting (avoiding) from the rest-house. [**apa**=taking off, by avoiding]

(2) **ā-**till, up to. • brahmalokā-the high heavens of Brahmā. saddo-the sound. abbhuggacchati-rises up.
i.e. The sound (of applause) rises up to the high heavens of Brahmā.

(3) **upari-**above. • pabbatā-the mountain. devo-the rain. vassati-pours. **i.e.** The rain pours above the mountain.

(4) • Buddhasmā-from Buddha. **pati-**on behalf of, representing. Sāriputto-Venerable Sāriputta. dhammadesanāya-for the purpose of teaching Dhamma. bhikkhū-monks. ālapati-addresses. temāsaṁ-for three months. **i.e.** Representing (from) Buddha, Venerable Sāriputta addresses the monks in order to teach Dhamma for three months.

(5) ghata'massa • telasmā **pati** dadāti.
[ghata'massa=ghataṁ+assa] ghataṁ-ghee. assa-to that person. • telasmā-from sesame oil. **pati**-instead of. dadāti-(he) gives. **i.e.** He gives him ghee instead of sesame oil.

(6) uppala'massa • padumasmā **pati** dadāti, uppalaṁ-white lotus. assa-to that person. • padumasmā-from red lotus. **pati**-instead of. dadāti-(he) gives. **i.e.** He gives him white lotus instead of red lotus.

(7) kanaka'massa • hiraññasmā **pati** dadāti. kanakaṁ-gold. assa-to that person. • hiraññsmā-from silver. **pati**-instead of. dadāti-(he) gives. **i.e.** He gives him gold instead of silver.

Ādiggahaṇena kārakamajjhe'pi pañcamī-vibhatti hoti.

By the word "ādi" in the Sutta, pañcamī vibatti can be applied in the midst of Kāraka (sentence parts).

Note: This word "**ādi**" comes from "upasaggayog**ā'dī**sva'pi ca" in Sutta. See "**ādi**" is shown in bold.

Examples:

(1) Ito-(starting) from this day. • pakkhasmā-from a pakkha of 15 days. vijjhati-shoots. migaṁ-deer. luddako-the hunter. Here, apādāna word "• pakkhasmā" is between "Ito" and "migaṁ", two Kārakas of ablative and accusative cases. **i.e.** Starting from today within 15 days, the hunter (is going to) shoot the deer and other games (in the forest).

(2) • kosā-from a distance of a Kosa. vijjhati-(he) shoots. kuñjaraṁ-the elephant. **i.e.** (He) shoots the elephant from (a distant of) a Kosa.

(3) • māsasmā-from a period of a month. bhuñjati-(he) eats. bhojanaṁ-food. **i.e.** (He) eats food from (since) a month.

Apiggahaṇena **nipāta**payoge'pi pañcamī-vibhatti hoti dutiyā ca tatiyā ca.

By the upasagga word "api" in Sutta, in addition to pañcamī vibatti, **dutiyā (accusative case)** and **tatiyā (instrumental case)** can also be applied for **apādāna** expression when used in context of certain nipāta words.

Note: This word "**api**" comes from "upasaggayogā'dīsv**a'pi** ca" in Sutta. The "**api**" is shown in bold.

(1) **Rahitā-**(रहिता) except/abandoning. • mātujā-from son. puññaṁ- meritorious deed. katvā-having done. dānaṁ-alms. deti-(he) gives.

i.e. Having done meritorious deed without son, he gives alms.

Note: Usually majority of apādāna words are in ablative case (pañcamī vibhatti). However, as an exception, in the following examples, **accusative (dutiyā)** and **instrumental (tatiyā)** cases are also applied. Please carefully note such words shown underlined below.

rahitā-Except, leaving or deserting. • mātujaṁ-the son, **i.e.** Leaving son or without son. **rahitā** • mātujena-with the son. vā.

Note: Though being translated in instrumental case, it does not mean "with the son" but without son. [rahitā-means without, except]

(2) **Rite** (ऋते) -except. • saddhammā-noble way of Dhamma. kuto-where. sukhaṁ-happiness. labhati-(one can) get. **i.e.** Where (one) can get happiness without(except) the noble way of Dhamma?

rite • saddhammaṁ, [Here apādāna word is in accusative case]

rite • saddhammena vā. [Here apādāna word is in instrumental case, with the same meaning, but in different case-ending]

(3) Te-those. bhikkhū-monks. nānā-leaving or deserting. • kulā-from families or Nānā Kulā-from various families and homes (two words together). pabbajitā-came forth (become) monks. **i.e.** Those monks (become) monks (after) leaving (various) families.

(4) **vinā-**except. • saddhammā-from noble Dhamma. natthañño [Sandhi@natthañño=natthi+añño] natthi-no. añño-other. koci-else, something. nātho-refuge/help. loke-in the world. vijjati-is. **i.e.** There is no other refuge/help in the world except the noble way of Dhamma.

Vinā • saddhammaṁ, vinā • saddhammena vā.

Vinā • Buddhasmā-from Buddha. vinā • Buddhaṁ vinā • Buddhena vā. [Meaning is easy to understand]

Caggahaṇena aññatthā'pi pañcamī-vibhatti hoti.

By means of the word "Ca", pañcamī vibatti can also be applied after various sabbanāma nouns.

Note: This word "**ca**" comes from "upasaggayogā'dīsva'pi **ca**" in Sutta. See "**ca**" is shown in bold.

• Yato'haṁ bhagini ariyāya jātiyā jāto. [yato'haṁ=yato+ahaṁ] Yato-since the time when. ahaṁ-I. bhagini-sister. ariyāya-by noble. jātiyā-birth. jāto-(was) born. **i.e.** Sister, since I was born the noble birth (by being enlightened).

• Yato-since. sarāmi-(I) remember. attānaṁ-oneself. **i.e.** Since or as far as I remember myself.

• Yato patto'smi viññutaṁ. [Sandhi@patto'smi=patto+asmi] Yato-since. patto-the one who attained. asmi-I am. viññutaṁ-to a state of being mature, wise. **i.e.** Since I reach a state of being wise (capable of knowing right and wrong, mature adulthood).

• Yatvā'dhikaraṇa'menaṁ cakkhu'ndriyaṁ asaṁvutaṁ viharantaṁ abhijjhā, domanassā pāpakā akusalā dhammā anvā'saveyyuṁ.

[Trans] Yato adhikaraṇaṁ-For the reason which. enaṁ-to that (person). cakkhundriyaṁ-[cakkhu+indriyaṁ] the faculty of eye. asaṁvutaṁ-without restraining. viharantaṁ-(to the one who is) living. abhijjhā, domanassā-desire and aversion etc. pāpakā-those which are bad. akusalā-unwholesome. dhammā-mental states. anvā'saveyyuṁ-may repeatedly arise. **i.e.** For (such a) reason of (casually) living without restraining one's eye, bad, unwholesome mental states (such as) desire, and aversion etc., may repeatedly arise to (the mind of) that person.

[Yatvā'dhikaraṇa'menaṁ=**yato**+**adhikaraṇaṁ**-reason+**enaṁ**]
[anvā'saveyyuṁ=**anu**-repeatedly, again and again+**āsaveyyuṁ**-may flow, increase. **ā**-intensifier√+**su**-to flow+**eyyuṁ**]

२७३, ३१०. रक्खणत्थान मिच्छितं

273, 310. Rakkhaṇa'tthāna'micchitaṁ.

[Rakkhaṇa-atthānaṁ+icchitaṁ. 2 words]

[V] Rakkhaṇatthānaṁ dhātūnaṁ payoge yaṁ icchitaṁ, taṁ kārakaṁ apādānasaññaṁ hoti.

When used in the context of verbs with the root meaning "to protect or prevent from", that noun (The object for which the protection is desired) can also be regarded as an "**apādāna**".

[See the examples. It is clear that the object for whom the protection is desired becomes an apādāna. Hence, that object is in ablative case.]

(1) Kāke-crows. rakkhanti-(people) prevent. • taṇḍulā-from (snatching) rice. **i.e.** People prevent crows from(eating) the rice.

(2) • yavā-from (eating) barley. paṭisedhenti-(people) prevent. gāvo-the cattle. **i.e.** People prevent cattle from (eating) the barley.

२७४, ३११. येन वा दस्सनं

274, 311. **Yena vā'dassanaṁ.** [Yena+vā+adassanaṁ. 3 words]

[V] Yena vā adassana'micchitaṁ, taṁ kārakaṁ apādānasaññaṁ hoti.

When one wishes not to be seen by someone, that person from which one wants to hide, can also be an "**apādāna**".

(1) • Upajjhāyā-from preceptor (teacher). antaradhāyati-hides. sisso-the pupil. **i.e.** The pupil hides from the preceptor.

(2) • mātarā ca-from mother also. • pitarā ca-from father also. antaradhāyati-hides. putto-son. **i.e.** The son hides from mother and father also.

Vā'ti kimatthaṁ?
What is the word "vā" for?
Sattamīvibhatyattaṁ.
It has some benefit for applying Sattamī Vibatti (Locative case) in some instances where disappearance is mentioned. (as in the example shown below).
* Jetavane-at Jetavana temple. antaradhāyati-disappears. bhagavā-Buddha. **i.e.** Lord Buddha disappears at Jetavana temple.

२७५, ३१२.दूरन्तिकद्धकाल निम्मान त्वालोप दिसायोग विभत्तारप्पयोग सुद्धप्पमोचन हेतु विवित्तप्पमाण पुब्बयोग बन्धन गुणवचन पञ्ह कथन थोकाकत्तूसु च

275, 312. **Dūra'ntika'ddhakāla, nimmāna, tvālopa, disāyoga, vibhattā'rappayoga, suddha' ppamocana, hetu, vivitta'ppamāṇa, pubbayoga, bandhana, guṇa-vacana, pañha, kathana, thokā'kattūsu ca.**

[Dūra, antika, addha, kāla-nimmāna, tvālopa, disāyoga, vibhatti, āra-payoga, suddha, pamocana, hetu, vivitta, pamāṇa, pubbayoga, bandhana, guṇa-vacana, pañha, kathana, thoka, akattūsu+ca. **2 words** only in this great Sutta]

[V] Dūratthe, antikatthe, addhanimmāne, kālanimmāne, tvālope, disāyoge, vibhatte, ārappayoge, suddhe, pamocane, hetva'tthe, vivitta'tthe, pamāṇe, pubbayoge, bandhana'tthe, guṇavacane, pañhe, kathane, thoke, akattari ca icce'te svatthesu, payogesu ca, taṁ kārakaṁ apādānasaññaṁ hoti.

It can also be named an "Apādāna" in many instances of expressions when (words expressive of Apādāna are) used in the context of the following:

[1] The word "dura" which means "distant and far" or any word synonymous with it,

[2] the word "antika", which means "near" or any synonymous word,

[3] In expressing measurement of distance,

[4] In expressing measurement of time,

[5] when used in the accusative and locative sense, without using a tvā-affixed ***Kita*** verb but the verb's implied meaning still evident in the sentence,

[6] when referring to direction between one location and other locations,

[7] when making an analytical comparison to highlight distinctive quality of superiority or seniority,

[8] when expressing abstinence using the words such as "ārati" or any synonymous word,
[9] when expressing purity and the state of being unadulterated,
[10] when expressing release and freedom,
[11] when expressing reason,
[12] when expressing dissociation or being free from,
[13] when expressing measurement,
[14] when used in context of the word "pubba" which means "before, prior to",
[15] when expressing of getting arrested,
[16] when expressing the result and benefit of a virtue,
[17] when questioning,
[18] When answering,
[19] when used in the context of the words meaning "a little, a small amount"
[20] when used in expressions with the sense of non-agent but the implied meaning of reason and result are more evident, **i.e.** reason-descriptive nouns which assumes the role of apādāna.

Dūra'tthe tāva-First, (here are the examples of apādāna) where the word **Dūra** (meaning "far") is used in the context:

(1) kīva-how much. dūro-(it is) far. • ito-from here. naḷakāragāmo-bamboo-crafter's village?
i.e. How far is from here to bamboo-crafter's village?

(2) • dūrato'vā'gamma
[Sandhi@ dūrato'vā'gamma=dūrato+eva+āgamma]
dūrato eva-from afar only. āgamma-having come.
i.e. Having come from a distant only.

Below are the examples of apādāna where the word "**āraka**", synonymous with **Dūra**, is used in the context:

(1) ārakā-are far. te-those. moghapurisā-empty men.
• imasmā-from this. • dhammavinayā-teaching of Buddha.
i.e. Those "empty men" are far from this noble teaching of Buddha.
Note: The term "empty men-**moghapurisa**" is used by Lord

Buddha when censuring someone for any improper action.

Dutiyā ca, tatiyā ca

Dutiyā (Accusative) and tatiyā (Instrumental) cases can also be applied in the Apādāna-expression words. For example:

(1) • dūraṁ • gāmaṁ-from distant village. āgato-come. [Here, it is in Dutiyā, accusative case]

(2) • dūrena • gāmena-from distant village. vā-as another example. āgato-come. [Here, Apādāna word is in tatitiyā, instrumental case]

(3) Ārakā-far. • imaṁ • dhammavinayaṁ-from this Buddha's teaching. [Here in Dutiyā, accusative case]

(4) • anena • dhammavinayena vā [Here is in tatitiyā, instrumental case] icce'va'mādi [iti+evaṁ+ādī]-and so on.

Antika'tthe–(Here is the example of apādāna) where the word **Antika** (meaning "near") is used in the context:

(1) antikaṁ-(is) near • gāmā-from village.

Below are the examples of apādāna where the two words "**āsanna, samīpa**" synonymous with **Antika** are used:

(1) āsannaṁ-(is) near • gāmā, [Meaning the same]

(2) samīpaṁ • gāmā,

(3) samīpaṁ • saddhammā-from noble Dhamma.

Dutiyā ca, tatiyā ca. Dutiyā and Tatiyā cases can also be applied in apādāna. Examples in the context of the word "**antika**"

(1) antikaṁ • gāmaṁ, [Dutiyā case]

(2) antikaṁ • gāmena vā. [Tatiyā case]

Examples with the word "**āsanna**"

(1) Āsannaṁ • gāmaṁ, [Dutiyā case]

(2) āsannaṁ • gāmena vā. [Tatiyā case]

Examples in the context of the word "**samīpa**"

(1) Samīpaṁ • gāmaṁ. [Dutiyā case]

(2) Samīpaṁ • gāmena vā. [Tatiyā case]

(3) Samīpaṁ • saddhammaṁ, [Dutiyā case]

(4) samīpaṁ • saddhammena vā [Tatiyā case]

icce'va'mādi.

Addhanimmāne–(Here is the example of apādāna) where **the measure of geographic distance** is expressed:

(1) • ito-from here. • mathurāya-from city of Mathura. catūsu-four. yojanesu-at "yojana". saṅkassaṁ nāma-named "saṅkassa". nagaraṁ-city. atthi-there is. tattha-there, at that city. bahū-many. janā-people. vasanti-live. **i.e.** At four "Yojana distance" from this city of Mathura, there is a city named "**saṅkassa**"**.** Many people live there. [**addha**-the distance+**nimmāna**-measure]

icce'va'mādi.

Note: A yojana is about four kosa (about 8 miles) distant.

Kālanimmāne–(Here are the examples of apādāna) where **the measure of time** is expressed:

(1) • ito-from now. bhikkhave-monks! ekanavutikappe-at a time of 91 eons. vipassī nāma-named Vipassī. bhagavā-Buddha. loke-in the world. udapādi-appeared. **i.e.** Monks! At a time of 91 eons from now, the Buddha named "**Vipassī**"**,** appeared in the world.

(2) • ito-from now. tiṇṇaṁ-of three. māsānaṁ-months. accayena-on passing (instrumental case in the locative sense. See Sutta 290). parinibbāyissati-(The Buddha) will expire.
i.e. On passing of three months from now, the Buddha will enter into Parinibbāna.

icce'va'mādi.

Tvālope kammā'dhikaraṇesu–

[**Tvā**-tvā-affixed *Kita*-verb+**lope**=elided, deleted. **i.e.** absent, not seen]
(Here are the examples of apādāna) where **tvā**-affixed gerund-verb is absent but the implied meaning thereof is evident and in the sense of accusative and locative.
There are **four set of examples**. In the first of each, there is no **tvā**-affixed gerund-verb. The meaning is implicit while in the second one it is explicit as there is a **tvā**-affixed gerund-verb being present.

(1) (a) • pāsādā-from mansion or palace. saṅkameyya-(he should) move. **i.e.** He should move from mansion. The meaning that he has been already on the mansion by going up there is implicit as there is no **tvā**-affixed gerund-verb.

(b) * pāsādaṁ-to the mansion or palace. abhiruhitvā-going up. vā-in other words.[This is an example of Kamma, accusative,

not apādāna example]
Here, **tvā**-affixed gerund-verb is already present. So, it is explicit. But this is not an apādāna example.

(2) (a) • Pabbatā-from mountain. saṅkameyya.
i.e. He should move from mountain.
(b) * pabbataṁ abhiruhitvā vā. [Similar to "pāsādaṁ abhiruhitvā"] [an example of Kamma, not apādāna]

(3) (a) • Hatthikkhandhā-from the back of elephant. saṅkameyya.
i.e. He should move from back of the elephant.
(b) * hatthikkhandhaṁ abhiruhitvā vā. [an example of Kamma, not apādāna]

(4) (a) • Āsanā-from seat. vuṭṭhaheyya-(he) should get up.
i.e. He should get up from seat.
(b) *Āsane-in the seat. nisīditvā-having seated. vā.
[an example of Okāsa-Locative, not apādāna]
icce'va'mādi.

Disāyoge–(The examples of apādāna) where words indicative of direction and physical points are used in the context:

(1) • avicito-from lowest hell. yāva-up to. upari bhavaggamantare-in between the highest heaven.
[upari bhavagga'mantare= **upari**-above, **bhava'gga**-the highest heaven+**antare**-in between]
bahū-many diverse. sattanikāyā-groups of living beings.
vasanti-live. **i.e.** Many diverse groups of beings live in between from the lowest hell (underneath) to the highest heaven above.

(2) • yato-where. khemaṁ-(it is) safe. • tato-there. bhayaṁ-(it is) unsafe. **i.e.** Where (it used to be) safe (before), is no longer safe.

(3) • puratthimato from the East, • dakkhiṇato-from the South, • pacchimato-from the West, • uttarato-from the North. aggī-the fires. pajjalanti-are aflame.

(4) • yato-since. assosuṁ-(they) heard. bhagavantaṁ-the Buddha.
i.e. Since they heard Buddha's (words).

(5) uddhaṁ-above. • pādatalā-from the feet. adho-down below.
• kesamatthakā-till the tip of hairs.
i.e. From the feet up till the tip of hairs and down below (to the feet)
icce'va'mādi.

Vibhatte–(The examples of apādāna) where the words indicative of comparison to highlight a distinction are used in the context:

(1) • yato-from which. paṇītataro vā-either the best. visiṭṭhataro vā-or the most outstanding thing. na'tthi-there is no. [natthi=**na**-not+**atthi**-is] **i.e.** From this Dhamma, there is nothing else which is either the best or more outstanding (than the Dhamma).

(2) Chaṭṭhī ca-Chaṭṭhī (genitive) case is also applicable for apādāna. **e.g.** • channavutīnaṁ-of ninety-six. • pāsaṇḍānaṁ-impious. dhammānaṁ-ideas. pavaraṁ-(is) the most excellent. yadidaṁ- that which is. sugatavinayo-the discipline of Buddha. **i.e.** Of the ninety-six impious ideas, the discipline (teaching) of Buddha is the most excellent.
icce'va'mādi.

Ārappayoge–(The examples of apādāna) where the words of abstinence are used in the context:

(1) • gāmadhammā-from the way of villagers. • vasaladhammā-from impious way. • asaddhammā-from ignoble way. ārati-(mentally) abstinence. virati-(physically) abstinence. paṭivirati-sustained abstinence.

(2) • pāṇātipātā-from killing. veramaṇī-abstinence.
icce'va'mādi.

Suddhe–(The examples of apādāna) where words indicative of the purity, are used in the context:

(1) • lobhaniyehi-from greed-causing. • dhammehi-phenomenon. suddho-(is) pure. asaṁsaṭṭho-(is) dissociated.
i.e. It is pure and dissociated from greed-causing phenomenon.

(2) • mātito ca-from mother's side also. • pitito ca- from father's side also. suddho-(is) pure. asaṁsaṭṭho-(is) not mixed (with other castes). anu'pakuddho-(is) not censured. agarahito-(is) not reproached. **i.e.** (He) is not to be censured nor to be reproached as he is pure and not racially mixed either from the mother's side or from the father's side.
icce'va'mādi.

Pamocane–(The examples of apādāna) where words indicative of freedom and release are used:

(1) parimutto-is free. • dukkhasmā'ti [dukkhasmā+iti]
  • dukkhasmā-from suffering. iti-as. vadāmi-(I) say.
  i.e. I say that it is freedom from suffering.

(2) mutto'smi [mutto'smi=mutto+asmi] mutto-free. asmi-(I) am.
  • mārabandhanā-from the snares of the devil.
  i.e. I am free from the snares of the devil.

(3) na-not. te-they. muccanti-are free. • maccunā-from death.
  i.e. They are not being free from death.
  icce'va'mādi.

Hetva'tthe–(The examples of apādāna) where the word indicative of the reason is used in the context:

(1) • kasmā • hetunā-for what reason, why, (ablative case example)

(2) • kena • hetunā-for what reason, (instrumental case example)

(3) • kissa • hetunā-for what reason, (genitive case example)

Note: See these examples from 1 to 3 in three different cases after the interrogative Sabbanāma word "**kiṁ**". This clearly shows a grammatical rule where an example word indicative of "reason" has to be in one of these three cases.

(4) • kasmā-why. nu-is a ***Nipāta*** particle which signifies a question and similar to such a question mark "?". tumhaṁ-of you, among you. daharā-the young ones. na mīyare-do not die. **i.e.** Why the young ones among you (in the family) do not die young?

(5) • kasmā-why. idhe'va[idhe'va=idha+eva] idha-here. eva-only. maraṇaṁ-death. bhavissati-will be. **i.e.** Why my death will be only here?
  icce'va'mādi.

Vivitta'tthe– (Here are the examples of apādāna) where words indicative of dissociation is used in the context:

(1) vivitto-is dissociated, being detached from. • pāpakā-unwholesome. • dhammā-mental states.
  i.e. Being detached from unwholesome mental states.

(2) vivicce'va [vivicce'va=vivicca+eva] vivicca-being detached. eva-only. • kāmehi-from sensual pleasures. vivicca- being detached.

• akusalehi-unwholesome. • dhammehi-mental states. **i.e.** Being detached from sensual pleasure and unwholesome mental states.
icce'va'mādi.

Pamāṇe–(The examples of apādāna) where the words indicative of measurement is used:

(1) • dīghaso-by length. navavidatthiyo-a measure of nine "vidatthi".
sugatavidatthiyā-by measure of Buddha's vidatthi. pamāṇikā-measurement. kāretabbā-should be made measured. majjhimassa-of medium height. purisassa-of man. aḍḍha-teḷasahatthā-half of thirteen feet. **i.e.** By measure of Buddha's Vidatthi measurement, nine vidatthi in length, half-thirteen feet by measure of a medium height man are to be measured.

Note: A **Vidatthi** is a length of measure of the distance between the extended thumb and the little finger while both are being stretched out.
icce'va'mādi.

Pubbayoge–(The example of apādāna) where the word "pubba" is used in the context.

(1) Pubbe'va [pubbe'va=pubbe+eva] Pubbe-before, previously. eva-only. • sammodhā-from (the time of) enlightenment. **i.e.** At the previous time from enlightenment. (Prior to enlightenment).
icce'va'mādi.

Bandhana'tthe–(Here are the example of apādāna) where the word meaning "to arrest" is used in the context.

(1) • satasmā-for (from the reason of) a hundred. bandho-arrested. naro-man. **i.e.** Man got arrested for a hundred.

Tatiyā ca- Tatiyā (Instrumental) case can also be applied. **e.g.**

(2) • satena-by a hundred. bandho naro raññā-by king. • iṇatthena-by reason of debt. **i.e.** Man was arrested by king for reasons of (unpaid) debt of a hundred.
icce'va'mādi.

Guṇavacane–(The examples of apādāna) when extolling the result or benefit of a virtue or a specific quality.

(1) • puññāya-by meritorious deeds. sugatiṁ-to good destiny (rebirth). yanti-(people) go. **i.e.** People go to a good (destiny of) rebirth by virtue of meritorious deed.

(2) • cāgāya-by alms. vipulaṁ-is abundant. dhanaṁ-wealth. **i.e.** Abundance of wealth is by virtue of alms.

(3) • paññāya-by wisdom. vimutti-is free. mano-the mind. **i.e.** The mind is free by virtue of wisdom.

(4) • issariyāya-by authority. janaṁ-people. rakkhati-protects or governs. rājā-the king. **i.e.** The king governs people by virtue of authority.

icce'va'mādi.

Pañhe tvālope kammā'dhikaraṇesu–(Here are the examples of apādāna) in case of questioning used together without a **tvā**-gerund ***Kita*** verb, in the sense of accusative and locative.

(1) • abhidhammā-from abhidhamma. pucchanti-(they) ask. [a **tvā**-affixed ***Kita***-verb is absent in this example] **i.e.** They ask question from (**i.e.** regarding) Abhidhamma.

* abhidhammaṁ sutvā-having listened. [This is a **tvā**-affixed ***Kita***-verb] **i.e.** Having listened to Abhidhamma, they ask question.

* abhidhamme ṭhatvā-standing (there as point of question) vā. [a **tvā**-affixed ***Kita***-verb is present] **i.e.** Standing on Abhidhamma, they ask question.

(2) • Vinayā-from vinaya. pucchanti, [a tvā-affixed ***Kita*** verb is absent]

* vinayaṁ sutvā, * vinaye ṭhatvā vā. [a tvā-affixed ***Kita***-verb is present]

Dutiyā ca tatiyā ca-Dutiyā case and Tatiyā cases are also applied too. **e.g.**

(1) • abhidhammaṁ, • abhidhammena vā.

(2) • Vinayaṁ, • vinayena vā.

Evaṁ-similarly in this way. • suttā-from Sutta, • geyyā-from stanza, • gāthāya-from verse, • veyyākaraṇā-from explanatory non-stanza discourses, • udānā-from joyous utterances, • itivuttakā-

from itivuttaka (re-narrated) discourses, • jātakā-from Buddha's former life stories, • abbhutadhammā-from inspirational discourses, • vedallā-from joyous sayings.
icce'va'mādi.

Kathane tvālope kammā'dhikaraṇesu–(the examples of apādāna) in regards of answering without a **tvā**-affixed ***Kita***-verb, in the sense of accusative and locative.

(1) • abhidhammā kathayanti-(they) answer. [a tvā-affixed ***Kita***-verb is absent here] **i.e.** They answer question from (regarding) Abhidhamma.
 * abhidhammaṁ sutvā,
 i.e. Having listened to Abhidhamma, they answer question.
 * abhidhamme ṭhatvā vā. [a tvā-affixed ***Kita***-verb is present here]
 i.e. Standing on Abhidhamma, they answer question.

(2) • Vinayā kathayanti, [a tvā-affixed ***Kita***-verb is absent]
 * vinayaṁ sutvā, * vinaye ṭhatvā vā. [a tvā-affixed ***Kita***-verb is present]

Dutiyā ca tatiyā ca- Dutiyā case and Tatiyā cases can also be applied too for apādāna word. (See the examples)

(1) • abhidhammaṁ, • abhidhammena vā.

(2) • Vinayaṁ • vinayena vā.

Evaṁ • suttā, • geyyā, • gāthāya, • veyyākaraṇā, • udānā, • itivuttakā, • jātakā, • abbhutadhammā, • vedallā icce'va'mādi.

Thoke–(the examples of apādāna) in the context of the words meaning "a little, a meagre amount".

(1) • thokā-from reasons of little (excuse). muccanti-(they) are free (from confinement). **i.e.** They are free by means of a little excuse.

(2) • Appamattakā-from little amount. muccanti,

(3) • kicchā-from being weary. muccanti.

Tatiyā ca.- A Tatiyā case can also be applied in apādāna word.

e.g. • Thokena-by little, • appamattakena, • kicchena vā icce'va'mādi.

Akattari ca–(the examples of apādāna) where non-agent words indicative of obvious reason, is an **apādāna.**

(1) kammassa-of (good) kamma. • katattā-for having done.
• upacitattā-for having collected. • ussannattā-for having accumulated. • vipulattā-for having increased.
cakkhuviññāṇaṁ-the eye-consciousness. uppannaṁ-act of arising. hoti-is.
i.e. for reasons of having done, for having collected, for having accumulated, for having increased the (good) Kamma, the eye-consciousness arises.
icce'va'mādi.

Caggahaṇena sesesu'pi ye mayā no'padiṭṭhā apādānapayogikā, te payogavicakkhaṇehi yathāyogaṁ yojetabbā.

By means of **"ca"** (included in this Sutta), the remaining instances and expressions of apādāna which are not explained by me, should also be applied by those skilled in the knowledge of grammatical examples wherever possible and applicable. (Refer to the last word "Ca" in Sutta)

२७६, ३०२. यस्स दातुकामो रोचते धारयते वा तं सम्पदानं

276, 302. **Yassa dātukāmo rocate dhārayate vā taṁ sampadānaṁ.**

[Yassa+dātukāmo+rocate+dhārayate+vā+taṁ+sampadānaṁ. 7 words]

[V] Yassa vā dātukāmo, yassa vā rocate, yassa vā dhārayate, taṁ kārakaṁ sampadānasaññaṁ hoti.

To whom one wishes to give something, to whom something adorns, or to whom one carries something for, such instances of expressions are called a "**sampadāna-**the recipient"**.**

(1) • Samaṇassa-of (to) the monk. cīvaraṁ-the robe. dadāti-(He) offers. **i.e.** He offers the robe to the monk. [Here, the monk is receiver. So, it has to be in dative case, thus signifying Sampadāna]

(2) • samaṇassa-of the monk. rocate-adorns. saccaṁ-truth. **i.e.** The truth adorns the monk. [Here, truth adorns the monk. So, the monk has to be in dative case]

(3) • devadattassa-of (for) Devadatta. suvaṇṇacchattaṁ-golden umbrella. dhārayate-carries. yaññadatto-Yaññadatta. **i.e.** Yaññadatta carries the golden-umbrella for (shielding) Devadatta.
[Here, Yaññadatta carries the umbrella for Devadatta's protection. So, Devadatta has to be in dative case as he is the recipient]

Sampadānamicca'ne'na kvattho? Sampadāne catutthī.
What is the benefit by terming "sampadāna"?
It has the benefit of ease of reference in such Suttas as: "Sampadāne catutthī" etc.

Vā'ti vikappana'tthaṁ.
dhātunāmānaṁ payoge vā upasaggappayoge vā nipātappayoge vā sati atthavikappanatthaṁ vā'ti padaṁ payujjati.

The word "**vā**" is included in Sutta to allow other instances of sampadāna (rather than those examples shown here) applicable in context of certain roots, or nouns, or upasagga words, or nipāta particles and wherever applicable.

२७७, ३०३. सिलाघ हनु ठा सप धार पिह कुधदुहिस्सोस्सूय राधिक्खपच्चासुण अनुपतिगिण पुब्बकत्तारोचनत्थ तदत्थ तुमत्थालमत्थ मञ्ञा नादरप्पाणिनि गत्यत्थकम्मनि आसिसत्थसम्मुति भिय्य सत्तम्यत्थेसु च

277, 303. **Silāgha, hanu, ṭhā, sapa, dhāra, piha, kudha, duhiss'osūya, rādh'ikkha, paccā'suṇa, anupatigiṇa, pubbakattā' rocana'ttha, ta'dattha, tumatthā'lamattha, maññā'nādara' ppāṇini, gatya'tthakammani, āsīsattha, sammuti, bhiyya, sattamya'tthesu ca.**

[Silāgha, hanu, ṭhā, sapa, dhāra, piha, kudha, duha, issa, usūya, rādha, ikkha, pati√ ā√suṇa, anu√pati√giṇa, pubbakattu, ārocana-attha, ta'dattha, tumattha, alaṁ-attha, mañña, anādara, apāṇini+gati-atthakammani+āsīsattha, sammuti, bhiyya, sattamī-atthesu+ca. **4 words.** Only four words in this long Sutta]

[V] Silāgha, hanu, ṭhā, sapa, dhāra, piha, kudha, duha, issa-icce'tesaṁ dhātūnaṁ payoge, usūya'tthānañ'ca payoge, rādha, ikkhappa-yoge, paccā'suṇa-anupatigiṇānaṁ pubbakattari, ārocana'tthe, ta'datthe, tuma'tthe,alama'tthe, maññati'ppayoge, anā'dare, a'ppāṇini, gatya'tthānaṁ dhātūnaṁ kammani, āsīsa'tthe ca, sammuti, bhiyya, sattamya'tthesu ca. taṁ kārakaṁ sampadānasaññaṁ hoti.

There are also many instances of expressions where it can be named as "sampadāna" when used in conjunction with the following:

[1] When used in the context of verbs with roots "**silāgha, hanu, ṭhā, sapa, dhara, piha, kudha, duha, issa,usūya, radha, ikkha,** the root "**su**" prefixed with **pati** and **ā** upasaggas, the root "**ge**" prefixed with **anu** and **pati** upassaga where preceding subject of the sentence assumes the position of "sampadāna" later on, the root

"**ruca**" prefixed with an "**ā**" upsagga which means "to tell" and other verbal roots of similar meaning,

[2] also, when expressing a purpose in the context of the word "**attha**" and or nouns in dative case with a morpheme "āya", expressive of a "to-infinitive purpose" similar to "**tuṁ-suffixed *Kita* verbs**",

[3] when used in the context of the Nipāta word "**alaṁ**" which has the meanings of worthiness and rejection,

[4] when expressing **disrespect** and sneering someone **as a lifeless stuff** in a contemptuous manner used in the context of the verbal word "**maññe-**I think", having the root "mana-to consider",

[5] when using a dative-case noun in the accusative sense of "to" in the context of verbs based in roots having the meaning of "**gati**-to move, to go", (That noun itself becomes a sampadāna)

[6] when expressing "**āsisa**" (wishing well-being for someone),

[7] when used in context of the words "**sammuti** (recognition), **bhiyya** (being in excess of or beyond measure) ",

[8] when used in the context of locative-sense words.

Silāghappayoge tāva–First, (here are examples of Sampadāna) in the context of verb with the root "**silāgha**-to praise"

(1) • Buddhassa-of the Buddha (to the Buddha). silāghate-(he) praises. **i.e.** He praises the Buddha.

(2) • dhammassa-of Dhamma. silāghate-(he) praises. **i.e.** He praises the Dhamma.

(3) • saṅghassa-of Sangha. silāghate-(he) praises. **i.e.** He praises the Sangha.

(4) sakaṁ-one's own. • upajjhāyassa-of preceptor. silāghate-(he) praises, **i.e.** He praises his own preceptor.

(5) • tava-you. silāghate-(he) praises. **i.e.** He praises you.

(6) • mama-me. silāghate-(he) praises. **i.e.** He praises me.

icce'va'mādi. and so on.

Note: Here, Sampadāna word in dative case is like that of accusative case having the meaning "to".

Hanu'ppayoge– Examples of Sampadāna used in context of verb with the root "**hanu**-to destroy or remove other's fault and shortcomings"

(1) Hanute • tuyha'meva, [tuyha'meva= tuyhaṁ+eva]
Hanute-(he) removes, hides. tuyhaṁ-your (faults). eva-only.
i.e. He hides your faults only.

(2) hanute • mayha'meva [Refer to the previous example for Sandhi] Hanute-(he) removes, hides. mayhaṁ-my (faults). eva-only
icce'va'mādi. and so on.

Ṭhā-payoge–Examples of Sampadāna in context of verb with the root "**ṭhā**-to stand"

(1) Upatiṭṭheyya-(should) stand nearby (to wait on). • sakyaputtānaṁ-to the sons of Sakyas. vaḍḍhakī-the carpenter.
i.e. The carpenter should stand near (to attend) to the sons of Sakyas (**i.e.** monks).

(2) • bhikkhussa-of the monk. • bhuñjantassa-while eating. Pānīyena vā-either by (passing) drinking-water. vidhūpanena vā-or by fanning (to keep him cool). upatiṭṭheyya-(should) stand by (to attend to). bhikkhunī-female monk. **i.e.** The female monk should wait on the monk while eating by passing water or by fanning.
icce'va'mādi.

Sapa-ppayoge– Examples of Sampadāna in the context of verb with the root "**sapa**-to curse, to swear"

(1) • Tuyhaṁ-your (to you). sapate-(he) curses. **i.e.** He curses you.

(2) • mayhaṁ-my (me). sapate. **i.e.** He curses me.

icce'va'mādi.

Dhāra-ppayoge– Examples of Sampadāna in context of verb with the root "**dhara**-to carry".

(1) Suvaṇṇaṁ-gold. • te-your. dhārayate-(He) carries.
i.e. (He, the debtor) carries your (the creditor's) gold. (It means that the debtor has to make repayment of gold to the creditor)
icce'va'mādi.

Piha-ppayoge–Examples of Sampadāna in the context of verb with the root "**piha**-to adore".
Sometimes other roots with the similar meanings can also necessitate the expression of Sampadāna. See examples in 2 and 3.
(a) In 2, the root "**Kamu**-to like, to wish" is found in the ***Kita*** noun verb "**dassanakāmā**". [**dassana**-see+**kāma**-want to]
(b) In example 3, the root "**isu**-to wish" is used in the ***ākhyāta*** verb "**Icchāmi**".

(1) • Buddhassa-the Buddha. aññatitthiyā-those having other belief and philosophies, heretics. pihayanti-adore.
i.e. Those having other belief and philosophies adore Buddha.
(2) devā-the deities. dassanakāmā-want to see. • te-you.
i.e. The deities (celestial beings) want to see you.
(3) yato-since. icchāmi-(I) prefer. • bhaddantassa-venerable one.
i.e. Since I prefer the Venerable one.
(4) • samiddhānaṁ-wealthy persons. pihayanti-adore. daliddā-poor people. **i.e.** The poor adore the rich people.
icce'va'mādi.

Kudha, duha, issa, usūya-ppayoge–Examples of the Sampadāna in the context of verb with the root "**kudha**-to be angry, **duha**-to spoil, **issa**-to be envious of, **usūya**-to be jealous of".
Kudha-root example:
(1) kodhayati-(he) is angry. • devadattassa-at Devadatta. **i.e.** (He is) angry at Devadatta.
(2) • tassa-to that king "kalābu". kujjha-(be) angry. mahāvīra-Oh respectable hermit of great effort. mā-do not. raṭṭhaṁ-the kingdom. vinassa-destroy. idaṁ-this. **i.e.** Oh respectable hermit of great effort! Be angry at that king "kalābu" (only). But, do not destroy this (whole) kingdom.

Duha-root example:
(1) Duhayati-spoils, destroys. • disānaṁ-directions. megho-rain.
i.e. The rains effect (the pleasant atmosphere of the) directions (for those wanting the clear skies).

Issa-root example:
(1) titthiyā-those having other views. • samaṇānaṁ-of the monks. issayanti-(are) envious. guṇagiddhena-craving for fame.

i.e. Craving for fame, those having other views, **i.e.** heretics, are envious of the monks.

(2) titthiyā • samaṇānaṁ issayanti lābhagiddhena-craving for offerings. **i.e.** Craving material-offerings, those having other views (**i.e.** heretics,) are envious of the monks.

Usūya-root example:

(1) dujjanā-bad people. • guṇavantānaṁ-of those having dignity. usūyanti-are jealous. guṇagiddhena-craving for dignity. **i.e.** Craving dignity, the bad guys are jealous of those with dignity.

(2) kā-of what (benefit is there). usūyā-being jealous. • vijānataṁ-of the wise. **i.e.** What benefit is there by being jealous of the wise!

icce'va'mādi.

Rādha, ikkha-icce'tesaṁ dhātūnaṁ payoge–Examples of Sampadāna in the context of verbs with the root "**rādha**-to accomplish, to be pleased (for verb in the first example), to injure (for verb in the second example). **ikkha**-to look at, to consider, to take into account". **Note:** Besides this root, other root of the similar meaning is also applied in the first example.

yassa akathitassa pucchanaṁ kammavikkhyāpanatthañ'ca, taṁ kārakaṁ sampadānasaññaṁ hoti, dutiyā ca.

When asking a question to the one who is muted (**Re:** the example No. 3, 4) and specifically telling one's emotions (kamma) to someone (**Re:** example No. 1, 2), that person being silent, that someone being talked to, is called "Sampadāna". (in such cases,) Dutiya (accusative) case is also applicable in addition to Catutthī (dative) case. See the examples carefully to clarify this explanatory sentence shown above.

rādha-root example:

(1) Ārādho'haṁ • rañño. [ārādho'haṁ=ārādho+ahaṁ] ārādho-(am pleased with). ahaṁ-I. • rañño-of the king.

(2) ārādho'haṁ • rājānaṁ-to King. [Here, accusative case is used as Sampadāna, meaning the same] **i.e.** I am pleased with king.

Note: "**of & to**" are only the meanings reflective of the case.

(3) Kyā'haṁ • ayyānaṁ aparajjhāmi. [kyā'haṁ=kiṁ+ahaṁ] Kiṁ-What (wrong). ahaṁ-do I. aparajjhāmi-offend.
• ayyānaṁ-to the Venerables. **i.e.** What do I offend against the Venerables?

(4) Kyā'haṁ • ayye aparajjhāmi. [Here, **accusative plural case, is**

applied for Sampadāna, meaning the same, in place of dative case]

Note: Both examples 3 & 4 are the types of usage and words said as a question of inquiry to the monks who remain silent without giving any polite response despite the repeated act of respectful greeting.

ikkha-root example:

(1) Cakkhuṁ • janassa dassanāya taṁ viya maññe. Cakkhuṁ viya-like the eye. • janassa-of people. dassanāya-to see. taṁ-that Venerable one. maññe-I think or it seems like. **i.e.** It seems that for people to see that Venerable one is like their only sight (at this moment).

(2) • āyasmato • upālittherassa upasampadā'pekkho upatisso. • āyasmato • upālittherassa-of Venerable Upāli, upasampad-ā'pekkho-considering to get ordained. upatisso-(the monk-to-be, a postulant) Venerable Upatissa.

i.e. The postulant Upatissa is considering(wanting) to get ordained (under the preceptorship) of Venerable Upāli.

Note: In this sentence, • **āyasmato** • **upālittherassa** are two words of Sampadāna in dative case. The word "**āyasmato**" is an adjective which modifies the next word. It equals to "Venerable", a form of respectful term used to address those senior ones. Its original base-word is actually "**āyasmā**". It is a **taddhita noun** with "**mantu**" affix which means "the one having long life". See **Sutta 371** for detail.

(3) • āyasmantaṁ vā [Sampadāna in accusative case]

icce'va'mādi.

Note: The word "• **upālitheraṁ**" is omitted in this example. In this example, Sampadāna word "• āyasmantaṁ" is **in accusative case though the meaning is the same. The next word "•upālittherassa"** of the first sentence **has to be in accusative case too.** So, it will be "**• āyasmantaṁ • upālitheraṁ**". Thus making two Sampadāna words to complete the meaning.

Paccā'suṇa anupatigiṇānaṁ pubbakattari–Examples of Sampadāna in the context of verb with the root "**su-**to listen to**,** prefixed with **pati** and **ā**", also the root "**ge-**to sing, prefixed with **anu** and **pati** Upasaggas".

suṇotissa paccā'yoge yassa kammuno pubbassa yo kattā, so sampadānasañño hoti.

The subject of first object, which is related to a verb with the root "**su-**to listen to**,** prefixed with **pati** and **ā**", is (to be herein) named a Sampadāna.

Taṁ yathā? For example,

Bhagavā bhikkhū eta'davoca [eta'davoca=etaṁ+avoca]
(An active voice sentence)
Bhagavā-the Lord Buddha. bhikkhū-monks. etaṁ-this word. avoca-said. **i.e.** Buddha said this discourse to the monks.

Note: In the above sentence, there are two objects (Kammas). They are **Bhikkhū** (the monks) and **etaṁ** (this word, **i.e.** Discourse).

Below is a grammatical explanation given by the great Grammarian Kaccāyana regarding the preceding sentence.
Bhikkhū'ti-the word "Bhikkhū". akathita kammaṁ-is called akathita kamma (non-principal object). **etan'**ti-the word "etaṁ". kathitakammaṁ-is called Kathita Kamma (the principal object).

Note: The student has to basically understand the nature of active and passive voice sentences in order to clearly understand "the principal and non-principal role of the subject and object which are determined according to the voice of a sentence. Please refer to "The formative system of Pāli Verbs" in Ākhyāta chapter, explained at the end of first section.

Yassa kammuno pubbassa yo kattā, so **bhagavā'**ti "yo karoti sa kattā" ti suttavacanena kattusañño.

Of the two Kammas (objects), the word "**Bhagavā**" which is subject of the first Kamma (Re: Bhikkhū) is named **Kattā** (doer, the one who does the action of saying the discourse to the monks) by the grammatical principle as stipulated by the Sutta "**yo karoti sa kattā**".

Evaṁ yassa kammuno pubbassa yo kattā,
so sampadānasañño hoti.

Thus, the subject of the first Kamma (after changing its role as a Subject) is named a Sampadāna. **i.e.** It becomes a Sampadāna.

Taṁ yathā? For example,
Note: Below, there are two examples.
In the first example, the verb is "**paccassosuṁ** (pati√ā√**su**+uṁ) **"**. Here, the root "**su**" is prefixed with **pati** and **ā.** In the second, the verb is "**āsuṇanti** (ā√**su**+ṇā-affix+anti) **"**. Here, the root word "**su**" is prefixed with an **ā.**
(1) Te bhikkhū • bhagavato paccassosuṁ.

Te-those. bhikkhū-monks. • bhagavato-(to the word) of Buddha. paccassosuṁ-listened or responded in affirmative.

i.e. Those monks listened (responded) to the Buddha.

Note: In this sentence, the word "**bhagavā**" in the first sentence becomes a Sampadāna by changing its case into dative case as "**bhaga vato**" as it receives the respectful attention (**i.e.** response) of the listener monks.

(2) āsuṇanti • Buddhassa bhikkhū.

āsuṇanti-(attentively) listen. • Buddhassa-of Buddha (to the Buddha). bhikkhū-monks.

i.e. The monks (attentively) listened to the Buddha.

Note: In this sentence, "**Budhassa**" is a synonymous with **bhagavato**.

Explanation

In the foregoing sentence "**Bhagavā bhikkhū eta'davoca**", the word "**Bhagavā**" is Subject. In the latter two sentences above, • **bhagavato** and • **Buddhassa** are **Sampadānas** in dative case. Now, it can be clearly seen that the word "**Bhagavā**", which had played the role of being a Subject in the first sentence, becomes a Sampadāna in next sentence when used in the context of the verb "**paccassosuṁ**" and here, the root "**su**" is prefixed with **pati** and **ā.**

In the second sentence, the Sampadāna word "**Buddhassa**" is a synonym of "**Bhagavato**" in the same case, playing the same grammatical role as a Sampadāna in the sentence used in the context of the verb "**āsuṇanti**". Here the root word "**su**" is prefixed with "**ā**".

Giṇassa anu, pati, yoge–Examples of Sampadāna in the context of verb with the root "**ge-**to sing., prefixed with **anu** and **pati** upasaggas".

yassa kammuno pubbassa yo kattā, so sampadānasañño hoti.

(Here too) the subject of the first Kamma word, is named Sampadāna.

Taṁ yathā? For example,

Bhikkhu janaṁ dhammaṁ sāveti.

Bhikkhu-monk. janaṁ-people. dhammaṁ-Dhamma. sāveti-cause it heard. **i.e.** The monk preaches dhamma to the devotees. [Causative sentence]

Note: In this sentence, the word "**Bhikkhu**" played the role of Subject. In next sentences below, it will become a Sampadāna word changing its case into dative as "**Bhikkhuno**". Please note that the word "**tassa**" also is a Sampadāna as it serves as an adjective of "**Bhikkhuno**".

(1) • tassa • bhikkhuno-(to the word) of that monk. jano-people. anugiṇāti-repeats after him. [anugiṇāti-anu√**ge**+ṇā+ti]
i.e. People repeat (say in chorus) after that preacher monk.

(2) • tassa • bhikkhuno jano patigiṇāti-rejoins in unison giving him (to the monk) appreciative words of Sādhu. **i.e.** People rejoin (in unison, giving) that monk appreciative words (such as saying Sādhu etc.). [patigiṇāti-pati√**ge**+ṇā+ti]

Explanatory Stanza

Yo vadeti sa **kattā**'ti, vuttaṁ **kamman**'ti vuccati.
yo paṭiggāhako tassa, **sampadānaṁ** vijāniyā.

The one who says, is to be known as **Kattā**, the subject.
That which is said, is called **Kamma**, the object.
The receiver of that said word, should be formally known as "**sampadāna**".
Icce'va'mādi. and so on.

Ārocana'tthe– Examples of Sampadāna in the context of verb with certain roots meaning "to announce, to summon, to make it known, to speak".

(1) ārocayāmi-(I) say. • vo-you. bhikkhave-Oh monks!
i.e. Oh monks! (I) tell you.

(2) āmantayāmi-(I) call on. • vo bhikkhave,
i.e. Oh monks! (I) call on you.

(3) paṭivedayāmi (I) let it be known. • vo bhikkhave,
i.e. Oh monks! (I) inform you.

(4) ārocayāmi • te-you. mahārāja-great king! **i.e.** I tell you great king!

(5) āmantayāmi • te mahārāja, **i.e.** (I) call on you great king.

(6) paṭivedayāmi • te mahārāja **i.e.** (I) inform you great king.
icce'va'mādi.

Ta'datthe– Examples of Sampadāna as dative-case nouns expressive of "to-infinitive". Here, the Sampadāna words are **āya** and **yā-ending nouns.** They are result-descriptive, formally called "**ta'dattha**" words. See all the examples carefully to clarify this grammatical concept of "**Ta'dattha Sampadāna**". [**ta'datthe**=**taṁ**-that+**atthe**-result]

(1) ūnassa-the need. • pāripūriyā-for the purpose of filling up. taṁ

cīvaraṁ-that emergency robe. nikkhipitabbaṁ-should keep.
i.e. That emergency robe should be kept to fulfil a (future) need.

(2) Buddhassa-of the Buddha. • atthāya-for the benefit,
i.e. For the benefit of Buddha.

(3) dhammassa-of the Dhamma. • atthāya-for the benefit,
i.e. For the benefit of Dhamma.

(4) saṅghassa-of the Sangha. • atthāya-for the benefit, jīvitaṁ-(one's) life. pariccajāmi-(I) sacrifice.
i.e. I sacrifice (my) life for the benefit of Sangha.

icce'va'mādi. so on.

Tum'atthe– Examples of Sampadāna in dative case nouns with "āya" whose meaning is similar to **tuṁ**-affixed ***kita*** verbs expressive of "to-infinitive, purpose". [**tumatthe**=tuṁ+atthe]

(1) • lokā'nukampāya-for compassion of the world. • atthāya-for the benefit. • hitāya-for the wellbeing. • sukhāya-for the happiness. devamanussānaṁ-of human and divine beings. Buddho-the Lord Buddha. loke-in the world. uppajjati-arises, emerges.
i.e. The Lord Buddha appears in the world for the compassionate action of the world, for the benefit, wellbeing and happiness of human and divine beings.

(2) Bhikkhūnaṁ-of the monks. • phāsuvihārāya-for purpose of living in peace. vinayo-the monastic codes (Rules and regulations). paññatto-clearly set out, set forth.
i.e. The monastic codes are imposed for (benefit of promoting) peaceful living of all the monks.

icce'va'mādi.

Note: The words ending in "**āya**" are Sampadāna, which are similar to **tuṁ**-affixed ***kita*** verbs expressive of purpose. See Sutta 109 for "**āya**". This is called "Tumattha Sampadāna".

Alama'tthappayoge–Examples of Sampadāna in the context of the **nipāta** particle "**alaṁ**"

alami'ti **arahati, paṭikkhitte**su.

The **nipāta** word "**alaṁ**" has two meanings: worthiness and rejection.

(Below are examples of Sampadāna in the context of the **nipāta** word "**alaṁ**" meaning worthiness. **Please carefully note that depending on the meaning, the case-ending (Vibatti) of the corresponding word, will change. In this meaning, the contextual word is in nominative case**)

(1) Alaṁ-deserves, is good. • me-to me. Buddho-Buddha.
i.e. I deserve (to see) Buddha.
(2) alaṁ • me rajjaṁ-kingdom. **i.e.** I deserve (to rule) the kingdom.
(3) alaṁ bhikkhu-monk. • pattassa-bowl.
i.e. The monk deserves (to have) bowl.
(4) alaṁ mallo-boxer. • mallassa-Boxer.
i.e. The boxer deserves (to wrestle with other) Boxer.
(5) arahati-deserves (to fight or play against.) mallo • mallassa.
i.e. The boxer deserves (to play against the other) Boxer.

Paṭikkhitte– (Examples) When the "alaṁ" means rejection. (Here, the contextual word is either in nominative or instrumental case.)
(1) alaṁ-of no use. • te-for you. rūpaṁ-beauty. karaṇīyaṁ-cosmetically made. **i.e.** Your cosmetically made beauty is of no use. (for the spiritual progress etc.)
(2) alaṁ • me-for me. hirañña, suvaṇṇena-by silver and gold.
i.e. Gold and silver is of no use for me (I do not need it)
icce'va'mādi.

Maññati-ppayoge, anādare, appāṇini– Examples of Sampadāna in context of the word "**maññe**" expressing disrespect, lifeless stuff.
(1) • kaṭṭhassa-(like) the wood. tuvaṁ-you. maññe-I Think.
i.e. I regard you (like a piece of) wood.
(2) • kaliṅgarassa-(like) useless chaff. tuvaṁ maññe.
i.e. I regard you (like useless) chaff.

Anādare'ti kimatthaṁ? What is the word "anādare" for? To show that the example below does not mean for "anādara-disrespect". So, it is inapplicable. (Catutthī Vibatti is not applied, Instead, Dutiyā only applied)
* Suvaṇṇaṁ-gold. viya-like. * taṁ-you. maññe.
i.e. I regard you like gold (You are like the precious gold).

Appāṇinī'ti kimatthaṁ? What is the word "appānini" for? To show that the example below is not an "appānini-a lifeless stuff" which is said in derogatory mode. So, it is inapplicable. (Hence, Dutiyā, accusative case only applied).
* Gadrabhaṁ-(like) mule. * tuvaṁ maññe. **i.e.** I think you as a mule.
icce'va'mādi.

Gatya'ttha'kammani–Examples of Sampadāna serving the role of Kamma (object) in the context of verbs with the root meaning "motion".

(1) • gāmassa-to village. pādena-by foot. gato-(he has) gone.
i.e. He has gone to village on foot.

(2) • nagarassa- to city. pādena gato.
i.e. He has gone to village on foot.

(3) appo-a few. • saggāya- to heaven. gacchati-goes.
i.e. A few go to heaven. [Here, the sampadāna word is with **āya**-function, in dative case]

• saggassa-to heaven.gamanena-by going. vā-in other usage.
[Here ordinary **sa**-vibatti, with no "āya" function]

(4) • mūlāya-to the original state of normalcy. paṭikasseyya-(should) pull. saṅgho-the community of Sangha. **i.e.** the Sangha (should) pull (reinstate that monk back) to the original state of normalcy.

Dutiyā ca, Examples where accusative (Dutiyā) case is applicable:

(1) * gāmaṁ-to village. pādena gato. **i.e.** He has gone to the village on foot.

(2) * nagaraṁ- to city. pādena gato. **i.e.** He has gone to the city on foot.

(3) appo * saggaṁ-to heaven. gacchati. **i.e.** A few go to the heaven.
* saggaṁ-to heaven. gamanena vā.

(4) * mūlaṁ- paṭikasseyya saṅgho. **i.e.** the Sangha (should) pull (reinstate that monk back) to the original state of normalcy.

icce'va'mādi.

Āsīsa'tthe– Examples of Sampadāna in the context of "wishing well".
Note: The Sampadāna, receiver of well-wishes is in dative case in all examples.

(1) • āyasmato-for Venerable. dīghāyuko-(being) long life. hotu-may it be! **i.e.** May you be of long-life !

(2) bhaddaṁ-good fortune or blessing. • bhavato-for your honorable. hotu! **i.e.** May there be good fortune or blessing for your honorable!

(3) kusalaṁ-wholesomeness . • bhavato hotu!
May there be wholesomeness (auspiciousness) for your honorable!

(4) anāmayaṁ-(being) healthy. • bhavato hotu!
May there be healthiness for your honorable!

(5) sukhaṁ-happiness. • bhavato hotu!
May there be happiness for your honorable!

(6) svāgataṁ-welcome. • bhavato hotu!
You are welcome your honorable!
(7) attho-benefit. • bhavato hotu!
May there be benefit for your honorable!
(8) hitaṁ-good. • bhavato hotu! May there be good for your honorable!
icce'va'mādi.

Sammuti-ppayoge– Examples of Sampadāna in context of the word "**sammuti**-to formally acknowledge,".
(1) aññatra-except for. saṅghasammutiyā-formal recognition of Sangha. • bhikkhussa-of a monk (for a monk). vippavatthuṁ-to live apart. na-not. vaṭṭati-permissible. **i.e.** Except through formal recognition of release from Sangha, a monk should not live apart (with his robes).
(2) sādhu-(it is) good. sammuti-giving formal recognition. • me-for me. tassa-that. bhagavato-Buddha. dassanāya-to see.
i.e. It is good giving me formal recognition to see that Buddha.
icce'va'mādi.

Bhiyya-ppayoge– Examples of Sampadāna in context of the word "**bhiyya**-beyond measure, excessively".
bhiyyoso-in excess, beyond. • mattāya-of measure. icce'va'mādi.

Sattamya'tthe– Examples of Sampadāna in the locative sense.
(1) • tuyhañ'ca'ssa āvi karomi, [tuyhañ'ca'ssa-tuyhaṁ+ca+assa]
Assa tuyhaṁ ca-in the presence of that you also. āvi-openly. karomi-(I) do, admit. **i.e.** I openly admit in the presence of that you.
(2) • tassa • me-to that me. sakko-the king of heaven. pātu'rahosi [pātu'rahosi=**pātu**-vividly, visible+**ahosi**-was] pātu-clearly visible. ahosi-was. The king of heaven appears to that me.
i.e. Sakka, the king of heaven appeared to me.
icce'va'mādi.

Note: "**tuyhaṁ assa**-that you", "**tassa me**-that me" are emphatic use of reference which used to be frequently found in the Pāli texts.

Atthaggahaṇena bahūsu akkharappayogesu dissati.

By the word "attha", [Refer to "attha" in "Sattamya'tthesu=Sattamī+**attha**esu"] sampadāna expression is also possible in the context of other "akkharā-words".

Taṁ yathā? For example,

(1) Upamaṁ-simile. • te-your. karissāmi-(I) will do.
i.e. I will do (**i.e.** show) you simile (for easy understanding).

(2) Dhammaṁ-Dhamma. • vo-you. desessāmi-(I) will preach.
i.e. I will preach you the Dhamma.

Sāra'tthe ca–(Here are some examples) related to noble meanings such as Buddha etc. too.

(1) desetu-teach. bhante-Venerable Lord. bhagavā-Buddha. dhammaṁ-Dhamma. • bhikkhūnaṁ-to the monks.
i.e. Lord Buddha!, teach Dhamma to the monks.

(2) • Tassa-for that person. phāsuvihārāya-for peaceful living. hoti-is.
i.e. (That) is for the purpose of peaceful living of that person.

(3) • etassa-this person. pahiṇeyya-(he) should send.
i.e. (He should) send that person.

(4) yathā-in which manner. • no-to us. bhagavā-Buddha. vyākareyya-would answer. tathā'pi-in that manner too. • tesaṁ-to them. vyākari-ssāma-(We are going to) tell.
i.e. We will tell them in the way Buddha would tell us.

(5) kappati-is permissible. • samaṇānaṁ-to the monks. āyogo-cloth-belt. **i.e.** Is a cloth-belt permissible for the monks? (to band around the waist to keep the upper robe in place firmly so as to prevent it from fluttering and slipping off)

(6) • amhākaṁ-for us. maṇinā-with ruby. attho-want.
i.e. We want ruby.

(7) ki'mattho • me. Buddhena. [kima'ttho=kiṁ+attho] kiṁ-what. attho-result. **i.e.** What benefit • me-for me. Buddhena- with Buddha.
i.e. Of what benefit for me with Buddha? or I have nothing to do with Buddha.

(8) seyyo-noble. • me-for me. attho-(May there be) the benefit.
i.e. (May there be) the noble benefit to me.

(9) bahū'pakārā-of great help. bhante-Lord Buddha! mahāpajāpati-gotamī-(Your aunt, foster mother) Mahāpajāpati Gotamī.
• bhagavato-for the lord Buddha.
i.e. Lord Buddha! (Your aunt) Mahāpajāpati Gotamī was of great help to you (when you were very young).

(10) bahū'pakārā-of much help. bhikkhave-monks. mātāpitaro-parents. • puttānaṁ-to children.
i.e. Monks! Parents are of great help to (their) children.

icce'va'mādi. Sesesu akkharappayogesu'pi aññe'pi payogā payogavicakkhaṇehi yojetabbā.

All those remaining examples of sampadāna expressions can also be applied by those skilled in the grammatical examples.

Caggahaṇaṁ vikappanattha, **vā**ggahaṇā'nukaḍḍhanatthaṁ.

The word "Ca" in Sutta has the purpose of pulling in the word "vā" which has a meaning of "**vikappana** (intellectual thinking on grammatical issues) " from the preceding Sutta to this Sutta.

Ye keci saddā sampadānappayogikā mayā no'padiṭṭhā. tesaṁ gahaṇatthaṁ idha vikappīyati vāsaddo.

Any instances of possible sampadāna examples yet unexplained by me in this Sutta, can also be applied. The word "vā" is included in this Sutta to allow such grammatical possibility.

Taṁ yathā? What are (some of) such examples?

(1) • Bhikkhusaṅghassa-of community of Monks. pabhū-is the lord. ayaṁ-this. bhagavā-Buddha.
i.e. This Buddha is the lord of community of monks.

(2) • desassa-of region. pabhū. ayaṁ rājā-this king.
i.e. This king is the lord of the region.

(3) • Khettassa-of the farming field. pabhū. ayaṁ gahapati-this householder. **i.e.** This householder is the lord of farming field.

(4) • araññassa-of the forest. pabhū. ayaṁ luddako-this hunter.
i.e. This hunter is the lord of forest.

icce'va'mādi. and so on.

What do these examples mean? It means that the use of the word "**Pabhu**" can also necessitates a Sampadāna. Its corresponding noun has to be in the dative case in the way certain English words like "want" or "listen" are to be usually used with the preposition "to" etc.

Kvaci dutiyā, tatiyā, pañcamī, chaṭṭhī, sattamya'tthesu ca.

In some instances, the expression of sampadāna can also happen in the sense of dutiyā (Accusative), tatiyā (Instrumental), pañcamī (Ablative), chaṭṭhī (Genitive) and sattamī (Locative).

२७८, ३२०. योधारो तमोकासं

278, 320. **Yo'dhāro ta'mokāsaṁ.**

[Yo+ādhāro+taṁ+okāsaṁ. 4 words]

[V] Yo ādhāro, taṁ **okāsa**saññaṁ hoti.

That which assumes the role of a location (in regard of time, things, events and other various conditions on which things come to pass) is to be named "**Okāsa** or **ādhāra** (Locative) ".

Svā'dhāro catubbidho: vyāpiko, opasilesiko, vesayiko sāmīpiko cā'ti.

That Ādhāra is of four kinds. Namely:

(1) **Vyāpika** ādhāra locative by means of permeation.
[vyāpika-**vi√apa+ṇika**, vyāpa-being permeated all over, ika- pertaining to. "**ā**" is a vuddhi vowel of "**a**" in the root **apa.**]

(2) **Opasilesika** ādhāra locative by being stuck closely (in a place or with something. **i.e.** contact. or by being related to in terms of time or any correlative situation.
[opasilesika-**upa√silisa+ṇika**, upasilisa-being closely stuck, in close contact with, related. **ika**-pertaining to. "**o**" is a vuddhi vowel of "**u**" in **upa.** There is also a vuddhi vowel "**e**" of the second "**i**" of the root **silisa**-to stick to.]

(3) **Vesayika** ādhāra, by mode of domaiṇ where one becomes a part of it or an integral element in it.
[Vesayika-**visaya+ṇika**, **visaya**-domain, **ika**-pertaining to. "**e**" is a vuddhi vowel of "**i**" in **visaya.**]

(4) **Sāmīpika** ādhāra, by mode of proximity, nearness.
[Sāmīpika-samīpa+ika, **samīpa**-near, proximity, **ṇika**-pertaining to. "**ā**" is a vuddhi vowel of the first "**a**" in **samīpa.**]

Tattha **vyāpiko** tāva–Of those four, at first (Here are the examples of) **vyāpika** ādhāra.

- jalesu-in the waters. khīraṁ-milk. tiṭṭhati-stands **i.e.** exists. **i.e.** The milk exists in the water.

- tilesu-in sesame seeds. telaṁ-oil. **i.e.** The oil is in the sesame.
- ucchūsu-in the sugar-cane plants. raso-the taste.
  i.e. The (sweet) taste is in the sugar-cane (being spread all over in it).

Opasilesiko–(Here are the examples of) **Opasilesika** ādhāra.

- pariyaṅke-on the royal couch. rājā-the king. seti-lies down.
  i.e. The king lies down on the couch.
- āsane-in (the assigned) seat. upaviṭṭho-dwells. saṅgho-the Sangha. **i.e.** The Sangha dwells in the seat.

Vesayiko–(Here are the examples of) **Vesayika** ādhāra.

- bhūmīsu-on the earth. manussā-humans. caranti-move about. **i.e.** The humans move on the earth (They cannot live being separated from it as the earth is their domain of life).
- antalikkhe-in the sky. vāyū-the winds. vāyanti-blow.
  i.e. The winds blow in the space.
- Ākāse-in the sky. sakuṇā-the birds. pakkhandanti-fly.
  i.e. The birds fly in the sky.

Sāmīpiko–(Here are examples of) **Sāmīpika** ādhāra.

- vane-in the forest. hatthino-the elephants. caranti-move about.
  i.e. The elephants move in the forest.
- gaṅgāyaṁ-in the river Ganges. ghoso-the noise. tiṭṭhati-exists.
  i.e. The noise exists in the river Ganges.
- vaje-in the cattle pen. gāvo-the cows. duhanti-(are) milked.
  i.e. The cows are milked in the cattle pen.
- sāvatthiyaṁ-in the city of Sāvatthi. viharati-(Buddha) lives.
- jetavane-in the Jeta grove temple. **i.e.** Buddha lives in the Jeta-grove temple in the city of Sāvatthi.

Okāsa'micca'nena kvattho? Okāse sattamī.
What is the benefit by terming "okāsa"?
It has the benefit of ease of reference in such Suttas as: "Okāse sattamī" etc.

२७९, २९२. येन वा कयिरते तं करणं

279, 292. **Yena vā kayirate taṁ karaṇaṁ.**

[Yena+vā+kayirate+taṁ+karaṇaṁ. 5 words]

[V] Yena vā kayirate, yena vā passati, yena vā suṇāti, taṁ kārakaṁ **karaṇa**saññaṁ hoti.

That by means of which an action is done, by means of which one sees or hears, is called "**karaṇa,** the instrumental". [See the karaṇa words in the instrumental cases]

- Dattena-by sickle. vihiṁ-the paddy plant. lunāti-(He) cuts.
  i.e. He cuts paddy by sickle.
- vāsiyā-by adze. kaṭṭhaṁ-the wood. tacchati-(He) chops (to shape).
  i.e. He chops (to shape) the wood by adze.
- pharasunā-by axe. rukkhaṁ-the tree. chindati-(He) cuts down.
  i.e. He cuts down the tree by axe.
- kudālena-by shovel. pathaviṁ-the soil. khaṇati-(He) digs.
  i.e. He digs the soil by shovel.
- satthena-by knife. kammaṁ-the work. karoti-(He) does.
  i.e. He does the work by means of the knife.
- Cakkhunā-by eye. rūpaṁ-the sight. passati-(He) sees.
  i.e. He sees the sight by the eye.

Karaṇa-micca'nena kvattho? Karaṇe tatiyā.
What is the benefit by terming "karaṇa"?
It has the benefit of ease of reference in such Suttas as: "Karaṇe tatiyā" etc.

२८०, २८५, यं करोति तं कम्मं

280, 285. **Yaṁ karoti taṁ kammaṁ.**

[Yaṁ+karoti+taṁ+kammaṁ. 4 words]

[V] Yaṁ vā karoti, yaṁ vā passati, yaṁ vā suṇāti, taṁ kārakaṁ **kamma**saññaṁ hoti.

That which is being done, or being seen or being heard etc. is called "**kamma,** the Object". [See Kamma words in the accusative case]

- Chattaṁ-umbrella. karoti-(He) makes. **i.e.** He makes an umbrella.
- rathaṁ-the chariot or vehicle. karoti-(He) makes.
  i.e. He makes the chariot.
- rūpaṁ-the sight. passati-(He) sees. **i.e.** He sees the sight.
- saddaṁ-the sound. suṇāti-(He) hears. **i.e.** He hears the sound.
- kaṇṭakaṁ-the thorn. maddati-(He) tramples on.
  i.e. He tramples on the thorn.
- visaṁ-poison. gilati-(He) swallows. **i.e.** He swallows the poison.

Kamma'micca'nena kva'ttho? Kammatthe dutiyā.
What is the benefit by terming "kamma"?
It has the benefit of ease of reference in such Suttas as "Kammatthe dutiyā" etc.

२८१, २९४. यो करोति स कत्ता

281, 294. **Yo karoti, sa' kattā.**

[Yo+karoti+so+kattā. 4 words]

[V] Yo karoti, so **kattu**saññо hoti.

Whoever does an action (or whichever facilitates to happen), is called a "**kattu or Kattā** (doer, **i.e.** the subject) ".
[See the Kattu words in instrumental case]

- Ahinā-by snake. daṭṭho-(is) bitten. naro-man.
  i.e. The man is bitten by snake.
- garuḷena-by Garuda bird. hato-(is) killed. nāgo-the dragon.
  i.e. The dragon is killed by Garuda bird.
- Buddhena-by Buddha. jito-(is) conquered. māro-the evil one.
  i.e. The evil one is conquered by Buddha.
- upaguttena-by Venerable Upagutta. māro-the evil one. bandho-(is) bound, restrained.
  i.e. The evil one is restrained by Venerable Upagutta.

Kattu-icca'nena kvattho? Kattari ca.
What is the benefit by terming "kattu (subject"?
It has the benefit of ease of reference in such Suttas as "Kattari ca" etc.

२८२, २९५. यो कारेति स हेतु

282, 295. **Yo kāreti. sa' hetu.** [Yo+kāreti+so+hetu. 4 words]

[V] Yo kattāraṁ kāreti, so **hetu**saññо hoti, kattā ca.

The one who prompts someone (while doing something) to do, (that prompter) is named "**hetu,** reason, prompter" as well as "**Kattā**-agent or subject".

Summary: This Sutta defines the nature of **Hetu Kattā** or **Causative subject** in a causative sentence.

(1) • So puriso-that man. taṁ purisaṁ-to that man, **i.e.** him. kammaṁ-work. kāreti-(causes) to do.
i.e. That man prompts him to do the work.

(2) • So puriso-that man. tena purisena-to that man. kammaṁ kāreti.[the same meaning]

(3) • So puriso-that man. tassa purisassa-to that man. kammaṁ kāreti. [the same meaning]

Evaṁ-in the same way,
hāreti-(causes) to bring, pāṭheti-(causes) to recite, pāceti-(causes) to cook, dhāreti-(causes) to carry.

Hetu-iccanena kvattho? Dhātūhi ṇe ṇaya ṇāpe ṇāpayā kāritāni hetvatthe.
What is the benefit by terming "hetu"?
It has the benefit of ease of reference in such Suttas as "Dhātūhi ṇe, ṇaya, ṇāpe, ṇāpayākāritāni hetvatthe" etc.

Note: The examples shown in this Sutta are **Causative sentence and verb examples**. Please note the structural patterns carefully. It will be seen that there is one causative subject, two objects and one causative verb. These will be the integral parts of a typical causative sentence. Also note the case-endings applicable in the subject and the objects.

२८३, ३१६. यस्स वा परिग्गहो तं सामी

283, 316. **Yassa vā pariggaho, taṁ sāmī.**

[Yassa+vā+pariggaho+taṁ+sāmī. 5 words]

[V] Yassa vā pariggaho, taṁ **sāmī**saññaṁ hoti.

The one who possesses something, is called "**sāmī** (the owner, possessive) ".
[See the "sāmi words" in the genitive case. This **Sāmi is non-kāraka**]

- Tassa bhikkhuno-of that monk. paṭivīso-share, portion. **i.e.** That monk's share.
- tassa bhikkhuno patto-bowl, **i.e.** That monk's bowl.
- tassa bhikkhuno cīvaraṁ-robe, **i.e.** That monk's robe.
- attano-of oneself. mukhaṁ-face. **i.e.** One's face.

Sāmī-iccanena kvattho? Sāmismiṁ chaṭṭhī.
What is the benefit by terming "sāmi"?
It has the benefit of ease of reference in such Suttas as "Sāmismiṁ chaṭṭhī" etc.

२८४, २८३. लिङ्गत्थे पठमा

284, 283. **Liṅga'tthe paṭhamā.**

[Liṅga-atthe+paṭhamā. 2 words]

[V] Liṅgatthā'bhidhānamatte paṭhamāvibhatti hoti.

The **paṭhamā** vibhatti (Nominative case) should be applied when signifying the definitive gender and its meaning (be it a masculine or a feminine or a neuter) in nominative sense.

[Plain nouns] • Puriso-man, • purisā-men,
[Numeral nouns] • eko-one, • dve-two,
[Nipāta, indeclinables] • ca-also, • vā-either or,
[Vocative indeclinable particles] • he, • ahe, • re, • are-hey, Hi!

Note: These examples show a wider variety of words where this paṭhamā vibatti is to be applied. But the vibatti applied after the indeclinable words such as Nipāta and other indeclinable words are usually to be elided while the Vibattis applied after other ordinary nouns undergo various forms of morphological changes.

२८५, ७०. आलपने च

285, 70. **Ālapane ca.** [Ālapane+ca. 2 words]

[V] Ālapana'tthā'dhike liṅgatthā'bhidhānamatte ca paṭhamāvibhatti hoti.

When addressing and signifying the meaning of mere gender, **paṭhamā** vibhatti is to be applied after that noun being addressed to (also after the vocative particles such as "**bho, he**" etc.).

[Singular] Bho • purisa-Oh man!
[Plural] bhavanto • purisā-Oh men!
[Singular] bho • rāja-Oh king!
[Plural] bhavanto • rājāno-Oh Kings!
[Singular] He • sakhe-Oh friend! [Plural] He • sakhino-Oh friends!
Note: This Ālapana (Vocative) is non-kāraka.

२८६, २९१. करणे ततिया

286, 291. **Karaṇe tatiyā.** [Karaṇe+tatiyā. 2 words]

[V] Karaṇakārake tatiyāvibhatti hoti.

When expressing a Karaṇa, **tatiyā** vibhatti (Instrumental case) is to be applied after the noun denoting it.

- Agginā-by fire. kuṭiṁ-the hut. jhāpeti-burns.
  i.e. The hut burns by fire.
- manasā-by mind. ce-if. • paduṭṭhena-unwholesome.
  i.e. If (committed) by unwholesome mind.
- manasā-by mind. ce-if. • pasannena-clean or wholesome.
  i.e. If (committed) by wholesome mind.
- kāyena-by body. kammaṁ-deed, work. karoti-(he) does.
  i.e. He does the deed or the work by (means of) body.

२८७, २९९, सहादियोगे च

287, 299. **Sahā'diyoge ca.** [Saha-ādiyoge+ca. 2 words]

[V] Sahādiyog'atthe ca tatiyāvibhatti hoti.

When used in the contexts of words such as "saha (together) and so on", a **tatiyā** vibhatti (Instrumental case) is to be applied after the noun related thereto.

(1) Sahā'pi-together also. • gaggena-with a monk named "Gagga". saṅgho-the Sangha. uposathaṁ-(twice monthly recital of the

vinaya rules called) uposatha. kareyya-should conduct. vinā'pi-without also, • gaggena-with a monk named "gagga". [Here the contextual Nipata is "**Saha**-with, **vinā**-without"]
i.e. Sangha should conduct Uposatha either with Venerable Gagga or without him in attendance.

(2) • Mahatā-with a large. • bhikkhusaṅghena-community of monks. saddhiṁ-together. **i.e.** Together with a large community of monks. [Here the contextual Nipata is "**Saddhiṁ**-together"]

(3) • Sahassena-with a thousand. samaṁ-equally. mitā-(are) measured.
i.e. (They) are equally measured with a thousand. [Here the Nipata is "**Samaṁ**-equal to".]

Note: This Sutta enjoins to apply Tatiyā vibatti (instrumental case) when certain Nipata particles which means "with, together, similar to, equal with, without" and so on are used in the context of a sentence.

२८८, २९३. कत्तरि च

288, 293. **Kattari ca.** [Kattari+ca. 2 words]

[V] Kattari ca tatiyāvibhatti hoti.

When expressing **a Kattā (subject) (in a** Kamma-dominant **passive voice sentence) tatiyā** vibhatti (Instrumental case) is to be applied after the noun denoting the subject.

Please note carefully that this Sutta enjoins to apply Tatiyā vibhatti only after a subject in a passive voice sentence. Not in an active voice sentence. This kind of subject is called "Avutta Kattā" which means non-principal subject in a Kamma-dominant passive voice sentence.

- Raññā-by king. hato-(is) killed. poso-man.
  i.e. The man is killed by the king.
- Yakkhena-by (a) spirit. dinno-(is) given, granted. varo-a boon.
  i.e. A boon is given (granted) by (the) spirit.
- Ahinā-by snake. daṭṭho-(is) bitten. naro-man.
  i.e. The man is bitten by the snake. [All are passive voice sentences]

२८९, २९७. हेत्वत्थे च

289, 297. **Hetva'tthe ca.** [Hetu-atthe+ca. 2 words]

[V] Hetva'tthe ca tatiyāvibhatti hoti.

When expressing a reason, **tatiyā** vibhatti (Instrumental case) is to be applied after the noun denoting the reason.
Note: This type of Vibatti is called "Instrumental of reason".

- Annena-by rice. vasati-(he) lives.
  i.e. He lives by (means of) rice.
- dhammena-by Dhamma. vasati-(he) lives.
  i.e. He lives by means of Dhamma.
- vijjāya-by knowledge. vasati-(he) lives.
  i.e. He lives by means of knowledge.
- sakkārena-by devotion. vasati-(he) lives.
  i.e. He lives by means of devotion.

२९०, २९८. सत्तम्यत्थे च

290, 298. **Sattamya'tthe ca.** [Sattamī-atthe+ca. 2 words]

[V] Sattamya'tthe ca tatiyāvibhatti hoti.

(As an exceptional usage,) **tatiyā** vibhatti (Instrumental case) can also be applied in the locative sense. [See the examples and meanings carefully as such examples are frequently found in the texts]

Examples of Instrumental case in the Locative sense:
- Tena kālena, • tena samayena-at that time, then.
- yena kālena, • yena samayena-at which time, when,
- tena kho pana • samayena-at that time, then.

["**kho** & **pana**" are two particles without meaning here though they may have meaning sometimes in some instances.]

२९१, २९९. येनङ्गविकारो

291, 299. **Yena'ṅgavikāro.** [Yena+aṅgavikāro. 2 words]

[V] Yena vyādhimatā aṅgena aṅgino vikāro lakkhīyate. Tattha tatiyāvibhatti hoti.

When expressing a physical defect, a **tatiyā** vibhatti (Instrumental case) is applied after the noun denoting the defective bodily part. [See the examples to clarify this injunction]

(1) • Akkhinā-by eye. kāṇo-is blind.
i.e. The one who is blind by eye.

(2) • hatthena-by hand. kuṇī-(the one who is) crooked.
i.e. The one who is crooked by hand.

(3) kāṇaṁ-(the one who is) blind. passati-(he) sees. • nettena-by eye. **i.e.** By eye, he sees the blind person.

(4) • pādena-by foot. khañjo-(the one who is) lame.
i.e. The one who is lame by foot.

(5) • piṭṭhiyā-by back. khujjo-(the one who is) bent.
i.e. The one who is bent by back, hunchbacked.

२९२, ३००. विसेसने च

292, 300. **Visesane ca.** [Visesane+ca. 2 words]

[V] Visesana'tthe ca tatiyāvibhatti hoti.

When expressing a modifying quality of adjective (visesana), **tatiyā** vibhatti (Instrumental case) is applied after that noun denoting the adjective of modification. [See Visesana words in instrumental case]

- Gottena-by race. gotamo-(is) gotama. nātho-Lord Buddha.
  i.e. Lord Buddha is Gotama by race.
- suvaṇṇena-by (having) golden complexion. abhirūpo-(is) handsome.
  i.e. (He) is handsome by (virtue of having) golden complexion.
- tapasā-by austerity. uttamo-(is) noble.
  i.e. (He) is noble by (the practice of) austerity.

Visesana

Here, the students should understand the Visesana, which means distinguishing attributive. There are two kinds of Visesanas. They are:

(1) Tulyā'dhikaraṇa Visesana [**Tulya**-similar+**adhikaraṇa** position, **i.e.** Vibatti case-ending. T**he appositional** Visesana]

(2) Binnā'dhikaraṇa Visesana [**Binna**-dissimilar+**adhikaraṇa**-position, **i.e.** Vibatti case-ending. N**on-appositional** Visesana]

Both play important roles in the structure of a sentence. Both are qualifier adjectives in different word-forms playing the same role.

The former qualifies a noun of similar case-ending while **the latter** qualifies a noun of different case-ending. In this Sutta, only the latter is to be taken as the referred Visesana to be applied with a Tatiyā (Instrumental case).

Gender and Number

A Visesana has its pair component-word known as "**Visesya or Visesitabba**" which means "the qualified". They are related to each other as the qualifier and the qualified in terms of syntactical relationship and have to be of similar gender and number for the Tulyā'dhikaraṇa Visesana. The gender and number are usually determined by "**Vesesya or Visesitabba** (The modified) " word.

In order to simplify and make it clearly understandable for the students, here is some more detailed explanation on practical aspects:

(a) If the word qualified is of masculine gender and singular, its qualifier word "Vesesana" has to be also of the same masculine gender and singular in number. If plural, both has to be plural.

Example:

(1) **Abhirūpo puriso**-the handsome man. (singular)

(2) **Abhirūpā purisā**-the handsome men. (plural)

Here, the qualified word or Visesya is **puriso,** a noun belonging to masculine gender and singular in number. The qualifier word (Visesana) is "**Abhirūpo**". So it has to follow gender and number of the word it qualifies. In example 2, the qualified word is plural. So, it has to be in plural too.

(b) If the qualified is of feminine gender and singular, its qualifier word "Vesesana" has to be of feminine gender and singular. If plural, both has to be of the same numbers.

Example:

(1) **Abhirūpā itthī**-the beautiful woman.

(2) **Abhirūpāyo itthiyo**-the beautiful women.

Here, the qualified word or Visesya is **itthī**, a noun belonging to feminine gender and singular in number. The qualifier word (Visesana) is "**Abhirūpā**". So, it has to follow gender and number of the word it qualifies. In example 2, the qualified word is plural. So, it has to be plural.

(c) If the qualified is of neuter gender and singular, its qualifier word "Vesesana" has to be of neuter gender and singular. If plural, both has to be of the same numbers.
Example:
(1) **Abhirūpaṁ pupphaṁ**-the beautiful flower.
(2) **Abhirūpāni pupphāni**-the beautiful flowers.
Here, the qualified word or Visesya is **pupphaṁ**, a noun belonging to neuter gender and singular in number. The qualifier word (Visesana) is "**Abhirūpaṁ**". So it has to follow the gender and number of the word it qualifies. In example 2, the qualified word is plural. So, it has to be plural. As **Binnā'dhikaraṇa Visesana is applicable Visesana in this Sutta,** it doesn't have to be of similar gender and numbers. The examples themselves will clarify this.

२९३, ३०१. सम्पदाने चतुत्थी

293, 301. Sampadāne catutthī. [Sampadāne+catutthī. 2 words]

[V] Sampadānakārake catutthīvibhatti hoti.

In cases of Sampadāna expression, **catutthī** vibatti (Dative case) is applied after the noun denoting it.

(1) • Buddhassa vā-either to the Buddha. • dhammassa vā-or to the Dhamma. • saṅghassa vā-or to the Sangha. dānaṁ-alms. deti-(He) offers. **i.e.** He offers alms either to Buddha, or to the Dhamma or to the Sangha.
(2) dātā-giver. hoti-(He) is • samaṇassa vā-either to the monk. • brāhmaṇassa vā-or to the Brāhmin.
i.e. (He is) the donor either to the monk or to the Brāhmin.

२९४, ३०५. नमोयोगादीस्वपि च

294, 305. Namoyogā'dīsva'pi ca.

[Namo, yoga-ādīsu+api+ca. 3 words]

[V] Namoyogā'dīsva'pi ca catutthīvibhatti hoti.

A **catutthī** vibhatti (Dative case) is also applicable in the context of the words "**namo** (to salute) " etc. after the noun "being saluted".

(1) Namo-(my) bowing. • te-to you. Buddha-Lord Buddha! vīra-the lord of great effort! or Brave one! atthu-(may it) be. [vīra'tthu= vīra+atthu] **i.e.** May my bowing (salutation) be to the Lord Buddha of great effort!

(2) Sotthi-blessing. • pajānaṁ-of beings. atthu-(may it) be. **i.e.** May blessings be to (all) beings!

(3) Namo-bowing. karohi-do. • nāgassa-to the monk. **i.e.** Do bowing to the monk! [Here, nāga means an enlightened holy monk, not dragon nor snake]

(4) Svāgataṁ-auspicious coming. • te-your. mahārāja-great king! **i.e.** Welcome the great king!

Note: the words **sotthi** (blessing), **svāgataṁ** (welcome) etc. are included in the context for the application of Catutthī.

२९५, ३०७. अपादाने पञ्चमी

295, 307. **Apādāne pañcamī.** [Apādāne+pañcamī. 2 words]

[V] Apādānakārake pañcamīvibhatti hoti.

In cases of an Apādāna expression, **pañcamī** vibhatti (Ablative case) is applied after the noun denoting it. [See the apādāna words in ablative case]

- Pāpā-from sin. cittaṁ-the mind. nivāraye-should restrain. **i.e.** One should restrain the mind from sin.
- Abbhā-from the cloud. mutto'va [mutto'va=mutto+iva] mutto-free. iva-like. candimā-moon. **i.e.** Like the moon being free from the clouds.
- Bhayā-from danger. muccati-is free. so naro-that man. **i.e.** That man is free from danger or fear.

२९६, ३१४. कारणत्थे च

296, 314. **Kāraṇa'tthe ca.** [Kāraṇa-atthe+ca. 2 words]

[V] Kāraṇa'tthe ca pañcamīvibhatti hoti.

Pañcamī vibhatti (Ablative case) is also used in expressing "the reason" after the noun denoting it. [See the words denoting the reason in the ablative case. Also refer to Sutta 108 for "ā" function]

• Ananubodhā-for not knowing. • appaṭivedhā-for not penetrating (by means of insight knowledge, path and fruition knowledge). catunnaṁ-four. ariyasaccānaṁ-noble truths. yathābhūtaṁ-rightly.

• adassanā-for not seeing.

i.e. For reasons of not knowing, not penetrating and not seeing four noble truths rightly.

Note: Also see another Sutta No. 289 regarding the applicable vibatti after such nouns denoting the reason. This Pañcamī is called "ablative of reason".

२९७, २८४. कम्मत्थे दुतिया

297, 284. **Kamma'tthe dutiyā.** [Kamma-atthe+dutiyā. 2 words]

[V] Kamma'tthe dutiyāvibhatti hoti.

To denote a Kamma, **dutiyā** vibhatti (Accusative case) is to be applied after the noun denoting Kamma (the object). [See the kamma words in accusative case, singular "aṁ"]

• Gāvaṁ-the cow. hanati-(He) kills.
• Vīhayo-the paddy plants. lunāti-(He) cuts.
• Satthaṁ-the weapon. karoti-(He) makes.
• Ghaṭaṁ-the ghee. karoti-(He) makes.
• Rathaṁ-the chariot. karoti-(He) makes.
• Dhammaṁ-the Dhamma. suṇāti-(He) listens.
• Buddhaṁ-the Buddha. pūjeti-(He) honors.
• Vācaṁ-the speech. bhāsatī-(He) says.
• Taṇḍulaṁ-the rice. pacati-(He) cooks.
• Coraṁ-the thief. ghāteti-(He causes to) kill

२९८. २८७. कालद्धानमच्चन्तसंयोगे

298, 287. **Kāla'ddhāna'maccantasaṁyoge.**

[Kāla, addhānaṁ+accanta-saṁyoge. 2 words]

[V] Kāla'ddhānaṁ accantasaṁyoge dutiyāvibhatti hoti.

When expressing a continuous, on-going action (or a situation or something) which occurs for a certain period or which lasts up to a certain distance, **dutiyā** vibhatti

(Accusative case) is applied after the noun denoting time or distance.

Examples of the Kāla Accantasaṁyoga
(Time-specific on-going incidence)

(1) • Māsaṁ-for a month. maṁsodanaṁ-the meat-mixed rice. bhuñjati-(He) eats. **i.e.** He eats the meat-mixed biryani rice for a month.

(2) • Saradaṁ-for autumn. ramaṇīyā-is pleasant. nadī-the river. The river is pleasant for the period of autumn.

(3) • Māsaṁ-for a month. sajjhāyati-(He) chants. He chants for a month.

Examples of the Addhāna Accantasaṁyoga
(Distance-specific on-going incidence)

(1) • Yojanaṁ-for (the distance of) a yojana. vanarāji-is the forest shadow. The forest-shadow is for (up to) the distant of a yojana. **i.e.** The shadowy length of forest is up to a yojana's distance.

(2) • Yojanaṁ-for (the distance of) a yojana. dīgho-is long. pabbato-mountain. **i.e.** The length of mountain is for a Yojana-distance long.

(3) • Kosaṁ--for (the distant of) a kosa. sajjhāyati-(He) chants. He chants for a Kosa. **i.e.** His chanting time lasts up to a Kosa's distance.

Accantasaṁyogeti kimatthaṁ?

What is the word "Accantasaṁyoge" for?

To show that there is no nature of "accantasaṁyoga" in the example shown below. So, no dutiyā vibatti is applied after it. [Only locative case is applied instead]

* Saṁvacchare-annually. bhojanaṁ-the food. bhuñjati-(He) eats.

Note: Kosa and **Yojana** are measurement units of geographic distance in ancient India.

Acca'nta=**ati**-beyond+**anta**-the end, the limit. **i.e.** continuously, without end. **saṁyoga**-being related to, involved.

२९९, २८८. कम्मप्पवचनीययुत्ते

299, 288. **Kamma’ppavacanīyayutte.**

[Kammappavacanīyayutte. 1 word]

[V] Kammappavacanīyayutte dutiyāvibhatti hoti.

When certain upasagga words complementary to a Kamma, are prefixed to a verb, **dutiyā** vibhatti (Accusative case) is to be applied after the Kamma-word which has a modified meaning afterwards.

[The **upasagga** prefixes such as **abhi** and **anu** in the examples called "Kammappavacanīya" are shown in bold, underlined.]

(1) • Taṁ kho pana-of that. • bhavantaṁ-honorable. • gotamaṁ-gotama. evaṁ-thus. kalyāṇo-good. kittisaddo-the sound of fame. **abbh**uggato-spread far and wide. [**abhi**-being spread+**uggato**-rises. **i.e.** The good sound of fame of Buddha (Referred to as Honorable Gotama) spread far and wide.

(2) • pabbajita’**manu**pabbajiṁsu.

[pabbajitaṁ+**anu**-following, in emulating+pabbajiṁsu]

pabbajitaṁ-to the Buddha (who had entered into) monkhood.

anupabbajiṁsu-(following him, his brethren too) become ordained.

i.e. To the Buddha entering monkhood, (his brethren too) ordained emulatively.

Note: Certain **Upasagga** particles which can distinctively change the meaning of a Kamma word by affecting to have specific meaning are called "**Kammappavacanīya**-the meaning-enhancer of Kamma". [**Kamma**-a Kamma, **i.e.** object+**pa**-specially+**vacanīya**-to indicate]

३००, २८६. गति बुद्धि भुज पठ हर कर सयादीनं कारिते वा
300, 286. **Gati buddhi bhuja paṭha hara kara sayā' dīnaṁ kārite vā.**

[Gati, buddhi, bhuja, paṭha, hara, kara, si-ādīnaṁ+kārite+vā. 3 words]

[V] **Gati, buddhi, bhuja, paṭha, hara, kara, sayā'**dīnaṁ payoge kārite dutiyāvibhatti hoti vā.

When certain verbs based in roots such as **Gamu, budha, bhuja, paṭha, hara, kara, si,** are used in a causative sentence, **dutiyā** vibhatti (Accusative case) is sometimes applied after the noun denoting the Kamma (a subordinate object of causative verb).

Note: The injunction of this Sutta reflects only a common pattern of case-endings applicable after sub-ordinate object in a causative sentence. This kind of object is called a causative-object or sub-ordinate object (Kārita-Kamma or payujjita-Kamma). In addition to Dutiyā-Vibatti (accusative) case, other cases such as **tatiyā** (instrumental) and **chaṭṭī** (Genitive) cases can also be applied after the causative-object. Please see the underlined words below which denote causative object in three case-endings. This is generally observed grammatical rule regarding applicable vibatti case-ending of the causative objects.

(1) Puriso-man. • purisaṁ-the other man. • gāmaṁ-to village. gāmayati-made (him) go, prompted to go.
i.e. The man made the other man (causes him to) go to the village. (also) The man prompts (**i.e.** orders) the other man (a servant) to go to the village.

(2) puriso * purisena vā, (Here the causative object is in instrumental case singular.)

(3) puriso * purisassa vā. (Here the causative object is in genitive case singular.)

Note: These two sentences have the same meaning, **except the case-endings of causative-object which is shown underlined.**

Evaṁ-in the same way.

bodhayati-cause him to know, bhojayati-cause him to eat, pāṭhayati-cause him to chant, hārayati-cause him to bring, kārayati-cause him to do, sayāpayati-cause him to lie down. Evaṁ-(one should know the same pattern of causative sentences) in this way. sabbattha-in all. kārite-(other) causative sentence(s) too.

३०१, ३१५. सामिस्मिं छट्ठी

301, 315. **Sāmismiṁ chaṭṭhī.** [Sāmismiṁ+chaṭṭhī. 2 words]

[V] Sāmismiṁ chaṭṭhīvibhatti hoti.

When expressing a sāmi (possessor or owner), **chaṭṭhī** vibhatti (Genitive case) is applied after the noun denoting it.

• Tassa • bhikkhuno paṭivīso. • Tassa • bhikkhuno patto.
• Tassa • bhikkhuno cīvaraṁ. • Attano mukhaṁ.
(Re: Sutta No. 283)

३०२, ३१९. ओकासे सत्तमी

302, 319. **Okāse sattamī.** [Okāse+sattamī. 2 words]

[V] Okāsakārake sattamīvibhatti hoti.

When expressing an okāsa (Locative), **sattamī** vibhatti (Locative case) is to be applied after the noun denoting it.

- Gambhīre-in deep. • odakantike-at the end of (underground) water. **i.e.** In the depth at the end of underground-water, (one keeps one's precious wealth as it is the custom in the ancient times.)
- Pāpasmiṁ-in sin. ramati-enjoys. mano-The mind. **i.e.** The mind enjoys in sin (unwholesome thoughts and things).
- Bhagavati-in (the presence of) Buddha. brahmacariyaṁ-the noble practice. vussati-practices. kulaputto-the son of noble family. **i.e.** The son of noble family practices the noble Dhamma in Buddha.

३०३, ३२१. सामिस्सराधिपति दायाद सक्खी पतिभू पसुत कुसलेहि च

303, 321. Sāmi'ssarā'dhipatidāyādasakkhīpatibhū pasutakusalehi ca.

[Sāmi, issara, adhipati, dāyāda, sakkhī, patibhū, pasuta, kusalehi+ca. 2 words]

[V] **Sāmī, issara, adhipati, dāyāda, sakkhī, patibhū, pasuta, kusala,** icce'tehi payoge **chaṭṭhī**vibhatti hoti **sattamī** ca.

Either a **chaṭṭhī** (Genitive case) or **sattamī** vibatti (Locative case) are applicable in the context of the words such as "**sāmī, issara, adhipati, dāyāda, sakkhī, patibhū, pasuta** and **kusala**" after the nouns corresponding to those words. [See each pair of examples shown in two applicable case-endings]

(1) • Goṇānaṁ-of cows. sāmī-master, owner, **i.e.** the master of cows. • goṇesu-in/over the cows. sāmī-master, owner, **i.e.** the master over cows.

(2) • Goṇānaṁ issaro-lord, **i.e.** the lord of cows. • goṇesu issaro. **i.e.** the lord over cows.

(3) • Goṇānaṁ adhipati-ruler, • goṇesu adhipati.

(4) • Goṇānaṁ dāyādo-heir, • goṇesu dāyādo.

(5) • Goṇānaṁ sakkhī-witness, • goṇesu sakkhī,

(6) • Goṇānaṁ patibhū-guarantor, • goṇesu patibhū.

(7) • Goṇānaṁ pasuto-progenitor, • goṇesu pasuto.

(8) • Goṇānaṁ kusalo-skillful, expert. • goṇesu kusalo.

३०४, ३२२. निद्धारणे च

304, 322. Niddhāraṇe ca. [Niddhāraṇe+ca. 2 words]

[V] **Niddhāraṇa**'tthe ca **chaṭṭhī**vibhatti hoti, **sattamī** ca.

When making a selection (out of many for the purpose of comparison to highlight a distinction), either **chaṭṭhī** (Genitive case) or **sattamī** vibatti (Locative case) is applied after the noun denoting "many" from which the selection is made.

Note: Please note that only **chaṭṭhī** or **sattamī** vibatti **in the plural number** can be used. As a rare exception, a singular in the locative case is found to be used in the Pāli texts. See the sample examples and sentences shown below.

(1) (a) Kaṇhā-the black one. • gāvīnaṁ-of all cows. sampannakhī-ratamā-(is of) more delicious milk. [Chaṭṭhī] Of all cows, the black cow is of the most delicious milk.

(b) kaṇhā • gāvīsu-in or among all cows. sampannakhīratamā. [Here is a Sattamī case-ending, of the same meaning.]

(2) (a) Sāmā-the gold-skinned one. • nārīnaṁ-of the women. dassanīyatamā-most attractive. [Chaṭṭhī]

(b) sāmā • nārīsu-in or among all women. dassanīyatamā. [Sattamī] Of all women, the gold-complexioned woman is the most attractive.

(3) (a) • Manussānaṁ-of all men. khattiyo-the warrior. sūratamo-the most brave. [Here is Chaṭṭhī]

(b) • manussesu-in or among all men. khattiyo sūratamo. [Sattamī] Of all men, the warrior is the most brave.

(4) (a) • Pathikānaṁ-of all wayfarers. dhāvanto-the runner. sīghatamo-(is) the quickest. [Chaṭṭhī]

(b) • pathikesu-in or among all the wayfarers. dhāvanto-the runner. sīghatamo-(is) the quickest. Of all the travelers, the runner is the quickest. [Sattamī]

Niddhāraṇa-Catukka
(Niddhāraṇa-quadriad)

According to traditional teaching of grammar devised by teachers, there are four Niddhāraṇa-related things which all students of Pāli grammar should understand. They are called Niddhāraṇa-Catukka. Namely:

(1) Niddhāraṇa-samudāya (The selection-group)
(2) Niddhāraṇa (Act of Selection)
(3) Niddhāraṇiya (The selected)
(4) Niddhāraṇa-hetu (The reason of selection)

Of the three,

(1) The group of people, animals or inanimate-things from which selection is being made is called **Niddhāraṇa samudāya.**

(2) Making selection by act of pointing out the distinctive quality of someone or something is **Niddhāraṇa.**

(3) Someone or something being selected for purpose of comparison is called **Niddhāraṇiya.**

(4) The distinctive qualities are **Niddhāraṇa-hetu** (the reason for selection). The function of this Sutta is applicable only after Niddhāraṇa-samudāya. This means that when making a selection for distinctive comparison, either Chaṭṭhī or Sattamī Vibattis in plural are to be applied after nouns which denote Niddhāraṇa-samudāya (Group from which selection is made).

Explanation

Example: Kaṇhā • gāvīnaṁ sampannakhīratamā.

(1) In the example above, the word "**gāvīnaṁ**" which indicates the group of cows, is **Niddhāraṇa-smudāya.** That is why a Chaṭṭhī Vibatti, plural number, is applied after it. [**niddhāraṇa**-selection+**samudāya**-group]

(2) The words indicative of selection "**sampannakhīratamā**" is **Niddhāraṇa,** which is a statement of distinction [**ni**-out+**dhara**-to take+**yu**-act of]

(3) The word "**Kaṇhā**" which indicates black cow is **Niddhāraṇiya** (the selected animal for its distinctive quality of milk) [ni+dhara+**anīya**-that which is being selected]

(4) The distinctively delicious sweet taste of the milk produced by black cow is **Niddhāraṇa-hetu** (Reason of selection. **Hetu**-reason)

Now, the students can also easily analyze other niddhāraṇa examples based on this clear and simple explanation.

३०५, ३२३. अनादरे च

305, 323. **Anā'dare ca.** [Anādare+ca. 2 words]

[V] Anādare **chaṭṭhī**vibhatti hoti, **sattamī** ca.

When expressing disrespect (in the context of two concurring actions, one being neglected, the other proceeding to perform an action regardless) either a **chaṭṭhī** (Genitive case) or **sattamī** vibatti (Locative case) can be applied after both the noun denoting "anādariya, the disrespected" and after its correlative word. [**anā'dara**=**na**-without+**ādara**-

respect, disregard]

Note: Please note that only one of **chaṭṭhī** or **sattamī** vibatti in the same number can be applied. See the sample sentences and examples below. Unlike in the Niddhāraṇa expression, both singular and plural numbers are applicable in this "anādara expression".

(1) • Rudato-while crying, ***cgs***. • dārakassa-the boy's (the boy), ***cgs***. pabbaji-(the father) renounces, ***āv***. [Chaṭṭhī, singular example] **i.e.** While the boy is crying, the father renounced (to become an ascetic or a monk).

(2) • Rudantasmiṁ-when crying, ***cls***. • dārake-the boy, ***cls***. pabbaji.***āv***. [Sattamī, singular, example] **i.e.** At the time (or as) the boy is crying, the father renounced (to become an ascetic or a monk).

Anā'dara-Catukka

(Anādara-quadriad)

Here too, there are four Anādara-related things the students of Pāli grammar should thoroughly understand. They are called Anādara-Catukka. Namely:

(1) Anādara (Act of neglect)
(2) Anādaravanta (Anādara-correlative)
(3) Anādariya (The neglected)
(4) Anādariyavanta (Anādariya-correlative)

Of the three components,

(1) The action of neglect to living things or inanimate-things is called **Anādara.** In this case, it is usually a verb, expressive of such action.
(2) Any word which is related to that act of anādara, such as the one who commit such act is called **Anādaravanta.** It is usually a subject or a word denoting it. [anādara+vanta. See Sutta 368 for this suffix "vantu"]
(3) Someone or something being neglected is called **Anādariya.** [anādara+iya]
(4) Any word syntactically related to it as a verb (usually an auxiliary verb) etc. is called **Anādariyavanta.** [anādariya+vanta]

The function of this Sutta is applicable only after Anādariya and its correlative. This means that Chaṭṭhī or Sattamī Vibattis are to be applied after the nouns which denote Anādariya and its correlative words.

Explanation

Example: • Rudato • dārakassa pitā pabbaji.

While the boy is crying, the father renounces. **i.e.** left (to become an ascetic). [The word "**pitā**-father" is added to make sentence more complete]

(1) In the example above, the word "**Dārakassa**" which indicates the neglected, crying boy, is "**Anādariya**-the disrespected or the neglected". That is why a Chaṭṭhī, singular "**sa**" Vibatti is applied after it.

(2) The word indicative of the boy's crying act "**Rudato**" is **Anādariya-correlative** which is related to "Dārakassa". A similar Chaṭṭhī Vibatti is to be applied after it as it is **Anādariya-correlative.** [Re: Sutta 187, 127, to understand the morphological procedure of this word]

(3) The word "**Pitā**-father" which indicates father who renounces home without compassionate regard for the crying boy is **Anādara-correlative** (the neglector, which plays the role as a subject)

(4) The word "**pabbaji**" which indicates "renouncing act" is **Anādara** (a verb
related to the subject as the doer of disrespectful act)

Now, Students can also easily analyze the second example by being based on the explanation of this example.

Note: Despite it may literally mean "non-respect", the actual purpose of this grammatical concept of "**Anādara**" is to describe two concurrent actions going on (sometimes in a pitiful, frustrating manner), not in the sense of intentional disrespect.

Here is one more relevant example to clarify this:

E.g. Ñātīnaṁ Pekkhataṁ Maccu ādāya gacchati.

While the relatives are looking on, the death goes (away) by snatching (the loved ones).

This example is very simple and vividly clear to understand. While relatives are looking on, or desperately thinking about what they can do for their sick, almost dying, beloved one who is lying on the bed, death invisibly takes away the loved ones as if snatching by force.

In this example,

(1) The words "ādāya gacchati-goes by snatching" are Anādara.

(2) The word "Maccu-death" is an Anādara-correlative.

(3) The word "Ñātīnaṁ-the relatives" is Anādriya.

(4) The word "Pekkhataṁ-while looking on" is its correlative (Anādriyavanta). Both are in Chaṭṭhī (genitive) plural case.
Regarding the word "Pekkha**taṁ**", please refer to Sutta No.187, 128 on how this word is brought to completion through due morphological procedures. It is hoped that the students will clearly understand this seemingly **complex grammatical concept** and will be able to write such sentences on their own without much difficulty.

३०६, २८९. क्वचि दुतिया छट्ठीन मत्थे

306, 289. **Kvaci dutiyā chaṭṭhīna'matthe.**

[Kvaci+dutiyā+chaṭṭhīnaṁ+atthe. 4 words]

[V] **Chaṭṭhī**na'matthe kvaci **dutiyā**vibhatti hoti.

(As an exceptional usage), **a dutiyā** vibatti sometimes can be applied **in chaṭṭhī** (genitive sense) **expression.**
Note: This kind of dutiyā(accusative) is called Accusative-in-genitive sense found in the Pāli texts.

Example of the Accusative case in Genitive sense:
Apissu-in fact. • maṁ-(in) my (mind). aggivessana-Oh Aggivessana! tisso-three. upamā-similes. paṭibhaṁsu-intuitively come up.
i.e. Oh Aggivessana! In fact, three similes come up in my mind intuitively (out of blue).

३०७, २९०. ततियासत्तमीनञ्च

307, 290. **Tatiyā, sattamīnañ'ca.**

[Tatiyā, sattamīnaṁ+ca. 2 words]

[V] **Tatiyā, sattamī**naṁ atthe ca kvaci **dutiyā**vibhatti hoti.

(As an exceptional usage), **a dutiyā** vibatti (an accusative) sometimes can be used **in tatiyā** (instrumental sense) and **sattamī** (locative sense) **expressions.**

Examples of the Accusative in Instrumental sense:
(1) Sace-if. • maṁ-with me. samaṇo gotamo-the monk Gotama. ālapissati-will talk. **i.e.** If the monk Gotama will talk with me.
(2) tvañ'ca [tvañca=tvaṁ+ca]-you too. • maṁ-with me. nābhibhāsasi-do not talk. **i.e.** You too do not talk with me.

Evaṁ tatiya'tthe. Thus, (these examples in the accusative case are) in the sense of instrumental.

Examples of the Accusative in Locative sense:

(1) • Pubbaṇhasamayaṁ-in the morning. nivāsetvā-having dressed. **i.e.** Having dressed in the morning.

(2) • ekaṁ-at one. • samayaṁ-time, **i.e.** on one occasion. bhagavā-the lord Buddha **i.e.** At one time, the Lord Buddha (is staying in such and such a place etc.)

Evaṁ sattamya'tthe. Thus, (these words in the accusative case) are in the sense of locative.

३०८, ३१७. छट्ठी च

308, 317. **Chaṭṭhī ca.** [Chaṭṭhī+ca. 2 words]

[V] **Tatiyā, sattamī**naṁ atthe ca kvaci **chaṭṭhī**vibhatti hoti.

(As an exceptional usage), a **chaṭṭhī** vibatti sometimes can be applied **in tatiyā** (instrumental, subject) and **sattamī** (locative) **sense expressions.**

Note: These kinds of Chaṭṭhī are called the genitive-in-instrumental, the genitive-in-locative sense, which are found the Pāli texts

Examples of the Genitive in Instrumental sense:

(1) Kato-done. • me-by me. kalyāṇo-the good deed (meritorious deed), **i.e.** The good deed (is) done by me.

(2) kataṁ • me pāpaṁ-unwholesome, bad deed. **i.e.** The bad deed (is) done by me.

Evaṁ tatiya'tthe. Thus, (these examples in genitive case) are in the sense of instrumental.

Note: Please do not be confused with ordinary instrumental which normally means "with". In this Sutta, it only means **instrumental subject** which means "by", mostly found as the meaning of subjects used in passive voice sentences. This type of word in genitive case, but whose meaning is the instrumental subject "by", is usually referred to as "Katv'attha-Chaṭṭhī" in grammatical terms. Such words usually play similar role of the subject in a passive voice sentence as the verbs they syntactically related to are structured using an affix of Kamma-sense only. This is one of a very delicate point of grammar.

[Katv'attha-Chaṭṭhī=**kattu**-Subject in instrumental+**attha**-sense. **Chaṭṭhī**-genitive-case word which has the sense and role of a Kattā, **i.e. Subject-genitive, or agent genitive**].

Examples of the Genitive in Locative sense:

(1) Kusalā-(are) skillful. • naccagītassa-in dancing and singing. sikkhitā-trained. cāturitthiyo [cāturitthiyo=cāturo+itthiyo], cāturo-beautiful (चातुर्य -shrewdness, lovely,). itthiyo-women. **i.e.** The pretty women skilled and trained in dancing and singing.

(2) kusalo-(are) skillful? tvaṁ-you. rathassa-of chariot. • aṅgapaccaṅgānaṁ-in (things related to) various components. **i.e.** Are you skilled in the chariot's component parts?

Evaṁ sattamya'tthe. Thus, (these examples of genitive case) are in the sense of locative.

Kvacī'ti kimatthaṁ?

What is the word "kvaci" for?

To show that in the example shown below, the function of Sutta is inapplicable as it is restricted by the word "kvaci".

(1) Yo-which. vo-you. ānanda-Oh Ānandā! * mayā-by me. dhammo ca- Dhamma also. vinayo ca-monastic discipline also. desito-have taught. paññatto- have promulgated,
i.e. Oh Ānandā! Dhamma which have been taught and Vinaya which had been prescribed by me (will be your teachers).

(2) ānando. Venerable Ānandā. * atthesu-in matters of meanings (of the various Dhamma). vicakkhaṇo-(is) wise.
i.e. Ānandā is wise in the matters of meanings of Dhamma.

३०९, ३१८. दुतियापञ्चमीनञ्च

309, 318. **Dutiyā, pañcamīnañ'ca.**

[Dutiyā, pañcamīnaṁ+ca. 2 words]

[V] **Dutiyāpañcamī**nañ'ca atthe kvaci **chaṭṭhī**vibhatti hoti.

(As an exceptional usage), **a chaṭṭhī** vibatti (genitive case) sometimes can be used **in dutiyā** (accusative) and **pañcamī** (ablative) **sense expressions.**

Examples of the Genitive in Accusative sense:

(1) • Tassa-to that person. bhavanti-will be. vattāro-those who censure.
i.e. There will be people censuring him. [vattāro-speakers, those who say in displeasure and disapproval]

(2) Sahasā-in a hurry. • kammassa-the action. kattāro-doers.
i.e. Those doing the action in a hurry.

Evaṁ dutiya'tthe. Thus, (these examples are) in the sense of accusative.

Note: This type of words in genitive case, but whose meaning is the accusative "to", is usually referred to as "**Kamma'ttha-chaṭṭhī**" in a typical formal grammatical term. Such words usually play a similar role of the object in any sentence of both voices. [Kamma'ttha-chaṭṭhī=**kamma**-Object in accusative+**attha**-sense. **Chaṭṭhī**-genitive case word**. i.e.** the **object-genitive or patient-genitive**]. This is also very delicate point of grammar.

Examples of the Genitive in Ablative sense:

(1) A'ssavanatā-for reason of not hearing. • dhammassa-from the Dhamma. parihāyanti-(they) lost.
i.e. They lost for not hearing Dhamma.
[**assavanatā**=**a**-not+**savana**-hearing+**tā**-suffix, due to a state of. See Sutta 360]

(2) Kinnu kho [Kinnu kho=Kiṁ+nu+kho] Kiṁ-why. ahaṁ-I. • tassa sukhassa-from that happiness. bhāyāmi-should be afraid of.
i.e. Why I should be afraid of that happiness?

(3) Sabbe-all. tasanti-are frightened • daṇḍassa-from punishment.
i.e. All are afraid of punishment.

(4) Sabbe bhāyanti-fear. • maccuno-from death.
i.e. All are afraid of death.

(5) Bhīto-feared. • catunnaṁ-from four. • āsīvisānaṁ-from quickly poisonous. • ghoravisānaṁ-from strongly poisonous.
i.e. Being fearful of four snakes of quick poison and strong poison.

(6) Bhāyāmi-(I) fear. • ghoravisassa-from strongly poisonous. • nāgassa-from snake.
i.e. I am afraid of snakes of quick poison and strong poison.

Evaṁ pañcamy'atthe. Thus, (these examples are) in the sense of ablative.

३१०, ३२४. कम्मकरणनिमित्तत्थेसु सत्तमी

310, 324. Kamma, karaṇa, nimitta'tthesu sattamī.

[Kamma, karaṇa, nimitta-atthesu+sattamī. 2 words]

[V] **Kamma, karaṇa, nimitta**'tthesu **sattamī**vibhatti hoti.

(As an exceptional usage), a **sattamī** vibatti (locative case) sometimes can be applied **in Kamma** (accusative), **karaṇa** (instrumental), and **nimitta** (reason-descriptive) **sense expressions.**

Note: These kinds of Sattamī are called the locative in accusative-sense, the locative in instrumental-sense, locative of reason(reason-descriptive sattamī, also called **nimitta-sattamī**, or **absolute-sattamī**) which are occasionally found in the canonical texts. The last kind of Sattamī is frequently found in many Suttas of this grammar text.

Example of the Locative in Accusative sense:

(1) Sundarā'vuso [Sundarā'vuso= Sundarā+āvuso] Sundarā-(are) nice. āvuso-Oh friends! ime-these. ājīvakā-heretics. • bhikkhūsu-to the monks. abhivādenti-bow (pay respect.)

i.e. Oh friends! These heretics are nice that they bow to the monks.

Evaṁ kammatthe.

Thus, (this example is) in the sense of kamma, accusative.

Examples of the Locative in Instrumental sense:

(1) • Hatthesu-by hands. piṇḍāya-for alms. caranti-go.

i.e. By hands (the monks) go for alms. (They put food in the hands as they do not have bowls).

(2) • Pattesu-by bowls. piṇḍāya caranti.

i.e. By bowls (the monks) go for alms.

(3) • Pathesu-by roads. gacchanti-go.

i.e. By (means of) roads, (people) go.

Evaṁ karaṇatthe.

Thus, (these examples are) in the sense of karaṇa, instrumental.

Examples of the Locative in Nimitta (Locative of reason) sense:

(1) Dīpi-the leopard. • cammesu-for the skins. haññate-(is) killed.

i.e. The leopard is killed for (its) hide.

(2) Kuñjaro-the elephant. • dantesu-for tusks. haññate-(is) killed.

i.e. The elephants are killed for (their) tusks (ivories).

evaṁ nimitta'tthe.
Thus, (these examples are) in the sense of nimitta, reason.

३११, ३२५. सम्पदाने च

311, 325. **Sampadāne ca.** [Sampadāne+ca. 2 words]

[V] **Sampadāne** ca **sattamī**vibhatti hoti.

(As an exceptional usage), a **sattamī** vibatti (Locative case) is applied **in the sampadāna** (Dative sense) **expression.**
Note: This kinds of Sattamī is called the locative in dative-sense, which is sometimes found in the canonical texts.

Examples of the Locative in Dative sense:

(1) • Saṅghe-of Sangha (community of monks as a whole). dinnaṁ-the offered charity. mahapphalaṁ-(is) of great result.
i.e. Alms donated to Sangha is of great benefit.

(2) • Saṅghe-of Sangha. tvaṁ-you. gotamī-Oh Gotamī! dehi-give.
i.e. Gotamī! (You) donate to the Sangha.

(3) • Saṅghe-of Sangha. te-by you. dinne-when given. ahañ'ce'va [ahaṁ+ca+eva]-to me also. pūjito-honored. bhavissāmi-will be.
i.e. When Sangha is offered by you, it is like honoring me (Buddha) too. (When you offer Sangha, it is like honoring me as well.)

३१२, ३२६. पञ्चम्यत्थे च

312, 326. **Pañcamya'tthe ca.** [Pañcamī-atthe+ca. 2 words]

[V] **Pañcamy**a'tthe ca **sattamī**vibhatti hoti.

(As an exceptional usage), a **sattamī** vibatti (Locative case) is applied **in the Pañcamī** (ablative sense) **expression.**
Note: This kind of Sattamī is called the locative in ablative-sense, which is found in the Pāli canon.

Examples of the Locative in Ablative sense:

• Kadalīsu-from (eating) banana plants. gaje-the elephants. rakkhanti-(people) prevent.
i.e. People prevent the elephants from eating banana plants.

३१३, ३२७. कालभावेसु च

313, 327. **Kālabhāvesu ca.** [Kāla, bhāvesu+ca. 2 words]

[V] Kāla, bhāvesu ca kattari payujjamāne **sattamī**vibhatti hoti.

When a subject is being engaged to time and action (of the two concurring incidences), a **Sattamī** vibatti (Locative case) is to be applied.

Explanation

When expressing two concurrent actions using time or action (an event) as a correlative marker, and with a subject being involved in the act, a **sattamī** vibatti is applied after the noun denoting time, or action along with the corresponding subject or the object of the action. This Sutta enjoins to apply a Sattamī vibatti after **the subject or the object** and **the verb** denoting coinciding action or event. In such a sentence, the verb is usually **nta, māna** or **ta**-suffixed **kita verbs** though Ākhyāta verbs are sometimes used to express the last action out of the two concurring actions in a precise and simple manner. See the examples below carefully to understand this seemingly complex grammatical concept and its applied function in the practical sentence.

Example of Kāla-lakkhaṇa
(Time-definitive concurrent action)

(1) • Pubbaṇhasamaye-in the morning. gato-(he) went. (First action)
• sāyanhasamaye-in the evening. āgato-(he) comes. (Subsequent incident) **i.e.** He went in the morning. In the evening, he came back.

Example of Bhāva-lakkhaṇa
(Action-definitive concurrent action)

(1) • Bhikkhūsu-(when) the monks, ***clp*** • bhojīyamānesu-(are still) eating, ***clp***. gato-(he) went, ***kv***. **i.e.** When the monks are still eating, he went. • bhuttesu-having eating (when they finished eating), ***clp***. āgato-(he) came back. ***kv***. **i.e.** When having eaten, he came. (When the monks finished eating, he came back)

(2) • Gosu-(when) cows. ***clp*** • duyhamānesu-(are being) milked. ***clp.***

gato-(he) goes, **i.e.** When the cows are still being milked, he goes.

• duddhāsu-when milked (when milking is done), ***clp***. āgato-(he) came back. **i.e.** When having milked, he came. (When milking is done, he came back).

Note: In these two examples, the **present passive participle** is used in the first incidence while the **past passive participle** is employed in the next incidence. Please note carefully this delicate mode of sentence structure.

Lakkhaṇa-Catukka

(Lakkhaṇa-quadriad)

There are four Lakkhaṇa-related things which all the students of Pāli grammar should understand so that they will have a clear and comprehensive understanding of this grammatical concept. They are called Lakkhaṇa-Catukka. Namely:

(1) Lakkhaṇa (The act of first Marking)
(2) Lakkhaṇavanta (Lakkhaṇa-correlative)
(3) Lakkhya (The concurring act called "the marked")
(4) Lakkhya-vanta (Lakkhya-correlative)

Of these four,

(1) When an ongoing primary event and another secondary incidence are taking place at the same time, the primary event is used as a marker of the secondary event. Such act of marking is called "**Lakkhaṇa**" by the ancient grammarians which means "the mark".

(2) Its correlative word, either it be a subject or an object that is syntactically related to it, is called "**the Lakkhaṇavanta**".

(3) The secondary incidence, is termed "**Lakkhya**".

(4) Its correlative word, either it be a subject or an object, is called "**Lakkhyavanta**".

The function of this Sutta is to apply Sattamī Vibatti (Locative case) after "Lakkhaṇa and Lakkhaṇa-correlative", so that it becomes a complete and meaningful sentence when expressing two concurrent actions.

Explanation

Example: • Bhikkhūsu • bhojīyamānesu puriso gato.

While or when the monks are eating, the man goes.

["**puriso**-man" is added for completeness's sake of the sentence]

Here, the man's going incidence is marked by the primary event of the monks' eating.

(1) In the example above, the word "**bhojīyamānesu**" which indicates the primary event of the monk's eating, is **Lakkhaṇa** by means of which the man's going is marked.

(2) The word "**Bhikkhūsu**" is its correlative object. Therefore, both are in the locative, plural case of Sattamī vibatti.

(3) the word "**gato**" which indicates the secondary action of man's going, is "**Lakkhya**".

(4) The word "**Puriso**" is its correlative which serves as a subject "goer". These two words are inapplicable by the rule of this Sutta.

The Injunction of Suttas 305, 313

The Sutta 305 and 313 enjoins the two prevalent grammatical rules regarding the expression of two simultaneous actions, one based on the concept of "anādara" and the other based on time and action as definitive markers. Regardless of what has been explained in two Suttas, the students should know that **there are also some methods of expressing two concurring incidences using relative pronouns and short sentences. The sentence structures based on the rules enjoined by these two Suttas are far more concise and needs less word.**

It should also be noted that even though there is no element of disrespect nor any definitive marker, one can still write the sentences based on the rules enjoined by these Suttas. Although it may at first seem a bit complex to the beginner, it is hoped that all the necessary simple explanation given thus far will suffice to make these two complex injunctions clear and simple to understand.

३१४, ३२८. उप'ध्याधिकिस्सरवचने

314, 328. **Upa'dhyā'dhiki'ssaravacane.**

[Upa, adhi+ādhika, issara, vacane. 2 words]

[V] **Upa, adhi**-iccetesaṁ payoge **adhika, issara**-vacane **sattamī**vibhatti hoti.

When used in the context of certain upasagga particles such as **upa** and **adhi,** meaning **over** and **the lord** respectively, a **sattamī** vibatti (Locative case) is applied (to its correlative noun qualified by those upasaggas).

Note: Upasagga words applied in the sentence have specific meanings which can thereby affect the case-ending of the nouns they are related to. See the case-endings of each example carefully to clearly understand this Sutta's function.

(1) **Upa**-(is) over, in excess. • khāriyaṁ-than a measure of "khāri". doṇo-a measure of "doṇa".
i.e. A measure of "doṇa" is in excess of a "khāri". (A "doṇa" is more than a "khāri")

Note: "khāri" and "doṇa" are measurement units of the grain in ancient India.

(2) **upa**- (is) over, in excess. • nikkhe-than a measure of "nikkha". kahāpaṇaṁ-the measure of "kahāpaṇa".
i.e. A measure of "kahāpaṇa" is in excess of a "Nikkha".
(A "Kahāpaṇa" is more than a "Nikkha")
Note: "nikkha" and "kahāpaṇa" are measurements of the monetary units in ancient India just as cents and dollar are common monetary units.

(3) **Adhi**-(is) the retinue. • brahmadatte-of the king Brahmadatta. pañcālā-(the people) of Pañcāla.
i.e. The people of Pañcāla are retinue of the king Brahmadatta.

Note: Though this example is mostly found in the texts, "Adhi brahmadatto pañcālesu. **i.e.** The king Brahmadatta is the lord of the people of Pañcāla" is also applicable text. In the grammatical rule, the word denoting the lordship or dominancy is in nominative case and the word denoting the subject of lordship or "the dominated" is usually in the locative case. Comparing with next two examples will clarify this fact which conform to this usage pattern and grammatical norm.

(4) **adhi**-(is) the lord. • naccesu-over the dancers. gotamī-(a lady named) Gotamī. **i.e.** Gotamī is the chief of all dancers. (She is the leader of the dance-ensemble)

(5) **adhi**-(is) the lord. • deve**su**-over all the celestial beings.
Buddho-the Lord Buddha. **i.e.** Buddha is the Lord over all celestial beings.

३१५, ३२९. मण्डितुस्सुक्केसु ततिया च

315, 329. **Maṇḍitu'ssukkesu tatiyā ca.**

[Maṇḍita, ussukkesu+tatiyā+ca. 3 words]

[V] **Maṇḍita-ussukka**-icce'tesva'tthesu **tatiyā**vibhatti hoti, **sattamī** ca.

When used in the context of the words **maṇḍita** (being clear and unobstructed), **ussukka** (to strive, or being strenuous) or any other synonymous word, either **tatiyā** (Instrumental case) or **sattamī** (Locative case) is to be applied after the nouns related to those words.

Examples of the word "maṇḍita"

(Here, a synonymous word "pasīdito" is used instead)

(a) • Ñāṇena-by intellect. pasīdito-(is) clear, unobstructed.
i.e. (Buddha or his disciple are) clear or unobstructed by (in terms of) intellect. [Tatiyā example]

(b) • ñāṇasmiṁ-in the intellect. vā-to show other applicable case-ending.
pasīdito-(is) clear, unobstructed. [Sattamī example]

Examples of the word "Ussuka"

(a) • ñāṇena-by intellect. ussukko-(is) strenuous.
i.e. (Buddha or his disciples are) strenuous by (in terms of) intellect.

(b) • ñāṇasmiṁ-in intellect. vā ussukko-(is) strenuous.
tathāgato vā-either Buddha. tathāgatagotto vā-or the one in lineage of Buddha. **i.e.** a disciple.
i.e. Either Buddha or Buddha's disciple are intellectually strenuous.

Iti nāmakappe kārakakappo chaṭṭho kaṇḍo.

Kāraka Chapter, the Sixth Section of Noun ends.

Kārakakappo niṭṭhito.

Kāraka Chapter ends.

4. Samāsa Kappa

Samāsa (Compound Noun) Chapter

Sattama Kaṇḍa

The Seventh Section of Noun

३१६, ३३१. नामानं समासो युत्तत्थो

316, 331. **Nāmānaṁ samāso yutta'ttho.**

[Nāmānaṁ+samāso+yuttattho. 3 words]

[V] Tesaṁ nāmānaṁ payujjamānapada'tthānaṁ yo yutta'ttho, so samāsasañño hoti.

Those nouns of the relevant and related meanings, when combined together, are called a **Samāsa** (Compound noun). **Summary:** This Sutta clearly defines the nature of Samāsa and explains what a Samāsa is. It explains that combining two or more nouns of the relevant, related and coherent meanings is called a Samāsa (Compound noun).

- Kathinadussaṁ-the robe reserved for Kathina. [Kathina+dussa, two nouns are compounded in this example]
- āgantukabhattaṁ-the food for guest. [āgantuka+batta]
- jīvitin'driyaṁ-the faculty of life. [jīvita+indriya]
- samaṇabrāhmaṇā-monk and Brāhmins. [samaṇa+brahmaṇa]
- sāriputtamoggallānā-Venerable Sāriputta and Venerable Moggalāna. [sāriputta+moggalāna]
- brāhmaṇagahapatikā-the Brāhmin and house-holders. [brāhmaṇa+gahapatika]

Nāmānami'ti kimatthaṁ?
What is the word "nāmānaṁ" for?
To show that the examples shown below are nouns and verbs in a sentence, not nouns which are relevant to be combined in a Samāsa process. So, there is no Samāsa.

Devadatto-Devadatta. pacati-cooks. **i.e.** Devadatta cooks.
Yaññadatto-yaññadatta. pacati-cooks. **i.e.** Devadatta cooks.

Yuttattho’ti kimatthaṁ?
What is the word “Yuttattho” for? [**Yutta**-related+**attho**-meaning]
To show that there is no “**yutattha, i.e.** having related meaning which are mutually relevant to each other in a compound process” of the words in the sentence shown below. So, there is no Samāsa.
* Bhato-servant. rañño-of king.
* putto-son. devadattassa-of Devadatta.

Samāsa-icca’nena kvattho?
“Kvaci samāsantagatāna’makāranto”.
What benefit is there by terming “samāsa”?
It has benefit of ease of reference in such Suttas as “Kvaci samāsantagatāna’makāranto” etc.

३१७, ३३२. तेसं विभत्तियो लोपा च
317, 332. **Tesaṁ vibhattiyo lopā ca.**

[Tesaṁ+vibhattiyo+lopā+ca. 4 words]

[V] Tesaṁ yutta’tthānaṁ samāsānaṁ vibhattiyo lopā ca honti.

Those vibattis applied after each component words during a compounding process of nouns, are to be elided (so that it becomes a complete compound noun with one single vibatti).
Summary: This Sutta enjoins elision of vibatti (case-endings) and related things. Before it becomes a complete Samāsa (compound) noun, there is a combining process of two or more nouns with different Vibattis (case-endings) which is called a Viggaha sentence (विग्रहवाक्य) abbreviated as ED. All those different Vibattis and related morphological remnant morphemes which are present during Viggaha process are required to be elided by injunction of this Sutta so that it will become a completed Samāsa (compound noun) with one single Vibatti. Students will not fully understand the function of this Sutta unless they study the

structural morphology of words in grammar called "Payogasiddhi or Padasiddhi". [See the appendices Section]

• Kathinadussaṁ, • āgantukabhattaṁ (Meaning shown).

Tesaṁgahaṇena samāsa, taddhitā'khyāta, kitakānaṁ vibhatti, paccaya, pada'kkharā'gamā ca lopā honti.

By means of the word "tesaṁ" in Sutta, all those vibattis, affixes, morphemes, inserted words (āgama) of samāsa nouns, any morpheme of Taddhita nouns, Ākhyata verbs and Kita nouns, which has been component parts of the ED, can also be elided (as necessary).
• Vāsiṭṭho-Vasiṭṭha's son. • Venateyyo-Vinata's son.

Caggahaṇa'mavadhāraṇa'tthaṁ.
The word "ca" in Sutta has a purpose of restricting the function of this Sutta in some examples shown below. (See that vibatti **aṁ** in the preceding component word "**Pabhaṅ**" of the compound noun "**Pabhaṅkaro**" is not elided. The "**ṅ**" is a Vagganta morpheme of **aṁ.** This kind of compound is sometimes called "**alutta samāsa**" where the vibatti remains intact and is not elided as prescribed by this Sutta).
• Pabhaṅ'karo-the light-maker, **i.e.** Sun.
• amataṅ'dado-the giver of deathlessness, **i.e.** Buddha.
• medhaṅ'karo-the wisdom-maker, or a Buddha so-named.
• dīpaṅ'karo-the wisdom-light-maker, or a Buddha so-named.

३१८, ३३३. पकति चस्स सरन्तस्स
318, 333. **Pakati ca'ssa sara'ntassa.**

[Pakati+ca+assa+sarantassa. 4 words]

[V] Luttāsu vibhattīsu assa sara'ntassa liṅgassa pakatirūpāni honti.

After the elision of vibattis and other related things are done in the process of a compound noun (as per preceding Sutta), all that is left after elision, has to be kept as a "Pakati". (Keep it as it is to further carry out necessary procedures of finalizing as a complete compound noun word).

• Cakkhusotaṁ-eye and ear. • mukhanāsikaṁ-face and nose.
• rājaputto-the king's son, **i.e.** the prince.
• rājapuriso-the king's man, **i.e.** the royal staff.
Note: The function of these two Suttas (317-318) are interrelated when performing morphological procedures. To clearly understand, please refer to the appendices section on the sample morphological procedures of a compound explained in this book.

३१९, ३३०. उपसग्गनिपातपुब्बको अब्ययीभावो
319, 330. **Upasagganipātapubbako abyayībhāvo.**

[Upasagga, nipāta, pubbako+abyayībhāvo. 2 words]

[V] **Upasagga, nipāta**pubbako samāso **abyayībhāva**saññо hoti.

A compound noun, when preceded by either an Upasagga or a Nipāta particle, is called an "**abyayībhāva-Adverbial compound**". [See the examples carefully. Those shown in bold are Upasagga or Nipāta words].

Summary: This Sutta outlines the basic characteristics and nature of "Abyayībhāva compound nouns" by explaining that any compound noun preceded in its structure by either an Upasagga or a Nipāta particle as the first component, is named "Abyayībhāva compound".

Note: Only those shown with this mark • are examples. The preceding words and phrases are called "Viggaha" or etymological definition and expansion of example word abbreviated as **ED.** The first example is translated in detail along with its Viggaha so as to make it more easily understandable for the students.

(1) Nagarassa samīpe pavattati kathā iti • **upa**nagaraṁ,
[Trans] Nagarassa-of the city. samīpe-in proximity. pavattati-is, arises. kathā-the talk. **i.e.** The talk arises in proximity of (regarding) city. iti-therefore. **upa**nagaraṁ-is called "**upa**nagaraṁ", [This is the translation of ED, the unfinished compounding process of the words]

• **upa**nagaraṁ-the talk which happens near the city. **i.e.** the talk whose general nature is concerning the city. (This is the meaning of completed compound noun) [**upa**-near+**nagaraṁ**-city. The talk relating to city]

(2) darathānaṁ-of worries. abhāvo-being absent. • **ni**ddarathaṁ-being absent of worries, **i.e.** worriless. [**ni**-without+**darathaṁ**-worry, one "d" reduplicated]

(3) makasānaṁ-of flies. abhāvo • **ni**mmakasaṁ-absent of flies, without flies, The fly-less. [**ni**-without+**makasaṁ**-fly, one "m" reduplicated]

(4) vuḍḍhānaṁ-of senior people. paṭipāṭi-serial order.
yathāvuḍḍhaṁ- in accordance with the seniority.
[**yathā**-according to+**vuḍḍhaṁ**-seniority]

(5) Ye ye-whosoever. vuḍḍhā-are senior. vā-to explain in another way.
• **yathā**vuḍḍhaṁ-whoever senior.

(6) jīvassa-of life. yattako-whatever. paricchedo-span.
• **yāva**jīvaṁ-for any span of life, **i.e.** for life. [**yāva**-indefinite measure+**jīvaṁ**-life]

(7) citta'madhikicca [cittaṁ+adhikicca] pavattanti te dhammā'ti [dhammā+iti] • **adhi**cittaṁ
[cittaṁ-consciousness, mind. adhikicca-on account of. pavattanti-arise. te dhammā-those phenomena. **i.e.** Those phenomena which arise on account of mind. iti-therefore. **adhi**cittaṁ-is so called.
• **adhi**cittaṁ-mind-related things. [**adhi**-related+**cittaṁ**-mind]

(8) pabbatassa-of the mountain. tiro-other side, yonder.
• **tiro**pabbataṁ-other side of mountain.
[**tiro**-beyond+**pabbataṁ**-mountain]

(9) sotassa-of the flow. pati-against. pavattati-is. nāvā-the boat. **i.e.** The boat is against the current.
iti-therefore. **pati**sotaṁ is so called. • **pati**sotaṁ-The boat against the current. **i.e.** upstream-moving boat.
[**pati**-against+**sotaṁ**-current]

(10) pāsādassa-of the mansion. anto-inside. • **anto**pāsādaṁ-the inside of mansion. [**anto**-inside+**pāsādaṁ**-mansion]

Abyayībhāva-micca'nena kvattho?
Aṁ vibhattīna makārantā abyayībhāvā.
What benefit is there by terming "abhyayībhāva"?
It has benefit of ease of reference in such Suttas as "Aṁ vibhattīna'makārantā abyayībhāvā" etc.

३२०, ३३५. सो नपुंसकलिङ्गो

320, 335. **So napuṁsakaliṅgo.**

[So+napuṁsakaliṅgo. 2 words]

[V] So abyayībhāvasamāso napuṁsakaliṅgo'va daṭṭhabbo.

That **abyayībhāva** compound is to be regarded as belonging to the neuter gender.
Summary: This Sutta defines the gender of "abyayībhāva compounds" as being neuter gender.

(1) Kumārīsu-in the girls. adhikicca-regarding. pavattati-arises. kathā iti.
• **adhi**kumāri-the talk regarding the girls.
[**adhi**-relating to+**kumāri**-girl]

(2) vadhuyā-of the daughter-in-law. samīpe pavattati kathā iti
• **upa**vadhu-the talk regarding the daughter-in-law.
[**upa**-near+**vadu**-daughter-in-law]

(3) gaṅgāya-of the river Ganges. samīpe pavattati kathā iti.
• **upa**gaṅgaṁ-the talk regarding the river Ganges.
[**upa**-near+**gaṅgaṁ**-the river Ganges]

(4) maṇikāya-of the big water pot. samīpe pavattati kathā iti.
• **upa**maṇikaṁ-the talk about big water-pot.
[**upa**-near+**maṇikā**-water-pot]

३२१. ३४९. दिगुस्सेकत्तं

321, 349. **Digusse'kattaṁ.** [Digussa+ekattaṁ. 2 words]

[V] Digussa samāsassa ekattaṁ hoti, napuṁsakaliṅgattañ'ca.

The "Digu" compound is to be recognized as of singular in number and belonging to neuter gender.
Summary: This Sutta marks the gender and number of "Digu compound noun" as being of neuter gender and singular in number. [Look at examples carefully to clarify this. All examples end in an "**aṁ**" which is a derivative morpheme of nominative singular "**si**", a common characteristic pattern of neuter gender nouns]

(1) Tayo-the three. lokā-worlds. • **ti**lokaṁ-three worlds, (of human, heaven and Brahma, Gods' worlds). [**ti**-three+**loka**-world]

(2) tayo daṇḍā-sticks. • **ti**daṇḍaṁ-three stick. [**ti**-three+**daṇḍa**-stick]

(3) tīṇi-three. nayanāni-eyes. • **ti**nayanaṁ-three eyes. [**ti**+**nayana**-eye]

(4) tayo siṅgā-horns. • **ti**siṅgaṁ-three horns. [**ti**+**siṅga**-horn]

(5) Catasso-four. disā-directions. • **catu**ddisaṁ-four direction. [**catu**-four+**disā**-direction]

(6) pañca-five. indriyāni-faculties. • **pañc**indriyaṁ-five faculty. [**pañca**-five+**indriya**-faculty]

३२२, ३५९. तथा द्वन्दे पाणि तूरिय योग्ग सेनङ्ग खुद्दजन्तुक विविधविरुद्ध विसभागत्थादीनञ्च

322, 359. **Tathā dvande pāṇi, tūriya, yogga, senaṅga, khuddajantuka, vividha viruddha, visabhāga'tthā'dīnañ'ca.**

[Tathā+dvande+pāṇi, tūriya, yogga, sena-aṅga, khuddajantuka, vividha viruddha, visabhāga-attha-ādīnaṁ+ca. 4 words]

[V] Tathā dvande samāse pāṇi, tūriya, yogga, sena'ṅga, khuddhajantuka, vividhaviruddha, visabhāga'ttha-icce'va'mādīnaṁ ekattaṁ hoti napuṁsakaliṅgattañ'ca.

When bodily parts, musical instruments, farming tools, accessories of military, small creatures, mutually hostile animals, mutually distinctive virtues are expressed together, an expression of Dvanda compound can takes place and it is also to be regarded as neuter gender and singular in number.

Taṁ yathā? For example,

(1) Cakkhu-eye. ca-also, sotañ'ca [sotañca=sotaṁ+ca. Refer to Sutta 31 to understand what happens to "ṁ"] sotaṁ ca-ear also, • cakkhusotaṁ-eye and ear.

(2) mukhañ'ca [mukhañca= mukhaṁ+ca] mukhaṁ ca-mouth also, nāsikā ca-nose also, • mukhanāsikaṁ-mouth and nose.

Note: The a-ending neuter gender nouns in the nominative singular usually have a morpheme "aṁ". So, they used to have this vagganta function "ñca"

(3) chavi ca-skin also, maṁsañ'ca [maṁsañca= maṁsaṁ+ca] lohitañ'ca [lohitañca= lohitaṁ+ca] maṁsaṁ ca-flesh also, lohitaṁ ca-blood also, • chavimaṁsalohitaṁ-skin, flesh and blood.

Evaṁ pāṇya'ṅgatthe. Thus, (are the examples regarding) parts of body.

(1) Saṅkho-conch. ca-also, paṇavo-drum. ca-also,
• saṅkhapaṇavaṁ-conch and drum.

(2) gītañ'ca-singing also, vāditañ'ca-playing of musical instruments also, • gītavāditaṁ-singing and playing of instruments.

(3) daddari ca-a kind of drum named "daddari" also, ḍiṇḍimo ca-a small drum so-named also,
• daddariḍiṇḍimaṁ-daddari drum and ḍiṇḍima drums.

Evaṁ tūriya'ṅgatthe. Thus, are the examples regarding musical instruments.

(1) Phālo ca-plow also, pācanañ'ca [pācanañca=pācanaṁ+ca] pācanaṁ ca-goad also, • phālapācanaṁ-plow and goad.

(2) yugañ'ca [yugañca= yugaṁ+ca] yugaṁ+ca-yoke also, naṅgalañ'ca [naṅgalañca= naṅgalaṁ+ca] naṅgalaṁ ca-plough also,
• yuganaṅgalaṁ-yoke and plough.

Evaṁ yogga'ṅgatthe. Thus, are the examples regarding farming tools.

(1) Asi ca-sword also, cammañ'ca [cammañca= cammaṁ+ca] cammaṁ ca-skin-armor also, • asicammaṁ-sword and skin-armor.

(2) dhanu ca-bow also, kalāpo ca-quiver also,
• dhanukalāpaṁ-bow and quiver.

(3) hatthī ca-elephant also, asso ca-horse also, • hatthiassaṁ-elephant and horse.

(4) ratho ca-chariot also, pattiko ca-infantry soldier also,
• rathapattikaṁ-chariot and infantry soldier.

Evaṁ sena'ṅgatthe. Thus, are the examples regarding military accessories.

(1) Ḍaṁsā ca-gnat also, makasā ca-mosquitoes also,
• ḍaṁsamakasaṁ-gnat and mosquito.
(2) kuntho ca-ant also, kipilliko ca-termite also,
• kunthakipillikaṁ-ant and termite.
(3) kīṭo ca-caterpillar also, sarīsapo ca-scorpion also,
• kīṭasarīsapaṁ-caterpillar and scorpion.

Evaṁ khuddajantuka'tthe. Thus, are the examples regarding small creatures.

(1) Ahi ca-snake also, nakulo ca-mongoose also,
• ahinakulaṁ-snake and mongoose.
(2) biḷāro ca-cat also, mūsiko ca-rat also,
• biḷāramīsikaṁ-cat and mouse.
(3) kāko ca-crow also, ulūko ca-owl also,
• kākolūkaṁ-crow and owl.

Evaṁ vividha-viruddha'tthe. Thus, are the examples regarding mutually hostile animals.

(1) Sīlañ'ca [sīlañ'ca=sīlaṁ+ca] sīlaṁ ca-morality also, paññāṇañ'ca [paññāṇañ'ca=paññāṇaṁ+ca] paññāṇaṁ ca-wisdom also,
• sīlapaññāṇaṁ-morality and wisdom.
(2) samatho ca-samatha meditation also, vipassanā ca-vipassanā meditation also,
• samathavipassanaṁ-samatha and vipassanā meditation.
(3) vijjā ca-knowledge also, caraṇañ'ca [caraṇañ'ca=caraṇaṁ+ca] caraṇaṁ ca-virtuous practices also,
• vijjācaraṇaṁ-knowledge and virtuous practice.

Evaṁ visabhāga'tthe. Thus, are the examples regarding distinctive virtues.

Ādiggahaṇaṁ kimatthaṁ?
What is the word "ādi" for?
It is to show that the following examples of **dvanda**

samāsa (Copulative compound) expressions are possible in many instances besides those explained herein.

(1) Dāsī ca-female-slave also, dāso ca-male-slave also,
• dāsidāsaṁ-female and male slave.

(2) itthī ca-woman also, pumā ca-man also,
• itthipumaṁ-woman and man.

(3) patto ca-bowl also, cīvarañ'ca [cīvarañ'ca=cīvaraṁ+ca] cīvaraṁ ca-robe also, • pattacīvaraṁ-bowl and robe.

(4) chattañ'ca [chattañ'ca=chattaṁ+ca] chattaṁ ca-umbrella also, upāhanā ca-slippers also, • chattupāhanaṁ-umbrella and slipper.

(5) tikañ'ca [tikañ'ca=tikaṁ+ca] tikaṁ ca-triad also, catukkañ'ca [catukkañ'ca=catukkaṁ+ca] catukkaṁ ca-quadriad also,
• tikacatukkaṁ-triad and quadriad.

(6) veno ca-bamboo-craftsman also, rathakāro ca-chariot-craftsman also, • venarathakāraṁ-bamboo-craftsman and chariot-craftsman.

(7) sākuṇiko ca-bird-hunter also, māgaviko ca-game-hunter also,
• sākuṇikamāgavikaṁ-bird-hunter and game-hunter.

(8) dīgho ca-the long also, majjhimo ca-the medium also,
• dīghamajjhimaṁ-the long and the medium.

icce'va'mādi.

३२३, ३६०. विभासा रुक्ख तिण पसु धन धञ्ञ जनपदादीनञ्च

323, 360. **Vibhāsā rukkha, tiṇa, pasu, dhana, dhañña, janapadā'dīnañ'ca.**

[Vibhāsā+rukkha, tiṇa, pasu, dhana, dhañña, janapada-ādīnaṁ+ca. 3 words]

[V] Rukkha, tiṇa, pasu, dhana, dhañña, janapada-icce'vamādīnaṁ vibhāsā ekattaṁ hoti napuṁsakaliṅgattañ'ca dvande samāse.

When expressing trees, grass, animals, wealth, grain, town and regions collectively, a dvanda samāsa in singular number sometimes can take place for that expression and it also belongs to neuter gender.

Note: there are two examples in each. The first is of neuter gender, singular. **The second, accompanied by a nipāta word "vā", is of plural.** The word "Vibhāsā" in Sutta is an equivalent of "vā" which signifies inconsistency of the function of the Sutta. By the word "Vibhāsā", it means that there will be some Dvanda compound nouns which may end in plural, not only in singular as prescribed in this Sutta.

(1) Assattho ca-holy fig tree also, kapītano ca-pipal tree also,
• assatthakapītanaṁ-holy fig tree and pipal tree. [neuter, singular]
* assatthakapītanā vā [neuter, plural, the same meaning].

(2) Usīrañ'ca [Usīrañ'ca=usīraṁ+ca] usīraṁ ca-a kind of grass named "usīra" also, bīraṇañ'ca [bīraṇañ'ca=bīraṇaṁ+ca] bīraṇaṁ ca-a kind of grass named "bīraṇa" also,
• usīrabīraṇaṁ-"usīra" and "bīraṇa" grass.
* usīrabīraṇā vā. [neuter gender, plural]

(3) Ajo ca-goat also. eḷako ca-sheep also, • ajeḷakaṁ-goat and sheep.
* ajeḷakā vā.

(4) Hiraññañ'ca [Hiraññañ'ca=Hiraññaṁ+ca] Hiraññaṁ ca-silver also, suvaṇṇañ'ca [suvaṇṇañ'ca=suvaṇṇaṁ+ca] suvaṇṇaṁ ca-gold also, • hiraññasuvaṇṇaṁ-silver and gold.
* hiraññasuvaṇṇā vā.

(5) Sāli ca-rice, yavo ca-barley also, • sāliyavaṁ-rice and barley.
* sāliyavā vā.

(6) Kāsī ca-the Kāsi region also, Kosalā ca-the Kosala region also,
• kāsikosalaṁ-the Kāsi and Kosala region. * Kāsikosalā vā.

Ādiggahaṇaṁ kimatthaṁ?
What is the word "ādi" for?
It has a purpose to show that the following examples of **dvanda samāsa** expressions are possible in many instances in addition to those explained above in Sutta.

(1) Sāvajjañ'ca [sāvajjañ'ca=sāvajjaṁ+ca] sāvajjaṁ ca-the blame-worthy thing (unwholesome) also, anavajjañ'ca [anavajjañ'ca=anavajjaṁ+ca] anavajjaṁ ca-the blameless thing (wholesome) also,

• sāvajjānavajjaṁ-the blame-worthy thing and the blameless things (**i.e.** the unwholesome and wholesome thing).
* sāvajjānavajjā vā.

(2) Hīnañ'ca [Hīnañ'ca=hīnaṁ+ca] hīnaṁ ca-the lowly thing also, paṇītañ'ca [paṇītañ'ca=paṇītaṁ+ca] paṇītaṁ ca--the holy thing also, • hīnapaṇītaṁ- the lowly and the holy thing.
* Hīnapaṇītā vā.

(3) Kaṇho ca-the black also, sukko ca-the white also,
• kaṇhasukkaṁ-the black and white. * kaṇhasukkā vā.

Note: Suttas 322, 323 show the natural characteristic of "Dvanda compound" nouns in two ways, one is that every Dvanda has to apply a Nipāta "ca" in its ED, and the other is that they used to be of neuter gender and singular. However, as an exception, there are also some Dvanda compounds in plural case.

३२४, ३३९. द्विपदे तुल्याधिकरणे कम्मधारयो

324, 339. **Dvipade tulyā'dhikaraṇe kammadhārayo.**

[Dvipade+tulya-adhikaraṇe+kammadhārayo. 3 words]

[V] Dve padāni tulyā'dhikaraṇāni yadā samasyante, tadā so samāso **kammadhāraya**sañño hoti.

When two component nouns of the related meaning and of similar case-endings are combined together, it is then called a "**kamma dhāraya-Appositional compound**".

Summary: This Sutta defines the two chief characteristics of a "Kammadhāraya" compound noun. They are:

(1) having two component words to be compounded,

(2) those words must be of Tulyādhikaraṇa, which means having the same base in terms of vibatti as well as in terms of relevant meaning each word imply.

[**Tulya**-similar+**adhikaraṇa**-base or position, being in apposition to each other in terms of having the same case ending, coherent meaning and syntactic as well as syntagmatic relation]

To clarify this fact, take a closer look at its EDs shown below. There is a "**ca**" after each component word which mutually pulls two words together and a Sabbanāma noun "**ta**" shown by means of "**so**-that" which signifies the harmony and collateral relationship of the implied meaning of the two words in addition to having the same Vibattis in nominative case.

(1) Mahanto ca-great also, so-that which is great, puriso cā'ti [ca+iti] puriso ca-(is) man also, iti-therefore, mahāpuriso-it is called "mahāpuriso". • mahāpuriso-the great man.
(2) Kaṇho ca-black also, so sappo cā'ti sappo ca-snake also, • kaṇhasappo-the black snake.
(3) Nīlañ'ca [Nīlaṁ+ca] Nīlaṁ ca-blue also, taṁ-that, uppalañ'cā'ti [uppalaṁ+ca+iti] uppalaṁ ca-lotus also, • nīluppalaṁ-the blue lotus.
(4) Lohitañ'ca [Lohitaṁ+ca] Lohitaṁ-red, taṁ candanañ'cā'ti [candanaṁ+ca+it] candanaṁ-sandal wood. • lohitacandanaṁ-the red sandal wood.
(5) Brāhmaṇī ca-female Brāhmin, sā-that woman, dārikā ca-girl, cā'ti • brāhmaṇadārikā-the Brāhmin girl.
(6) Khattiyā ca-a female of warrior (क्षत्रिय) caste, sā kaññā ca-girl, cā'ti. • khattiyakaññā-the khattiya girl.

Kammadhāraya-icca'nena kva'ttho?
What benefit is there by terming "kammadhāraya"?
Kammadhārayasaññe ca.
It has the benefit of ease of reference in such Suttas as "Kammadhārayasaññe ca" etc.

३२५, ३४८. सङ्ख्यापुब्बो दिगु
325, 348. **Saṅkhyāpubbo digu.**

[Saṅkhyā-pubbo+digu. 2 words]

[V] Saṅkhyāpubbo kammadhārayasamāso **digu**sañño hoti.

A Kammadhāraya compound noun, when preceded by the words of numerical values (**i.e.** a numerical noun), is called "**digu-Numeral Appositional compound**".
Summary: This Sutta simply and clearly defines the characteristic of "Digu" compound by pointing to the fact

that a Kammadhāraya compound when preceded by a word of the numerical value in its combination is called "Digu". See both EDs and examples carefully to clarify this.

(1) Tīṇi-three, malāni-impurities, **ti**malaṁ-three (kinds of) impurities. [the word "**mala**" is of neuter gender]
(2) Tīṇi phalāni-fruits, • **ti**phalaṁ-three fruit. [**phala** is of neuter gender]
(3) Tayo lokā • **ti**lokaṁ. [**loka** is of masculine gender]
(4) Tayo daṇḍā • **ti**daṇḍaṁ. [**daṇḍa** is of masculine gender]
(5) Catasso disā • **catu**ddisaṁ. [**disā** is of feminine gender]
(6) Pañca indriyāni • **pañc**indriyaṁ. [**indriya** is of neuter gender]
(7) Satta-seven, godāvariyo-Godāvarī rivers, • **satta**godāvaraṁ-seven Godāvarī rivers. [The word **Godāvarī** is of feminine gender]

Digu-icca'nena kva'ttho? Digusse'kattaṁ.
What benefit is there by terming "digu"?
It has the benefit of ease of reference in Suttas like "Digusse' kattaṁ" etc.

३२६, ३४१. उभे तप्पुरिसा

326, 341. **Ubhe tappurisā.** [Ubhe+tappurisā. 2 words]

[V] Ubhe **digu, kammadhāraya**samāsā **tappurisa**saññā honti.

The two **Digu, Kammadhāraya** samāsas are called "Tappurisa".
Summary: This Sutta simply defines a combination of Digu and Kammadhāraya as a Tappurisa when it is preceded by a negative particle nipāta word "**na**" which means "not". See both EDs and examples carefully to clarify this. "**na**" morphs into either "**a**" or "**an**" later on when it becomes a completed compound noun. (Refer to Sutta 333, 334 for changing into "a" or "an")

(1) Na-not, Brāhmaṇo-the Brāhmin, • abrāhmaṇo-non-Brāhmin. **i.e.** the bogus Brāhmin.
(2) na vasalo-a wretch, vile person. • avasalo-not a wretch, **i.e.** noble.

(3) na bhikkhu-monk, • abhikkhu-non-monk, **i.e.** bogus monk.
(4) na pañcavassaṁ-five year, • apañcavassaṁ-not five years.
[pañca-five+vassa-year]
(5) na pañcapūlī-five packet, • apañcapuli-not five packet.
[pañca-five+puli-packet]
(6) na sattagodāvaraṁ-seven Godāvarī rivers,
• asattagodāvaraṁ-not seven Godāvarī rivers.
(7) na dasagavaṁ-ten cows, • adasagavaṁ-not ten cows.
[dasa-ten+gava-cow]
(8) na pañcagavaṁ-five cows, • apañcagavaṁ-not five cows.

Tappurisa-icca'nena kva'ttho? Attaṁ nassa tappurise.
What benefit is there by terming "tappurisa"?
It has the benefit of ease of reference in such Suttas as "Attaṁ nassa tappurise" etc.

Note: This Tappurisa is called Paṭhmā Tappurisa (Tappurisa in nominative case) as well as Ubhe Tappurisa (Tappurisa of dual nature as referred to in this Sutta) by Pāli grammarians. In the Sanskrit grammars, it is called (नञ तपुरुष) by the Sanskrit grammarians.

३२७, ३५१. अमादयो परपदेभि

327, 351. A'mādayo parapadebhi.

[Aṁ-ādayo+parapadebhi. 2 words]

[V] Tā amā'dayo nāmehi parapadebhi yadā samasyante, tadā so samāso **tappurisa**sañño hoti.

When those Dutiyā (accusative) "**aṁ** vibatti" and similar vibattis (except nominative and vocative) are joined with the other component words together, it is then called a "**Tappurisa-Determinative compound**" samāsa.

Summary: This Sutta defines Tappurisa Samasa. When one of **Dutiyā, Tatiyā, Catutthī, Pañcamī, Chaṭṭī, and Sattamī Vibattis are applied after the front component nouns with its corresponding component noun ending in nominative case, it is then called "Tappurisa Samāsa".** In a Tappurisa compound, <u>the front component word</u>

usually ends in one of these six vibattis while the other component word ends in nominative. This is a basic structural pattern of most of Tappurisa compounds. Look at the EDs of examples shown below carefully. Each Vibatti applied after the front word is clearly shown underlined in the ED of each example. If students are quite familiar with morphological patterns explained in the Nouns section, they will understand the nature of this Samāsa without much difficulty.

[Dutiyā Tappurisa]

["**ṁ**" "**aṁ**" after the front component word, shown underlined, is indicative of the accusative case, singular]

(1) Bhūmiṁ-to the earth, gato-goer, • bhūmigato-the earth-goer, **i.e.** the one who walks on earth.

(2) Sabbarattiṁ-for the whole night, sobhaṇo-beautiful, • sabbarattisobhaṇo-beautiful for the whole night.

(3) Apāyaṁ-to four apāyas, gato-goer, gone, • apāyagato-the one who has gone to apāyas (woeful states).

[Tatiyā Tappurisa]

["**ena**" behind the front component word is indicative of the instrumental case, singular, Re: Sutta 103]

(1) Issarena-by powerful, kataṁ-done, • issarakataṁ-done by powerful, an act done by a person of authority, or God-made if Issara-means God.

(2) Sallena-by arrow, viddho-hurt, penetrated, • sallaviddho-hurt or penetrated by arrow, a person hit by arrow.

[Catutthī Tappurisa]

["**ssa**" behind the front component word is indicative of the dative case, singular, Re: Sutta 61]

(1) Kathinassa-for Kathina, dussaṁ-(designed & offered) robe, • kathinadussaṁ-Kathina-robe.

(2) Āgantukassa-for the guest, bhattaṁ-reserved food, • āgantukabhattaṁ-the guest-food.

[Pañcamī Tappurisa]

["**ā**" behind the front component word
is indicative of the ablative case, singular, Re: 108]

(1) Methunā-from sexual intercourse, apeto-abstaining,
• methunāpeto-abstinence from the sexual intercourse.

(2) Corā-from thief, bhayaṁ-fear, • corabhayaṁ-fear of thief.

[Chaṭṭhī Tappurisa]

[For "**Rañño**", Re: Sutta 135. "**naṁ**" behind the front component word
is indicative of the genitive case, plural]

(1) Rañño-of king, putto-son, • rājaputto-the king's son. **i.e.** the prince.

(2) Dhaññānaṁ-of grains, rāsi-heap, • dhaññarāsi-the heap of grain.

[Sattamī Tappurisa]

["**e**" behind the front component word
is indicative of the locative case, singular, Re: 108]

(1) Rūpe-in the form, saññā-concept, • rūpasaññā-the form-concept.

(2) Saṁsāre-in the Samsarā, dukkhaṁ-suffering,
• saṁsāradukkhaṁ-suffering of the Samsarā.

३२८, ३५२. अञ्ञपदत्थेसु बहुब्बीहि
328, 352. **Aññapada'tthesu bahubbīhi.**

[Aññapada-atthesu+bahubbīhi. 2 words]

[V] Aññesaṁ padānaṁ atthesu dve nāmāni bahūni vā nāmāni yadā samasyante. tadā so samāso **bahubbīhi**-sañño hoti.

When the meaning of (an external) other word is predominant in a combination of two or more nouns, it is then called a "**Bahubbīhi-Attributive** compound".

Summary

When an **external Sabbanāma noun** word, such as "**ya, ima**" etc. rather than component words included in the compound, plays a dominant role in determining the qualified collective meaning of the completed compound noun, it is then called a "**Bahubbīhi**" samāsa compound.

To clarify this, please refer to the first example "Āgatasamaṇo" shown below. In it, the collective meaning of complete compound as a whole is not the coming monks as implied by two component words "Āgata and samaṇa", but the temple where the monks had arrived which is shown by the external word "ima (imaṁ) " in the ED. That external word is called "**Aññapada**" and the meaning of it is known as "**Aññapadattha**". This meaning is usually a predominant character of the whole Bahubbīhi compound when completed no matter how short or how long it may be. In the end of most examples shown in this grammar, the "**Aññapadattha**" of each Bahubbīhi compound is directly indicated by the great grammarian himself. [**Añña**-other+**pada**-word+**attha**-meaning. **i.e.** the meaning of other word.]

Why it is called "Bahubbīhi"?
Because any compound noun in this category of compounds has the same nature of having the same implied meaning of an external, foreign word like the word "bahubbīhi". [**bahu**-much, abundant+**vīhi**-rice. Here, it does not literally mean "the abundant rice" as meant by the combination of these two words. but it only means **a district where the rice is abundant**.]

How many kinds of "**Bahubbīhi**" are there?
Basically, there are altogether seven kinds of Bahubbīhi which are determined based on the Vibatti (case-ending) being applied after an "**Aññapada-(i.e.** The other foreign word) such as **ya, ta, eta** and **ima**". They are: Pathamā, Dutiyā, Tatiyā, Catutthī, Pañcamī, Chaṭṭhī and Sāttamī. (7)

Note: There are other forms of Bahubbīhi as explained by eminent Pāli grammarian **Buddha piyā'cariya,** the author of **Rūpasiddhi-vyākaraṇaṁ.** However, all those forms, despite some slight differences, are also based on the case-ending of Aññapada. The vibatti-based classification is much easier to learn and remember for the beginners in the beginning process. Therefore, a student needs to carefully look out for what Vibatti case-ending is applied after an "**Aññapada**" in the ED of a

"**Bahubbīhi compound**". By knowing its vibatti case-ending, they will be able to determine it according to its case-ending. This will not be quite difficult if a student has already studied the nouns chapter very well as **all the chapters of grammar, except Sandhi and Ākhyāta, are mostly nouns** in various forms. **For the ease of study, all the case-endings of aññapada will be shown <u>in bold, underlined</u> in the ED of each compound with the exception of its correlative word located next to it which have the same vibatti case-ending throughout this Bahubbīhi section.** This way, the students will easily notice and clearly understand its relevant category according to its vibatti case-ending.

How long a "**Bahubbīhi**" compound can be?
It rather depends on how many different kinds of word are to be joined into a would-be Bahubbīhi compound until it becomes a completed Bahubbīhi. Before it becomes a Bahubbīhi, all the different words are to be first joined into relevant compounds such as Tappurisa, Kammadhāraya, Dvanda and so on. It is very interesting to study this compounding process till it becomes a complete Bahubbīhi compound. In the forthcoming pages, different Bahubbīhi compounds, some quite long, some longer and some being the longest, will be shown and explained. The students will even see some long Bahubbīhi compounds with the beautiful poetic expressions of idyllic nature coupled with the spiritual element of undying respect and pure devotion toward the Buddha, the appreciation of spiritual life of the forest-dwelling ascetics, masterfully woven together by the great grammarian Mahā Kaccāyana.

Āgatasamaṇo

[**Āgata**-those arrived, came+**samaṇa**-monk. "**o**" is the derivative of "si"]

Āgatā-had come. samaṇā-monks. **<u>imaṁ</u>**-to this. saṅghārāmaṁ-monk's place, monastery. **i.e.** The monks had come to this monastery.

so'yaṁ [so'yaṁ=so+ayaṁ] so-that. ayaṁ-this place.

āgatasamaṇo-is called "āgatasamaṇo". [The meaning of the whole ED] [the meaning of completed Samāsa] • āgatasamaṇo-the monastery where the monks came. **i.e.** have arrived. [This is a Dutiyā Bahubbīhi compound. The temple is **aññapadattha** or the exact final sense of the whole compound] saṅghārāmo-"the monastery where the monks have come to" is to be taken as "āgatasamaṇo". **Note:** so'yaṁ is a redundant use of two sabbanāma words "ta" and "ima". The meaning has to be either "that or this". Sometimes it is quite similar to emphatic usage of "this very place" in the English language.

Jiti'ndriyo

[**Jita**-conquered+**indriya**-faculty]

Jitāni-had conquered. indriyāni-faculties (**i.e.** eye etc.) **anena**-by this. samaṇena-monk. **i.e.** Faculties are conquered by this monk. so'yaṁ-that monk. jitin'driyo-is called "jitindriyo".

• jitin'driyo-the monk who has conquered (his own) faculties. **i.e.** the monk who can restrain his senses completely. [This is a tatiyā Bahubbīhi compound] [Aññapadattha] samaṇo-the monk is to be taken or regarded as "jitindriyo".

Dinnasuṅko

[**Dinna**-paid+**suṅka**-revenue]

Dinno-had been given, paid (by people). suṅko-revenue or tax. **yassa**-of whom. rañño-of the king. **i.e.** The king for whom the revenue is paid by people. so'yaṁ-that king. dinnasuṅko-is called "dinnasuṅko",

• dinnasuṅko-the king who has revenues paid by people. [This is a Catutthī Bahubbīhi compound] [Aññapadattha] rājā-the king is to be taken as the meaning of this compound noun

Niggatajano

[**Niggata**-departed+**jana**-people]

Niggatā-had come out. janā-people. **asmā**-from that. gāmā-from village. **i.e.** people had come out from that village. so'yaṁ-that village. niggatajano-is called "niggatajano", • niggatajano- the village from where people left. [This is a Pañcamī Bahubbīhi compound] [Aññapadattha] gāmo-the village is the meaning of this compound noun.

Chinnahattho

[**Chinna**-cut, amputated+**hattha**-hand]

Chinno-is cut. hatto-hand. **yassa**-of which, whose. purisassa-man. **i.e.** The man whose hand is cut. so'yaṁ-that man. chinnahattho-is called "chinnahattho", • chinnahattho- the man whose hand is cut (amputated). [This is a Chaṭṭhī Bahubbīhi compound] [Aññapadattha] puriso-the amputee man is to be regarded as the directly implied meaning of this compound.

Sampannasasso

[**Sampanna**-abundant+**sassa**-rice]

Sampannāni-(are) abundant. sassāni-the rice, paddy. **yasmiṁ**-in which, where. janapade-district. **i.e.** The district where the rice plants or paddy are abundant and thriving. so'yaṁ-that district. sampannasasso-is called "sampannasasso". • sampannasasso-the district where the rice is abundant. [This is a Sattamī Bahubbīhi compound] [Aññapadattha] janapado-the district is to be taken as the meaning of this compound noun.

Nigrodhaparimaṇḍalo

[**Nigrodha**-banyan tree+**parimaṇḍala**-circle, diameter]

(1) Nigrodhassa-of banyan tree. parimaṇḍalo-circumference.
• nigrodhaparimaṇḍalo-the circumference of banyan tree.
[Chaṭṭhī Tappurisa compound]

(2) nigrodhaparimaṇḍalo iva-(is) like the circumference of banyan tree. parimaṇḍalo-(the proportionate) bodily figure. **yo**-whosoever. rājakumāro-the prince. **i.e.** The prince who has body-figure like that of a banyan tree. so'yaṁ-that prince. nigrodhaparimaṇḍalo-is called "nigrodhaparimaṇḍalo". [This is a Paṭhamā Bahubbīhi compound]
• nigrodhaparimaṇḍalo- the prince who has the proportionate, shapely bodily figure like that of a banyan tree.

Atha vā-(Here is to explain this compound in) other method: nigrodhaparimaṇḍalo iva-like the circumference of banyan tree. parimaṇḍalo-(the proportionate) bodily figure. **yassa**-whose. rājakumārassa-of the prince. **i.e.** The prince, whose proportionate bodily figure is like that of symmetrically shaped Banyan tree. so'yaṁ • nigrodhaparimaṇḍalo- the prince whose proportionate, shapely bodily

figure is like that of a banyan tree. [This is a Chaṭṭhī Bahubbīhi compound. Catutthī is also possible] [Aññapadattha] rājakumāro-the prince is to be taken as the meaning of this compound noun.
Note: iva and **viya** are two ***Nipāta*** particles which mean "like". In this second method ED, a genitive case is applied after Aññapada.

Cakkhubhūto

[**Cakkhu**-eye+**bhūto**-that was, that has arisen]

(1) Cakkhuno-of the eye. bhūto-the arisen nature. • cakkhubhūto-the arisen nature of eye. [Chaṭṭhī Tappurisa compound]

(2) cakkhubhūto iva-like the arisen nature of eye. bhūto-has arisen. **yo**-whosoever. bhagavā-the lord Buddha. **i.e.** The lord Buddha has arisen like the eye. so'yaṁ-that lord Buddha. cakkhubhūto-is called "cakkhubhūto", • cakkhubhūto-The lord Buddha who has arisen (like the guiding) eye of the worldlings. [This is a Paṭhamā Bahubbīhi compound] [Aññapadattha] bhagavā-The Lord Buddha is to be taken as the meaning of this compound noun.
Note: This term "Bhūto" means only a state, a condition. e.g. **Cakkhubhūto**-being like an eye. **Manussabhūto**-being a human.

Suvaṇṇavaṇṇo

[**Suvaṇṇa**-gold+**vaṇṇa**-color]

(1) Suvaṇṇassa-of the gold. vaṇṇo-color. • suvaṇṇavaṇṇo-the gold's color. **[Chaṭṭhī Tappurisa compound]**

(2) suvaṇṇavaṇṇo viya-(is) like the gold's color. vaṇṇo-the skin complexion. **yassa** bhagavato-of the lord Buddha. so'yaṁ suvaṇṇa- vaṇṇo-is called "suvaṇṇavaṇṇo". • suvaṇṇavaṇṇo-The Lord Buddha whose skin complexion is like that of gold. [This is a Chaṭṭhī Bahubbīhi compound. The catutthī is also applicable] [Aññapadattha] bhagavā-The Lord Buddha is to be taken as the meaning of this compound noun.

Brahmassaro

[**Brahma**-Brahmā, **i.e.** God+**sara**-voice. One "s" is augmented]

(1) Brahmuno-of Brahmā. saro-the voice. • brahmassaro-The Brahmā's voice. **[Chaṭṭhī Tappurisa]**

(2) brahmassaro viya- like the Brahmā's voice. saro-the voice. **yassa**-whose. bhagavato-of Lord Buddha. so'yaṁ. brahmassaro-is called

Brahmassaro. • Brahmassaro-The Lord Buddha whose voice is like that of Brahmā's voice. [This is a Chaṭṭhī Bahubbīhi compound, Catutthī is also applicable]

[Aññapadattha] bhagavā-The Lord Buddha is to be taken as the meaning of this compound noun.

Sayaṁ patita paṇṇa pupphaphalavāyutoyā'hārā

[**Sayaṁ**-self. **patita**-fallen. **paṇṇa**-leave. **puppha**-flower. **phala**-fruit. **vāyu**-air. **toya**-water. **āhārā**-food.]

"Sayaṁ patita paṇṇa pupphaphalavāyutoyā'hārā"

In this long Bahubbīhi compound noun, how the graduated series of relevant compounds are first combined in order to become **a final Bahubbīhi Samāsa** will be explained step by step by joining different words into applicable compounds according to their relevant meaning and correlation of each word. Here, it will be seen that **there are five, separate compounds occurred** according to the relevant and coherent meanings of each word, being combined into various appropriate compounds. Please study carefully.

"Sayaṁ patita paṇṇa pupphaphalavāyutoyā'hārā"ti–

Now, this compound containing above "**Sayaṁ patita paṇṇa pupphaphalavāyutoyā'hārā**" words, will be explained (on how it finally becomes a perfect Bahubbīhi after combining various words into relevant compounds) :

(1) paṇṇañ'ca-leave also, pupphañ'ca-flower also. phalañ'ca-fruit also. • paṇṇapupphaphalāni-the leaves, flowers and fruits.
[This is a **Dvanda**, copulative compound, See "ca" in the ED]

(2) saya'meva [saya'meva=sayaṁ+eva] patitāni • sayaṁpatitāni,
sayaṁ-itself. eva-only. patitāni-fallen. sayaṁpatitāni-fallen itself.
[Kammadhāraya. Due to usage of a Nipāta particle "**eva**-only", it is called "**Ava-dhāraṇa** Kammadhāraya compound"]

(3) sayaṁpatitāni ca tāni paṇṇapupphaphalāni ce'ti
• sayaṁpatitapaṇṇapupphaphalāni **[Kammadhāraya]**
sayaṁpatitāni ca-fallen itself also. tāni-those fallen. paṇṇapupphaphalāni ce'ti [ceti=ca+iti] paṇṇapupphaphalāni ca-(are) leaves, flowers and fruits. sayaṁpatitapaṇṇapupphaphalāni-self-fallen leaves, flowers and fruits.

(4) vāyu ca toyañ'ca [toyaṁ+ca] • vāyutoyāni. [**Dvanda Compound]**
vāyu ca-air also. toyaṁ ca-water also. • vāyutoyāni-air and waters.

(5) sayaṁpatitapaṇṇapupphaphalāni ca-self-fallen leaves, flowers, fruits also. vāyutoyāni ca-air and waters also.

• sayaṁpatitapaṇṇapupphaphalavāyutoyāni-self-fallen leaves, flowers, fruits, air and waters. **[Dvanda Compound]**

(B) Sayaṁpatitapaṇṇapupphaphalavāyutoyāni-self-fallen leaves, flowers, fruits, air and waters. āhārā-(are) foods or nourishments. **yesaṁ**-whose. te-they. sayaṁpatitapaṇṇapupphaphalavāyutoyāhārā-are called "sayaṁpatitapaṇṇapupphaphalavāyutoyāhārā".

• sayaṁpatitapaṇṇapupphaphalavāyutoyā'hārā-the hermits whose foods are self-fallen (natural) leaves, flowers, fruits and air, waters. [Aññapadattha] isayo-(the forest-living) hermits are to be taken as the final sense of this compound.

Ya'mettha [Ya'mettha=yaṁ+ettha] yaṁ-whatever. ettha-here (regarding the nature of this Bahubbīhi compound) vattabbaṁ-should be said, taṁ-that. heṭṭhā-below (**i.e.** previously). vutta'meva [vuttaṁ+eva]. vuttaṁ-(I have already) said. eva-only. **i.e.** Whatever should be said on the nature of this compound, had already been said before in the beginning of Sutta. Ayaṁ-this compound noun. pana-a nipāta with no meaning. **dvanda, kammadhāraya,** gabbho-dvanda and Kammadhāraya compounds concealed inside. **tulyā'dhikaraṇa**bahubbīhi-(is called) **tulyādhikaraṇa**bahubbīhi compound. [This is so-called because the two words, **sayaṁpatitapaṇṇapupphaphalavāyutoyāni** and **āhārā** have the same case-endings in the nominative plural]

Atha vā–Here is another method of combining: sayaṁpatitapaṇṇapupphaphalavāyutoyehi-by (means of consuming) self-fallen leaves, flowers, fruit, (fresh) air and waters). āhārā-(daily) foods. **yesaṁ**-of whom. **i.e.** the daily foods of whom are by means of consuming self-fallen leave, flowers, fruit, fresh air and waters. te-they. sayaṁpatitapaṇṇapupphaphalavāyutoyāhārā-are called "sayaṁpatitapaṇṇapupphaphalavāyutoyāhārā ".

• sayaṁpatitapaṇṇapupphaphalavāyutoyā'hārā-the hermits whose foods are by means of self-fallen leaves, flowers, fruit, (fresh) air and waters. **Note:** There is a slight difference in translation of this completed compound as it has to be translated in strict accordance with the second ED.

Ayaṁ pana-this Bahubbīhi compound.

bhinnā'dhikaraṇabahubbīhi-is called **bhinnā'dhikaraṇa**bahubbīhi.

Note: "B" means Bahubbīhi.
This is called **bhinnā'dhikaraṇa**bahubbīhi because the two words, one "**sayaṁpatitapaṇṇapupphaphalavāyutoyehi**" and the other "**āhārā**" have

different case-endings, one in instrumental and the other in nominative plural. Please refer to Sutta 292 for explanation regarding these two words **Tulyā'dhikaraṇa** and **bhinnā'dhikaraṇa.** [binna+adhikaraṇa]

Nānā dumapatita pupphavāsita sānu

[**Nānā**-various. **duma**-tree. **patita**-fallen. **puppha**-flower. **vāsita**-scented. **sānū**-hill-surface of the peak]

Nānā dumapatita pupphavāsita sānū'ti–Now, it will be explained this Bahubbīhi which contains above words:

(1) nānā pakārā-various kinds of. dumā-trees. • nānādumā-various kinds of trees. **[Kammadhāraya]**

(2) nānādumehi-from various trees. patitāni-fallen. • nānādumapatitāni-fallen from various trees, **[Pañcamī Tappurisa]**

(3) nānādumapatitāni ca-fallen from various tree also. tāni-those fallen. pupphāni ce'ti [ca+iti] pupphāni ca-are flowers also. iti-therefore. nānādumapatitapupphāni-is called "nānādumapatitapupphāni". • nānādumapatitapupphāni-flowers fallen from various-trees. **[Kammadhāraya]**

(4) nānādumapatitapupphehi-by flowers fallen from various trees. vāsitā-are scented. • nānādumapatitapupphavāsitā-scented by the flowers fallen from various trees. **[Tatiyā Tappurisa]**

(B) nānādumapatitapupphavāsitā-(is) scented with flowers fallen from various trees. sānū-the level surface of mountain peak. **yassa**-of which. pabbatarājassa-mountain king (**i.e.** great mountain). so'yaṁ-that peak. nānādumapatitapupphavāsitasānu-is so-called.

• nānādumapatitapupphavāsitasānu-the mountain peak which is scented with flowers fallen from various trees. [This is a Chaṭṭhī Bahubbīhi compound. Catutthī is also applicable]

[Aññapadattha] pabbatarājā-the great mountain (whose peak is fragrant) is to be regarded as the final meaning of this compound.

Ayaṁ pana **kammadhāraya, tappurisa**gabbho **tulyādhikara-ṇa**bahubbīhi-This Bahubbīhi is a **tulyādhikaraṇa**bahubbīhi with **kammadhāraya, tappurisa** concealed inside.

Atha vā–Here is another method:

(1) vāsitā-The scented. sānū-mountain peak. • vāsitasānu-the scented peak. **[Kammadhāraya]**

sā'pekkhatte sati'pi gamakattā samāso.

Despite different syntactical relation of the word "vāsita" to an external word "pupphehi"(See next procedure), there is Bahubbīhi samāsa process as the implied meaning is still relevant and related between "**vāsita**" and "**sānu**". [This is an explanation of some subtle complexity in the foregoing ED, In the next examples, this statement will be left untranslated. **sā'pekkhatte**=sa+apekkha+tte-being syntactically related. **sati'pi**=sati+api-despite. **gamakattā**=gamaka+ttā-due to understandability. **gamaka** doesn't mean "to go". Here, it means "to easily know".]

(B) Nānādumapatitapupphehi-with flowers fallen from various trees. vāsitasānū-scented peak. **yassa**-of which. pabbatarājassa-great mountain. **i.e.** The great mountain whose peak is scented with flowers fallen from various trees. so'yaṁ-that peak. nānādumapatitapupphavāsitasānu-is so-called.

• nānādumapatitapupphavāsitasānu-The great mountain whose peak is scented with flowers fallen from various trees.

[Aññapadattha] pabbatarājā-the king of mountains, **i.e.** the great mountain.

Ayaṁ pana **bhinnā'dhikaraṇa**bahubbīhi.
This is a **bhinnā'dhikaraṇa** bahubbīhi.

Vyā'lamba'mbudharabinducumbitakūṭo

[**Vyālamba**-variously hanging. **ambudhara**-rain-cloud. **bindu**-drop. **cumbita**-sprayed, kissed. **kūṭo**-mountain-peak]

Vyā'lamba'mbudharabinducumbitakūṭo'ti–Now, it will be explained this Bahubbīhi which contains these words:

(1) ambuṁ-the water. dhāretī'ti [dhāretī'ti=dhāreti+iti] dhāreti-carries. iti-therefore. ambudharo-is so called, • ambudharo-the water-carrying. **[Dutiyā Tappurisa]** ko-what. so-that? What is that? Pajjunno-the rain clouds (are called ambudharo.)

Note: This word is called "samudāya'ttha-ekavacana", collective singular though it may mean many clouds. [**ambu**-water+**dhara**-to carry, carrier]

(2) Vividhā-by various ways. ālambo-is hanging (dangling in the sky)
• vyā'lambo-hanging variously. [Vyālambo=**vi**-variously+**ālambo**-hanging in the sky] **[Kammadhāraya]**

(3) vyā'lambo ca-variously hanging also. so-that hanging thing. ambudharo cā'ti [ca+iti] ambudharo ca-(is) the water-carrying rain-cloud. iti-therefore. vyālambambudharo-is so-called.

• vyā'lambambudharo-The variously hanging, water-carrying rain-cloud. **[Kammadhāraya]**

(4) vyā'lambambudharassa-of variously hanging, water-carrying rain cloud, bindū-drops. • vyā'lambambudharabindū-the rain-drops of variously hanging, water-carrying cloud. **[Chaṭṭhī Tappurisa]**

(5) vyā'lambambudharabindūhi-by the rain-drops of variously hanging, water-carrying clouds. cumbito-sprayed, kissed.

• vyā'lambambudharabinducumbito-sprayed or kissed by the rain-drops of variously hanging, water-carrying clouds. **[Tatiyā Tappurisa]**

(B) vyā'lambambudharabinducumbito-(is) sprayed or kissed by the rain-drops of variously hanging, water-carrying cloud, kūṭo-the peak. **yassa**-of which. pabbatarājassa-great mountain. so'yaṁ-that peak. vyā'lambambudharabinducumbitakūṭo-is so-called.

• vyā'lambambudharabinducumbitakūṭo-the peak which is sprayed or kissed by the rain-drops of variously hanging, water-carrying clouds.

Ayaṁ pana kammadhāraya, tappurisagabbho **tulyā'dhikaraṇa**bahubbīhi.
This Bahubbīhi is a **tulyā'dhikaraṇa**bahubbīhi with **kammadhāraya, tappurisa compounds** concealed inside.

Atha vā–Here is another method of combining into necessary Samāsa:

(1) cumbito-the sprayed. kūṭo-peak. • cumbitakūṭo-the sprayed peak. **[Kammadhāraya]**

sā'pekkhatte sati'pi gamakattā samāso.

(B) Vyā'lambambudharabindūhi-by drops of variously hanging, water carrying rain-clouds. cumbitakūṭo-the sprayed peak. **yassa**-of which. pabbatarājassa-great mountain. so'yaṁ-that peak. vyā'lambambudharabinducumbitakūṭo is so-called

• vyā'lambambudharabinducumbitakūṭo-the mountain whose peak is sprayed by the drops of variously hanging, water-carrying rain-clouds.

Ayaṁ pana **bhinnā'dhikaraṇa**bahubbīhi.
This Bahubbīhi is a **bhinnā'dhikaraṇa**bahubbīhi.

Amitabalaparakkamajuti

[**Amita**-immeasurable. **bala**-strength. **parakkama**-effort. **juti**-light, or glory]

Amitabalaparakkamajutī'ti–Now, it will be explained this Bahubbīhi which contains these words:

(1) na-not (Negative particle). mitā-measurable. • amitā-immeasurable. **[Ubhe Tappurisa]**

(2) balañ'ca [balaṁ+ca] balaṁ ca-strength also. parakkamo ca-effort also. juti ca-glory also. • balaparakkamajutiyo-strength, effort and glories. [Dvanda]

(B) amitā-(are) immeasurable. balaparakkamajutiyo-strength, effort and glories. <u>yassa</u>-of whom. so'yaṁ-that Buddha. amitabalaparakkamajuti-is so called.

• amitabalaparakkamajuti-The Buddha whose strength, effort and glories are immeasurable.

ayaṁ pana **kammadhāraya, dvanda**gabbho **tulyā'dhikaraṇa**bahubbīhi.

This Bahubbīhi is a **tulyā'dhikaraṇa**bahubbīhi with **kammadhāraya, dvanda compounds** concealed inside.

Pīṇo'rakkhaṁsa bāhū

[**Pīṇa**-full, **i.e.** having attractively plump body-mass. **ura**-chest. **akkha**-collar bones. **aṁsa**-shoulder. **bāhū**-arms]

Pīṇo'rakkhaṁsa bāhū'ti–Now, it will be explained this Bahubbīhi which contains these "**Pīṇo'rakkhaṁsa bāhu**" words:

(1) uro ca-chest also. akkhañ'ca [akkaṁ+ca] akkhaṁ ca-collar bone also. aṁso ca-shoulder also. bāhu ca-arm also.
• ura'kkha'ṁsabāhavo-chest, collar-bone, shoulder and arms. **[Dvanda]**

(B) pīṇā-(are) full, plump. urakkhaṁ'sabāhavo-chest, collar-bone, shoulder and arms. <u>yassa</u>-whose. bhagavato-Lord Buddha. so'yaṁ- that Buddha. pīṇo'rakkha'ṁsabāhu-is so-called.

• pīṇo'rakkha'ṁsabāhu-The Buddha whose chest, collar-bone, shoulder and arms are full (with appropriate body-mass, being plump).

Ayaṁ pana **dvanda**gabbho **tulyā'dhikaraṇa**bahubbīhi.

This Bahubbīhi is a **tulyā'dhikaraṇa**bahubbīhi with **dvanda** inside.

Pīṇa gaṇḍa vadana thanū'ru jaghanā

[**Pīṇa**-full. **gaṇḍa**-cheek. **vadana**-mouth. **thanu**-breast. **ūru**-thigh. **jaghanā**-waist]

Pīṇa gaṇḍa vadana thanū'rujaghanā'ti–Now, it will be explained this Bahubbīhi which contains these "**Pīṇagaṇḍa vadanathanū'rujaghanā**" words:

(1) gaṇḍo ca-cheek also. vadanañ'ca [vadanaṁ+ca] vadanaṁ ca-mouth also. thano ca-breast also. ūru ca-thigh also. jaghanañ'ca [jaghanaṁ+ca] jaghanaṁ-waist also.

- gaṇḍavadanathanū'rujaghanā-cheek, mouth, breast, thigh and waists. **[Dvanda compound]**

(B) pīṇā-(are) full, plump. gaṇḍavadanathanū'rujaghanā-cheek, mouth, breast, thigh and waists. **yassā**-of whose (woman). sā'yaṁ [sā+ayaṁ] sā ayaṁ-that woman. pīṇagaṇḍavadanathanū'rujaghanā-is so called.

- pīṇagaṇḍavadanathanū'rujaghanā-the woman whose cheek, mouth, breast, thigh and waists are (attractively) full, plump.

Ayam'pi [**ayaṁ**-this+**api**-also, too]
dvandagabbho tulyā'dhikaraṇabahubbīhi.
This Bahubbīhi too is a **tulyā'dhikaraṇa** bahubbīhi with a **dvanda** hidden inside.

Pavara surā'sura garuḍa manuja bhujaga gandhabba makuṭa kūṭa cumbita sela, saṅghaṭṭita caraṇo

[**Pavara**-noble. **surā**-gods. **asura**-demons. **garuḍa**-mythical birds (griffon). **manuja**-human. **bhujaga**-dragons. **gandhabba**-celestial artiste. **makuṭa**-crown. **kūṭa**-peak. **cumbita**-fixed. **sela**-precious-stones, **saṅghaṭṭita**-touched. **caraṇo**-feet] (* This Bahubbīhi compound noun is the longest one)

Pavara surā'sura garuḍa manuja bhujaga gandhabba makuṭa kūṭa cumbita sela, saṅghaṭṭita caraṇo'ti–
Now, it will be explained this Bahubbīhi which contains the words "**Pavara**" **etc.**

(1) surā ca-gods also. asurā ca-demons. garuḍā ca-garuḍa birds. manujā ca-humans. bhujagā ca-dragons. gandhabbā ca-celestial artiste also. • surā'suragaruḍamanujabhujagagandhabbā-gods, demons, garuḍa birds, humans, dragons and celestial artistes. **[Dvanda compound]**

(2) pavarā ca-(are) noble. te-those noble ones are.
surā'suragaruḍamanujabhujaga gandhabbā ca- gods, demons, garuḍa birds, humans, dragons and celestial artistes. ceti [ceti=ca+iti]
• pavarasurā'suragaruḍamanujabhujagagandhabbā-the noble gods, demons, garuḍa birds, humans, dragons and celestial artistes. **[Kammadhāraya]**

(3) pavarasurā'suragaruḍamanujabhujagagandhabbānaṁ-of the noble gods, demons, garuḍa birds, humans, dragons and celestial artistes. makuṭāni-crowns.
• pavarasurā'suragaruḍamanujabhujagagandhabbamakuṭāni-the crowns of the noble gods, demons, garuḍa birds, humans, dragons and celestial artistes. **[Chaṭṭhī Tappurisa]**

(4) pavarasurā'suragaruḍamanujabhujagagandhabbamakuṭānaṁ-of the crowns of noble gods, demons, garuḍa birds, humans, dragons and celestial artistes. kūṭāni-the tips.
•pavarasurāsuragaruḍamanujabhujagagandhabbamakuṭa-kūṭāni- the tip of crowns of noble gods, demons, garuḍa birds, humans, dragons and celestial artistes. **[Chaṭṭhī Tappurisa]**

(5) pavarasurā'suragaruḍamanujabhujagagandhabbamakuṭakūṭe-su-on the tip of crowns of noble gods, demons, garuḍa birds, humans, dragons and celestial artistes. cumbitā-studded.
• pavarasuā'surā'suragaruḍamanujabhujagagandhabbamakuṭa-kūṭacumbitā-studded on the tip of crowns of noble gods, demons, garuḍa birds, humans, dragons and celestial artistes. [**Sattamī Tappurisa]**

(6) pavarasurā'suragaruḍamanujabhujagagandhabbamakuṭakūṭa-cumbitā ca- studded on the tip of crowns of noble gods, demons, garuḍa birds, humans, dragons and celestial artistes. te-those (studded). selā ca-(are the precious) stones. cā'ti [ca+iti] iti-therefore.
pavarasurā'suragaruḍamanujabhujagagandhabbamakuṭa-kūṭacumbitaselā-are so called.
• pavarasurā'suragaruḍamanujabhujagagandhabbamakuṭa-kūṭacumbitaselā-The precious stones studded on tip of the crowns of noble gods, demons, garuḍa birds, humans, dragons and celestial artistes. **[Kammadhāraya]**

(7)
pavarasurāsuragaruḍamanujabhujagagandhabbamakuṭakūṭacumbitaselehi-by the precious stones studded on tip of the crowns of

noble gods, demons, garuḍa birds, humans, dragons and celestial artistes.
saṅghaṭṭitā-(are) touched.

• pavarasurā'suragaruḍamanujabhujagagandhabbamakuṭa-kūṭacumbitaselasaṅghaṭṭitā-touched by precious stones studded on tip of the crowns of noble gods, demons, garuḍa birds, humans, dragons and celestial artistes. **[Tatiyā Tappurisa]**

(B)

pavarasurā'suragaruḍamanujabhujagagandhabbamakuṭakūṭa-cumbitaselasaṅghaṭṭitā-touched by precious stones studded on tip of the crowns of noble gods, demons, garuḍa birds, humans, dragons and celestial artistes. caraṇā-a pair of feet. **yassa** tathāgatassa-of which Buddha. so'yaṁ-that Buddha. pavarasurāsuragaruḍamanujabhujagagandhabbamakuṭakūṭacumbita selasaṅghaṭṭitacaraṇo-is so called.

• pavarasurā'suragaruḍamanujabhujagagandhabbamakuṭakū-ṭacumbitaselasaṅghaṭṭitacaraṇo-The Buddha whose pair of feet are touched by precious stones studded on tip of the crowns of noble gods, demons, garuḍa birds, humans, dragons and celestial artistes.

[Aññapadattha] tathāgato-the Buddha is to be taken as the final meaning of this Bahubbīhi.

Ayaṁ pana **dvanda, kammadhāraya, tappurisa**-gabbho **tulyā'dhikaraṇa**bahubbīhi.

This Bahubbīhi is a **tulyādhikaraṇa**bahubbīhi with **dvanda, kammadhāraya, tappurisa compounds** concealed inside.

Atha vā-

(1) saṅghaṭṭitā-touched. caraṇā-feet. saṅghaṭṭitacaraṇā-touched feet. **[Kammadhāraya]**

sā'pekkhatte sati'pi gamakattā samāso.

Pavarasurāsura garuḍamanujabhujaga gandhabbamakuṭakūṭa-cumbitaselehi- by precious stones studded on the tip of the crowns of noble gods, demons, garuḍa birds, humans, dragons and celestial artistes. saṅghaṭṭitacaraṇā-touched feet. **yassa** tathāgatassa so'yaṁ.

• pavarasurāsuragaruḍamanujabhujagagandhabbamakuṭakūṭa-cumbitaselasaṅghaṭṭitacaraṇo-Buddha who has the feet touched with precious stones studded on the tip of crowns of noble gods, demons, garuḍa birds, humans, dragons and celestial artistes (whenever they paid respects to the Buddha).

Ayaṁ pana **bhinnā'dhikaraṇa**bahubbīhi.
This Bahubbīhi is a **bhinnā'dhikaraṇa**bahubbīhi.

Catu'ddiso

[**Catu**-four. **disā**-directions]

Catu'ddiso'ti–Now, it will be explained this Bahubbīhi which contain the words "**Catu'ddiso**":
catasso-(are unobstructed) four. disā-directions. **yassa**-whose. so'yaṁ-that Buddha. catu'ddiso-is called "catu'disso",
• catuddiso-the Lord Buddha for whom all the four directions are unobstr-ucted (as he has the all-penetrating, all-knowing omniscient knowledge). [Aññapadattha] bhagavā-Buddha is to be taken as the meaning of this Bahubbīhi compound noun.

Pañcacakkhu

[**Pañca**-five. **cakkhu**-eyes]

Pañcacakkhū'ti–Now, it will b explained this Bahubbīhi which contain the words "**Pañca cakkhu**":
pañca-(have) the five. cakkhūni-eyes. **yassa**-of which, whose. tathāgatassa-Lord Buddha. so'yaṁ-that Buddha. pañcacakkhu-is called "pañcacakkhu",
• pañcacakkhu-the Buddha who has five kinds of eyes. [Aññapadattha] tathāgato-Buddha is to be taken as the sense of this Bahubbīhi compound noun.

Dasabalo

[**Dasa**-ten. **bala**-powers of super-knowledge]

Dasabalo'ti–Now, it will be explained this Bahubbīhi which contain the words "**Dasabalo**":
dasa-(have) the ten. balāni-powers. **yassa** so'yaṁ dasabalo-is so-called. • dasabalo-the Buddha who has ten kinds of powers. [Aññapadattha] bhagavā-Buddha is to be taken as the implied meaning of this Bahubbīhi compound noun.

Ana'ntañāṇo

[**Ana'nta**-unlimited, infinite. **ñāṇa**-knowledge.]

Ana'ntañāṇo'ti–Now, it will be explained this Bahubbīhi which contain the words "**Anantañāṇo**":

(1) na'ssa [na+assa]. na-(There is) no, **assa**-for that knowledge (of Buddha). anto-the end, the limit. iti-therefore. anantaṁ-is called "ananta". • anantaṁ-the knowledge which has no limit. [**Ananta**=**na**-no+**anta**-limit]

(2) anantaṁ-(is) limitless. ñāṇaṁ-knowledge. **yassa** tathāgatassa- of Buddha. so'yaṁ-that Buddha. anantañāṇo-is called "anantañāṇo", • anantañāṇo-Buddha who has limitless (infinite) knowledge. [Aññapadattha] tathāgato-Buddha is to be taken as the sense of this Bahubbīhi compound noun.

Note: This compound is a unique noun since both of its combinations are not other compounds, but Bahubbīhi only.

Amita ghana sarīro

[**Amita**-immeasurable. **ghana**-solid. **sarīra**-body]
[**Amita**=**na**-not+**mita**-measured. **i.e.** immeasurable]

Amita ghana sarīro'ti–Now, it will be explained this Bahubbīhi which contain the words "**Amitaghanasarīro**":

(1) na-not. mitaṁ-measured. • amitaṁ-unmeasured. **[Ubhe Tappurisa]**

(2) ghanaṁ eva-the Solid only. sarīraṁ-body. • ghanasarīraṁ-the solid body. **[Avadhāraṇa-Kammadhāraya]**

(B) amitaṁ-(is) not measurable. ghanasarīraṁ-the strong, solid body. **yassa** tathāgatassa-of Buddha. so'yaṁ-that Buddha. amitaghanasarīro-is so called. • amitaghanasarīro-Lord Buddha who has immeasurable solid body. (immeasurable means in terms of strength, and proportionate body-mass) [Aññapadattha] tathāgato-Buddha is to be taken as the meaning of this Bahubbīhi compound noun.

Amita bala parakkama patto

[**Amita**-immeasurable. **bala**-power. **parakkama**-effort. **patta**-achieved]

Amitabalaparakkamapatto'ti–Now, it will be explained this Bahubbīhi which contain the words "**Amitabala parakkamapatto**":

(1) na-not. mitā-measured. • amitā-un-measured. **[Ubhe Tappurisa]**

(2) balañ'ca [balaṁ+ca] balaṁ ca-power also. parakkamo ca-effort also. • balaparakkamā-power and effort, **[Dvanda]**

(3) amitā eva-immeasurable only. balaparakkamā-power and efforts.
• amitabalaparakkamā-immeasurable power and effort, **[Avadhāraṇa-Kammadhāraya]**

(B) amitabalaparakkamā-(to) immeasurable power and efforts. pattā-had achieved or attained. **yena**-by whom (**i.e.** Lord Buddha). so'yaṁ amitabalaparakkamapatto-is so-called. • amitabalaparakkamapatto-The Lord Buddha who had attained the immeasurable power and effort. [Aññapadattha] bhagavā-Buddha is the referred meaning of this compound.

Ayaṁ pana **kammadhāraya, dvanda**gabbho **tulyā'dhikaraṇa**bahubbīhi.
This Bahubbīhi is a **tulyā'dhikaraṇa**bahubbīhi with **kammadhāraya, dvanda** concealed inside.

Matta bhamara gaṇa cumbita vikasita puppha vallināga-rukkho'pasobhitakandaro

[**Matta**-inebriated. **bhamara**-bee. **gaṇa**-group. **cumbita**-kissed. **vikasita**-blooming. **puppha**-flower. **valli**-vines. **nāgarukkha**-mesua ferrea=iron wood tree, **upasobhita**-adorned. **kandaro**-valley]

Matta bhamara gaṇa cumbita vikasitapupphavallināga-rukkho'pasobhitakandaro'ti–Now, it will be explained this Bahubbīhi which contain the words "**Matta...etc.**":

(1) mattā eva-inebriated. bhamarā-bees. • mattabhamarā-the inebriated bees. **[Avadhāraṇa-Kammadhāraya]**

(2) mattabhamarānaṁ-of the inebriated bees. gaṇā-groups. • mattabhamaragaṇā-the groups of inebriated bees. **[Chaṭṭhī Tappurisa]**

(3) mattabhamaragaṇehi-by groups of inebriated bees. cumbitāni-(are) kissed (**i.e.** touched). • mattabhamaraṇacumbitāni-kissed by the groups of inebriated bees. **[Tatiyā Tappurisa]**

(4) vikasitāni eva-the blooming only. pupphāni-flowers. • vikasitapupphāni-the blooming flowers. [Avadhāraṇa-Kammadhāraya]

(5-B) mattabhamaragaṇacumbitāni-(are) kissed by groups of inebriated bees. vikasitapupphāni-the blooming flowers. **yesaṁ**-of which (vines, trees etc.) te'ti [te+iti] te-those (vines and mesua ferrea trees) iti-therefore. mattabhamaragaṇacumbitavikasitapupphā-

are so called. • mattabhamaragaṇacumbitavikasitapupphā-the trees whose blooming flowers are kissed by the groups of inebriated bees. [Bahubbīhi]

(6) valli ca-vine also. nāgarukkho ca-mesua ferrea tree also.
• vallināgarukkhā-vine and mesua ferrea trees. **[Dvanda]**

(7) mattabhamaragaṇacumbitavikasitapupphā ca-the plants whose blooming flowers are kissed by groups of inebriated bees. te-those plants. vallināgarukkhā ce'ti [ca+iti] vallināgarukkhā ca-vine and mesua ferrea trees also. iti-therefore. mattabhamaragaṇacumbitavikasitapupphavallināgarukkhā-are so-called. • mattabhamaragaṇacumbitavikasitapupphavallināgarukkhā-vine and mesua ferrea trees whose blooming flowers are kissed by groups of inebriated bees. **[Kammadhāraya]**

(8) mattabhamaragaṇacumbitavikasitapupphavallināgarukkhehi-by vine and mesua ferrea trees whose blooming flowers are kissed by groups of inebriated bees. upasobhitāni-(are) adorned. •mattabhamaragaṇacumbitavikasitapupphavallināgarukkho' pasobhitāni-adorned by vine, and mesua ferrea trees whose blooming flowers are kissed by groups of inebriated bees. **[Tatiyā Tappurisa]**

(B) mattabhamaragaṇacumbitavikasitapupphavallināgarukkho' pasobhitāni-(are) adorned by vine and mesua ferrea trees whose blooming flowers are kissed by groups of inebriated bees. kandarāni-valleys. **yassa** pabbatarājassa-of which great mountain. so'yaṁ-that mountain. mattabhamaragaṇacumbitavikasitapupphavallināgarukkho'pa sobhitakandaro-is so called.
• mattabhamaragaṇacumbitavikasitapupphavallināgarukkho' pasobhitakandaro-the mountain whose valleys are adorned with vines, mesua ferrea trees, the blooming flowers, which are kissed by groups of inebriated bees.
[Aññapadattha] pabbatarājā-the mountain (with such beautiful valleys) is to be taken as the final sense of this compound noun.

Ayaṁ pana **dvanda, kammadhāraya, tappurisa**gabbho **tulyā'dhikaraṇa**bahubbīhi.
This Bahubbīhi is a **tulyā'dhikaraṇa**bahubbīhi with **dvanda, kammadhāraya, tappurisa** compounds concealed inside.

Atha vā–Here is another method of compounding:
(1) upasobhitāni-beautiful. kandarāni-valleys. upasobhitakandarāni-beautiful valleys. [Kammadhāraya]
sā'pekkhatte sati'pi gamakattā samāso.
Mattabhamaragaṇacumbitavikasitapupphavallināgarukkhehi-by vine and mesua ferrea trees whose blooming flowers are kissed by groups of inebriated bees.
upasobhitakandarāni-(have) beautiful valleys.
yassa pabbatarājassa-of which mountain. so'yaṁ.
mattabhamaragaṇacumbitavikasitapupphavallināgarukkho'pasobhitakandaro-is so-called.
•mattabhamaragaṇacumbitavikasitapupphavallināgarukkho'pasobhitakandaro-the mountain which have beautiful valleys with vines and mesua ferrea trees, the blooming flowers of which are kissed by inebriated bees.
[Aññapadattha] pabbatarājā- the mountain (with such beautiful valleys) is the final sense of this compound.

Ayaṁ pana **bhinnā'dhikaraṇa**bahubbīhi.
This Bahubbīhi is a **bhinnā'dhikaraṇa**bahubbīhi.

Nānā rukkha tiṇa patita puppho'pasobhita kandaro

[**Nānā**-various. **rukkha**-tree. **tiṇa**-grass. **patita**-fallen. **puppha**-flower. **upasobhita**-adorned. **kandaro**-valley]
Nānā rukkha tiṇa patita puppho'pasobhita kandaro'ti– Now, it will be explained this Bahubbīhi which contain the words "**Nānā...etc.**":
(1) rukkho ca-the tree also. tiṇañ'ca [tiṇaṁ+ca] tiṇaṁ ca-the grass also. • rukkhatiṇāni-the tree and grass. **[Dvanda]**
(2) nānā pakārāni eva-various only. rukkhatiṇāni-tree and grass.
• nānārukkhatiṇāni-various tree and grass. [**Kammadhāraya]**
(3) nānārukkhatiṇehi-from various tree and grass. patitāni-fallen.
• nānārukkhatiṇapatitāni-fallen from various tree and grass. **[Pañcamī Tappurisa]**

(4) nānārukkhatiṇapatitāni ca-fallen from various tree and grass. tāni-those that fall. pupphāni ca-(are) the flowers too. ce'ti [ca+iti] iti-therefore. nānārukkhatiṇapatitapupphāni-are so called,

• nānārukkhatiṇapatitapupphāni-the flowers fallen from various tree and grass. **[Kammadhāraya]**

(5) nānārukkhatiṇapatitapupphehi-with the flowers fallen from various tree and grass. upasobhitāni-are adorned. • nānārukkhatiṇapatitapuppho'pasobhitāni-adorned with the flowers fallen from various trees and grass. **[Tatiyā Tappurisa]**

(B) nānārukkhatiṇapatitapuppho'pasobhitāni- adorned with the flowers fallen from various trees and grass. kandarāni-valleys. **yassa** pabbatarājassa-of which mountain. so'yaṁ-that mountain. nānārukkhatiṇapatitapuppho'pasobhitakandaro-is so called.

• nānārukkhatiṇapatitapuppho'pasobhitakandaro-the mountain which has valleys adorned with the flowers fallen from various trees and grass. [Aññapadattha] pabbatarājā.

Ayaṁ pana **dvanda, kammadhāraya, tappurisa**gabbho **tulyādhikaraṇa**bahubbīhi.
This Bahubbīhi is a **tulyādhikaraṇa**bahubbīhi with **dvanda, kammadhāraya, tappurisa** concealed inside.

Atha vā–upasobhitāni eva-adorned only. kandarāni-valleys. upasobhitakandarāni-adorned valleys. [Kammadhāraya] sā'pekkhatte sati'pi gamakattā samāso.

(B) Nānārukkhatiṇapatitapupphehi-by flowers fallen from various trees and grass. upasobhitakandarāni-(are) adorned valleys. **yassa** pabbatarājassa-of which mountain. so'yaṁ-that mountain. nānārukkhatiṇapatitapupphopasobhitakandaro-is so called.

• nānārukkhatiṇapatitapupphopasobhitakandaro-the mountain whose valleys are adorned with flowers fallen from various trees and grass. [Aññapadattha] pabbatarājā.

Ayaṁ pana **bhinnā'dhikaraṇa**bahubbīhi.
This Bahubbīhi is a **bhinnā'dhikaraṇa**bahubbīhi.

Nānāmusalaphālapabbatatarukaliṅgarasaradhanugadā'si-tomarahatthā.

[**Nānā**-various. **musala**-pestle. **phāla**-ploughshare. **pabbata**-mount. **taru**-tree. **kaliṅgara**-pieces of wood such as twigs and branches. **sara**-arrow. **dhanu**-bow. **gada**-javelin. **asi**-sword. **tomara**-lance. **hatthā**-hands]

Nānāmusalaphālapabbatatarukaliṅgarasaradhanugadā'si tomarahatthā'ti–Now, it will be explained this Bahubbīhi which contain the words "**Nānā...etc.**":

(1) musalo ca-pestle also. phālo ca-ploughshare also. pabbato ca-mount also. taru ca-tree also. kaliṅgaro ca-piece of wood also. saro ca-arrow also. dhanu ca-bow also. gadā ca-javelin also. asi ca-sword also. tomaro ca-lance also. • musalaphālapabbatatarukaliṅgarasaradhanugadāsitomarā-pestle, ploughshare, mount, tree, piece of wood, arrow, bow, javelin, sword and lance. **[Dvanda compound]**

(2) nānā pakārā eva-various only. musalaphālapabbatatarukaliṅgarasaradhanugadāsitomarā-pestle, ploughshare, mount, tree, piece of wood, arrow, bow, javelin, sword, and lance. • nānāmusalaphālapabbatatarukaliṅgarasaradhanugadāsi tomarā-various pestle, ploughshare, mount, tree, piece of wood, arrow, bow, javelin, sword and lance. **[Avadhāraṇa-Kammadhāraya]**

(B) nānāmusalaphālapabbatatarukaliṅgarasaradhanugadāsitomarā - (are) various pestle, ploughshare, mount, tree, piece of wood, arrow, bow, javelin, sword, and lances. hatthesu-(held) in the hands. **yesaṁ**-of whose (the companions of Māra, the evil one). te-those companions. nānāmusalaphālapabbatatarukaliṅgarasaradhanugadāsi-tomarahatthā-are so called. • nānāmusalaphālapabbatatarukaliṅgarasara-dhanugadāsitomara hatthā-the companions of Māra, the evil one, in whose hands are various pestle, ploughshare, mount, tree, piece of wood, arrow, bow, javelin, sword and lances (preparing to launch an assault on Buddha so as to disrupt his efforts to attain enlightenment under the Bodhi tree).

Ayaṁ pana **dvanda, kammadhārayagabbho** gabbho
bhinnā'dhikaraṇabahubbīhi.
This Bahubbīhi is a **bhinnā'dhikaraṇa**bahubbīhi with **Dvanda, Kamma dhāraya compounds** concealed inside.

Note: This Bahubbīhi is called a **bhinnā'dhikaraṇa**bahubbīhi because (1) the word "**nānāmusalaphālapabbatatarukaliṅgarasaradhanugadā'sitomarā**" is in nominative plural while its correlative word "hatta" ends in the locative plural as "**hatthesu**"**.** So, they are not **tulyā'dhikaraṇa** as both component words are in different case-endings.

Bahubbīhi-icca'nena kvattho? Bahubbīhimhi ca.
What benefit is there by terming "Bahubbīhi"?
It has the benefit of making easy reference in such Suttas as "Bahubbīhimhi ca" etc.

३२९, ३५७. नामानं समुच्चयो द्वन्दो

329, 357. **Nāmānaṁ samuccayo dvando.**

[Nāmānaṁ+samuccayo+dvando. 3 words]

[V] Nāmānaṁ ekavibhattikānaṁ yo samuccayo. so **dvanda**sañño hoti.

When multiple nouns of different meanings but with the same vibattis are joined together, it is called "**dvanda**-Copulative compound".

Summary: This Sutta defines a Dvanda Samāsa. The two chief distinctive marks of a Dvanda are:

(1) having a Nipāta "ca" after every component word,

(2) all the component words including nipāta particle "Ca" end in the nominative-case in the ED. [See the EDs and examples to validate this]

(1) Candimā ca-moon also, sūriyo ca-sun also,
• candimasūriyā-moon and suns.

(2) samaṇo ca-monk also, brāhmaṇo ca-the Brāhmin also,
• samaṇabrāhmaṇā- the monk and Brāhmins.

(3) sāriputto ca-Venerable Sāriputta also, moggallāno ca-Venerable Moggalāna also, • sāriputtamoggallānā-

Venerable Sāriputta and Venerable Moggalānas.

(4) brāhmaṇo ca-the Brāhmin also, gahapatiko ca-householder also, • brāhmaṇagahapatikā- the Brāhmin and householders.

(5) yamo ca-yama also, varuṇo ca-varuṇa also,
• Yamavaruṇā-(two deities named) Yama and Varuṇas.

(6) kuvero ca-kuvera also, vāsavo ca-vāsava also,
• Kuveravāsavā- Kuvera and Vāsavas. (two guardian deities so-named)

Dvanda-icca'nena kvattho? Dvandaṭṭhā vā.
What benefit is there by terming "dvanda"?
It has the benefit of making easy reference in such Suttas as "Dvandaṭṭhā vā" etc.

३३०, ३४०. महतं महा तुल्याधिकरणे पदे
330, 340. **Mahataṁ mahā tulyā'dhikaraṇe pade.**

[Mahataṁ+mahā+tulyādhikaraṇe+pade. 4 words]

[V] Tesaṁ **mahanta**saddānaṁ **mahā-**ādeso hoti tulyādhikaraṇe pade.

The word "mahanta" in a Kammadhāraya compound, changes to "mahā".

Note: The front word always has to follow the gender of next word.

(1) Mahanto ca-great also. so-that great. puriso ca-is man also. cā'ti [ca+iti] iti-therefore. mahāpuriso-is called "mahāpuriso",
• mahāpuriso-the great man.

(2) mahantī ca-great. sā-that woman. devī-is queen. cā'ti
• mahādevī-the great queen.

(3) mahantañ'ca [mahantaṁ+ca] mahantaṁ ca-great. taṁ-that great. balañcā'ti [balaṁ+ca+iti] balaṁ ca-power. iti.
• mahābalaṁ-the great power.

(4) mahanto ca so nāgo ca-dragon. cā'ti • mahānāgo-the great dragon, the great elephant or great saint (three possible meanings).

(5) mahanto ca so yaso ca-fame or retinue. cā'ti • mahāyaso-the great fame or retinue (two possible meanings),

(6) mahantañ'ca taṁ padumavanañ'cā'ti [padumavanaṁ+ca+iti] padumavanaṁ ca-red lotus grove. [**paduma**-lotus+**vanaṁ**-

grove]
• mahāpadumavanaṁ-the great red lotus-grove.
(7) mahantī ca sā nadī-river. cā'ti • mahānadī-the great river.
(8) mahanto ca so maṇi-ruby. cā'ti • mahāmaṇi-the great ruby.
(9) mahanto ca so gahapatiko-householder or the wealthy man. cā'ti • mahāgahapatiko-the great house-holder or the great wealthy man.
(10) mahantañ'ca taṁ dhanañ'cā'ti [dhanaṁ+ca+iti] dhanaṁ-wealth. • mahādhanaṁ-the great wealth.
(11) mahanto ca so puñño ca-virtuous. cā'ti
• mahāpuñño-the great virtuous.

Bahuvacanaggahaṇena kvaci mahantasaddassa mahā-deso hoti.

By means of Bahuvacana (plural number indicated by the word "mahataṁ" in Sutta), changing of "mahanta" into "**maha**" can occur in some Kammadhāraya compound nouns. [Please note that it is with a short vowel "**maha**". See the examples. Augmentation with either a similar or dissimilar consonant is also occurred in each example which is shown in bold]
(1) Mahantañ'ca [mahantaṁ+ca] mahantaṁ ca taṁ phalañ'cā'ti [phalaṁ+ca+iti] phalaṁ ca-fruit or result.
• maha**p**phalaṁ-the great fruit or the great result.
(2) • maha**b**balaṁ-the great power.[No ED in these examples, just only examples] **evaṁ-**similarly in this way.
(3) • maha**d**dhanaṁ-the great wealth.
(4) • maha**b**bhayaṁ-the great danger or the great fear.

३३१, ३५३. इत्थियं भासितपुमित्थी पुमाव चे

331, 353. **Itthiyaṁ bhāsitapumi'tthī pumā'va ce.**

[Itthiyaṁ+bhāsitapumā+itthī+pumā+iva+ce.6]

[V] Itthiyaṁ tulyā'dhikaraṇe pade ce bhāsitapumi'tthī pumā'va daṭṭhabbā.

In a Bahubbīhi compound, the last component word which once used to belong to feminine gender, has to be assumed as that of a masculine gender of the completed compound. (when it becomes a complete word)

(1) Dīghā-long. jaṅghā-legs. **yassa**-of whose. so'yaṁ
• dīghajaṅgho-the one who has long legs.
(2) • kalyāṇabhariyo-the one who has good wife.
(3) • pahūtapañño-the one who has much wisdom.
[All three are Bahubbīhi]

Explanation

In these three examples, the last component words "**Jaṅgā**-calf or leg, **Bhariyā**-wife, **paññā**-wisdom" are permanent feminine gender nouns. So, they can still assume feminine gender in the compounding process of ED. But, when the word becomes a complete word, they have become of masculine gender as the meaning of completed compound noun refers to only the man who has long leg, good wife and much wisdom.

Bhāsitapume'ti kimatthaṁ?
What is the word "bhāsitapume" for?
To show that the last component word "bhariyā-(wife) " in the example below is not a "bhāsitapuma-word". It is always a feminine gender. Hence, it does not need to be assumed as a masculine noun.
Brāhmaṇabandhu ca-of the Brāhmin caste also. sā-that woman. bhariyā ca-(is) wife also. cāti * Brāhmaṇabandhubhariyā-the Brāhmin-caste wife. [Kammadhāraya]

३३२, ३४३. कम्मधारयसञ्ञे च
332, 343. **Kammadhārayasaññe ca.**

[Kammadhārayasaññe+ca. 2 words]

[V] Kammadhārayasaññe ca samāse itthiyaṁ tulyā'dhikaraṇe pade pubbe bhāsitapumi'tthī ce. pumā'va daṭṭhabbā.

In a Kammadhāraya compound, the first component word, which is currently a modifier adjective to the latter in feminine gender, has to be assumed as that of a masculine gender when the compound becomes a completed word. (It means that the first word serving as a modifier adjective to the latter of feminine gender has to be in the same feminine gender as per the grammatical rule in the pending etymological process of compound. It is the rule of syntax that the qualifier and the qualified has to be in the same gender and of same vibatti. But, when completed, the preceding word must re-assume its masculine gender, no longer of feminine gender which it has once been conformed to during the compounding process of ED.)

(1) • Brāhmaṇadārikā-the Brāhmin girl,
(2) • khattiyakaññā-the Khattiya girl,
(3) • khattiyakumārikā-the Khattiya little girl.

Explanation

In these three examples, the first component words "**Brahmaṇa**-Brāhmin, **Khattiya**-warrior" are usually of masculine genders. So, they can still assume feminine gender in the compounding process of ED by being "Brahmaṇī, Khattiyā" as per the grammatical rule. See the possible ED of the example words shown below.

(1) Brāhmaṇī ca sā dārikā cā'ti • Brāhmaṇadārikā [This is ED]

Here is the Meaning of ED:

Brāhmaṇī ca-(is) the Brāhmin caste also. Sā-that woman. Dārikā Ca-is also the girl. iti-therefore • Brāhmaṇadārikā-the Brāhmin caste girl.

[The EDs are **not shown in the original grammatical text**. This is a sample of possible ED shown as correctly as possible. In the ED, See the word "Brahmaṇī" which ends in an "ī-affix" indicating the feminine gender. This first word has to follow the feminine gender of the last word "Dārikā" as it is of feminine gender]

In the meaning of completed word, the first component words re-assume their masculine gender as the meaning of completed compound noun refers to only the one whose caste or family back-ground is that of a Brāhmin or Khattiya caste system.

Bhāsitapume'ti kimatthaṁ?

What is the word "bhāsitapume" for?

To show that the last component word "dārikā-the young girl" in the example shown below is not a "bhāsitapuma-word". It is always of a feminine gender. Hence, it does not need to be assumed as a masculine noun.

[**bhāsita**-said before, **i.e.** being indicative of. **puma**-literally means male, **i.e.** masculine gender]

(1) * Khattiyabandhudārikā-the young girl of Khattiya caste.

(2) * brāhmaṇabandhudārikā-the young girl of Brāhmin caste.
[All examples are Kammadhāraya compounds]

३३३, ३४४. अत्तं नस्स तप्पुरिसे

333, 344. **Attaṁ nassa tappurise.**

[Attaṁ+nassa+tappurise. 3 words]

[V] **N**assa padassa tappurise uttarapade **a**ttaṁ hoti.

The word "**na** (meaning "not) " which is the first component part in a tappurisa compound, changes into an "**a**".

(1) Na brāhmaṇo [ED] • abrāhmaṇo. [Complete word]
(2) • avasalo. (3) • abhikkhu.
(4) • apañcavassaṁ. (5) • apañcagavaṁ. (Refer to Sutta 326)
[All examples are Ube-tappurisa compounds]

३३४, ३४५. सरे अन

334, 345. **Sare an.** [Sare+an. 2 words]

[V] **N**assa padassa tappurise **an**-ādeso hoti sare pare.

In an Ubhe-tappurisa compound when the "**na**" is followed by a vowel of the vowel-initial-component word, it changes into an "**an**".

Note: The function of previous Sutta is applicable for **the consonant-initial** Ubhe-tappurisa compounds. The function of this Sutta is applicable for **the vowel-initial** Ubhe tappurisa compounds such as "asso, issaro, ariyo" and so forth. See the examples carefully to clarify this.

(1) Na-not. asso-horse. • **an**asso-non-horse.
(2) • **an**issaro-not Lord, uncontrolled, undominated.
(3) • **an**ariyo-not noble. [All are Ube-tappurisa compounds]

३३५, ३४६. कद कुस्स

335, 346. **Kad kussa.** [Kad+kussa. 2 words]

[V] **Ku**-icce'tassa **kad** hoti sare pare.

In a Kammadhāraya compound where the "**ku** (means bad or disgusting) " is the first component part of the compound, it is then to be changed into "**kad**". ["ku" is substituted with "kad"]

(1) Kucchitaṁ-disgusting, or of poor taste. annaṁ-rice. [ED]
 • **kad**annaṁ-the disgusting or poorly-cooked rice.
 [The complete word]
(2) kucchitaṁ-bad. asanaṁ-food.
 • **kad**assanaṁ-bad food (without taste.)

Sare'ti kimatthaṁ?
What is the word "sare" for?
To show that examples shown below are inapplicable as they do not have sara (vowels) in the initial of them.
(See the last component words: **Dāra**-wife, **jana**-people, **putta**-son, **geha**-home, **vattha**-cloth, **dāsa**-servant. The initial letter in them is not a vowel, but consonants "**d, j, p, g, v** and **d**". Hence, are inapplicable.)

(1) Kucchitā-disgusting. dārā-wife. **yesaṁ**-of whose. (apuññakārānaṁ-those who have done unwholesome deeds). te-those. hontī'ti [honti+iti] honti-are. iti-therefore.
 i.e. those who had done unwholesome deeds in the past have bad wife. They are called "kudārā". * kudārā-those who have bad wife.
(2) * **ku**janā-those who have bad people (friends).

Evaṁ

(1) * **ku**puttā-those who have bad son.
(2) * **ku**gehā-those who have bad home.
(3) * **ku**vatthā-those who have bad (poor-quality) cloth.
(4) * **ku**dāsā-those who have bad servant [All Bahubbīhi compounds]

३३६, ३४७. का'प्पत्थेसु च

336, 347. **Kā'ppa'tthesu ca.** [Kā+appa-atthesu+ca. 3 words]

[V] **Ku**-icce'tassa **kā** hoti appa'tthesu ca.

In a Kammadhāraya compound where "**ku** (Here it means little amount, small in size) " is the first component part of the compound, it changes into "**kā**". ["ku" is substituted with "kā"]

• Kālavaṇaṁ-little salt. [**Kā**-little+**lavaṇa**-salt]
• kāpupphaṁ-small flower. [**Kā**-small+**puppha**-flower]

Bahuvacanaggahaṇaṁ kimatthaṁ?
What is the use of Bahuvacana(refer to the word "Kā'ppa'tthesu" in Sutta which is in locative, plural number "su") for?

Ku-icce'tassa ana'ppatatthesu'pi kvaci **kā** hoti.

To show that changing "ku" into "kā" can also happen in some words with other meaning (such as being bad or evil etc.).
• kāpurisā-bad men. [**Kā**-bad+**purisa**-man] [Kammadhāraya compound]

Note: (a) The function of previous Sutta 335 is applicable for compounds which begins with a vowel.
(b) The function of this Sutta is applicable for compounds which begins with consonants such as "lavaṇaṁ", "pupphaṁ" and so on. See the examples carefully to clarify this difference.

३३७, ३५०. क्वचि समासन्त गतानमकारन्तो
337, 350. **Kvaci samāsa'ntagatāna'makāra'nto.**

[Kvaci+samāsa-antagatānaṁ+akāro+anto. 4 words]

[V] Samāsa'ntagatānaṁ nāmāna'manto saro kvaci **a**kāro hoti.

The last component vowel at the end of a compound, changes into an "a".

[This Sutta changes the end-vowel of the last word of some compound nouns into an "a". For example, the end vowels "a" of **rāja**-king etc. will remain in "a" while "i" of **akkhi**-eye etc. will change into "a". See the examples 1 and 8 to clarify this function]

(1) Devānaṁ-of deities. rājā-king. • devarājo, • devarājā-the king of deities. [Chaṭṭhī-tappurisa]
(2) Devānaṁ sakhā-friend. • devasakho, • devasakhā-the friend of deities. [Chaṭṭhī-tappurisa]
(3) Pañca-five. ahāni-days. • pañcā'haṁ-five day. [pañca+ahaṁ, Digu]
(4) • sattā'haṁ-seven day. [satta+ahaṁ, Digu]
(5) • pañcagavaṁ-five cow. [Digu]

(6) • chattu'pāhanaṁ-umbrella and slipper. [Dvanda]
(7) • **upa**saradaṁ-the talk regarding autumn. [Abyayībhāva]
(8) • visālakkho-the wide-eyed person. [Bahubbīhi]
(9) • vimukho-the person who has unsightly face. [Bahubbīhi]

Kāraggahaṇaṁ kimatthaṁ? Ākāranta ikārantā ca honti,
What is the word "kāra" for?
[Refer to the word "Kāra" in "makāranto" in Sutta]
It is to show that by the word "Kāra" in Sutta, the last component vowel of some compound nouns can also be changed into "**ā** or **i**".

The example of "ā-function". ("ā" shown underlined in the example)
(1) paccakkhā-attained, known. dhammā-the dhamma. **yassa** so'yan'ti [ED] • paccakkhadhammā-the who has attained Dhamma. [Complete word, Bahubbīhi compound]

The example of "i-function" ("i" shown underlined).
(1) surabhino-of pleasant flower. gandho-odor.
• surabhigandhi-the odor of pleasant flower.[Chaṭṭhī-tappurisa]
(2) sundaro-good. gandho-smell. • sugandhi-the good smell. [Kammadhāraya]
(3) pūtino-foul. gandho-smell. • pūtigandhi-the foul smell. [Kammadhāraya]
(4) kucchito-disgusting. gandho • kugandhi-disgusting smell. [Kammadhāraya]
(5) duṭṭhu-bad. gandho-smell. **yassa** so'yan'ti [so+ayaṁ+iti]
• dugandhi-something which has a bad smell. [Bahubbīhi]
(6) pūti eva-foul only. gandho-smell. • pūtigandhi-the foul smell. [Kammadhāraya]

Nadī-antā ca kattuantā ca kapaccayo hoti samāsa'nte.

The "ka" affix can be applied at the end of "nadī" and "kattu-doer" in the bahubbīhi compound nouns.
(1) Bahū-(are) plenty. nadiyo-rivers. **yasmiṁ**-in which (district). so'yaṁ-that district. bahunadiko-is so called.
• bahunadiko-the district where there are a lot of rivers, [Bahubbīhi]

[Aññapadattha] janapado-the district is to be regarded as the final sense of this compound.

(2) Bahavo-(are) plenty. kattāro-doers, **i.e.** workers. **yassa**-whose (employer). so'yaṁ-that man (employer). bahukattuko-is so called. • bahukattuko-the man who has many workers. [Bahubbīhi] puriso-the man (employer) who has many workers, is to be taken as the sense of this compound noun.

३३८, ३५६. नदिम्हा च

338, 356. **Nadimhā ca.** [Nadimhā+ca. 2 words]

[V] **Nadi**mhā ca **ka**paccayo hoti samāsa'nte.

The affix "ka" has to be added after the last component word "nadī" in a Bahubbīhi compound. [This function was already shown in the preceding Sutta. It is shown here again to show the consistency of the function. The applied **"ka"** is shown underlined]

(1) Bahū nadiyo **yasmiṁ** so'yan'ti • bahunadiko.
(Refer to the preceding Sutta)

(2) Bahū kantiyo-pleasures. **yassa** so'yan'ti • bahukantiko-the man who has a lot of pleasures (amenities). [Bahubbīhi]

(2) • Bahunāriko-the man who has a lot of women. [Bahubbīhi]

३३९, ३५८. जायाय तु दं जानि पतिम्हि

339, 358. **Jāyāya tu daṁ, jāni patimhi.**

[Jāyāya+tu+daṁ, jāni+patimhi. 4 words]

[V] **Jāyā**-icce'tāya tu **daṁ, jāni**-icce'te ādesā honti **pati**mhi pare. [The particle "tu" is an expletive without specific meaning]

The front word "**jāyā**-wife" changes into "**daṁ**" and "**jāni**" when the word "**pati**-husband" follows in a dvanda compound. (See the function shown underlined.)

• Daṁpati (दंपति) • jānipati-wife and husband.

[Both examples are of the same meaning. Dvanda compound]

३४०, ३५५. धनुम्हा च

340, 355. **Dhanumhā ca.** [Dhanumhā+ca. 2 words]

[V] **Dhanu**mhā ca **ā-**paccayo hoti samāsa'nte.

An "**ā**" is be added after the word "**dhanu** (arrow) " in a Bahubbīhi compound.

Gaṇḍīvo-noded. dhanu-bow. yassa so'yaṁ gāṇḍīvadhanvā-is so called. • gāṇḍīvadhanvā-the one who has knotted-bow. [Bahubbīhi] **Note:** This example word (गाण्डवधन्वा) is also found in the Paṇinī, Sutta Number 5-4-132.

३४१, ३३६. अंविभत्तीनमकारन्ता अब्ययीभावा

341, 336. **Aṁ vibhattīna'makārantā abyayībhāvā.**
[Aṁ+vibhattīnaṁ+akārantā+abyayībhāvā. 4 words]

[V] Tasmā **a**kāra'ntā abyayībhāvasamāsā parāsaṁ vibhattīnaṁ kvaci **aṁ** hoti.

In a-ending Abyayībhāva compounds, the vibattis applied after them sometimes changes into "**ṁ**".
(See the examples carefully to clarify it. "ṁ" is shown underlined)

- **Adhi**cittaṁ-the mind-related thing.
- **yath**āvuḍḍhaṁ-according to seniority.
- **upa**kumbhaṁ-the talk about pot.
- **yāva**jīvaṁ-for lifetime.
- **tiro**pabbataṁ-beyond the mountain.
- **tiro**pākāraṁ-beyond the fence.
- **tiro**kuṭṭaṁ beyond the wall.
- **anto**pāsādaṁ-inside the mansion.

Kvacī'ti kimatthaṁ?
What is the word "kvaci" for? To show that in some examples like the ones shown below, the function of Sutta is not applied as restricted by the word "kvaci".
* Adhicittassa-the one striving for mental development.
bhikkhuno-of the monk.

What does the function of "kvaci" mean?
It means that when such compound nouns are used as an adjective in the wider areas of Buddhist texts based on the context, different case-endings are applied. Thus, the rule of Sutta is only a statement of the general pattern of such nouns.

Note: Though it is said in Sutta as only a-ending Abyayībhāva is applicable, it should be noted that ā-ending abyayībhāva compound is also applicable by the function of this Sutta after "ā" is shortened by the next Sutta 342. See ā-ending abyayībhāva example "upagaṅgaṁ" shown in the next Sutta to clarify this fact.

३४२, ३३७. सरो रस्सो नपुंसके

342, 337. **Saro rasso napuṁsake.**

[Saro+rasso+napuṁsake. 3 words]

[V] Napuṁsake vattamānassa abyayībhāvasamāsassa liṅgassa saro rasso hoti.

In Abyayībhāva compounds of neuter gender, the end dīgha (long vowels) "**ā, ī, ū**", change into "**rassa** (short vowels) ".

(1) Kumārīsu-in the girls. adhikicca-regarding. pavattati-arises. kathā-talk. **i.e.** the talk arises regarding the young the girls. iti-therefore. • **adhi**kumāri-the talk regarding young girls.
[Here, the last vowel "ī" of "**Kumārī**-young girl" is shortened into "**i**"]

(2) • **Upa**vadhu-the talk regarding daughter-in-law, [Here, the last vowel "**ū**" of "**vadhū**-daughter in law" is shortened into "**u**"]

(3) • **upa**gaṅgaṁ-the talk regarding the river Ganges. [Here, the last vowel "**ā**" of "**gaṅgā**-river Ganges" is shortened into an "**a**"]

(4) • **upa**maṇikaṁ-the talk regarding big-water-pot. [Here, the last vowel "**ā**" of "**maṇikā**-big water pot" is shortened into an "**a**"]

३४३, ३३८. अञ्ञस्मा लोपो च

343, 338. **Aññasmā lopo ca.** [Aññasmā+lopo+ca. 3 words]

[V] Aññasmā abyayībhāvasamāsā anakāra'ntā parāsaṁ vibhattīnaṁ lopo ca hoti.

Except the vibatti (case-endings) applied after **a**-ending abyayībhāva compounds, the vibattis which have been applied after those **ī, ū**-ending abyayībhāva compounds**,** are to be elided.

- **Adhi**'tthi-the talk regarding woman. [Adhi+itthī]
- **adhi**kumāri. [Adhi+kumārī]
- **upa**vadhu. [Upa+vadhū] (Refer to previous Sutta for the meaning)

Explanation: The vibatti applied after a-ending abyayībhāva is not elided as it undergoes morphological procedure of changing into "aṁ" by Sutta 341. Also, in **ā**-ending abyayībhāva compounds, ā is shortened by the preceding Sutta and then undergoes similar procedure by Sutta 341. In **ī, ū**-ending abyayībhāva compounds, the vibattis applied after them are to be elided as they do not need to undergo any further morphological function. Compare similar functions enjoined for those plain, non-compound nouns ending in "ī, ū" by Suttas 118, 220 in the nouns chapter.

Endings of Abyayībhāva Compound

(The Endings of compound is usually to be determined by the gender and ending of the last word after the first preceding Upasagga or Nipāta word)

(a) The Abyayībhāva compound nouns ending in "**a**"

- **adhi**cittaṁ. [Adhi+citta]
- **Upa**nagaraṁ. [Upa+nagara]
- **Tiro**pabbataṁ, etc. [Tiro+pabbata]

(b) The Abyayībhāva compound nouns ending in "**ā**",

- **upa**gaṅgaṁ [Upa+gaṇgā]
- **upa**maṇikaṁ, etc. [Upa+maṇikā]

(c) The Abyayībhāva compound nouns ending in "**ī**",

- **Adhi**'tthi, [Adhi+itthī]
- **adhi**kumāri etc. [Adhi+kumārī]

(d) The Abyayībhāva compound nouns ending in "**ū**",

- **upa**vadhu etc. [Upa+vadhū]

Iti nāmakappe samāsakappo sattamo kaṇḍo.
Samāsa Chapter, the Seventh Section of Noun ends.

Samāsakappo niṭṭhito.
Samāsa Chapter ends.

5. Taddhita Kappa

Taddhita[24] Chapter

(Nouns in *Taddhita* Affixes)

Aṭṭhama Kaṇḍa

The Eighth Section of Noun

Apacca Taddhita

[**Apacca**-son, offspring, descendant]

(Nouns in Patronymic-affixes)

Note: Suttas 344, 345, 346, 347, 348, 349 apply the affixes which are expressive of family lineage or ancestry of a proper noun.

३४४, ३६१. वा णा'पच्चे

344, 361. **Vā ṇā'pacce.** [Vā+ṇa+apacce. 3 words]

[V] **Ṇ**apaccayo hoti vā "**tassā'pacca**" micce'tasmiṁ atthe.

To signify "the son or descendant of someone", an affix "**ṇa**" is sometimes added after that noun denoting it. [The affix "ṇa" is invisible in the examples]

Note: There are **three types of endings** in each example: ending in "**o**, **aṁ**, and **ī**". The "**o**" and "**aṁ**", are vibatti-derivative morphemes of masculine and neuter genders respectively while "**ī**" is an affix for the feminine gender. The "**o**" is morpheme of nominative singular "**si**" for any nouns of masculine gender while "**aṁ**" is derivative morpheme of "**si**" for nouns of neuter gender. The "**ī**" represents nouns belonging to feminine gender which has

[24] Taddhita=**ta**-of that noun+**hita**-the well-being & meaning enhancer. All the affixes such as **ṇa** etc. are formally called "taddhita" as they enhance as well as complement the meaning of nouns. "h" is substituted with "dha" and augmented with a "da". Thus it becomes "**taddhita**" in stead of "tahita".

no morpheme as applied "**si**" is elided. Such type of word-endings will be found not only in Taddhita, but also in Samāsa, Kita and Uṇādi chapters as those words are also nouns in different genders. To highlight this, the word "si" is included in the WA of each Taddhita nouns. The word analysis [WA] is shown only where necessary. WA for most examples is quite easy to study in Taddhita. In WA, there will be slight changes of vowels between the example and word analysis. For example, in the example, it will be **ā, e** or **o** though it is shown as **a, i,** or **u** in the word analysis. This is due to the **Vuddhi** procedure occurred in the example as a result of having an ṇ-conjoined affix. [Refer to Sutta 400, 404]

(1) (a) Vasiṭṭhassa-of a person named Vasiṭṭha, apaccaṁ-son or male descendant. vāsiṭṭho-Vasiṭṭha's son or descendant. [Masculine noun]

[wa] • vāsiṭṭho=vasiṭṭha+ṇa+si. (**ā** is a lengthened Vuddhi vowel)

* Vasiṭṭhassa apaccaṁ vā.

Note: This is not an example. It is rather an incomplete sentence which signifies as being inapplicable. Throughout this grammar text, any inapplicability will be sometimes shown by means of such incomplete sentences which may also contain a Nipāta particle "vā".]

(b) vasiṭṭhassa apaccaṁ-daughter or female descendant.

• vāsiṭṭhī-Vasiṭṭha's daughter or female descendant. [Feminine Taddhita-noun] [wa] vāsiṭṭhī=vasiṭṭha+ṇa+ī+si ["si" is elided. "ā" @vā is a vuddhi vowel]

(c) vasiṭṭhassa apaccaṁ-descendant race as a whole.

• vāsiṭṭhaṁ- Vasiṭṭha's race. [Taddhita-noun, Neuter gender]

[wa] • vāsiṭṭhaṁ=vasiṭṭha+ṇa+si ["si" becomes "aṁ"]

Note: As WA of All three examples in three genders are quite easy to understand, only the first one's WA will be shown.

Evaṁ-similarly in this way.

(2) • bhāradvājo-bhāradvāja m-descendant.

[wa] bhāradvājo=bhāradvāja+ṇa+si.

• bhāradvājī-bhāradvāja f-descendant.

[wa] bhāradvājī=bhāradvāja+ṇa+ī+si.

• bhāradvājaṁ-bhāradvāja race.

[wa] bhāradvājaṁ=bhāradvāja+ṇa+si.

Note: In next examples, only WA of one example will be shown as it is easy to understand.

(3) • Gotamo-Gotama m-descendant.

• gotamī-Gotama f-descendant.

• gotamaṁ-Gotama race.

[wa] Gotamo=Gotama+ṇa+si.

(4) • Vāsudevo-Vasudeva m-descendant.

• vāsudevī-Vasudeva f-descendant.

• vāsudevaṁ-Vasudeva race.

[wa] Vāsudevo=Vasudeva+ṇa+si.

(5) • Bāladevo-Baladeva m-descendant.

• bāladevī-Baladeva f- descendant. • bāladevaṁ-Baladeva race.

[wa] Bāladevo=Baladeva+ṇa+si.

(6) • Vesāmitto-Vesāmitta m-descendant. • vesāmittī-Vesāmitta f- descendant. • vesāmittaṁ-Vesāmitta race.

[wa] Vesāmitto=Vesāmitta+ṇa+si.

Note: Please note that **m-descendant** means male-descendant while **f-descendant** means female-descendant.

३४५, ३६६. णायन णान वच्छादितो

345, 366. Ṇāyana, ṇāna vacchā'dito.

[Ṇāyana, ṇāna+vaccha-ādito. 2 words]

[V] Tasmā **vacchā**'dito gottagaṇato **ṇāyana, ṇāna**paccayā honti vā "tassā'pacca" micce'tasmiṁ atthe.

To express "the son or descendant of someone", affixes "**ṇāyana, ṇāna**" are added after the race-descriptive noun "**vaccha** (a man so-named) etc.".

Note: "**ṇ**" of **ṇāyana, ṇāna** is usually elided. Hence, only "**āyana** and **āna**" will be left. This pattern is clearly shown underlined in the first set of examples. Please look carefully to understand it.

(1) (a) Vacchassa-of Vaccha. apaccaṁ • vacchāyano,

vacchāno-Vaccha m-descendant. [M-gender]
* vacchassa apaccaṁ vā.
[wa] vacchāyano=vaccha+ṇāyana+si
[wa] vacchāno=vaccha+ṇāna+si
(b) Vacchassa apaccaṁ • vacchāyanī, • vacchānī-Vaccha f-descendant. [F-gender]
[wa] vacchāyanī=vaccha+ṇāyana+ī+si
[wa] vacchānī=vaccha+ṇāna+ī+si
(c) Vacchassa apaccaṁ • vacchāyanaṁ, • vacchānaṁ-Vaccha race. [N-gender]
[wa] vacchāyanaṁ=vaccha+ṇāyana+si
[wa] vacchānaṁ=vaccha+ṇāna+si
(2) Sakaṭassa apaccaṁ • sākaṭāyano, • sākaṭāno-Sākata m-descendant.
* Sakaṭassa apaccaṁ vā.
• Sākaṭāyanī, • sākaṭānī-Sākata f-descendant.
• sākaṭāyanaṁ, • sākaṭānaṁ-Sākata race.
[wa] sākaṭāyano=sakaṭa+ṇāyana+si
[wa] sākaṭāno=sakaṭa+ṇāna+si ["ā" @Sākata is a Vuddhi vowel. Only WA of masculine gender words will be shown.]

Evaṁ---

(3) • kaṇhāyano, • kaṇhāno-Kaṇha m-descendant.
* kaṇhassa apaccaṁ vā.
• Kaṇhāyanī, • kaṇhānī-Kaṇha f-descendant.
• Kaṇhāyanaṁ, • kaṇhānaṁ-Kaṇha race.
[wa] kaṇhāyano=kaṇha+ṇāyana+si
[wa] kaṇhāno=kaṇha+ṇāna+si
(4) • Aggivessāyano, • aggivessāno-Aggivessa m-descendant.
• Aggivessāyanī, • aggivessānī-Aggivessa f-descendant.
• Aggivessāyanaṁ, • aggivessānaṁ-Aggivessa race.
[wa] Aggivessāyano=Aggivessa+ṇāyana+si
[wa] Aggivessāno=Aggivessa+ṇāna+si
(5) • Gacchāyano, • gacchāno-Gaccha m-descendant.
• Gacchāyanī, • gacchānī-Gaccha f-descendant.
• Gacchāyanaṁ, • gacchānaṁ-Gaccha race.

[wa] Gacchāyano=Gaccha+ṇāyana+si
[wa] Gacchāno=Gaccha+ṇāna+si
(6) • Kappāyano, • kappāno-Kappa m-descendant.
• Kappāyanī, • kappānī-Kappa f-descendant.
• Kappāyanaṁ, • Kappānaṁ-Kappa race.
[wa] Kappāyano=Kappa+ṇāyana+si
[wa] Kappāno=Kappa+ṇāna+si
(7) • Moggallāyano, • Moggallāno-Moggalla m-descendant.
• Moggallāyanī, • Moggallānī-Moggalla f-descendant.
• Moggallāyanaṁ, • moggallānaṁ-Moggalla race.
[wa] Moggalāyano=Moggala+ṇāyana+si
[wa] Moggalāno=Moggala+ṇāna+si
(8) • Muñcāyano, • muñcāno-Muñca m-descendant.
• Muñcāyanī, • muñcānī-Muñca f-descendant.
• Muñcāyanaṁ, • muñcānaṁ-Muñca race.
[wa] Muñcāyano=Muñca+ṇāyana+si
[wa] Muñcāno=Muñca+ṇāna+si
(9) • Saṅghāyano, • saṅghāno-Saṅgha m-descendant.
• Saṅghāyanī, • saṅghānī-Saṅgha f-descendant.
• Saṅghāyanaṁ, • saṅghānaṁ-Saṅgha race.
[wa] Saṅghāyano=Saṅgha+ṇāyana+si
[wa] Saṅghāno=Saṅgha+ṇāna+si
(10) • Lomāyano, • lomāno-Loma m-descendant.
• Lomāyanī, • lomānī-Loma f-descendant.
• Lomāyanaṁ, • lomānaṁ-Loma race.
[wa] Lomāyano=Loma+ṇāyana+si
[wa] Lomāno=Loma+ṇāna+si
(11) • Sākamāyano, • sākamāno-Sākama m-descendant.
• Sākamāyanī, • sākamānī-Sākama f-descendant.
• Sākamāyanaṁ, • sākamānaṁ-Sākama race.
[wa] Sākamāyano=Sakama+ṇāyana+si
[wa] Sākamāno=Sakama+ṇāna+si
["ā" @Sākama is a vuddhi vowel]
(12) • Nārāyano, • nārāno-Nara m-descendant.
• Nārāyanī, • nārānī-Nara f-descendant.

• Nārāyanaṁ, • nārānaṁ-Nara race.
[wa] Nārāyano= Nara+ṇāyana+si
[wa] Nārāno=nara+ṇāna+si [first "ā"@ nārā is a vuddhi vowel]
(13) • Corāyano, • corāno-Cora m-descendant.
• Corāyanī, • corānī-Cora f-descendant.
• Corāyanaṁ, • corānaṁ-Cora race.
[wa] Corāyano=Cora+ṇāyana+si
[wa] Corāno=Cora+ṇāna+si
(14) • Āvasālāyano, • āvasālāno-Avasāla m-descendant.
• Āvasālāyanī, • āvasālānī-Avasāla f-descendant.
• Āvasālāyanaṁ, • āvasālānaṁ-Avasāla race.
[wa] Āvasālāyano=Avasāla+ṇāyana+si
[wa] Āvasālāno=Avasāla+ṇāna+si ["ā" @āva is vuddhi vowel]
(15) • Dvepāyano, • dvepāno-Dvipa m-descendant.
• Dvepāyanī, • dvepānī-Dvipa f-descendant.
• Dvepāyanaṁ, • dvepānaṁ-Dvipa race.
[wa] Dvepāyano= Dvipa+ṇāyana+si
[wa] Dvepāno= Dvipa+ṇāna+si ["e" @dve is a vuddhi vowel]
(16) • Kuñcāyano, • kuñcāno-Kuñca m-descendant.
• Kuñcāyanī, • kuñcānī-Kuñca f-descendant.
• Kuñcāyanaṁ, • kuñcānaṁ-Kuñca race.
[wa] Kuñcāyano=Kuñca+ṇāyana+si
[wa] Kuñcāno=Kuñca+ṇāna+si
(17) • Kaccāyano, • kaccāno-Kacca m-descendant.
• Kaccāyanī, • kaccānī-Kacca f-descendant.
• Kaccāyanaṁ, • kaccānaṁ-Kacca race.
[wa] Kaccāyano=Kacca+ṇāyana+si
[wa] Kaccāno=Kacca+ṇāna+si

३४६, ३६७. णेय्यो कत्तिकादीहि

346, 367. Ṇeyyo kattikā'dīhi. [Ṇeyyo+kattika-ādīhi. 2 words]

[V] Tehi gottagaṇehi **kattikā**'dīhi **ṇeyya**paccayo hoti vā "tassā'pacca" micce'tasmiṁ atthe.

When expressing " the son or descendant of someone", an affix "**ṇeyya**" is sometimes added after the feminine noun word "**kattikā** etc.".

Note: "**ṇ**" of **ṇeyya**, is usually elided. Hence, only "**eyya**" will be left. See this pattern shown underlined in the examples.

(1) Kattikāya apaccaṁ • kattikeyyo-a woman named Kattikā's m-descendant.

[wa] kattikeyyo=kattikā+ṇeyya+si

* Kattikāya apaccaṁ vā.

Evaṁ

(2) • Venateyyo-a woman named Vinatā's m-descendant.

[wa] Venateyyo=vinatā+ṇeyya+si ["e" @ve is a vuddhi vowel]

(3) • Rohiṇeyyo-a woman named Rohiṇī's m-descendant.

[wa] Rohiṇeyyo=Rohiṇī+ṇeyya+si

(4) • Gaṅgeyyo-a woman named Gaṅgā's m-descendant.

[wa] Gaṅgeyyo=Gaṅgā+ṇeyya+si

(5) • Kaddameyyo-a woman named Kaddamā's m-descendant.

[wa] kaddameyyo=kaddamā+ṇeyya+si

(6) • Nādeyyo-a woman named Nadī's m-descendant.

[wa] Nādeyyo=nadī+ṇeyya+si ["ā" @nā is a vuddhi vowel]

(7) • Āleyyo-a woman named Ālī's m-descendant.

[wa] Āleyyo=ālī+ṇeyya+si

(8) • Āheyyo-a woman named Āhī's m-descendant.

[wa] Āheyyo=āhī+ṇeyya+si

(9) • Kāmeyyo-a woman named Kāmī's m-descendant.

[wa] kāmeyyo=kāmī+ṇeyya+si

(10) • Suciyā-a woman named Suci or of a pure woman. apaccaṁ

• Soceyyo-a woman named Suci's m-descendant or a pure woman's son. [wa] Soceyyo=suci+ṇeyya+si ["o" @So is a vuddhi vowel]

(11) • Sāle̲y̲y̲o-a woman named Sālā's m-descendant.
[wa] Sāleyyo=Sālā+ṇeyya+si
(12) • Bāle̲y̲y̲o-a woman named Bālā's m-descendant.
[wa] Bāleyyo=Bālā+ṇeyya+si
(13) • Māle̲y̲y̲o-a woman named Mālā's m-descendant.
[wa] Māleyyo=Mālā+ṇeyya+si
(14) • Kāle̲y̲y̲o-a woman named Kalā's m-descendant.
[wa] kāleyyo=kalā+ṇeyya+si

३४७, ३६८. अतो णि वा
347, 368. Ato ṇi vā. [Ato+ṇi+vā. 3 words]
[V] Tasmā akārato ṇipaccayo hoti vā
"tassā'pacca" micce'tasmiṁ atthe.

An affix "ṇi" is added after that a-ending noun to signify "the son or descendant of someone".
Note: ṇ of "ṇi" is usually elided. Hence, only "i" will be left. See this pattern shown in bold, underlined in the examples.

(1) Dakkhassa-of a person named "Dakkha". apaccaṁ
• dakkh<u>i</u>- Dakkha's son or descendant.
[wa] Dakkhi=dakkha+ṇi+si ("Si" is elided)
* dakkhassa apaccaṁ vā.
(2) Duṇassa apaccaṁ • Doṇ<u>i</u>-Doṇa's son or descendant.
[wa] Doṇi=duṇa+ṇi+si ["o" @do is a vuddhi vowel]
* duṇassa apaccaṁ vā.

Evaṁ
(3) • Vāsav<u>i</u>-Vāsava's son or descendant.
[wa] Vāsavi=Vāsava+ṇi+si
(4) • Sakyaputt<u>i</u>-Sakya's son or descendant.
[wa] sakyaputti=Sakyaputta+ṇi+si
(5) • Nāṭaputt<u>i</u>-Nāṭa's son or descendant.
[wa] Naṭaputti=Nāṭaputta+ṇi+si ["ā" @Nā is a vuddhi vowel]

(6) • Dāsaputti-Dāsa's son or descendant.
[wa] Dāsaputti=dāsaputta+ṇi+si

(7) • Dāsavi-Dāsava's son or descendant.
[wa] Dāsavi=dāsava+ṇi+si

(8) • Vāruṇi-Varuṇa's son or descendant.
[wa] Vāruṇi=Varuṇa+ṇi+si ["ā" @Vā is a vuddhi vowel]

(9) • Gaṇḍi-Gaṇḍa's son or descendant.
[wa] Gaṇdi=Gaṇda+ṇi+si

(10) • Bāladevi-Baladeva's son or descendant.
[wa] Bāladevi=Baladeva+ṇi+si

(11) • Pāvaki-Pāvaka's son or descendant.
[wa] Pāvaki=Pāvaka+ṇi+si

(12) • Jenadatti-Jinadatta's son or descendant.
[wa] Jenadatti=Jinadatta+ṇi+si ["e" @Je is a vuddhi vowel]

(13) • Buddhi-Buddha's son or descendant.
[wa] Buddhi=Buddha+ṇi+si

(14) • Dhammi-Dhamma's son or descendant.
[wa] Dhammi=dhamma+ṇi+si

(15) • Saṅghi-Sangha's son or descendant.
[wa] Saṅghi=Saṅgha+ṇi+si

(16) • Kappi-Kappa's son or descendant.
[wa] Kappi=Kappa+ṇi+si

(17) • Anuruddhi-Anuruddha's son or descendant.
[wa] Anuruddhi=Anuruddha+ṇi+si

Vā'ti vikappanatthena **ṇika**paccayo hoti
"tassāpacca" miccetasmiṁ atthe.

By means of the word "vā" which has a "vikappana" meaning, a "**ṇika**" affix is also applied after some nouns when expressing "the son or descendants of someone". [**Vikappana**- speculative possibility of grammatical application. See the affix shown underlined]

(1) Sakyaputtassa apaccaṁ • Sakyaputtiko-Sakyaputta's son or descendant.
[wa] Sakyaputtiko=Sakyaputta+ṇika+si

Evaṁ

(2) • Nāṭaputtiko-Nāṭaputta's son or descendant.
[wa] Nāṭaputtiko=Naṭaputta+ṇika+si
(3) • Jenadattiko-Jinadatta's son or descendant.
[wa] Jenadattiko=Jinadatta+ṇika+si

३४८, ३७१. णवोपक्वादीहि

348, 371. Ṇavo'pakvā'dīhi. [Ṇavo+upaku-ādīhi. 2 words]

[V] **Upaku**-icce'va'mādīhi **ṇava**paccayo hoti vā "tassā'pacca" micce'tasmiṁ atthe.

An affix "**ṇava**" is added after the nouns "**upaku** (a person so-named) " etc. to express "the son or descendant of someone".

Note: "**ṇ**" of ṇava is usually elided. Hence only "**ava**" will be left. See this pattern shown underlined in the first example. The same should be noted in subsequent Suttas.

(1) Upakussa-of a man named Upaku. apaccaṁ
• Opakavo-Upaku's son or descendant.
[wa] Opakavo=Upaku+ṇava+si ["o" @Opa is a vuddhi]
* upakussa apaccaṁ vā.
(2) Manuno apaccaṁ • Mānavo-Manu's son or descendant.
[wa] Mānavo=Manu+ṇava+si
* manuno apaccaṁ vā.
(3) Bhaggussa apaccaṁ • Bhaggavo-Bhaggu's son or descendant.
[wa] Bhaggavo=Bhaggu+ṇava+si
* bhaggussa apaccaṁ vā.
(4) Paṇḍussa apaccaṁ • Paṇḍavo-Paṇḍu's son or descendant.
[wa] Paṇḍavo=Paṇḍu+ṇava+si
* paṇḍussa apaccaṁ vā.
(5) Bahussa apaccaṁ • Bāhavo-Bāhu's son or descendant.
[wa] Bāhavo=Bāhu+ṇava+si
* bahussa apaccaṁ vā.

३४९, ३७२. णेर विधवादितो

349, 372. **Ṇera vidhavā'dito.** [Ṇera+vidhava-ādito. 2 words]

[V] Tasmā **vidhavā**'dito **ṇera**paccayo hoti vā "tassā'pacca" micce'tasmiṁ atthe.

An affix "**ṇera**" is sometimes added after the nouns "**vidhavā** (a widow) etc." to express "the son or descendant of someone". (**vi**-without+**dhava**-spouse, husband, **i.e.** widow)

(1) Vidhavāya-of widow. apaccaṁ-son. • Vedhavero-Widow's son or descendant.

[wa] Vedhavero=Vidhavā+ṇera+si ["e" @Ve is a vuddhi]

* vidhavāya apaccaṁ vā.

(2) Bandhukiyā-of a person named Bandhuki. apaccaṁ

• Bandhukero-Bandhuki's son or descendant.

[wa] Bandukero=Banduki+ṇera+si

* bandhukiyā apaccaṁ vā.

(3) Samaṇassa apaccaṁ • Sāmaṇero-Samaṇa's son, **i.e.** A novice who is like the preceptor's son.

[wa] Sāmaṇero=Samaṇa+ṇera+si ["ā" @Sā is a vuddhi]

* samaṇassa apaccaṁ vā.

Evaṁ-in this way.

• Sāmaṇerī-Samaṇa's daughter or **i.e.** A female-novice who is like the preceptor's daughter.

[wa] Sāmaṇeri=Samaṇa+ṇera+ī+si

• Sāmaṇeraṁ-Samaṇa's race.

[wa] Sāmaṇeraṁ=Samaṇa+ṇera+si

(4) • Nāḷikero-Nāḷika's son or m-descendant.

[wa] Nāḷikero=Nāḷika+ṇera+si

• Nāḷikerī-Nāḷika's daughter or f-descendant.

[wa] Nāḷikeri=Nāḷika+ṇera+ī+si

• Nāḷikeraṁ-Nāḷika's race.

[wa] Nāḷikeraṁ=Nāḷika+ṇera+si

Ane'ka'ttha Taddhita

[**Aneka**=**na**-not+**eka**-one, **i.e.** not one but many, various+**attha**-meaning]

(Nouns in affixes expressive of various meanings)

Note: Suttas 350, 351, 352, 353 apply affixes expressive of various meanings.

३५०, ३७३. येन वा संसट्ठं तरति चरति वहति णिको

350, 373. **Yena vā saṁsaṭṭhaṁ tarati carati vahati ṇiko.**

[Yena+vā+saṁsaṭṭhaṁ+tarati+carati+vahati+ṇiko. 7 words]

[V] Yena vā saṁsaṭṭhaṁ, yena vā tarati, yena vā carati, yena vā vahati-icce'tesva'tthesu **ṇika**paccayo hoti vā.

To express "being mixed in something as an ingredient, mode of crossing a river, mode of travel, mode of carrying something etc., an affix "**ṇika**" is sometimes added after the nouns.

Note: Only "**ika**" will be left when "**ṇ**" of **ṇika** is elided which is somewhat similar to English suffix "**ic**" or "**ical**". The applied affix is shown underlined.

Examples of "saṁsaṭṭha" which means "being mixed in as an ingredient":

(1) Tilena-with sesame, saṁsaṭṭhaṁ-mixed, bhojanaṁ-food,
• tel<u>ikaṁ</u>-food mixed with sesame.
[wa] Telikaṁ=tila+ṇika+si
* tilena saṁsaṭṭhaṁ vā. (Inapplicable example sentence)

Evaṁ

(2) • goḷ<u>ikaṁ</u>-food mixed with guḷa (molasses or jaggery).
[wa] Goḷikaṁ=Guḷa+ṇika+si

(3) • ghāt<u>ikaṁ</u>-food mixed with ghee.
[wa] Ghatikaṁ=ghata+ṇika+si

Examples of "tarati" which means "mode of crossing a river etc.":

(1) Nāvāya-by boat, taratī'ti [tarati+iti] tarati-crosses, iti-so, nāviko-is called "nāviko". • nāv<u>iko</u>-traveler by boat.
[wa] • Nāviko=Nāvā+ṇika+si
* nāvāya tarati vā.

Note: Other connotations such as boat operator, owner or anyone connected with the Boat such as sailors can also be termed as nāviko.

Evaṁ

(2) • oḷumpiko-traveller by raft (Uḷumpa).

[wa] Oḷumpiko=Uḷumpa+ṇika+si ["u" changes into "o" through Vuddhi. So, "o" is a vuddhi vowel]

Examples of "carati" which means "mode of travel or practice":

(1) Sakaṭena-by ox-drawn cart, caratī'ti [carati+iti] carati-travels,

• sākaṭiko-bullock-cart-traveler.

[wa] Sākaṭiko=Sakaṭa+ṇika+si

* sakaṭena carati vā.

Evaṁ-similarly in this way.

(2) • pattiko-wing-traveler, bird.

[wa] • Pattiko=patta+ṇika+si

(3) • daṇḍiko-the one moving with stick.

[wa] • Daṇḍiko=Daṇḍa+ṇika+si

(4) • dhammiko-the one who practices Dhamma, the religious.

[wa] • Dhammiko=Dhamma+ṇika+si

(5) • pādiko-foot-traveller, pedestrian.

[wa] • Pādiko=Pāda+ṇika+si

Examples of "Vahati" which means "mode of carriage":

(1) Sīsena-by head, vahatī'ti [vahati+iti] vahati-carries,

• sīsiko-one who carries (something) on head.

[wa] • Sīsiko=Sīsa+ṇika+si

* sīsena vahati vā.

(2) Aṁsena-by shoulder, vahatī'ti • aṁsiko-shoulder-carrier.

[wa] • Aṁsiko=aṁsa+ṇika+si

* aṁsena vahati vā.

Evaṁ-similarly in this way.

(3) • khandhiko-shoulder-carrier.

[wa] Khandiko=Khanda+ṇika+si

(4) • aṅguliko-finger-carrier.

[wa] Aṅguliko=aṅgula+ṇika+si

Vā'ti vikappanatthena aññesu'pi ṇikapaccayo hoti.

By means of the word "vā" of "vikappana meaning", a "**ṇika**" affix is also applied after some nouns.

(1) Rājagahe-in the city of Rājagaha, vasatīti [vasati+iti] vasati-dwells, iti-therefore, • rājagahiko-is called the resident of Rājagaha city.
[wa] • Rājagahiko=Rājagaha+ṇika+si
* rājagahe vasati vā.

(2) Rājagahe jāto-born, • rājagahiko-the native of Rājagaha city.
* rājagahe jāto vā.

Evaṁ

(3) • māgadhiko-the resident or native of Magadha.
[wa] • Māgadhiko=magadha+ṇika+si

(4) • sāvatthiko-the resident or native of Sāvatthi city.
[wa] • Sāvatthiko=Sāvatthi+ṇika+si

(5) • kāpilavatthiko-the resident or native of Kapilavattu city.
[wa] • Kāpilavatthiko=Kapilavatthu+ṇika+si

(6) • pāṭaliputtiko-the resident or native of Pāṭaliputta city.
[wa] • Pāṭaliputtiko=Pāṭaliputta+ṇika+si

(7) • vesāliko-the resident or native of Vesālī city.
[wa] • Vesāliko=Vesāli+ṇika+si

३५१, ३७४. तमधीते तेनकतादि सन्निधाननियोग सिप्प भण्ड जीविकत्थेसु च

351, 374. Ta'madhīte tena katādi, sannidhāna, niyoga, sippa, bhaṇḍa, jīvika'tthesu ca.

[Taṁ+adhīte+tena katādi, sannidhāna, niyoga, sippa, bhaṇḍa, jīvika-atthesu+ca. 4 words]

[V] Ta'madhīte, tena katā'di-atthe, tamhi sannidhānā, tattha niyutto, ta'massa sippaṁ, ta'massa bhaṇḍaṁ, ta'massa jīvikaṁ, icce'tesva'tthesu ca **ṇika**paccayo hoti vā.

To express "the subject of study", "the mode or means by which something is done", "that in which something is originated", "where one is involved as a duty", "skill of science", "that which is possessed", "livelihood", etc. an affix "**ṇika**" is sometimes added after the nouns to which the meaning is to be affected.

Examples of "Adhīte" which means "learning or subject of study":

(1) Vinaya'madhīte [Vinayaṁ+adhīte] Vinayaṁ-Vinaya texts, adhīte-(he) learns, iti-therefore, venayiko-is so called.

• Venayiko-Vinaya-learner. **i.e.** the student of Vinaya texts.

[wa] • Venayiko=Vinaya+ṇika+si

* Vinaya'madhīte vā.

Evaṁ

(2) • Suttantiko-Suttanta-learner. **i.e.** Suttanta Student.

[wa] Suttantiko=Suttanta+ṇika+si

(3) • ābhidhammiko-Abhidhamma-learner. **i.e.** an Abhidhamma Student.

[wa] ābhidhammiko=abhidhamma+ṇika+si

(4) • veyyākaraṇiko-Veyākaraṇa-learner. **i.e.** Veyākaraṇa-the grammar Student. (Veyākaraṇa means grammar)

[wa] Veyākaraṇiko=Veyākaraṇa+ṇika+si

Note: Although it is said in Sutta the word "adhīte" and its related ED, the meaning thus implied can also be broadly taken as contextually variable and applicable. For example, when it refers to those who not only learn Suttanta, but also those who chant, teach or those who are expert in any respective subjects of Suttanta, Abhidhamma or Vinaya, it can be usually referred to as "Suttantika, Ābhidhammika, or Vinayika" and so on.

Examples of "tena Kataṁ" which means "modes of action":

(1) Kāyena-by body, kataṁ-done, kammaṁ-action,

• kāyikaṁ- bodily action. [wa] Kāyikaṁ=Kāya+ṇika+si

* kāyena kataṁ kammaṁ vā.

Evaṁ

(2) • vācasikaṁ-verbal action.

[wa] Vācasikaṁ=Vaca+ṇika+si

(3) • mānasikaṁ-mental action.

[wa] Mānasikaṁ=mana+ṇika+si

Examples of "Sannidhāna" which means "originated in":

(1) Sarīre-in the body, sannidhānā-existing, vedanā-feeling,

• sārīrikā-the bodily feeling. **i.e.** bodily pain etc.

[wa] Sārīrikā=Sarīra+ṇika+si

* sarīre sannidhānā vā.

Evaṁ

(2) • mānasikā-mental feeling.

[wa] Mānasikā=mana+ṇika+si

Examples of "Niyutta" which means "being involved in or related to":

(1) Dvāre-in the door, niyutto-involved (as a responsibility etc.,),

• dovāriko-the door-keeper, guard.

[wa] Dovāriko=Dvāra+ṇika+si

* dvāre niyutto vā.

Evaṁ

(2) • bhaṇḍāgāriko-the store-keeper or treasurer.

[wa] Baṇḍāgāriko=Baṇḍāgāra+ṇika+si

(3) • nāgariko-the city-keeper. **i.e.** mayor, city-resident etc.

[wa] Nāgariko=Nagara+ṇika+si

(4) • nāvakammiko-the new-deed keeper. **i.e.** one who is involved in a new project or action.

[wa] Nāvakammiko=Navakamma+ṇika+si

Examples of "Sippa" which means "profession or knowledge":

(1) Vīṇā-(playing) harp, assa-of that person, sippaṁ-is profession,

• veṇiko-the Harp-professional. the harpist.

[wa] Veṇiko=Vīṇā+ṇika+si

* vīṇā assa sippaṁ vā.

Evaṁ

(2) • pāṇaviko-the Drum-professional, drummer.

[wa] Pāṇviko=paṇava+ṇika+si

(3) • modiṅgiko-the tambourine-professional, tambourinist.

[wa] Modiṅgiko=mudiṅga+ṇika+si

(4) • vaṁsiko-the Flute-professional, Flutist.

[wa] Vaṁsiko=vaṁsa+ṇika+si

Examples of "bhaṇḍaṁ" which means "merchandise":

(1) Gandho-perfume or fragrance, assa-of that person, bhaṇḍaṁ-(is) the merchandise, • gandhiko-the perfume-trader, perfumer.

[wa] Gandhiko=Gandha+ṇika+si

* gandho assa bhaṇḍaṁ vā.

Evaṁ

(2) • teliko-the cooking-oil trader.

[wa] Teliko=Tila+ṇika+si

(3) • goḷiko-the molasses-trader.

[wa] Goḷiko=Guḷa+ṇika+si

Examples of "Jīvika" which means "livelihood":

(1) Urabbhaṁ-sheep, hantvā-having killed, jīvatī'ti-lives (makes a living), • orabbhiko-sheep-butcher.

[wa] Orabbhiko=Urabbha+ṇika+si

* urabbhaṁ hantvā jīvati vā.

(2) Magaṁ hantvā jīvatī'ti • māgaviko-deer-butcher, hunter.

[wa] Māgaviko=maga+ṇika+si

* magaṁ hantvā jīvati vā.

Evaṁ

(3) • sokariko-pig-butcher, Pig-farmer,

[wa] Sokariko=Sūkara+ṇika+si

(4) • sākuṇiko-bird-butcher.

[wa] Sākuṇiko=sakuṇa+ṇika+si

Ādiggahaṇena aññatthā'pi **ṇika**paccayo yojetabbo.

By means of the word "ādi" in Sutta, "**ṇika**" affix can also be applied after some nouns (of other meanings).

Below is a list of examples applicable by means of the word "ādi".

Examples of "hata" which means "mode of killing for a living":

(1) Jālena-by (casting) net, hato-(one) kills, • jāliko-fisher-man

* jālena hato vā.

[wa] Jāliko=Jāla+ṇika+si

(2) Suttena-by thread, bandho-(one) binds, • suttiko-the thread-trapper. (who sets traps by thread or strings to catch small creatures such as birds and wild rabbits etc.),

[wa] Suttiko=Sutta+ṇika+si
* suttena bandho vā.

Examples of "āvudha" which means "weapon":

(1) Cāpo-bow, assa-of that person, āvudho-(is) weapon,
• cāpiko- archer.
[wa] Cāpiko=cāpa+ṇika+si
* cāpo assa āvudho vā.

Evaṁ

(2) • tomariko-lance-armed.
[wa] Tomariko=Tomara+ṇika+si

(3) • muggariko-club-bearer, club-armed.
[wa] Muggariko=muggara+ṇika+si

(4) • mosaliko-pestle-armed, or pestle-bearer.
[wa] Mosaliko=musala+ṇika+si

Examples of "ābādha" which means "disease or pain":

(1) Vāto-the wind (gas), assa ābādho-(is) disease or pain,
• vātiko- gas-pain-sufferer.
[wa] Vātiko=vāta+ṇika+si
* vāto assa ābādho vā.

Evaṁ

(2) • semhiko-phlegm-caused pain sufferer.
[wa] Semhiko=semha+ṇika+si

(3) • pittiko-bile-based pain-sufferer.
[wa] Pittiko=Pitta+ṇika+si

Examples of "pasanna" which means "being pleased with or being devoted to":

(1) Buddhe-in the Buddha, pasanno-(is) pleased, • Buddhiko-the one who is pleased in Buddha. **i.e.** a devotee of Buddha.
[wa] Buddhiko=Buddha+ṇika+si
* Buddhe pasanno vā.

Evaṁ

(2) Dhammiko-the one who is pleased in Dhamma. **i.e.** a religious devotee. [wa] Dhammiko=Dhamma+ṇika+si

(3) • Saṅghiko-the one who is pleased in Sangha.
i.e. a Sangha-supporter devotee.
[wa] Saṅghiko=Saṅgha+ṇika+si

Examples of "santakaṁ" which means "possession, being owned by":

(1) Buddhassa-of Buddha, santakaṁ-(is) possession,
• Buddhikaṁ- Buddha's possession such as funds meant for shrine-renovation etc. [wa] Buddhikaṁ=Buddha+ṇika+si
* Buddhassa santakaṁ vā.

Evaṁ

(2) • Dhammikaṁ-Dhamma's possession such as funds to print Dhamma-books etc.
[wa] Dhammikaṁ=Dhamma+ṇika+si

(3) • Saṅghikaṁ-Sangha's possession such as temple building etc.
[wa] Saṅghikaṁ=saṅgha+ṇika+si

Examples of "kītaṁ" which means "mode of purchase, being bartered with":

(1) Vatthena-by cloth, kītaṁ-bought, bhaṇḍaṁ-things,
• vatthikaṁ- the thing bought by means of bartering with cloth.
[wa] Vatthikaṁ=vattha+ṇika+si
* vatthena kītaṁ bhaṇḍaṁ vā.

Evaṁ

(2) • kumbhikaṁ-anything bought with a measure of Kumbha.
[wa] Kumbhikaṁ=Kumbha+ṇika+si

(3) • phālikaṁ-anything bought with cotton.
[wa] phālikaṁ=phāla+ṇika+si

(4) • kiṁkaṇikaṁ-anything bought with small bell.
[wa] Kiṁkaṇikaṁ=Kiṁkaṇa+ṇika+si

(5) • sovaṇṇikaṁ-anything bought with gold.
[wa] Sovaṇṇikaṁ=Suvaṇṇa+ṇika+si

Examples of "parimāṇa" which means "measurement":

(1) Kumbho-one measure of Kumbha, assa-of that thing, parimāṇaṁ- (is) measure, • kumbhikaṁ-a thing of one Kumbha measure of grain.
[wa] kumbhikaṁ=kumbha+ṇika+si

* kumbho assa parimāṇaṁ vā.

Examples of "rāsi" which means "heap":
(1) Kumbha'ssa [kumbho+assa] kumbho assa rāsi-the heap,
• kumbh<u>ika</u>ṁ-one-kumbha-measured heap of grains.
kumbhassa rāsi vā. [wa] is the same.

Examples of "arahati" which means "deserve":
(1) Kumbhaṁ-for one Kumbha, arahatīti [arahati+iti] arahati-(he) deserves, iti-therefore, • kumbh<u>ik</u>o-someone deserving one-Kumbha of grains.
[wa] Kumbhiko=Kumbha+ṇika+si
* kumbhaṁ arahati vā.

Examples of "dibbati" which means "to play a game of luck":
(1) Akkhena-by (throwing) dice, dibbatī'ti [dibbati+iti] dibbati-(he) plays or gambles, iti • akkh<u>ik</u>o-dice-player, gambler.
[wa] Akkhiko=akkha+ṇika+si
* akkhena dibbati vā.

Evaṁ
(2) • sālāk<u>ik</u>o-the one who plays by using a small piece of cut-bamboo. [wa] Sālākiko=Salāka+ṇika+si
(3) • tinduk<u>ik</u>o-the one who plays using a *tinduka* seed, (**tinduka**-Diospyros Embryopteris, also called Indian persimmon or wild persimmon whose fruits are edible when ripe)
[wa] Tindukiko=Tinduka+ṇika+si
(4) • ambaphal<u>ik</u>o-the one who plays using mango seed.
[wa] ambaphaliko=ambaphala+ṇika+si
(5) • Kapiṭṭhaphal<u>ik</u>o-the one who plays using the seed of a fruit called "***Kapiṭṭha***-Limonia Acidissima, also called wood apple".
[wa] Kapiṭṭhaphaliko=kapiṭṭhaphala+ṇika+si
(6) • nāḷiker<u>ik</u>o-the one who plays using coconut shell.
[wa] Nāḷikeriko=Nāḷikera+ṇika+si
icce'va'mādi.

३५२, ३७६. ण रागा तस्सेदमञ्ञत्थेसु च

352, 376. Ṇa rāgā tasse'da'maññatthesu ca.

[Ṇa+rāgā+tassa+idaṁ+aññatthesu+ca.6]

[V] **Ṇa**paccayo hoti vā rāgamhā "tena rattaṁ" iccetasmiṁ atthe, "tasse'daṁ" aññatthesu ca.

To express "that by which a specific color is dyed with, "that which it belongs to" etc, an affix "**ṇa**" is sometimes added after the nouns.

Note: "**ṇa**" affix is invisible in the examples.

Examples of "Rāga-dye":

(1) Kasāvena-by yellow color, rattaṁ-dyed, vatthaṁ-the cloth,
• kāsāvaṁ-yellow-colored robe.
[wa] Kāsāvaṁ=Kasāva+ṇa+si
* kasāvena rattaṁ vatthaṁ vā.

Evaṁ

(1) • kosumbhaṁ-Safflower-colored cloth.
[wa] Kosumbhaṁ=Kusumbha+ṇa+si

(2) • hāliddaṁ-tumeric-colored cloth.
[wa] Hāliddhaṁ=haliddha+ṇa+si

(3) • pāṭaṅgaṁ-Red-colored cloth whose dye is available from the Sappan-wood tree (पतंग). [wa] Pāṭaṅgaṁ=Paṭaṅga+ṇa+si

(4) • rattaṅgaṁ-Hibiscus rosa sinensis-flower-colored cloth.
[wa] Rattaṅgaṁ=rattaṅga+ṇa+si

(5) • mañjiṭṭhaṁ-crimson-colored cloth (whose color is available from plants such as Indian madder plant).
[wa] Mañjiṭṭhaṁ= Mañjiṭṭha +ṇa+si

(6) • kuṅkumaṁ-saffron-colored cloth.
[wa] Kuṅkumaṁ=Kuṅkuma+ṇa+si

Examples of "Idaṁ-(this) belongs to":

(1) Sūkarassa-(is) of pig, idaṁ-this, maṁsaṁ-meat, • sokaraṁ-pig's meat, **i.e.** pork.
[wa] Sokaraṁ=Sūkara+ṇa+si
* sūkarassa idaṁ maṁsaṁ vā.

Evaṁ

(2) • māhiṁsaṁ-meat of buffalo.

[wa] Māhisaṁ=Mahiṁsa+ṇa+si

Examples of "Avidūra-not far off, in proximity":

(1) Udumbarassa-(of) fig tree, avidūre-near, pavattaṁ-that exists, vimānaṁ-the mansion, • odumbaraṁ-the mansion near fig tree.

[wa] Odumbaraṁ=Udumbara+ṇa+si

* udumbarassa avidūre pavattaṁ vimānaṁ vā.

(2) Vidisāya-(of) the corner or a city so-named, avidūre-nearby, nivāso-the residence, • vediso-the residence near corner or near a city so-named.

[wa] Vediso=Vidisā+ṇa+si

vidisāya avidūre nivāso vā.

Note: Vedisa (वैदिशम) is translated as a city so-named located in the neighbourhood where the river Vidisa flows. [Siddhanta Kaumudi by Srīsa Chandra Vasu, Sutta Number 1282]

Examples of "jāta-native":

(1) Mathurāya-at the city of Mathura, jāto-(he) was born,

• māthuro-the native of Mathura.

[wa] Māthuro=Mathura+ṇa+si

* mathurāya jāto vā.

Examples of "āgata-comer":

(1) Mathurāya-from the city of Mathura, āgato-came, māthuro-the person coming from the city of Mathura.

* mathurāya āgato vā.

The Names of Twelve Months

Examples of "Niyutta-being related to or with":

Kattikāya-with the star named "Kattika", niyutto-(prominently) related, māso-the month, **i.e.** The month when a star named Kattika is prominent.

(1) • kattiko-the month when the star named "Kattika (Krittika) " is prominent. [wa] Kattiko=Kattikā+ṇa+si

* kattikāya niyutto māso vā.

Evaṁ

(2) • māgasiro-the month when the star named "migasira (Mrugasi ra) " is prominent.
[wa] māgasiro=Magasira+ṇa+si

(3) • phusso-the month when the star named "phussa (Pushyami) " is prominent. [wa] Phusso=phussa+ṇa+si

(4) • māgho-the month when the star named "magha" is prominent.
[wa] Māgho=magha+ṇa+si

(5) • phagguno-the month when the star named "phagguna (Phal gunī) " is prominent. [wa] Phagguno=phagguna+ṇa+si

(6) • citto-the month when the star named "cittra (Chitra) " is prominent. [wa] Citto=Citta+ṇa+si

(7) • vesākho-the month when the star named "Visākha" is prominent. [wa] Vesākho=Visākha+ṇa+si

(8) • jeṭṭho-the month when the star named "Jeṭṭha (Jyestha) " is prominent.
[wa] Jeṭṭho=Jeṭṭha+ṇa+si

(9) • āsaḷho-the month when the star named "Āsalha (ashadha) " is prominent.
[wa] āsaḷho=āsaḷha+ṇa+si

(10) • sāvaṇo-the month when the star named "Sāvaṇa (Sravana) " is prominent
[wa] Sāvaṇo=savaṇa+ṇa+si

(11) • bhaddo-the month when the star named "bhaddra (bhadrapada) " is prominent
[wa] bhaddo=Bhadda+ṇa+si

(12) • assayujo-the month when the star named "assayuja (Asvini) " is
prominent
[wa] assayujo=assayuja+ṇa+si

Na vuddhi **nīla, pītā**'do, paccaye saṇakārake.
Phakāro **phussa**saddassa, "**siro**" ti **sirasaṁ** vade.

No Vuddhi function is applied in the words "**Nīla**" and "**Pīta**", though an ṇ-joined-affix is present.
No Vuddhi ever occurs in the "**pha**" of "**Phussa**",

No extra "sa" is ever inserted after the word "**Siro**",
So it is not said as "**Sirasaṁ**".

Explanation

This stanza shows that there can never be an absolute rule regarding the rules of morphological procedures as prescribed in Suttas. Sometimes, in some instances, that rule is not applied. Thus leaving room for any exception for variable outcome of the words as pattern of common spoken language may prevail sometimes despite the prescribed grammatical rules. In the examples of words cited, all the three words have an ṇ-joined-**ṇa** affix applied as per this Sutta. With an **ṇ-joined-affix** being present in the words, both "ī" of **Nīla**-red-dyed cloth) and **Pīta**-yellow-dyed cloth, also the vowel "u" of **Phusso**, should have seen a Vuddhi process occurred. Thus possibly affecting to change into other word-forms such as **Nela, Peta** and **Phossa**. But it never had occurred as common usage pattern of the language is only **Nīla, Pīta** and **Phussa.** Similarly, if an additional consonant "**s**" is to be attached to the **aṁ**-vibatti-ending word "**siro**-head", then it should have become "**sirasaṁ**" instead. But it remained unchanged though. Therefore, sometimes **there may be some exceptions to any prescribed grammatical rule** as and when dictated by prevalent common norms and patterns of the language in the society. This is what the stanza means.

Examples of "Samūha-collective grouping":

(1) Sikkhānaṁ-of the precepts, samūho-collection,
• sikkho-collection of precepts
[wa] Sikkho=Sikkhā+ṇa+si

(2) bhikkhānaṁ-of dishes, samūho • bhikkho-motley of dishes.
[wa] Bhikkho=Bhikkhā+ṇa+si

Evaṁ

(3) • kāpoto-group of pigeons.
[wa] Kāpoto=Kapota+ṇa+si

(4) • māyūro-group of peacocks.
[wa] Māyūro=mayūra+ṇa+si

(5) • kokilo-group of koel birds (i.e. black cuckoo, which has a sweet voice.)
[wa] Kokilo=Kokila+ṇa+si

Examples of "devatā-being devoted like a deity":

(1) Buddho-Buddha. assa-of that person. devatā-(is like) deity.

• Buddho-the one who devotes Buddha like a deity.

[wa] Buddho=Buddha+ṇa+si

Evaṁ

(2) • bhaddo-the one who devotes Bhadda like a deity.

[wa] Bhaddo=Bhadda+ṇa+si

(3) • māro the one who devotes Māra like a deity.

[wa] Māro=māra+ṇa+si

(4) • māhindo the one who devotes a deity named Mahinda.

[wa] Māhindo=Mahinda+ṇa+si

(5) • vessavaṇo the one who devotes a deity named Vessavaṇa.

[wa] Vessavaṇo=Vessavaṇa+ṇa+si

(6) • yāmo the one who devotes a deity named Yama.

[wa] Yāmo=Yama+ṇa+si

(7) • somo the one who devotes a deity named Soma.

[wa] Somo=Soma+ṇa+si

(8) • nārāyaṇo the one who devotes a deity named Nārāyaṇa.

[wa] Nārāyaṇo=nārāyaṇa+ṇa+si

Examples of "being related for a certain period such as a year etc. or being related to a skill of knowledge":

(1) Saṁvacchara'madhīte [Saṁvaccharaṁ+adhīte]

Saṁvaccharaṁ-for (the whole) year. adhīte-(he) learns.

• saṁvaccharo-annual learner, yearly student.

[wa] Saṁvaccharo=Saṁvacchara+ṇa+si

Evaṁ

(2) • mohutto-the one who studies for a moment, part-time student.

[wa] Mohutto=muhutta+ṇa+si

(3) • nemitto-the one who studies about interpreting various omens and signs.

[wa] Nemitto=Nimitta+ṇa+si

(4) • aṅgavijjo-the one who studies physiognomy.

[wa] Aṅgavijjo=aṅgavijja+ṇa+si

(5) • veyyākaraṇo-the one who studies grammar, The grammar-

student.

[wa] Veyyākaraṇo=Veyyākaraṇa+ṇa+si

(6) • chando-the one who studies prosody and the art of writing metrical stanzas, The student of prosody.

[wa] Chando=Chanda+ṇa+si

(7) • bhāsso-the one who studies commentaries.

[wa] Bhāsso=bhāssa+ṇa+si

(8) • cando-the one who studies a text named Canda.

[wa] Cando=Canda+ṇa+si

Examples of "Visaya-domain or a specifically reserved place etc.":

(1) Vasādānaṁ-of lions, visayo-domain, deso-location,

• vāsādo-the lion's den.

[wa] Vāsādo=Vasāda+ṇa+si

Evaṁ

(2) • kumbho-the place of pots.

[wa] kumbo=kumba+ṇa+si

(3) • sākunto-the place of birds.

[wa] Sākunto=Sakunta+ṇa+si

(4) • ātisāro-the place of guests.

[wa] ātisāro=atisāra+ṇa+si

(5) Udumbarā-fig trees. asmiṁ-at that. padese-location. santī'ti [santi+iti] santi-(there) are. • odumbaro-the place where there are fig trees.

[wa] Odumbaro=Udumbra+ṇa+si

The following examples are of different meanings.

(1) Sāgarehi-by the princes called Sāgara, nibbatto-made,

• sāgaro-the place made by Sāgara, **i.e.** ocean.

[wa] Sāgaro=sāgara+ṇa+si

The examples with meaning of "being resident and chief".

(1) Sāgala'massa [sāgalaṁ+assa] sāgalaṁ-city of Sāgala, assa-of that person, nivāso-(is) residence, • Sāgalo-the resident of Sāgala. [wa] Sāgalo=sāgala+ṇa+si

(2) (a) Mathurā assa nivāso • māthuro-the resident of Mathurā.

[wa] Māthuro=Mathura+ṇa+si

(b) Mathurāya-at Mathurā, issaro-(is) chief, • māthuro-the

chief of Mathurā. **Note:** WA is similar.

Icce'va'mādayo yojetabbā.

Icce'va'mādayo-such examples. yojetabbā-should be applied.

३५३, ३७८. जातादीनमिमिया च

353, 378. **Jātā'dīna'mi'mi'yā ca.**

[Jāta-ādīnaṁ+ima, iyā+ca. 3 words]

[V] **Jāta-**icce'va'mā'dīna'matthe **ima, iya**paccayā honti.

To express "when and where it happens or in which species one is born into etc. the affixes "**ima, iya**" are added after the nouns to denote it. [See the applied affixes shown underlined.]

Ima-affix examples:

(1) Pacchā-in the back or at a later time, jāto-(it) was,

• pacchimo- that which happens later, the latter, the last.

[wa] Pacchimo=Pacchā+ima+si

Evaṁ

(2) • antimo-that which happens in the end, the last.

[wa] Antimo=Anta+ima+si

(3) • majjhimo-that which happens in the center, the middle.

[wa] Majjimo=Majja+ima+si

(4) • purimo-that which happens in the beginning, the first.

[wa] Purimo=Pura+ima+si

(5) • uparimo-that which happens above.

[wa] Uparimo=Upari+ima+si

(6) • heṭṭhimo-that which happens down below.

[wa] Heṭṭhimo=Heṭṭhā+ima+si

(7) • gopphimo-that which happens on metatarsal surface of the feet.

[wa] Gophimo=Goppha+ima+si`

Iya-affix examples:

(1) Bodhisattajātiyā-by birth as Bodhisatta, jāto-was born,

• bodhisattajātiyo-the one who was born as a Bodhisatta.

[wa] Bodhisattajātiyo=Bodhisattajāti+iya+si

Evaṁ

(2) • assajātiyo-the one which was born as a horse, **i.e.** horse-species.
[wa] Assajātiyo=assajāti+iya+si

(3) • hatthijātiyo-the one which was born as an elephant.
[wa] Hatthijātiyo=Hatthijāti+iya+si

(4) • manussajātiyo-the one who was born as a human.
[wa] Manussajātiyo=Manussajāti+iya+si

Ādiggahaṇena **niyutta**tthā'dito'pi **tadassatthā**'dito'pi **ima, iya, ika-**icce'te paccayā honti.

By means of the word "ādi" in Sutta, the "**ima, iya, ika**" affixes can also be applied after some nouns to express "pertaining to" and "a qualitative inherent characteristic or a possession".

Examples of "pertaining to":

(1) Ante-in the end, niyutto-(is) related, • antimo-that which is related to the end. **i.e.** the end, the final.
[wa] Antimo=Anta+ima+si

Evaṁ

• antiyo, • antiko-that which is related to the end. **i.e.** the end, the final. (the same meaning, but with different affix)
[wa] Antiyo=Anta+iya+si [wa] Antiko=Anta+ika+si

Examples of "having something as an inherent quality etc.":

(2) Putto-son, assa-of that person, atthi-(there) is, tasmiṁ-in that person, vā-in other way, vijjatī'ti [vijjati+iti] vijjati-has, iti-therefore, puttimo-is so called. • puttimo-the one who has son (child). [wa] Puttimo=Putta+ima+si

Note: The words "**tasmiṁ vā vijjatī'ti**" themselves show one more possible ED of "puttimo". See such similar EDs in Suttas starting from 364 to 371. The Nipāta word "**vā**" indicates other possible method.

Evaṁ

• puttiyo, • puttiko-the one who has son (child). (the same meaning but with different affix)

[wa] Puttiyo=putta+iya+si [wa] Puttiko=puttta+ika+si

(3) • kappimo, • kappiyo, • kappiko-the one who has plan and

thought.

[wa] Kappimo=Kappa+ima+si

[wa] Kappiyo=Kappa+iya+si

[wa] Kappiko=Kappa+ika+si

Caggahaṇena **kiya**paccayo hoti niyutta'tthe.

By means of the word "ca" in Sutta, the affix "**kiya**" can also be applied after some nouns in the sense of "pertaining to".

Examples:

(1) Jātiyaṁ-in the conception or in birth, niyutto-(is) related,
 • jātikiyo-birth-related, inborn, innate.
 [wa] Jātikiyo=Jāti+kiya+si

(2) Andhe-in being blind, niyutto-(is) related, • andhakiyo-blindness-related.
 [wa] Andhakiyo=Andha+kiya+si

(3) Jātiyā-by birth, andho-(is) blind, • Jaccandho-blind by birth. **i.e.** an inborn blindness. [Tatiyā Tappurisa, this is called a minor ED shown for partial word "Jaccandhao", an incomplete ED]
 jaccandhe-in being born blind, niyutto-(is) related,
 • Jaccandhakiyo-the one who is born blind.
 [This is final complete ED for the whole word, 2 EDs for this word]
 [wa] Jaccandhakiyo=Jaccandha+kiya+si

Samūha Taddhita

(Nouns in Affixes expressive of collective grouping)

Note: Suttas 354, 355 apply the affixes expressive of collective grouping.

३५४, ३७९. समूहत्थे कण णा

354, 379. **Samūha'tthe kaṇ, ṇā.**

[Samūha-atthe+kaṇ, ṇā. 2 words]

[V] **Samūha**'tthe **kaṇ, ṇa**-iccete paccayā honti.

When expressing a collective assembly, the affixes "**kaṇ, ṇa**" are added after the nouns to denote it.

Note: In the affix "**kaṇ**", only "**k**" will be seen in the example while the affix "**ṇ**" is almost unnoticeable. See two examples in each set. the first is "**kaṇ**-affixed" example where "**k**" is shown underlined. The second is an ṇ-affixed example where the applied affix is invisible. [**Samūha**-collective group]

(1) Rājaputtānaṁ-of the king's son, **i.e.** of the princes, samūho-group, • rājaputtako-the collective group of princes.
[wa] Rājaputtako=Rājaputta+kaṇ+si

Evaṁ

• rājaputto-the collective group of princes.
[wa] Rājaputto=Rājaputta+ṇa+si

(2) • mānussako, • mānusso-the collective group of men.
[wa] Mānussako=manussa+kaṇ+si
[wa] Mānusso=manussa+ṇa+si

(3) • māyūrako, • māyūro-the collective group of peacocks.
[wa] Māyūrako=mayūra+kaṇ+si
[wa] Māyūro=mayūra+ṇa+si

(4) • māhiṁsako, • māhiṁso-the collective group of buffaloes.
[wa] Māhiṁsako=mahiṁsa+kaṇ+si
[wa] Māhiṁso=Mahiṁsa+ṇa+si

३५५, ३८०. गाम जन बन्धु सहायादीहि ता

355, 380. Gāma, jana, bandhu, sahāyā'dīhi tā.

[Gāma, jana, bandhu, sahāya-ādīhi+tā. 2 words]

[V] **Gāma, jana, bandhu, sahāya,** icce'va'mādīhi **tā**-paccayo hoti **samūha**'tthe.

To express a collective grouping, an affix "**tā**" is added after the nouns "**gāma** (villages), **jana** (people), **bandhu** (relatives), **sahāya** (friends) etc. to denote it.
[See the affix shown underlined in the examples]

(1) Gāmānaṁ-of the villages, samūho-group,
• gāmatā-the collective group of villages.
[wa] Gāmatā=gāma+tā+si ("si" is to be elided)

Evaṁ

(2) • janatā-the collective group of people.
[wa] Janatā=Jana+tā+si

(3) • bandhutā-the collective group of relatives.
[wa] Bandhutā=bandhu+tā+si

(4) • sahāyatā-the collective group of friends.
[wa] Sahāyatā=sahāya+tā+si

(5) • nagaratā-the collective group of cities.
[wa] Nagaratā=Nagara+tā+si

Ta'dassaṭhāna Taddhita

(Nouns in Affixes expressive of the source or the cause)

३५६, ३८१. तदस्स ठानमियो च

356, 381. **Ta'dassa ṭhāna'miyo ca.**

[Taṁ+assa+ṭhānaṁ+iyo+ca. 5 words]

[V] "Tadassa ṭhāna" micce'tasmiṁ atthe **iya**paccayo hoti.

When expressing an instigating source or a cause for passion, arrest, release, joy, etc. an affix "**iya**" is added after the nouns to denote it. (The affix is shown underlined in the examples) [Ta'dassaṭhāna=**Taṁ**-that+**assa**-of that infatuation etc.+ **ṭhāna**-is the source. Here, "**ṁ**" becomes "**d**" as per Sutta 31]

(1) Madanassa-of being infatuated or inebriated, ṭhānaṁ-(is) cause or source, • madaniyaṁ-the source of infatuation or inebriation, something alluring or extremely tempting or attractive thus causing lust or madness etc.
[wa] Madaniyaṁ=madana+iya+si

(2) Bandhanassa-of getting arrested, ṭhānaṁ • bandhaniyaṁ-the cause of imprisonment.
[wa] Bandaniyaṁ=Bandana+iya+si

(3) Mucchanassa-of intoxication, ṭhānaṁ • mucchaniyaṁ-the source of intoxication. **i.e.** sensual pleasures, alcohol and something very confusing etc.
[wa] Mucchaniyaṁ=mucchana+iya+si

Note: In some texts, it is found as "Muccaniyaṁ". The meaning is "the cause of freedom". [wa] Muccaniyaṁ=muccana+iya+si

Evaṁ

(4) • rajaniyaṁ-the source of desire or craving, the thing which

arouses desire, lust etc.

[wa] Rajaniyaṁ=rajana+iya+si

(5) • kamaniyaṁ-the source of pleasure, pleasing.

[wa] Kamaniyaṁ=Kamana+iya+si

(6) • gamaniyaṁ-the source of going, somewhere one should go and see, worth going to see.

[wa] Gamaniyaṁ=Gamana+iya+si

(7) • dussaniyaṁ-the source of anger, causing anger.

[wa] Dussaniyaṁ=Dussana+iya+si

(8) • dassaniyaṁ-the source of seeing, something deserving to see, attractive.

[wa] Dassaniyaṁ=dassana+iya+si

Note: This affix is somewhat confusable with a **Kita-affix** "anīya" applied by Sutta 540. Remember the distinction between two affixes. The Kita affix has an "**ī**" and this affix has a shortened "**i**".

Upamā Taddhita

(Nouns in the Affix expressive of analogous similitude)

३५७, ३८२. उपमत्थायितत्तं

357, 382. Upamatthā'yitattaṁ.

[Upamā-atthe+āyitattaṁ. 2 words]

[V] **Upama**'tthe **āyitatta**paccayo hoti.

When expressing a simile or a metaphoric likeness, an "**āyitatta**" affix is added after the noun to denote it.

[**Upamā**-comparing, likening by means of an analogy or a metaphor] (See the affix "āyitatta" shown underlined.)

(1) Dhūmo-smoke, viya-like, dissati-looks, aduṁ-that, vanaṁ-forest. **i.e.** That forest looks like smoke. ta'didaṁ [taṁ+idaṁ] taṁ idaṁ-that forest, dhūmāyitattaṁ-is so called.

• dhūmāyitattaṁ- the smoky forest (whose color is like green-greyish when seen from a distant).

[wa] Dūmāyitattaṁ=Dūma+āyitatta+si

(2) Timiraṁ viya-like darkness, dissati aduṁ vanaṁ ta'didaṁ

• timirāyitattaṁ-the darkish-looking forest.

[wa] Timirāyitattaṁ=Timira+āyitatta+si

Tannissita Taddhita

(Nouns in affix expressive of "dependent nature and source")

३५८, ३८३. तन्निस्सितत्थे लो

358, 383. **Tannissita'tthe lo.** [Tannissita-atthe+lo. 2 words]

[V] "**Tannissitatthe, tadassa ṭhāna**" micce'tasmiṁ atthe ca **la**paccayo hoti.

To express that "on which something depends or being associated to or being the source of ", the "**la**" affix is to be added after the noun to denote it.

[**Taṁ**-to that+**nissita**-dependent. The "**ṁ**" becomes "**n**" by Sutta 31 word. See affix "**l**" with one more reduplicated "**l**" together in the examples shown in bold, underlined. "aṁ" is derivative morpheme of "si"]

(1) Duṭṭhu-bad or indecent nature, nissitaṁ-related to,
• duṭṭhu**<u>ll</u>a**ṁ-related to bad nature, indecent, obscene.
[wa] Duṭṭhullaṁ=Duṭṭhu+la+si

(2) Vedaṁ-joy, nissitaṁ • veda**<u>ll</u>a**ṁ-relating to joy, joyous.
[wa] Vedallaṁ=Veda+la+si

The following are different EDs of the same examples. Note that in the EDs, the word "**ṭhāna**-cause" is used in place of "nissita":

(1) Duṭṭhu-of bad or indecent nature, ṭhānaṁ-(is) the cause, the point,
• duṭṭhu**lla**ṁ-the cause or the point of bad, indecent.

(2) Vedassa-of joy, ṭhānaṁ • veda**lla**ṁ-the cause of joy.
[wa] is very much the same.

Tabbahula Taddhita

(Nouns in affix expressive of the prominent nature)

३५९, ३८४. आलु तब्बहुले

359, 384. **Ālu tabbahule.** [Ālu+tabbahule. 2 words]

[V] **Ālu**paccayo hoti **tabbahula**'tthe.

To express "a state of being a common prominent nature", an "**ālu**" affix is added after the noun to denote it. [**Ta**-that nature+**bahula**-being much, prominent. One "b" augmented. See the affix shown underlined.]

(1) Abhijjhā-covetousness. assa-of that person, pakati-(is) nature, **i.e.** covetousness is the nature of that person. • abhijjh<u>ālu</u>-the one whose nature is covetousness. (This ED is different which uses the word "pakati-nature") Abhijjhā assa bahulā-(is) usual nature. vā-to explain other method. • abhijjh<u>ālu</u>-the one who is usually covetous. (This ED is different as it uses the word "bahulā-usually much")
[wa] Abhijjhālu=Abhijjhā+ālu+si [Abhijjhā is permanently a feminine gender noun word ending in "ā"]

Evaṁ

(2) • sīt<u>ālu</u>-One whose nature is cold, or the one who is usually cold. **i.e.** the one who is intolerant of cold and used to catch cold easily due to such a weak bodily nature.
[wa] Sītālu=Sīta-cold+ālu+si

(3) • dhaj<u>ālu</u>-the place or building where there are a lot of banners.
[wa] Dhajālu=dhaja-bannar+ālu+si

(4) • day<u>ālu</u>-the one whose nature is compassion, or the one who is usually compassionate.
[wa] Dayālu=Dayā-kindness+ālu+si

Bhāva Taddhita
(Nouns in Affix expressive of the abstract condition)
Note: Suttas 360, 361, 362 apply affixes to form abstract nouns expressive of condition or state or a qualitative character of someone or something. The affixes are similar to English affixes such as "**hood, ship**" from the words "boyhood, lordship" etc.

३६०, ३८७. ण्यत्तता भावे तु
360, 387. Ṇya, tta, tā bhāve tu.
[Ṇya, tta, tā+bhāve+tu. 3 words]
[V] **Ṇya, tta, tā**-icce'te paccayā honti **bhāva**'tthe.

When expressing a **bhāva**, (a state of being so and so, a situation, or a qualitative character of someone or something), the affixes "**ṇya, tta, tā**" are added after the noun to denote it. [Applied affixes are shown underlined.]

ṇya-affix example:

(1) Alasassa-of being lazy, bhāvo-is state, • Ālasyaṁ-the state of being lazy, the laziness.

[wa] Ālasyaṁ=Alasa+ṇya+si [**alasa**-being lazy]

(2) Arogassa-of being healthy, bhāvo-is state, • Ārogyaṁ-the state of being healthy, the healthiness.

[wa] Ārogyaṁ=Aroga+ṇya+si [**a**-without+**roga**-disease]

tta-affix example:

(1) Paṁsukūlikassa-of being a practitioner of Paṁsukūlika austerity-practice, bhāvo-is state, • paṁsukūlikattaṁ-practitioner-hood of Paṁsukūlika austerity-practice.

[wa] Paṁsukūlikattaṁ=Paṁsukūlika+tta+si

Note: Paṁsu-earth, dusty+**kūla**=edges of cloth+**ika** & **tta** are two affixes. The word refers to an austerity practice done by monks in ancient times of Buddha who wear the robes made up of rag clothes discarded by people and stitched together and dyed in maroon or saffron color.

(2) Anodarikassa-of being an anodarika, bhāvo-is state, • anodarikattaṁ-the state of being an anodarika.

[wa] Anodarikattaṁ=anodarika+tta+si

Note: Anodarika=**Na**-not+**Odarika**-stomach-caring. **i.e.** always caring and paying priority to fill up one's stomach. It is more of an analogical statement figuratively referring to the one who cares only about material needs of this life, not about spiritual progress nor moral integrity. [**Odarika**=**Udara**-stomach+**ika**-concerned, pertaining to. "**U**" is transformed into "**O**" through **Vuddhi** procedure.]

tā-affix example:

(1) Saṅgaṇikā'rāmassa-of being gregarious, bhāvo-is state, • saṅgaṇikā'rāmatā-gregariousness, being fond of socializing.

[wa] Saṅgaṇikārāmatā=Saṅgaṇikārāma+tā+si

Note: Saṅ'gaṇikā'rāma=**saṁ**-being together+**gaṇika**-friendship, being social+**ārāma**-enjoying. **i.e.** spending more of one's time in socializing and paying priority to it rather than important things.

(2) Niddā'rāmassa-of being indolent, bhāvo-is state,

• niddā'rāmatā-state of being indolent, slothfulness.

[wa] Niddārāmatā=Niddārāma+tā+si

Note: Niddā=sleep+**ārāma**-enjoying. **i.e.** always spending time sleeping, no meditation, nor any study nor doing anything worthwhile.

Tuggahaṇena ttanapaccayo hoti.

By means of the word "tu" in Sutta, the affix "**ttana**" can also be applied after some nouns in the sense of bhāva.

(1) • Puthujjanattanaṁ-state of being unenlightened, a common worldling who is still a victim of defilements.

[wa] Puthujjanattanaṁ=Puthujjana+ttana+si

(2) • Vedanattanaṁ-the state of feeling.

[wa] Vedanattanaṁ=Vedanā+ttana+si

३६१, ३८८. ण विसमादीहि

361, 388. **Ṇa visamā'dīhi.** [Ṇa+visama-ādīhi. 2 words]

[V] **Ṇa**paccayo hoti **visamā'**dīhi "tassa bhāvo" iccetasmiṁ atthe.

To express a **bhāva**, (a state of being so and so, a situation or a qualitative character of someone or something) an affix "**ṇa**" is added after the words **visama** (non-level land) etc.

[**Note:** The affix "**ṇa**" is invisible in the examples.]

(1) Visamassa-of being uneven, bhāvo-is state, • vesamaṁ-state of being uneven, ruggedness, uneven-ness, non-level place of the earth.

[wa] Vesamaṁ=Visama+ṇa+si

Note: Sometimes, this word is figuratively used to express crookedness of mind or actions of being dishonest.

(2) Sucissa-of being pure, bhāvo-is state, • socaṁ-state of purity.

[wa] Socaṁ=Suci+ṇa+si

३६२, ३८९. रमणीयादितो कण

362, 389. Ramaṇīyā'dito kaṇ. [Ramaṇīya-ādito+kaṇ. 2 words]

[V] **Ramaṇīya**-icce'va'mādito **kaṇ**paccayo hoti "tassa bhāvo" icce'tasmiṁ atthe.

When expressing a **bhāva**, (a state of being so and so, a situation or a qualitative character), an affix "**kaṇ**" is added after the words "**ramaṇīya** (being pleasant) " etc. to denote it.
Note: In the affix "**kaṇ**", the joint word "**aṇ**" has to be elided. So, only "**k**" is visible. It is shown in bold, underlined.

(1) Ramaṇīyassa-of being pleasant, bhāvo-is state,
• rāmaṇīya**k**aṁ- pleasantness.
[wa] Rāmaṇīyakaṁ=Ramaṇīya+kaṇ+si

(2) Manuññassa-of being enjoyable, bhāvo-is state,
• mānuñña**k**aṁ- enjoyability.
[wa] Mānuññakaṁ=Manuñña+kaṇ+si

Visesa Taddhita
(Nouns in Affix expressive of Superlative-comparison)

३६३, ३९०. विसेसे तरतमिसिकियिट्ठा

363, 390. Visese tara, tami'siki'yiṭṭhā.
[Visese+tara, tama, isika, iya, iṭṭhā. 2 words]

[V] **Visesa**'tthe **tara, tama, isika, iya, iṭṭha**-icce'te paccayā honti.

To express a **visesa** (a comparative comparison for the superlative), the affixes "**tara, tama, isika, iya, iṭṭha**" are to be added after the nouns to denote it. [**Visesa**-distinction]
Note: The affixes are to be grouped into two:
(a) **Tara, tama** are the first group.
(b) **isika, iya and iṭṭha** are the second group.
The order of superlative degree is as per the sequence of each affix. For example, **tara** is positive while **tama** is superlative. Similarly, **isika** is positive. **iya** is comparative and **iṭṭha** is superlative. Sometimes, the words in a combination of two superlative affixes are found to be used frequently. E.g. **Seṭṭhataro**-the most best. [Here, both **iṭṭha** and **tara**

affixes are applied. See all the affixes shown underlined in the examples below.]

The examples of first group affixes.

(1) Sabbe-all, ime-these, pāpā-(are) bad, aya'mimesaṁ [ayaṁ+imesaṁ] ayaṁ-this one, imesaṁ-among or of these, visesena-especially, pāpo'ti [pāpo+iti] pāpo-(is) bad, iti-therefore, pāpataro-is so called. **i.e.** These are bad. Of all these bad, this one is especially bad. So, it is called "pāpataro". [tara]

• pāpataro-specially bad among the bad. **i.e.** especially bad of the bad.

[wa] Pāpataro=Pāpa+tara+si

Evaṁ-in this way.

(2) [tama] • pāpatamo-the most bad, the worst.

[wa] Pāpatamo=Pāpa+tama+si

The second group affixes.

(1) [isika] • pāpisiko-specially bad.

[wa] Pāpisiko=Pāpa+isika+si

(2) [iya] • pāpiyo-more bad.

[wa] Pāpiyo=Pāpa+iya+si

(3) [iṭṭha] • pāpiṭṭho-the most bad or the worst.

[wa] Pāpiṭṭho=Pāpa+iṭṭha+si

Ta'dassa'tthi Taddhita

(Nouns in Affixes expressive of possessed quality or inherent nature)

Note: Suttas 364, 365, 366, 367, 368, 369, 370, apply affixes expressive of quality or nature possessed by someone or inherent in something.

३६४, ३९८. तदस्सत्थीति वी च

364, 398. Ta'dassa'tthī'ti vī ca.

[Taṁ+assa+atthi+iti+vī+ca. 6 words]

[V] "**Ta'dassatthi**" icce'tasmiṁ atthe **vī**paccayo hoti.

When expressing a "**ta'dassa'tthi**", a quality being possessed by someone (or something), the affix "**vī**" is added after the noun denoting the quality or character.

(See the affix shown underlined)
Note:[ta'dassa'tthi=**taṁ**-that quality or nature+**assa**-of that person or thing+**atthi**-is]

(1) Medhā-intellect or wisdom, yassa-of whose, atthi-there is, tasmiṁ-in that person, vā-to show another method, vijjatī'ti. [vijjati+iti] vijjati-has, iti-therefore, medhāvī-is so called.

• medhāvī-the one who has intellect or wisdom, the wise.

[wa] Medhāvī=Medhā+vī+si

Note: There are two methods of ED for this word "medhāvī".

(a) One uses dative-case word "**assa**" and an ***ākyāta*** verb "**atthi**".

(b) The other uses locative-case word "**tasmiṁ**" and ***ākhyāta*** verb "**vijjati**". There is not much difference in the meaning of both EDs. Throughout this category of "**ta'dassa'tthi**" taddhita, there will be such kind of EDs shown in both methods.

Evaṁ

(2) • māyāvī-the one who has deceit, deceitful.

[wa] Māyāvī=Māyā+vī+si

Caggahaṇena so-paccayo hoti.

By means of the word "Ca" in Sutta, the affix "**so**" can also be applied after some nouns in expressing a "**tadassatthi**". (See the affix underlined.)

Sumedhā-good intellect, yassa atthi, tasmiṁ vā vijjatī'ti.

• sumedhaso-the one who has good intellect.

[wa] Sumedhaso=Sumedhā+so+si

३६५, ३९९. तपादितो सी

365, 399. **Tapā'dito sī.** [Tapa-ādito+sī. 2 words]

[V] **Tapā**'dito **sī**paccayo hoti "**ta'dassa'tthi**" icce'tasmiṁ atthe.

To express a "**ta'dassatthi**", a quality being possessed, the affix "**sī**" is added after the words "**tapa** (austerity practice) " etc.

(1) Tapo-austerity, yassa atthi tasmiṁ vā vijjatī'ti. • tapassī-the one having austerity practices, an ascetic, a hermit.
[wa] Tapassī=Tapa+ssī+si

Evaṁ

(2) • yasassī-the one who has fame, famous.
[wa] Yasassī=Yasa+ssī+si

(3) • tejassī-the one who has power, powerful.
[wa] Tejassī=Teja+ssī+si

३६६, ४००. दण्डादितो इक ई

366, 400. **Daṇḍā'dito ika, ī.** [Daṇḍa-ādito+ika, ī. 2 words]

[V] **Daṇḍā'**dito **ika, ī**-icce'te paccayā honti "**ta'dassa'tthi**" icce'tasmiṁ atthe.

To express a "**tadassatthi**", a quality being possessed by someone or in something, the affixes "**ika, ī**" are added after nouns "**daṇḍa** (stick) " etc.

(1) Daṇḍo-stick, yassa atthi, tasmiṁ vā vijjatī'ti. • daṇḍiko, • daṇḍī-the one having stick.
[wa] Daṇḍiko=Daṇḍa+ika+si [wa] Daṇḍī=Daṇḍa+ī+si

Evaṁ

(2) • māliko, • mālī-the one having flower, a florist.
[wa] Māliko=Mālā+ika+si [wa] Mālī=Mālā+ī+si

३६७, ४०१. मध्वादितो रो

367, 401. **Madhvā'dito ro.** [Madhu-ādito+ro. 2 words]

[V] **Madhu-**icce'va'mādito **ra**paccayo hoti "**ta'dassa'tthi**" icce'tasmiṁ atthe.

To express a "**tadassatthi**", a quality being possessed, an affix "**ra**" is added after the words "**madhu** (of sweet taste) " etc. (See the affix "**r**" shown in bold, underlined)

(1) Madhu-sweet taste, yassa atthi, tasmiṁ vā vijjatī'ti.
• madhuro-something having sweet taste, sweet.
[wa] Madhuro=Madhu+ra+si

Evaṁ

(2) • kuñjaro-the one having jaws, **i.e.** elephant, [**kuñja**-jaw]
[wa] Kuñjaro=Kuñja+ra+si

(3) • muggaro-the one having bean. [**mugga**-bean]
[wa] Muggaro=Mugga+ra+si

(4) • mukharo-the one having bad-mouth, rude. [**mukha**-mouth]
[wa] Mukharo=Mukha+ra+si

(5) • susiro-something having hollow. [**susi**-hollow]
[wa] Susiro=Susi+ra+si

(6) • sīsaro-the one having head. [**sīsa**-head]
[wa] Sīsaro=Sīsa+ra+si

(7) • sukaro-the one having arrow. [**suka**-arrow.A dubious word]
[wa] Sukaro=Suka+ra+si

(8) • suṅkaro-the one having revenue, a king. [**suṅka**-revenue]
[wa] Suṅkaro=Suṅka+ra+si

(9) • subharo-the one having beauty. [**subha**-beauty]
[wa] Subharo=Subha+ra+si

(10) • suciro-the one having purity, pure. [**suci**-purity]
[wa] Suciro=Suci+ra+si

(11) • ruciro-the one having light. [**ruci**-light, shine, beauty]
[wa] Ruciro=Ruci+ra+si

३६८, ४०२. गुणादितो वन्तु

368, 402. **Guṇā'dito vantu.** [Guṇa-ādito+vantu. 2 words]

[V] **Guṇa-**icce'va'mā'dito **vantu-**paccayo hoti "**ta'dassa'tthi**" icce'tasmiṁ atthe.

To express a "**tadassatthi**", a quality being possessed by someone or in something, the affix "**vantu**" is added after the words "**guṇa** (virtue or dignity) " etc.

Note: Due to necessary morphological procedure, only "**vā**" will be left in the affix which is shown underlined. See Sutta 124 for clarification.

(1) Guṇo-virtue or dignity, yassa atthi, tasmiṁ vā vijjatī'ti.

• guṇavā-virtuous or a dignitary.
[wa] Guṇavā=Guṇa+vantu+si

Evaṁ

(2) • yasav<u>ā</u>-the one having fame, the famous.
    [wa] Yasavā=Yasa+vantu+si
(3) • dhanav<u>ā</u>-the one having wealth, the wealthy.
    [wa] Dhanavā=Dhana+vantu+si
(4) • paññav<u>ā</u>-the one having wisdom, the wise.
    [wa] Paññavā= Paññā +vantu+si
(5) • balav<u>ā</u>-the one having power, the powerful.
    [wa] Balavā=Bala+vantu+si
(6) • bhagav<u>ā</u>-the one having auspiciousness, the glorious.
    [wa] Bhagavā=Bhaga+vantu+si

३६९, ४०३. सत्यादीहि मन्तु
369, 403. Satyā'dīhi mantu. [Sati-ādīhi+mantu. 2 words]
[V] **Sati**-iccevamādīhi **mantu**-paccayo hoti "**ta'dassa'tthi**" icce'tasmiṁ atthe.

To signify "**tadassatthi**", a quality being possessed by someone or in something), the affix "**mantu**" is added after the words "**sati** (mindfulness or memory) " etc.
Note: Due to necessary morphological procedure, only "**mā**" will be visible in the affix which is shown underlined. Also see Sutta 124.

(1) Sati-mindfulness, yassa atthi, tasmiṁ vā vijjatī'ti. • satim<u>ā</u>-the one having mindfulness, mindful.
    [wa] Satimā=Sati+mantu+si

Evaṁ

(2) • jutim<u>ā</u>-the one having light, the bright.
    [wa] Jutimā=Juti+mantu+si
(3) • rucim<u>ā</u>-the one having light, the illustrious.
    [wa] Rucimā=Ruci+mantu+si
(4) • thutim<u>ā</u>-the one having praise, the praised.
    [wa] Thutimā=Thuti+mantu+si
(5) • dhitim<u>ā</u>-the one having wisdom or integrity, the wise.
    [wa] Dhitimā=Dhiti+mantu+si

(6) • matimā-the one having intellect, intelligent.
[wa] Matimā=Mati+mantu+si

(7) • bhāṇumā-the one having shine, **i.e.** the sun.
[wa] Bhāṇumā=Bhāṇu+mantu+si

३७०, ४०५. सद्धादितो ण

370, 405. Saddhā'dito ṇa. [Saddhā-ādito+ṇa. 2 words]

[V] **Saddhā**-icce'va'mādito **ṇa**paccayo hoti "**ta'dassa'tthi**" icce'tasmiṁ atthe.

When expressing "**tadassatthi**", a quality being possessed by someone, the affix "**ṇa**" is added after the words "**saddhā** (faith) " etc. [This affix is invisible]

(1) Saddhā-faith, yassa atthi, tasmiṁ vā vijjatī'ti • saddho-the one having faith, the faithful. [wa] Saddho=Saddhā+ṇa+si

Evaṁ

(2) • pañño-the one having wisdom, the wise.
[wa] Pañño=Paññā+ṇa+si

(3) • amaccharo-the one having non-stinginess, the generous.
[wa] Amaccharo=Amacchara+ṇa+si

Note: "**a**" in the last example is a morpheme of negative particle "**na**" which means "**without, not**".[**na**-without+**macchara**-stinginess. See Sutta 333 to understand the procedure of changing "**na**" into "**a**"]

३७१, ४०४. आयुस्सुकारास मन्तुम्हि

371, 404. Āyussu'kārā'sa mantumhi.

[Āyussa+u-kāro+āsa+mantumhi. 4 words]

[V] **Āyu**ssa anto **u**kāro **asā**'deso hoti **mantu**mhi paccaye pare.

The component vowel "**u**" of the word "**Āyu** (life) " changes into "**asa**" when the affix "**mantu**" is affixed after it.

Āyu-life, assa atthi, tasmiṁ vā vijjatīti • āyasmā-the one having life, [wa] āyasmā=āyu+mantu+si

Note: This term "**āyasmā**" is a very polite form of address used among monastics which means "the one having a long life-span".

Ta'ppakati Taddhita

(Nouns in Affix expressing "made up of something")

३७२, ३८५. तप्पकतिवचने मयो

372, 385. **Ta'ppakativacane mayo.**

[Tappakativacane+mayo. 2 words]

[V] **Tappakati**vacana'tthe **maya**paccayo hoti.

To express "**tappakati**", "by means of which something is made up of, or crafted with", an affix "**maya**" is added after the noun to denote it. See the affix shown underlined. [**Ta**-by that+**pakati**-done, made of, crafted with]

(1) Suvaṇṇena-with gold, pakataṁ-made, crafted, kammaṁ-deed or craft, **i.e.** The craft made with gold or made up of gold.
• sovaṇṇamayaṁ-made of gold.
[wa] Sovṇṇamayaṁ=Suvaṇṇa+maya+si

Evaṁ

(2) • rūpiyamayaṁ-made of silver.
[wa] Rūpiyamayaṁ=Rūpiya+maya+si

(3) • jatumayaṁ-made of lac.
[wa] Jatumayaṁ=Jatu+maya+si

(4) • rajatamayaṁ-made of silver.
[wa] Rajatamayaṁ=Rajata+maya+si

(5) • iṭṭhakamayaṁ-made of brick.
[wa] Iṭṭakamayaṁ=Iṭṭakā+maya+si

(6) • ayomayaṁ-made of iron,
[wa] Ayomayaṁ=Aya+maya+si

(7) • mattikāmayaṁ-made of clay or mud.
[wa] Mattikāmayaṁ=Mattikā+maya+si

(8) • dārumayaṁ-made of wood.
[wa] Dārumayaṁ=Dāru+maya+si

(9) • gomayaṁ-originated from cow, **i.e.** cow-dung.
[wa] Gomayaṁ=Go+maya+si

Saṅkhyā Taddhita

(Numerical Nouns in Taddhita-affix)

Note: Suttas 373, 374, 375, 376, 377, 378, 379, 380, 381, 382, 383, 384, 385, 386, 387, 388, 389, 390, 391, 392, 393, 394, 395, these twenty-three Suttas deal with numerical nouns. Of these, five Suttas 373, 375, 384, 385, 392, apply various affixes.

Of various numerical nouns:

(a) The cardinal numbers from "**one to ten**" are **independent numerical nouns.**

(b) **Upward numerical nouns** such as **Visa** (twenty) to **Navuti** (ninety) and **mixed-value numerical nouns,** which are made up of numerical nouns of lesser and higher value, such as from eleven to nineteen, ninety-one to ninety-nine, are mostly **Samāsa (Compound) nouns.**

(c) Other numerical nouns of higher to the highest value, starting from **Sata** (hundred) to **Koṭi** (crore) to **Asaṅkhyeya** (infinity, aeon) are **nouns with numerical values of progressive multiplication** which have specific gender and numbers.

३७३, ४०६. सङ्ख्यापूरणे मो

373, 406. Saṅkhyāpūraṇe mo. [Saṅkhyāpūraṇe+mo. 2 words]

[V] **Saṅkhyāpūraṇa**'tthe **ma-**paccayo hoti.

To express "full completeness of the value" in the ordinal numbers, an affix "**ma**" is added after the numerical nouns. [See the affix "**ma**" shown in bold, underlined. Note that "**o**" is derivative morpheme of nominative singular "**Si**" applied after the word.]

(1) Pañcannaṁ-of five, pūraṇo-fullness, • pañca**ma**o-the fullness of five, the fifth. [Chaṭṭhī Tappurisa]
[wa] Pañcamo=Pañca+ma+si

Evaṁ

(2) • satta**m**o-fullness of seven, the seventh
[wa] Sattamo=Satta+ma+si

(3) • aṭṭha**m**o-fullness of eight, the eighth
[wa] Aṭṭhamo=Aṭṭha+ma+si

(4) • nava**m**o-fullness of nine, the ninth.
[wa] Navamo=Nava+ma+si

(5) • dasamo-fullness of ten, the tenth.
[wa] Dasamo=Dasa+ma+si [All are Chaṭṭhī Tappurisa]

३७४, ४०८. स छस्स वा

374, 408. **Sa chassa vā.** [Sa+chassa+vā. 3 words]

[V] **Cha**ssa **sa**kārādeso hoti vā saṅkhyāpūraṇa'tthe.

The numerical word "**cha**-six" sometimes changes into "**sa**" in the order of ordinal numbers. [See "sa" shown underlined]

(1) Channaṁ-of six, pūraṇo • saṭṭho-fullness of six, the sixth. [Chaṭṭhī Tappurisa]
[wa] Saṭṭho=Cha+ṭṭha+si

(2) * chaṭṭho-fullness of six, the sixth. vā-also. (This one is inapplicable example)
[wa] Chaṭṭho=Cha+ṭṭha+si

Note: "chaṭṭho vā" means that there are two forms of usage for this numerical word, one with "**sa**" and one with its original "cha" where the function of Sutta is not applied.

३७५, ४१२. एकादितो दसस्सी

375, 412. **Ekā'dito dasassī'.** [Eka-ādito+dasassa+ī. 3 words]

[V] **Ekā**'dito **dasa**ssa ante **ī**-paccayo hoti vā saṅkhyāpūraṇatthe.

When signifying fullness of numerical value, an affix "**ī**" is added after the word "**dasa** (ten) " (which is positioned after "**eka** (one) " etc.

Note: This affix also **signifies feminine gender.** See the affix "**ī**" shown in bold, underlined in the examples.

(1) Eko ca-one also, dasa ca-ten also, ekādasa-one and ten or one plus ten, the eleven. [Dvanda. This is minor ED which combines "eka and dasa"]
ekādasannaṁ-of one and ten, pūraṇī-is fullness, • ekādasī-fullness of one and ten, **i.e.** the eleventh. [Chaṭṭhī Tappurisa, final complete ED]
[wa] Ekādasī=Ekādasa+ī+si

(2) Pañca ca-five also, dasa ca pañcadasa-five and ten, the fifteen. [Dvanda] pañcadasannaṁ-of five and ten, pūraṇī-is fullness,

• pañcadasī-fullness of five and ten, the fifteenth. [Chaṭṭhī Tappurisa]

[wa] Pañcadasī=Pañcadasa+ī+si

(3) Cattāro ca-four also, dasa ca catuddasa-four and ten. [Dvanda]

catuddasannaṁ-of four and ten, pūraṇī-is fullness,

• cātuddasī- fullness of four and ten, **i.e.** the fourteenth. [Chaṭṭhī Tappurisa]

[wa] Cātudasī=Catudasa+ī+si

Pūraṇe'ti kimatthaṁ?

What is the word "puraṇe" for?

To show that numerical nouns shown below are not a "puraṇa-signifying the fullness", So, inapplicable.

(No need to affix with "ī" affix)

* Ekādasa-one and ten, eleven. * pañcadasa-five and ten, the fifteen. [Dvanda compounds]

३७६, २५७. दसे सो निच्चञ्च

376, 257. **Dase so niccañ'ca.** [Dase+so+niccaṁ+ca. 4 words]

[V] **Dasa**sadde pare niccaṁ **cha**ssa **so** hoti.

When the word "**dasa**" follows (in a numerical compound noun), the front word "**cha** (six) " always changes into "**so**".

["**so**" shown underlined]

• Soḷasa-six and ten, sixteen. [Dvanda]

३७७, ०. अन्ते निग्गहितञ्च

377,...**Ante niggahitañ'ca.** [Ante+niggahitaṁ+ca. 3 words]

[V] Tāsaṁ saṅkhyānaṁ ante niggahitā'gamo hoti.

At the ends of numerical compounds (such as Pañcadasa-fifteen, cātuddasa-sixteen), there comes a "**niggahita-ṁ**".

[This Sutta enjoins to insert an "**ṁ**" after certain numerical nouns. See the added "**ṁ**" in the examples shown in bold, underlined]

(1) • Pañcadasi**ṁ**-on the fifteenth day or for fifteen days.

(2) • cātuddasi**ṁ**-on fourteenth day or for fourteen days.

Note: An Accusative singular "aṁ" in the sense of Accanta-saṁyoga or Locative can also be applied to complete this word properly if the function of this Sutta is not applied.

३७८, ४१४. ति च

378, 414. **Ti ca.** [Ti+ca. 2 words]

[V] Tāsaṁ saṅkhyānaṁ ante **ti**kārā'gamo hoti.

(In numerical nouns like **vīsa** and **tiṁsa**), there is a "**ti**" affix to be added after them.
[See "ti" in the examples shown in bold, underlined.]

(1) • Vīsa**ti**-twenty.
(2) • Tiṁsa**ti**-thirty. [Dvanda compound]

Note: Note that the "ti-affixed numerical nouns" are usually of **feminine gender, singular.**

३७९, २५८. ळ द,रानं

379, 258. **La da, rānaṁ.** [La+da, rānaṁ. 2 words]

[V] **D**akāra, **r**akārānaṁ saṅkhyānaṁ **l**akārā'deso hoti.

The consonants "**d**" and "**r**" of numerical nouns changes into "**ḷ or l**". [**i.e.** It is substituted with "ḷ-l", shown in bold]

Explanation: In the numerical words "Chadasa (sixteen) and Cattārīsa (forty) ", the consonants "**d**" of **Chadasa** and "**r**" of **Cattārīsa** changes into "**l**" in the morphological process of those words. See "**ḷ** and **l**" shown in bold in the examples. In the grammatical parlance, both "**ḷ** and **l**" are not different except in the shape of writing as they are interchangeable.
[Reference Text] Laḷāna'maviseso (Sandhi, Sutta 34, Rūpasiddhi text)

(1) • So**ḷ**asa-sixteen.
(2) • cattā**l**īsaṁ-forty. [Dvanda Compound]

३८०, २५५. वीसति दसेसु बा द्विस्स तु

380, 255. **Vīsati, dasesu bā dvissa tu.**

[Vīsati, dasesu+bā+dvissa+tu. 4 words]

[V] **Vīsati, dasa,** icce'tesu **dvi**ssa **bā** hoti.

The numerical word "**dvi**" changes into "**bā**" (where **vīsa** or **dasa** are after it in a numerical compound).
[See the applied-function "**bā**" shown in bold, underlined. This "**bā**" is similar to the English prefix "**by, bi**"]

(1) • B**ā**vīsati'ndriyāni-twenty-two faculties. [Bāvīsati+indriyāni] [Dvigu]

(2) • b**ā**rasa-twelve. manussā-men. [Dvanda]

Tuggahaṇena **dvissa du, di, do**-ādesā ca honti.

By virtue of the word "Tu" in Sutta, the numerical word "**dvi**" also changes into "**du, di, do**". [See the applied functions shown in bold, underlined.]

[Du-function] • **Du**rattaṁ-two night. [Dvigu]

[Di-function] • **di**rattaṁ-two night.

• **di**guṇaṁ-two layered or two times. [Dvigu]

[Do-function] • **do**haḷinī-craving of a pregnant woman (which used to occur during pregnancy). [Ta'dassa'tthi Taddhita]

३८१, २५४. एकादितो दस्स र सङ्ख्याने

381, 254. **Ekā'dito dassa ra saṅkhyāne.**

[Eka-ādito+dassa+ra+saṅkhyāne. 4 words]

[V] **Ekā'**dito **das**assa **da**kārassa **ra**kāro hoti vā saṅkhyāne.

In the numerical compound noun "ekādasa (eleven) etc.," the consonant "**d**" of the word "dasa" located after "eka" etc. sometimes changes into an "**r**". [The changed "**r**" is shown in bold, underlined. The second is inapplicable example]

(1) • Ekā**r**asa, * ekādasa-eleven. (Both are of the same meaning)

(2) • bā**r**asa, * dvādasa-twelve. [Dvanda]

Saṅkhyāne'ti kimatthaṁ?
What is the word "saṅkhyāne" for?

To show that the example below is inapplicable as it does not signify a numerical noun, but only a numerical qualifier (an adjective).
* Dvādasā'yatanāni-twelve bases. [Dvādasa+āyatanāni]

३८२, २५९. अट्ठादितो च

382,259. **Aṭṭhā'dito ca.** [Aṭṭha-ādito+ca. 2 words]

[V] **Aṭṭha**-icce'va'mādito ca **dasa**saddassa **da**kārassa **ra**kārā'deso hoti vā saṅkhyāne.

In the numerical nouns "Aṭṭhādasa (eighteen) etc.", the consonant "**d**" of numerical word "dasa" placed after "aṭṭha", sometimes changes into an "**r**". [The changed "**r**" is shown in bold, underlined.]

• Aṭṭhā**r**asa-eight and ten, the eighteen.
* aṭṭhadasa-eighteen. [Second is inapplicable example] [Dvanda]

Aṭṭhādito'ti kimatthaṁ?
What is the word "Aṭṭhādito" for?
To show that the examples below are inapplicable as they are not in "Aṭṭhādi-the 18s group".
* Pañcadasa-fifteen. * soḷasa-sixteen [Dvanda compound].

Saṅkhyāne'ti kimatthaṁ?
What is the word "saṅkhyāne" for?
To show that the example shown below is inapplicable as it is not a numerical noun, but a numeral adjective.
* Aṭṭhadasiko-something of eighteen parts. [Ta'dass'atthi Taddhita]
[wa] Aṭṭhādasiko=Aṭṭhādasa+ika+si

३८३, २५३. द्वेकट्ठानमाकारो वा

383, 253. **Dve'ka'ṭṭhāna'mākāro vā.**

[Dvi, eka, aṭṭhānaṁ+ākāro+vā. 3 words]

[V] **Dvi, eka, aṭṭha**icce'tesa'manto **ā**kāro hoti vā saṅkhyāne.

The last component vowels "**i, a**" of the numerical words **dvi, eka, aṭṭha,** change into "**ā**" sometimes. (It all becomes **dvā, ekā, aṭṭhā.** See the applied functions shown in bold).

• **Dvā**dasa-twelve. • **ekā**dasa-eleven. • **aṭṭhā**rasa-eighteen. [Dvanda compounds]

Saṅkhyāne'ti kimatthaṁ?
What is the word "saṅkhyāne" for?
To show that the examples shown are inapplicable as they are not numerical nouns, but numeral adjectives of the "Bahubbīhi compound nouns".

* Dvidanto-someone having two stick.[**dvi**-two+**danta**-teeth+**o**]
* ekadanto-someone having one tooth. [**eka**-one+**danta**+**o**]
* ekacchanno-the building having one roof. [**eka**+**channa**-roofed,covered+**o,** one "c" augmented]
* aṭṭhatthambho-the building having eight pillars. [**aṭṭha**-eight+**thamba**-pillar+**o,** "t" augmented] [All are Bahubbīhi Compounds]

३८४, ४०७. चतुच्छेहि थ ठा

384, 407. **Catu, cchehī tha, ṭhā.**

[Catu, cchehī+tha, ṭhā. 2 words]

[V] **Catu, cha**-icce'tehi **tha, ṭha**icce'te paccayā honti saṅkhyāpūraṇa'tthe.

When expressing ordinal numbers, the affixes "**tha, ṭha**" should be added after numerical words **catu** (four), **cha** (six) respectively. [See the affixes shown in bold.]

(1) • Catut**tha**o-the fourth.
[wa] Catuttho=Catu+tha+si (one dissimilar "**t**" augmented)

(2) • chaṭ**ṭh**o-the sixth. [Chaṭṭhī Tappurisa]
[wa] Chaṭṭho=Cha+ṭha+si (one similar "**ṭ**" augmented)

३८५, ४०९. द्वितीहि तियो

385, 409. **Dvi, tīhi tiyo.** [Dvi, tīhi+tiyo. 2 words]

[V] **Dvi ti-**icce'tehi **tiya**paccayo hoti saṅkhyāpūraṇa'tthe.

When expressing ordinal numbers, the affix "**tiya**" is added after numerical nouns **dvi** (two) and **ti** (three) respectively. [See the applied affix in bold, underlined.]

- Du**tiy**o-the second. (See next Sutta for "**du**" function) [wa] Dutiyo=Dvi+tiya+si
- ta**tiy**o-the third. [Chaṭṭhī Tappurisa] (See next Sutta for "**ta**" function) [wa] Tatiyo=Ti+tiya+si

३८६, ४१०. तिये दुतापि च

386, 410. **Tiye dutā'pi ca.** [Tiye+dutā+api+ca. 4 words]

[V] **Dvi, ti,** icce'tesaṁ **du, ta-**icce'te ādesā honti **tiya**paccaye pare.

Dvi changes into "**du**" and **ti** changes into "**ta**" when the affix "**tiya**" is added after them. [See the applied function displayed in bold.]

- **Du**tiyo. • **ta**tiyo. (Refer to 385)

Apiggahaṇena aññesu'pi **dvi-**iccetassa **du-**ādeso hoti.

By means of the word "**api**" in Sutta, The numerical word "**dvi**" also changes into "**du**" in the other instances of words. [See the applied function displayed in bold.]

- **Du**rattaṁ-two night. [Compare the function prescribed by "tu" in Sutta 380] [Dvigu]

Caggahaṇena **dvi-**icce'tassa **di**kāro hoti.

By means of the word "**Ca**" in Sutta, the numerical word "**dvi**" also changes into "**di**".

- **Di**rattaṁ-two night.
- **di**guṇaṁ-two-layered, saṅghāṭiṁ-cover robe, pārupetvā-having clothed. **i.e.** Having covered with two-layered robe. [Compare the function prescribed by "tu" in Sutta 380. This seems like a redundant function]

३८७, ४११. तेस मड्ढूपपदेन अड्ढुड्ढ दिवड्ढ दियड्ढ’ ड्ढतिया

387, 411. **Tesa’maḍḍh’ūpapadena aḍḍhuḍḍha, divaḍḍha, diyaḍḍha’ḍḍhatiyā.**

[Tesaṁ+aḍḍha-ūpapadena+aḍḍhuḍḍha, divaḍḍha, diyaḍḍha, aḍḍhatiyā. 3 words]

[V] Tesaṁ **catuttha, dutiya, tatiyā**naṁ **aḍḍh**’ūpapadānaṁ **aḍḍhuḍḍha, divaḍḍha, diyaḍḍha, aḍḍhatiyā’**desā honti, aḍḍhū’papadena saha nippajjante.

Those numerical words **catuttha** (fourth), **dutiya** (second), **tatiya** (third) which has a penultimate word **aḍḍha** (half) before them, respectively change into **aḍḍhuḍḍha, divaḍḍha, diyaḍḍhha, aḍḍhatiya,** along with the word “**aḍḍha**”. [Function is quite simple and easy to understand]

The Order of Functions

aḍḍha+catuttha (half & fourth) >aḍḍhuḍḍha.
aḍḍha+dutiya (half & second) >divaḍḍha, diyaḍḍha.[Two functions]
aḍḍha+tatiya (half & third) >aḍḍhatiya.

(1) Aḍḍhena-together with half, catuttho-the four or fourth,
- aḍḍhuḍḍho-(is called) four and half.

(2) aḍḍhena-together with half, dutiyo-the two or second,
- divaḍḍho-(is called) two and half.

(3) aḍḍhena-together with half, dutiyo-the two or second,
- diyaḍḍho-(is called) two and half.

(4) aḍḍhena-together with half, tatiyo- the three or third,
- aḍḍhatiyo-(is called) three and half.

[All examples are Tatiyā Tappurisa compounds]

३८८, ६८. सरूपान मेकसेस्वसकिं

388, 68. **Sarūpāna’mekasesva’sakiṁ.**

[Sarūpānaṁ+ekaseso+asakiṁ. 3 words]

[V] **Sarūpā**naṁ **pada, byañjanā**naṁ **ekaseso** hoti asakiṁ.

When repeatedly expressing multiple words of the same shape and meaning, a procedure called “**ekasesa**” is to be performed, making all those words into one and retaining only one word. [**eka**-one+**sesa**-left, to remain, to retain]

Puriso ca-man also, puriso ca-man also, • purisā-men [Dvanda]. **Note:** Here, two of the same word "Purisa" are made into one by "ekasesa" procedure of this Sutta, making all those words of similar form into one.

Sarūpānami'ti kimatthaṁ?
What is the word "sarupānaṁ" for? To show that the example words of dvanda compound nouns shown below are words of dissimilar forms and meanings, not "sarūpa-words of similar forms and meanings". Hence, they are inapplicable here. [**sarūpa**=words of similar forms and meaning]
Hatthī ca-elephant also, asso ca-horse also, ratho ca-chariot also, pattiko ca-infantry man also,* hatthi, assa, ratha, pattikā-the elephant, horse, chariot and infantry man. [Dvanda Compound]

Asakin'ti kimatthaṁ? [asakiṁ+iti+kimatthaṁ]
What is the word "asakiṁ" for?
To show that the example below is meant for only one time, not "asakim-many times". So, it is inapplicable.
* Puriso-man.

३८९, ४१३. गणने दसस्स द्वितिचतुपञ्चछसत्तअट्ठनवकानं वीतिचत्तार पञ्ञाछसत्तासनवा योसु योनञ्चीसमासंठिरितीतुति

389, 413. **Gaṇane dasassa dvi, ti, catu, pañca, cha, satta,aṭṭha, navakānaṁ vī, ti, cattāra, paññā, cha, sattā'sa, navā yosu, yonañ'cī'sa'māsaṁ, ṭhi, ri, tī'tu'ti.**

[Gaṇane+dasassa+Dvi, ti, catu, pañca, cha, satta'aṭṭha, navakānaṁ+vī, ti, cattāra, paññā, cha, satta, asa, navā+yosu+ yonaṁ+ca+īsaṁ, āsaṁ, ṭhi, ri, ti, īti, uti. 8 words]

[V] Gaṇane dasassa **dvika, tika, catukka, pañcaka, chakka, sattaka, aṭṭhaka, navakā**naṁ sarūpānaṁ kate'kasesānaṁ yathāsaṅkhyaṁ **vī, ti, cattāra, paññā, cha, satta, asa, nava**-iccā' desā honti asakiṁ yosu, **Yo**nañ'ca **īsaṁ, āsaṁ, ṭhi, ri, ti, īti, uti**-iccā'desā honti. Pacchā puna nippajjante.

In numerical nouns, the numerical word "dasa", with "yo" vibattis duly applied after it, also having made it into an "ekasesa" after being multiplied by times **dvika** (two), **tika** (three), **catukka** (four), **pañcaka** (five), **chakka** (six), **sattaka** (seven), **aṭṭhaka** (eight), **navaka** (nine), changes into "**vī, ti, cattāra, paññā, cha, satta, asa, nava**" respectively. All the applied "yo" vibattis after them also change into "**īsaṁ, āsaṁ, ṭhi, ri, ti, īti, uti**" respectively.

Explanation

(on the morphological procedure as prescribed in the Sutta)

When a **dasa** (a numerical value in **ten**) is multiplied by times in a Dvanda: **dvika** (two), **tika** (three), **catukka** (four), **pañcaka** (five), **chakka** (six), **sattaka** (seven), **aṭṭhaka** (eight), **navaka** (nine), all the resultant times of the same **dasa** in the dvanda compound process has to be made into "**ekasesa**", thereby having only one "**dasa**" left, but the resultant numerical value of each multiplication is to remain accordingly unchanged. Afterwards, it will look like this:

(1) **Dasa** [multiplied x in two times=twenty]

(2) **Dasa** [multiplied x in three times=thirty]

(3) **Dasa** [multiplied x in four times=forty]

(4) **Dasa** [multiplied x in five times=fifty]

(5) **Dasa** [multiplied x in six times=sixty]
(6) **Dasa** [multiplied x in seven times=seventy]
(7) **Dasa** [multiplied x in eight times=eighty]
(8) **Dasa** [multiplied x in nine times=ninety]

Now, next stage of morphological procedure is like this:
Here, Paṭhmā "yo" vibatti (Nominative plural) is to be applied after each dasa. So, there will be a "yo" after each of eight "dasa".
Example: (1) dasa+yo.....(8) dasa+yo

By injunction of this Sutta, each of eight "**dasa**" are to be respectively changed into **vī, ti, cattāra, paññā, cha, satta, asa, nava** respectively. Then it will look like this:
(1) **vī+yo,** (2) **ti+yo,** (3) **cattāra+yo,** (4) **paññā+yo,** (5) **cha+yo,** (6) (a) **satta+yo,** (b) **satta+yo,** (7) **asa+yo,** (8) **nava+yo.**

Then, all the applied "**yo**" after each of eight "**dasa**" are to be changed into **īsaṁ** (for three initial words), **āsaṁ, ṭhi, ri, ti, īti, uti** respectively. Now, here is what it will look like: (when all preceding morphological procedures are done)

(1) **vī+īsaṁ** (elide **ī** after **v** and then, join **v** to **ī**) **vīsaṁ**=20
(2) **ti+īsaṁ** ("i" of "**ti**" is elided. A niggahita **ṁ** has to be inserted after **ti**, "**ī**" is shortened) **tiṁsaṁ**=30
(3) **cattāra+īsaṁ** (elide **a** behind **r** and change "**r**" into "**l**" by 379. join **l** to **ī**) **cattālīsaṁ**=40 ["**īsam**" function for examples 1,2,3,]
(4) **paññā+āsaṁ** (elide **ā** after **ñ** and join **ñ** to next **ā**) **paññāsaṁ**=50
(5) **cha+ṭhi** (change "cha" into "sa". Reduplicate with one ṭ) **Saṭṭhi**=60
(6) (a) **satta+ri**=(no further action needed) **sattari**=70
(b) **satta+ti**=(no further action needed) **sattati**=70
[2 examples for the 70]
(7) **asa+īti**=(delete **a** after **s** and join **s** to next **ī**) **asīti**=80
(8) **nava+uti**=(elide **a** after **v** and then join **v** to next **u**) **navuti**=90

Now, let's see the examples of Sutta as finished words:
• Vīsaṁ-Twenty. • tiṁsaṁ-Thirty. • cattālīsaṁ-Forty.
• paññāsaṁ-Fifty. • saṭṭhi-Sixty. • sattari-Seventy. • sattati-Seventy. • asīti-Eighty. • navuti-Ninety. [All these words are Dvanda compound nouns]

Asakin'ti kimatthaṁ?
What is the word "asakiṁ" for?
To show that the example below is meant for only one time, not "asakim-many times". So, it is inapplicable.
[This word "**asakiṁ**" is to be found in the Vutti of Sutta]
* Dasa-ten.

Gaṇane'ti kimatthaṁ?
What is the word "gaṇane" for?
To show that the example below is meant for the statement of a fact, not for numerical counting. So, it is inapplicable.
* Dasadasakā-ten multiplied by ten. purisā-men (a hundred men).

३९०, २५६. चतूपपदस्स लोपो तु'त्तरपदादिचस्स चु चोपि नवा

390, 256. Catū'papadassa lopo tu'ttarapadā'dicassa cuco'pi navā.

[Catu-upapadassa+lopo+tu+uttarapada-ādicassa+cu, co+api+navā. 7 words]

[V] **Catū**'papadassa gaṇane pariyāpannassa **tu**kārassa lopo hoti. uttarapadā'di**ca**kārassa **cu, co'p**i ādesā honti navā.

Of the numerical word "**catu** (four) ", "**tu**" has to be deleted and the initial "**ca**" thereof also changes into "**cu, co**". [See the applied function which is shown in bold, underlined. **Only the first two examples are applicable.** The third is inapplicable.]

(1) • C**u**ddasa,
(2) • C**o**ddasa.
(3) *Catuddasa-fourteen.
[One "d" is augmented in example words, all Dvanda compounds]

Apiggahaṇena anu'papadassāpi padā'di**ca**kārassa lopo hoti navā. **ca**ssa **cu, co'**pi honti.

By means of the word "Api" in Sutta, the initial word "ca" which has no penultima, is occasionally elided while in some words, that initial "ca" changes into "**cu** or **co**". [See the applied function in bold, underlined]
(1) • Tālīsaṁ (The initial **Ca** is elided in this example).

(2) * Cattālīsaṁ (Ca is not elided in this example)

(3) • **Cu**ttālīsaṁ ("Cu" function).

(4) • **Co**ttālīsaṁ-Forty. ("Co" function. All have the same meaning. All examples are Dvanda compounds without any penultima)

३९१, ४२३. यदनुपपन्ना निपातना सिज्झन्ति

391, 423. Ya'danu'papannā nipātanā sijjhanti.

[Yaṁ+ana-upapannā+nipātanā+sijjhanti. 4 words]

[V] Ye saddā aniddiṭṭhalakkhaṇā

[1] akkhara, pada, byañjanato,

[2] itthi, puma, napuṁsakaliṅgato,

[3] nāmu'pasagga, nipātato,

[4] abyayībhāva samāsa, taddhitā'khyātato,

[5] gaṇana, saṅkhyā, kāla, kāraka'ppayoga saññāto,

[6] sandhi, pakati, vuddhi, lopā'gama, vikāra, viparitato,

[7] vibhattivibhajanato ca,

te nipātanā sijjhanti.

Any Pāli word, structural characteristic of which are as yet morphologically unexplained herein:

[1] by mode of letter, completed word form and consonant,

[2] by means of feminine, masculine and neuter genders,

[3] by Noun, Upasagga, Nipāta,

[4] by means of Samāsa nouns such as Abyayībhāva etc. Taddhita noun and Ākhyāta verbs,

[5] By numerical terms, time, Kāraka (parts of sentences in any specific case-endings) and example words and grammatical terms,

[6] Sandhi (euphonic combination), Pakati (keeping a word as it is. **i.e.** holding off any morphological procedure), vuddhi, Lopa-elision, insertion, vikāra and viparita procedures,

[7] by analysis of Vibatti-(Noun case-endings and Verb-terminations), can be brought to completion by this Sutta.

३९२, ४१८. द्वादितो को'नेकत्थे च

392, 418. **Dvā'dito ko'neka'tthe ca.**

[Dvi-ādito+ko+aneka-atthe+ca. 4 words]

[V] **Dvi-**icce'va'mādito **ka**paccayo hoti aneka'tthe ca, nipātanā sijjhanti.

There should come a "**ka**" to be affixed after the numerical word "**dvi**" and so on when expressing a sense of the multitude. (Those shown with mark • only are examples. See "**k**" shown in bold, underlined. The "**aṁ**" is a vibatti morpheme of the nominative singular "si" for neuter gender nouns)

(1) Satassa-of a hundred, • dvi**k**aṁ-two times, dvisataṁ-(is called) two hundred, 200. [wa] Dvikaṁ=Dvi+ka+si (WA of all the examples are the same except the preceding numeral component word such as "**ti, catu**" etc.)

(2) satassa-of a hundred, • ti**k**aṁ-three times, tisataṁ-(is called) three hundred, 300.

(3) satassa • catuk**k**aṁ-four times, (One "k" augmented). catusataṁ-(is called) four hundred, 400.

(4) satassa • pañca**k**aṁ-five times, pañcasataṁ-(is called) five hundred, 500.

(5) satassa • chak**k**aṁ-six times, (One "k" augmented). chasataṁ-(is called) six hundred, 600.

(6) satassa • satta**k**aṁ-seven times, sattasataṁ-(is called) seven hundred, 700.

(7) satassa • aṭṭha**k**aṁ-eight times, aṭṭhasataṁ-(is called) eight hundred, 800.

(8) satassa • nava**k**aṁ-nine times, navasataṁ-(is called) nine hundred, 900. [wa] Navakaṁ=Nava+ka+si

(9) satassa-of a hundred, • dasa**k**aṁ-ten times, dasasataṁ-(is called) ten hundred, 1000, sahassaṁ-(is also called) one thousand. hoti-(the term) is.

[wa] Dasakaṁ=Dasa+ka+si

Note: The same examples are shown in Rūpasiddhi grammar though there are some differing views regarding the way the examples are shown and explained by some scholars.

३९३, ४१५. दसदसकं सतं दसकानं सतं सहस्सञ्च योम्हि

393, 415. **Dasadasakaṁ sataṁ dasakānaṁ sataṁ sahassañ'ca yomhi.**

[Dasadasakaṁ+sataṁ+dasakānaṁ+sataṁ+sahassaṁ+ca+ yomhi. 7 words]

[V] Gaṇane pariyāpannassa **dasadasaka**ssa **sataṁ** hoti, **sata-dasaka**ssa **sahassaṁ** hoti, **yo**mhi pare.

In matters of counting, when a "**dasa** (ten) " is multiplied by ten (**dasadasaka** means ten times by ten), it becomes "**sata** (a hundred) " and a sata multiplied further by ten becomes a **sahassaṁ** (one thousand) with "**yo**" applied after those numerical nouns. ("**Yo**" is applied only after "multiple dasa" before it becomes a **sata or sahassa.** It is to be deleted afterwards.)

(1) • Sataṁ-hundred. (2) • sahassaṁ-thousand.

Dvikā'dīnaṁ **ta'duttarapadā**nañ'ca nippajjante yathāsaṅkhyaṁ.

By progressive multiplication of **Dvika** (two times) and so on, all upward numerical terms can be duly formulated in order of value.

(1) Satassa-of a hundred, dvikaṁ-two times, (ta'didaṁ-that, hoti-is) • dvisataṁ-two hundred. **i.e.** A hundred by two times is called two-hundred.

Evaṁ-thus in the same way,

(2) • tisataṁ-three hundred.

(3) • catusataṁ-four hundred.

(4) • pañcasataṁ-five hundred.

(5) • chasataṁ-six hundred.

(6) • sattasataṁ-seven hundred.

(7) • aṭṭhasataṁ-eight hundred.

(8) • navasataṁ-nine hundred.

(9) • dasasataṁ-ten hundred.

(10) • sahassaṁ-thousand. hoti-is.

(9 & 10 are two terms for a thousand).

३९४, ४१६. याव तदुत्तरि दसगुणितञ्च

394, 416. **Yāva ta'duttari dasaguṇitañ'ca.**

[Yāva+taṁ-uttari+dasaguṇitaṁ+ca. 4 words]

[V] Yāva tāsaṁ saṅkhyānaṁ uttari dasaguṇitañ'ca kātabbaṁ.

(For numerical words starting from a hundred and upwards to a **koṭi**-ten million or one crores), it is to be multiplied by ten.

Taṁ yathā? For example,

(1) Dasassa-of ten, gaṇanassa-the numerical value, dasaguṇitaṁ-ten-times multiplication, katvā-having done, • **sataṁ-**a hundred, hoti- is. **i.e.** Having done multiplication of the numerical value ten by ten times, (it) becomes a hundred.

(2) satassa-of a hundred, dasaguṇitaṁ katvā • **sahassaṁ-**a thousand, hoti. **i.e.** Having done multiplication of a hundred by ten times, (it) becomes a thousand.

(3) sahassassa-of a thousand, dasaguṇitaṁ katvā • **dasasahassaṁ**-ten thousand, hoti. **i.e.** Having done multiplication of a thousand by ten times, (it) becomes ten thousand.

(4) dasasahassassa-of ten thousand, dasaguṇitaṁ katvā • **satasahassaṁ**-a hundred thousand, hoti. **i.e.** Having done multiplication of ten thousand by ten times, (it) becomes a hundred thousand.

(5) satasahassassa-of a hundred thousand, dasaguṇitaṁ katvā • **dasasatasahassaṁ**-ten hundred-thousand, hoti. **i.e.** Having done multiplication of a hundred thousand by ten times, (it) becomes ten-hundred thousand, (one million).

(6) dasasatasahassassa-of ten hundred-thousand, dasaguṇitaṁ katvā • **koṭi**-a crore or ten million, hoti. **i.e.** Having done multiplication of ten-hundred thousand by ten times, (it) becomes a **koṭi** (a crore, Ten million)

(7) koṭisatasahassassa-of a hundred-thousand crores, sataguṇitaṁ-a hundred-times multiplication, katvā • **pakoṭi**-a pakoṭi, hoti. **i.e.** Having done multiplication of a hundred thousand **koṭi** by hundred times, (it) becomes a **pakoṭi**. [Here, multiplication is by a hundred]

Evaṁ sesā'pi yojetabbā.
Evaṁ-thus, sesā'pi [sesā+api]-the remaining numerical terms also, yojetabbā-should be engaged or formulated.

Caggahaṇaṁ visesana'tthaṁ.
The word "Ca" in Sutta has a purpose for allowing "visesana" (any applicable specific mathematical formulation).

३९५, ४१७. सकनामेहि

395, 417. **Sakanāmehi.** [Sakanāmehi. 1 word]

[V] Yāsaṁ pana saṅkhyānaṁ aniddiṭṭhanāmadheyyānaṁ sakehi sakehi nāmehi nippajjante.

Those numerical words whose names are not yet shown, are to be completed by their individual names.

(1) Satasahassānaṁ-of a hundred-thousands, sataṁ-a hundred, • **koṭi-**is a **koṭi**. A hundred-thousand (multiplied by) times a hundred is a **koṭi**.
(2) koṭisatasahassānaṁ sataṁ • **pakoṭi.** A hundred-thousand **koṭi**, (multiplied by) times a hundred is a **pakoṭi**.
(3) pakoṭisatasahassānaṁ sataṁ • **koṭipakoṭi.** A hundred-thousand **pakoṭi**, (multiplied by) times a hundred is a **koṭipakoṭi**.
(4) koṭipakoṭisatasahassānaṁ sataṁ • **nahutaṁ.** A hundred-thousand **koṭipakoṭi**, (multiplied by) times a hundred is a **nahuta**.
(5) nahutasatasahassānaṁ sataṁ • **ninnahutaṁ.** A hundred-thousand **nahuta**, (multiplied by) times a hundred is a **ninnahuta**.
(6) ninnahutasatasahassānaṁ sataṁ • **akkhobhiṇī.** A hundred-thousand **ninnahuta**, (multiplied by) times a hundred is an **akkhobhiṇī**.

Tathā-multiply similarly in that manner (for the following terms) :
• bindu, • abbudaṁ, • nirabbudaṁ, • ahahaṁ, • ababaṁ, • aṭaṭaṁ, • sogandhikaṁ, • uppalaṁ, • Kumudaṁ, • Padumaṁ, • Puṇḍarikaṁ, • Kathānaṁ, • Mahākathānaṁ, • asaṅkhyeyyaṁ.

Note: Each upward numeral terms such as **bindu, abbuda** and up to **asaṅkhyeyya (infinity** or **aeon)** are to be multiplied by a hundred times progressively.

३९६, ३६३. तेसं णो लोपं

396, 363. **Tesaṁ ṇo lopaṁ.** [Tesaṁ+ṇo+lopaṁ. 3 words]

[V] Tesaṁ paccayānaṁ **ṇo** lopa'mā'pajjate.

The "**ṇ**" of all taddhita affixes containing "**ṇ**" is to be elided.

Gotamassa-of a person named Gotama, apaccaṁ-son,
• gotamo-Gotama's son. [See Sutta 344]
Evaṁ
• vāsiṭṭho. • Venateyyo. • ālasyaṁ. • ārogyaṁ.
(These examples are shown already).

Note: "**ṇa, ṇāyana, ṇāna, ṇeyya, ṇi, ṇika, nva, ṇera, ṇya,** etc are called "**ṇ**-containing affixes". After elision procedure, only "**a, āyana, āna, eyya, i, ika, ava, era, ya,** will be left in the examples.

Abyaya Taddhita
(Nouns in indeclinable affixes)

Note: Suttas 397, 398, 399 apply indeclinable affixes. Any word applied with one of these affixes becomes indeclinable which has no gender, nor any change of word-form through a specific morphological procedure. Although some appropriate Vibattis are applicable depending on the context, they have to be elided though without undergoing any form of change. [**a**-not+**byaya**-change. **i.e.** Changeless]

३९७, ४२०. विभागे धा च

397, 420. **Vibhāge dhā ca.** [Vibhāge+dhā+ca. 3 words]

[V] **Vibhāga'**tthe ca **dhā**-paccayo hoti.

To signify distributive expressions, an affix "**dhā**" is added. [See the "**dhā**" affix shown underlined in examples. This affix can be applied after numerical nouns and also after other common nouns. It is an indeclinable affix and has no gender. It serves as a distributive adjective or adverb. See the affix shown underlined in the examples]

Ekena-by one, vibhāgena-division of portion, • eka<u>dhā</u>-by one portion, in one kind. [wa] Ekadhā=eka+dhā ["**Nā**" Vibatti is applicable but to be deleted. All examples are the same]
Evaṁ

- dvidhā-by two portions, in two kinds.
- tidhā-by three portions, in three kinds.
- catudhā-by four portions, in four kinds
- pañcadhā-by five portions, in five kinds.
- chadhā-by six portions, in six kinds.

[wa] Chadhā=cha+dhā
(WA of all examples are the same except the preceding numbers)

Ce'ti kimatthaṁ?
What is the word "Ca" in Sutta for?

So-paccayo hoti.

To show that an affix "**so**" can be applied after other non-numerical words. [See the "**so**" affix shown underlined]

- Suttaso-by means of Sutta. [wa] Suttaso=Sutta+so
- Byañjanaso-by means of byañjana (consonants).

[wa] byañjanaso=byañjana+so
- padaso-by means of pada (word). [wa] Padaso=Pada+so

Note: This affix "**so**" usually means "by means of". It is an indeclinable affix which serves as an equivalent of the instrumental case.

३९८, ४२१. सब्बनामेहि पकारवचने तु था
398, 421. **Sabbanāmehi pakāravacane tu thā.**

[Sabbanāmehi+pakāravacane+tu+thā. 4 words]

[V] Sabbanāmehi **pakāra**vacana'tthe **thā**paccayo hoti.

After sabbanāma nouns, the affix "**thā**" is added to express manner and mode. [**pakāra**-mannar+**vacana**-expression]
Look at the following EDs of nouns affixed with "**thā**" "**thaṁ**" of Sutta 398-399. All the seven Vibatti (case endings) are shown being applied by the great Grammarian. However, it should be noted that the most widely used one in the majority of Buddhist text is only instrumental case. See the "**thā**" affix shown underlined in examples.

(1) So pakāro-that manner, • tathā-that manner.
(2) taṁ pakāraṁ-to that manner, • tathā-to that manner.
(3) tena pakārena-by that manner, • tathā-by that manner.
(4) tassa pakārassa-of that manner, • tathā-of that manner.

(5) tasmā pakārā-from that manner, • tathā-from that manner.
(6) tassa pakārassa-of that manner, • tathā-of that manner.
(7) tasmiṁ pakāre-at, in that manner, • tathā-in that manner.
[wa] Tathā=Ta+thā

Evaṁ

• yathā-by which manner. [wa] Yathā=Ya+thā
• sabbathā-by all manner, after all.
[wa] Sabbathā=Sabba+thā
• aññathā-by other manner, otherwise, or else.
[wa] aññthā=añña+thā
• itarathā-by another manner, to speak other way or otherwise.
[wa] Itarathā=Itara+thā (All examples are similar in WA)

Tuggahaṇaṁ kimatthaṁ?
What is the word "tu" in Sutta for?

Tatthā-paccayo hoti.

By it, an affix "**tatthā**" can also be applied after some words.

So pakāro • tatatthā-by that manner.

Evaṁ

• yatatthā-by which manner. • Sabbatatthā-by all manner.
• aññatatthā-by other manner. • itaratatthā-by other manner.
[wa] • Itaratatthā=Itara+tatthā (All examples are similar in WA)

Note: The words in this affix "**tatthā**" are seldom found in majority of Pāli texts.

३९९, ४२२. किमिमेहि थं

399, 422. **Ki'mimehi thaṁ.** [Kiṁ, imehi+thaṁ. 2 words]

[V] **Kiṁ, ima**-icce'tehi **thaṁ**paccayo hoti **pakāra**vacana'tthe.

The affix "**thaṁ**" is added after **Kiṁ** (what) and **ima**(this) sabbanāma nouns when expressing manner and mode.
[See "**thaṁ**" affix shown underlined in the examples. Also note seven case-endings applied in each ED of the examples.]

Examples of "**kiṁ**"

(1) Ko pakāro-what manner, • kathaṁ-what manner. How? [wa] Kathaṁ=Kiṁ+thaṁ
(2) kaṁ pakāraṁ-to what manner, • kathaṁ-to what manner.
(3) kena pakārena-by what manner, • kathaṁ-by what manner, how?
(4) Kassa pakārassa • kathaṁ-of what manner.
(5) kasmā pakārā • kathaṁ-from what manner.
(6) Kassa pakārassa • kathaṁ-of what manner.
(7) kasmiṁ pakāre • kathaṁ-in what manner.

Examples of "**ima**"

(1) Ayaṁ pakāro-this manner, • itthaṁ-this manner. [one similar "t" is augmented by Sutta 28]. [wa] Itthaṁ=ima+thaṁ
(2) imaṁ pakāraṁ • itthaṁ-to this manner.
(3) iminā pakārena-by this manner, • itthaṁ-by this manner, in this way.
(4) Imassa pakārassa • itthaṁ-of this manner.
(5) imasmā pakārā • itthaṁ-from this manner.
(6) Imassa pakārassa • itthaṁ-of this manner.
(7) imasmiṁ pakāre • itthaṁ-in this manner.

४००, ३६४. वुद्धादिसरस्स वा'संयोगन्तस्स सणे च

400, 364. **Vuddhā'disarassa vā'saṁyogantassa saṇe ca.**

[Vuddhi+ādisarassa+vā+a-saṁyoga-antassa+saṇe+ca. 6 words]

[V] Ādisarassa vā asaṁyogantassa ādibyañjanassa vā sarassa vuddhi hoti saṇakārake paccaye pare.

When an "**ṇ**-conjoined affix" is present in a Taddhita noun without any conjunct word, either the initial vowel or the vowel of a certain consonant is to undergo a morphological process called "**vuddhi**".

[Vowels where Vuddhi-function is applied are shown underlined]

• Ābhidhammiko. • venateyyo. • vāsiṭṭho. • ālasyaṁ.
• ārogyaṁ. [These examples already shown]

Asaṁyogantasse'ti kimatthaṁ?
What is the word "asaṁyogantassa" for?
To show that examples below are not "asaṁyogantassa-single consonant taddhita-nouns". Instead, they are taddhita-nouns with conjunct-consonants. So, they are inapplicable.
(See **bold-faced, underlined conjuncts** in the example words below)
* Bha**gg**avo-the son of a person named Bhaggu.
* ma**nt**eyyo-the son of a woman named Mantī.
[wa] Manteyyo=Mantī+ṇeyya+si
* ku**nt**eyyo-the son of a woman named Kuntī.
[wa] Kunteyyo=Kuntī+ṇeyya+si
Note: The WA of most examples are already shown.

४०१, ३७५. मा यूनमागमो ठाने
401, 375. Mā 'yūna'māgamo ṭhāne.

[Mā+iū-naṁ+āgamo+ṭhāne. 4 words]

[V] **I, u**-icce'tesaṁ ādibhūtānaṁ mā vuddhi hoti.
Tesu ca **e, o**-vuddhā'gamo hoti ṭhāne.

The **vuddhi** procedure on the initial vowels "**i, u**" of certain Taddhita nouns is debarred. Instead, the vowel "**e, o**" are to come(insert) and be replaced in the place of "**i, u**" where appropriate. [Replacing "**i**" with "**e**" can be applied only when it is followed by "**y**", while replacing "**u**" with "**o**" is applicable only when followed by a "**v**"]
Note: In **examples 1, 2, 3,** "**e**" is inserted in the front of "**i**" and "**i**" is changed into "**y**".
In **example 4,** "**o**" is inserted in front of "**u**" and that "**u**" is changed into "**v**". The substituted vowels are shown in bold, underlined. In WA, a process of applicable expansion called **saṁpasāraṇa** (सम्प्रसारण) is shown in bold, underlined to clearly understand somewhat complex function of this Sutta.

(1) Vyākaraṇa'madhīte [Vyākaraṇaṁ+adhīte] Vyākaraṇaṁ-grammar, adhīte-(he) learns, • v**e**yyākaraṇiko-the one who learns grammar, a grammar-student.
[wa] Veyyākaraṇiko=V**i**-**ā**karaṇa+ṇika+si

(2) nyāya'madhīte [nyāyaṁ+adhīte] nyāyaṁ-the logic, adhīte
• N<u>e</u>yyāyiko-the one who learns logic, a logic-student.
[wa] Neyyāyiko=N<u>i</u>-<u>ā</u>ya+ṇika+si

(3) vyāvacchassa-of a person named vyāvaccha, apaccaṁ-son,
• v<u>e</u>yyāvaccho-the son of vyāvaccha.
[wa] Veyyāvaccho=V<u>i</u>-<u>ā</u>vaccha+ṇika+si

(4) dvāre-at the door, niyutto-(is) involved, • d<u>o</u>vāriko-door-keeper, security-man at the door.
[wa] dovāriko=d<u>u</u>-<u>ā</u>ra+ṇika+si

४०२. ३७७. आत्तञ्च

402, 377. **Āttañ'ca.** [Āttaṁ+ca. 2 words]

[V] **I, u**-icce'tesaṁ **ā**ttañ'ca hoti. **ri**-kārā'gamo ca ṭhāne.

The vowels "**i, u**" changes into "**ā**". The "**ri**" also comes to be inserted in some Taddhita nouns where appropriate.
Note: (a) The two vowels "**I**" and "**U**", which form part of the basic front component of each word are included in the ED of examples. Those vowels and the changed "**ā**" are shown in bold, underlined. **In examples 1 & 2,** "**I**" changes into "**ā**". The coming of "**ri**-function" is applied and "**ri**" is inserted after the changed "**ā**" in the first example only. (b) **In examples 3 & 4,** "**U**" changes into "**ā**". But the changed "**ā**" is shortened in example 4. (All examples shown are Bhāva Taddhita)

(1) Isissa-of hermit, bhāvo-state, • ā**ri**syaṁ-the state of hermit, the hermit-hood.
[wa] Ārisyaṁ=Isi+ṇya+si ["**i**" of "**isi**" becomes "**ā**", "**ri**" is inserted after it in this example]

(2) Iṇassa-of debt, bhāvo-state, • āṇyaṁ-state of debt, being in-debted.
[wa] Āṇyaṁ=Iṇa+ṇya+si ["**i**" of "**iṇa**" becomes "**ā**" in this example]
Note: Also "**ānaṇyaṁ**" is found in the Pāli texts.
[**1. anaṇa**-being debt-free+ṇya, ***tn***. **2. anaṇa**=**na**-without+**iṇa**-debt. ***cn***]

(3) Usabhassa-of being brave like a strong bull, bhāvo • āsabhaṁ-bravery, fearlessness.
[wa] Āsabhaṁ=Usabha+ṇa+si ["**u**" of "**usabha**" becomes "**ā**" in this example]

(4) Ujuno-of being upright, bhāvo • ajjavaṁ-uprightness.
[wa] Ajjavaṁ=Uju+ṇa+si

Note on morphological procedure of example 4:
(1) "**u**" of "**uju**" becomes "**ā**" in this example>**āju**.
(2) One "**j**" is augmented>**ājju**. The second "**u**" changed into "**āv**">**ājjāv.**
(3) The "**ā**" is shortened later on. >Thus, it becomes "**ajjava**" and "**si**" is applied after it. **[ajjav+si]** .
(4) That "**si**" is again changed into an "**aṁ**". **[ajjav+aṁ]**.
The word is thus completed after all due procedures are done.

icce'va'mādī yojetabbā.

Yūnami'ti kimatthaṁ?
What is the word "yūnaṁ" for?
To show that in the example below, there is no "**i-u,** which is grammatically known as "**yū**". So, it is inapplicable. Instead, it undergoes only a normal Vuddhi procedure. (The applied Vuddhi-vowel is shown underlined).
Apāyesu-in woeful states of Apāya, jāto-born,
* āpāyiko-the one who was born in woeful states, the Apāya-born.
[wa] āpāyiko=apāya+ṇika+si

Ṭhāne'ti kimatthaṁ?
What is the word "ṭhāne" for?
To show that the example shown below is a point of the ordinary "vuddhi". So they are inapplicable. Only a normal Vuddhi procedure occurred. (The applied Vuddhi-vowel is shown underlined. In the first example "**i**" becomes "**e**"**.** In the other three examples, "**u**" becomes "**o**")
* Vematiko-doubt-related, doubtful.
[wa] Vematiko=vimati+ṇika+si
* opanayiko--inference-related, accessible, being logical.
[wa] Opanayiko=Upanaya+ṇika+si
* opamāyiko-simile-related, analogous.
[wa] Opamāyiko=Upamā+ṇika+si
* opāyiko-method-related, methodical.
[wa] Opāyiko=Upāya+ṇika+si

४०३, ३५४. क्वचादिमज्झुत्तरानं दीघरस्सा पच्चयेसु च

403, 354. **Kvacā'di, majjhu'ttarānaṁ dīgha, rassā paccayesu ca.**

[Kvaci+ādi, majjha, uttarānaṁ+dīgha, rassā+paccayesu+ca. 5 words]

[V] Kvaci ādimajjha-uttara-icce'tesaṁ dīgharassā honti paccayesu ca apaccayesu ca.

When paccaya (Vibattis and affixes) or non-paccaya (Upasagga and Nipāta particles etc.) are present in the words, the process of changing into "dīgha" or "rassa" can sometimes be performed at the beginning, or in the middle, or at the end of the words.

Ādidīgho tāva–First, (here are examples where) "**Dīgha-lengthening**" process takes place in the beginning:
[Look at the examples carefully. The long vowels **ā** and **ī** shown in bold and underlined in the beginning of words, are the lengthened vowels.]

• p**ā**kāro-fence. • n**ī**vāro-hindrance. [The word **Nīvaraṇaṁ** is a frequently found word in the texts]. • p**ā**sādo-mansion. • p**ā**kaṭo-well-known. • p**ā**timokkho-monastic discipline. • p**ā**ṭikaṅkho-wanted, or surely to happen (two meanings).
icce'va'mādi.

Majjhedīgho tāva–First, (here are examples where) "**Dīgha-lengthening**" process takes place in the middle:
[The long vowel **ā** shown in bold and underlined in the middle of the words is the lengthened vowel.]

• aṅgam**ā**gadhiko-the resident of aṅga and magadha regions.
[wa] aṅgamāgadhiko=aṅgamagadha+ṇika+si
• orabbham**ā**gaviko-sheep and game hunter.
[wa] Orabbhamāgaviko=Urabbha,magava+ṇika+si
iccevamādi.

Uttaradīgho tāva–First, (here are examples where) "**Dīgha-lengthening**" process takes place in the end:
[The long vowels **ī** and **ā** shown in bold and underlined in the end of the words are the lengthened vowels.]

• khant**ī**-the practice of patience, paramaṁ-noble, tapo-(is) the

highest ethics, titikkhā-a quality called titikkhā,
i.e. The practice of patience, a quality called "titikkhā" is the noble and highest ethic.

- añjan**ā**-so-called, giri-mountain.
- koṭar**ā**-which has cave or hollowed trees (कोटर). vanaṁ-forest.
- aṅgul**ī**-finger.

icce'va'mādi.

Ādirasso tāva–First, (here are examples where) "**Rassa-shortening**" process takes place in the beginning:
[Look at example carefully. The short vowel **a** shown in bold and underlined in the beginning of the word is the shortened vowel.]

- p**a**geva [pā+eva] pageva-early in the morning.

icce'va'mādi.

Majjhe rasso tāva–First, (here are examples where) "**Rassa-shortening**" process takes place in the middle: [The short vowel **a** shown in bold and underlined in the middle of the words is the shortened vowel.]

- sumedh**a**so-the one who has good intellect.
- suvaṇṇadh**a**rehi-by the flows of molten-gold.

icce'va'mādi.

Uttararasso tāva–First, (here are examples where) "**Rassa-shortening**" process takes place in the end:
[Look at examples carefully. The short vowel **i** shown in bold, underlined in the end of the words is the shortened vowel.]

- bhovād**i** nāma-named "bhovādī", so-that person, hoti-is.
- yathābhāv**i**-is called "yathābhāvī", guṇena-by virtue, so-that person.

icce'va'mādi.
Aññe'pi yathājinavacanā'nuparodhena yojetabbā.
Other similar examples should be applied in a way not contravening the prevalent usage of Tipiṭaka Pāli canon.

Caggahaṇena apaccayesu cā'ti atthaṁ samucceti.

By the word "Ca" in Sutta, it also shows that the function of Sutta can also be applied in cases of non-paccaya words.

४०४, ३७०. तेसु वुद्धि लोपागम विकार विपरितादेसा च

404, 370. **Tesu vuddhi, lopā'gama, vikāra, viparītā' desā ca.**

[Tesu+vuddhi, lopa, āgama, vikāra, viparīta, ādesā+ca. 3 words]

[V] Tesu ādimajjhu'ttaresu yathājinavacanā'nuparodhena kvaci **vuddhi** hoti. kvaci **lopo** hoti. kvaci **āgamo** hoti. kvaci **vikāro** hoti. kvaci **viparīto** hoti. kvaci **ādeso** hoti.

At the beginning, or in the middle or in the end of various words, the morphological procedures of **vuddhi, Lopa, āgama, vikāra, viparīta** and **ādesa** are applicable in a way not contravening the usages of the canonical Buddhist texts.

Note: Some examples and most of the procedures have been already shown before in the preceding chapters. See underlined vowels in each example shown in bold. It is where the respective procedure takes place.

Vuddhi Procedure

(1) Changing of "**a**" into "**ā**",
(2) changing of "**i-ī**" into "**e**",
(3) changing of "**u-ū**" into "**o**" is called "**Vuddhi**-to increase".

Ādivuddhi tāva– First, (here are examples where) "**vuddhi**" process takes place in the beginning:

- ābhidhammiko-the Abhidhamma scholar or student [Here, "**a**" becomes "**ā**"].
- venateyyo-the son of someone named Vinatā. [Here, "**i**" becomes "**e**"]

icce'va'mādi.

Majjhe vuddhi tāva– First, (here are examples where) "**vuddhi**" process takes place in the middle:

- sukhaseyyaṁ-happily sleeping [Here, "**i**" becomes "**e**"],
- sukhakāri-happiness-creating. dānaṁ-charity, **i.e.** charitable deed which creates happiness.
- sukhakāri-happiness-creating. sīlaṁ-morality [In these two examples, "**a**" becomes "**ā**"].

icce'va'mādi.

Uttaravuddhi tāva– First, (here are examples where) "**vuddhi**" process takes place at the end:

• kāliṅgo-the resident of Kaliṅga, • māgadhiko-the resident of Magadha

[In these two examples, the applied vibatti nominative singular "**si**" becomes "**o**". This function is redundant as it was already shown in the nouns section]

• paccakkhadhammā-the one who have witnessed (realized) Dhamma

[Here, component vowel "**a**" of the last word "**ma**" becomes "**ā**". **Note:** This function is also redundant as "**yo**" applied after it can be changed into "**ā**" by normal procedure as prescribed in the previous sections of noun and Samāsa. [**ādi**-in the beginning. **majje**-in the middle, **uttara**-at the last point]

icce'va'mādi.

Lopa Procedure

Disappearance of a visible, pre-existing syllable by procedure of elision is called "Lopa".

Ādilopo tāva– First, (here are examples where) "**Lopa-**elision" process takes place in the beginning:

• tālīsaṁ-forty. [Here, "**ca**" before "**tā**" is elided]

icce'va'mādi.

Majjhelopo Tāva– First, (here are examples where) "**Lopa**" process takes place in the middle:

• kattukāmo-the one wanting to do. [Here, "**ṁ**" before "**kā**" is elided. If left unelided, it will be "**Kattuṁ kāmo**"].

• kumbhakāraputto-the son of potter. [Here, "**ṁ**" before "**kā**" is elided. If unelided, it will be "**Kumbhaṁ kāraputto**"].

• vedallaṁ-joy-related. [Here, "**ṁ**" before "**ll**" is elided. If left unelided, it will be "**vedaṁ llaṁ**"].

icce'va'mādi.

Uttaralopo tāva– First, (here are examples where) "**lopa**" process takes place at the end:

• bhikkhu-male-monk.

• bhikkhunī-female-monk. [In these examples, "**si**" vibatti applied after them is elided. As this procedure was also shown in the Nouns section, it is a redundant function]

icce'va'mādi.

Āgama Procedure

Appearance of non-existent syllable by procedure of Āgama-'coming', this insertion process is called "Āgama".

Ādi-āgamo tāva– First, (here are examples where) "**āgama**-coming & inserting of new alphabet" process takes place in the beginning:

- vutto-said, bhagavatā-by lord Buddha. [Here, "**v**" is inserted before "u"]

icce'va'mādi.

Majjhe-āgamo tāva–First, (here are examples where) "**āgama**" process takes place in the middle:

- sa sīlavā [so+sīlavā] so-that person, sīlavā-has Sīla (morality). [Here, "**a**" is inserted between two "**s**"]
- sa paññavā [so+paññvā] so paññvā-has paññā (wisdom). [Here, "**a**" is inserted between "**s** and **p**".

Note: In both examples, this procedure was already shown in Sutta 27, the Sandhi section.

icce'va'mādi.

Uttara-āgamo tāva– First, (here are examples where) "**āgama**" process takes place at the end:

- vedallaṁ-joy-related. [Here, "**si**" is inserted in the end of the word and transformed it into an "**aṁ**"].

Note: This procedure of changing "**si**" into "**aṁ**" was already shown in the nouns section.

icce'va'mādi.

Vikāra Procedure

The transformation of a visible syllable into other different form of syllable is called "Vikāra".

Ādivikāro Tāva– First, (here are examples where) "**vikāra**-changing into different forms" process takes place in the beginning:

- ārisyaṁ [Here, "**i**" changed into "**ā**" and "**ri**" is inserted after it].
- āṇyaṁ [Here, "**i**" changed into "**ā**"].
- āsabhaṁ [Here, "**u**" changed into "**ā**"].
- ajjavaṁ [Here, "**u**" changed into "**ā**" and shortened] (The functions already shown in Sutta 402)

icce'va'mādi.

Majjhe vikāro tāva–First, (here are examples where) "**vikāra**" process takes place in the middle:

- varārisyaṁ-the state of holy ascetic.
  [wa] Varārisyaṁ=Vara-isi+ṇya+si
- parārisyaṁ--the state of other ascetic. [In both examples, "**i**" changed into "**ā**" and "**ri**" is inserted in the middle].
  [wa] Parārisyaṁ=para-isi+ṇya+si

iccevamādi.

Uttaravikāro tāva– First, (here are examples where) "**vikāra**" process takes place at the end:

- yā**ni**-those which. • tā**ni**-those. • sukhā**ni**-those joys.
  [In all these examples, "**Yo**" vibatti after them transformed into "**ni**". This function was already shown in the Nouns section]

icce'va'mādi.

Viparīta Procedure

Changing of a visible syllable such as "**O** or **ava**" into "**u**" and vice versa is called "Viparīta".

Ādiviparīto tāva–First, (here are examples where) "**viparīta-reversal**" process takes place in the beginning:

- **u**ggate-when arisen, sūriye-the sun. **i.e.** When the sun arises.
- **u**ggacchati-(it) rises up.

[In both examples, the initial vowel "**ava**" transforms into "**u**"] .

icce'va'mādi.

Majjhe viparīto tāva– First, (here are examples where) "**viparīta**" process takes place in the middle:

- sa'm**u**ggacchati [saṁ+uggacchati], saṁuggacchati-(it) rises up well.
- sa'm**u**ggate[saṁ+uggate] saṁuggate-when well-arisen. sūri-ye-the sun.

[In both examples, the middle vowel "**u**" between "**m**" and "**g**", which is shown underlined, is a reversed morpheme of "**ava**". This function was already shown in Sutta 79, Nouns chapter].

icce'va'mādi.

Uttaraviparīto tāva– First, (here are examples where) "**viparīta**" process takes place at the end:

- dig**u**-two cows.[Here, the last vowel "**o**" of "**go**-cow" transforms into "**u**"]
- diguṇ**aṁ**-two-layered.[Here, the applied vibatti "**si**" transforms into "**aṁ**"]

icce'va'mādi.

Ādesa Procedure

Changing of an existing syllable to another form of syllable is called "Ādesa".

Ādi-ādeso tāva–First, (here are examples where) "**ādesa-**the process of changing the vowel into consonant and vice versa" takes place in the beginning:

- **yū**naṁ-of "**i and u**"

Note: The word "**Yūnaṁ**" is to be initially based as: "**iu**"**.** Then, by this Sutta, "**i**" transforms into "**y**">**yu.** Then, apply a genitive plural "naṁ" after it>**yu+naṁ.** After "u" is lengthened by Sutta 89, it eventually becomes a complete word "**Yūnaṁ**"**.**

icce'va'mādi.

Majjhe-ādeso tāva– First, (here are examples where) "**ādesa**" process takes place in the middle:

- n**y**āyogo-being always involved, constant effort. [Here, the original word is "ni+āyogo". "**i**" transforms into "**y**" by means of this Sutta and later it becomes a completed word. The example shown in Sutta 51].

icce'va'mādi.

Uttara-ādeso tāva–First, (here are examples where) "**ādesa**" process takes place at the end:

- sabbaseyy**o**-the noblest of all.
- sabbaseṭṭh**o**-the best of all. [In both examples, "**si**" Vibatti applied after these words transforms into "**o**" by this Sutta].
- citt**aṁ**-the amazing, the mind. [Here, "**si**" Vibatti applied after the word transforms into "**aṁ**" by this Sutta. The function of all three examples have been already shown in the Nouns section. The word "Citta" originally means wonderful, amazing].

icce'va'mādi.

Evaṁ yathājinavacanānuparodhena sabbattha yojetabbā.

Thus, appropriate procedures should be applied in all examples by not contravening to Buddha's words.

Note: Some functions, although shown previously, are included in this Sutta again in order to show that all those various kinds of morphological procedures and functions can also be performed by means of invoking the injunction of this great Sutta.

४०५, ३६५. अयुवण्णानञ्चायो वुद्धि

405, 365. A'yu, vaṇṇānañ'cā'yo vuddhi.

[**1.** A, yu, vaṇṇānaṁ+ca+āyo+vuddhi. 4 words]
[**2.** A, i, u, vaṇṇānaṁ+ca+ā, e, o+vuddhi.]
(The second is a **more detailed parsing** of the Sutta)

[V] **A**-iti **a**kāro, **i-ī**-iti **ivaṇṇo**, **u-ū**-iti **uvaṇṇo,** tesaṁ **a**kāra, **ivaṇṇu'vaṇṇā**naṁ **ā, e, o,** vuddhiyo honti yathāsaṅkhyaṁ. **ā, ī, ū**-vuddhi ca.

(1) **A**-is to be known as **a**kāra (**a**-alphabet).
(2) **i** and **ī** are to be known as **ivaṇṇa.**
(3) **u** and **ū** are to be known as **uvaṇṇa.**
Changing into "**ā, e, o,"** of all these **a, i-ī, u-ū,** vowels respectively, are formally called the process of "**vuddhi**".

Note: As shown in translation, the vowel "a" changes into "**ā**". "**i or ī**" changes into "**e**". "**u or ū**" changes into "**o**". This is what is formally called "vuddhi". This Sutta clearly defines the process of "vuddhi" in a very simple explanation.

- Ābhidhammiko
  [Here "A" becomes "Ā" as a result of vuddhi procedure. Re: 351].
- venateyyo [Here "i" becomes "e". Re: 346]
- oḷumpiko [Here "u" becomes "o". Re: 350. The meanings of words shown already in the preceding relevant Suttas]

Puna **vuddhi**ggahaṇaṁ kimatthaṁ?
What is the purpose of using the word "vuddhi" again in this Sutta for?

Uttarapadavuddhibhāvatthaṁ.
To apply performing of vuddhi function at the end of the words too.

(**See the underlined vowels** at the end of each example shown in bold. They are the result of vuddhi procedure. **Note that in the majority of examples previously shown thus far, Vuddhi occurs only in the beginning or in the middle**. Here, it occurs also at the end of the word through the injunction of Sutta 404.

(1) aṅgamagadhehi-from Aṅga and Magada regions, āgatā'ti [āgatā+iti] āgatā-come, iti • aṅgam**ā**gadhik**ā**-those coming from Aṅga and Magada. [Here, "a" becomes "ā". Vuddhi occurs at

two points in this example]

[wa] aṅgamāgadhikā=aṅgamagadha+ṇika+yo

(2) Nigamajanapadesu-in big village and districts, jātā'ti [jātā+iti] jātā-born, iti • negamajānapadā-the native of big village and districts.

[Here, "i" becomes "e" and "a" becomes "ā". Vuddhi occurs at three points in this word]

[wa] Negamajānapadā=nigamajanapada+ṇika+yo

(3) Purimajanapadesu-in the Eastern districts, jātā'ti [jātā+iti] jātā-born, iti-therefore, • porimajānapadā-the native of Eastern districts.

[Here, "U" becomes "o" and "a" becomes "ā". Vuddhi occurs at three points in this example]

[wa] Porimajānapadā=Purimajanapada+ṇika+yo

(4) Sattā'he [**satta**+**ahe**] Sattā'he-in seven days, niyutto'ti [niyutto+iti] niyutto-engaged, iti • sattāhikā-seven-dayers.

[Here, "a" becomes "ā". Vuddhi occurs at one point in this example]

[Sattāhikā=**satta**-seven+**aha**-day+**ika**-the one who has]

[wa] Sattāhikā=Sattāha+ṇika+yo

(5) catuvijje-in four (kinds of) sciences, niyutto'ti [niyutto+iti] niyutto-involved, iti-therefore, cātuvijjikā-are so called "cātu vijjikā".

• cātuvijjikā-those expert in four kinds of science.

[Vuddhi occurs at two points in this example.]

[Cātuvijjikā=**catu**-four+**vijjā**-knowledge+**ika**-the one who is involved with]

[wa] Cātuvijjikā=Catuvijja+ṇika+yo

Icce'va'mādī yojetabbā.

Note: All the lengthened long vowels at the very end of each example are the function expressly and specifically applied by Sutta 404. Besides, it should be known that any morphological procedure which was prescribed in the Nouns section can also be applied.

Vuddhi-icca'nena kvattho?

Vuddhā'disarassa vā'saṁyogantassa saṇe ca.

What benefit is there by this term "vuddhi"?

It has the benefit of making easy reference in such Suttas as "Vuddhā'disarassa vā'saṁyogantassa saṇe ca" etc.

Iti nāmakappe taddhitakappo aṭṭhamo kaṇḍo.
Taddhita Chapter, the Eight Section of Noun ends.

Taddhitakappo niṭṭhito.
Taddhita Chapter ends.

6. Ākhyāta Kappa
Ākhyāta Verbs Chapter

Paṭhama Kaṇḍa
The First Section

(a) Ākhyātasāgara'mathajjatanītaraṅgaṁ,
Dhātujjalaṁ vikaraṇā'gamakālamīnaṁ.
Lopā'nubandhariya'matthavibhāgatīraṁ,
Dhīrā taranti kavino puthubuddhināvā.

The wise of eloquent speech,
Navigate the vast ocean of verbs,
By big ship of broad grammatical wisdom,
On the waves of Aorist vibattis,
Thro' ocean water of the roots,
Vikaraṇa affixes, Āgama and tenses.
Resembling its aquatic creatures,
Elision of ṇ-conjoined-affix, like its mud,
whose shore is the grammatical skill of words.

(b) Vicittasaṅkhāraparikkhitaṁ imaṁ,
Ākhyātasaddaṁ vipulaṁ asesato.
Paṇamya sambuddha'manantagocaraṁ,
Sugocaraṁ yaṁ vadato suṇātha me.

Having bowed down to the Lord Buddha,
Of infinite wisdom of boundless domain,
Whose mind is set on the Nibbānic-bliss,
Ye! Hearken this entire Ākhyāta section
Adorned with verbs of unique nature,
Which is going to be explained by me.

(c) Adhikāre maṅgale ce'va, nipphanne cā'vadhāraṇe,
Anantare cā'pādāne, **atha**saddo pavattati.

The Nipāta particle [25] "**atha**" has various connotations, such as in the senses of:

(1) **Adhikāra** (Introductory particle placed at the beginning of a text),

(2) **Mangala** (as a word of auspiciousness said at the beginning of performance of rites and rituals),

(3) **Nipphanna** (Conclusion),

(4) **Avadhārana** (Restriction or limitation),

(5) **Anantara** (Disjunctive particle meaning "then, afterwards, after the section of") and

(6) **Apādāna** (Besides, moreover, apart from that).

४०६, ४२९. अथ पुब्बानि विभत्तीनं छ परस्सपदानि

406, 429. **Atha pubbāni vibhattīnaṁ cha parassapadāni.**

[Atha+pubbāni+vibhattīnaṁ+cha+parassapadāni. 5 words]

[V] Atha sabbāsaṁ vibhattīnaṁ yāni yāni pubbakāni cha padāni, tāni tāni parassapadasaññāni honti.

After Taddhita-nouns section, out of twelve in each of the eight Ākhyāta Vibatti (Verb-terminations), the first pairs of six are called "parassapada".

Summary: There are **eight group** of Ākhyāta Vibattis for all Pāli verbs known as Ākhyāta. **Each Vibatti comprises twelve**. This Sutta **names the first pair of six** which are **out of that twelve, as the "Parassapada"** group.

Here in this section, a **Vibatti is a form of verb-endings or verb-terminations to be applied after the roots** in order to form a Verb. **In the nouns section, a Vibatti is a case-**

---

[25] This Nipāta particle "**atha**" has various meanings in addition to the meanings shown in this verse. Here in the first Sutta, the word "**atha**" means "**after the section of**" serving as a disjunctive conjunction. Some of other meanings are (1) or (2) if (3) otherwise (4) Despite, in spite of, usually accompanied by either **ca,** or **pana** or **api** Nipāta particles.

ending to be applied after the nouns. Note this distinctive role of two types of Vibattis carefully.
Taṁ yathā? For example.
Ti-anti, si-tha, mi-ma.
They are "**Ti-anti, si-tha, mi-ma**". **(6)**

Parassapada'micca'nena kva'ttho? Kattari parassapadaṁ.
What is the benefit by terming "parassapada"?
It has the benefit of making easy reference in such Suttas as "Kattari parassapadaṁ" etc.

४०७, ४३९. पराण्यत्तनोपदानि

407, 439. **Parāṇya'ttanopadāni.**

[Parāṇi+attanopadāni. 2 words]

[V] Sabbāsaṁ vibhattīnaṁ yāni yāni parāni cha padāni.
Tāni tāni attanopadasaññāni honti.

Of all the Ākhyāta vibattis, the other six (out of twelve in each of the eight Ākhyāta Vibatti) are called "Attanopada".

Taṁ yathā? For example,
Te ante, se vhe, e mhe.
They are "**Te ante, se vhe, e mhe**". **(6)**

Attanopada'micca'nena kva'ttho?
Attanopadāni bhāve ca kammani.
What is the benefit by terming "attanopada"?
It has the benefit of making easy reference in such Suttas as "Attanopadani bhāve ca kammani " etc.

Summary: This Sutta names other six pairs as "**Attanopada**". By both Suttas 406-407, the Ākhyāta verbs are divided into **two main groups**. Viz.
(1) **Parassapada** verbs and
(2) **Attanopada** verbs.
The purpose is to make a clear distinction between the two groups in terms of voice and the way they are used in a sentence. **The voice of each vibatti groups will be explained in Sutta No. 453 and 456.**

४०८, ४३१. द्वे द्वे पठममज्झिमुत्तमपुरिसा

408, 431. **Dve dve paṭhama, majjhimu'ttama, purisā.**

[Dve, dve+paṭhama, majjhima, uttama, purisā. 2 words]

[V] Tāsaṁ sabbāsaṁ vibhattīnaṁ parassapadānaṁ attanopadānañ'ca **dve dve** padāni **paṭhama, majjhim'uttama**-purisasaññāni honti.

Of all the eight Vibattis which have been grouped into six prassapada and six attanopada, a pair of two in each of those two groups, are called **paṭhama purisa, majjhima purisa and uttama purisa** respectively.

Taṁ yathā? For example:

Among the first six parassapada Vibattis:

Ti, anti, iti **paṭhama**purisā. (The first pair)

Ti and **anti** are called **paṭhama**purisa (The first person, **i.e.** Third person).

si, tha, iti **majjhima**purisā. (The second pair)

Si and **tha** are called **majjhima**purisa (The middle person. **i.e.** Second person).

mi, ma, iti **uttama**purisā. (The third pair)

mi and **ma** are called **uttama**purisa (The * high person. **i.e.** First person).

Note: * It is translated as the high person as the word "uttama" implies.

Attanopadānam'pi.

Of (next six) attanopada vibattis:

te, ante, iti **paṭhama**purisā,

te and **ante** are called **paṭhama**purisa (The first person).

se, vhe, iti **majjhima**purisā,

Se and **Vhe** are called **majjhima**purisa (The middle person).

e, mhe, iti **uttama**purisā.

e and **mhe** are called **uttama**purisa (The high person).

Evaṁ-(It should be noted) thus. sabbattha-in all eight Vibattis.

Paṭhamamajjhimuttamapurisa'micca'nena kva'ttho? Nāmamhi payujjamāne'pi tulyādhikaraṇe paṭhamo, Tumhe majjhimo, Amhe uttamo.

What is the benefit by terming " Paṭhama, majjhima, uttama-purisa"?
It has the benefit of making easy reference in such Suttas as "Nāmamhi payujjamānepi tulyādhikaraṇe paṭhamo, Tumhe majjhimo and Amhe uttamo" etc.

Note: This Sutta clearly sets out a pair of two in each vibatti group to three persons (Purisas) assigning each pair to their respective Purisas. Please note it carefully because the assigned pairs of vibattis are to be conjugated with their respective verbs and persons accordingly. Only when one correctly knows with what vibatti and Purisa (persons) are to be used together, one will then be able to write and understand Pāli easily.

४०९, ४४१. सब्बेसमेकाभिधाने परो पुरिसो

409, 441. **Sabbesa'mekā'bhidhāne paro puriso.**

[Sabbesaṁ+eka-abhidhāne+paro+puriso. 4 words]

[V] Sabbesaṁ tiṇṇaṁ paṭhama, majjhimu'ttama-purisānaṁ ekā'bhidhāne paro puriso gahetabbo.

When all two or three Purisas (as possible subjects) specify the same action in a sentence, the last one is to determine the purisa of the sentence.
It means that only relevant vibatti and number that conforms to the last purisa (person, **i.e.** subject) shall be used in the verb when multiple subjects are involved in the same action (**i.e.** verb). Look at example sentences (a) and (b) shown below carefully. In (a), two different persons with their relevant verbs. In (b), only the last person's plural termination "tha" is applied thus combining both. Purisa and vibattis are shown in bold-faced letters.

[a] **So**-that person, ca-also, paṭha**ti**-recites.
tvañ'ca [tvañ'ca=tvaṁ+ca]-you also, paṭha**si**-recites.
Here two purisas are concurrently shown for the same action of a verb. See that the second person singular "tvaṁ" is the last purisa. This will determine as the purisa to be used in a sentence of combined purisas. See the final sentence here:

[b] **tumhe**-you (both that person and you), paṭha**tha**-recite.
(Two purisa, **i.e.** persons are combined into one second person plural in this last sentence. Only the last purisa, second person, plural

number is used in the verb. It is to be assumed that the first purisa "So" is included in the second person plural form "tumhe-you both". This example shows how the last purisa, **i.e.** person, is to determine the verb of combined purisa. Next example is the same except the action of verb).

[a] **So** ca paca**ti**-cooks, **tvañ**'ca [tvañ'ca=tvaṁ+ca] paca**si.**

[b] Tumhe-you (both that person and you), paca**tha**-cook.

Evaṁ sesāsu vibhattīsu paro puriso yojetabbo.
In this way, in the remaining vibattis, the last person should be applied.

The Three Persons

Note: The following **three Suttas from No. 410, 411 to 412 will explain three persons**, called **"purisa"**, which are used in Pāli grammar. Note them carefully as it is one of very important fundamental aspects of the grammar.

४१०, ४३२. नामम्हि पयुज्जमानेपि तुल्याधिकरणे पठमो

410, 432. **Nāmamhi payujjamāne'pi tulyā'dhikaraṇe paṭhamo.**

[Nāmamhi+payujjamāne+api+tulya-adhikaraṇe+paṭhamo. 5 words]

[V] Nāmamhi payujjamāne'pi appayujjamāne'pi tulyādhikaraṇe paṭhamapuriso hoti.

When a noun [as a subject] is either directly present or implicit in a sentence which is of a tulyādhikaraṇa (being appositional) nature, it is called **paṭhamapurisa** (The first person). **[paṭhama**=first+**purisa**=person**]**

(1) [Singular subject & verb] So-that person, or he, gaccha**ti**-goes.

(2) [Plural Subject & Verb] Te-those persons, or they, gacch**anti**-go. (In these two sentences, both subject and verb are present.)

Appayujjamāne'pi–example where subject is implicit (not directly shown) :

(1) [Singular verb only] gacchati-(he) goes.

(2) [Plural verb only] gacchanti-(they) go. (In these two sentences, only the verb is shown. The subject is not shown)

Tulyādhikaraṇe’ti ki’matthaṁ?
What is the word “tulyādhikaraṇe” for? To show that in the example shown below, there is no “tulyādhikaraṇa”. So, it is inapplicable.

Tena-by that, haññase-(are) killed, tvaṁ-you, devadattena-Devadatta. **i.e.** You are killed by that Devadatta. (passive voice, in the 2nd person)

Note: Tulyā’dhikaraṇe-means of being in the same position. The relationship of the subject and verb has to be directly related to each other in terms of meaning as well as in direct syntactic relation of voice. Here, subject, the killer "tena Devadattena" has no direct syntactic relationship, but the killed "tvaṁ" only has direct link to the verb as the main principal object of passive voice verb. Hence, no tulyādhikaraṇa. As a result, the first person verb termination "**ti** or **anti**" is inapplicable in this sentence.

४११, ४३६. तुम्हे मज्झिमो

411, 436. **Tumhe majjhimo.** [Tumhe+majjhimo. 2 words]

[V] Tumhe payujjamāne’pi appayujjamāne’pi tulyādhikaraṇe majjhimapuriso hoti.

When a **tumha** (you) pronoun [as a subject] is either directly present or implicit in a sentence of tulyādhikaraṇa, it is called **majjimapurisa** (The middle person, **i.e.** the second person). [**majjima**=middle+**purisa**=person]

(1) [Singular subject & verb] Tvaṁ-you (singular), yā**si**-go.
(2) [Plural subject & verb] Tumhe-you (plural), yā**tha**-go.

Appayujjamāne’pi–example where subject is implicit (not directly shown) :
(1) [Singular verb only] yāsi-(you) go,
(2) [Plural verb only] yātha-(you-plural) go.

Tulyādhikaraṇe’ti ki’matthaṁ?
What is the word “tulyādhikaraṇe” for? To show that in the example shown below, there is no “tulyādhikaraṇa”. So, it is inapplicable.

Tayā-by you, paccate-(is) cooked, odano-the rice.
i.e. The rice is cooked by you.

४१२, ४३७. अम्हे उत्तमो

412, 437. **Amhe uttamo.** [Amhe+uttamo. 2 words]

[V] Amhe payujjamāne'pi appayujjamāne'pi tulyā'dhikaraṇe uttamapuriso hoti.

When an **amha** (me) pronoun [as a subject] is either directly present or implicit in a sentence of tulyādhikaraṇa nature, it is called **uttamapurisa** (The high person, "**Uttama**" means noble or high or the last.).

Note: Terming persons is a bit different from the English grammar. Here **in Pāli grammar, the third person is the first. The last person is the first in English grammar.** Despite such minor differences, the role of each person remain the same in terms of actual usage in each language**. [uttama**=high, noble, last+**purisa**=person**]**

(1) [Singular subject & verb] Ahaṁ-I, yajā**mi**-worship.

(2) [Plural subject & verb] Mayaṁ-we, yajā**ma**-worship.

Appayujjamāne'pi–example where subject is implicit (not directly shown) :

(1) [Singular verb only] yajāmi-(I) worship.

(2) [Plural verb only] yajāma-(We) worship.

Tulyādhikaraṇe'ti kimatthaṁ?
What is the word "tulyādhikaraṇe" for? To show that in the example shown below, there is no "tulyādhikaraṇa".
Mayā-by me, ijjate-(is) worshipped, buddho-Buddha.
i.e. The Buddha is worshipped by me.

४१३, ४२७. काले

413, 427. **Kāle.** [Kāle. 1 word]

[V] "Kāle" icce'taṁ adhikāratthaṁ veditabbaṁ.

This "kāle" Sutta is to be regarded as an adhikāra Sutta. (This means that this Sutta influences next Suttas from 414 to 422, in indicating a specific time and tense of all the Ākhyāta vibattis as shown by those forthcoming Suttas.)

The Eight Modes of Ākhyāta Pāli Verbs

Note: In these Suttas from 414 to 422, (a) the eight modes and tenses of Ākhyāta Pāli Verbs, and (b) when and where they are to be applied, are briefly explained.

४१४, ४२८. वत्तमाना पच्चुप्पन्ने

414, 428. **Vattamānā paccuppanne.**

[Vattamānā+paccuppanne. 2 words]

[V] Paccuppanne kāle vattamānā vibhatti hoti.

Vattamānā vibatti (the present termination) is (used to express actions or events which occur) at the present.

(1) Pāṭaliputtaṁ-to the city of Pāṭaliputta, gaccha**ti**-(he) goes.
i.e. He goes to the city of Pāṭaliputta.

(2) sāvatthiṁ-to the city of Sāvatthi, pavisa**ti**-(he) enters.
i.e. He enters into the city of Sāvatthi.

Note: From this Sutta No.414 to 422, see bold-faced letters such as "**ti, tu**" at the end of example verbs carefully. They are called **the Ākhyāta Vibattis** or **Verb-endings** which have to be applied after the roots. [Verb-ending or verb-termination refers to Ākhyāta Vibattis]

४१५, ४५१. आणत्यासिट्ठे'नुत्तकाले पञ्चमी

415, 451. **Āṇatyā'siṭṭhe'nuttakāle pañcamī.**

[Āṇati, āsiṭṭhe+ana-uttakāle+pañcamī. 3 words]

[V] Āṇatyā'tthe ca āsīsa'tthe ca anuttakāle pañcamī vibhatti hoti.

Pañcamī vibatti (the imperative) is (used to express) āṇatti (command), āsīsa (wish) at a non-specific time-frame mode (anuttakāla).

(1) Karo**tu**-(please) do, kusalaṁ-meritorious deed.
i.e. Do meritorious deed. (**āṇatti**-command)

(2) sukhaṁ-happiness, te-for you, ho**tu**-be.

May happiness be for you, **i.e.** May you be happy. (**āsīsa**-wish, prayer)

४१६, ४५४. अनुमतिपरिकप्पत्थेसु सत्तमी

416, 454. **Anumatiparikappa'tthesu sattamī.**

[Anumati, parikappa-atthesu+sattamī. 2 words]

[V] Anumatya'tthe ca parikappa'tthe ca anuttakāle sattamī vibhatti hoti.

Sattamī vibatti (the optative) is applied (to express) anumati (permission), prikappa (thought) at a non-specific time (anuttakāla).

(1) Tvaṁ-you, gacch**eyyāsi-**should go or can go.

i.e. You should go or You can go. (**anumati**-permission)

(2) Ki'mahaṁ [Kiṁ+ahaṁ] Kiṁ-what, ahaṁ-I, kar**eyyāmi-**should do.

i.e. What I should do? (This is **parikappa**-thinking about what to do).

४१७, ४६०. अपच्चक्खे परोक्खा'तीते

417, 460. **Apaccakkhe parokkhā'tīte.**

[Apaccakkhe+parokkhā+atīte. 3 words]

[V] Apaccakkhe atīte kāle parokkhāvibhatti hoti.

Prokkhā vibatti (the past perfect) is (to be applied to express things happened in one's absence, in a situation where the speaker is not a witness to) at a past time-frame mode. (atīta-past)

(1) Supine-in the dream, kila'māh**a** [kila+āha] kila āha-(he is supposed to have) said. **i.e.** (He is supposed to have) said in the dream.

(2) Evaṁ-thus, kila porāṇā'h**u** [porāṇā+āhu] porāṇā-ancient sages, āhu-(are supposed to) have said.

i.e. Ancient sages (are supposed to) have said thus.

Note: Paro'kkhā=para-beyond, **i.e.** past+**akkha**-physical senses. **i.e.** something which had occurred without one's knowledge

+**ā**=a feminine noun affix.
"**Kila**" is Nipāta particle used in indirect hearsay where the speaker is uncertain of truthfulness of what he heard or nor a witness to the actual event occurred. Sometimes it means an asseveration or an emphasis.

४१८, ४५६. हिय्योपभुति पच्चक्खे हिय्यत्तनी

418, 456. Hiyyopabhuti paccakkhe hiyyattanī.

[Hiyyopabhuti+paccakkhe+hiyyattanī. 3 words]

[V] Hiyyopabhuti atīte kāle paccakkhe vā apaccakkhe vā hiyyattanī vibhatti hoti.

Hiyattanī vibatti (the past imperfect) is (used to express events that took place) in past time starting from yesterday, either being witnessed or not witnessed (by the speaker).

(1) So-that person, or he, agam**ā**-went, maggaṁ-to the road.
i.e. He went to the road. (Singular verb)

(2) Te-those persons, or they, agam**ū**-went (plural), maggaṁ.
i.e. They went to the road. (Plural Verb)

Note: Hiyyattanī=**hiyya**-yesterday, **i.e.** a somewhat distant past+ **ttana**-having occurred. A bhāva affix applicable by means of particle "tu" in Sutta 360 +**ī**-feminine affix.

४१९, ४६९. समीपे'ज्जतनी

419, 469. Samīpe'jjatanī. [Samīpe+ajjatanī. 2 words]

[V] Ajjappabhuti atīte kāle paccakkhe vā apaccakkhe vā samīpe ajjatanīvibhatti hoti.

Ajjattanī vibatti (the aorist) is (used to express things happened) in the near past starting from today, either being witnessed or not witnessed (by the speaker).

(1) So maggaṁ agam**ī**-went, gone.
i.e. He has (just) gone to the road.

(2) Te maggaṁ agam**uṁ**-went, gone. (plural verb)
i.e. They have (just) gone to the road.

Note: Ajjattanī=**ajja**-today, **i.e.** recent past+**ttana**-having occurred. A bhāva affix applicable by means of particle "tu" in Sutta 360 +**ī**-a feminine-gender noun affix.

४२०, ४७१. मायोगे सब्बकाले च

420, 471. **Māyoge sabbakāle ca.**

[Māyoge+sabbakāle+ca. 3 words]

[V] **Hiyyattanī, ajjatanī**-icce'tā vibhattiyo yadā māyogā, tadā sabbakāle ca honti.

When **Hiyyattanī, Ajjatanī** vibattis are used in the context of a Nipāta word "mā" (barring the action), they then assume all tenses. [**mā**-means "do not", a particle of prohibition]

(1) [Hiyyattanī] Mā-do not, gam**ā-**be gone. (Do not go)
mā-do not, vac**ā-**be said. (Do not say)

(2) [Ajjattanī] mā-do not, gam**ī-**be gone. (Do not go)
mā-do not, vac**ī-**be said. (Do not say)

Caggahaṇena pañcamīvibhatti'pi hoti.

By the word "Ca" in Sutta, pañcamī vibatti can also be applied (in the context of mā, assuming all tenses).
[Pañcamī] Mā gacchāhi. (You) (do not go).

४२१, ४७३. अनागते भविस्सन्ती

421, 473. **Anāgate bhavissanti.** [Anāgate+bhavissanti. 2 words]

[V] Anāgate kāle bhavissanti vibhatti hoti.

Bhavissanti vibatti (the future) is (to be used) in the (expression of) future.
Note: Anāgata means that which has not yet come to pass. **i.e.** future.[**anā'gata**=**na**-not+**āgata**-coming yet. **i.e.** not happening]

(1) So-that person, gacchi**ssati-**will go. kari**ssati-**will do.
i.e. He will go. He will do. (Singular verbs)

(2) Te gacchi**ssanti-**will go (plural). kari**ssanti-**will do (plural).
i.e. They will go. They will do. (Plural verbs)

४२२, ४७५. क्रियातिपन्ने'तीते कालातिपत्ति

422, 475. **Kriyā'tipanne'tīte kālā'tipatti.**

[Kriyā-atipanne+atīte+kālā'tipatti. 3 words]

[V] Kriyā'tipannamatte atīte kāle kālātipatti vibhatti hoti.

Kālātipatti vibhatti (the conditional) is (to be used) in (the expression of) an action that was past (without being materialized due to adverse conditions or lack of the supporting causes).

(1) So ce taṁ yānaṁ alabhi**ssā,** agacchi**ssā** (Singular)
[So-that person or he, ce-if, taṁ-that, yānaṁ-vehicle, alabhi**ssā**-should have got, agacchi**ssā**-(he) might have gone already.]
i.e. If he should have got that vehicle, he might have gone already. **Actually, he did not have that vehicle.** [supporting cause absent, **reason**] **and as a result, he did not go.** [action of going not materialized, the **result**]

(2) Te ce taṁ yānaṁ alabhi**ssaṁsu,** agacchi**ssaṁsu**. (Plural Verbs)
[Te-they, ce-if, taṁ-that, yānaṁ-vehicle, alabhi**ssaṁsu**-should have got, agacchi**ssaṁsu**-would have gone already.]
i.e. Had they got that vehicle, they might have gone already. **Actually, they did not get that vehicle** [supporting cause absent, **reason**] **and as a result, they did not go.** [action not materialized, the **result**]

Note: Kālā'tipatti=kāla-time+**ati**-past beyond+**patti**-to happen.
The term literally means "something timed out".

The Eight Ākhyāta Vibattis

The Pāli Ākhyāta Verb-terminations

Note: All Ākhyāta vibattis are clearly shown in **the following eight Suttas** starting from 423 to 430. **The Students should try to familiarize with these vibattis, twelve in each, by all means** if they want to learn Pāli successfully and efficiently. These are the ending-forms of Pāli verbs which need to be familiar at all times.

४२३, ४२६. वत्तमाना ती अन्ति, सि थ, मि म , ते अन्ते, से व्हे, ए म्हे

423, 426. **Vattamānā ti anti, si tha, mi ma, te ante, se vhe, e mhe.**

[Vattamānā+ti anti, si tha, mi ma, te ante, se vhe, e mhe. 2 words]

[V] **Vattamānā** icce'sā saññā hoti ti anti, si tha, mi ma, te ante, se vhe, e mhe icce'tesaṁ dvādasannaṁ padānaṁ.

"Ti anti, si tha, mi ma,
te ante, se vhe, e mhe" all these twelve are called
"**Vattamāna**"(the present).

Vattamānā icca'nena kva'ttho? Vattamānā paccuppanne.
What is the benefit by terming "vattamāna" ?
It has the benefit of making easy reference in Suttas as "Vattamānā paccuppanne" etc.

४२४, ४५०. पञ्चमी तु अन्तु, हि थ, मि म, तं अन्तं, स्सु व्हो, ए आमसे

424, 450. **Pañcamī tu antu, hi tha, mi ma, taṁ antaṁ, ssu vho, e āmase.**

[Pañcamī+tu antu, hi tha, mi ma, taṁ antaṁ, ssu vho, e āmase. 2 words]

[V] **Pañcamī**icce'sā saññā hoti tu antu, hi tha, mi ma, taṁ antaṁ, ssu vho, e āmase icce'tesaṁ dvādasannaṁ padānaṁ.

"tu antu, hi tha, mi ma,
taṁ antaṁ, ssu vho, e āmase" all these twelve are called
"**Pañcamī** (The imperative) ".

Pañcamīicca'nena kva'ttho?
Āṇatyā'siṭṭhe nuttakāle pañcamī.
What is the benefit by terming "Pañcamī"?
It has the benefit of making easy reference in Suttas as "Āṇatyāsiṭṭhe nuttakāle pañcamī" etc.

४२५, ४५३. सत्तमी एय्य एय्युं, एय्यासि एय्याथ, एय्यामि एय्याम,
एथ एरं, एथो एय्याव्हो, एय्यं एय्याम्हे

425, 453. **Sattamī eyya-eyyuṁ, eyyāsi-eyyātha, eyyāmi-eyyāma, etha-eraṁ, etho-eyyāvho, eyyaṁ-eyyāmhe.**

[Sattamī+eyya-eyyuṁ, eyyāsi-eyyā tha, eyyāmi-eyyāma, etha-eraṁ, etho-eyyāvho, eyyaṁ-eyyāmhe. 2 words]

[V] **Sattamī**iccesā saññā hoti eyya-eyyuṁ, eyyāsi-eyyātha, eyyāmi-eyyāma, etha-eraṁ, etho-eyyāvho, eyyaṁ-eyyāmhe icce'tesaṁ dvādasannaṁ padānaṁ.

"eyya-eyyuṁ, eyyāsi-eyyātha, eyyāmi-eyyāma, etha-eraṁ, etho-eyyāvho, eyyaṁ-eyyāmhe", all these twelve are called "**Sattamī** (the optative) ".

Sattamī icca'nena kva'ttho?
Anumatiparikappatthesu sattamī.
What is the benefit by terming "sattamī"?
It has the benefit of making due reference in Suttas as "Anumatiparikappatthesu sattamī" etc.

४२६, ४५९. परोक्खा अ उ, ए त्थ, अं म्ह, त्थ रे, त्थो व्हो, इं म्हे
426, 459. **Parokkhā a-u, e-ttha, aṁ-mha, ttha-re, ttho-vho, iṁ-mhe.**

[Parokkhā+a-u, e-ttha, aṁ-mha, ttha-re, ttho-vho, iṁ-mhe. 2 words]

[V] **Parokkhā**icce'sā saññā hoti a-u, e-ttha, aṁ-mha, ttha-re ttho-vho, iṁ-mhe icce'tesaṁ dvādasannaṁ padānaṁ.

"a-u, e ttha, aṁ mha,
ttha re, ttho vho, iṁ mhe", all these twelve are called "**Parokkhā** (the past imperfect) ".

Parokkhā icca'nena kva'ttho? Apaccakkhe parokkhā'tīte.
What is the benefit by terming "Parokkhā"?
It has the benefit of making easy reference in Suttas as "Apaccakkhe parokkhā'tīte" etc.

४२७, ४५५. हिय्यत्तनी आ ऊ, ओ त्थ, अं म्हा, त्थ त्थुं, से व्हं, इं म्हसे
427, 455. **Hiyyattanī ā-ū, o-ttha, aṁ-mhā, ttha-tthuṁ, se-vhaṁ, iṁ-mhase.**

[Hiyyattanī+ā-ū, o-ttha, aṁ-mhā, ttha-tthuṁ, se-vhaṁ, iṁ-mhase. 2 words]

[V] **Hiyyattanī** icce'sā saññā hoti ā-ū, o-ttha, aṁ-mhā, ttha-tthuṁ, se-vhaṁ, iṁ-mhase icce'tesaṁ dvādasannaṁ padānaṁ.

"ā-ū, o ttha, aṁ mhā,
ttha tthuṁ, se vhaṁ, iṁ mhase", all these twelve are called "**Hiyyattanī** (The past perfect) ".

Hiyyattanī icca'nena kva'ttho?
Hiyyopabhuti paccakkhe hiyyattanī.
What is the benefit by terming "hiyyattanī"?
It has the benefit of making easy reference in Suttas as "Hiyyopabhuti paccakkhe hiyyattanī " etc.

४२७, ४६८. अज्जतनी ई उं, ओत्थ, इं म्हा, आ ऊ, से व्हं, अं म्हे

428, 468. Ajjatanī ī-uṁ, o-ttha, iṁ-mhā, ā-ū, se-vhaṁ, aṁ-mhe.

[Ajjatanī+ī-uṁ, o-ttha, iṁ-mhā, ā-ū, se-vhaṁ, aṁ-mhe. 2 words]

[V] **Ajjatanī** icce'sā saññā hoti ī-uṁ, o-ttha, iṁ-mhā, ā-ū, se-vhaṁ, aṁ-mhe icce'tesaṁ dvādasannaṁ padānaṁ.

"ī uṁ, o ttha, iṁ mhā,
ā-ū, se vhaṁ, aṁ mhe", all these twelve are called "**Ajjatanī** (Aorist) ".

Ajjatanī icca'nena kva'ttho? Samīpe'jjatanī.
What is the benefit by terming " ajjattanī "?
It has the benefit of making easy reference in Suttas as "Samīpe'jjatanī" etc.

४२९, ४७२. भविस्सन्ति स्सति स्सन्ति, स्ससि स्सथ, स्सामि स्साम, स्सते स्सन्ते, स्ससे स्सव्हे, स्सं स्साम्हे

429, 472. Bhavissanti ssati-ssanti, ssasi-ssatha, ssāmi-ssāma, ssate-ssante, ssase-ssavhe, ssaṁ-ssāmhe.

[Bhavissanti+ssati-ssanti, ssasi-ssatha, ssāmi-ssāma, ssate-ssante, ssase-ssavhe, ssaṁ-ssāmhe. 2 words]

[V] **Bhavissanti** icce'sā saññā hoti ssati-ssanti, ssasi-ssatha, ssāmi-ssāma, ssate-ssante, ssase-ssavhe, ssaṁ-ssāmhe icce'tesaṁ dvādasannaṁ padānaṁ.

"ssati-ssanti, ssasi-ssatha, ssāmi-ssāma,
ssate-ssante, ssase-ssavhe, ssaṁ-ssāmhe", all these twelve are called "**Bhavissanti** (Future) ".

Bhavissanti icca'nena kva'ttho? Anāgate bhavissantī.
What is the benefit by terming "bhavissanti"?
It has the benefit of making easy reference in Suttas as "Anāgate bhavissantī" etc.

४३०, ४७४. कालातिपत्ति स्सा स्संसु, स्से स्सथ, स्सं स्साम्हा,
स्सथ स्सिंसु, स्ससे स्सव्हे, स्सं स्साम्हसे

430, 474. **Kālātipatti ssā-ssaṁsu, sse-ssatha, ssaṁ-ssāmhā, ssatha-ssiṁssu, ssase-ssavhe, ssaṁ-ssāmhase.**

[Kālātipatti+ssā-ssaṁsu, sse-ssatha, ssaṁ-ssāmhā, ssatha-siṁssu, ssase-ssavhe, ssaṁ-ssāmhase. 2 words]

[V] **Kālātipatti** icce'sā saññā hoti ssā-ssaṁsu, sse-ssatha, ssaṁ-ssāmhā, ssatha-ssiṁsu, ssase-ssavhe, ssaṁ-ssāmhase icce'tesaṁ dvādasannaṁ padānaṁ.

"ssā-ssaṁsu, sse-ssatha, ssaṁ-ssāmhā, ssatha-ssiṁsu, ssase-ssavhe, ssaṁ-ssāmhase", all these twelve are called "**Kālātipatti** (Conditional) ".

Kālātipatti icca'nena kva'ttho?
Kriyātipanne'tīte kālātipatti.
What is the benefit by terming "kālātipatti"?
It has the benefit of making easy reference in Suttas as "Kriyātipanne'tīte kālātipatti" etc.

४३१, ४५८. हिय्यत्तनी सत्तमी पञ्चमी वत्तमाना सब्बधातुकं

431, 458. **Hiyyattanī sattamī pañcamī vattamānā sabbadhātukaṁ[26].**

[Hiyyattanī, sattamī, pañcamī, vattamānā+sabbadhātukaṁ. 2 words]

[V] Hiyyattanā'dayo catasso vibhattiyo **sabbadhātuka**saññā honti.

---

[26] **Note:** By naming these four as "Sabba dhātuka vibatti", the remaining four should be conversely known as "Asabbadhātuka vibatti". So, **Parokkhā, Ajjattanī, Bhavissanti, Kālātipatti** are to be known as "**Asabba dhātuka vibatti".** The purpose of dividing into two group is to make each group of verbs a bit distinctive from each other. See Suttas 516-519 to clarify.

"**Hiyyattanī, sattamī, pañcamī, vattamāna**", all these four vibattis are called "**sabbadhātuka vibatti**".
[Hiyyattanī] Agam**ā**-(he) went. [Sattamī] gacch**eyya**-(he should) go. [pañcamī] gaccha**tu**-(Let him) go. [vattamāna] gaccha**ti**-(he) goes.

Sabbadhātuka iccanena kvattho?
Ikārāgamo asabbadhātukamhi.
What is the benefit by terming "sabbadhātuka"?
It has the benefit of making easy reference in Suttas like "Ikārāgamo asabbadhātukamhi" etc.
[**Sabba**-all+**dhātu**-roots+**ka**-related to]

Iti ākhyātakappe paṭhamo kaṇḍo.
The First Section of Ākhyāta Verb ends.

****

ĀKHYĀTA VIBATTI TABLES

The Verb-termination and three persons,
How they are to be conjugated and used according to their relevant Purisa (persons) and Numbers.

Please carefully study the two tables shown alongside in next pages to clearly understand as to (a) how each Purisa (person) is related to an individual Ākhyāta vibatti (Verb-terminations) and how they are to be used together accordingly and (b) what are the relevant three persons among various kinds of Pāli nouns.
Once the students clearly understand all the necessary basics for the correct conjugation, only then they will be able to correctly conjugate and use three Purisas with their respective relevant vibatti (verb-terminations) together in a sentence. Note that those two vibattis shown with this *mark are not widely and frequently used in the scriptures.

The Formative System of Pāli Verbs

"The Roots and Ākhyāta Verb-terminations"

How to conjugate them together to form a Pāli verb.

The roots

The students should understand the important role of the roots as they are the bases of the verbs on which verbs are built. There are three kinds of roots. They are:

(a) Single stem or one-word roots such as:

vā-to move**, yā-**to go**, pā-**to drink**, ji-**to conquer**, nī-**to carry**, su-**to flow**, bhū-**to be, etc.

(b) dual-word roots such as: **gamu-**to go**, paca-**to cook**, vada-**to speak etc.

(c) multiple-stem or three word roots such as **vāyama-**to attempt**, araha-**to deserve**, kilisa-**to torment, etc.

Note: Only the roots with a maximum of three words are found to be in use in the scriptural texts.

The Vibattis

(The Verb-terminations)

Before studying conjugation, it is necessary to understand various nature of vibattis. There are three kinds of vibattis based on their initials. They are:

(a) **consonant-initial** vibatti such as **ti, se, tu, ssati, ssā** etc.

(b) **vowel-initial vibatti** such as **anti, ante, aṁ, āmase** etc.

(c) **complete-vowel vibatti** such as **e, a, ā, ī, u, ū,** etc.

Method: For consonant-initial vibattis, just put the root before the vibatti. It is quite easy.

For the vowel-initial or complete vowels roots, delete the last component vowel of the root and only the last vowel-less consonant of the root should be attached to the vibatti by placing it before a vibatti.

The form of Verbs

There are three factors which play an integral part in shaping the form of a verb. They are:

(a) The vibatti,

(b) The component vowel of the root,

(c) The affix which is applied after the root.

Explanation

It is quite easy to understand a verb by looking at the applied Vibatti (verb-termination) if the student knows all the eight groups of Ākhyāta-Vibattis thoroughly well.

Component vowels of the root

(a) For the roots comprising only an "**a**" such as **paca-**to cook**,** **vasa**-to dwell. and **vada-**to speak**,** there is not much different in the shape of verbs as it has only one "a" in it. Therefore, it is quite easy and simple to form a verb using those roots.

(b) For the single-word roots with an "**ā**", it may retain its natural vowel sometimes. But that "ā" may sometimes change into an "āya" in most instances of verbs.

(c) For the single-word roots with an "**e**", it may keep its natural vowel sometimes. But that "e" may change into an "āya" in some instances of verbs.

(d) For the roots comprising either of "**i, ī, u, ū**" vowels in a root, regardless of being a single or a dual or a multiple word root, there used to be a slight change in the form of the verb. This happens due to a morphological process known as "**vuddhi**" and its follow-up procedure. According to this procedure, "**i, ī**" used to be changed into an "**e**". In some cases, "e" changes into an "**aya**" and even that "aya" further changes into an "**āya**" in some instances of verbs. For the roots containing "**u** or **ū**", it may change into an "**o**". In some cases, it may further change into an "**ava**". In some cases, it may still continue to change into an "**āva**".

Examples:

(1) The single-stem root with "ā"

Vā-to blow, to move. Here "ā" does not undergo any change thus retaining its natural vowel. e.g., **Vāti** (The wind blows). When this "ā" further changes into "āya", a new verb form emerges. e.g., **Vāyati** (The wind blows).

(2) The single-stem root with "i"

Ji- to win, to conquer.

Here " i" changes into "e". e.g. **Jeti** (he wins).

When this "e" further changes into "aya", a new verb form emerges. e.g., **Jayati** (he wins).

(3) The single-stem root with "ī"

Nī-to carry. Here "ī" changes into "e". e.g. **Neti** (he carries). When this "e" further changes into "aya", a new verb form emerges as **Nayati** (he carries).

(4) The single-stem root with "u"

Su-to flow.

Here "u" changes into "o". This "o" further changes into "ava" resulting in a new verb form as **Savati** (The river) flows.

Hu-to sacrifice.

Here "u" changes into "o". This "o" further changes into "ava" resulting in a new verb form as **Havati** (He) sacrifices.

(5) The single-stem root with "ū"

Hū-to be.

Here "ū" changes into "o". e.g. **Hoti** (it is).

Bhū- to be. Here "ū" changes into "o". This "o" further changes into "ava", resulting in a new verb form as **Bhavati** (It is).

(6) The single-word root with "e"

For the single-word roots with an "e", it usually changes into an "āya" in most instances.

Example: **Ge**-to sing. e.g. **Gāyati** (He) sings.

Jhe-to burn, to contemplate. e.g. **Jhāyati** (The fire) burns or (he) contemplates.

The Affix and its impact
on the verb forms

When an affix such as a **Kārita (causative affix) or other affix** is applied after the root in a verb, it can usually affect the vuddhi process and some subsequent follow-up morphological procedures occur. Examples:

Lū-to cut,

Base structure: lū+ṇe+ti

(with causative affix ṇe & ti. "ṇ" is deleted leaving only "e">lū+e+ti)

Here "ū" changes into "o" as a "vuddhi" procedure. This "o" further changes into an "āva"> lāv+e+ti, resulting in a new verb form as **Lāveti** (It causes to cut)

Nī- to carry. **Base structure:** nī+ṇe+ti

Here "ī" changes into "e" as a "vuddhi" procedure. This "e" further changes into an "āya", resulting in a new verb form as **Nāyeti** (It causes to carry).

The Conjugation of Dual-word Roots

Of the three roots mentioned above, conjugation of the dual-word roots is quite simple and easy for beginners to understand. Study the following example of the root "**gamu**-to go". Note that the last component vowel "u" is to be elided as per Sutta No.521 thus having the root-form as "gam" and consonant "**m**" of the root changes into "**cch**" as per Sutta 476. So, the steps of change for this root is=**gamu**>gam>gacch. See below.

Example: **gamu>gam>gacch**-to go

(a) Now, let's attach this root to consonant-initial vibattis "**ti, si** and **tha**". It is quite easy as there is nothing complex to do except to conjugate everything together.

Gacch+a+ti= Gacchati (He) goes.

Gacch+a+si=Gacchasi (You) go.

Gacch+a+tha=Gacchatha (You, plural) go.

Note: An affix "a" is applied as per Sutta 445. When conjugating with vibattis like **mi, ma** and **mhe,** follow the rule

prescribed in Sutta No.478. The rule stipulates that the front vowel in front of **mi, ma** and **mhe** must be lengthened.
So, it will look like "Gacchā".
Now, let's attach this morphed root-structure to "mi" "ma" and "mhe".
Gacchā+mi= Gacchāmi. (I) go.
Gacchā+ma= Gacchāma. (we) go.
Gacchā+mhe= Gacchāmhe. (we) go.

(b) Let's attach this "gacch" to vowel-initial vibattis "**anti, ante, aṁ** and **āmase**". Don't forget to remove the affix vowel "a" because one consonant can be combined to one vowels only, not to two vowels. So, we have to delete it before combining. Look at examples below carefully.
Gacch+anti=Gacchanti (They) go.
Gacch+ante=Gacchante (They) go.
Gacch+aṁ=Gacchaṁ (I) went.
Gacch+āmase=Gacchāmase (We must) go.

(c) Now, again, let's attach this same thing to complete-vowel vibattis "**e, a, ā, ī, u** and **ū**". Remember that the same rule of removing the last component vowel applies. Also keep in mind that as per the rule set forth in Sutta No.519, there should be an **"a"** in the front of verbs applied with **ā, ī, ū,** vibattis. There can also be verbs without "a" as the rule is optional, not a consistent injunction.
So, there will be two example of the verbs.
Gacch+e=Gacche. (I) go.
Gacch+a=Gaccha, (he) have gone.
Gacch+ā=Agacchā, gacchā. (he) has gone.
Gacch+ī=Agacchī, gacchī, (he) had gone.
Gacch+ī=Agacchi, gacchi, (he) had gone. (When "ī" is shortened as "i")
Gacch+u=Gacchu. (they) have gone.
Gacch+ū=Agacchū, gacchū. (They) have gone.

SAMPLE COMBINATION OF THE ROOTS WITH ĀKHYĀTA VIBATTIS

The following is a completely detailed form of various verbs conjugated with all eight Ākhyāta vibattis. The sample verbs of each Vibatti will be shown here so that the students will be able to try conjugating other roots with all of the eight vibattis easily. All the vibattis, except Parokkhā, Hiyyattanī and Ajjattanī, are quite easy to conjugate with any root. However, **it may be a challenge for the student to conjugate verbs using Parokkhā, Hiyyattanī and Ajjattanī vibattis.** But, with determination and practice, the student will find it a bit easy later on. Please note that the Verbs shown with this *mark are **irregular-verbs** different from their original vibatti forms. Please see the explanations carefully so that students will not be confused with the irregular verb forms. It is recommended that any serious student who wants to learn and master the Pāli efficiently should study these sample verb-forms repeatedly until they become quite familiar with all verb forms.

Note: The verb-forms shown below are **plain verbs in the active voice mode** which are easier for the beginners. For the **Passive voice verb forms** and **causative verb forms,** only a few samples will be shown. All detailed treatment of this subject are dealt with in a separate book.

THE PLAIN VERBS
(Active Voice)
Vattamāna Vibatti

(Present Indicative)

Root: Gamu-to go. The "**m**" of the root changes into "**ccha**" (Re Sutta 476).

[Parassa-pada]

(ti) Gacchati, *Gacche **(anti)** Gacchanti, *Gacchare

("anti" changes into "**re**" sometimes)

(si) Gacchasi **(tha)** Gacchatha.

(mi) Gacchāmi, *Gacche. ("ti, mi" sometimes changes into "**e**")
(ma) Gacchāma.

[Attano pada]

(te) Gacchate. **(ante)** Gacchante, *Gacchare. ("ante" sometimes change into "**re**")
(se) Gacchase. (**vhe)** Gacchavhe.
(e) Gacche. **(mhe)** Gacchāmhe.

Note: Please note carefully that there is a dīgha "ā" in "mi, ma and mhe" vibatti verbs as per injunction of Sutta No.478.

Pañcamī Vibatti (Imperative)

[Parassapada]

(tu) Gacchatu, *Gacche. **(antu)** Gacchantu.
(hi) Gacchāhi, *Gaccha ("hi" elided), *Gacchassu.
(tha) Gacchatha,
(mi) Gacchāmi, *Gacche. ("tu, mi" sometimes changes into "**e**").
(ma) Gacchāma.

[Attanopada]

(taṁ) Gacchataṁ. **(antaṁ)** Gacchantaṁ.
(ssu) Gacchassu. **(vho)** Gacchavho.
(e) Gacche. **(āmase)** Gacchāmase.

Note: Please note carefully that there are three examples in "hi-vibatti", one without "hi" (Re: Sutta 479), the other with a "hi" and another with "ssu" function (Re: Sutta 571). Also note a dīgha in "mi, ma-vibatti" verbs.

Sattamī Vibatti (Optative)

[Parassapada]

(eyya) Gaccheyya, *Gacche. **(eyyuṁ)** Gaccheyyuṁ.
(eyyāsi) Gaccheyyāsi, *Gacche. **(eyyātha)** Gaccheyyātha.
(eyyāmi) Gaccheyyāmi, *Gacche. **(eyyāma)** Gaccheyyāma.

[Attanopada]

(etha) Gacchetha. (**eraṁ)** Gaccheraṁ.
(etho) Gacchetho. **(eyyāvho)** Gaccheyyāvho.
(eyyaṁ) Gaccheyyaṁ, *Gacche.
(eyyāmhe) Gaccheyyāmhe.

Note: Note the irregular verb form "**e**" in "**eyya, eyyāsi, eyyāmi, eyyaṁ**" **vibattis** as these sometimes changes into "e" in the canonical Pāli texts.

Parokkhā Vibatti (Past Perfect)

[Parassapada]

(a) Jagama, jagāma. **(u)** Jagamu.
(e) Jagame. **(ttha)** Jagamittha.
(aṁ) Jagamaṁ. **(amha)** Jagamimha.

[Attanopada]

(ttha) Jagam**i**ttha. **(re)** Jagam**i**re.
(ttho) Jagam**i**ttho. **(vho)** Jagam**i**vho.
(iṁ) Jagamiṁ. **(mhe)** Jagam**i**mhe.
Note: In this Vibatti group, there is some reduplication of the initial word of root as per Sutta 458. See "ja" as the effect of this function. Also, in the Parokkhā, Ajjattanī, Bhavissanti, Kālātipatti vibattis, there is an "**i**" behind the root of some verbs as per Sutta No.516. To clarify this, see the verbs in **ttha, re, ttho, vho, mhe** vibattis where an "**i**" is shown in bold. [See Sutta 467 "Kavaggassa cavaggo", Rūpasiddhi Pāli grammar text].

Hiyyattanī Vibatti (Imperfect)

[Parassapada]

(ā) Agacchā-Gacchā, *Agaccha-Gaccha. ("ā" shortened)
(ū) Agacchū-Gacchū, *Agacchu-Gacchu. ("ū" shortened),
(o) Agaccho-Gaccho, *Agaccha-Gaccha. *Agacchi-Gacchi,
(ttha) Agacchattha Gacchattha, *Agacchatha, Gacchatha.
(aṁ) Agacchaṁ-Gacchaṁ.
(mhā) Agacchamhā-Gacchamhā.

[Attanopada]

(ttha) Agacchattha-Gacchattha,
(tthuṁ) Agacchatthuṁ-Gacchatthuṁ.
(se) Agacchase-Gacchase. **(vhaṁ)** Agacchavhaṁ-Gacchavhaṁ.
(iṁ) Agacchiṁ-Gacchiṁ.
(mhase) Agacchamhase-Gacchamhase.

Note: Please carefully note that there are two types of verbs in each vibatti, one with an "a" in front and the other without it. It is as per the rule set forth in Sutta No.519, but is not a consistent pattern. Also note carefully that in "**o**-vibatti" verb, there are extra two pairs of verbs: **Agaccha-Gaccha, Agacchi-Gacchi** which is seen frequently in the Pāli texts. The vibatti "o" changes into "a" or "i" sometimes. It is **quite rare to see verbs in the original structure of "o" vibatti in the scriptures.** Instead, it is seen in changed state of **"a" or "i".** Regarding this, there is a grammatical rule in Moggālaṇa Vyākaraṇa which specifically stipulated that the "o" changes into either **"a" or "i" or "ttha" or "ttho"** by a procedure of Sutta named **"Ossa a, i, ttha, ttho".** Also in Rūpasiddhi, a very well-known, highly respected grammar, it is said: **"Kvacidhātūti ādina Okarassa A-ādeso vā".** It means that by applying the function of "Kvaci dhātu" Sutta (No.517), "**o**-vibatti" changes into an "**a**" in some instances. Although two pairs of extra examples are shown, all the examples can be found in the scriptures.

Ajjattanī Vibatti (Aorist)

[Parassapada]

(ī) Agacchī-Gacchī, *Agacchi-Gacchi.
("ī" is shortened in this second pair of verbs),
(uṁ) Agacchuṁ-Gacchuṁ, *Agacchiṁsu-Gacchiṁsu.
("uṁ" changed into "iṁsu" in this pair of verbs. Re: Sutta 504)
(o) Agaccho-Gaccho, *Agaccha-Gaccha, *Agacchi-Gacchi.
(See foregoing notes for explanation regarding irregular verb forms different from the original verb-form)
(ttha) Agacch**i**ttha-Gacch**i**ttha.
(iṁ) Agacchiṁ-Gacchiṁ. **(mhā)** Agacch**i**mhā-Gacch**i**mhā.
*Agacchimha-Gacchimha. ("ā" of mhā is shortened)

[Attanopada]

(ā) Agacchā-Gacchā, *Agacchittha-Gacchittha.
("ā" changed into "ttha" in this pair of verbs)
(ū) Agacchū-Gacchū. **(se)** Agacch**i**se-Gacch**i**se.
(vhaṁ) Agacch**i**vhaṁ-Gacch**i**vhaṁ.
(aṁ) Agacchaṁ-Gacchaṁ, *Agaccha-Gaccha.
("aṁ" changed into "a" in this pair of verbs).
(mhe) Agacch**i**mhe-Gacch**i**mhe.

Note: Please note that there is an "i" after the root of some verbs in **ttha, mhā, se, vhaṁ, mhe** vibatti-terminations as per the rule of Sutta No.516.

Bhavissanti Vibatti (Future)

[Parassapada]

(ssati) Gacchissati. **(ssanti)** Gacchissanti, *Gacchissare.

(ssasi) Gacchissasi. **(ssatha)** Gacchissatha.

(ssāmi) Gacchissāmi. **(ssāma)** Gacchissāma.

[Attanopada]

(ssate) Gacchissate. **(ssante)** Gacchissante, *Gacchissare. **(ssa-se)** Gacchissase. (**ssavhe)** Gacchissavhe.

(ssaṁ) Gacchissaṁ. **(ssāmhe)** Gacchissāmhe.

Note: There is an "i" added after the root of all verbs in all Bhavissanti vibatti-terminations as per the rule of Sutta No.516.

Kālātipatti Vibatti (Conditional)

[Parassapada]

(ssā) Agacchissā-Gacchissā, *Agacchissa-Gacchissa.
("ā" is shortened in this second pair of verbs),

(ssaṁsu) Agacchissaṁsu-Gacchissaṁsu.

(sse) Agacchisse-Gacchisse, Agacchissa-Gacchissa. (The "e" of "sse" is changed into "a" in this second pair of verb-forms by Sutta 517),

(ssatha) Agacchissatha-Gacchissatha.

(ssaṁ) Agacchissaṁ-Gacchissaṁ.

(ssāmhā) Agacchissāmhā-Gacchissāmhā.
*Agacchissāmha-Gacchissāmha ("ā" is shortened in this pair)

[Attanopada]

(ssatha) Agacchissatha-Gacchissatha.

(ssiṁsu) Agacchissiṁsu-Gacchissiṁsu.

(ssase) Gacchissase-Gacchissase.

(ssavhe) Agacchissavhe-Gacchissavhe.

(ssaṁ) Agacchissaṁ-Gacchissaṁ.

(ssāmhase) Agacchissāmhase-Gacchissāmhase.

Note: In the Kālātipatti vibattis, there is an "i" behind the root of all verbs as per rule of Sutta No.516.

THE PLAIN VERBS
(Passive Voice)
Vattamāna Vibatti

To build passive voice verb-forms, students should understand two mainly important things. They are:

(1) The passive voice verb forms are mainly Kamma-specific in nature. As such, they have to be in Kamma-specific vibattis. This means that no other vibattis, except Kamma-specific **six Attanopada-vibattis** only can be used in the passive voice.

(2) Next, those verbs are to be affixed with **Kamma-specific affixes only**. This means that no other affixes can be used in the passive voice structure.

The Kamma-specific Vibatti and affixes

Out of twelve Verb-terminations in each of eight Ākhyāta vibattis, **only six Attanopada have Kamma** (passive) **and bhāva** (Impersonal) **voices.** (Refer to Sutta 453)
However, they may be Kattu-specific sometimes. (See Sutta 454).
As for Kamma-specific affixes, only one "ya" affix applied by Sutta 440 is eligible to be used in the passive voice structure of Ākhyāta verbs. This basic rule is quite easy to understand and apply in the sentence structure. Therefore, Pāli is quite simple to learn.

The Practical Method

Method:
(1) Begin with six attnopada Vattamāna Vibattis.
(2) Use only "**ya**" affix.
Please note that **the verbs affixed with "ya" have some distinctive forms** which may be a bit challenging for the beginners. Therefore, **only more simple structure** and easy to build verb-form **will be shown** here.

The formula of passive voice form is: (Try to remember)
Root+**i** or **ī** +**ya**+relevant attanopada vibatti. (4 parts)
Now, Let's start building verbs in Passive voice:

Root: Paca=to cook.
Affix: ya

Attanopada-termination
Kamma-specific

(te) Pacīyate. **(ante)** Pacīyante, *Pacīyare.
(se) Pacīyase. **(vhe)** Pacīyavhe. **(e)** Pacīye. **(mhe)** Pacīyāmhe.

Parassapada-termination (Reversed)

Now, Let's try building the Passive Voice verb-forms using "the Parassapada vibattis". This is made possible by Sutta 518. Please remember that these "parassapada" are actually "attanopada vibattis" being reversed to look like "parassapada", not the original ones. Therefore, the voice will still remain Kamma-specific (**i.e.** passive voice) though.
Also please know that the actual "Parassapada vibattis" never signify the sense of Kamma in any way. **They have only one voice of Kattu (active voice).** Therefore, they are always to be used in the active voice only. This is an important grammatical rule to be remembered.

Sample Passive Voice Verb
in the reversed Parassapada-termination

(ti) Pacīyati. *Pacīye. **(anti)** Pacīyanti,*Pacīyare.
(si) Pacīyasi. **(tha)** Pacīyatha.
(mi) Pacīyāmi, *Pacīye. ("ti, mi" sometimes changes into "e")
(ma) Pacīyāma.

****

CAUSATIVE VERBS

Like the plain verbs, there are two types of causative verbs. They are:

(a) Causative verb in the active voice

(b) Causative verb in the passive voice.

To be able to build causative Verbs and to understand them well, the students need to understand two things which are fundamental to the core structural pattern of a causative verb. They are:

(1) the causative affixes.

(2) Subsequent Vuddhi procedures resulting from causative affix. [This needs much study and practice].

Method
Causative Verb in the Active Voice

It will be explained here in a way as simple as possible for the students. First, there are four causative affixes which are mainly used in the causative verbs. They are "**ṇe, ṇaya, ṇāpe** and **ṇāpaya**". Please refer to **Sutta 438**. It is also important to understand that "**ṇ**" has to be removed from all the causative affixes as per **Sutta 523.** There will remain only "**e, aya, āpe, āpaya**". One of these affixes will be used in the sample causative verbs. Regarding the Vuddhi procedure, refer to **Sutta 483.** It may at first seems like a big challenge for a beginner. But, it is not that much difficult if simple guidelines are understood. The Vuddhi procedure usually occurs in the initial vowel of the root if that is a two-stem root. As an exception, there are some roots such as **jīva**-to live, **katha**-to speak, **kilamu**-to be weary, which never undergo a Vuddhi procedure in a causative or even in the plain verb forms.

Now, Here is the formula of causative verb to remember:

The root with an initial vowel being in a Vuddhi+**one of the four causative affixes**+relevant **Vibatti.** (3 integral parts)

Now, Let's work out that formula here:

The root: **Paca**-to cook.

See the table below. All the complex structural patterns of causative verbs are shown in the table in a very simple way.
[(1) Vuddhi procedure in the initial vowel of the root **"a"** as **"ā"**, (2) the last component vowel of the root deleted, (3) the component consonant "ṇ" of affix elided. Three important procedures]

Base Structure	After three Procedures	The completed verb
Paca+ṇe+ti>	Pāc+e+ti>	Pāc+e+ti. (He) causes to cook
Paca+ṇaya+ti>	Pāc+aya+ti>	Pāc+aya+ti.
Paca+ṇāpe+ti>	Pāc+āpe+ti>	Pāc+āpe+ti.
Paca+ṇāpaya+ti>	Pāc+āpaya+ti>	Pāc+āpaya+ti.

Sample Causative Verb in the Active Voice [Parassapada]

Now, Let's start building causative verbs in the active voice:
Root: Paca=to cook.
(1st) **Affix:** "ṇe"
(ti) Pāceti. **(anti)** Pācenti.
(si) Pācesi. **(tha)** Pācetha.
(mi) Pācemi. **(ma)** Pācema. [No dīgha procedure in "mi & ma"]
(2nd) **Affix:** "ṇaya"
(ti) Pācayati. **(anti)** Pācayanti.
(si) Pācayasi. **(tha)** Pācayatha.
(mi) Pācayāmi. **(ma)** Pācayāma.[Dīgha procedure in "mi & ma"]
Note: In verbs with 3rd and 4th affixes, there can be some verb forms with no Vuddhi function occurred on the initial vowel. So, two examples of verb forms are shown below.
(3rd) **Affix:** "ṇāpe"
(ti) Pācāpeti, pacāpeti. **(anti)** Pācāpenti, pacāpenti.
(si) Pācāpesi, pacāpesi. **(tha)** Pācāpetha, pacāpetha.
(mi) Pācāpemi, pacāpemi. **(ma)** Pācāpema, pacāpema.
[No dīgha procedure in "mi & ma"]

(4th) **Affix:** "ṇāpaya"
(ti) Pācāpayati, pacāpayati. **(anti)** Pācāpayanti, pacāpayanti.

(si) Pācāpayasi, pacāpayasi.**(tha)** Pācāpayatha, pacāpayatha.
(mi) Pācāpayāmi, pacāpayāmi.
(ma) Pācāpayāma, pacāpayāma.[Dīgha procedure in "mi & ma"]
Note: Please note that verbs in "ṇe and ṇāpe" affixes are slightly similar to each other while verbs in "ṇaya and ṇāpaya" affixes share some similar morphological traits.

Causative Verb in the Passive Voice

This too may be a bit challenging. But remember that it is very much similar to the plain verbs in respect of the passive voice structural pattern. It only **needs to insert one more affix "ya" signifying the Kamma (passive voice).** Here is one thing to be mindful that not all causative affixes are used in the passive voice structure. Only a few causative affixes, mostly "ṇe" and "ṇāpe" are found to be used in the Pāli literature. This does not mean that the remaining ones are not used at all. There could be some instances of usage. Please note that <u>in the passive voice causative verbs, there used to be two or sometimes even three affixes</u> though some traces of the causative affixes are not easily noticeable.

Here is the formula to remember: **the root** with an initial vowel being a vuddhi+**e** or **āpe**+**i** or **ī**+**ya**+the relevant **Vibatti.**
(5 integral parts)

Now, Let's practically work out that formula here:
The root: Paca-to cook
Affix: ṇe or ṇāpe+ya.
Assume that all three basic procedures have already been done. So, it will be:
(a) Pāca+e+i+ya+ti > Pāciyati.[The trace of causative affix unnoticeable in this verb with the **"ṇe"** affix, as its residual vowel "e" is already absent except a Vuddhi vowel "ā" representing it]
(b) Pāca+āpe+ya+ti >Pācāpiyati. [The trace of causative affix is slightly noticeable in this verb with the **"ṇāpe"** affix]

Verbs with Affix: "ṇe"

(ti) Pāciyati. **(anti)** Pāciyanti.

(si) Pāciyasi. **(tha)** Pāciyatha.

(mi) Pāciyāmi. **(ma)** Pāciyāma.[Dīgha procedure in "mi & ma"]

Verbs with affix: "ṇāpe"

(ti) Pācāpiyati. **(anti)** Pācāpiyanti.

(si) Pācāpiyasi. **(tha)** Pācāpiyatha.

(mi) Pācāpiyāmi. **(ma)** Pācāpiyāma. [Dīgha procedure in "mi & ma"]

Note: These samples are to orient the student with the basic causative verb forms. It is important to study and familiarize with these sample verb forms as explained here.

****

THE BASIC PĀLI SENTENCE STRUCTURE

Based on conjugation of the verbs and various verb-forms which have been explained thus far in some detail, some basic sentence structure and the relevant rules will be explained here for the benefit of all serious students of the Pāli grammar. There are, as a matter of the grammatical fact stated in Suttas, three voices in the Pāli grammar. They are:
(a) the active voice (Kattu),
(b) the passive voice (Kamma) and
(c) the impersonal voice (bhāva).

Of the three, bhāva voice is rarely used in the actual usage of Pāli texts and a wider area of the Pāli literature except in the etymological definition of words in the Pāli grammar and some instances of the commentary and subcommentary texts where some detailed and delicate explanation is necessary regarding a word or a phrase. Even in this Kaccāyana's grammar, especially in Kita and Uṇādi chapters, bhāva voice known as Bhāva Sādhana is widely applied to explain some etymological definition of the example words using either an Ākhyāta verb or a Kita verb of bhāva sense and voice. Only active and passive voices are used in the majority of written Pāli texts. Therefore, fundamental rules and the writing-method of these two voices only will be explained.

The Rules of Active Voice Sentence

An active voice sentence is called in grammatical parlance as "Kattu-vācaka Vākya" which means the subject-principal sentence where Kattā (the agent, doer subject) is much more dominant. Such a subject is called "Kathita Kattā" or "Vutta-kattā" which means a predominant-subject. The object (Kamma) in such a sentence plays a secondary role. Hence it is called an "Akathita-kamma" or "Avutta-kamma" which means a non-principal object.

Here are the rules of an active voice sentence:

In an active voice sentence,

(1) The subject must be in the nominative case.

(2) The object has to be in the accusative case.

(3) The verb must be either in the parassapada-termination in most cases or in the attnopada-termination with or without an affix of Kattu-sense.

[But affixes of Kamma sense such as **ya**, **tabba**, **ta**, etc. are absolutely inapplicable.] (Tabba & Ta are ***Kita*** affixes not to be used with ākhyāta verbs)

(4) The persons (subjects) and verbs should be concordant.

Note: The rule numbers 3 and 4, are not required when writing active voice sentences using ***Kita*** verbs and ***kita*** affixes of Kattu-sense or past perfect such as "**ta**". (Refer to Sutta 555, 557).

Formula:

Subject+**O**bject+**V**erb [S+V+O is possible and permissible although majority style is S+O+V]

Now, let us study the sample sentences shown in the table.

SAMPLE ACTIVE VOICE SENTENCE

Subject (nominative)	**Object** (accusative)	**Verb** (in kattu-affix "a")	**Meaning**
Puriso	Odanaṁ	Pacati	Man, the rice, cooks. (Man cooks the rice).
Purisā	Odanaṁ	Pacanti	Men, the rice, cook. (Men cook the rice).
Buddho	Dhammaṁ	Deseti Disa-to teach.	Buddha, the Dhamma, teaches. (Buddha teaches the Dhamma).
Buddhā	Dhammaṁ	Desenti	Buddhas, the Dhamma, teach. (Buddhas teach the Dhamma).
Tvaṁ	Odanaṁ	Pacasi	You, cook, the rice.
Tumhe	Odanaṁ	Pacatha	You (plural) cook the rice.
Ahaṁ	Odanaṁ	Pacāmi	I cook the rice.
Mayaṁ	Odanaṁ	Pacāma	We cook the rice.

Please note that all the relevant subject (person), verbs and their numbers are to be in perfect agreement.

The Rules of Passive Voice Sentence

A passive voice sentence is called in grammatical parlance as "Kamma-vācaka Vākya" which means the object-principal sentence where the Kamma (the thing being done, the object) is more visibly dominant by being in the nominative case. Such an object is called "Kathita Kamma" or "Vutta-kamma" which means the predominant-object. The subject (Kattā) in such a sentence is called an "Akathita-kattā" or an "Avutta-kattā" which means the non-principal subject.

The rules in a passive voice sentence are:

(1) The subject has to be in the instrumental case.

(2) The object has to be in the nominative case.

(3) The verb should be mainly in the attnopada-termination or it can be in a reversed Parassapada form with an affix which has a Kamma-sense only.
[Refer to the verb and verb-forms shown in Suttas 440, 441 442 and 443. The easiest verb-form to use is the type of verb affixed with a "**ya**" preceded by either an "**i** or **ī**".]

(4) The obbject (not the Subject!) and verb should be in agreement.

Note: The rule number four is a major distinction of Sanskrit and Pāli passive voice sentences which is different from other grammars of modern languages such as English.
In Sanskrit and Pāli grammar, the Subject is dominant in the active voice. In the passive voice sentence, the object is dominant. So, the verb has to follow them accordingly.
In English grammar, the Subject is more emphasized in both active and passive voices. Therefore, the Subject and verb are to be in perfect agreement with each other in both voices.

SAMPLE PASSIVE VOICE SENTENCE

Subject (instrumental)	**Object** (nominative)	**Verb** (Kamma-affix "**ya**" and "ī")	**Meaning**
Purisena	Odano	Pacīyate	By man, the rice, is cooked (The rice is cooked by man)
Purisehi	Odano	Pacīyante	By men, the rice, is cooked (The rice is cooked by men)
Buddhena	Dhammo	Desīyate	By Buddha, the Dhamma, is taught (The Dhamma is taught by Buddha)
Buddhehi	Dhammo	Desīyante	By Buddhas, the Dhamma, is taught (The Dhamma is taught by Buddhas)
Rājena	tvaṁ	Dīyase	By king, you are given
Rājūhi	tumhe	Dīyavhe	By king, you are given
Raññā	ahaṁ	Dīye	By king, I am given
Rājūhi	mayaṁ	Dīyāmhe	By kings, we are given

****

THE IMPERSONAL VOICE

Q: What does an **impersonal voice (Bhāva) sentence** looks like in terms of the sentence structure?

A: It is much more like a passive voice sentence in the structural pattern except that **it conveys a bhāva sense of expressing just mere action**. Neither the doer (subject) nor the thing being done (Kamma) is in fact implied as a principal focus or the subject matter of the sentence.

The Applicable Person and Number

According to the most Venerable Buddhapiyācariya, the great grammarian of Rūpasiddhi Vyākaraṇa Pāli grammar, it is said that in a Bhāva (impersonal voice) sentence, **only the paṭhama Purisa (third person), singular** number is applicable. No other (purisa) persons are applicable because **Bhāva itself singularly**

signifies just mere action, not any materiality nor the physical tangibility of any sort as implied by the relevant roots of the verb.

Re: Ākhyāta chapter, Rūpasiddhi Vyākaraṇa, Pāli grammar, in Sutta **No. 446,** (Attanopadāni parassapadattaṁ) which said:

"Bhāve Adabbavuttino Bhāvass'ekattā Ekavacana'meva. Tañ'ca Paṭhamapurisasse'va" .

THE SAMPLE SENTENCES OF IMPERSONAL VOICE

(1) Devadattena (Devadatta, the subject) Būyate. [**Bū**-to be] (by Devadatta, became. **i.e.** Devadatta's being)

(2) Pabbatena (the mountain, the subject) ṭṭhīyate. [**ṭhā**-to stand] (by the mountain, standing, **i.e.** The mountain's standing)

(3) Purisena (by man, the subject) kathīyate. [**katha**-to speak] (by the man, said. **i.e.** The man speaks, or man's speaking)

Note: Please note that strictly there is no applicable Kamma word (the object) in an impersonal voice sentence though it can not be ruled out the likely presence of a Kamma word in a verb with sakammaka roots(transitive verb) of a Bhāva structure.

Sometimes, **genitive case is also found to be employed in place of a subject** in some Pāli writings although it is not a consistent pattern.

Re: Kaccāyana Vyākaraṇa, Sutta No. 556: "Bhāve tāva, Tassa Gītaṁ" etc. Here genitive case is used in the context of a ***Kita*** verb to signify a Bhāva voice and most possibly "the mere action".

****

SAMPLE CAUSATIVE SENTENCE

There are **four integral parts** in a causative sentence. They are:

(1) Causative subject (grammatically known as Hetu-kattā, or Payojaka-kattā, the prompter or the mover, abbreviated as CS)

(2) Subordinate Object (also called Kārita-kamma, causative object, CO)

(3) The root-object (also called Dhātu-kamma, the object of the root which has direct connection to the root in terms of having direct relationship with the meaning of the root, RO),

(4) The causative verb, CV.

Note that there used to be two objects in an ordinary causative sentence although sometimes there may be some more additional objects depending on nature of the root. For example, if the root is a dual-kamma-indicative root(dvikammaka) such as **Nī**-to carry, **Duha**-to milk, then there can be three objects.

Now, here is a sample of a normal causative sentence:

Causative Subject (nominative)	**Subordinate Object** (accusative)	**The root-object** (accusative)	**Causative Verb** (one causative affix	**Meaning**
Puriso (cs) the man	Purisaṁ (co) to the other man	Odanaṁ (ro) the rice	Pāceti (cv) causes to cook	Man causes the other man to cook the rice.
Purisā (cs) the men	Purise (co) to the other men	Odanaṁ (ro) the rice	Pācenti (cv) cause to cook	Men cause the other men to cook the rice.

This is a very simple causative sentence which is quite easy to understand. It is hoped that all the explanation given regarding the verbs and basic types of Pāli sentence structures thus far is sufficient for all keen students at this point to make the study of the next sections of the Pāli grammar much more easier and understandable for them.

EXERCISES

By studying the example of verbs shown in all of Ākhyāta vibattis along with sample active and passive voice sentences, it is hoped that the students will be able to do some practical drills by themselves using the following roots.

(a) Now, please try conjugating one of the roots with any two or more Vibatti of your choice:

(1) **Paca**-to cook. (2) **Vasa**-to dwell, to live. (3) **Vada**-to speak.
(4) **Labha**-to get, to obtain. (5) **Sara**-to remember.

(b) Please translate the following sentences and determine the voice of each sentence and the kind of possible sentence correctly.

(1) Buddho Vihāraṁ (the temple) Gacchati.
(2) Buddhā Vihāraṁ (the temple) Gacchanti.
(3) Puriso Gāmaṁ (the village) Gacchati.
(4) Purisā Gāmaṁ (the village) Gacchanti.
(5) Purisena Gāmo (the village) Gacchiyate.
(6) Purisehi Dhammo cariyante. (the root "**cara**-to practice")
(7) Puriso Dhanaṁ (wealth) Labhati. (the root "**labha**-to get")
(8) Upāsako (the devotee) Saggaṁ (Heaven) Gacchati.
(9) * Puriso purisaṁ Gāmaṁ Gacchāpeti.
[Please also determine the type of sentence after translating this]
(10) * Purisā purise Gāmaṁ Gacchāpenti.
[Please also determine the type of sentence after translating]

Dutiya Kaṇḍa

The Second Section

४३२, ३६२. धातुलिङ्गेहि परा पच्चया

432, 362. **Dhātuliṅgehi parā paccayā**[27].

[Dhātuliṅgehi+parā+paccayā. 3 words]

[V] **Dhātu, liṅga**-icce'tehi parā **paccayā** honti.

"**paccaya**-the affixes" are to be applied after "**Dhātu** (roots) and **liṅga** (words of the specific gender) ".

Summary: This Sutta enjoins to apply "paccaya":

(a) after the "**Dhātu**-roots" in the case of verbs and kita-nouns structured with roots.

(b) after "**liṅga**-gender-specific words" in the case of various kinds of nouns such as plain common nouns, Sabbanāma Nouns, Samāsa nouns, Taddhita nouns and Kita nouns.

What are the "**Paccayas**"?

Vibattis and various *taddhita, ākhyāta* and *kita* **affixes** are called "paccaya".

Here is how to apply each relevant "paccaya":

(a) First, **noun-vibattis** (noun case-endings) such as **paṭhamā** (Nominative case) etc. are to be applied after gender-specific nouns (Samāsa, Taddhita and Kita words are also included as they are classified as nouns).

---

[27]"paccaya" means those through which any specific meaning of the words are known. It refers to the affixes and vibattis applied after the roots of the verbs and gender-specific nouns (*liṅga* does not mean mere gender). Note that Ākhyāta affixes, Ākhyāta vibattis and kita affixes are to be applied after the roots while noun vibattis (refer to Sutta No. 55) are to be applied after the crude-nouns. This Sutta enjoins one preliminary procedure in carrying out basic morphological process of the Pāli words.

[Reference text] *Patīyanti anena atthā'ti vā paccayo* (Rūpasiddhi, Sutta 362)

(b) Ākhyāta Vibattis such as "**ti, anti**" and so forth, together with various **Ākhyāta affixes** are to be applied after the roots of Ākhyāta verbs.

(c) Kita affixes and **noun-Vibattis** are to be applied after the Kita-nouns.

(d) Those **Taddhita-affixes** and **noun-Vibattis** are to be applied after Taddhita-nouns according to their respective meanings as prescribed in the relevant Taddhita Suttas.

Ākhyāta Verb Examples cited in Sutta

(1) [Plain Verb] • Karoti-(he) does. • gacchati-(he) goes.

(2) [Causative Verb] Yo koci-whoever. karoti-does (an action), taṁ-to that person. añño-the other person. "karohi-do! karohi-do!" icce'vaṁ-as such. bravīti-says. **i.e.** Suppose someone is doing something. Then someone come and says "do it, do it". This act of prompting is called a causative motive **(Payojaka vyāpāra)** which is expressed by such verbs as "**Kāreti, Kārenti**" etc. atha vā-in other words, karontaṁ-(while one is) doing (something), payojayati-prompts. This act of prompting or urging results in such a causative verb as: • kāreti-(he) causes to do.

(3) [Nominal Verb] (a) Saṅgho-the Sangha, monks, pabbata'miva [**pabbataṁ**-mountain+**iva**-like] pabbataṁ iva-like mountain, attāna'mācarati [**attānaṁ**-oneself+**ācarati**-practises] attānaṁ-oneself, ācarati-conducts(being unshaken by temptations).

• pabbatāyati-The Sangha conducts itself like mountain (when faced with temptations and defilements without being emotionally upset).

(b) Taḷākaṁ-the reservoir. samudda'miva [**samuddaṁ**-sea+**iva**-like] samuddaṁ iva-like the sea. attāna'mācarati [attānaṁ+ācarati]

• samuddāyati-(The reservoir) behaves itself like an ocean. **i.e.** The reservoir is so wide and big. As such, it seems like an ocean for its own size.

(c) saddo-the sound. ciccita'miva [**cicciṭaṁ**-sizzling sound+**iva**] cicciṭaṁ iva-like a sizzling sound. attāna'mācarati. attānaṁ-itself. ācarati-acts. • ciccitāyati-The sound acts itself like a sizzling sound.

Taddhita noun Example in ṇ-affix & noun-vibatti

(4) vasiṭṭhassa apaccaṁ • vāsiṭṭho. (Refer to Sutta 344)
Eva'maññe'pi [**evaṁ**-thus+**aññe**-other examples+**api**-also] yojetabbā-should be engaged, **i.e.** applied.

४३३, ५२८. तिजगुपकितमानेहि खछसा वा

433, 528. **Tija, gupa, kita, mānehi kha, cha, sā vā.**

[Tija, gupa, kita, mānehi+kha, cha, sā+vā. 3 words]

[V] **Tija, gupa, kita, māna**-icce'tehi dhātūhi **kha, cha, sa**-icce'te paccayā honti vā.

The affixes "**kha, cha, sa**" are sometimes applied after the roots "**Tija, gupa, kita, māna**". [The applied affixes are shown underlined in the examples]

- Titik<u>kha</u>ti-(He) forbears, endures. [wa] tija+kha+ti
- jiguc<u>cha</u>ti-(He) detests. [wa] gupa+cha+ti
- tikic<u>cha</u>ti-(He) treats, cures (a patient by medicine). [wa] kita+cha+ti
- vīmaṁ<u>sa</u>ti-(He) inquires. [wa] māna+sa+ti

Vā'ti kimatthaṁ?
What is the word "vā" for?
To show that in examples shown below, no "kha, cha, sa" affixes are applied to them as restricted by the word "vā".
* Tejati-(He) sharpens. [wa] tija+a+ti
* gopati-(He) protects. [wa] gupa+a+ti
* māneti-(He) adores. [wa] māna+a+ti

४३४, ५३४. भुजघसहरसुपादीहि तुमिच्छत्थेसु

434, 534. **Bhuja, ghasa, hara, su, pā'dīhi tu'micchatthesu**[28]**.**

[Bhuja, ghasa, hara, su, pā-ādīhi+tuṁ, icchā-atthesu. 2 words]

[V] **Bhuja, ghasa, hara, su, pā**-icce'va'mādīhi dhātūhi tu'miccha'tthesu **kha, cha, sa**-iccete paccayā honti vā.

The affixes "**kha, cha, sa**" are sometimes applied after the roots "**Bhuja, ghasa, hara, su, pā** etc." when expressing a wish (to-infinitive)

Note: Only those examples shown with the mark • are examples. The other preceding words are etymological explanations of the verb which is not an ED. The affixes applied by this Sutta are shown underlined.

(1) Bhottu'micchati [Bhottuṁ+icchati] Bhottuṁ-to eat. icchati-(He) wants.= • bubhuk<u>kha</u>ti-(He) wants to eat. [wa] bhuja+kha+ti

(2) ghasitu'micchati [ghasituṁ+icchati] ghasituṁ-to eat. icchati=• jighac<u>cha</u>ti-(He) wants to eat. [wa] ghasa+cha+ti

(3) haritu'micchati [harituṁ+icchati] harituṁ-to carry. icchati= • jigī<u>sa</u>ti-(He) wants to carry. [wa] hara+sa+ti

(4) sotu'micchati [sotuṁ+icchati] sotuṁ-to hear. icchati=• sussu<u>sa</u>ti-(He) wants to hear. [wa] su+sa+ti

(5) pātu'micchati [pātuṁ+icchati] pātuṁ-to drink. icchati=• pivā<u>sa</u>ti-(He) wants to drink. [wa] Pā+sa+ti

Vā'ti kimatthaṁ?

What is the word "vā" for?

To show that the example shown below, is inapplicable as restricted by "vā".

Bhottu'micchati. [Bhottuṁ+icchati] Bhottuṁ-to eat, *icchati-(He) wants. [wa] *isu+a+ti.

---

[28] The verbs applied with affixes by this Sutta are called "**tu'micchatta verbs**" which means verbs expressive of wish or purpose by hint of a "**tuṁ-suffix**". It is also called the **desiderative verb** in English.

Tu'micchatthesū'ti kimatthaṁ?
What is the word "tumicchattesu" for?
To show that the example shown below has no expression of purpose "tumicchatta". So, it is inapplicable here. (Hence, no "kha, cha, sa" affixes are applied in it, only an ordinary "a" affix is applied)
* Bhuñjati-(He) eats. [wa] bhuja+a+ti

४३५, ५३६. आय नामतो कत्तूपमाना दाचारे

435, 536. **Āya nāmato[29] kattū'pamānā'dācāre.**

[Āya+nāmato+kattu-upamānā+ācāre. 4 words]

[V] **Nāma**to kattū'pamānā ācāra'tthe **āya**paccayo hoti.

An affix "āya" is applied after the noun likened to a doer (kattā-agent), being expressed as a metaphorical analogy. [Affixes are shown underlined]

(1) Saṅgho pabbata'miva attāna'mācarati=• pabbatāyati, [wa] pabbata+āya+ti
(2) taḷākaṁ samudda'miva attāna'mācarati=• samuddāyati, [wa] Smudda+āya+ti
(3) saddo ciccita'miva attāna'mācarati=• ciccitāyati. [wa] ciccita+āya+ti

Eva'maññe'pi yojetabbā. (Please refer to Sutta 432)

---

[29]**Nāmato**-refers to ordinary nouns assuming the role of a root in a verb. All the affixes in Suttas 435, 436, 437 are to be applied after nouns which have a specific meaning. These nouns are also called "**Nāma-dhātu**-the root-like nouns" and verbs thereof are known as "**Nāma-dhātu kiriyā**" meaning nominal-stem verbs. The affix of verbs shown in Sutta 435 have usually **onomatopoetic expressions**. Such verbs are often found in the Pāli texts.

४३६, ५३७. ईयू'पमाना च

436, 537. **Īyū'pamānā ca.** [Īya+upamānā+ca. 3 words]

[V] **Nāma**to upamānā ācāra'tthe ca **īya**paccayo hoti.

An affix "īya" is to be applied after a noun which has a meaning of behaving in a specific manner in an analogous expression. [The affix "īya" is shown underlined in the examples]

(1) Achattaṁ-Despite being not umbrella, chatta'miva [chattaṁ+iva] chattaṁ iva-like umbrella, ācarati-(he) treats=
• chattīyati-He treats (a big leave) as if it was like an umbrella. **i.e.** He uses it like an umbrella. [wa] chatta+īya+ti

(2) aputtaṁ-Despite being not (one's own) son. putta'miva [puttaṁ+iva] puttattaṁ iva=like one's own son. ācarati=
• puttīyati-(He) treats (him) like a son (even though not a son). [wa] putta+īya+ti

Upamānā'ti kimatthaṁ?
What is the word "upamānā" for?
To show that example below is inapplicable as it is not expressive of simile.
Dhammaṁ-Dhamma, * ācarati-(he) practices.
i.e. He practices Dhamma. [wa]* ā+cara+a+ti

Ācāre'ti kimatthaṁ?
What is the word "ācāre" for?
To show that example below is inapplicable as the verb and its meaning meant in sentence is irrelevant to the word "ācāra"
Achattaṁ chattam'iva * rakkhati-protects.
i.e. He protects non-umbrella stuff like an umbrella though it is not an umbrella. [wa] * rakkha+a+ti
Eva'maññe'pi yojetabbā.

४३७, ५३८. नामम्हा'त्तिच्छत्थे

437, 538. **Nāmamhā'tticchatthe.**

[Nāmamhā+atta-icchā-atthe. 2 words]

[V] **Nāma**mhā attano iccha'tthe **īya**paccayo hoti.

When expressing wanting something for oneself, an affix "īya" is applied after a noun denoting that thing being wished for. [The affix "īya" is shown underlined in the examples]

(1) Attano-for oneself, patta'micchati [pattaṁ+icchati] pattaṁ-the bowl, icchati-(He) wants. • pattīyati-(He) wants bowl for himself. [wa] patta+īya+ti

Evaṁ-similarly.

(2) • vatthīyati-(He) wants cloth for himself. [wa] vatha+īya+ti

(3) • parikkhārīyati-(He) wants accessories for himself. [wa] parikkhāra+īya+ti

(4) • cīvarīyati-(He) wants robe for himself. [wa] cīvara+īya+ti

(5) • dhanīyati-(He) wants wealth for himself. [wa] dhana+īya+ti

(6) • ghaṭīyati-(He) wants ghee for himself. [wa] ghaṭa+īya+ti

Atticchatthe'ti kimatthaṁ?

What is the word "atticchatthe" for?

To show that the example below is expressive of wishing for others, not for oneself. So, it is inapplicable.

* Aññassa-for other person. patta'micchati. [pattaṁ+icchati]

Eva'maññe'pi yojetabbā.

४३८, ५४०. धातूहि णे णय णापे णापया कारितानि हेत्वत्थे

438, 540. **Dhātūhi ṇe, ṇaya, ṇāpe, ṇāpayā kāritāni hetva'tthe**[30].

[Dhātūhi+ṇe, ṇaya, ṇāpe, ṇāpayā+kāritāni+hetu-atthe. 4 words]

[V] Sabbehi **dhātūhi ṇe, ṇaya, ṇāpe, ṇāpaya**-icce'te paccayā honti **kārita**saññā ca hetva'tthe.

When expressing a "prompting causative mode action", the affixes "**ṇe, ṇaya, ṇāpe, ṇāpaya**" are applied after the roots of the verb. The affixes thus applied are to be also formally termed as "**kārita-**the causative affix".

Example of Causative Singular verb, using the root "Kara-to do"
(Please also refer to Sutta 432)

See all four affixes "**ṇe, ṇaya, ṇāpe, ṇāpaya**" are applied in each verb, However, as the conjoined "**ṇ**" is to be elided as per morphological procedures, only "**e, aya, āpe, āpaya**" can be seen in the verbs (See these affixes underlined in the first set of examples. Also see the long vowel "**ā**" in the initial point of the verb which is a result of **vuddhi procedure** affected by "**ṇ**" affix).

Yo koci karoti, taṁ añño "karohi karohi" icce'vaṁ bravīti, **atha vā** karontaṁ payojayati [Re: Sutta 432]

In other words, (he) prompts (while someone is) doing. This act of prompting or urging results in causative verb expressions as shown below:

• kāreti. • kārayati. • kārāpeti. • kārāpayati-(he) causes to do.

[Causative Verbs in singular, all are of the same meaning]

[wa] kara+ṇe+ti [wa] kara+ṇaya+ti [wa] kara+ṇāpe+ti

---

[30]**Kārita**-literally means the prompter. **i.e.** Causative. The affixes applied in the Suttas 438, 439, 452 are called "**Kārita Paccaya, or causative affixes**". Please note that only those affixes applied through Sutta 438 have a strong sense of "**Payojaka Vyāpara**-prompting or causative nature" while the rest are only a putative formal term in the nomenclature of Pāli grammar. The conjoining "**ṇ**" of these affixes is to be elided (Refer: Sutta No. 523) later leaving only component words without "ṇ". The elision is for initiating necessary procedure of "**vuddhi**" of the verbs in morphological process. (Refer to Sutta No. 483).

[wa] kara+ṇāpaya+ti (WA is shown in order of example verbs)

Example of Causative Plural verb, using the root "Kara-to do"

Ye keci karonti, te aññe "karotha karotha" icce'vaṁ bruvanti.
i.e. Suppose people are doing. (Then) other people tell them "do! do!".

• kārenti, • kārayanti, • kārāpenti, • kārāpayanti-(they) cause to do. [Causative Verbs in plural]

[wa] kara+ṇe+anti [wa] kara+ṇaya+anti [wa] kara+ṇāpe+anti [wa] kara+ṇāpaya+anti

Example of Causative Singular verb, using the root "paca-to cook"

Yo koci pacati-cooks, taṁ añño" pacāhi-cook! pacāhi-cook!" icce'vaṁ bravīti, **i.e.** Suppose someone is cooking. (Then) someone tells him "cook!, cook!".

atha vā pacantaṁ payojayati.
In other words, (he) prompts (while one is) cooking. This act of prompting or urging results in a causative verb expression as these:

• pāceti, • pācayati, • pācāpeti, • pācāpayati-(He) causes to cook. [Causative Verbs in singular]

[wa] paca+ṇe+ti [wa] paca+ṇaya+ti [wa] paca+ṇāpe+ti [wa] paca+ṇāpaya+ti

Example of Causative Plural verb, using the root "paca-to cook"

Ye keci pacanti, te aññe "pacatha pacatha" icce'vaṁ bruvanti.
Whoever are cooking. (Then) other people tell them "cook! cook! ".

• pācenti, • pācayanti, • pācāpenti. • Pācāpayanti-(They) cause to cook. [Causative Verbs in plural]

[wa] paca+ṇe+anti [wa] paca+ṇaya+anti [wa] paca+ṇāpe+anti [wa] paca+ṇāpaya+anti

Evaṁ-similarly in this manner, [In a different root "**bhaṇa-**to talk"]

• bhaṇeti, • bhaṇayati, • bhaṇāpeti, • bhaṇāpayati-(He) causes to speak. [Causative Verbs in singular]

[wa] baṇa+ṇe+ti [wa] baṇa+ṇaya+ti [wa] baṇa+ṇāpe+ti [wa] baṇa+ṇāpaya+ti

• Bhaṇenti, • bhaṇayanti, • bhaṇāpenti, • bhaṇāpayanti-(They) causes to speak. [Causative Verbs in plural]

[wa] baṇa+ṇe+anti [wa] baṇa+ṇaya+anti [wa] baṇa+ṇāpe+anti [wa] baṇa+ṇāpaya+anti

Tatha'riva [Tathā+iva] Tathā-in that way, iva-like, aññe'pi-other examples (using various roots) too, yojetabbā-should be applied.
i.e. other causative-examples should also be similarly applied.

Hetvatthe'ti kimatthaṁ?
What is the word "hetvatthe" for?
To show that examples below are inapplicable as they have no meaning of "hetu-the prompting". It is only a statement, a plain verb.
* Karoti-(He) does. * pacati-(He) cooks. (wa of these example will be shown later)

Atthaggahaṇena **ala-**paccayo hoti.
By the use of the word "attha (refer to hetv**a'tthe**) " in Sutta, an "**ala**" affix can be applied after some roots. [The affix is shown in bold, underlined]
• jot**ala**ti-(It causes to) shine or (it) shines. [wa] juta+ala+ti

४३९, ५३९. धातुरूपे नामस्मा णयो च
439, 539. Dhāturūpe nāmasmā ṇayo ca.

[Dhāturūpe+nāmasmā+ṇayo+ca. 4 words]

[V] Tasmā **nāma**smā **ṇaya**paccayo hoti kāritasañño ca dhāturūpe sati.

A "**ṇaya**" affix is to be added after that noun when it functions like an actual "**dhātu**-the root". [The affix is shown underlined]

(1) Hatthinā-by the elephant. atikkamati-(he) passes. maggaṁ-the road. • atihatthayati-(He) passes the road by (riding on an) elephant. [wa] atihattī+ṇaya+ti

(2) vīṇāya-by harp. upagāyati-(he) sings along. gītaṁ-the music. • upavīṇayati-(He) sings along with (playing) a harp. [wa] upavīṇā+ṇaya+ti

(3) daḷhaṁ-firmly. karoti-(He) does. vīriyaṁ-effort. • daḷhayati-(He) makes firm effort. [wa] daḷha+ṇaya+ti

(4) visuddhā-clear. hoti-is. ratti-the night. • visuddhayati-the

night is clear (as being free from clouds).
[wa] Visuddha+ṇaya+ti

Caggahaṇena āra, āla-iccete paccayā honti.

By the word "Ca" in Sutta, "**āra, āla**" affixes can be applied (after nominal stems).

(1) Santaṁ-to be peaceful, karoti-(He) does. • santārati-(He) makes it calm. [wa] Santa+āra+ti

(2) upakkamaṁ-the effort, karoti • upakkamālati-(He) exerts effort. [wa] upakkama+āla+ti

४४०, ४४५. भावकम्मेसु यो

440, 445. **Bhāvakammesu yo**[31]**.** [Bhāvakammesu+yo. 2 words]

[V] Sabbehi dhātūhi bhāvakammesu **ya**paccayo hoti.

A "**ya**" affix is added after all roots when signifying the senses of "**Bhāva** (impersonal voice) **and Kamma** (passive voice)".

Note: The verbs affixed with "**ya**" applied by this Sutta play very important role as passive voice verbs in the Pāli texts.[See also Sutta No.447 for a similar kind of "ya" affix. The verbs affixed with it are the active voice verbs]

---

[31] The "ya" affix applied by this Sutta is distinctive in shaping the verb forms and voice. By carefully learning its characteristics as shown in **Suttas** 440, 441, 442, 443, 444, the student will understand any verb affixed with "ya". There are two kinds of "ya", one being applied by Sutta 440 and one being applied by Sutta 447. Of the two "ya", The former is of two voices: Kamma (passive) and Bhāva (impersonal) while the latter is only of Kattu (active) voice. **Note the distinction of these two "ya" affixes in terms of voice** despite they share similar shapes and structure. In canonical Buddhist texts, the verbs in active and passive voices are widely used while Bhāva voice is seldom used in sentences except in matters of etymological definition of words.

There are two kinds of ya-affixed verbs. They are:
(a) The simple "ya-affixed" verbs,
(b) The complex "ya-affixed" Verbs augmented with similar or dissimilar syllables.

Explanation

(a) The first type of verbs are simple and easy to build and to understand as they do not have any complex morphological changes. They are usually structured by simply inserting either a "ya" affix only or putting one more vowel "**i**" or "**ī**" in front of "**ya**". They are usually one single-stem (one word) roots such as "**nī**" "**dā**" or ordinary double-stem or multiple-stem roots. [Refer to Sutta Nos.442, 502]

Example: Single-stem root verbs:
Nīyati, (No morphological change in this verb except a "**ya**" affix being inserted between the root **"nī"** and vibatti **"ti"**)
Dīyati, here, besides inserting "**ya**" affix, the vowel of the root is changed into an "**ī**". [Refer to Sutta No.502 to clarify this change]

Multiple-stem root verbs:
Karīyati, (Double-stem root, here, both "**ī**" an "**ya**" affixes are inserted. Refer to Sutta No.442 to understand this function) The examples (1) & (5) shown in Sutta are such simple type of verbs.

(b) The verb-type "b" is a bit complex as the affix "**ya**" itself undergoes a word-form change and it is further augmented with either similar word of that changed letter or with a rather dissimilar word. As a result of complex morphologic changes, the affix "ya" becomes invisible in these verbs. [Refer to Suttas 441, 443, 444, 487, 488 for more clarification].

Examples (3) (6) (7) below are augmented with similar words while examples (2) and (4) are augmented with dissimilar words. If one carefully studies the examples below, it will be easy to understand these different structural patterns of **ya**-affixed verbs. To highlight these unique patterns, all the examples are shown underlined.

(1) • Ṭhīyate-act of standing. [wa] ṭhā+ya+te
(2) • bujjhate-act of eating, (It is) eaten. [wa] bhuja+ya+te
(3) • paccate-act of cooking, (It is) cooked. [wa] paca+ya+te
(4) • labbhate-act of obtaining, (It is) obtained. [wa] laba+ya+te
(5) • karīyate-act of doing, (It is) done. [wa] kara+ya+te
(6) • yujjate-act of beating or yoking. (It is) beaten, or is bound. [wa] yudha or yuja+ya+te (2 possible roots)
(7) • uccate-act of speaking, (It is) spoken. [wa] uca+ya+te

Note: There are two types of translations in each example. The first is a "**Bhāva translation**" while the second signifies "**Kamma translation**". In the next sections, only the relevant type of one translation will be shown to avoid redundancy and confusion.

Bhāvakammesū'ti kimatthaṁ?
What is the word "bhāvakammesu" for?
To show that the examples shown below are inapplicable as they have only **Kattu-voice**.
* Karoti. * pacati. * paṭhati-(He) recites.
[wa] kara+o+ti [wa] paca+a+ti [wa] paṭha+a+ti

४४१, ४४७. तस्स चवग्गयकारवकारत्तं सधात्वन्तस्स

441, 447. **Tassa cavagga yakāravakārattaṁ sadhātvantassa.**

[Tassa+cavagga, yakāra, vakārattaṁ+sa-dhātvantassa. 3 words]

[V] Tassa **ya**paccayassa **ca**vagga, **ya**kāra, **va**kārattaṁ hoti dhātūnaṁ antena saha yathāsambhavaṁ.

That "**ya**" affix, together with the last component consonant of the root word, changes into "**ca**-group consonants or **ya** or **va** as per relevant applicability.

(1) • Vuccate-(It is) said. ***sl*** [wa] uca, vaca+ya+te

• vuccante-(These) are said, ***pl***, [wa] uca, vaca+ya+ante

[two possible roots for both set of examples in 1 and 2]

(2) • uccate-(It is) said. ***sl***, [wa] uca+ya+te

• uccante-(these) are said. ***pl*** [wa] uca+ya+ante

(3) • paccate-(It is) cooked. ***sl*** [wa] paca+ya+te

• paccante-(Those) are cooked. ***pl*** [wa] paca+ya+ante

In these examples above, the last consonant of the root "**c**" and the consonant "**y**" of the affix merged into one single "**c**" and later augmented with similar "**c**" and it thus becomes "**cca**"

(4) • Majjate-(He is) intoxicated or (He is) massaged, rubbed. ***sl*** [wa] mada or maja+ya+te (the root for 1st meaning),

• majjante. ***pl***, [wa] mada or maja+ya+ante

(Note that there are two roots based on different meaning)

(5) • yujjate-(It is) tied, engaged. ***sl.*** [wa] yuja+ya+te

• yujjante. ***pl.*** [wa] yuja+ya+ante

In the examples above, the last consonant of the root "**j**" and the affix "**y**" merged into one single "**j**" and later augmented with a similar "**j**".

(6) • Bujjhate-(It is) known. ***sl***, [wa] budha+ya+te

• bujjhante. ***pl***, [wa] budha+ya+ante

(7) • kujjhate-(He is) angry. ***sl***. [wa] kudha+ya+te

• kujjhante. ***pl***. [wa] kudha+ya+ante

(8) • ujjhate-(It is) abandoned, or discarded. ***Sl***. [wa] udha+ya+te

• ujjhante. ***pl.*** [wa] udha+ya+ante

In the examples above, the last consonant of the root "**dh**" and the affix "**y**" merged into one single "**jh**" and later augmented with a dissimilar "**j**".

(9) • Haññate-(It is) killed. ***sl***. [wa] hana+ya+te

• haññante. ***pl***. [wa] hana+ya+ante

In the example above, the last consonant of the root "**n**" and the affix "**y**" merged into one single "**ñ**" and later augmented with a similar "**ñ**".

(10) • Kayyate-(It is) done. ***sl***. [wa] kara+ya+te

• kayyante. ***pl***. [wa] kara+ya+ante

In the example above, the last consonant of the root "**r**" and the affix "**y**" merged into one single "**y**" and later augmented with a similar "**y**".

(11) • Dibbate-(It is) shined. ***sl.*** [wa] divu+ya+te

• dibbante. ***pl.*** [wa] divu+ya+ante

In the example above, the last consonant of the root "v" and the affix "y" merged into one single "b" and later augmented with a similar "b".

४४२, ४४८. इवण्णागमो वा

442, 448. **Ivaṇṇā'gamo vā.** [Ivaṇṇa-āgamo+vā. 2 words]

[V] Sabbehi dhātūhi **ya**mhi paccaye pare **ivaṇṇā**'gamo hoti vā.

Either "**i** or **ī**" is to be inserted after all roots when a "ya" affix follows (after the root). [Usually in front of "ya" affix].

(1) • Karīyate, • karīyati-(It is) done. [wa] kara+ya+te (Both are the same but the second is a Prassapada-reversed verb)

(2) • gacchīyate, • gacchīyati-(It's) gone. [wa] gamu+ya+te (Both are the same)

Note: Please keep in mind that in each pair of verbs, the first is of Attanopada verb-group while **the second verb form is a reversed verb-form of Attanopada into Parassapada.** However, the voice still remains only in passive mode regardless of change. Of also greatly important is to note that these **verb-forms applied by the function of this Sutta are for purely passive voice use only.** They are **never to be used in the active voice mode** like the verbs where the functions prescribed by Sutta 441, 443, 442. They can be used interchangeably either as active or passive voice depending on the sense and voice of affix "ya" in addition to contextual nature of sentence. For example, being in the presence or absence of an Avutta-kattā (**i.e.** non-principal subject) in a sentence. This means that:

(a) If the sense and voice of the affix "ya" is Kamma as per Sutta 440, and have a non-principal subject (Avutta-kattā) in the sentence, then it will surely be a passive voice verb.

(b) If it is a "ya" affix as per Sutta 447 without the presence of an Avutta-kattā (non-principal subject) in the sentence, then it will be an active voice verb.

Vā'ti kimatthaṁ?
What is the word "vā" for?
To show that as restricted by the word "vā", there is no "i or ī" applied in the example below.
* Kayyate. [wa] kara+ya+te

४४३, ४४९. पुब्बरूपञ्च

443, 449. **Pubbarūpañ'ca.** [Pubbarūpaṁ+ca. 2 words]

[V] Sabbehi dhātūhi **ya**paccayo **pubbarūpa**'māpajjate vā.

A "ya" affix sometimes undergoes a morphological procedure of **pubbarūpa,** (changing into a consonant similar to the last consonant of the root.) [**Pubba**-of front, the preceding letter of the root. **i.e.** the last consonant of root+**rūpa**-shape. **i.e.** assimilation].

Note: Example verb (1) and (5) are anomalous verbs.

(1) • Vuḍḍhate-(It's) grown. [wa] vaḍha+ya+te
In the example above, the affix "**y**" changed into "ḍh"**.** So it becomes "vaḍh+ḍha+te" [It is still a pubbarūpa, similar words]. Later on, the last word of the root has to be changed into a "ḍ" by Sutta 612. The "a" of "va" further changes into an "u" by Sutta 517 bringing the word to completion. (This is an anomalous verb of dissimilar words whose morphological procedure is a bit complex for the beginners)

(2) • phallate-(It is) finished or come to fruition.
[wa] phala+ya+te
In this example, the affix "**y**" changed into "l"**.** [This is a simple pubbarūpa verb of similar words]

(3) • dammate-(It is) tamed. [wa] damu+ya+te
In this example, the affix "**y**" changed into "m"**.** [This is a simple pubbarūpa verb of similar words]

(4) • sakkate-(It is) honored. [wa] saka+ya+te
In this example, the affix "**y**" changed into "k"**.** [This is a simple pubbarūpa verb of similar words]

(5) • labbhate-(It is) obtained. [wa] labha+ya+te
In this example, the affix "**y**" changed into "**bh**"**.** Later on, the last consonant "**bh**" of the root is to be changed into "**b**" by Sutta 20 or 517 [This is an anomalous verb with dissimilar augmentation]

(6) • dissate-(It is) seen. [wa] disa+ya+te
In this example, the affix "**y**" changed into "s"**.** [This is a simple pubbarūpa verb of similar words or assimilation]

४४४, ५११. तथा कत्तरि च

444, 511. **Tathā kattari ca.** [Tathā+kattari+ca. 3 words]

[V] Yathā heṭṭhā bhāvakammesu **ya**paccayassa ādeso hoti. tathā kattari'pi yapaccayassa ādeso kātabbo.

The morphological procedures on "ya" affix prescribed in previous Suttas are to be similarly applied to "ya" affix (of active voice as prescribed in forthcoming Sutta 447 "Divā' dito yo").

Note: This Sutta enjoins that the two functions of Sutta 441, 443 are to be similarly applied on the "ya-affixed verbs" of Sutta 447 too. So, the function of all examples are easily understandable. The only difference is that these verbs are not applicable for the reversal procedure into Parassapada as they themselves are basically of the Parassapadas whose voice is always "active voice". This is the reason why the Verb-ending is only Parassapada "**ti**", not "**te**"**.** (See the applied-functions in the examples shown underlined.)

(1) • Bujjhati-(He) knows. [wa] budha+ya+ti

(2) • vijjhati-(It) penetrates. (as with a sharp object or by means of sharp intellect) [wa] vidha+ya+ti
[These verbs are augmented with dissimilar word]

(3) • maññati-(He) knows. [wa] mana+ya+ti

(4) • sibbati-(He) sews. [wa] sivu+ya+ti
[These verbs are augmented with similar syllables]

४४५, ४३३. भूवादितो अ

445, 433. **Bhūvā'dito a**[32]**.** [Bhū-ādito+a. 2 words]

[V] **Bhū**-icce'vamādito dhātugaṇato **a**paccayo hoti kattari.

An "**a**" affix is to be added after the roots "**bhū**" etc. in the sense of active voice of Kattā (the agent).
[The applied affix "a" is shown in bold, underlined.]

- Bhav**a**ti-(It) becomes. [wa] bhū+a+ti
- paṭh**a**ti-(He) recites. [wa] paṭha+a+ti
- pac**a**ti-(He) cooks. [wa] paca+a+ti
- jay**a**ti-(He) conquers. [wa] ji+a+ti

४४६, ५०९. रुधादितो निग्गहितपुब्बञ्च

446, 509. **Rudhā'dito niggahitapubbañ'ca.**

[Rudha-ādito+niggahita-pubbaṁ+ca. 3 words]

[V] **Rudha**-icce'va'mādito dhātugaṇato **a**paccayo hoti kattari. pubbe **niggahitā**'gamo hoti.

An "**a**" affix is to be added after the root "**rudha**" etc. in the sense of the active voice (Kattā). Besides, a "**niggahita**" is also to be put on top of the first component consonant of the root.
Note: That Niggahita later changes into one of "ṅ, ñ, ṇ, n, m" based on

---

[32]All the affixes applied by eight Suttas from 445 to 452 are called "**Vikaraṇa Paccaya**" which means the **distinctive affixes**. In the word "Vikaraṇa", "**Vi**=means special, to be distinctive, **kraṇa**-doing, **i.e.** the affixes that make each verb distinctive. All the **Ākhyāta verbs are classified into eight groups based on those eight affixes.** They are: **Būvādi gana** (Bhū-group Verbs), **Rudādi gana** (Rudha-group Verbs), **Divādi gana** (Divu-group Verbs), **Svādi gana** (Su-group Verbs), **Kīyādi gana** (Kī-group Verbs), **Gahādi gana** (Gaha-group Verbs), **Tanādi gana** (Tanu-group Verbs), **Curādi gana** (Cura-group Verbs). All verbs of each group are to be used as active Voice verbs. **As for those "ya-affixed verbs"** per Sutta 440, **they are to be regarded as the passive voice verbs of those eight groups and other verbs.**

next consonant it precedes as prescribed in Sutta 31. The transformed "n" of niggahita is shown in bold, underlined.

- Ru**n**dhati-(He) obstructs. [wa] Rudha+a+ti
- chi**n**dati-(He) cuts. [wa] chida+a+ti
- bhi**n**dati-(He) breaks. [wa] bhida+a+ti.

Caggahaṇena **i, ī, e, o-**iccete paccayā honti niggahitapubbañ'ca.

By the word "Ca" in Sutta, "**i, ī, e, o**" affixes can also be applied while a nigghita is inserted on top of initial letter of the root.

Note: The transformed "**n**" and "**m**" of niggahita and all four affixes are shown in bold, underlined.

- Ru**n**dh**i**ti, [wa] rudha+i+ti
- ru**n**dh**ī**ti, [wa] rudha+ī+ti
- ru**n**dh**e**ti, [wa] rudha+e+ti
- ru**n**dh**o**ti-(He) obstructs. [wa] rudha+o+ti
- su**m**bh**o**ti-(he) beats. [wa] subha+o+ti
- parisu**m**bh**o**ti-(He) beats. [wa] pari√subha+o+ti.

४४७, ५१०. दिवादितो यो

447, 510. **Divā'dito yo.** [Divu-ādito+yo. 2 words]

[V] **Divu**-icce'va'mādito dhātugaṇato **ya**paccayo hoti kattari.

A "**ya**" affix is to be added after the roots "**divu**" etc. in the sense of the active voice (Kattā).

- Dibbati-(It) shines or (He) plays. [wa] divu+ya+ti
- Sibbati-(He) sews. [wa] sivu+ya+ti
- yujjhati-(He) fights or engages. [wa] yuja+ya+ti
- vijjhati-(It) penetrates. [wa] vidha+ya+ti
- bujjhati-(He) knows. [wa] budha+ya+ti.

Note: All the verbs affixed with "ya" applied by this Sutta are the active voice only. The meanings of verb are translated based on possible meaning of the root.

४४८, ५१२. स्वादितो णुणा उणा च

448, 512. **Svā'dito ṇu, ṇā, uṇā ca.**

[Su-ādito+ṇu, ṇā, uṇā+ca. 3 words]

[V] **Su**-icce'va'mādito dhātugaṇato **ṇu, ṇā, uṇā**-icce'te paccayā honti kattari.

The affixes "**ṇu, ṇā, uṇā**" are added after the roots "**su**" etc. in the sense of the active voice of Kattā.

Note: The affixes are shown in bold. The "**u**" of affix "**ṇu**" changes into "**o**" through Vuddhi procedure. There are two verbs with different affixes for each root, but of the same meaning.

(1) [ṇu] • Abhisu**ṇo**ti, [wa] abhi-√su+ṇu+ti
[ṇā] • abhisu**ṇā**ti-(He attentively) listens. [wa] abhi√su+ṇā+ti
(2) [ṇu] • saṁvu**ṇo**ti, [wa] saṁ-√vu+ṇu+ti
[ṇā] • saṁvu**ṇā**ti-(He) protects or prevents.[wa]saṁ√vu+ṇā+ti
(3) [ṇu] • āvu**ṇo**ti, [wa] ā-√vu+ṇu+ti
[ṇā] • āvu**ṇā**ti-(He) protects or prevents. [wa] ā-√vu+ṇā+ti
(4) [ṇu] • pāpu**ṇo**ti, [wa] pa-√apa+ṇu+ti.
[uṇā] • pāpu**ṇā**ti-(He) reaches. [wa] pa-√apa+uṇā+ti.

४४९, ५१३. कीयादितो ना

449, 513. **Kī'yādito nā.** [Kī-ādito+nā. 2 words]

[V] **Kī**-icce'va'mādito dhātugaṇato **nā**-paccayo hoti kattari.

A "**nā**" affix is to be added after the roots "**Kī**" etc. in the sense of the active voice (Kattā).

Note: The affix is shown in bold. The "**n'** of affix "**nā**" changes into "**ṇ**" in the first example. "**ī**" of the root "kī" is sometimes shortened into "**i**".

- Ki**ṇā**ti-(He) purchases. [wa] Kī+nā+ti.
- ji**nā**ti-(He) conquers. [wa] ji+nā+ti.
- dhu**nā**ti-(It) shakes. [wa] dhu+nā+ti.
- mu**nā**ti-(He) knows. [wa] muna+nā+ti.
  [The last "n" of the root is to be elided]
- lu**nā**ti-(He) cuts or harvests. [wa] lu+nā+ti.
- pu**nā**ti-(It) cleanses. [wa] pu+nā+ti.

४५०, ५१७. गहादितो प्पण्हा

450, 517. **Gahā'dito ppa, ṇhā.** [Gaha-ādito+ppa, ṇhā. 2 words]

[V] **Gaha**-icce'va'mādito dhātugaṇato **ppa, ṇhā,** icce'te paccayā honti kattari.

The "**ppa, ṇhā**" affixes are added to the root "**gaha**" etc. in the sense of the active voice (Kattā). (The affixes are shown in bold.)

- Ghe**ppa**ti, [wa] gaha+ppa+ti.
- ga**ṇhā**ti-(He) takes. [wa] gaha+ṇhā+ti.

४५१, ५२०. तनादितो ओ यिरा

451, 520. **Tanā'dito o, yirā.** [Tanu-ādito+o, yirā. 2 words]

[V] **Tanu**-icce'va'mādito dhātugaṇato **o, yira**-icce'te paccayā honti kattari.

The "**o, yira**" affixes are added after the roots "**tanu**" etc. in the sense of the active voice (Kattā). (The affixes are shown in bold, underlined.)

- Tan**o**ti-(It) expands or stretches. [wa] tanu+o+ti.
- tan**o**hi-Expand! (command). [wa] tanu+o+hi.
- kar**o**ti-(He) does. [wa] kara+o+ti.
- kar**o**hi-Do! (command). [wa] kara+o+hi.
- ka**yira**ti-(He) does. [wa] kara+yira+ti.
- ka**yir**āhi-Do!(command). [wa] kara+yira+hi.

४५२, ५२५. चुरादितो णे णया

452, 525. **Curā'dito ṇe, ṇayā.** [Cura-ādito+ṇe, ṇayā. 2 words]

[V] **Cura**-icce'va'mādito dhātugaṇato **ṇe, ṇaya**-icce'te paccayā honti kattari, kāritasaññā ca.

The "**ṇe, ṇaya**" affixes are added after the roots "**cura**" etc. in the sense of the active voice (Kattā). Those affixes are also to be formally termed as "**kārita**".
(The affixes are shown underlined.)
Note: Although formally named as "**kārita**", these affixes have no

nature of "payojaka-vyāpāra-the prompting". The purpose of naming as "Kārita" is to initiate Vuddhi procedure and to serve as distinctive mark of the Curādi-verb-groups.

(1) • Cor<u>e</u>ti, [wa] cura+ṇe+ti.
 • cor<u>ay</u>ati-(He) steals. [wa] cura+ṇaya+ti.
(2) • cint<u>e</u>ti, [wa] cinta+ṇe+ti.
 • cint<u>ay</u>ati-(He) thinks. [wa] cinta+ṇaya+ti.
(3) • mant<u>e</u>ti, [wa] manta+ṇe+ti.
 • mant<u>ay</u>ati-(He) consults or speaks. [wa] manta+ṇaya+ti

४५३, ४४४. अत्तनोपदानि भावे च कम्मनि
453, 444. [33]Attanopadāni bhāve ca kammani.
[Attanopadāni+bhāve+ca+kammani. 4 words]
[V] Bhāve ca kammani ca attanopadāni honti.

The Vibattis of "**attanopada-group**" are in the sense of "**bhāva and Kamma**" voice.

• Uccate, • uccante, • majjate, • majjante, • yujjate,
• yujjante, • kujjhate, • kujjhante, (Refer to Sutta 441)
• labbhate, [wa] labha+ya+te. • labbhante,
 [wa] labha+ya+ante. (Refer to Sutta 443)
• kayyate, • kayyante. (Refer to Sutta 441)

---

[33]This Sutta clearly defines the voice of all Attanopada Ākhyāta verbs. When those Ākhyāta verbs in Attanopada vibatti-termination signify one of these two voices, they used to have a "**ya**-affix"(per Sutta 440) in them. As such, any sentence structure using those verbs should follow relevant grammatical rules regarding the voices they signify.

४५४, ४४०. कत्तरि च

454, 440. **Kattari**[34] **ca.** [Kattari+ca. 2 words]

[V] Kattari ca attanopadāni honti.

The "**attanopada-group**" Vibattis can also be in "**kattā**" the active voice.

Summary: This Sutta indicates that verbs in "Attanopada-terminations" can also be in the sense of Kattā, as the active voice verbs.

(1) • Maññate-(He) knows or thinks. [wa] mana+ya+te.

(2) • rocate-(It) shines. [wa] ruca+a+te.

(3) • socate-(He) worries. [wa] suca+a+te.

(4) • bujjhate-(He) knows. [wa] budha+ya+te.

(5) • jāyate-(It) arises. [wa] jana+ya+te. [The last "n" of the root elided and "a" of the root lengthened]

---

[34]The Sutta No. 454 indicates again that the Ākhyāta verbs of Attanopada vibatti-termination can also sometimes signify Kattu (active) voice. **Please do not be confused by injunction of this Sutta.** The Ākhyāta verbs in Attanopada vibatti group signify active voice on condition that the verbs are either be affixed in kattu-voiced affixes or be without it, **but no Kamma-voiced affix** in them. Otherwise they will be only in passive voice. **Studying the examples shown in Sutta will clarify** this fact more clearly. Here, examples 1,4,5 are applied with kattu-voiced "**ya**" affix as per Sutta No. 447, while 2,3 are applied with a kattu-voiced "**a**" affix per Sutta No. 445.

४५५, ५३०. धातुप्पच्चयेहि विभत्तियो

455, 530. **Dhātuppaccayehi[35] vibhattiyo.**

[Dhātuppaccayehi+vibhattiyo. 2 words]

[V] Dhātuniddiṭṭhehi paccayehi khā'dikārita'ntehi vibhattiyo honti.

The vibattis are applied only after the affixes starting with "**kha** and ending in kārita **causative affixes**", formally known as "**Dhātuni- ddiṭṭha affixes**" have been first applied.

• Titikkhati, • jigucchati, • vīmaṁsati, • samuddāyati, • puttīyati, • kāreti, • pāceti. (Refer to Sutta 433, 435, 438)

४५६, ४३०. कत्तरि परस्सपदं

456, 430. **Kattari parassapadaṁ[36].**

[Kattari+parassapadaṁ. 2 words]

[V] Kattari parassapadaṁ hoti.

The "**prassapada-**group vibattis" are in the sense and voice of the "**kattā** (agent or active) "

Summary: This Sutta indicates that "Verbs of Parassapada-vibatti termination" are to be applied in the active voice only.

---

[35]This Sutta enjoins that all the "**Dhātu-paccaya affixes**" has to be applied first after the roots prior to any ākhyāta vibattis are applied. Normally, in a morphological procedure of an ākhyāta verb, setting up the root, eliding the last component vowel of the root and then applying relevant ākhyāta vibatti are standard procedures. Application of the affixes is next in the order of common procedure. What are "dhātu paccaya" affixes? **They are: kha, cha, sa, āya, īya, ṇe, ṇaya, ṇāpe, ṇāpaya, ala, āra and āla.** All these affixes are applied through Suttas 433, 434, 435, 436, 437, 438, 439. These are also called "**Dhātu niddiṭṭha affixes**".

[36]This Sutta sets forth the voice of the Ākhyāta verbs in Parassapada group termination as the Kattu (active) voice. Studying the examples carefully will show that they are affixed in Kattu-voiced affixes. This is a consistent rule and morphological pattern being applied in every Ākhyāta verbs of the active voice.

• Karoti, • pacati, • paṭhati, • gacchati.
[Refer to the preceding Suttas]

४५७, ४२४. भूवादयो धातवो

457, 424. **Bhūvā'dayo**[37] **dhātavo.**

[Bhū-ādayo+dhātavo. 2 words]

[V] **Bhū-**icceva'mādayo ye saddagaṇā, te **dhātu**saññā honti.

The root words such as "**bhū**" and so forth are formally called "**dhātu**".

(1) • Bhavati-(It) is, becomes. ***sl.*** [wa] bhū+a+ti.
• bhavanti-(they) are, become. ***pl.*** [wa] bhū+a+anti.
(2) • carati-(He) practices or moves. ***sl.*** [wa] cara+a+ti.
• caranti, ***pl***, [wa] cara+a+anti.
(3) • pacati-(He) cooks. ***sl.*** [wa] paca+a+ti.
• pacanti, ***pl***. [wa] paca+a+anti.
(4) • cintayati-(He) thinks. ***sl.*** [wa] cinta+ṇaya+ti.
• cintayanti, ***pl***. [wa] cinta+ṇaya+anti.
(5) • hoti-(It) is. ***sl.*** [wa] hū+a+ti.
• honti, ***pl***. [wa] hū+a+anti.
(6) • gacchati-(He) goes. ***sl.*** [wa] gamu+a+ti.
• gacchanti ***pl***. [wa] gamu+a+anti.

Iti ākhyātakappe dutiyo kaṇḍo.
The Second Section of Ākhyāta Verb ends.

---

[37]This Sutta **formally names** the words such as "**Bū**" etc, as **dhātu** (the root) of all verbs in the Pāli language and its grammar. **The roots play greatly important role as the building blocks of verbs and various words.** Therefore, studying the roots and their meaning is also an important part of the grammar study. With broader understanding of the roots, one can multiply different word-structures.

Tatiya Kaṇḍa
The Third Section

४५८, ४६१. क्वचादिवण्णान मेकस्सरानं द्वेभावो
458, 461. Kvacā'divaṇṇāna'mekassarānaṁ dvebhāvo[38].

[Kvaci+ādivaṇṇānaṁ+ekassarānaṁ+dvebhāvo. 4 words]

[V] Ādibhūtānaṁ vaṇṇānaṁ ekassarānaṁ kvaci dvebhāvo hoti.

The initial consonant of the root is sometimes reduplicated with a similar word of the same vowel.

Note: See the reduplicated words shown in bold underlined. Due to morphological changes after reduplication procedure, there are some examples which have dissimilar syllables in different forms.

- **Ti**tikkhati-(he) bears or is patient with. • **ji**gucchati-(he) detests.
- **ti**kicchati-(he) cures. • **vī**maṁsati-(he) investigates.
- **bu**bhukkhati-(He) wants to eat. • **pi**vāsati-(He) wants to drink. [Refer to Sutta 433-434 for WA of these examples]
- **da**ddallati-(It) shines. [wa] dala+a+ti.
- **da**dāti-(He) gives. [wa] dā+a+ti.
- **ja**hāti-(He) abandons. [wa] hā+a+ti.
- **ca**ṅkamati-(He) paces up and down. [wa] kamu+a+ti.

Kvacī'ti kimatthaṁ?

What is the word "kvaci" for?

To show that "reduplication procedure" is not applied in some examples shown below as restricted by the word "kvaci".

* Kampati, [wa] kapi+a+ti. * calati-(He) trembles. (Both verbs are of same meaning) [wa] cala+a+ti.

---

[38]This reduplication procedure is usually applicable only in verbs applied with affixes shown in Suttas 433-434. Other Ākhyāta verbs applied with "vikranṇa" affixes can also be redoubled when they are in Prokkhā vibatti and in a few other vibatti-terminations too.

४५९, ४६२. पुब्बो’ ब्भासो

459, 462. **Pubbo’bbhāso.** [Pubbo+abbhāso. 2 words]

[V] Dvebhūtassa dhātussa yo pubbo, so **abbhāsa**sañño[39] hoti.

The duplicated initial consonant (as per previous Sutta) is to be formally named as an "**abbhāsa**".
Summary: This Sutta enjoins to name the reduplicated word as an "**abbhāsa**".

- Dadhāti-(He) carries. [wa] dhā+a+ti. • dadāti, [Re: Sutta 458]
- babhūva-(It) was. [wa] bhū+a ("a" is a Parokkā Vibatti, not affix)

४६०, ५०६. रस्सो

460, 506. **Rasso.** [Rasso. 1 word]

[V] Abbhāse vattamānassa sarassa rasso hoti.

The component dīgha vowel of duplicated consonant named as "**abbhāsa**" is shortened.
Summary: This Sutta shortens a long vowel of reduplicated "**abbhāsa**". [See the shortened vowel in the examples shown underlined.]

- Dadhāti, • jahāti.

[39]**Abbhāsa** means "something additionally said, **i.e.** an extra word. [**ā**-additionally+**bhāsa**-said, an extra-word. The initial "ā" is shortened with one dissimilar "b" augmented.]

४६१, ४६४. दुतियचतुत्थानं पठमततिया

461, 464. **Dutiyacatutthānaṁ paṭhamatatiyā**[40]**.**

[Dutiya, catutthānaṁ+paṭhama, tatiyā. 2 words]

[V] Abbhāsagatānaṁ **dutiya, catutthā**naṁ **paṭhama, tatiyā** honti.

Those **abbhāsa** consonants which are **dutiya** (The Second), **catuttha** (the fourth) in the vagga groups, are to be changed into **paṭhama** (the first), **tatiyā** (the third) consonant of vagga groups respectively.

Note: dutiya-the second becomes> paṭhama (the first).
catuttha-the fourth becomes> tatiyā (the third).
The changed words are shown in bold, underlined.

- C̲iccheda-(It was) cut. [wa] chida+a (Parokkā Vibatti) [Here, the second "cha" changes into the first "c"]
- **b̲**ubhukkhati, • babhūva, [Here, the fourth "bha" changes into the third "b"]
- **d̲**adhāti-(He) carries. [Here, the fourth "dha" changes into the third "d"]

४६२, ४६७. कवग्गस्स चवग्गो

462, 467. **Kavaggassa cavaggo.**

[Kavaggassa+cavaggo. 2 words]

[V] Abbhāse vattamānassa **ka**vaggassa **ca**vaggo hoti.

Those "abbhāsa consonants" belonging to **Ka**-vagga group are to be changed into **ca**-vagga group consonants.
[Changed consonants are shown underlined]

- C̲ikicchati-(He) cures. [wa] kita+cha+ti.
  [Here, "k" changes into "c"]
- J̲igucchati-(He) detests. [wa] gupa+cha+ti.
  [Here, "g" changes into "j"]

[40] Only by exactly knowing the initial word of the root and its position in the vagga will make the function of this Sutta easily understandable.

- Jighacchati-(He) wants to eat. [wa] ghasa+sa+ti.
  [Here, "gha" changes into "j"]
- Jigīsati-(He) wants to carry. [wa] hara+sa+ti.
  [This is **an anomalous example.** First, the root "hara" changes into "gī" and "g" of it further changes into "j"]
- Jaṅgamati-(He) goes. [wa] gamu+a+ti.
  [Here, "g" changes into "j"]
- Caṅkamati. (He) paces up and down. [wa] kamu+a+ti.
  [Here, "k" changes into "c"]

४६३, ५३२. मानकितानं व तत्तं वा

463, 532. **Mānakitānaṁ va, ta-ttaṁ vā.**

[Mānakitānaṁ+va, ta-ttaṁ+vā. 3 words]

[V] **Māna, kita**-icce'tesaṁ dhātūnaṁ abbhāsagatānaṁ **va**kāra, **ta**kārattaṁ hoti vā yathāsaṅkhyaṁ.

Those "abbhāsa consonants **m** and **k**" which are part of the roots "**māna, kita**", sometimes change into consonants "**v**" and "**t**" respectively. (The duplicated abbhāsa **m** of **māna** becomes "**v**" and **k** of the root **kita** becomes "**t**". Shown underlined below)

- Vīmaṁsati-(He) investigates, • Tikicchati.

Vā'ti kimatthaṁ? What is the word "vā" for?
To show that function of this Sutta is not always applied in some examples shown below as restricted by the word "vā".
* Cikicchati.

४६४, ५०४. हस्स जो

464, 504. **Hassa jo.** [Hassa+jo. 2 words]

[V] Abbhāse vattamānassa **ha**kārassa **j**o hoti.
The reduplicated abbhāsa consonant "**h**" changes into "**j**".
(The applied function shown in bold, underlined)

- **J**ahāti, [wa] hā+a+ti.
- **J**uhvati-(He) sacrifices. [wa] hu+a+ti.
- **J**uhoti-(He) sacrifices. [wa] hu+a+ti.
- **J**ahāra-(He had) carried. [wa] hara+a (Parokkhā Vibatti, not an affix).

४६५, ४६३. अन्तस्सिवण्णाकारो वा

465, 463. **Antassi'vaṇṇā'kāro vā.**

[1.Antassa+ivaṇṇa, akāro+vā. 3 words.
2.Antassa+ivaṇṇo+akāro+vā. 4 words.]

[V] Abbhāsassa antassa **i**vaṇṇo hoti, **a**kāro vā.

The component vowels of abbhāsa consonants sometimes changes into "**i** or **ī**" or "**a**". (The applied functions are shown in bold, underlined)

- J**i**gucchati, [Here, "u" of "gu" changes into "i"]
- p**i**vāsati, [Here, "ā" of "pā" changes into "i"]
- v**ī**maṁsati, [Here, "ā" of "mā" changes into "ī"]
- j**i**ghacchati, [Here, "a" of "gha" changes into "i"]
- b**a**bhūva, [Here, "ū" of "bhū" changes into "a"]
- d**a**dhāti. [Here, "ā" of "dhā" changes into "a"] [wa shown already]

Vā'ti kimatthaṁ? What is the word "vā" for?
To show that function of this Sutta is not always applied in some examples as restricted by the word "vā".
[Hence, there is no "Babhukkhati", but "bubhukkhati".]
* Bubhukkhati-(He) wants to eat.

४६६, ४८९. निग्गहितञ्च

466, 489. **Niggahitañ'ca.** [Niggahitaṁ+ca. 2 words]

[V] Abbhāsassa ante niggahitā'gamo hoti vā.

Sometimes, there has to come a "niggahita" by the end of an abbhāsa consonant. ["by the end of" is a literal translation which means "after". The applied "niggahita-**ṁ**" is invisible except its derivative morpheme "**ṅ**" or "**ñ**" in its place shown in bold, underlined]

- Ca**ṅ**kamati,
- ca**ñ**calati-(He) shakes, [wa] cala+a+ti.
- ja**ṅ**gamati.

Vā'ti kimatthaṁ? What is the word "vā" for?
To show that function of this Sutta is not always applied in

some examples shown below as restricted by the word "vā".
* Pivāsati, * daddallati.

४६७, ५३३. ततो पामानानं वामं सेसु

467, 533. **Tato pā, mānānaṁ vā, maṁ sesu.**
[Tato+pā, mānānaṁ+vā, maṁ+sesu. 4 words]

[V] Tato abbhāsato **pā, māna**-icce'tesaṁ dhātūnaṁ **vā, maṁ**-icce'te ādesā honti yathāsaṅkhyaṁ **sa**paccaye pare.

When "**sa**" affix follows, the root **pā** and **māna,** located after an abbhāsa word, changes into "**vā**" and **maṁ**" respectively [This Sutta changes **Pā** into **Vā** and the root **māna** into **maṁ**. The applied functions are shown in bold, underlined]

• Pi**vā**sati, • vī**maṁ**sati.

४६८, ४९२. ठा तिट्ठो

468, 492. **Ṭhā tiṭṭho.** [Ṭhā+tiṭṭho. 2 words]

[V] **Ṭhā**-icce'tassa dhātussa **tiṭṭhā**'deso hoti vā.

The root word "**ṭhā**" sometimes changes into "**tiṭṭha**".
[The applied function is shown in bold]

• **Tiṭṭh**ati-(He) stands. [wa] ṭhā+a+ti.
• **tiṭṭh**atu-(Let it) stand. [wa] ṭhā+a+tu.
• **tiṭṭh**eyya-(He) should stand. [wa] ṭhā+eyya.
• **tiṭṭh**eyyuṁ-(They) should stand. [wa] ṭhā+eyyuṁ.

Vā'ti kimatthaṁ? What is the word "vā" for?
To show that function of this Sutta is not always applied in some examples shown below as restricted by the word "vā".
* Ṭhāti-(It) stands. [wa] ṭhā+a+ti.

Note: In Sutta 468, 469, the structures of verbs are so simple that sometimes it may be unnecessary to apply an affix such as "a". But, some teachers used to hold the strict view that there should be an affix of Kattu sense in it to signify the relevant voice. Even if the affix is applied, it has to be elided by Sutta 510. In WA of examples, some are shown with an affix and some are not. This is a delicate minor grammatical matter. However, the golden rule is that it makes a grammatical sense to have at least one appropriate affix even though without an affix, the applied Vibattis can still signify the voice (Refer to Suttas 453, 456). As such, in cases where the structure of the verb is so simple and does not require any complex morphological procedure, it is still possible for such simple verbs without an affix.

४६९, ४९४. पा पिवो

469, 494. **Pā pivo.** [Pā+pivo. 2 words]

[V] **Pā-**icce'tassa dhātussa **pivā**'deso hoti vā.

The root "**pā**" sometimes changes into "**piva**".
[The applied function is shown in bold, underlined]

- **Piva**ti-(He) drinks. [wa] pā+a+ti.
- **piva**tu-(Let him) drink. [wa] pā+a+tu.
- **piv**eyya-(He) should drink. [wa] pā+eyya.
- **piv**eyyuṁ. p*l*. [wa] pā+eyyuṁ.

Vā'ti kimatthaṁ? What is the word "vā" for?
To show that function of this Sutta is not always applied in some examples shown below as restricted by the word "vā".
* Pāti-(He) drinks. [wa] pā+a+ti.

४७०, ५१४. ञास्स जाजंना

470, 514. **Ñāssa jā, jaṁ, nā.** [Ñāssa+jā, jaṁ, nā. 2 words]

[V] **Ñā-**icce'tassa dhātussa **jā, jaṁ, nā-**ādesā honti vā.

The root "**ñā**" sometimes changes into "**jā, jaṁ, nā**".
[The applied functions are shown underlined]

[jā-function] • Jānāti-(He) knows. [wa] ñā+nā+ti.
• jāneyya • jāniyā-(He) should know or he may know.
[jaṁ-function] • jaññā-(He) should know. [wa] ñā+nā+eyya
(**Please note** that **jāneyya, jāniyā, jaññā** all have the same WA).
[nā-function] • nāyati-(He) knows. [wa] ñā+nā+ti.
Note:(1) "**jā**" function is applied only when "**nā**" affix is applied after the root.

(2) "**jaṁ**" function is applied when "**ñā**" morphological function is present behind (**i.e.** after this function has been done by Sutta 508)
(3) "**nā**" function is applied when changing of affix "nā" into "**ya**" is done by Sutta 509.

४७१, ४८३. दिसस्स पस्स दिस्स दक्खा वा

471, 483. **Disassa passa, dissa, dakkhā vā.**

[Disassa+passa, dissa, dakkhā+vā. 3 words]

[V] **Disa**-icce'tassa dhātussa **passa, dissa, dakkha**-icce'te ādesā honti vā.

The root "**disa**" sometimes changes into "**passa, dissa, dakkha**". [The applied functions are shown underlined]

• Passati, • dissati, • dakkhati-(He) sees.
[wa] disa+a+ti. (All three have the same wa)
• adakkha-(He) saw.
[wa] disa+ā (A shortened Hiyyattanī "ā" Vibatti).

Vā'ti kimatthaṁ? What is the word "vā" for?
To show that function of this Sutta is not always applied in some instances shown below as restricted by the word "vā".
* Addasa-(He) saw. [wa] disa+ā (A shortened Hiyyattanī "ā" Vibatti).

४७२, ५३१. ब्यञ्जनन्तस्स चो छप्पच्चयेसु च

472, 531. **Byañjana'ntassa co chapaccayesu ca.**

[Byañjana-antassa+co+chapaccayesu+ca. 4 words]

[V] Byañjanantassa dhātussa **co** hoti **cha**paccayesu paresu.

The last component consonant of a root changes into "**ca**" when a "**cha**" affix follows. [The applied function "c" is shown in bold, underlined]

(1) • Jigucchati. (Here, the last consonant "**p**" of the root "**gupa**" changes into "**c**")
(2) • tikicchati. (Here, the last consonant "**t**" of the root "**kita**" changes into "**c**")

(3) • jighaccchati. (Here, the last consonant "**s**" of the root "**ghasa**" changes into "**c**") [Refer to 434]

४७३, ५२९. को खे च

473, 529. **Ko khe ca.** [Ko+khe+ca. 3 words]

[V] Byañjana'ntassa dhātussa **ko** hoti **kha**paccaye pare.

The last component consonant of the root changes into "**ka**" when a "**kha**" affix is applied after the root.
[The applied function "k" is shown in bold, underlined]

(1) • Titi**k**khati. (Here, the last consonant "**j**" of the root "**tija**" changes into "**k**")

(2) • bubhu**k**khati. (Here, the last consonant "**j**" of the root "**bhuja**" changes into "**k**") [Re: 433-434]

४७४, ५३५. हरस्स गी से

474, 535. **Harassa gī se.** [Harassa+gī+se. 3 words]

[V] **Hara-**icce'tassa dhātussa sabbasse'va **gī-**ādeso hoti **sa**paccaye pare.

The entire root "**hara**" changes into "**gī**" when an affix "**sa**" is applied after the root.
[The applied function "gī" is shown in bold, underlined]

• Ji**gī**sati-(He) wants to carry. [This verb has other root such as "**esa**-to search"] [wa] hara or esa+sa+ti [Re: 434]

४७५, ४६५. ब्रूभून माहभूवा परोक्खायं

475, 465. **Brū, bhū, na'māha, bhūvā parokkhāyaṁ.**
[Brū, bhū, naṁ+āha, bhūvā+parokkhāyaṁ. 3 words]

[V] **Brū, bhū-**icce'tesaṁ dhātūnaṁ **āha, bhūva-**icce'te ādesā honti yathāsaṅkhyaṁ parokkhāyaṁ vibhattiyaṁ.

The root words "**brū, bhū**" changes into "**āha, bhūva**" respectively when Parokkhā vibattis are applied after them.
[Brū>āha. Bhū>bhūva. The applied functions shown underlined]

• Āha-(He) said. *sl.*[wa] brū+a (Parokkhā Vibatti.)
• āhu-(They) said. *pl*, [wa] brū+u (Parokkhā Vibatti)
• babhūva-(It) has been. *sl.* [wa] bhū+a (Parokkhā Vibatti)
• babhūvu *pl.* [wa] bhū+u (Parokkhā Vibatti. No affixes)

Parokkhāyami'ti kimatthaṁ?
What is the word "prokkhāyaṁ" for?
To show that the example below is not a parokkhā vibatti.
So, it is inapplicable.

• Abravuṁ-(they) said. [wa] brū+uṁ (Ajjattanī Vibatti, "a" is inserted in front of the verb by Sutta 519)

४७६, ४४२. गमिस्सन्तो च्छो वा सब्बासु
476, 442. **Gamissa'nto ccho vā sabbāsu.**

[Gamissa+anto+ccho+vā+sabbāsu. 5 words]

[V] **Gamu-**icce'tassa dhātussa anto **ma**kāro **cch**o hoti vā sabbāsu paccaya, vibhattīsu.
The component consonant "**m**" of the root "**gamu**" sometimes changes into "**cch**" in verbs of all vibattis and affixes. [The applied function "cch" is shown in bold, underlined]

• Ga**<u>ccha</u>**māno-(While he is) going. [wa] gamu+"a+māna"+si.
Note: This example has two affixes. Those inside the quotation mark " " are two affixes.
• ga**<u>ccha</u>**nto-(While he is) going. [wa] gamu+anta+si.

In each set of examples below, the second is inapplicable one.

• Ga**<u>ccha</u>**ti, * gameti-(He) goes. (In second * example, affix "a" becomes "e" by Sutta 510)
[wa] gamu+a+ti (Both are Vattamāna Vibatti verbs, same WA).
• Ga**<u>ccha</u>**tu, * gametu-(Let him) go. (Here, "a" becomes "e" by 510)
[wa] gamu+a+tu (Both are Pañcamī Vibatti verbs, same WA).
• Ga**<u>cch</u>**eyya. * Gameyya-(He should) go.
[wa] gamu+eyya (Both are Sattamī Vibatti verbs, the same wa).
• Aga**<u>cch</u>**ā, * Agamā-(He) has gone.
[wa] gamu+ā (Both Hiyyattanī Vibatti verbs, the same WA, with no affix).

- Aga**cch**ī, * Agamī-(He) has gone.
  [wa] gamu+ī (Both Ajjattanī Vibatti verbs, the same WA).
- Ga**cch**issati, * Gamissati-(He) will go.
  [wa] gamu+ssati (Both Bhavissanti Vibatti verbs, same WA).
- Aga**cch**issā, * Agamissā-(He might have) gone (Actually he didn't).
  [wa] gamu+ssā (Both Kālātipatti Vibatti verbs, same WA).

Gamisse'ti kimatthaṁ?
What is the word "gamissa" for?
To show that the example below is not of the root "gamu", but the other root word "isu". So it is inapplicable.
* Icchati-(He) wants. [wa] isu+a+ti.

४७७, ४७९. वचस्स'ज्जतनिम्हि मकारा ओ

477, 479. **Vacassa'jjatanimhi'makāro o.**

[Vacassa+ajjatanimhi+akāro+o. 4 words]

[V] **Vaca**-icce'tassa dhātussa **a**kāro **o**tta'māpajjate ajjatanimhi vibhattimhi.

The initial component vowel of the root "**vaca**" changes into "**o**" when an Ajjattanī vibatti is applied after the root.
[The applied function is shown in bold, underlined]

- Av**o**ca-(He) said. ***sl.*** [wa] vaca+ā(Ajjattanī Attanopada Vibatti verb).
- Av**o**cuṁ-(They) said. ***pl.*** [wa] vaca+uṁ(Ajjattanī Parassapada verb).

Ajjatanimhī'ti kimatthaṁ?
What is the word "ajjattanimhi" for?
To show that examples below are not of "ajjattanī", but of "Hiyyattanī". So, they are inapplicable.
* Avaca-(He) said. ***sl.*** [wa] vaca+ā [Vibatti "ā" is shortened]
* avacū-(they) said. ***pl.*** [wa] vaca+ū

४७८, ४३८. अकारो दीघं हिमिमेसु

478, 438. **Akāro dīghaṁ hi, mi, mesu.**
[Akāro+dīghaṁ+hi, mi, mesu. 3 words]

[V] Akāro **dīgha**'māpajjate **hi, mi, ma-**icce'tesu vibhattīsu.

When "**hi, mi, ma**" vibattis are applied in a verb, the vowel before them is to be made into **a dīgha** (**i.e.** lengthened). ["**mhe**" vibatti is also applicable for the function of this Sutta. The applied function is shown in bold, underlined]

- Gacch**<u>ā</u>**hi-(you) go. [wa] gamu+a+hi
- gacch**<u>ā</u>**mi-(I) go. [wa] gamu+a+mi
- gacch**<u>ā</u>**ma-(We) go. [wa] gamu+a+ma
- gacch**<u>ā</u>**mhe-(We) go. [wa] gamu+a+mhe

Mikāraggahaṇena **hi**vibhattimhi **a**kāro kvaci **na dīgha**'māpajjate.

By means of "mi" in Sutta, the dīgha procedure is inapplicable in some words (even if "hi" is applied).
* Gacchahi-(you) go. [wa] gamu+a+hi

४७९, ४५२. हि लोपं वा

479, 452. **Hi lopaṁ vā.** [Hi+lopaṁ+vā. 3 words]

[V] **Hi**vibhatti **lopa**'māpajjate vā.

The "**hi**" vibatti (belonging to pañcamī vibatti group) is sometimes elided.
[Only the first is applied example. The second is inapplicable in each set.]

- Gaccha, * gacchāhi-(you) go. [wa] gamu+a+hi
- gama, * gamāhi-(you) go. [wa] gamu+a+hi (wa of both set of examples are the same)
- gamaya, * gamayāhi-(you causes to) go. (You prompt him to go. Causative verbs). [wa] gamu+ṇaya+hi

Hī'ti kimatthaṁ?
What is the word "hi" for?
To show that examples shown below are not of "hi", but of

"ti". So they are inapplicable.
* Gacchati-he goes. [wa] gamu+a+ti
* gamayati-(He causes to) go. [wa] gamu+ṇaya+ti

४८०, ४९०. होतिस्सरे' हो'हे भविस्सन्तिम्हि सस्स च

480, 490. Hotissare'ho'he' bhavissantimhi ssassa ca.

[Hotissaro+eha, oha, e+bhavissantimhi+ssassa+ca. 5 words]

[V] **Hū**-icce'tassa dhātussa saro **eha, oha, e**-tta'māpajjate bhavissantimhi, **ss**assa ca **lopo** hoti vā.

The component vowel "**ū**" of the root word "**hū**" sometimes changes into "**eha, oha, e**" when bhavissanti vibatti is applied after the root. Besides, the component consonants "**ss**" of the vibatti are also elided. [Two functions] In three set of examples below, all two functions are applied. Shown in bold, underlined.

[eh] • H**eh**iti-(It) will be. [wa] hū+ssati
• h**eh**inti-(They) will be. p*l*. [wa] hū+ssanti
[oh] • h**oh**iti, [wa] hū+ssati • h**oh**inti, ***pl***. [wa] hū+ssanti
[e] • h**e**ti, [wa] hū+ssati • h**e**nti, ***pl***. [wa] hū+ssanti

In three set of examples below, only the first function is applied. Eliding of "**ss**", the second function, is not applied.
[eh] • h**eh**issati, [wa] hū+ssati • h**eh**issanti, ***pl***. [wa] hū+ssanti
[oh] • h**oh**issati,[wa] hū+ssati • h**oh**issanti, ***pl***. [wa] hū+ssanti
[e] • h**e**ssati, [wa] hū+ssati • h**e**ssanti. ***pl***. [wa] hū+ssanti
Note: No affix in these examples though there can be an "a" affix applicable. There will be an "i" to be inserted before Vibatti which renders any extra vowel unnecessary to complete the word.

Hū'ti kimatthaṁ? What is the word "hū" for?
To show that the examples below are not of the root word "hū", but of "bhū". So, they are inapplicable.
* Bhavissati-(It) will be. [wa] bhū+ssati
* bhavissanti-(they) will be. p*l*. [wa] bhū+ssanti

Bhavissantimhī'ti kimatthaṁ?
What is the word "bhavissantimhi" for?

To show that the example below is not of "bhavissanti", but of "vattamāna-**ti**". So, it is inapplicable.
* Hoti-(It) is. [wa] hū+a+ti

४८१, ५२४. करस्स सप्पच्चयस्स काहो

481, 524. **Karassa sapaccayassa kāho.**

[Karassa+sa-paccayassa+kāho. 3 words]

[V] **Kara**-icce'tassa dhātussa sapaccayassa **kāhā'**deso hoti vā bhavissantimhi vibhattimhi, **sas**sa ca niccaṁ **lopo** hoti.

When a bhavissanti is applied, the root "**kara**", along with the component consonant "**ss**" of the applied vibatti, sometimes changes into "**kāha**". Besides, the component consonants "**ss**" of the vibatti are always elided.
[Applied functions are shown in bold, underlined.]

- **Kāh**ati, • **kāh**iti-(He) will do. [wa] kara+a+ssati (Both are the same)
- **kāha**si, • **kāh**isi-(you) will do. [wa] kara+a+ssasi (Both are the same)
- **kāh**āmi-(I) will do. [wa] kara+a+ssāmi
- **kāh**āma-(We) will do. [wa] kara+a+ssāma

Vā'ti kimatthaṁ? What is the word "vā" for?
To show that function of this Sutta is not always applied in some examples shown below as restricted by the word "vā".
* Karissati-(He) will do. [wa] kara+a+ssati
* karissanti-(they) will do. [wa] kara+a+ssanti

Sapaccayaggahaṇena aññehi'pi bhavissantiyā vibhattiyā **khāmi, khāma, chāmi, chāma**-iccā'dayo ādesā honti.

By means of the word "**sapaccaya**" in Sutta, the "**ssāmi, ssāma**" of bhavissanti vibatti applied after other roots, can also change into "**khāmi, khāma, chāmi, chāma**" respectively. [Functions are shown underlined]

(1) • Vakkhāmi-(I) will say. [wa] vaca+a+ssāmi
• vakkhāma-(we) will say. [wa] vaca+a+ssāma

Note: The last consonant "c" of the root changes into "k" by Sutta 473 in these examples and later combined it to next "kh".

(2) • vacchāmi-(I) will stay. [wa] vasa+a+ssāmi

• vacchāma-(we) will stay. [wa] vasa+a+ssāma

Note: The last consonant "s" of the root changes into "c" by Sutta 472 in these examples. It is later combined to next "ch" to become a complete word.

Iti ākhyātakappe tatiyo kaṇḍo.

The Third Section of Ākhyāta Verb ends.

Catuttha Kaṇḍa
The Fourth Section

४८२, ५०८. दादन्तस्सं मिमेसु

482, 508. **Dā'dantassa'ṁ mi, mesu.**

[Dā-antassa+aṁ+mi, mesu. 3 words]

[V] **Dā**-icce'tassa dhātussa antassa **aṁ** hoti **mi, ma**-icce'tesu.

The component vowel "**ā**" of the root "**dā**" changes into "**aṁ**" when "**mi, ma**" vibattis are applied after it. [See the function shown underlined below]

- Dammi-(I) give. [wa] dā+mi
- damma-(We) give. [wa] dā+ma

Note: The applied "**ṁ**" becomes ordinary "**m**" by the rule of sutta 31.

४८३, ५२७. असंयोगन्तस्स वुद्धि कारिते

483, 527. **Asaṁyogantassa vuddhi**[41] **kārite.**

[Asaṁyogantassa+vuddhi+kārite. 3 words]

[V] Asaṁyogantassa[42] dhātussa kārite **vuddhi** hoti.

The component vowel of non-conjunct root undergoes the process of "**vuddhi**" in verbs where causative affixes are applied after them. [The applied Vuddhi vowels are shown in bold]

- K**ā**reti-(he) causes to do. • k**ā**renti-(they) causes to do.
- k**ā**rayati, • k**ā**rayanti,
- k**ā**rāpeti, • k**ā**rāpenti,
- k**ā**rāpayati, • k**ā**rāpayanti. [Refer to Sutta 438]

Asaṁyogantasse'ti kimatthaṁ?
What is the word "asaṁyogantassa" for?
To show that the examples shown below are not

---

[41]**Vuddhi** means an increase in the metrical nature of the word. Through this procedure, "**a**" changes into "**ā**", "**i**" changes into "**ī**", "**U**" changes into "**ū**". This may seems like similar to "digha-the lengthening process" of rassa **i.e.** short vowels. But it is somewhat different in terms of how it takes place. In addition, "**i and ī**" changes into "**e**", while "**u & ū**" changes into "**o**". **This process of morphing into another different vowel form is called** "**vuddhi**". Furthermore, "**e**" becomes either "**aya or āya**" while "**o**" also becomes "**ava or āva**" by means of another follow-up procedure called "**anuvuddhi**"(**anu**-means following, **i.e.** a follow-up procedure after vuddhi has been applied in some words). All three Suttas from 483, 484, 485, perform vuddhi function. Only 483-485 have a wider application while Sutta 484 is confined to only a few roots in its function.

[42] "**Asaṁyoganta**" means ending in non-conjunct.[**A**-not, **saṁyoga**-being well-joined in a cluster of words, **i.e.** conjunct, **anta**-ending] The conjunct-consonants are clearly noticeable in the oriental Asian scripts which used to be written in vertical order in the languages such as Devanāgari and Burmese etc. In the Romanized Pāli which used to be written in horizontal mode, it may not be easily noticeable. However, when **double, vowel-less consonants of similar or dissimilar shape are present** in the root, it can be easily assumed as "**saṁyoganta dhātu** (the conjunct-ending root) ".

"asaṁyoganta-single consonant words", but "saṁyoganta-conjunct-consonants words". So, they are inapplicable. (See conjuncts in the verbs shown in bold, underlined)
* Ci**nt**ayati-(he) thinks. * ma**nt**ayati-(he) consults or calls. [Refer to Sutta 452]

४८४, ५४२. घटादीनं वा

484, 542. **Ghaṭā'dīnaṁ vā.** [Ghaṭa-ādīnaṁ+vā. 2 words]

[V] **Ghaṭā**'dīnaṁ dhātūnaṁ asaṁyogantānaṁ **vuddhi** hoti vā kārite.

The component vowel of the non-conjunct root "**ghaṭa**" etc. sometimes undergoes the process of "**vuddhi**" when followed by a causative affix.
[The applied Vuddhi vowels are shown in bold. The second example in each pair is inapplicable]

- Gh**ā**ṭeti, * ghaṭeti-(he) causes to make effort. [wa] ghaṭa+ṇe+ti
- gh**ā**ṭayati,* ghaṭayati. [wa] ghaṭa+ṇaya+ti
- gh**ā**ṭāpeti, * ghaṭāpeti. [wa] ghaṭa+ṇāpe+ti
- gh**ā**ṭāpayati, * ghaṭāpayati. [wa] ghaṭa+ṇāpaya+ti
- g**ā**meti, * gameti-(he) causes to go. [wa] gamu+ṇe+ti
- g**ā**mayati, * gamayati, [wa] gamu+ṇaya+ti
- g**ā**māpeti, * gamāpeti. [wa] gamu+ṇāpe+ti
- g**ā**māpayati, * gamāpayati. [wa] gamu+ṇāpaya+ti

Ghaṭādīnami'ti kimatthaṁ?
What is the word "ghaṭādīnaṁ" for?
To show that the example below is inapplicable as it is not the root "ghaṭa", but "kara".
* Kāreti.

४८५, ४३४. अञ्ञेसु च

485, 434. **Aññesu ca.** [Aññesu+ca. 2 words]

[V] Aññesu ca paccayesu sabbesaṁ dhātūnaṁ asaṁyogantānaṁ **vuddhi** hoti.

The component vowel of non-conjunct roots usually undergoes the process of "**vuddhi**" in verbs when other non-causative affixes and vibattis follow. [The result of applied point of Vuddhi are shown underlined]

• Jayati-(he) conquers. • hoti, [wa] hū+a+ti • bhavati. [Refer to Sutta 445]

Caggahaṇena **ṇu-**paccayassā'pi **vuddhi** hoti.

By the word "Ca", the affix "**ṇu**" can become **a Vuddhi,** (**i.e.** the component vowel "**u**" of the affix changes into "**o**".) [See "**o**" in the example shown in bold, underlined]

• Abhisuṇ**o**ti-(he) listens. [Refer to Sutta 448]

४८६, ५४३. गुहदुसानं दीघं

486, 543. **Guha, dusānaṁ dīghaṁ.**

[Guha, dusānaṁ+dīghaṁ. 2 words]

[V] **Guha, dusa**-icce'tesaṁ dhātūnaṁ saro **dīgha'**māpajjate kārite.

The component vowel "**u**" of root words "**guha, dusa**" changes into a dīgha "**ū**" when causative affixes are applied after them. [See the applied dīgha vowels shown in bold]

• G**ū**hayati-(It) cause to protect, hides. [wa] guha+ṇaya+ti
• d**ū**sayati-(he) causes to spoil. [wa] dusa+ṇaya+ti

४८७, ४७८. वचवसवहादीन मुकारो वस्स ये

487, 478. Vaca, vasa, vahā'dīna'mukāro vassa ye.

[Vaca, vasa, vaha-ādīnaṁ+ukāro+vassa+ye. 4 words]

[V] **Vaca, vasa, vaha**-icce'va'mādīnaṁ dhātūnaṁ **va**kārassa **u**kāro hoti **ya**paccaye pare.

The component vowel "**a**" and sometimes consonant "**v**" of the roots "**vaca, vasa, vaha**" changes into "**u**" when a "**ya**" affix follows. (**i.e.** is present in the verb).

Note: Two ways of changing into "u": In the first example, the whole "va" changes into "u". In the rest, only "a" of "va" changes into "u". The applied vowel "u" is shown in bold, underlined.

- **U**ccate, [wa] vaca+ya+te [Here, "**Va**" changes into "**u**"]
- V**u**ccati, [wa] vaca+ya+te [Refer to Sutta 441, both are the same]
- V**u**ssati-(has) stayed. [wa] vasa+ya+te
- V**u**yhati-(It is) carried away (as in river currents). [wa] vaha+ya+te

४८८, ४८१. ह विपरिययो लो वा

488, 481. Ha vipariyayo[43] lo vā.

[Ha-vipariyayo+lo+vā. 3 words]

[V] **Ha**kārassa **vipariyayo** hoti **ya**paccaye pare, **ya**paccayassa ca **l**o hoti vā.

In the roots such as "vaha" etc. with "ya" affix being applied after it, the consonants "h (of the root) " and "y (of the affix) " are to be reversed in their positions (**i.e**. **y** of the affix "ya" moved to front. Hence, it looks like "**yha**"). In addition, "**ya**" changes into "**la**" in some instances of verbs. [The words being reversed are shown in bold, underlined]

---

[43] **Vipariyāya** means reversing the position of two letters from back to forth and vice versa. It is one form of grammatical procedure in the morphology. [**Vi**-specially+**pari**-being reversed+**aya**-happening]

- Vu**lh**ati,
- vu**yh**ati-(It is) carried away (as by river currents, same meaning).
  [wa] vaha+ya+te

Note: In first example, the affix "y" becomes "l" after reversal.
In the second, only "h" and "y" are reversed.

४८९, ५१९. गहस्स घे प्पे

489, 519. **Gahassa ghe ppe.** [Gahassa+ghe+ppe. 3 words]

[V] **Gaha**-icce'tassa dhātussa sabbassa **ghe**kāro hoti **ppa**-paccaye pare.

The entire root "**gaha**" changes into "**ghe**" when the affix "**ppa**" is applied after the root. [See the applied function shown underlined]

- Gheppati-(he) takes. [Refer to Sutta 450]

४९०, ५१८. हलोपो ण्हाम्हि

490, 518. **Halopo ṇhāmhi.** [Halopo+ṇhāmhi. 2 words]

[V] **Gaha**-icce'tassa dhātussa **ha**kārassa **lopo** hoti **ṇhā**-mhi paccaye pare.

The consonant "**ha**" of the root word "**gaha**" is elided when the affix "**ṇhā**" follows it. [See the elided "**ha**" of the root "**gaha**" is no longer visible which is shown underlined].

- Gaṇhāti-(he) takes. [Refer to Sutta 450]

४९१, ५२३. करस्स कासत्तमज्जतनिम्हि

491, 523. **Karassa kāsatta'majjatanimhi.**

[Karassa+kāsattaṁ+ajjatanimhi. 3 words]

[V] **Kara**-icce'tassa dhātussa sabbassa **kāsa**-ttaṁ hoti vā ajjatanimhi vibhattimhi.

The entire root word "**kara**" sometimes changes into "**kāsa**" in verbs when an ajjattanī vibatti is applied. [The applied function "**kāsa**" is shown in bold, underlined]

• Akāsi-(he) did. [wa] kara+ī
• akāsuṁ-(they) did. [wa] kara+uṁ
* Akari-(he) did. [wa] kara+ī
* akaruṁ-(they) did. [wa] kara+uṁ (These are inapplicable examples)

Kāsatta'mitibhāvaniddesena aññatthā'pi sā'gamo hoti.

By using the Bhāva-taddhita expression "kāsattaṁ", an "**s**" is to be inserted (before the vibatti) applied after other roots rather than the root "kara". [The applied function "**s**" is shown in bold, underlined. The vibatti "ī" is shortened]

• Ahosi-(It) was. [wa] hū+ī • adāsi-(he) gave. [wa] dā+ī

४९२, ४९९. असस्मा मिमानं मिम्हा'न्तलोपो च

492, 499. **Asasmā mi, mā, naṁ mhimhā'ntalopo ca.**

[Asasmā+mi, mā, naṁ+mhi, mhā+antalopo+ca. 5 words]

[V] **Asa-**icce'tāya dhātuyā **mi, ma,** icce'tesaṁ vibhattīnaṁ **mhi, mhā**'desā honti vā, dhātva'ntassa lopo ca.

The vibattis "**mi, ma**" applied after the root word "**asa**" sometimes changes into "**mhi, mha**" respectively. In addition, the component consonant "s" of the root is also elided. [Two functions. See applied function "**mhi**" "**mha**" shown underlined.]

• Amhi-(I) am. [wa] asa+mi • amha-(we) are. [wa] asa+ma
* asmi-(I) am. [wa] asa+mi * asma-(we) are. [wa] asa+ma

४९३, ४९८. थस्स त्थत्तं

493, 498. **Thassa tthattaṁ.** [Thassa+tthattaṁ. 2 words]

[V] **Asa-**icce'tāya dhātuyā **tha**ssa vibhattissa **ttha**ttaṁ hoti, dhātva'ntassa lopo ca.

The vibatti "**tha**" applied after the root word "**asa**" sometimes changes into "**ttha**". Besides, the component consonant "s" of the root is also elided.
[Two functions. See the applied function "**ttha**" shown underlined]

• Attha-(you, ***pl***) are. [wa] asa+tha

४९४, ४९५. तिस्स त्थित्तं

494, 495. **Tissa tthittaṁ.** [Tissa+tthittaṁ. 2 words]

[V] **Asa-**icce'tāya dhātuyā **ti**ssa vibhattissa **tthi**ttaṁ hoti, dhātva'ntassa lopo ca.

The vibatti "**ti**" applied after the root word "**asa**" sometimes changes into "**tthi**". Besides, the component consonant "s" of the root is also elided.
(See the applied function "**tthi**" shown underlined).

- Atthi-(There) is. [wa] asa+ti

४९५, ५००. तुस्स त्थुत्तं

495, 500. **Tussa tthuttaṁ.** [Tussa+tthuttaṁ. 2 words]

[V] **Asa-**icce'tāya dhātuyā **tu**ssa vibhattissa **tthu**ttaṁ hoti, dhātva'ntassa lopo ca.

The vibatti "**tu**" applied after the root "**asa**" sometimes changes into "**tthu**" . In addition, the component consonant "s" of the root is also elided.
[See the applied function "**tthu**" shown underlined.]

- Atthu-(Let it) be. [wa] asa+tu

४९६, ४९७. सिम्हि च

496, 497. **Simhi ca.** [Simhi+ca. 2 words]

[V] **Asa**sse'va dhātussa **si**mhi vibhattimhi antassa **lopo** ca hoti.

The component consonant "**s**" of the root word "**asa**" is elided when "**si**" vibatti is applied after the root. (The applied function is understandable only through morphological procedure.)

Ko nu tva'masi mārisa?
Ko-who, nu-?, tva'masi [tvaṁ+asi] tvaṁ-you, • asi-(you) are. mārisa-friend, **i.e.** Friend, who are you? [wa] asa+si
Note: "**Nu**" is a Nipāta particle equal to a question mark "**?**". It is used to be syntactically related to the verb. Here, it is related to the verb "**asi+nu**" which can be translated as "**are you**".

४९७, ४७७. लभस्मा ईइंनं त्थ, त्थं

497, 477. **Labhasmā ī, iṁnaṁ ttha, tthaṁ.**

[Labhasmā+ī, iṁnaṁ+ttha, tthaṁ. 3 words]

[V] **Labha**-icce'tāya dhātuyā **ī, iṁ**naṁ vibhattīnaṁ **ttha, tthaṁ**-ādesā honti, dhātva'ntassa lopo ca.

The ajjattanī vibattis "**ī, iṁ**" applied after the root "**labha**" respectively changes into "**ttha, tthaṁ**". Additionally, the component consonant "**bh**" of the root is also elided.
[Two functions. See the applied functions "**ttha**" "**tthaṁ**" shown underlined.]

- Alattha-(he) got, obtained. [wa] labha+ī
- Alatthaṁ-(I) got, obtained. [wa] labha+iṁ

४९८, ४८०. कुसस्मा दी च्छि

498, 480. **Kusasmā'dī cchi.** [Kusasmā+ī+cchi. 3 words]

[V] **Kusa**-icce'tāya dhātuyā **ī**-vibhattissa **cchi** hoti, dhātva'ntassa lopo ca.

The ajjattanī vibatti "**ī**" applied after the root word "**kusa**" changes into "**cchi**" and the component consonant "**sa**" of the root is also elided.
[Two functions. See applied function "**cchi**" shown underlined.]

- Akkocchi-(he) reviles (by saying abusive words etc.). [wa] kusa+ī

४९९, ५०७. दा धातुस्स दज्जं

499, 507. **Dādhātussa dajjaṁ.** [Dā-dhātussa+dajjaṁ. 2 words]

[V] **Dā**-icce'tassa dhātussa sabbassa **dajjā**'deso hoti vā.

The whole "**dā**" of the root "**dā**" sometimes changes into "**dajja**". [See the applied function of "**dajja**" shown underlined.]

- Dajjāmi-(I) give. [wa] dā+a+mi
- dajjeyya-(he) should give. [wa] dā+eyya

* dadāmi-(I) give. [wa] dā+a+mi
* dadeyya-(he) should give. [wa] dā+eyya (Inapplicable examples)

५००, ४८६. वदस्स वज्जं

500, 486. **Vadassa vajjaṁ.** [Vadassa+vajjaṁ. 2 words]

[V] **Vada**-icce'tassa dhātussa sabbassa **vajjā**'deso hoti vā.

The entire root "**vada**" sometimes changes into "**vajja**". [See applied function "**vajja**" shown underlined. The second pair is inapplicable]

• Vajjāmi-(I) say. [wa] vada+a+mi
• vajjeyya-(he) should say. [wa] vada+eyya
* vadāmi-(I) say. [wa] vada+a+mi
* vadeyya-(he) should say. [wa] vada+eyya.

५०१, ४४३. गमिस्स घम्मं

501, 443. **Gamissa ghammaṁ.** [Gamissa+ghammaṁ. 2 words]

[V] **Gamu**-icce'tassa dhātussa sabbassa **ghammā**'deso hoti vā.

The entire root "**gamu**" sometimes changes into "**ghamma**". [See the applied function "**ghamma**" shown underlined.]

• ghammatu-(let him) go. [wa] gamu+a+tu
• Ghammāhi-(you) go. [wa] gamu+a+hi
• ghammāmi-(I) go. [wa] gamu+a+mi

Note: These ghamma-function applied verbs are seldom found in the canonical texts.

Vā'ti kimatthaṁ? What is the word "vā" for?
To show that the function of Sutta is not applied as restricted by the word "vā" in the examples below.
* Gacchatu-(let him) go. * gacchāhi-(you) go.
* gacchāmi-(I) go. [WA as shown above]

५०२, ४९३. यम्हि दा धा मा ठा हा पा मह मथादीन मी

502, 493. **Yamhi dā, dhā, mā, ṭhā, hā, pā, maha, mathā'dīna'mī.**

[Yamhi+dā, dhā, mā, ṭhā, hā, pā, maha, matha-ādīnaṁ+ī. 3 words]

[V] **Ya**mhi paccaye pare **dā, dhā, mā, ṭhā, hā, pā, maha, matha**-icce'va'mādīnaṁ dhātūnaṁ anto **ī**-kāra'māpajjate.

The component vowel of the roots "**dā, dhā, mā, ṭhā, hā, pā, maha, matha**" etc, changes into "**ī**" when a "**ya**" affix is applied after the roots. [See the applied function "**ī**" shown in bold in front of "ya" affix. This affix is applicable by Sutta 440 only, not by 447. As such, these verbs are only in Kamma, Bhāva senses and voices. However, verbs of active voice prefixed with some Upasagga and structured in this pattern are sometimes found in the Pāli texts. **e.g.** Ohīyati-(he) loses, Nilīyati-(he) hides. Pidhīyati-(It) blocks]

- D**ī**yati-(It is) given. [wa] dā+ya+te
- dh**ī**yati-(It is) carried. [wa] dhā+ya+te
- m**ī**yati-(It is) measured. [wa] mā+ya+te
- ṭh**ī**yati-(It is) stood . [wa] ṭhā+ya+te
- h**ī**yati-(It is) abandoned. [wa] hā+ya+te
- p**ī**yati-(It is) drunk. [wa] pā+ya+te
- mah**ī**yati-(It is) honored. [wa] maha+ya+te
- math**ī**yati-(It is) churned. [wa] matha+ya+te

५०३, ४८५. यजस्सादिस्सि

503, 485. **Yajassā'dissi'.** [Yajassa+ādissa+i. 3 words]

[V] **Yaja**-icce'tassa dhātussa ādissa **i**-kārādeso hoti **ya**paccaye pare.

The initial consonant "**y**" of "**ya**" of the root word "**yaja**" changes into "**i**" when a "**ya**" affix is applied after it. [See the applied function "**i**" shown in bold. One "**j**" is augmented]

- **I**jjate-(is) worshiped, mayā-by me, Buddho-Buddha, **i.e.** Buddha is worshipped by me (Passive voice verb). [wa] yaja+ya+te

५०४, ४७०. सब्बतो उं इंसु

504, 470. **Sabbato uṁ iṁsu.** [Sabbato+uṁ+iṁsu. 3 words]

[V] Sabbehi dhātūhi **uṁ**-vibhattissa **iṁsu**ādeso hoti.

An ajjattanī vibatti "**uṁ**" applied after the roots of all verbs, changes into "**iṁsu**". [See applied function "**iṁsu**" shown underlined.]

- Upasaṅkamiṁsu-(they) approached, came near. [wa] upa√saṁ√kamu+uṁ.
- Nisīdiṁsu-(they) sat. [wa] ni√sada+uṁ.

५०५, ४८२. जरमरानं जीर जीय्य मीय्या वा

505, 482. **Jara, marānaṁ jīra, jiyya, miyyā vā.**

[Jara, marānaṁ+jīra, jiyya, miyyā+vā. 3 words]

[V] **Jara, mara**-icce'tesaṁ dhātūnaṁ **jīra, jiyya, miyyā'**desā honti vā.

The root words "**Jara, mara**" sometimes changes into "**jīra, jiyya, miyya**".

Note: The root "**Jara**" changes into "**jīra, jiyya**" and the root "**mara**" changes into "**miyya**".

[**jīra**-function] • Jīrati-(he) gets old. [wa] jara+a+ti.
• jīranti-(they) get old. [wa] jara+a+anti.

[**jiyya**-function] • jiyyati-(he) gets old. • jiyyanti-(they) get old
[WA same as before]

[**miyya**-function] • miyyati-(he) dies. [wa] mara+a+ti.
• miyyanti-(they) die. [wa] mara+a+anti.
* marati-(he) dies. * maranti-(they) die.

[The last two are inapplicable examples as restricted by "**vā**"]

५०६, ४९६. सब्बत्था'सस्सादिलोपो च

506, 496. **Sabbatthā'sassā'dilopo ca.**

[Sabbattha+asassa+ādilopo+ca. 4 words]

[V] Sabbattha vibhatti, paccayesu **asa-**icce'tassa dhātussa ādissa lopo hoti vā.

In instances of all vibattis and affixes, the initial vowel "**a**" of the root "**asa**" is sometimes elided.
[The function is clearly noticeable as there is no more "a" of the root "asa". These examples are widely found in the Pāli texts.]

- Siyā-(It) should be. [wa] asa+eyya.
- Santi-(There) are. [wa] asa+a+anti.
- Sante-(while it) is being, that being so. ***kv.***
  [wa] asa+anta+smiṁ.
- Samāno-(while it) is, if being so. ***kv.***
  [wa] asa+"a+māna"+si.

Note: Both **Sante** and **Samāno** are auxiliary Kita-verbs with multiple-uses. They are frequently used as ***present participle*** or ***cls*** **or** ***adv*** **or** ***adj.***

Vā'ti kimatthaṁ?
What is the word "vā" for?
To show that the function of Sutta is not applied as restricted by the word "vā".
* Asi-(you) are. [wa] asa+a+si.

५०७, ५०१. असब्बधातुके भू

507, 501. **Asabbadhātuke bhū.** [Asabbadhātuke+bhū. 2 words]

[V] **Asa**sse'va dhātussa bhū hoti vā asabbadhātuke.

The whole root "**asa**" sometimes changes into "**bhū**" in verbs where asabbadhātuka vibattis are applied. (The applied function can be seen in the same form of verbs structured with the root "bhū". This is the only injunction in the grammar where a root is changed into the verb-form of the other root "bhū" in instances of verbs with Asabbadhātuka-terminations.)

- Bhavissati-(it) will be. [wa] asa+a+ssati.
- Bhavissanti-(they) will be. [wa] asa+a+ssanti.

Vā'ti kimatthaṁ? What is the word "vā" for?
To show that the function of Sutta is not applied as restricted by the word "vā".
* Āsuṁ-(they) were. [wa] asa+uṁ.

५०८, ५१५. एय्यस्स ञातो इया ञा

508, 515. **Eyyassa ñāto iyā, ñā.**

[Eyyassa+ñāto+iyā, ñā. 3 words]

[V] **Eyya**ssa vibhattissa **ñā-**icce'tāya dhātuyā parassa **iyā, ñā-**ādesā honti vā.

A Sattamī vibatti "**eyya**" applied after the root word "**ñā**" sometimes changes into "**iyā, ñā**".
[The applied functions "**iyā**" and "**ñā**" are shown underlined]

- Jāniyā, • jaññā-(he) should know or it should be known. [One "**ñ**" is augmented in the second example. Refer to Sutta 470]

Vā'ti kimatthaṁ? What is the word "vā" for?
To show that the function of Sutta is not applied in the example below as being restricted by the word "vā".
* Jāneyya-(he) should know. [Refer to Sutta 470]

५०९, ५१६. नास्स लोपो यकारत्तं

509, 516. **Nāssa lopo yakārattaṁ.**

[Nāssa+lopo+yakārattaṁ. 3 words]

[V] **Ñā-**icce'tāya dhātuyā parassa **nā**paccayassa **lopo** hoti vā, **ya**kārattañ'ca.

The affix "**nā**" applied after the root word "**ñā**" is elided. Sometimes, the affix "**nā**" changes into "**ya**". [Two functions, one function for each example below]

- Jaññā-(he) should know, [Eliding of affix "nā" is applied]
- ñāyati-(he) knows. [Changing of the affix "nā" into "ya" is applied. Refer to Sutta 470]

Vā'ti kimatthaṁ? What is the word "vā" for?
To show that the function of Sutta is not applied as being restricted by the word "vā".
* Jānāti-(he) knows.

५१०, ४८७. लोपञ्चेत्तमकारो

510, 487. **Lopañ'ce'tta'makāro.**

[Lopaṁ+ca+ettaṁ+akāro. 4 words]

[V] Akārapaccayo **lopa'**māpajjate, **e**ttañ'ca hoti vā.

The affix "**a**"(per Sutta 445) is sometimes either elided or if unelided, it changes into an "**e**".
[This Sutta changes the affix "**a**" into "**e**" sometimes or elides it in most cases of "Bhū-group" verbs.]

• Vajjemi, • vademi-(I) say. [Here, "**a**" changes into "**e**"**.** See "**e**" shown in bold, underlined]
• vajjāmi, • vadāmi-(I) say. [Here, "**a**" is lengthened into "**ā**"]
[wa] vada+a+mi [Refer to Sutta 500]

५११, ५२१. उत्तमोकारो

511, 521. **Utta'mokāro.** [Uttaṁ+okāro. 2 words]

[V] **O**kārapaccayo **u**tta'māpajjate vā.

The affix "**o**" applied after the root word "**kara**" sometimes changes into "**u**"**.** [See the applied "u" function shown in bold, underlined in the first example. The second is inapplicable one]

• Kurumc-(hc) does. [wa] kara+o+te.
* karoti-(he) does. [wa] kara+o+ti.

Okāro'ti kimatthaṁ? What is the word "okāro" for?
To show that here "o" means an affix, not a "**vuddhi** morpheme **o**" as shown in example below. Hence, it is inapplicable here.
* Hoti. [wa] hū+a+ti.

५१२, ५२२. करस्साकारो च

512, 522. **Karassā'kāro ca.** [Karassa+akāro+ca. 3 words]

[V] **Kara**-icce'tassa dhātussa **a**kāro **u**tta'māpajjate vā.

The component vowel "**a**" of "**ka**" in the root word "**kara**", sometimes changes into "**u**". [See the applied "u" function shown in bold, underlined in the two examples]

• K**u**rute, * Karoti, [WA shown in the preceding Sutta]
• K**u**bbanti-(they) do. [wa] kara+o+anti.
* Kayirati-(he) does. [wa] kara+yira+ti.

Karasse'ti kimatthaṁ? What is the word "karassa" for?
To show that the examples below are not of the root "kara", but of the root "sara, & mara". So, they are inapplicable.
* Sarati-(he) remembers. [wa] sara+a+ti.
* marati-(he) dies. [wa] mara+a+ti.

५१३, ४३५. ओ अव सरे

513, 435. **O ava sare.** [O+ava+sare. 3 words]

[V] **O**kārassa dhātva'ntassa sare pare **avā'**deso hoti.

A Vuddhi morpheme "**o**" (of root words such as "**cu, bhū**" etc.) changes into "**ava**" when a vowel follows it. ["a vowel follows it" here means the affix "a"]
Note: "**o**" is a morpheme derivative of Vuddhi procedure performed on "**u-ū**" of roots "**cu, bhū**". See the applied function shown in bold, underlined.

• C**av**ati-(It) moves or dies. [wa] cu+a+ti.
• Bh**av**ati-(It) is. [wa] bhū+a+ti.

O'ti kimatthaṁ? What is the word "o" for?
To show that in the example below, there is no "o", but only a **vuddhi** morpheme "e", So it is inapplicable here.
* Jayati-(he) conquers. [wa] ji+a+ti.

५१४, ४९१. ए अय

514, 491. **E aya.** [E+aya. 2 words]

[V] **E**kārassa dhātva'ntassa sare pare **ayā'**deso hoti.

A Vuddhi morpheme "**e**" (of root words such as "**nī, ji**" etc) changes into "**aya**" when a vowel follows.[**i.e.** present behind in a verb. See the applied function shown in bold, underlined]
Note: "**o**" is a morpheme derivative of Vuddhi procedure performed on "**i-ī**" of roots "**Ji** and **Nī** ". See the applied function shown in bold, underlined.

• N**<u>ay</u>**ati-(he) carries. [wa] nī+a+ti. • j**<u>aya</u>**ti. [wa] ji+a+ti.

५१५, ५४१. ते आवाया कारिते

515, 541. **Te āvā'yā kārite.** [Te+āva, āyā+kārite. 3 words]

[V] Te **o, e**-icce'te **āva, āyā'**dese pāpuṇanti kārite.

Those vowels "**o** and **e**" respectively change into "**āva** and **āya**" when a causative affix follows. [See the applied functions of "**āva** and **āya**" shown in bold, underlined]
Note: "**o** and **e**" are morpheme derivatives of Vuddhi procedure performed on "**ū-ī**" of the roots "**Lū** and **Nī** ". See the applied function shown in bold, underlined.

• L**<u>āv</u>**eti-(he) causes to cut. [wa] lū+ṇe+ti.
• n**<u>āy</u>**eti-(he) causes to carry. [wa] nī+ṇe+ti.

Yogavibhāgena aññasmim'pi **e**kārassa **āyā'**deso hoti.

By means of **yogavibhāga** procedure, the component vowel "**e**" changes into "**āya**" in verbs where a non-causative affix is applied. [See the applied function shown in bold, underlined]

• G**<u>āy</u>**ati-(he) sings. [wa] ge+a+ti.
• g**<u>āy</u>**anti-(they) sing. [wa] ge+a+anti.

Note: A **yogavibhāga** means splitting Sutta without the word "kārite", So, in this Split-Sutta function, the word Kārite is excluded. [**yoga**=Sutta, **vibhāga**=splitting]

५१६, ४६६. इकारागमो असब्बधातुकम्हि
516, 466. **I-kārā'gamo asabbadhātukamhi**[44].

[I-kāra-āgamo+asabbadhātukamhi. 2 words]

[V] Sabbasmiṁ **asabbadhātuka**mhi **i**-kārā'gamo hoti.

In verbs with **asabbadhātuka** vibatti-terminations, there should come an "**i**" after the last consonant of the root and be joined to it. (See the inserted "**I**" shown in bold, underlined in the examples. See the footnote of Sutta 431 for Asabbadhātuka Vibatti)

- Gam**i**ssati-(he) will go. [wa] gamu+ssati.
- kar**i**ssati-(he) will do. [wa] kara+ssati.
- labh**i**ssati-(he) will obtain. [wa] labha+ssati.
- pac**i**ssati-(he) will cook. [wa] paca+ssati.

Asabbadhātukamhī'ti kimatthaṁ?
What is the word "asabbadhātukamhi" for?
To show that as the vibattis in the examples below do not belong to "asabbadhātuka" group, the function is therefore not applied.
* Gacchati-(he) goes.
* karoti-(he) does, [WA shown already]
* labhati-(he) obtains. [wa] labha+a+ti.
* pacati-(he) cooks. [wa] paca+a+ti.

[44] This Sutta enjoins to mark a very definitive form of Ākhyāta **verbs in the asabbadhātuka vibatti-terminations** by requiring an "i" to be inserted after the root and to attach that vowel to the last consonant of root.

५१७, ४८८. क्वचि धातुविभत्तिप्पच्चयानं दीघविपरीतादेस लोपागमा च

517, 488. Kvaci[45] dhātuvibhattipaccayānaṁ dīgha, viparītā'desa, lopā'gamā ca.

[Kvaci+dhātu, vibhatti, paccayānaṁ+dīgha, viparīta, ādesa, lopa, āgamā+ca. 4 words]

[V] Idha ākhyāte aniddiṭṭhesu sādhanesu kvaci dhātu, vibhatti, paccayānaṁ dīgha, viparītā'desa, lopā'gama-icce'tāni kāriyāni jinavacanānurūpāni kātabbāni.

All the necessary morphological procedures such as **dīgha, viparīta, ādesa, lopa** and **āgama** which conforms to usage in Buddhist texts, can be occasionally performed as necessary for verbs of all roots, vibattis and affixes whose morphological procedures were not explained in this Ākhyāta section.

(1) • Jāyati-(It) borns, arises. [wa] jana+a+ti.

(2) • kareyya-(he) should do. [wa] kara+o+eyya.
["o" affix is elided by this Sutta.]

(3) • jāniyā-(It) should be known. [For wa, Re:508]

(4) • siyā-(It) is or should be. [For wa, Re:506]

(5) • kare-(he) should do. [wa] kara+eyya.

---

[45] This is one of mahāvisaya Suttas in this grammar. [**mahā**-great+**visaya**-domain of influence in affecting various morphological procedures.]
There are four Mahā-visaya Suttas according to the following verse:

Mahāsuttā [1]tesu vuddhi, [2]kvaci dhātu ca [3]paccayā
'daniṭṭhā [4]yadanupā'ti, cattāri'pi nipātanā.

They are: (1) Tesu Vuddhi (Sutta No. 404) (2) Kvaci dhātu (Sutta No. 517) (3) Paccayā'daniṭṭhā (Sutta No. 571) (4) Ya'danuppannā (Sutta No.391). The role of a mahāvisaya Sutta is to invoke the power of any necessary morphological procedure required for the completion of a word whose procedures are not directly mentioned through injunction of a specific Sutta in the grammatical text. This grammatical concept of having such Suttas is one unique aspect of the Pāli grammar to allow any applicable morphological procedure for any word not shown in the grammar text.

(6) • gacche-(he) should go. [wa] gamu+eyya. ["eyya" is substituted with "e" by this Sutta in examples 5 and 6.]

(7) • jaññā-(he) should know or (it) should be known. [Re: 508]

(8) • vakkhetha-(you) should say. ***pl***, [wa] vaca+tha. [Component word "ca" of the root changed into "khe" by this Sutta]

(9) • dakkhetha-(you) should see. ***pl***, [wa] disa+tha. [Component word "sa" of the root changed into "khe" by this Sutta and "i" of the root "disa" changed into "a"]

(10) • dicchati-(he) sees. [wa] disa+ti. [Component word "sa" of the root changed into "ccha" by this Sutta]

(11) • agacchi-(he) went. [wa] gamu+ī. (Ajjattanī) [The "ī" shortened into "i" by this Sutta. Also refer to 476, 519]

(12) • agacchuṁ-(they) went. [wa] gamu+uṁ. [Re:476, 519]

(13) • ahosi-(It) was. [wa] hū+ī ["ī" changed into "si" by this Sutta]

(14) • ahesuṁ-(they) were. [wa] hū+uṁ.

Icce'va'mādīni-so on, aññāni'pi-others also, sādhanāni-example words of Sādhana, yojetabbāni-should be applied.

५१८, ४४६. अत्तनोपदानि परस्सपदत्तं

518, 446. **Attanopadāni parassapadattaṁ.**

[Attanopadāni+parassapadattaṁ. 2 words]

[V] Attanopadāni kvaci parassapadatta'māpajjante.

Sometimes, the Attanopada vibattis assume the physical mode of Prassapada vibattis (except in terms of actual voice.)

This means that they can take physical appearance of the Parassapada vibattis by having all six prassapada-terminations at the end of verbs as if they are Prassapada. However, the voice still remains in passive voice. Sometimes it is referred to as **reversal of Attanopada Vibattis into Parassapada Vibattis.** In the examples below, see the underlined Parassapada verb-endings shown in bold. Actually, they are reversed from Attanopada verb-ending "**te**" to "**ti**". Therefore, In WA, it has to be shown as "**te**" to represent its true Vibatti.

• Vuccat**i**-(is) said. [wa] vaca+ya+te.
• labbhat**i**-(is) obtained. [wa] labha+ya+te.
• paccat**i**-(is) cooked. [wa] paca+ya+te.

Kvacī'ti kimatthaṁ?
What is the word "kvaci" for?
It shows that as restricted by the word "kvaci", the function of Sutta is not applied in some examples shown below.
(Hence, Attanopada verb-ending "te" remains without being reversed. See the underlined verb-endings shown in bold, underlined).
* Karīya**te**-(is) done. [wa] kara+ya+te.
* labbha**te**-(is) obtained. [wa] labha+ya+te.
* pacca**te**-(is) cooked. [wa] paca+ya+te.

५१९, ४५७. अकारागमो हिय्यत्तनीअज्जतनीकालातिपत्तीसु

519, 457. **Akārā'gamo[46] hiyyattanī, ajjatanī, kālātipattīsu.**

[Akāra-āgamo+hiyyattanī, ajjatanī, kālātipattīsu. 2 words]

[V] Kvaci **a**kārāgamo hoti **hiyyattanī, ajjatanī, kālātipatti**-icce'tāsu vibhattīsu.

In verbs with **Hiyyattanī, Ajjatanī, Kālātipatti** vibatti-terminations, there should sometimes come an "**a**" and be inserted at the initial point of such verbs.
(See the added "**a**" shown in bold, underlined. This "**a**" has no meaning except that it is a distinctive symbolic mark of **Hiyyattanī, Ajjatanī** and **Kālātipatti** vibatti-applied verbs)

---

[46] The function of this Sutta clearly marks a salient form of ākhyāta verbs in **Hiyyattanī, Ajjatanī, Kālātipatti** vibatti-terminations by requiring an "**a**" to be placed before the verbs. However, this function is not a consistent feature. Sometimes there are verbs without an "a" being applied before them. See the examples of "kvaci" to clarify this. Note that this "a" has no meaning at all except to denote the past of action as implied by the verb.

- Agamā-(he) went. [wa] gamu+ā.
- agamī-(he) went. [wa] gamu+ī
- agamissā-(he) might have gone (but did not). [wa] gamu+ssā.

Kvacī'ti kimatthaṁ?
What is the word "kvaci" for?
It shows that as restricted by the word "kvaci", the function of Sutta is not applied in some examples shown below though they are in Hiyyattanī, Ajjatanī, Kālātipatti vibattis.
* Gamā, * gamī, * gamissā. (The same meaning and **wa** as those preceding three examples shown in this Sutta)

५२०, ५०२. ब्रूतो ई तिम्हि

520, 502. **Brūto ī timhi.** [Brūto+ī+timhi. 3 words]

[V] **Brū**-icce'tāya dhātuyā **ī**kārā'gamo hoti **ti**mhi vibhattimhi.

There should come an "**ī**" after the root word "**brū**" when a "**ti**" vibatti is applied.
Note: In the example, the vowel "**ū**" of "brū" changes into "**o**" through Vuddhi process and it further changes into "**av**" and "**ī**" is then inserted by this Sutta. The inserted "ī" is shown in bold, underlined.

- Brav**<u>ī</u>**ti-(he) says. [wa] brū+a+ti

५२१, ४२५. धातुस्सन्तो लोपो' नेकसरस्स
521, 425. **Dhātussa'nto[47] lopo'nekasarassa.**

[Dhātussa+anto+lopo+ana-ekasarassa. 4 words]

[V] Dhātussa anto kvaci lopo hoti ane'kasarassa.

The last component vowel of the multiple-stem roots having multiple-vowels, is usually elided except a few roots.

Note: This Sutta deletes the last vowel in multi-stem roots as a basic morphological standard procedure before other procedures are performed.

• Gacchati-(he) goes. • sarati-(he) remembers. • marati-(he) dies.

Anekasarasse'ti kimatthaṁ?
What is the word "anekasarassa" for?
To show that the function of Sutta is not applied in the examples shown below as they are of single-vowel, one letter (single-stem) roots.
* Pāti-(he) drinks. [wa] pā+a+ti.
* yāti-(he) goes. [wa] yā+a+ti.
* vāti-(It) goes. [wa] vā+a+ti.

Kvacī'ti kimatthaṁ?
What is the word "kvaci" for?
It shows that as restricted by the word "kvaci", the function of Sutta is not applied in some examples as those shown below even though they are multiple-stem roots.
* Mahīyati-(is) honored. [wa] maha+ya+te.
* mathīyati-(is) churned. [wa] matha+ya+te.

---

47 When carrying out the morphological procedures, the function of this Sutta is usually applied in almost all Ākhyāta and Kita verbs except some verbs such as single-stem roots and some two or multiple-stem roots like those shown as restricted by "kvaci".

५२२, ४७६. इसुयमूनमन्तो च्छो वा

522, 476. **Isu, yamūna'manto ccho vā.**

[Isu, yamūnaṁ+anto+ccho+vā. 4 words]

[V] **Isu, yamu**-icce'tesaṁ dhātūnaṁ anto **cch**o hoti vā.

The last component consonants "**s** and **m**" of the roots "**isu, yamu**" sometimes changes into "**cch**".
[See the applied function "**cch**" shown in bold, underlined]

- I**<u>cch</u>**ati-(he) wants. (Here, "s" becomes "ch") [wa] isu+a+ti.
- niya**<u>cch</u>**ati-(he) abstains, restrains. (Here, "m" becomes "ch".) [wa] ni-√yamu+a+ti.

Vā'ti kimatthaṁ?
What is the word "vā" for?
To shows that as restricted by the word "vā", the function of Sutta is not applied in some examples shown below.

* Esati-(he) wants or searches. "**E**" is vuddhi-vowel of "i" in the root "**isu**-to want, to search for". [wa] isu+a+ti.

* niyamati-(he) abstains. [wa] ni√yamu+a+ti.

५२३, ५२६. कारितानं णो लोपं

523, 526. **Kāritānaṁ ṇo**[48] **lopaṁ.**

[Kāritānaṁ+ṇo+lopaṁ. 3 words]

[V] **Kārita**-icce'tesaṁ **paccayā**naṁ **ṇo** lopa'māpajjate.

The "**ṇ**" of all causative affixes called "**kārita**" is (always) to be elided.

• Kāreti, • kārayati, • kārāpeti, • kārāpayati.

(Refer to Sutta 438)

Nigama Gāthā

The Concluding Verses

Sāsana'tthaṁ sa'muddiṭṭhaṁ,
mayā'khyātaṁ samāsato.
sakaṁ buddhivisesena,
cintayantu vicakkhaṇā.

"For the benefit of Buddha's Sāsana,
Ākhyāta section was explained briefly by me.
By one's own special intelligence,
May the wise study and analyze it".

Iti ākhyātakappe catuttho kaṇḍo.

The Fourth Section of Ākhyāta Verb ends.

Ākhyātakappo niṭṭhito.

Ākhyāta Chapter ends.

---

[48] "**ṇ**" means those causative affixes which has an "**ṇ**" in them.
They are: **ṇe, ṇaya, ṇāpe, ṇāpaya.** See Sutta No. 438, 452.
When these affixes are applied after the root in a verb, "**ṇ**" has to be elided, only component vowels such as **e, aya, āpe, āpaya** will be left. Then **Vuddhi** procedure is usually performed either in the initial or the middle vowel of the verb. The purpose of eliding by this Sutta is to enable vuddhi process and thereby leading to the completion of the word.

7. Kibbidhāna Kappa

Kita Chapter

Paṭhama Kaṇḍa

The First Section

(a) Buddhaṁ ñāṇasamuddaṁ,
sabbaññuṁ lokahetu'khīṇamatiṁ,
vanditvā pubba'mahaṁ,
vakkhāmi sasādhanaṁ hi kitakappaṁ.

Having first prostrated to the Buddha
Of the vast ocean of infinite wisdom,
Inexhaustible in guiding the world,
I am going to expound the Kita section,
Which indeed comprises Sādanas.

(b) Sādhanamūlaṁ hi payogaṁ.
āhu payogamūla'matthañ'ca.
atthesu visāradamatayo,
sāsanassudharā jinassa matā.

"The words are of Sādhana origin,
The meaning too is of word origin"
So said by the sages,
Bearers of Buddha's noble teachings,
Who have erudite wisdom,
On the meaning of words.

(c) Andho desakavikalo,
ghata, madhu, telāni bhājanena vinā;
naṭṭho naṭṭhāni yathā,
payogavikalo tathā attho.

Just as the blind without a guide,
clarified butter, honey and oil without vessel,
Will perish and disappear.
So will the meanings without example words.

(d) Tasmā saṁrakkhaṇatthaṁ,
munivacana'tthassa dullabhassā'haṁ;
vakkhāmi sissakahitaṁ,
kitakappaṁ sādhanena yutaṁ.

Therefore, to well preserve the meaning
Of rarely available teachings of the holy sage,
Will I expound the Kita section related to Sādhanas[49],
Benefiting the generations of Students.

५२४, ५६१. धातुया कम्मादिम्हि णो
524, 561. **Dhātuyā kammā'dimhi ṇo.**

[Dhātuyā+kamma-ādimhi+ṇo. 3 words]

[V] **Dhātuyā** kammā'dimhi **ṇa**paccayo hoti.

An affix "**ṇa**" is to be applied after the root which is preceded by a Kamma (an object in accusative case). **Summary:** This Sutta applies a "**ṇa**" affix after the roots preceded by a Kamma (a noun in accusative case).

This noun in accusative case is known as "saddūppada" which means a near-by word, closely located in front of the

[49] There are seven **Sādhanas**. They are Kattu, Kamma, Karaṇa, Sampadāna, Apādāna, Adhikaraṇa and Bhāva. In Kāraka chapter, the first six, except Bhāva, are shown as six Kārakas. There is some significant difference between Kāraka and Sādhana. While Kāraka means that which facilitates an action, Sādhana rather means something which helps complete the word and defines the meaning of an individual *kita* or *uṇādi*-affixed word whose affix is being classified into one of these seven Sādhanas. Depending on specific Sādhana of the affix, the ED as well as the meaning of that word is affected in a very subtle way. However, **it can not affect the case-ending of the word in the same way a specific Kāraka can** do. [Refer to the table in Kāraka chapter to clarify]. The words affixed in **Kattu, Kamma** and **Bhāva sādhana-specific affixes have significant impact** in a sentence-structure while other four Sādhanas have no significant effect. See the Appendix on the Kāraka and Sādhana for a detailed explanation.

roots "kara" etc. [saddū'ppada=**sadda**-syllable+**upa**-near+**pada**-word]
Actually, the words shown as examples in Suttas 524, 525 are compound nouns known grammatically as "Kita'ntogadha Dutiyā Tappurisa". Therefore, in the word analysis of each example, the front component parts of the words such as **Kamma-**work**, kumbha-**pot**, mālā-**flower and so forth are to be regarded as Saddūpapada, **i.e.** the preceding near-by words. "Kara, gaha" and so on are the roots after which an affix "**ṇa**" is to be applied.
[Kita'ntogadha=**Kita**-a kita-noun+**antogadha**-inside. **i.e.** compound noun with a kita-word inside as a component]

(1) [Kammaṁ-work. karotī'ti [karoti+iti] karoti-does. iti-for this reason] kammakāro-is called "kammakāra".• kammakāro-the one who does work, **i.e.** worker, laborer.

[wa] kamma-saddūpapada+kara+ṇa

Note: Always refer the front word as "saddūppada" for all similar examples. The words inside bracket are called ED. All EDs are Kattu-sādhana ones in this Sutta.

Evaṁ-similarly,

(2) • kumbhakāro-the one who makes pots, **i.e.** potter.
[wa] kumbha+kara+ṇa

(3) • mālākāro-the one who makes flowers, **i.e.** florist.
[wa] mālā+kara+ṇa ["**mālā**" is permanently feminine gender word]

(4) • kaṭṭhakāro-the one who makes fire-wood, **i.e.** fire-wood maker.
[wa] kaṭṭha-wood+kara+ṇa

(5) • rathakāro-the one who makes chariot, **i.e.** chariot-maker.
[wa] ratha-chariot+kara+ṇa

(6) • rajatakāro-the one who does silver-craft, **i.e.** the silver-smith.
[wa] rajata-silver+kara+ṇa

(7) • suvaṇṇakāro-the one who makes gold-craft., **i.e.** the gold-smith.
[wa] suvaṇṇa+kara+ṇa

(8) • pattaggāho-the one who holds bowl, **i.e.** the beggar.
[wa] patta+gaha+ṇa

(9) • tantavāyo-the one who weaves thread, **i.e.** the weaver, textile-worker. [wa] tanta+vā+ṇa

(10) • dhaññamāyo-the one who measures grains, **i.e.** the grain-measurer. [wa] dhañña+mā+ṇa

(11) • dhammakāmo-the one who prefers Dhamma, **i.e.** the Dhamma-admirer, a spiritual person. [wa] dhamma+kamu+ṇa

(12) • dhammacāro-the one who practices Dhamma, **i.e.** the Dhamma- practitioner. [wa] dhamma+cara+ṇa

५२५, ५६५. सञ्ञायमनु

525, 565. **Saññāya'ma nu.** [Saññāyaṁ+a+nu. 3 words]

[V] **Saññā**ya'mabhidheyyāyaṁ **dhātu**yā kammā'dimhi **a**kārapaccayo hoti. **nāma**mhi ca **nu**kārā'gamo hoti.

When denoting a personal name, an affix "**a**" is applied after the roots preceded by a Kamma word and a "**nu**" is also placed after the word denoting name.

[Two functions. The "nu" changes into a niggahita "ṁ" later on by Sutta 537. See it shown in bold, underlined]

(1) Ariṁ-enemy, dametī'ti [dameti+iti] dameti-subdues, iti-therefore, arindamo-is so called, • ar**<u>i</u>**ndamo-the one who subdues enemies. rājā-the king who subdues enemies is to be regarded as "**arindamo**". [wa] ari-saddūpapada+damu+a

(2) Vessaṁ-the merchant road, taratī'ti [tarati+iti] tarati-passes, iti-so, • vessa**<u>n</u>**taro-is so called, rājā-the king who was born past merchant road, is to be regarded as such. (Here, "ṁ" changed into "n") [wa] vessa+tara+a

(3) Taṇhaṁ-the craving, karotī'ti [karoti+iti] karoti-overcomes, iti • taṇha**<u>ṅ</u>**karo-is so called, bhagavā-the Buddha who overcomes craving is to be regarded as "taṇhaṅkaro". [wa] taṇhā+kara+a

Note: Here, the root "kara" does not mean "to do". It means "to overwhelm, to kill".

(4) Medhaṁ-wisdom, karotī'ti [karoti+iti] karoti-makes, iti • medha**<u>ṅ</u>**karo-the wisdom-maker, the one who can lead to development of wisdom for all, bhagavā-the Buddha who makes (promotes) wisdom (in other beings), is to be regarded as "medhaṅkaro". [wa] medhā+kara+a

(5) Saraṇaṁ-refuge or sanctuary, karotī'ti • saraṇa**ṅ**karo-the one who creates refuge or sanctuary, bhagavā-the Buddha who makes refuge or sanctuary (for all beings) is to be regarded as "saraṇaṅkaro". [wa] Saraṇa+kara+a

(6) Dīpaṁ-the light of wisdom, karotī'ti • dīpa**ṅ**karo-the light of wisdom maker, bhagavā-the Buddha who makes the light of wisdom is to be regarded as "dīpaṅkaro". [wa] dīpa+kara+a

Note: All EDs in this Sutta are Kattu-sādhana EDs.

५२६, ५६७. पुरे ददा च इं

526, 567. **Pure dadā ca iṁ.** [Pure+dadā+ca+iṁ. 4 words]

[V] **Pura**sadde ādimhi **dada-**icce'tāya dhātuyā **akāra**paccayo hoti, **pura**saddassa **akā**rassa ca **iṁ** hoti.

An affix "**a**" is added after the root word "**dada**" prefixed with the word "**pure**". In addition, the last component vowel "**a**" of "**pura**" changes into "**iṁ**". (Later that "**ṁ** excluding-i" becomes "**n**")

Pure-in the previous past, dānaṁ-alms, charitable giving, adāsī'ti [adāsi+iti] adāsi-gave, iti-so, • purindado-the one who gave alms in the previous past lives. devarājā-the king of heaven is to be regarded as "purindado". [Kattu-sādhana ED]
[wa] Pura-saddūpapada+dada+a

५२७, ५६८. सब्बतो ण्वुत्वा'वी वा

527, 568. **Sabbato ṇvu tvā'vī vā.**

[Sabbato+ṇvu, tu, āvī+vā. 3 words]

[V] Sabbato dhātuto kammā'dimhi vā akammā'dimhi vā **akāra, ṇvu, tu, āvī** icce'te paccayā honti.

Either being preceded by a Kamma (object) word or not, the affixes "**a, ṇvu, tu, āvī**" are applied after all roots. [This Sutta applies these four affixes after the roots whether there is a preceding Kamma word or not]

Examples of a-affixed words

(1) Taṁ-that deed, karotī'ti [karoti+iti] • takkaro-the one who does that deed, [wa] Ta-saddūpapada+kara+a

(2) Hitaṁ-wellbeing, karotī'ti • hitakaro the one who creates wellbeing.[Both 1 and 2 are Kattu-sādhana EDs]
[wa] hita-saddūpapada+kara+a

(3) Vineti-(It) disciplines, ettha-in this precept, etenā'ti [etena+iti] etena-by this code of conduct, iti. vā-to show other method of Viggaha. vinayo-is called "vinaya". • vinayo-the discipline where one is trained in or by which one is regulated (to conduct properly).[Adhikaraṇa and Karaṇa-sādhana EDs for this word]
[wa] Vi√nī+a

Note: Please study the ED of this word "Vinayo". It is shown in two methods, one using an "adhikaraṇa (Locative case) "**ettha**" and the other using a Karaṇa (Instrumental case) "**etena**". The first is called **adhikaraṇa Sādana** and the second ED is called **Karaṇa Sādhana**. The complete meaning of "Vinayo" also has to be systematically translated in accordance with the ED explanation of the word.

(4) Nissāya-being dependent on, naṁ-to that person or that thing, vasatī'ti [vasati+iti] vasati-(one) lives, iti • nissayo-supporting person or things such as teacher and requisites on which one depends. [Kamma sādhana ED] [wa] Ni√sī+a

Examples of ṇvu-affixed words

Ṇvumhi–(Here are examples of) **ṇvu**-affixed words.

(1) rathaṁ-chariot, karotī'ti • rathakārako-the one who makes chariot. The chariot-maker.
[wa] ratha-saddūpapada+kara+ṇvu

(2) Annaṁ-food, dadātī'ti [dadāt+iti] dadāti-(one) gives, iti • annadāyako-the one who gives food. food-giver.
[wa] anna-saddūpapada+dā+ṇvu

(3) Vineti-(one) leads, satte'ti [satte+iti] satte-beings, iti • vināyako-the one who leads others, the leader.
[wa] Vi√nī+ṇvu

(4) Karotī'ti [karoti+iti] • kārako-the one who makes, maker, the doer. [wa] kara+ṇvu

(5) Dadātī'ti [dadāti+iti] • dāyako-the one who donates, the donor.
[wa] dā+ṇvu

(6) Netī'ti [neti+iti] neti-(one) leads, iti • nāyako-the one who leads, the leader. [All Kattu-sādhana EDs] [wa] nī+ṇvu

Examples of tu-affixed words

Tumhi–(Here are examples of) **tu**-affixed words.

(1) (a) taṁ-that deed, karotī'ti • takkattā-the one who does that deed. (one "k" and "t" is augmented)

(b) Tassa kattā'ti vā • takkattā-the one who does that deed. (2 EDs. In ED-a, the word "**ta**-that" is shown in accusative case "taṁ". In ED-b, it is shown in genitive case "tassa".)

[wa] ta-saddūpapada+kara+tu

(2) (a) Bhojanaṁ-food, dadātī'ti • bhojanadātā-the one who gives food, the food-giver.

(b) Bhojanassa dātā'ti vā bhojanadātā-the one who gives food, the food-donor (2 EDs).

[wa] Bhojana-saddūpapada+dā+tu

(3) Karotī'ti • kattā-the one who makes. The maker,. [wa] kara+tu

(4) Saratī'ti • saritā-the one who remembers. [wa] sara+tu

Examples of āvī-affixed words

Āvīmhi–(Here are examples of) **āvī**-affixed words.

(1) Bhayaṁ-danger, passatī'ti [passati+iti] passati-(one) sees, iti • bhayadassāvī-the one who sees danger.

[wa] bhaya-saddūpapada+disa+āvī [All are Kattusādhana EDs.]

icce'va'mādi-and so on.

५२८, ५७७. विस रुज पदादितो ण

528, 577. **Visa, ruja, padā'dito ṇa.**

[Visa, ruja, pada-ādito+ṇa. 2 words]

[V] **Visa, ruja, pada**-icce'va'mādīhi dhātūhi **ṇa**paccayo hoti.

An affix "**ṇa**" is applied after various roots such as **visa, ruja, pada** and so on.

(1) Pavisatī'ti [pavisati+iti] pavisati-(one) enters, iti • paveso-the one who enters. [wa] pa√visa+ṇa

(2) rujatī'ti [rujati+iti] rujati-(It) afflicts, iti • rogo-that which afflicts, pain or disease. [wa] ruja+ṇa

(3) uppajjatī'ti [uppajjati+iti] uppajjati-(It) arises, iti • uppādo-that which arises, the process of arising. [wa] u√pada+ṇa

(4) phusatī'ti [phusati+iti] phusati-(it) touches, iti • phasso-that which touches, contact. [wa] phusa+ṇa

(5) ucatī'ti [ucati+iti] ucati-(It) emerges (as a whole), iti • oko-that which emerges as a whole (from a state of small pieces). **i.e.** a house etc. [wa] uca+ṇa

(6) bhavatī'ti [bhavati+iti] bhavati-(It) arises, iti • bhāvo-that which arises, act of arising. [wa] bhū+ṇa

(7) ayatī'ti [ayati+iti] ayati-(It) arises. iti • āyo-that which arises (as an income), revenue. [wa] aya+ṇa

(8) sammā-well, bujjhatī'ti [bujjati+iti] bujjhati-(one) knows, iti • sambodho-the one who knows well, A Buddha. [wa] saṁ√budha+ṇa

(9) viharatī'ti[viharati+iti] viharati-(It) removes (physical tensions), iti • vihāro-that which removes physical tensions. An act of dwelling at a place (where one can relax one's bodily tensions either by lying down, or sitting or choosing whatever alternative bodily mode is comfortable.) [wa] vi√ hara+ṇa

[All are Kattu sādhana EDs]

५२९, ५८०. भावे च

529, 580. **Bhāve ca.** [Bhāve+ca. 2 words]

[V] Bhāvatthā'bhidheyye sabbadhātūhi **ṇa**paccayo hoti.

An affix "**ṇa**" is applied after all roots in the sense of bhāva(action).

(1) [a] Paccate, [b] pacanaṁ-cooking, vā-to show other method. • pāko-act of cooking. [wa] paca+ṇa

(2) [a] cajate-sharing, [b] cajanaṁ-sharing, vā • cāgo-act of sharing, giving charity. [Bhāva-sādhana] [wa] caja+ṇa

Note: The numbers indicate two modes of ED, one using an Ākhyāta verb of Bhāva voice and the other being a Kita verb of Bhāva sense. However, both verbs signify "Bhāva". Both EDs are similar in meaning except the verb-forms.

Evaṁ-similarly in this way.

(3) • yāgo-act of sacrifice, the sacrifice. [wa] yaja+ṇa
(4) • yogo-act of tying up, or making effort. [wa] yuja+ṇa
(5) • bhāgo-act of dividing or sharing of portions. [wa] bhaja+ṇa
(6) • paridāho-act of burning (as with heat, desire or emotions etc.). [All Bhāva sādhana EDs] [wa] pari-√daha+ṇa

५३०, ५८४. क्वि च

530, 584. **Kvi ca.** [Kvi+ca. 2 words]

[V] Sabbadhātūhi **kvi**paccayo hoti.

An affix "**kvi**" is applied after all roots.

(1) Sambhavatī'ti [sambhavati+iti] sambhavati-(one) which happens well or arises well, iti • sambhū-the one which happens or arises well. [wa] saṁ√bhū+kvi
(2) visesena-specially, bhavatī'ti [bhavati+iti] bhavati-(one) arises, iti • vibhū-the one which specially happens or arises. [wa] vi√bhū+kvi
(3) bhujena-by being in zigzag twists, wiggling, gacchatī'ti [gacchati+iti] gacchati-(one) goes, iti • bhujago-the one which moves in twists. a snake or a reptile which moves sinuously. [wa] bhuja-saddūpapada+gamu+kvi
(4) [a] saṁ attānaṁ-oneself, khanati-(it) digs,
[b] saṁ saṭṭhu-well, khanatī'ti [khanati+iti] khanati iti vā-to show other form of ED.
• saṅkho-the sea creature which digs itself or which burrows well (into the sand), conch, marine gastropod mollusks. [2 EDs, All Kattu-sādhana EDs] [wa] Saṁ√khanu+kvi

५३१, ५८९. धरादीहि रम्मो

531, 589. **Dharā'dīhi rammo.** [Dhara-ādīhi+rammo. 2 words]

[V] **Dhara**-icce'vamādīhi dhātūhi **ramma**-paccayo hoti.

An affix "**ramma**" is applied after the roots such as **dhara** etc.

(1) Dharati-carries (good results), tenā'ti [tena+iti] tena-by virtue of that wholesome meritorious deed, iti • dhammo-the wholesome righteous Dhamma by which good-result are carried. [Karaṇa-sādhana ED] [wa] dhara+ramma

(2) Karīyate-(is) done, tan'ti [taṁ+iti] taṁ-that action, iti • kammaṁ-that which is being done, an action. [Kamma-sādhana ED] [wa] kara+ramma

५३२, ५९०. तस्सीलादीसु णी त्वा वी च

532, 590. **Tassīlā'dīsu ṇītvā'vī ca.**

[Tassīla-ādīsu+ṇī, tu, āvī+ca. 3 words]

[V] Sabbehi dhātūhi **tassīlā**'dīsva'tthesu **ṇī, tu, āvī**-icce'te paccayā honti.

In expressing (either) a habitual pattern etc., (an ingrained nature or a dedicated habit of doing things well), "**ṇī, tu, āvī**" affixes are applied after all roots.

Note: The words within parenthesis are included for the sake of completeness as implied by the word "ādi" contained in the word "Tassīlādīsu". By that word "**ādi**-etc", (1) Taddhamma and (2) Tassādhukārī are implied.

(1) **Tassila**=ta-that+sīla-habit. **i.e.** a habit, habitual pattern, a consistent character.

(2) **Taddhamma**=ta-that+Dhamma-nature. **i.e.** an ingrained, innate nature.

(3) **Tassādhukārī**=ta-that+sadhu-well+karī-used to do. **i.e.** The one who used to do efficiently in doing something.

All three affixes applied by this Sutta signify one of these three meanings. The words in these affixes are widely found in the Pāli texts.

Examples

(1) Piyaṁ-to whom one loves, pasaṁsituṁ-to praise, sīlaṁ-(is) the habit, yassa rañño-of whoever king, so-that, hoti-is. rājā-king (syntactically related to the word "so-that"), **i.e.** The king whose habit is only to praise the loved one, that (type of) king. piyapasaṁsī-is called "piyapasaṁsī". • piyapasaṁsī-the king who used to praise the loved ones.

[wa] piya-saddūpapada+pa√saṁsa+ṇī [**pa** is a prefix of the root]

(2) Brahmaṁ-the holy practice, carituṁ-to practice, sīlaṁ-(is) the habit, yassa puggalassa-of any individual, so-that, hoti-is, puggalo-individual, • brahmacārī-the individual who used to practice holy practice. [wa] brahma-saddūpapada+cara+ṇī

(3) Pasayha-by overbearing, pavattituṁ-to behave, sīlaṁ yassa rañño, so hoti rājā • pasayhapavatthā-the king who used to behave overbearingly. [wa] pasayha-saddūpapada+pa√vatu+ṇī

(4) Bhayaṁ-the danger, passituṁ-to see, sīlaṁ yassa samaṇassa-of any monastic, so hoti samaṇo-monastic, • bhayadassāvī-the monk who used to see dangers (of unwholesome actions).

[wa] bhaya-saddūpapada+disa+ṇī

Note: All are Kattu-sādhana EDs.

icce'va'mādi.

५३३, ५९१. सद्द कुध चल मण्डत्थ रुचादीहि यु

533, 591. **Sadda, kudha, cala, maṇḍa'ttha, rucā'dīhi yu.** [Sadda, kudha, cala, maṇḍa'ttha, ruca-ādīhi+yu. 2 words]

[V] **Sadda, kudha, cala, maṇḍa**tthehi ca **rucā**'dīhi ca dhātūhi **yu**paccayo hoti **tassīlā**'dīsva'tthesu.

When expressing a habitual pattern etc, a "**yu**" affix is applied after the roots "**Sadda, kudha, cala, maṇḍa**, **ruca**" etc.

(1) Ghosanasīlo-the one whose habit is to be vocal, • ghosano-the vocal one, noisy talker. [wa] ghusa+yu

(2) bhāsanasīlo-the one used to talk, • bhāsano-the talkative.
[wa] bhāsa+yu

Evaṁ-thus. viggaho-the ED, kātabbo-should be done.
i.e. the EDs of the remaining examples should be done similarly.

(3) • Kodhano-the one who used to get angry, temperamental person.
[wa] kudha+yu

(4) • dosano-the one who used to spoil. the spoiler . [wa] dusa+yu

(5) • calano-the one used to shake. the fickle person. [wa] cala+yu

(6) • kampano (same meaning as "calano") [wa] kapi+yu

(7) • phandano (same meaning as "calano"). [wa] phadi+yu

(8) • maṇḍano-the one who used to adorn. [wa] maḍi+yu

(9) • vibhūsano-the one who used to beautify. [wa] vi√bhūsa+yu

(10) • rocano-the one which used to be bright and shiny.
[wa] ruca+yu

(11) • jotano-the one which used to be bright and flashy.
[wa] juta+yu

(12) • vaḍḍhano-the one which used to be progressive.
[wa] vaḍḍha+yu

५३४, ५९२. पारादिगमिम्हा रू

534, 592. **Pārā'digamimhā rū.** [Pāra-ādigamimhā+rū. 2 words]

[V] **Gamu**-icce'tamhā dhātumhā **pāra**saddā'dimhā **rū**paccayo hoti **tassīlā**'dīsva'tthesu.

When expressing a habitual pattern etc. a "**rū**" affix is applied after the root word "**gamu**" prefixed with the word "**pāra**-shore".

Bhavassa-of life, pāraṁ-other shore or side, bhavapāraṁ-the other shore of life. [This is a minor partial ED, Chaṭṭhī tappurisa] bhavapāraṁ-to the other shore of life, gantuṁ-to go, sīlaṁ yassa purisassa-of man, so hoti puriso • bhavapāragū-the man whose habit is to go the other shore of life. **i.e.** an enlightened *Arahanta* monk. [This is complete ED of the example. Kattu-sādhana ED]
[wa] bhavapāra-saddūpapada+gamu+rū

Note: All syllables "am" of the root "gamu" and "r" of the affix are elided by Sutta 539. "u" of the root is already elided by Sutta 521. Thus, it becomes a complete word as "Bhavapāragū".

Tassīlādīsvī'ti kimatthaṁ?
What is the word "tassilādīsu" for?
To show that the example shown below is inapplicable as it does not have an expression of "tassīla-a habitual pattern" in it. (So, the affix "rū" is not applied)
* Pāraṅgato-the one who had gone to the other shore of life.
[wa] pāra-saddūpapada+gamu+ta [Re Sutta 555 for this affix]

Pārādigamimhā'ti kimatthaṁ?
What is the word "pārādigamimhā" for?
To show that the example below is not prefixed with "pāra" as indicated in Sutta, but prefixed with "anu". So it is inapplicable. (So, the affix "rū" is not applied.)
* Anugāmī-the one who used to follow. [wa] anu√gamu+ṇī

५३५, ५९३. भिक्खादितो च

535, 593. **Bhikkhā'dito ca.** [Bhikkha-ādito+ca. 2 words]

[V] **Bhikkha**-icce'va'mādīhi dhātūhi **rū**paccayo hoti **tassīlā**'dīsva'tthesu.

When expressing a habitual pattern etc. a "**rū**" affix is applied after the roots "**bhikkha**" etc.

(1) Bhikkhanasīlo yācanasīlo-the one who used to beg,
• bhikkhu-the one used to begging. [wa] bhikkha+rū
Note: Yācanasīlo is synonymous with Bhikkhanasīlo.
(2) Vijānanasīlo-the one used to analytically understand,
• viññū-the wise person, an analyst. [wa] vi-ñā+rū

५३६, ५९४. हनत्यादीनं णुको
536, 594. **Hanatyā'dīnaṁ ṇuko.**

[Hana-iti-ādīnaṁ+ṇuko. 2 words]

[V] **Hana**tyā'dīnaṁ dhātūnaṁ ante **ṇuka**paccayo hoti **tassīlā**'dīsva'tthesu.

When expressing a habitual pattern etc. a "**ṇuka**" affix is applied after the roots "**hana**" etc.

(1) Āhananasīlo-the one used to kill or hurt, • āghātuko-the executioner, killer. [wa] ā√hana+ṇuka

(2) karaṇasīlo-the one used to do (crafts), • kāruko-the artisan, carpenter, craftsman etc. [wa] kara+ṇuka

५३७, ५६६. नु निग्गहितं पदन्ते
537, 566. **Nu niggahitaṁ pada'nte.**

[Nu+niggahitaṁ+pada-ante. 3 words]

[V] Pada'nte **nu**kārā'gamo **niggahita'**māpajjate.

The word "nu", which has been applied at the end of a kamma word (by Sutta 525), changes into a "niggahita-**ṁ**". [This "**ṁ**" further changes into "**n**" or "**ṅ**" or "**ñ**".]

(1) Ariṁ dametī'ti • arindamo. rājā.
[wa] ari-saddūpapada+damu+a

(2) Vessaṁ taratī'ti • vessantaro. rājā. (Refer to Sutta 525)
[wa] vessa-saddūpapada+tara+a

(3) Pabhaṁ-the light, karotī'ti [karoti+iti] karoti-makes, iti • pabhaṅkaro-the light-maker. Bhagavā-the Buddha who makes the light of wisdom is to be regarded as "pabhaṅkaro".
[wa] pabhā-saddūpapada+kara+a

५३८, ५९५. संहना'ञ्ञाय वा रो घो
538, 595. Saṁhanā'ññāya vā ro gho.

[Saṁhanā+aññāya+vā+ro+gho. 5 words]

[V] **Saṁ**pubbāya **hana-**iccetāya dhātuyā, aññāya vā dhātuyā **ra-**paccayo, **hana**ssa ca **gh**o hoti.

A "**ra**" affix is to be added after the root "**hana**" prefixed with an upasagga "**saṁ**" and other roots. Besides, that root word "**hana**" changes into "**gh**". [Two functions]

(1) Samaggaṁ-being united, kammaṁ-to the activities, sa'mupagacchatī'ti [saṁ+upa+gacchati+iti] saṁupagacchati-congregates, iti-therefore, saṅgho-is called "Saṅgho". [**saṁ**=well, unitedly+**upa**=closely+**gacchati**=goes, **i.e.** gathering together unitedly]

• saṅgho-the community of brethren who congregates to (conduct) the sacred activities unitedly. [Kattu-sādhana]

[wa] saṁ√-hana+ra

(2) Samantato-from all around, nagarassa-of the city, bāhire-outside, khaññatī'ti [khaññati+iti] khaññati-(is) dug, iti-so,

• parikhā-that which is dug outside city (filled with water to provide security), a moat. [Kamma-sādhana]

[wa] pari√-khanu+ra

(3) antaṁ-the ending, karotī'ti [karoti+iti] karoti-(It) does, iti

• antako-the end-maker, terminator of life. **i.e.** the devil or death. [Kattu-sādhana ED] [wa] anta-saddūpapada-kara+ra

Saṁi'ti kimatthaṁ? What is the word "saṁ" for?
To show that example shown here is inapplicable as it is not prefixed with "saṁ", but with an "upa" instead. So, it is inapplicable.
Upahananaṁ-hurting closely,* upaghāto-closely hurting, a close irritant such as bodily or mental pain or fear etc.
[wa] upa√hana+ṇa [Bhāva-sādhana ED]

५३९, ५५८. रम्हि रन्तो रादि नो

539, 558. **Ramhi ra'nto rā'di no.**

[Ramhi+ra-anto+ra-ādi+no. 4 words]

[V] **Ra**mhi paccaye pare sabbo dhātva'nto **ra**-kārā'di **lopo** hoti.

When either a "**ra**" affix or any **r**-containing morpheme is present in a word, the first component vowel preceding the last vowel-less consonant of the root and that last consonant of the root too are usually to be elided along with the vowel of the "**r-containing affix**" as well as any **r**-containing morphemes.

Summary: This Sutta deletes:

(1) the component **vowel** in front of the last vowel-less consonant of the root

(2) the vowel-less **consonant** of the root (It is referred to as vowel-less as its vowel was already elided by Sutta 521 in the initial procedure) and

(3) the vowel of any of "**r-containing affix**"

(4) any **r**-contained morphemes such as those applied by Sutta 572. (Examples 1,2, and 3 have r-containing affixes while example 4 contains **r**-morphemes)

The list of r-containing affixes (8)

ramma (531), rū (534), Ra (538), ricca (542), ririya (554), ratthu (566), ritu (567), rātu (568).

The list of r-containing functions (4)

riṭṭha (572), raṭṭha, raṭṭhuṁ (These two functions are applied by means of "ca" of 572), racca (598).

(1) • Antako-the end-maker, terminator, **i.e.** the devil or death.
[wa] anta-saddūpapada-kara+ra (**Anta**-the end+**kara**-to do)

(2) • pāragū-the one who have reached the shore (the climax of something), also an expert. [wa] pāra-saddūpapada-gamu+rū

(3) • satthā-the one who instructs. **i.e.** a teacher. [wa] sāsa+ratthu

(4) • diṭṭho-seen. [wa] disa+ta

icce'va'mādi.

Detailed Explanation

[As the rule of Sutta and the related morphological procedures are a bit complex for uninitiated beginner, a simple explanation is given below.]
First, look at the WA of the word "**Antako**" as shown above.

(a) Here, the root is "**kara**". The first "**a**" after "k" as well as the vowel-less "**r**" are to be deleted along with the applied affix "**ra**" leaving only the words "**Anta+k**".

Note: Assume that "**r**" is vowel-less as its "a" had been already elided by Sutta 521 in the initial procedure of morphology for this word. It will then look like this=**anta+k.**

(b) Then, this pending incomplete word "**anta+k**" is to be formally recognized as a noun by means of Sutta 601.

(c) Only after this formal recognition procedure, a nominative singular "si" can be applied. Thus,>**anta+k+si.**

(d) Then, that "**si**" is to be changed into "**o**" by 104>**antak+o** (complete) [Through such a detailed step-by-step morphological process, this word becomes a complete word]

५४०, ५४५. भावकम्मेसु तब्बा'नीया

540, 545. **Bhāvakammesu tabbā'nīyā.**

[Bhāva, kammesu+tabba, anīyā. 2 words]

[V] **Bhāva, kamma-**icce'tesva'tthesu **tabba-anīya**iccete paccayā honti sabbadhātūhi.

The affixes "**tabba, anīya**" are applied after all roots in the sense of both Bhāva and Kamma voices.

Note: Any word affixed with these "**tabba, anīya**" affixes are to be regarded as belonging to Bhāva and Kamma sense verbs and verbal nouns. See each pairs of examples.

(1) [a]• Bhavitabbaṁ-(It) should be (Kamma sense), or the state of being (Bhāva sense). [wa] bhū+tabba
[b]• bhavanīyaṁ-(It) should be (Kamma), or state of being (Bhāva). [wa] bhū+anīya

(2) [a]• āsitabbaṁ-(It should be) entered, or act of entering. [wa] āsa+tabba [b]• āsanīyaṁ. [wa] āsa+anīya

(3) [a]• pajjitabbaṁ-(It) should be reached, moved, or act of reaching, moving. [wa] pada+tabba
[b]• pajjanīyaṁ [wa] pada+anīya

(4) [a]• kattabbaṁ-(It) should be done or act of doing.
[wa] kara+tabba [b] • karaṇīyaṁ [wa] kara+anīya
(5) [a]• gantabbaṁ-(It) should be gone or act of going.
[wa] gamu+tabba [b] • gamanīyaṁ [wa] gamu+anīya

५४१, ५५२. ण्यो च

541, 552. **Ṇyo ca.** [Ṇyo+ca. 2 words]

[V] **Bhāva, kamme**su sabbadhātūhi **ṇya**paccayo hoti.

An affix "**ṇya**" is applied after all roots in the sense of both Bhāva and Kamma voices.
Note: Any word affixed with this "**ṇya**" affix is to be regarded as belonging to Bhāva and Kamma sense verbs and nouns.

(1) Kattabbaṁ • kāriyaṁ- (It) should be done or act of doing, an act. (Two translations, one as a verb, other as a verbal noun)
[wa] kara+ṇya
(2) jetabbaṁ • jeyyaṁ-(It) should be conquered or act of winning.
[wa] ji+ṇya
(3) netabbaṁ • neyyaṁ-(It) should be carried or act of carriage. (Sometimes it means "knowing".) [wa] nī+ṇya
icce'va'mādi.

Caggahaṇena **teyya**paccayo hoti.

By the word "Ca" in Sutta, a "**teyya**" affix is similarly applied (in the sense of Bhāva and Kamma. This affix is also used either as verb or verbal noun).
(1) Ñātabbaṁ-(should be) known. • ñāteyyaṁ-it should be known or act of knowing. [wa] ñā+teyya
(2) • daṭṭheyyaṁ-it should be seen, or act of seeing.
[wa] disa+teyya
(3) • patteyyaṁ-it should be reached or act of reaching.
[wa] pada+teyya
iccevamādi. [All are Kamma and Bhāva sādhana EDs]

Note: The kita verbs such as "**Kattabbaṁ, Jettabbaṁ**" etc. shown before actual examples are EDs, not examples.

५४२, ५५७. करम्हा रिच्च

542, 557. **Karamhā ricca.** [Karamhā+ricca. 2 words]

[V] **Kara-**icce'tamhā dhātumhā **ricca**paccayo hoti **bhāva, kamme**su.

An affix "**ricca**" is applied after the root "kara" in the sense of Bhāva and Kamma.

Kattabbaṁ-(should be) done, • kiccaṁ-something that should be done, **i.e.** a matter or a case or a duty to do. [Kamma-sādhana] [wa] kara+ricca

५४३, ५५५. भूतो'ब्ब

543, 555. **Bhūto'bba.** [Bhūto+abba. 2 words]

[V] **Bhū-**icce'tāya dhātuyā **ṇya**paccayassa **ū**kārena saha **abbā**'deso hoti **bhāvakamme**su.

An affix "**ṇya**" applied after the root "bhū" changes into "abba" together with component vowel "ū" of the root in the bhāva and Kamma senses of the word.
Summary: This Sutta changes the "**ū**" of bhū and the affix "**ṇya**" into "**abba**">**b+abba>babba.**

(1) Bhavitabbo-(It should) be, • bhabbo-likely to happen, likely to occur. [wa] bhū+ṇya
(2) bhavitabbaṁ-(It should) be, • bhabbaṁ-possibly to happen, likely to occur. [Both Kamma and Bhāva sādhana] [wa] bhū+ṇya

५४४, ५५६. वद मद गमु युज गरहाकारादीहि ज्जम्मग्गय्हेय्यागारो वा

544, 556. **Vada, mada, gamu, yuja, garahā'kārā'dīhi jja, mma, gga, yhe'yyā'gāro vā.**

[Vada, mada, gamu, yuja, garaha, ākāra-ādīhi+jja, mma, gga, yha, eyyā+gāro+vā. 4 words]

[V] **Vada, mada, gamu, yuja, garahā**'kāranta-icce'va'mādīhi dhātūhi **ṇya**paccayassa yathāsaṅkhyaṁ **jja, mma, gga, yha, eyyā**'desā honti vā dhātva'ntena saha, **gara**ssa ca **gār**o hoti **bhāvakamme**su.

Translation of Sutta's Vutti:

[1] The affix "**ṇya**" applied after the roots "**vada, mada, gamu, yuja, garaha**", along with the last component consonants "**d, m, j, h**" of the roots, changes into "**jja, mma, gga, yha** respectively,

[2] Also, the **ā**-of ā-ending roots such as "**dā, pā, hā, mā, ñā**", together with affix "**ṇya**" applied after them, changes into an "**eyya**" and

[3] the word "**gara**" of the root "**garaha**-to censure" changes into "**gāra**" in cases of the words which are affixed with "**ṇya**" in Bhāva and Kamma senses.

[This Sutta has **three functions.** Please look at examples below carefully to clarify all the functions. Look at explanatory words shown inside parenthesis]

The examples of d, m, j-ending roots:

(d+ṇya>**jja)**

(1) Vattabbaṁ-(that should be) said.

- vajjaṁ-something said. **i.e.** A fault to be censured or the talk. [wa] vada+ṇya

(2) madanīyaṁ-(that which causes) being drunk or inebriated.

- majjaṁ-liquor, narcotics. [wa] mada+ṇya

(m+ṇya>**mma)**

(1) gamanīyaṁ-(It should be) gone.

- gammaṁ-act of going or a place to be. [wa] gamu+ṇya

(j+ṇya>gga)

(1) yojanīyaṁ-(It should be) bound or engaged.

• yoggaṁ-yoke, act of involvement. [wa] yuja+ṇya

The examples of h-ending root "garaha":

(h+ṇya>yha, gara>gāra>gāra+yha, [2 functions for this word]

(1) garahitabbaṁ-(that should be) censured. • gārayhaṁ-deserving censure. **i.e.** an offence, a wrong-doing to be censured. [wa] graha+ṇya

The examples of ā-ending roots:

(ā+ṇya>eyya)

(1) dātabbaṁ-(that should be) given. • deyyaṁ-something to give. [wa] dā+ṇya

(2) pātabbaṁ-(that which should be) drunk. • peyyaṁ-something to drink, beverage. [wa] pā+ṇya

(3) hātabbaṁ-(that which should be) abandoned. • heyyaṁ-something to abandon. [wa] hā+ṇya

(4) mātabbaṁ-(that which should be) measured. meyyaṁ-something to measure. [wa] mā+ṇya

(5) ñātabbaṁ-(that which should be) known. • ñeyyaṁ-something to know. [wa] ñā+ṇya

icce'va'mādi. [All are Kamma-sādhana EDs]

५४५, ५४८. ते किच्चा

545, 548. **Te kiccā.** [Te+kiccā. 2 words]

[V] Ye paccayā **tabbā**'dayo **ricca**'ntā, te **kicca**saññā'ti veditabbā.

Those affixes starting from "**tabba**" up to "**ricca**" are to be formally known as "**kicca affixes**".

Kiccasaññāya kiṁpayojanaṁ?
Bhāvakammesu kiccattakhatthā.
What is the benefit by terming "kicca"?
It has the benefit of making due reference in Suttas such as "Bhāvakammesu kiccattakhatthā" etc.

Note: "Tabba, anīya, ṇya, teya, ricca", these five affixes are called **"Kicca"** affixes

५४६, ५६२. अञ्ञे कित

546, 562. **Aññe kitā.** [Aññe+kitā. 2 words]

[V] **Aññe** paccayā **kitā**'eva saññā honti.

All the remaining other affixes (shown in this Kita section) are to be formally termed "**kita affixes**".

Kitasaññāya kiṁ payojanaṁ? Kattari kitā.
What is the benefit by terming "kita"?
It has the benefit of making due reference in such Suttas as "Kattari Kitā" etc.

Note: Below is a list of **Kita-affixes**:
ṇa, a, ṇvu, tu, āvī, kvi, ramma, ṇī, yu, rū, ṇuka, ra, i, ti, ririya, ta, tavantu, tāvī, ina, kha, tave, tuṁ, tuna, tvāna, tvā, māna, anta, ratthu, ritu, rātu, tuka, ika, kāra. (33 affixes)

५४७, ५९६. नन्दादीहि यु

547, 596. **Nandā'dīhi yu.** [Nanda-ādīhi+yu. 2 words]

[V] **Nandā**'dīhi dhātūhi **yu**paccayo hoti **bhāvakamme**su.

The "**yu**" affix is applied after the root "**nanda**" etc. in the senses of Bhāva and Kamma.

(1) (a) Nandīyate-act of liking, • nandanaṁ-act of liking. the pleasure (Bhāva Sādhana ED) [wa] nanda+yu
(b) Nanditabbaṁ-(that which should be) pleased, vā • nandanaṁ- something which should be pleased with. Being pleasant or such a thing. (Kamma Sādhana ED) [wa] nanda+yu

(2) Gahaṇīyaṁ-(that which should be) taken, • gahaṇaṁ- something to take. act of grabbing. [wa] gaha+yu

(3) Caritabbaṁ-(that which should be) practiced, • caraṇaṁ- something to practice. the practice of Dhamma etc. [wa] cara+yu
[All are Bhāva & Kamma-sādhana EDs which use ākhyāta and kita verbs]

Evaṁ sabbattha yojetabbā.

५४८, ५९७. कत्तुकरणपदेसेसु च

548, 597. **Kattu, karaṇa, padesesu ca.**

[Kattu, karaṇa, padesesu+ca. 2 words]

[V] **Kattu, karaṇa, padesa**-icce'tesva'tthesu ca **yu**paccayo hoti.

The "yu" affix is also applied in the senses of **Kattu** (agent), **karaṇa** (Instrumental) and **padesa** (Locative).

Kattari tāva–(Here is) the example in the Kattu (Subject, agent) sense:

(1) rajaṁ-the dust, haratī'ti [harati+iti] harati-(it) removes, iti • rajoharaṇaṁ-the dust-remover. toyaṁ-the water (is to be regarded as such). In some cases, it refers to handkerchief or a napkin. [Kattu-sādhana] [wa] raja-saddūpapada+hara+yu

Karaṇe tāva—(Here is) the example in the Karaṇa (Instrumental) sense:

(2) karoti-(it) does (to finish), tenā'ti [tena+iti] tena-by means of that cause, iti • karaṇaṁ-a supporting cause. A means or an instrument by which actions are accomplished. [Karaṇa-sādhana ED] [wa] kara+yu

Padese tāva–(Here is) the example in the Padesa (Locative) sense:

(3) **tiṭṭhanti**-(they) stand, tasmin'ti [tasmiṁ+iti] tasmiṁ-at that point, iti • ṭhānaṁ-point or location on which things stand or exist.

[wa] ṭhā+yu [Adhikaraṇa-sādhana ED.

Note: The term "**padesa**" in Sutta means **Adhikaraṇa**. Sometimes also called as "**Okāsa**" or "**ādhāra**". These four terms refer to "Locative"]

Evaṁ sabbattha yojetabbā-This way, it should be applied at all applicable instances.

५४९, ५५०. रहादितो ण

549, 550. **Ra, hā'dito ṇa.** [Ra, ha-ādito+ṇa. 2 words]

[V] **Ra**kāra, **ha**kārādya'ntehi dhātūhi **anā**'desassa **na**ssa **ṇ**o hoti.

The "**n**" of morpheme "**ana**" derived from affix "**yu**", which has been applied after "**r, h-ending** roots", usually changes into an "**ṇ**".
Summary: This Sutta enjoins the morpheme "**n**" of "**ana**" to be changed into an "**ṇ**". [So, it becomes an "**aṇa**"] The rule is **applicable after r, h**-ending **roots** only. The "**ana**" function is applied by Sutta 622. The function of Sutta is slightly similar to the function of Sutta "रषाभ्यं नोणः समानपदे" in the Pāṇinī Sanskrit grammar. [See the applied "**ṇ**" shown in bold in the examples below.]

(1) Karoti tenā'ti • kara**ṇ**aṁ. [wa] kara+yu [Re: The previous Sutta]
(2) pūreti-(causes) to fill, tenā'ti [tena+iti] tena-by that, iti • pūra**ṇ**aṁ-an addition which causes to fill. [wa] pūra+yu
(3) Gahaṇīyaṁ-(should be) taken, tenā'ti • gaha**ṇ**aṁ-the cause of grabbing. [wa] gaha+yu [All are Karaṇa-sādhana EDs
Eva'maññe'pi yojetabbā-Thus, other examples should be applied.

Iti [50]kibbidhānakappe paṭhamo kaṇḍo.
The First Section of Kita ends.

[50] Kibbidhāna=**kita**-of those kita-suffixed words+**vidhāna**-plan, section. "ta" is elided with one more "b" being augmented.

Dutiya Kaṇḍa
The Second Section

५५०, ५४६. णादयो तेकालिका

550, 546. **Ṇā'dayo tekālikā.**

[Ṇa-ādayo+tekālikā. 2 words]

[V] **Ṇā**'dayo paccayā **yu**paccaya'ntā tekālikā'ti veditabbā.

The affixes starting from "**ṇa**" to "**yu**", are to be known as "tekālika" which means belonging to three tenses.
Note: Please carefully see the EDs of the examples. All numbered verbs in three tenses signify three tenses of those affixes. WA of examples are already shown in the first section. [Tekālika=**ti**-three+**kāla**-time+**ṇika**-relating to. "**e**" is a vuddhi-vowel. **i.e.** Affixes the meanings of which are related to three tenses]

(1) Kumbhaṁ-the pot, [1] karoti-makes (This present verb signifies present), [2] akāsi-made (This signifies past), [3] karissatī'ti [ka rissati+iti] (This signifies future) karissati-will make, iti-therefore, kumbhakāro-is so called, • kumbhakāro-the potter who makes pot (at present), who made pot (in the past), who will make pot (in the future).

(2) [1] Karoti [2] akāsi [3] karissati tenā'ti [tena+iti] tena-by that cause, iti • karaṇaṁ-a supporting cause or an instrument by which actions are accomplished at present, had been accomplished in the past and will also be accomplished in the future. (To understand the tenses of verbs, refer to relevant Suttas in the first section of Ākyāta)

Eva'maññe'pi yojetabbā-Thus, other examples should be applied.

५५१, ५९८. सञ्ञायं दाधातो इ

551, 598. **Saññāyaṁ dādhāto i.**

[Saññāyaṁ+dādhāto+i. 3 words]

[V] **Saññāya**'mabhidheyyāyaṁ **dā**dhāto **i-**paccayo hoti.

When denoting a name (proper noun), an "**i**" affix is to be applied after the root "**dā**".

(1) Paṭhamaṁ-initially, ādīyatī'ti [ādīyati+iti] ādīyati-(is) taken, iti • ādi-something taken initially. A beginning, an inception, a starting point. [Kamma-sādhana] [wa] ā√-dā+i
(2) Udakaṁ-water, dadhātī'ti [dadhāti+iti] dadhāti-(it) carries, iti • udadhi-that which carries water, an ocean.
[wa] udaka-saddūpapada-dhā+i
(3) Maho'dakāni [**mahā**-great+**udakāni**-waters]-the great (amount of) water, dadhātī'ti • mahodadhi-that which carries great (amount of) water, an ocean. [Both 2, 3 are Kattu-sādhana EDs]
[wa] mahodaka-saddūpapada-dhā+i
(4) Vālāni-hairs, dadhāti-(it) carries, tasmin'ti [tasmiṁ+iti] tasmiṁ-in that tail, iti • vāladhi-the body part where it carries hairs. the tail of an animal. [Adhikaraṇa-sādhana]
[wa] vāla-saddūpapada-dhā+i
(5) Sammā-well, dhīyatī'ti [dhīyati+iti] dhīyati-(is) kept combined, iti • sandhi-act of combining well. [Kamma-sādhana]
[wa] saṁ√-dhā+i

५५२, ६०९. ति किच्चा'सिट्ठे

552, 609. Ti kitā cā'siṭṭhe.

[Ti+kitā+ca+āsiṭṭhe. 4 words]

[V] **Saññāya'**mabhidheyyāyaṁ sabbadhātūhi **ti-**paccayo hoti, kitā ca āsiṭṭhe.

When denoting the name (proper noun) with an expression of well-wishes, a "**ti**" affix as well as other "kita" affixes are applied after the roots denoting the proper noun.

(1) Jino-Buddha, enaṁ-that person, bujjhatū'ti [bujjhatu+iti] bujjhatu-let be known!, iti-for this reason, jinabuddhi-is so called. • jinabuddhi-the name "Jinabuddhi" meaning "may the Buddha know him". [wa] jina-saddūpapada-budha+ti
(2) Dhanaṁ-wealth, assa-for that son, bhavatū'ti [bhavatu+iti] bhavatu-may there be!, iti • dhanabhūti-the name "dhanabhūti" meaning "may he be prosperous or wealthy".
[wa] dhana-saddūpapada-bhū+ti

(3) Bhavatū'ti [bhavatu+iti] bhavatu-may there be, iti • bhūto-the name "bhūto" meaning "may be, **i.e.** Grow". [wa] bhū+ta

(4) bhavatū'ti • bhāvo-the name "bhāvo". [wa] bhū+ṇa

(5) Dhammo-the Dhamma, enaṁ-to that person, dadātū'ti [dadātu+iti] dadātu-may give (happiness) !, iti • dhammadinno-the name "Dhammadinno" meaning "may the Dhamma give him (happiness) ". [wa] dhamma-saddūpapada-dā+ta

(6) Vaḍḍhatū'ti [Vaḍḍhatu+iti] Vaḍḍhatu-May he prosper!, iti • vaḍḍhamāno-the name so called meaning "prosperous". [wa] vaḍḍha+māna

Eva'maññe'pi yojetabbā.

५५३, ५९९. इत्थिय मतियवो वा

553, 599. **Itthiya'matiyavo vā.**

[Itthiyaṁ+a, ti, yu, vo+vā. 3 words]

[V] **Itthiya'**mabhidheyyāyaṁ sabbadhātūhi **a**kāra**, ti, yu**-icce'te paccayā honti vā.

The affixes "**a, ti, yu**" are sometimes applied after the roots and such "**a, ti, yu-affixed words**" belong to feminine gender.

Note: Only affix "**ti**" is of permanent feminine gender. The "**a, yu**" affixes applied through other Suttas can also be of variable genders.

[**a**-affix] Jīratī'tī [jirati+iti] jirati-(it) degenerates, iti • jarā-that which degenerates. decaying, the old-age. [wa] jara+a

[**ti**-affix] Maññatī'ti [Maññati+iti] Maññati-(It) thinks, iti • mati-that which thinks. thought, view, opinion. [wa] mana+ti

[**yu**-affix] (1) Cetayatī'ti [Cetayati+iti] Cetayati-(it) motivates, iti • cetanā-that which motivates, motive, volition, intent. [wa] citi+yu

(2) Vedayatī'ti [Vedayati+iti] Vedayati-(it) feels, iti • vedanā-that which feels, feeling. [All Kattu-sādhana EDs] [wa] vida+yu

Eva'maññe'pi yojetabbā.

५५४, ६०१. करतो रिरिय

554, 601. **Karato ririya.** [Karato+ririya. 2 words]

[V] **Kara**to **itthiya'manitthiyaṁ** vā abhidheyyāyaṁ **rirīya-**paccayo hoti vā.

The affix "**ririya**", which may be of feminine gender or not, is sometimes applied after the root "**kara**".

(1) Kattabbā-(it) should be done, • kiriyā-an action. [Feminine gender word] [wa] kara+ririya

(2) Karaṇīyaṁ-(it) should be done, • kiriyaṁ-an action. [Neuter gender word] [Both Kamma-sādhana EDs] [wa] kara+ririya

५५५, ६१२. अतीते त तवन्तु तावी

555, 612. **Atīte ta, tavantu, tāvī.**

[Atīte+ta, tavantu, tāvī. 2 words]

[V] Atīte kāle sabbadhātūhi **ta, tavantu, tāvī**-icce'te paccayā honti.

The affixes "**ta, tavantu, tāvī**" are applied after all roots in the sense of past.

Note: The affixes applied by this Sutta usually signify a past tense. So, any word affixed with these "**ta, tavantu, tāvī**" affixes are to be regarded as belonging to past perfect verbs and verbal nouns. These affixes are also referred to as "past participles". [See three pairs of examples for each affix in three roots]

(1) (a) • Huto. [wa] hu+ta
 (b) • hutavā. [wa] hu+tavantu
 (c) • hutāvī-given, sacrificed. [wa] hu+tāvī

(2) (a) • Vusito. [wa] vasa+ta
 (b) • vusitavā. [wa] vasa+tavantu
 (c) • vusitāvī-lived. [wa] vasa+tāvī

(3) (a) • Bhutto, [wa] bhuja+ta
 (b) • bhuttavā [wa] bhuja+tavantu
 (c) • bhuttāvī-eaten. [wa] bhuja+tāvī

५५६, ६२२. भावकम्मेसु त

556, 622. **Bhāvakammesu ta.**

[Bhāvakammesu+ta. 2 words]

[V] **Bhāvakamme**su atīte kāle **ta**paccayo hoti sabbadhātūhi.

The affix "**ta**" is applied in the sense of bhāva (action), kamma (passive voice) and past tense.

Note: Any word affixed with this "**ta**" affix is to be regarded as having either Bhāva or Kamma sense (passive voice verb) or past tense verbs according to context.

Bhāve tāva–(Here are) examples in the sense of Bhāva.

(1) tassa-of that person,(This word in genitive case signifies Bhāva-sense of the example). • gītaṁ-singing. **i.e.** The singing act of that person. [wa] ge+ta

(2) • naccaṁ-dancing. [wa] naṭa+ta

(3) • naṭṭaṁ-dancing, [wa] naṭa+ta (2 words of the same root but different word-forms)

(4) • hasitaṁ-laughing. [wa] hasa+ta

Kammani tāva—(Here are) examples in the sense of Kamma (passive voice).

(1) tena-by that person, (this word in instrumental case signifies Kamma-sense of the example, indicative of non-principal subject).
• bhāsitaṁ-is said, **i.e.** Said by that person. [wa] bhāsa+ta

(2) • desitaṁ-is taught or proclaimed. [wa] disa+ta

५५७, ६०६. बुधगमादित्थे कत्तरि

557, 606. **Budha, gamā'ditthe kattari.**

[Budha, gamu-ādi-atthe+kattari. 2 words]

[V] **Budha, gamu-**icce'va'mādīhi dhātūhi ta'datthe gamyamāne **ta**paccayo hoti **katta**ri sabbakāle.

The affix "ta" is applied after the roots "budha, gamu" etc. in the sense of Kattā (an active voice) at all tense modes.
Note: Any word affixed with this "**ta**" affix is to be regarded as belonging to Kattu-sense, active voice verb.

(1) Sabbe-all, saṅkhatā'saṅkhate-the conditioned and uncondi

tioned, dhamme-phenomena, [1] bujjhati-knows, [2] abujjhi-knew, [3] bujjhissatī'ti [bujjhissati+iti] bujjhissati-will know, iti-therefore, Buddho-is called Buddha. • Buddho-the one who knows, who knew and who will know all conditioned and unconditioned phenomena. The Buddha. [Kattu-sādhana ED]

[wa] Budha+ta

(2) • saraṇaṅgato-the one who went/goes/will go to refuge.

[wa] saraṇa-saddūpapada gamu+ta

(3) • samathaṅgato-the one who attained/attains/will attain peace.

[wa] samatha-saddūpapada gamu+ta

(4) • amathaṅgato-the one who attained/attains/will attain *amata* (deathlessness). [wa] amata-saddūpapada gamu+ta

(5) [1] jānāti-(He) knows, [2] ajāni-knew, [3] jānissatī'ti [jānissati+iti] jānissati-will know, iti • ñāto-the one who knows, knew, will know. [Kattu-sādhana] [wa] ñā+ta

icce'va'mādi.

Note: The numbered three verbs in the ED indicate all three tense modes of the words affixed with "**ta**".

In view of Suttas 555, 556 and 557, it should be noted that there are four senses of Pāli words affixed with a "ta". They are:

(1) Atīta (past), (2) the Bhāva (impersonal voice), (3) Kamma (Passive voice) and (4) Kattu (Active voice). Knowing this basic fact will help in the understanding of Pāli texts and words suffixed with this "ta" affix.

५५८, ६०२. जितो इन सब्बत्थ

558, 602. **Jito ina sabbattha.** [Jito+ina+sabbattha. 3 words]

[V] **Ji-**iccetāya dhātuyā **ina-**paccayo hoti sabbakāle **katta**ri.

An "**ina**" affix is applied after the root "**ji**" in the sense of Kattā in all tenses.

(1) Pāpake-evil, akusale-unwholesome, dhamme-phenomena, [1] jināti-subjugates, [2] ajini-subjugated, [3] jinissatī'ti [jinissati+iti] jinissati-will subjugate, iti-therefore, jino-is called jina.

• jino-the one who subjugates, subjugated and will subjugate the evil, bad, unwholesome mental states. Buddha, the victor of evil. [Kattu-sādhana ED] [wa] ji+ina

५५९, ६०३. सुपतो च

559, 603. **Supato ca.** [Supato+ca. 2 words]

[V] **Supa**-iccetāya dhātuyā **ina**paccayo hoti kattari, bhāve ca.

A similar "**ina**" affix is applied after the root "**supa**" in the sense not only of Kattā but also of bhāva.

(1) (a) Supatī'ti [supati+iti] supati-(it) sleeps, iti-therefore.
• supinaṁ-dream, (seen while sleeping) [Kattu-sādhana].
(b) Supīyate-act of sleeping, • supinaṁ-sleep.
[Bhāva-sādhana ED] [wa] supa+ina

५६०, ६०४. ईसंदुसूहि ख

560, 604. **Īsaṁ, du, sū, hi kha.**

[Īsaṁ, du, sū, hi+kha. 2 words]

[V] **Īsaṁ, du, su**-saddā'dīhi sabbadhātūhi **kha**paccayo hoti.

A "**kha**" affix is applied after the roots prefixed with Upasagga and Nipāta particles such as "**Īsaṁ** (small, little), **du** (badly), **su** (well) ".

Note: The affix "**Kha**" is only a **kh**-conjoined affix "**a**". So, only "**a**" will be shown in WA as the actual affix in the examples below.

Examples in the root "si"

(1) • īsassayo-little-sleeping, a nap. [wa] īsaṁ-saddhūpapada, si+a

(2) • dussayo-badly-sleeping, bad sleep. [wa] du√si+a

(3) • sussayo-well-sleeping. bhavatā-by your honorable [This word in instrumental case signifies bhāva and Kamma senses of the affix and all these Kita-verbs and verbal nouns affixed with it]
[wa] su√si+a

Examples in the root "kara"

(1) īsakkaraṁ-little-doing. [one "k" augmented]
[wa] īsaṁ-saddhūpapada, kara+kh-conjoined a

(2) • dukkaraṁ-being not easy to do. badly-done, hard to do. [one "k" augmented] [wa] du√kara+a

(3) • sukaraṁ-easily done. well-done, bhavatā-by your honorable. [wa] su√kara+a

५६१, ६३६. इच्छत्थेसु समानकत्तुकेसु तवे तुं वा

561, 636. Iccha'tthesu samānakattukesu tave tuṁ vā.

[Icchā-atthesu+samānakattukesu+tave, tuṁ+vā. 4 words]

[V] **Iccha'tthe**su **samānakattu**kesu sabbadhātūhi **tave, tuṁ**icce'te paccayā honti **sabbakāle kattar**i.

When expressing "**wish or purpose**" in a sentence having one same Kattā (subject), the affixes "**tave, tuṁ**" are applied after all roots in all tenses.

(1) Puññāni-meritorious deeds, • kātave-to do, **i.e.** for the purpose of doing meritorious deeds. [wa] kara+tave

(2) saddhammaṁ-the noble teachings, • sotu'micchati [sotuṁ+icchati] sotuṁ-to listen, icchati-(he) wants. **i.e.** He wants to listen to noble Dhamma. [wa] su+tuṁ

५६२, ६३८. अरहसक्कादीसु च

562, 638. Araha, sakkā'dīsu ca.

[Araha, sakka-ādīsu+ca. 2 words]

[V] **Araha, sakkā'**dīsu ca atthesu sabbadhātūhi **tuṁ-**paccayo hoti.

When expressing worthiness and ability, the affix "**tuṁ**" is applied after all roots.

(1) Ko-who, taṁ-to that person, him. • ninditum'arahati [ninditum+arahati] ninditum-to blame, arahati-deserves? **i.e.** Who deserves to blame that person? [wa] ninda+tuṁ

(2) sakkā-can be, • jetuṁ-to conquer, dhanena-by wealth, vā-also, **i.e.** It may be possible to conquer by means of wealth also. [wa] ji+tuṁ

Eva'maññe'pi yojetabbā.

५६३, ६३९. पत्तवचने अलमत्थेसु च

563, 639. **Pattavacane ala'matthesu ca.**

[Pattavacane+alaṁ, atthesu+ca. 3 words]

[V] **Pattavacane alama'tthe**su sabbadhātūhi **tuṁ-**paccayo hoti.

To express "appropriateness" to do something, which is one of the meanings of the word "alaṁ", an affix "**tuṁ**" is applied after all roots.

Summary: This Sutta enjoins to apply "**tuṁ**" affix after all roots of the verb used in the context of "**alaṁ**" which has the meaning of suitability and appropriateness.

(1) Ala'meva [alaṁ+eva] alaṁ-(is) appropriate, eva-only, dānāni-alms, • dātuṁ-to offer, **i.e.** It is only appropriate to offer alms (as it can enrich one in many ways). [wa] dā+tuṁ

(2) ala'meva [alaṁ+eva] alaṁ eva puññāni-meritorious deeds, • kātuṁ-to do, **i.e.** It is fitting or suitable to do meritorious deeds (as it can lead to wholesome results). [wa] kara+tuṁ

५६४, ६४०. पुब्बकाले'ककत्तुकानं तुन त्वान त्वा वा

564, 640. **Pubbakāle'kakattukānaṁ tuna, tvāna, tvā vā.**

[Pubbakāle+ekakattukānaṁ+tuna, tvāna, tvā+vā. 4 words]

[V] **Pubbakāle ekakattu**kānaṁ dhātūnaṁ **tuna, tvāna, tvā-**icce'te paccayā honti vā.

To express concurrent actions of a single doer, one being a preceding action and the other being next subsequent action, the affixes "**tuna, tvāna, tvā**" are sometimes applied after the root (of the verb denoting the preceding action.)

Note: The verbs suffixed with these three affixes applied by this Sutta are called **"gerund or absolutive"** which have no gender.

(1) • Kātuna-having done, [the preceding action]. kammaṁ-work, gacchati-(he) goes [the subsequent action]. **i.e.** He goes (after) having done work. [wa] kara+tuna

(2) • akātuna-not having done,("**a**" is a morpheme of negative particle "**na**" which means "**not**"). puññaṁ-meritorious deed, kilissati-will suffer. **i.e.** (He) will suffer for not having done meritorious deeds. [wa] na-√kara+tuna

(3) Sattā-living beings, • sutvāna-having heard, dhammaṁ-the Dhamma, modanti-are delighted, **i.e.** Having heard Dhamma, the living beings are delighted. [wa] su+tvāna

(4) Ripuṁ-the enemy, • jitvāna-having conquered, vasati-(he) lives. **i.e.** Having conquered the enemy, (he) lives. [wa] ji+tvāna

(5) Dhammaṁ-Dhamma, • sutvāna'ssa [sutvāna+assa] sutvāna-having heard, assa-of that person, eta'dahosi [etaṁ+ahosi] etaṁ-this (thought), ahosi-was, arose. **i.e.** Having heard Dhamma, this thought arose in him (in his mind). [wa] su+tvāna

(6) Ito-from this place, • sutvāna-having heard, amutra-at that place, there, kathayanti-(they) say. **i.e.** Having heard here, they say there (what they heard). [wa] su+tvāna

(7) • Sutvā-after having heard, jānissāma-(we) must know. **i.e.** We must know (how to respond) (only after) having heard (from you). [wa] su+tvā

Evaṁ sabbattha yojetabbā.

५६५, ६४६. वत्तमाने मान'न्ता

565, 646. Vattamāne māna'ntā.

[Vattamāne+māna, antā. 2 words]

[V] **Vattamāne Kāle** sabbadhātūhi **māna, anta**-icce'te paccayā honti.

To express an on-going action being done or still taking place at present, (**i.e.** as yet unfinished action), the affixes "**māna** or **anta**" are applied after all roots.

Note: These two affixes are often referred to as the present participle and play various roles in a sentence.

[māna affix] • Saramāno-while remembering, rodati-(he) cries.
[wa] sara+a+māna (two affixes)

[anta affix] • Gacchanto-while going, gaṇhāti-(he) takes or grabs.
[wa] gamu+anta

५६६, ५७४. सासादीहि रत्थु

566, 574. **Sāsā'dīhi ratthu.** [Sāsa-ādīhi+ratthu. 2 words]

[V] **Sāsa**-icce'va'mādīhi dhātūhi **ratthu**paccayo hoti.

The affix "**ratthu**" is applied after the roots "**sāsa**" etc.

(a) Sāsatī'ti [Sāsati+iti] Sāsati-(he) teaches, iti • satthā-the one who teaches, teacher.

(b) sāsati hiṁsatī'ti [hiṁsati+iti] hiṁsati-(he) hurts defilements, iti vā • satthā-the one who hurts the defilements, Buddha who hurts defilements. [Kattu-sādhana ED] [wa] sāsa+ratthu

Note: In the second ED, the verb "**hiṁsati**" is another possible meaning of the previous verb "**sāsati**". It means that the root word "**sāsa**" in the verb "**sāsati**" does not only mean to teach, but it also means to hurt, as shown by another verb "**hiṁsati**"**.** Such explanation by means of a substitute verb of different meaning or the same meaning will be frequently found in the EDs of forthcoming sections of Kita and Uṇādi chapters. The students need to be familiar with such explanatory verbs and words in the EDs.

५६७, ५७५. पातितो रितु

567, 575. **Pātito ritu.** [Pātito+ritu. 2 words]

[V] **Pā**-icce'tāya dhātuyā **ritu-**paccayo hoti.

The affix "**ritu**" is applied after the root "**pā**".

Pāti-(One) protects, puttanti [puttaṁ+iti] puttaṁ-son or offspring, iti • pitā-the one who protects one's offspring, father.
[Kattu-sādhana ED] [wa] pā+ritu

५६८, ५७६. मानादीहि रातु

568, 576. **Mānā'dīhi rātu.** [Māna-ādīhi+rātu. 2 words]

[V] **Māna**-icce'va'mādīhi dhātūhi **rātu**-paccayo hoti, **ritu**-paccayo ca.

The affix "**rātu**", as well as the affix "**ritu**", is applied after the roots "**māna**" etc.

(1) Dhammena-justly, puttaṁ-son or offspring, mānetī'ti [māneti+iti] māneti-adores. iti • mātā-the one who justly adores (her) offspring, a mother. [wa] māna+rātu

(2) pubbe-before (other young siblings), bhāsatī'ti [bhāsati+iti] bhāsati-speaks. iti • bhātā-the one who speaks (first before other young siblings) **i.e.** Brother. [Both Kattu-sādhana]
[wa] bhāsa+rātu

(3) mātāpitūhi-by mother and father, dhāṛīyatī'ti [dhārīyati+iti] dhārīyati-(is) carried or protected. iti • dhītā-the one protected by mother and father. **i.e.** a daughter. [Kamma-sādhana]
[wa] dhara+ritu

५६९, ६१०. आगमा तुको

569, 610. **Āgamā tuko.** [Āgamā+tuko. 2 words]

[V] **Ā**-iccā'dimhā **gam**ito **tuka**paccayo hoti.

The affix "**tuka**" is applied after the root "**gamu**" prefixed with an upasagga particle "ā".

Āgacchatī'ti [Āgacchati+iti] Āgacchati-(he) comes (to visit), iti • āgantuko-the one who comes (to visit). bhikkhu-the guest monk. [Kattu-sādhana] [wa] ā-√gamu+tuka

Note: Any guest is also implied by the word.

५७०, ६११. भब्बे इक

570, 611. Bhabbe ika. [Bhabbe+ika. 2 words]

[V] **Gamu-**icce'tamhā dhātumhā **ika**paccayo hoti bhabbe.

The affix "**ika**" is applied after the root "**gamu**" in the sense of expressing a future possibility or prospect.

[1] Gamissati-will go. [2] gantuṁ-to go (on a trip), bhabbo'ti [bhabbo+iti] bhabbo-is likely, iti • gamiko-the one who will go or who is likely (be going on a trip), the would-be-traveler, the tourist. bhikkhu-the traveler monk is here to be known as a "Gamiko".

[wa] gamu+ika

Note: Any traveler is also implied by the word. The numbered verb and phrases indicate two possible EDs of this word.

Iti kibbidhānakappe dutiyo kaṇḍo.

The Second Section of Kita ends.

Tatiya Kaṇḍa
The Third Section

५७१, ६२४. पच्चयादनिट्ठा निपातना सिज्झन्ति

571, 624. **Paccayā'daniṭṭhā nipātanā sijjhanti.**

[Paccayā+aniṭṭhā+nipātanā+sijjhanti. 4 words]

[V] Saṅkhyā, nāma, samāsa, taddhitā'khyāta, kitakappamhi sappaccayā ye saddā aniṭṭhaṅgatā, te sādhanena nirakkhitvā sakehi sakehi nāmehi nipātanā sijjhanti.

Any uncompleted word of Saṅkhyā (numerical nouns), or nāma (noun words), or samāsa (compound noun words), or Taddhita (nouns in Taddhita affixes), or ākhyāta (verbs), or Kita (nouns in Kita affixes), all those words can be completed by means of this great Sutta.

Some functions on Numerical Nouns

Saṅkhyāyaṁ tāva–First, are some examples of numerical nouns (which can also be completed by this Sutta).

(1) ekassa ekā hoti. **dasa**ssa ca **da**kārassa **ra**kārā'deso hoti.

The numerical word "**eka**-one" becomes "**ekā**". The syllable "**d**" of the word "**dasa**-ten" changes into "**r**".
Eko ca-one also. dasa ca-ten also. • Ekārasa-one and ten, **i.e.** Eleven.

(2) **Dvi**ssa **bā** hoti. **dasa**ssa ca **da**kārassa **ra**kārā'deso hoti.

The numerical word "**Dvi**-two" becomes "**bā**". The syllable "**d**" of the word "**dasa**-ten" changes into "**r**".
dve ca-two also. dasa ca • Bārasa-two and ten, **i.e.** Twelve.

(3) **Dvi**ssa **bā** hoti. **dasa**ssa ca **vīsaṁ** hoti.

The numerical word "**Dvi**-two" becomes "**bā**". The word "**dasa**-ten" changes into "**vīsaṁ**".
Dve ca-two also. vīsañca [vīsaṁ+ca] vīsaṁ ca-twenty also.
• Bāvīsaṁ-two and twenty, **i.e.** Twenty-two.

(4) **Cha**ssa **so** hoti. **dasa**ssa ca **da**kārassa **ḷo** hoti.

The numerical word "**Cha**-six" becomes "**so**". The syllable "**d**" of the word "**dasa**-ten" changes into "**ḷ**".

Cha ca-six also. dasa ca • Soḷasa-six and ten. **i.e.** Sixteen.

(5) Cha-āyatanamhi **cha**ssa **saḷo** hoti.

In the example word "Cha-āyatana" The numerical word "**Cha**-six" becomes "**saḷa**".

• Saḷāyatanaṁ-Six base.

Evaṁ sesā saṅkhyā kātabbā.
Thus, the remaining numerical nouns should be applied.
Note: The functions for most of these examples are already shown in relevant Suttas in the Saṅkhyā Taddhita section.

Some functions on Nouns

Nāmike tāva-Here are some examples of nouns.

ima, samāna, apara-iccetehi **jja, jju**-paccayā honti.
ima, samāna-saddānañ'ca **a**kāra, **sa**kārā'desā honti.

The "**jja, jju**" affixes are applied after the words **ima** (this), **samāna** (similar) and **apara** (other). Besides, "**ima**" changes into "**a**" and "**samāna**" changes into "**sa**".

(1) Imasmiṁ kāle-at this time, • ajja, • ajju-at this time, **i.e.** Today. [wa] ajja=ima+jja [wa] ajju=ima+jju
(2) samāne kāle-at the same time, • sajja, • sajju-at the same time, at once, simultaneously.
[wa] sajja=smāna+jja [wa] sajju=smāna+jju
(3) aparasmiṁ kāle-at other time, • aparajja, • aparajju-the other day, on the following day.
[wa] aparajja=apara+jja [wa] aparajju=apara+jju

Note: The words affixed with "jja, jju" are indeclinable, which have no gender nor number except that it signifies a locative sense. The words "Imasmiṁ kāle" etc. are EDs for the examples.

Some functions on Compound Nouns

Samāse tāva–Here are some examples of compound nouns.
• bhūmigato. • apāyagato. • issarakataṁ. • Sallaviddho.
• kathinadussaṁ. • corabhayaṁ. • dhaññarāsi.
• saṁsāradukkhaṁ. [Tappurisa compounds]
• pubbā'paraṁ-front and back (This is a Dvanda compound). [Pubbañ'ca aparañ'ca **Pubbā'paraṁ** .ED].

Some functions on Taddhita-nouns

Taddhite tāva–Here are some examples of Taddhita nouns.
• vāsiṭṭho. • bhāradvājo. • bhaggavo. • paṇḍavo. • kāleyyo.

Note: All examples shown in Samāsa and Taddhita section of this Sutta have been already shown in their respective Suttas of the relevant chapters. The purpose of showing again here by the great grammarian is to show that these words too can be completed by means of this great Sutta wherever necessary by invoking necessary morphological procedures.

Some functions on ākhyāta-Verbs

Ākhyāte tāva-Here are some examples of Ākhyāta (Verbs).

"**asa** bhāve" ti dhātuto vattamānesu ekavacana, bahuvacanesu **ekavacana**ssa **ti**ssa **sso** hoti antena saha, **bahuvacana**ssa **anti**ssa **ssu** hoti antena saha.

The Vattamāna singular vibatti "**ti**" applied after the root "**asa**-to be", changes into "**ssa**" while the plural vibatti "**anti**" changes into "**ssu**" together with last component word "**sa**" of the root. [**Ti**>**ssa**, **Anti**>**ssu.**]

(1) Eva'• ma**ssa** [Evaṁ+assa] Evaṁ-thus, assa-should be, vacanīyo- said. **i.e.** It should be said thus. [wa] assa=asa+ti

(2) eva'• ma**ssu** [Evaṁ+assu] evaṁ assu-should be, ***pl.*** vacanīyā, ***pl.*** [wa] assu=asa+anti

Āṇattiyaṁ hissa **ssu** hoti vā.

In expression of command, the pañcamī vibatti "**hi**" is substituted with "**ssu**" sometimes.

• gaccha**ssu**-go. * gacchāhi-go. (The second is inapplicable example). [wa] gamu+hi (Both are the same)

Some functions on Kita-nouns

Kitake tāva– Here are some examples of nouns in Kita-affixes.

vada hana-icce'va'mādīhi dhātūhi **ka**paccayo hoti.

An affix "Ka" is applied after the roots "**vada**-to speak" and "**hana**-to kill".

vadassa ca **vādo** hoti.

The root "vada" becomes "vāda".

hanassa ca **ghāto** hoti.

The root "hana" becomes "ghāta".

(1) • Vādako-speaker. [wa] vada+ka [No "ṇvu" affix in these words]

(2) • ghātako-killer. [wa] hana+ka

Note: These two examples can also be completed by applying "**ṇvu**" affix as per the standard morphological procedures prescribed in Suttas 527, 622.

Naṭadhātuto **ta**paccayassa **cca, ṭṭā'**desā honti antena saha.

Also, the affix "**ta**", applied after the root "**naṭa-**to dance", changes into "**cca** and **ṭṭa**" along with the last consonant "**ṭ**" of the root.

• Naccaṁ-dancing. • naṭṭaṁ-dancing. [wa] naṭa+ta (two different word-forms of the same meaning & basic structure)

Icce'va'mādayo nipātanā sijjhanti.

Such example of words can be completed by means of this Sutta.

५७२, ६२५. सासदिसतो तस्स रिट्ठो च

572, 625. **Sāsa, disato tassa riṭṭho ca.**

[Sāsa, disa-to+tassa+riṭṭho+ca. 4 words]

[V] **Sāsa, disa**-icce'va'mādīhi dhātūhi **ta**paccayassa **riṭṭhā**'deso hoti ṭhāne.

The affix "**ta**" applied after the roots "**sāsa, disa**" etc. changes into "**riṭṭha**" at some appropriate instances of words.

(1) • Anusiṭṭho-(have) instructed. so-that person, mayā-by me, **i.e.** That person was instructed by me. [wa] anu-√sāsa+ta

(2) • diṭṭhaṁ-(have) seen. me-by me, rūpaṁ-the sight, **i.e.** The sight was seen by me. [wa] disa+ta

Caggahaṇena kicca**ta**kārassa ca **tuṁ**-paccayassa ca **raṭṭha, raṭṭhuṁ,** ādesā honti.

By means of "Ca" in Sutta, "**ta**" of **tabba** affix and the whole "**tuṁ**-affix" changes into "**raṭṭha, raṭṭhuṁ**".

Note: (a) "Ta" of tabba>**raṭṭha**> **raṭṭhabba,**

(b) Tuṁ>**raṭṭhuṁ.**

(See the examples below. The function is shown in bold. The "**r**" is deleted by Sutta 539)

(1) Dassanīyaṁ-(should be) seen or known, • **daṭṭha**bbaṁ-should see or know. [wa] daṭṭhabbaṁ=disa+tabba

(2) • **Daṭṭhuṁ**-to see, vihāraṁ-to the temple, gacchanti-(they) go. samaṇānaṁ-the monks, **i.e.** (They) go to the temple in order to see the monks. [wa] daṭṭhuṁ=disa+tuṁ

५७३, ६२६. सादिसन्त पुच्छ भन्ज हन्तादीहि ट्ठो

573, 626. **Sā'di sa'nta, puccha, bhanja, hansā'dīhi ṭṭho.**

[Sa-ādi+sa-anta, puccha, bhanja, hansa-ādīhi+ṭṭho. 3 words]

[V] **Sa**kāranta **puccha, bhanja, hansa-**icce'va'mādīhi dhātūhi **ta**paccayassa sahā'dibyañjanena **ṭṭh**ā'deso hoti ṭhāne.

The affix "ta" applied after the roots **puccha, bhanja, hansa** and the roots ending in "**s**" etc. together with the last component consonant of the root, changes into "**ṭṭha**" in some instances. [See the function shown in bold]

(1) • Tu**ṭṭh**o-pleased. [wa] tusa+ta

(2) ahinā-by the snake, • da**ṭṭh**o-(had) bitten. naro-the man, **i.e.** The man is bitten by snake. [wa] daṁsa+ta

(3) mayā-by me, • pu**ṭṭh**o-(have) asked. [wa] puccha+ta

(4) • bha**ṭṭh**o. [wa] bhanja+ta

(5) • pabha**ṭṭh**o-(have) thrashed or slipped down. [wa] pa√bhanja+ta

Note: 4, and 5 have the same root and meaning except the prefix.

(6) • ha**ṭṭh**o. [wa] haṁsa+ta

(7) • paha**ṭṭh**o-(have) delighted, laughed. [wa] pa-√haṁsa+ta

Note: 6 and 7 have the same root and meaning except the prefix.

(8) • yi**ṭṭh**o-(have) sacrificed. [wa] yaja+ta

Eva'maññe'pi dhātavo sabbattha yojetabbā.

Thus, similar examples of other roots should be applied.

५७४, ६१३. वसतो उत्थ

574, 613. **Vasato uṭṭha.** [Vasato+uṭṭha. 2 words]

[V] **Vasa-**icce'tamhā dhātumhā **ta**kārapaccayassa sahā'dibyañjanena **uṭṭh**ā'deso hoti ṭhāne.

The affix "**ta**" applied after the root "**vasa**", together with the last consonant "**s**" of the root, changes into "**uṭṭha**" where applicable.

Vassaṁ-for three month of rains retreat (Vassa), • vuṭṭho-(have) lived. **i.e.** (A monk who have) lived three month's rains retreat. [wa] vasa+ta

५७५, ६१४. वस वा वु

575, 614. **Vassa vā vu'.** [Vassa+vā+u. 3 words]

[V] **Vasa**-sse'va dhātussa **ta**paccaye pare **va**kārassa **u**kārā'deso hoti vā.

The component consonant "**v**" of the root "**vasa**", sometimes changes into "**u**" when a "**ta**" affix is applied. [This Sutta changes "**v**" of "**vasa**-to stay" into "**u**". Function shown in bold, underlined]

(1) • V**u**sitaṁ-(have) lived. **i.e.** completed. brahmacariyaṁ-the noble practice, [Here, "**v**" of "**vasa**-to stay" becomes "**u**" and "**v**" is inserted before it by Sutta 404] [wa] vasa+ta

(2) • **U**ṭṭho [Here, "**v**" of "**vasa**-to stay" becomes "**u**" and affix "**ta**" along with the root-end consonant "**s**" changes into "ṭṭha" by 573]. [wa] vasa+ta

(3) • V**u**ṭṭho-(have) lived. vā-also, as another possible example found in texts. [wa] vasa+ta

Note: "vā" means another possible example although being inapplicable by the function of this Sutta, but usually found in the Pāli texts.

५७६, ६०७. धढभहेहि धड्ढा च

576, 607. **Dha, ḍha, bha, hehi dha, ḍhā ca.**

[Dha, ḍha, bha, hehi+dha, ḍhā+ca. 3 words]

[V] **Dha, ḍha, bha, ha**-icce'va'mantehi dhātūhi **ta**kārapaccayassa yathākkamaṁ **dha, ḍhā'**desā honti.

The affix "ta" applied after the roots ending in consonants "**dha, ḍha, bha, ha**" changes into "**dha, ḍha**" respectively. **Note:** Affix "**ta**" after **dha, bha**-ending roots becomes **dha** while affix "**ta**" after **ḍha, ha**-ending roots becomes **ḍha**.

Yathā? For example,

(1) • Buddho-enlightened. bhagavā-Buddha. [Here, affix "**ta**" changes into "**dha**"] [wa] budha+ta

(2) • vaḍḍho-grown-up, old. bhikkhu-monk. **i.e.** Senior monk. [Here, affix "**ta**" becomes "**ḍha**"] [wa] vaḍha+ta

Note: The morphological procedure of this example is a bit complex.

(3) • laddhaṁ-obtained. me-by me, pattacīvaraṁ-bowl and robe, **i.e.** I have got my bowl and robes. [Here, affix "**ta**" changes into "**dha**"] [wa] labha+ta

(4) agginā-by fire, • daḍḍhaṁ-was burnt. vanaṁ-the forest, **i.e.** The forest was burnt by fire. [Here, affix "**ta**" changes into "**ḍha**"] [wa] daha+ta

५७७, ६२८. भन्जतो ग्गो च

577, 628. **Bhanjato ggo ca.** [Bhanjato+ggo+ca. 3 words]

[V] **Bhanja**to dhātumhā **ta**kārapaccayassa **ggo**-ādeso hoti sahā'dibyañjanena.

The affix "**ta**" applied after the root "**bhanja**", together with its last component consonant "**j**" changes into "**gga**".

• Bha**ggo**-(have) broken. [wa] bhanja+ta

५७८, ५६०. भुजादीनमन्तो नो द्वि च

578, 560. **Bhujā'dīna'manto no dvi ca.**

[Bhuja-ādīnaṁ+anto+no+dvi+ca. 5 words]

[V] **Bhuja**icce'va'mādīnaṁ dhātūnaṁ anto **no** hoti, **ta**paccayassa ca **dvibhāvo** hoti.

The last component consonant of the roots "**bhuja**" etc. is elided, while the affix "**ta**" applied after them is duplicated too. [Eliding the root consonant and augmenting the affix "ta". Two functions]

(1) • Bhutto-he had eaten. [wa] bhuja+ta

(2) • bhuttāvī-he ate. [wa] bhuja+tāvī

(3) • catto-given up, abandoned, sacrificed. [wa] caja+ta

(4) • satto-clung to, attached to. [wa] Sanja+ta

(5) • ratto-attached to (as with desire or lust), enamored of. [wa] Ranja+ta

(6) • yutto-tied, engaged, bound. [wa] yuja+ta

(7) • vivitto-retired by being secluded. [wa] vi-√vica+ta

Note: All examples shown here have the roots ending in consonants "**j**" and "**c**".

५७९, ६२९. वच वा वु

579, 629. **Vaca vā'vu.**

[**1.**Vaca+vā+u. 3 words or **2.** Vaca+vā+va+u. 4 words.]
(This Sutta is structurally somewhat similar to 575)

[V] **Vaca**-icce'tassa dhātussa **va**kārassa **u**kārā'deso hoti. anto **ca**kāro **no** hoti, **ta**-paccayassa ca **dvebhāvo** hoti vā.

The entire component letters "**va**" of the root "**vaca**", sometimes changes into "**u**" while component consonant "**c**" of the root is elided. Besides, the applied affix "ta" is also reduplicated. [Three functions]

(1) • V<u>u</u>ttaṁ-(is) said. bhagavatā-by Buddha, [Here, "**va**" becomes "**u**" and a "**v**" is inserted] [wa] vaca+ta

(2) • <u>U</u>ttaṁ-(is) said. vā. [Here, "**v**" is not inserted leaving "**u**" as it is.] [wa] vaca+ta

Note: Compare the function of Sutta numbers 487, 575, 579, as they are somewhat similar to each other.

५८०, ६३०. गुपादीनञ्च

580, 630. **Gupā'dīnañ'ca.** [Gupa-ādīnaṁ+ca. 2 words]

[V] **Gupa**-icceva'mādīnaṁ dhātūnaṁ anto ca byañjano **no** hoti, **ta**-paccayassa ca **dvebhāvo** hoti.

The last component consonant of the roots "**gupa**" etc. is elided while the affix "**ta**" applied after them is also reduplicated. [Two functions]

(1) • Sugutto-well-protected, well-kept. [wa] su-√gupa+ta

(2) • catto (Re: 578).

(3) • litto-anointed. [wa] lipa+ta

(4) • santatto-well-heated. [wa] saṁ-√tapa+ta
(5) • utto (Re: 579).
(6) • vivitto (Re: 578).
(7) • sitto-poured (as with liquid). [wa] sica+ta
Eva'maññe'pi yojetabbā.

५८१, ६१६. तरादीहि इण्णो

581, 616. Tarā'dīhi iṇṇo. [Tara-ādīhi+iṇṇo. 2 words]

[V] **Tara**-icce'vamādīhi dhātūhi **ta**-paccayassa **iṇṇā'**deso hoti, anto ca byañjano **no** hoti.

The affix "**ta**" applied after the roots "**tara**" etc. changes into "**iṇṇa**" and the last component consonant of the root is also elided. [Two functions]

(1) Taratī'ti [tarati+iti] tarati-crossed over, iti • tiṇṇo-(had) crossed, overcome (such as river, obstacles etc,). [wa] tara+ta
(2) uttaratī'ti [uttarati+iti] uttarati-move beyond, iti • uttiṇṇo-moved beyond. [wa] u-√tara+ta
(3) saṁpūratī'ti [saṁpūrati+iti] saṁpūrati-well-filled, iti • sampuṇṇo-well filled, full. [wa] saṁ-√pūra+ta
(4) turatī'ti [turati+it] turati-dashes off, iti • tuṇṇo-hurried. [wa] tura+ta
(5) parijīratī'ti [parijīrati+iti] parijīrati-degenerates, iti. • parijiṇṇo- degenerated, old. [wa] pari-√jara+ta
(6) ākiratī'ti [ākirati+iti] ākirati-mingles, iti • ākiṇṇo-mingled, mixed. [All Kattu-sādhana EDs] [wa] ā-√kira+ta

५८२, ६३१. भिदादितो इन्न अन्न ईणा वा

582, 631. Bhidā'dito inna, anna, īṇā vā.

[Bhida-ādito+inna, anna, īṇā+vā. 3 words]

[V] **Bhidi**-icce'va'mādīhi dhātūhi **ta**-paccayassa **inna, anna, īṇā'**desā honti vā, anto ca byañjano no hoti.

The affix "**ta**" applied after the roots "**bhida**" etc. sometimes changes into "**inna, anna, īṇa**" and the last component consonant of the root is also elided. [Two functions]

inna-function examples:

(1) Bhinditabbo'ti [Bhinditabbo+iti] Bhinditabbo-should break apart, iti • bhinno-split, broken. [Kamma-sādhana] [wa] bhida+ta

(2) chindīyatī'ti [chindīyati+iti] chindīyati-(is) cut, iti • chinno-cut. [wa] chidi+ta

(3) ucchindīyitthā'ti [ucchindīyittha+iti] ucchindīyittha-(was) totally cut, iti • ucchinno-cut. [wa] u-√chidi+ta

(4) dīyatī'ti [dīyati+iti] dīyati-(is) given, iti • dinno-given. [All Kamma-sādhana EDs] [wa] dā+ta

(5) nisīdatī'ti [nisīdati+iti] nisīdati-sits, iti • nisinno-sat. [Kattu-sādhana] [wa] Ni-√sada+ta

anna-function examples:

(1) suṭṭhu-well, chādīyatī'ti [chādīyati+iti] chādīyati-(is) covered, iti • suchanno-well-covered. [Kamma-sādhana] [wa] su-√chada+ta

(2) khidatī'ti [khidati+iti] khidati-exhausts, wears out, iti • khinno- exhausted, fatigued, feared. [wa] khida+ta

Note: There is another possible root as "**Khiṭa**-to fear"

(3) rodatī'ti [rodati+iti] rodati-weeps, iti • runno-wept. [Both Kattu-sādhana] [wa] ruda+ta

īṇa-function example:

(1) • khīṇā-(is) finished up, nothing left. jāti-rebirth. [wa] khī+ta

Vā'ti kimatthaṁ?

What is the word "vā" for?

To show that the examples below are inapplicable for function of this Sutta as restricted by the word "vā".

Bhijjatī'ti [Bhijjati+iti] Bhijjati-(it) breaks, iti * bhitti-wall (made of breakable materials). [Kattu-sādhana] [wa] bhida+ti

५८३, ६१७. सुस पच सकतो क्ख क्का च

583, 617. **Susa, paca, sakato kkha, kkā ca.**

[Susa, paca, sakato+kkha, kkā+ca. 3 words]

[V] **Susa, paca, saka-**icce'va'mādīhi dhātūhi **ta-**paccayassa **kkha, kkā'**desā honti, anto ca byañjano **no** hoti.

The affix "**ta**" applied after the roots "**susa, paca, saka**" etc. changes into "**kkha, kka**" and the last component consonant of the root is also elided. [Two functions]

kkha-function example:

(1) Sussatī'ti [Sussati+iti] Sussati-(it) dries, iti • sukkhaṁ-dried. kaṭṭhaṁ-wood, the dry timber. [Kattu-sādhana] [wa] susa+ta

kka-function examples:

(1) paccatī'ti [paccati+iti] paccati-(is) ripe, iti • pakkaṁ-ripened. phalaṁ-fruit. the ripe fruit. [Kamma-sādhana] [wa] paca+ta

(2) [1] Sakati samattheti-(is) able,
[2] pūjetī'ti [pūjeti+iti] pūjeti-honors, iti vā • sakko-an able being or an honored being, **i.e.** the king of heaven. sujampati-the husband of a deity named "Sujā" is to be regarded as "sakko". [Kattu-sādhana] [wa] saka+ta

Note: There are two EDs for the word **Sakko.** The first is shown by "**Sakati samattheti-**is able". The second is explained by "**pūjeti**". These two EDs show two different meanings of the root "saka" in the word "Sakko".

५८४, ६१८. पक्कमादीहि न्तो च

584, 618. **Pa'kkamā'dīhi nto ca.**

[Pa-kamu-ādīhi+nto+ca. 3 words]

[V] **Pa'kkama-**icce'va'mādīhi dhātūhi **ta-**paccayassa **nto-**ādeso hoti, **anto** ca **no** hoti.

The affix "**ta**" applied after the roots "**kamu** prefixed with **pa**" etc. changes into "**nta**" and the last component consonant of the root is also elided. [Two functions]

(1) Pakkamatī'ti [Pakkamati+iti] Pakkamati-goes away, iti
• pakkanto-gone away.[**pa**-away+**kanta**-gone.]
[wa] pa-√kamu+ta

(2) Vibbhamatī'ti [Vibbhamati+iti] Vibbhamati-totters, iti
• vibbhanto-tottered, disrobed (as a wavering monk being no longer able to maintain pious life).[Both Kattu-sādhana]
[wa] vi-√bhamu+ta

(3) • saṅkanto-moved (to somewhere else). [wa] saṁ-√kamu+ta
(4) • khanto-endured with patience, being patient. [wa] khamu+ta
(5) • santo-calmed, calm. [wa] samu+ta
(6) • danto-trained, tame. [wa] damu+ta
(7) • vanto-vomitted. [wa] vamu+ta

Caggahaṇaṁ kimatthaṁ?
Tehe'va dhātūhi **ti**-paccayassa **nti** hoti. Anto ca no hoti.

What does the extra word "Ca" in Sutta meant for?
By means of the word "Ca" in Sutta, the affix "**ti** (Re: Sutta 553) " applied after those roots changes into "**nti**" while the last consonant of the root is also elided.

(1) • Kanti-act of liking, joy. [wa] kamu+ti
(2) • Khanti-act of endurance, patience. [wa] khamu+ti
Evaṁ sabbattha.

५८५, ६१९. जनादीन मा तिम्हि च

585, 619. Janā'dī'na'mā timhi ca.

[Jana-ādīnaṁ+ā+timhi+ca. 4 words]

[V] **Jana**-icce'va'mādīnaṁ dhātūnaṁ antassa byañjanassa **ā**ttaṁ hoti **ta**-paccaye pare, **ti**mhi ca.

The vowel of the initial consonant of the root "**jana**" changes into "**ā**" when the affix "**ta**" or "**ti**" is applied after it. ["**a**" of "**ja**" changes into "**ā**". See it shown in bold]

(1) Ajanī'ti [Ajani+iti] Ajani-(was) born, arisen, iti • j**ā**to-born, arisen. [Kattu-sādhana] [wa] jana+ta

(2) jananaṁ-act of arising or being born, • jāti-arising, the birth. [Bhāva-sādhana ED] [wa] jana+ti

Timhī'ti kimatthaṁ?
Aññasmim'pi paccaye pare **ā**kāra-nivattanatthaṁ.

What is the word "timhi" in Sutta for?
This function of changing into "ā" is debarred in words where other affixes are applied. [See examples]

(1) Janitvā-having arisen. [wa] jana+tvā
(2) janitā-that which arises. [wa] jana+ta
(3) janituṁ-to arise, for arising. [wa] jana+tuṁ
(4) janitabbaṁ-should arise. [wa] jana+tabba
icce'va'mādi.

५८६, ६००. गम खन हन रमादीन मन्तो

586, 600. **Gama, khana, hana, ramā'dīna'manto.**

[Gama, khana, hana, ramu-ādīnaṁ+anto. 2 words]

[V] **Gama, khana, hana, ramu**-icce'va'mādīnaṁ dhātūnaṁ **anto** byañjano **no** hoti vā **ta**-paccaye pare, **ti**mhi ca.

The last consonants of the roots "**gamu, khana, hana, ramu**" etc, is sometimes elided when affixes "**ta**" or "**ti**" follow. [This Sutta elides the last consonants "**m, n**" of the roots "ga**m**u, kha**n**a, etc" when affixed with either "**ta**" or "**ti**" affix after them.]

(1) Sundaraṁ-to the good, nibbānaṁ-Nibbāna, gacchatī'ti [gacchati+iti] gacchati-goes. iti • sugato-Lord Buddha who goes to good destiny of Nibbāna. [wa] su√gamu+ta
(2) Sundaraṁ nibbānaṁ gacchatī'ti • sugati [Meaning the same, except different affix "ti"], [Kattu-sādhana] [wa] su√gamu+ti
(3) • khataṁ-dug. [wa] khanu+ta
(4) • khati-digging. [wa] khanu+ti
(5) • Upahataṁ-killed, hurt. [wa] upa√hana+ta
(6) • upahati-killing, hurting. [wa] upa√hana+ti
(7) • Rato-rejoiced. [wa] ramu+ta

(8) • rati-rejoicing. [wa] ramu+ti
(9) • mato-knew. [wa] mana+ta
(10) • mati-knowing, knowledge, view, idea. [wa] mana+ti

Vā'ti kimatthaṁ? What is the word "vā" for?
To show that examples below are inapplicable for function of this Sutta as restricted by the word "vā".
(1) * Ramato-of the one who rejoices. [wa] ramu+anta+sa (Noun in genitive case, not a verb)
(2) * ramati-(He) rejoices. [wa] ramu+a+ti (an ākhyāta verb)

५८७, ६३२. रकारो च

587, 632. **Rakāro ca.** [Rakāro+ca. 2 words]

[V] **Ra**kāro ca dhātūna'mantabhūto **no** hoti **ta**paccaye pare **ti**mhi ca.

The last component consonant "**r**" of roots "**kara, sara**" etc. is elided when a "**ta** or **ti**" affix is applied after them.

(1) Pakārena-by various manner, karīyatī'ti [karīyati+iti] karīyati-(is) done. iti • pakato-done variously. [wa] pa√kara+ta
(2) paṭhamaṁ-initially, karīyatī'ti • pakati-act of initial state, The natural. [wa] pa√kara+ti
(3) visarīyatī'ti [visarīyati+iti] visarīyati-moves disorderly. iti • visato-moving disorderly, being spread. [wa] vi√sara+ta
(4) • visati-disorderly move or being spread as poison or water or effect of medicine etc. [All Kamma-sādhana EDs]
[wa] vi√sara+ti

५८८,६२० ठापान मिई च

588, 620.**Ṭhā, pā, na'mi, ī ca.** [Ṭhā, pā, naṁ+i, ī+ca. 3 words]

[V] **Ṭhā, pā**-icce'tesaṁ dhātūnaṁ antassa **ākārassa i**-kāra, **ī**-kārā'desā honti yathāsaṅkhyaṁ **ta**paccaye pare, **ti**mhi ca.

The component vowel "**ā**" of the roots "**ṭhā, pā**" etc. changes into "**i, ī**" respectively when "**ta** or **ti**" affixes are applied after them. **[ā of ṭhā>i, pā>ī.]**

(1) Yatra-where, • ṭhito-stood. [wa] ṭhā+ta

(2) • ṭhiti-act of standing. [wa] ṭhā+ti

(3) • pīto-(he was) drunk, being drunk. [wa] pā+ta

(4) • pīti-act of drinking. [wa] pā+ti

Note: When the root is different as "**pī**", the word "**pīti**" has a different meaning as "**joy**"**.** It is also inapplicable by the function of this Sutta. Just apply the affix "**ti**" after the root. No other procedure is required in such case of a word in this root.

५८९, ६२१. हन्तेहि हो हस्स ळो वा अदहनहानं

589, 621. **Ha'ntehi ho hassa ḷo vā a-daha, nahānaṁ.**

[Ha-antehi+ho+hassa+ḷo+vā+a-daha, nahānaṁ. 6 words]

[V] **Ha**kāra'ntehi dhātūhi **ta-**paccayassa **ha**kārā'deso hoti, **ha**kārassa dhātva'ntassa **ḷ**o hoti vā adaha, nahānaṁ.

The affix "**ta**" applied after "**ha-ending roots**", (except "daha and naha"), changes into "**ha**". In addition, the component consonant "**h**" of the root changes into "**ḷ**" in some words. [Two functions, the affix "ta" changes into "**h**" and the last consonant "**h**" of the root becomes "**ḷ**">**ḷh**]

(1) Āruhitthā'ti [Āruhittha+iti] Āruhittha-climbed up, rode. iti • āruḷho-climbed, rode.[Kamma-sādhana ED] [wa] ā√ruha+ta

(2) • Gāḷho-plunged, entered deeply into, unfathomable (This is figurative meaning). [wa] gaha+ta

(3) • bāḷho-grown, increased, intense (adj). [wa] baha+ta

Note: This word is mainly used as an adjective meaning "severe and intense".

(4) • Mūḷho-confused, being ignorant (adj). [wa] muha+ta

Adaha, nahānami'ti kimatthaṁ?
What is the word "adaha, nahānaṁ" for?
To show that the examples below are inapplicable as they have the roots "daha & naha" in them. (This word "adaha, nahānaṁ" means "except the roots daha & naha").

(1) Dayhatī'ti [Dayhati+iti] Dayhati-(is) burnt, iti * daḍḍho-burnt. [wa] daha+ta

(2) Saṁ suṭṭhu-well, nayhatī'ti [nayhati+iti] nayhati-(is) tied, bound. Iti. * sannaddho-well-tied, entangled. [Both Kamma-sādhana EDs] [wa] saṁ√naha+ta

Note: Suṭṭhu is a synonym of the Nipāta word "**Saṁ**"**.** In the EDs, it is natural to give explanation of the less-understandable word by using more understandable word of similar meaning.

Iti kibbidhānakappe tatiyo kaṇḍo.
The Third Section of Kita ends.

Catuttha Kaṇḍa
The Fourth Section

५९०, ५७९. णम्हि रन्जस्स जो भावकरणेसु

590, 579. **Ṇamhi ranjassa jo bhāvakaraṇesu.**
[Ṇamhi+ranjassa+jo+bhāvakaraṇesu. 4 words]

[V] **Ṇa**mhi paccaye pare **ranja-**icce'tassa dhātussa antabhūtassa **nja-**kārassa **j**o-ādeso hoti bhāvakaraṇesu.

The "**nja**" of the root "**ranja**" changes into "**j**" when an affix "**ṇ**" of bhāva and karaṇa senses is applied after the root.

(1) Rañjanaṁ-act of coloring, also act of craving, • rāgo-dyeing (Literal meaning, said of clothes or linen), craving or lust (figurative meaning, said of mind). [Bhāva-sādhana]

(2) ranjanti-dyes. etenā'ti [etena+iti] etena-by that dye, iti • rāgo-that by which things get dyed, dye, any coloring agent, lust. [Karaṇa-sādhana ED] [wa] ranja+ṇa

Bhāvakaraṇesū'ti kimatthaṁ?
What is the word "bhāvakaraṇesu" for?
To show that the example below is inapplicable as the "ṇa-affix" of the word has only a sense of **kattu** in it, not **bhāva** or **karaṇa** senses. [Kattu sense of affix shown by its ED]
Ranjatī'ti [Ranjati+iti] Ranjati-(it) dyes, iti * raṅgo-dye, coloring agent. [Kattu-sādhana] [wa] ranja+ṇa

५९१, ५४४. हनस्स घातो

591, 544. **Hanassa ghāto.** [Hanassa+ghāto. 2 words]

[V] **Hana-**icce'tassa dhātussa sabbassa **ghātā**'deso hoti **ṇa**mhi paccaye pare.

The root "**hana**" changes into "**ghāta**" when a "**ṇa**" affix is applied after the root.

(1) Upahanatī'ti [Upahanati+iti] Upahanati-(It) hurts closely, iti
• upaghāto-hurting closely. [wa] upa√hana+ṇa

(1) gāvo-the cows, hanatī'ti [hanati+iti] hanati-(he) kills. Iti
• goghātako-the one who kills cows. **i.e.** Butcher.
[Both Kattu-sādhana] [wa] Go-saddūpapada-hana+ṇvu

५९२, ५०३. वधो वा सब्बत्थ

592, 503. **Vadho vā sabbattha.**

[Vadho+vā+sabbattha. 3 words]

[V] **Hana**-icce'tassa dhātussa **vadhā**'deso hoti vā sabbattha ṭhānesu.

The root "**hana**" sometimes changes into "**vadha**" when a "**ṇa**" affix is applied at all instances.

(1) Hanatī'ti. hanati-(One) kills or hurts, iti • vadho-the one who hurts or kills. [wa] hana+ṇa

(2) • vadhako-the one who hurts or kills, killer. [ED for Both are the same Kattu-sādhana] [wa] hana+ṇvu

(3) • avadhi-(he) killed. * ahani-(He) killed. vā. [wa] hana+ī
(Ākhyāta verb, these two examples show that the function is applicable not only in Kita-affixed words, but also in a wide range of words including such Ākhyāta verbs shown here.)

५९३, ५६४. आकारन्तान मायो

593, 564. **Ākārantāna'māyo.** [Ākāra-antānaṁ+āyo. 2 words]

[V] Ākārantānaṁ dhātūnaṁ antassa **ākārassa āyā'**deso hoti **ṇa**mhi paccaye pare.

The component vowel "ā" of "ā-ending roots" changes into an "**āya**" when a "**ṇa**-containing" affix is applied after the roots. [The ā-ending roots are such as **dā**-to give, **vā**-to move, etc.]

(1) Dadātī'ti [Dadāti+iti] Dadāti-(one) gives. iti • dāyako-the one who gives, a donor. [wa] dā+ṇvu

(2) dānaṁ-alms, dātuṁ-to give, sīlaṁ-(is) the habit, yassā'ti [yassa+iti] yassa-of whatever person, iti • dānadāyī-the one

whose habit is to give alms. A generous habitual alms-donor.
[wa] dāna-saddūpapada-dā+ṇī

(3) majjaṁ-intoxicants, dātuṁ sīlaṁ yassā'ti • majjadāyī-the one whose habit is to give intoxicants. An intoxicant-sponsor.
[wa] majja-saddūpapada-dā+ṇī

(4) nagaraṁ-to the city, yātuṁ-to go, sīlaṁ yassā'ti • nagarayāyī- the one whose habit is to go to city. A habitual city-goer. [Kattu-sādhana EDs] [wa] nagara-saddūpapada-yā+ṇī

Note: Even though it is said "**ṇa**mhi paccaye pare" in Vutti of Sutta, the function is not limited to only ṇa-affixed words. It is also applicable for any word applied with **ṇ**-containing affix. Please refer to Sutta 532 for similar examples expressive of the habitual nature.

५९४, ५८२. पुरसमुपपरीहि करोतिस्स ख खरा वा तप्पच्चयेसु च

594, 582. **Pura, sa'mupa, parīhi karotissa kha, kharā vā ta-paccayesu ca.**

[Pura, saṁ, upa, parīhi+karotissa+kha, kharā+vā+ta-paccayesu+ca. 6 words]

[V] **Pura, saṁ, upa, pari**-icce'tehi **kar**otissa dhātussa **kha, kharā**'desā honti vā **ta**-paccaye pare, **ṇa**mhi ca.

The root "**kara**" prefixed with "**pura** (front), **saṁ** (well), **upa** (near), **pari** (around) " sometimes changes into "**kha** or **khara**" when either "**ta**" or "**ṇa**" affixes etc. are applied after it.

(1) Pure-at the front, karīyatī'ti [karīyati+iti] karīyati-(is) done or kept. iti • purakkhato-done or kept at the front. **i.e.** preferred, honored. [wa] pura-saddūpapada-kara+ta

(2) sammā-well, karīyatī'ti • saṅkhato-well-done. **i.e.** all conditioned things. [wa] saṁ-√kara+ta

(3) upagantvā-having approached, karīyatī'ti • upakkhato-done in proximity. [1,2,3 are Kamma-sādhana EDs]
[wa] upa-√kara+ta

(4) parisamantato-from all around, karotī'ti [karoti+iti] karoti-(it) does. **i.e.** keeps. iti • parikkhāro-things kept around oneself. **i.e.**

Accessories of daily need, personal effects. [Kattu-sādhana ED]
[wa] pari-√kara+ṇa

Note: In the word "**parisamantato**", **samantato** is a synonymous explanation for "**pari**" as Upasagga word "**pari**" alone is not enough to convey the meaning.

(5) saṁkarīyatī'ti [saṁkarīyati+iti] saṁkarīyati-(is) well-done, iti • saṅkhāro-well-done. **i.e.** conditioned things. [Kamma-sādhana ED] [wa] saṁ-√kara+ṇa

Vā'ti kimatthaṁ?

What is the word "vā" for?

To show that the example is inapplicable as restricted by the word "vā". (There is "ṇ" affix in it. The root is also "kara", but no function of the Sutta. What does it all mean? It means that in Buddhist scriptures, you will find words with "kha or khara" morphemes while you will also find words without it. So, don't be confused whenever you come across such a wide diversity of words for the same root word "kara")

Upagantvā karotī'ti * upakāro-an act done nearby. **i.e.** help or any act of good-will done by parents, teachers, best friends or good-willed strangers etc. [Kattu-sādhana] [wa] upa-√kara+ṇa

५९५, ६३७. तवेतुनादीसु का

595, 637. **Tave, tunā'dīsu kā.** [Tave, tunā'dīsu+kā. 2 words]

[V] **Tave, tuna**-icce'va'mādīsu paccayesu karotissa dhātussa **kā**-ādeso hoti vā.

The root "**kara**" sometimes changes into "**kā**" when "**tave, tuna**" affixes are applied after it.

(1) • Kātave-to do. [wa] kara+tave

(2) • kātuṁ-to do. [wa] kara+tuṁ

* kattuṁ-to do. vā [Inapplicable example] [wa] kara+tuṁ

(3) • kātuna-having done. [wa] kara+tuna

* kattuna-having done. vā. [Inapplicable example] [wa] kara+tuna (Both are the same)

५९६, ५५१. गमखनहनादीनं तुंतब्बादीसु न

596, 551. **Gama, khana, hanā'dīnaṁ tuṁ, tabbā'dīsu na.**

[Gama, khana, hana-ādīnaṁ+tuṁ, tabba-ādīsu+na. 3 words]

[V] **Gama, khana, hana-**icce'va'mādīnaṁ dhātūnaṁ antassa **na**kāro hoti vā **tuṁ, tabbā**'dīsu paccayesu.

The last component consonants "**m, n**" of roots "**gamu, khanu, hana**" etc. sometimes changes into an "**n**" when "**tuṁ, tabba**" affixes are applied after them.

Note: In each pair of examples, the "**n**" is shown in bold underlined, and clearly visible in the first example. The second is inapplicable example where an "**i**" is inserted.

(1) • Ga**n**tuṁ, * gamituṁ-to go. [wa] gamu+tuṁ

(2) • ga**n**tabbaṁ,* gamitabbaṁ-should go. [wa] gamu+tabba

(3) • Kha**n**tuṁ. " Khanituṁ-to dig. [wa] khanu+tuṁ

(4) • kha**n**tabbaṁ * khanitabbaṁ-should dig. [wa] khanu+tabba

(5) • Ha**n**tuṁ, * hanituṁ-to kill, to hurt. [wa] hana+tuṁ

(6) • ha**n**tabbaṁ. " Hanitabbaṁ-should kill or hurt. [wa] hana+tabba

(7) • Ma**n**tuṁ, * manituṁ-to know. [wa] mana+tuṁ

(8) • ma**n**tabbaṁ, * manitabbaṁ-should know. [wa] mana+tabba

Ādiggahaṇaṁ kimatthaṁ? **Tuna**ggahaṇatthaṁ.
What is the word "ādi" for?
For the purpose of including the affix "**tuna**" (for application of the function of this Sutta in **tuna**-affixed verbs too).

• Ga**n**tuna-having gone. [wa] gamu+tuna
• kha**n**tuna-having dug. [wa] khanu+tuna
• ha**n**tuna-having hurt. [wa] hana+tuna
• ma**n**tuna-having known. [wa] mana+tuna

Note: Many verbs with other affixes are also found to be applicable as per the rule of this Sutta in the canonical texts.

५९७, ६४१. सब्बेहि तुनादीनं यो

597, 641. **Sabbehi tunā'dīnaṁ yo.**

[Sabbehi+tuna-ādīnaṁ+yo. 3 words]

[V] Sabbehi dhātūhi **tunā'**dīnaṁ paccayānaṁ **ya**kārā'deso hoti vā.

The affixes "**tuna, tvāna, tvā**" etc, applied after all roots sometimes changes into "**ya**". [See "ya" shown in bold. In each set of examples, the second one is inapplicable]

(1) • Abhivandi**ya** * abhivanditvā-having bowed. [wa] abhi√vanda+tvā

(2) • ohā**ya**, * ohitvā-having abandoned. [wa] ava-√hā+tvā

(3) • upanī**ya**, * upanetvā-having carried along. [wa] upa√nī+tvā

(4) • passi**ya**, * passitvā-having seen. [wa] disa+tvā

(5) • uddi**ss**a, ["tvā" changes into "y" by this Sutta. "**y**" morphs into "**s**" by assimilation procedure of 443 in this example] * uddisitvā-having directed. [wa] u√disa+tvā

(6) • ādā**ya**, * ādiyitvā-having taken. [wa] ā√dā+tvā

५९८, ६४३. चनन्तेहि रच्चं

598, 643. **Ca, na'ntehi raccaṁ.**

[Ca, na-antehi+raccaṁ. 2 words]

[V] **Ca**kāra, **na**kāra'ntehi dhātūhi **tunā**'dīnaṁ paccayānaṁ **raccā**'deso hoti vā.

All the affixes "**tuna, tvāna, tvā**" etc. applied after all "**ca, na**-ending roots" sometimes changes into "**racca**". ["r" is to be elided as per Sutta 539 thus leaving only "acca" shown underlined]

(1) • Viv<u>icca</u>-having renounced, being away from. [wa] vi√vica+tvā

(2) • āh<u>acca</u>-having hurt or having touched. [wa] ā√hana+tvā

(3) • upah<u>acca</u>-having hurt or having touched closely. [wa] upa√hana+tvā

Vā'ti kimatthaṁ? What is the word "vā" for?
To show the example below is inapplicable as restricted by the word "vā".
* Hantvā-having killed. [wa] hana+tvā

५९९, ६४४. दिसा स्वानस्वन्तलोपो च

599, 644. **Disā svāna, svā'ntalopo ca.**

[Disā+svāna, svā+antalopo+ca. 4 words]

[V] **Disa**-icce'tāya dhātuyā **tunā**'dīnaṁ paccayānaṁ **svāna, svā'**desā honti, antalopo ca.

The affixes "**tuna**" etc. applied after the root word "disa" changes into "**svāna, svā**" and the last consonant "**s**" of the root is also elided. [See the applied function shown underlined]

(1) • Disvāna-having seen. [wa] disa+tuna or tvāna [one of these affixes are applicable]
(2) • disvā-having seen, after seeing. [wa] disa+tvā

६००, ६४५. महदभेहि म्म य्ह ज्ज ब्भ द्धा च

600, 645. **Ma, ha, da, bhehi mma, yha, jja, bbha, ddhā ca.**

[Ma, ha, da, bhehi+mma, yha, jja, bbha, ddhā+ca. 3 words]

[V] **Ma, ha, da, bha**-icce'va'mantehi dhātūhi **tunā'**dīnaṁ paccayānaṁ **mma, yha, jja, bbha, ddha**-ādesā honti vā . antalopo ca.

All the affixes "**tuna, tvāna, tvā**" etc. applied after all "**ma, ha, da, bha-ending roots**", sometimes changes into "**mma, yha, jja, bbha, ddha**" respectively. In addition, the last component consonants of the root are also elided. [See the applied functions shown underlined. The second is inapplicable example.]

(1) [**mma**-function] • Āgamma, * āgamitvā-having come. [wa] ā√gamu+tvā
(2) • okkamma. * Okkamitvā-having gone downward, or plunging into (as into a pond or a problem). [wa] ava√kamu+tvā

(3) [**yha**-function] • paggayha, * paggaṇhitvā-having lifted up, (by act or words of encouragement or courtesy when someone did well).
[wa] pa√gaha+tvā (First example WA)
[wa] * pa√gaha+ṇhā+tvā (Second example, dual affixes)

(4) [**jja**-function] • uppajja, * uppajjitvā-having arisen.
[wa] u√pada+tvā

(5) [**bbha**-function] • ārabbha, * ārabhitvā-having exerted, after having made effort. [wa] ā√rabha+tvā

(6) [**ddha**-function] • āraddha, * ārabhitvā-having exerted.
[wa] ā√rabha+tvā

६०१, ३३४. तद्धितसमासकितका नामं वा'तवेतुनादीसु च

601, 334. Taddhita, samāsa, kitakā nāmaṁ'vā' tave, tunā'dīsu ca.

[Taddhita, samāsa, kitakā+nāmaṁ+iva+a-tave, tunā'dīsu+ca. 5 words]

[V] **Taddhita, samāsa, kitaka-**icce'va'mantā saddā **nāmaṁ'va daṭṭhabbā tave, tuna, tvāna, tvā**dipaccaya'nte vajjetvā.

All the words processed by due morphological procedures as prescribed in relevant Suttas and explained in the sections of Taddhita, Samāsa and Kitaka, except those words ending in affixes "**tave, tuna, tvāna and tvā** etc.", are to be recognized as nouns.

Summary: This Sutta enjoins to formally recognize all Samāsa words, Taddhita-affixed words, Kita-affixed words as nouns except those Kita-words suffixed with "tave, tuna, tvāna and tvā" affixes.

The Benefit of Recognition

After this formal recognition as nouns, the noun-vibatti (case-terminations) can be applied after them. Then, all the necessary steps of morphological procedures are carried out and thus these formally recognized nouns become complete words to convey the relevant meanings in a sentence.

Note: All other indeclinable affixes such as **tuṁ, khattuṁ, thaṁ, dhā, to, dā, dāni** and so on are to be excluded. This exclusion means that words affixed with such indeclinable affixes are neither required to formalize as nouns nor any specific morphological procedure be performed on them. As a result, such words with indeclinable affixes will remain unchanged without any specific declension contingent on case-ending of nouns.

• Vāsiṭṭho (Re Sutta 344).

• pattadhammo-the one who have attained Dhamma. [Tatiyā Bahubbhīhi compound] • kumbhakāro. (Re Sutta 524)

icce'va'mādi.

Note: Those ending in affixes "**tave, tuna, tvāna** and **tvā**" are indeclinable. They do not have any gender and numbers. As such, do not require to be recognized as nouns. That is why they are excluded.

Q: Why compound-nouns, words in Taddhita-affixes and Kita-affixes are to be formally recognized as nouns by this Sutta?

A: The purpose is to bring such kind of words to completion in the same way as ordinary nouns are completed by applying all necessary Vibattis (noun-case endings) and performing due morphological procedures on them.

This Sutta is a proof which affirms the fact that all Taddhita, Samāsa and Kita words too are actually nouns in different forms.

६०२, ६. दुम्हि गरु

602, 6. **Dumhi garu.** [Dumhi+garu. 2 words]

[V] **Du**mhi akkhare yo **pubbo** akkharo, so **garu**ko'va daṭṭhabbo.

When two syllables (**i.e.** conjunct-consonants) follow, the front word in a short vowel is to be regarded as "**garu**".

[The preceding short vowel is shown in bold and succeeding conjunct consonants are shown underlined. See the examples carefully to clarify]

(1) • Bhitvā-having broken. [wa] bhida+tvā

(2) • chitvā-having cut. [wa] chidi+tvā

(3) • datvā-having given. [wa] dā+tvā
(4) • hutvā-having been. [wa] hū+tvā

६०३, ७. दीघो च

603, 7. **Dīgho ca.** [Dīgho+ca. 2 words]

[V] **Dīgho** ca saro **garu**ko'va daṭṭhabbo.

Any **dīgha** (long) vowel is also to be regarded as "**garu**". [See dīgha-long vowels shown underlined below.]

- Āhāro-food. [wa] ā-√hara+ṇa (a Kita-affixed noun)
- nadī-river. • vadhū-daughters-in-law. te-those.
- dhammā-Dhamma. (These words are nouns in Dīgha)
- opanayiko-deserved to understand closely as well as logically.

[wa] upanaya+ṇika (This word is a Taddhita noun)

Q: Why it has to be regarded as "**garu**-heavy syllable" and "**lahu**-light syllable"?

A: To make the students understand a very basic matter of metrical measurement of the garu and lahu, which has to be applied in the art of composing Pāli verses. It further provides the student with basic knowledge in the study of Pāli prosody and learning of the necessary stress, rhythm and intonation so that reciting of Pāli proses and texts can be done correctly.

Note: The recitation period of a garu syllable is two morae while it is one mora for reciting a lahu syllable.

६०४, ६८४. अक्खरेहि कार

604, 684. **Akkharehi kāra.**

[Akkharehi+kāra. 2 words]

[V] Akkhara'tthehi akkharā'bhidheyyehi **kāra**paccayo hoti payoge sati.

To signify an alphabet, the suffix "**kāra**" is to be applied after that alphabet denoting and referring to it.

A-eva-"a" only. • akāro-the a-alphabet, syllable "a" [wa] a+kāra
ā-eva-"ā" only. • ākāro-the ā-alphabet, syllable "ā" [wa] ā+kāra
ya-eva-"ya" only. • yakāro-the ya-alphabet, syllable "ya" [wa] ya+kāra

६०५, ५४७. यथागम मिकारो

605, 547. **Yathāgama'mikāro.** [Yathā-āgamaṁ+ikāro. 2 words]

[V] Yathā'gamaṁ sabbadhātūhi sabbapaccayesu **i**-kārā'gamo hoti.

An "**i**" has to be added after the roots in all affixes in a way that conforms to scriptural usage of Buddhist texts. [See the added "**i**" in each examples shown in bold]

- Kār**i**yaṁ-(it) should be done. [wa] kara+ririya
- bhav**i**tabbaṁ-(it) should be. [wa] bhū+tabba
- jan**i**tabbaṁ-(it) should happen. [wa] jana+tabba

Note: In major Pāli texts, another word form is found as "jān**i**tabbaṁ" which means "it should be known. In this case, wa is with dual affixes. [wa] ñā+"nā+tabba"

- vid**i**tabbaṁ-(it) should be known. [wa] vida+tabba
- kar**i**tvā-having done. [wa] kara+tvā
- icch**i**taṁ-(is) wanted. [wa] isu+ta

६०६, ६४२. दधन्ततो यो क्वचि

606, 642. **Da, dha'ntato yo kvaci.**

[Da, dha-antato+yo+kvaci. 3 words]

[V] **Da**kāra, **dha**kārantāya dhātuyā yathāgamaṁ **ya**kārā'gamo hoti kvaci **tunā'**dīsu paccayesu.

A "**ya**" is sometimes to be added after "**da, dha**-ending roots" when "**tuna, tvāna, tvā**" **affixes** are applied. ("y" should be inserted between the root and affix. Later that "**y**", along with the last consonant of the root, changes into "**j**" and is reduplicated. See the augmented "**jj**" in the examples shown in bold.)

(1) Buddho-the Buddha, loke-in the world, • uppa**jj**itvā-having arisen. [wa] u√pada+tvā

(2) Dhammaṁ-the Dhamma, • bujjhitvā-having known.
[wa] budha+tvā

Dadhantato'ti kimatthaṁ?
What is the word "dadhantato" for?
To show that the example below is inapplicable as it is the root "labha" which ends in a "bha", not in "da, dha".
* Labhitvā-having obtained. [wa] labha+tvā

Kvacī'ti kimatthaṁ?
What is the word "kvaci" for?
To show that the example below is inapplicable as restricted by the word "kvaci".
* Uppādetvā-having caused to arise, causing it to happen.
[wa] u√pada+ṇe+tvā (Dual affixes, please note this.)

Note: This gerund verb (also referred to as absolutive) is a special kind of gerund called **causative gerund verb.** As a result of having a causative affix, there is a Vuddhi vowel "**ā**" in the verb after the last "**p**" of "**upa**". Also see one more "**p**" is reduplicated.

Iti kibbidhānakappe catuttho kaṇḍo.
The Fourth Section of Kita ends.

Pañcama Kaṇḍa
The Fifth Section

६०७, ५७८. निग्गहित संयोगादि नो
607, 578. **Niggahita saṁyogā'di no.**
[Niggahita+saṁyoga-ādi+no. 3 words]

[V] Saṁyogā'dibhūto **na**kāro **niggahita**'māpajjate.

The "**n**" which used to be the initial syllable of two conjunct-consonants of some roots, changes into a "**niggahita-ṁ**".

[In the root "**Ranja**-to dye", "**nj**" is a conjunct, double consonants joined in the root. The "n" is said to be in the initial point. That "**n**" is to be changed into "a niggahita-**ṁ**" by this Sutta. That "**ṁ**" further changes into "**ṅ**" by Sutta 31. See the examples below to clarify this evolving process of word and the related function of Sutta]

(1) • Raṅgo-act of coloring. [wa] ranja+ṇa

(2) • bhaṅgo-act of breaking, tearing apart. [wa] bhanja+ṇa

(3) • saṅgo-act of clinging. [wa] sanja+ṇa

६०८, ६२३. सब्बत्थ गे गी
608, 623. **Sabbattha ge gī.** [Sabbattha+ge+gī. 3 words]

[V] **Ge**-icce'tassa dhātussa **gī**-ādeso hoti sabbattha ṭhāne.

The root word "**ge-**to sing" changes into "**gī**" wherever appropriate in all instances.

• Gītaṁ-sung, the music. [wa] ge+ta [This is a Kita Verbal-noun]

* gāyati-(He) sings. **i.e.** He sings the music. [wa] ge+a+ti
[This is an Ākhyāta Verb]

६०९, ४८४. सदस्स सीदत्तं

609, 484. **Sadassa sīdattaṁ.** [Sadassa+sīdattaṁ. 2 words]

[V] **Sada**-icce'tassa dhātussa **sīdā**'deso hoti sabbattha ṭhāne.

The root "**sada**" changes into "**sīda**" at all instances.

- Nisinno-sat. [wa] Ni√sada+ta [This is a Kita Verb]
- nisīdati-(He) sits. [wa] ni√sada+a+ti [This is an Ākhyāta Verb]

६१०, ६२७. यजस्स सरस्सि ट्ठे

610, 627. **Yajassa sarassi'ṭṭhe.**

[Yajassa+sarassa+i+ṭṭhe. 4 words]

[V] **Yaja**-icce'tassa dhātussa sarassa **i**-kārā'deso hoti **ṭṭh**e pare.

The component vowel "**a**" of "**ya**" in the root "**yaja**" changes into "**i**" when the "**ṭṭha**", a derivative morpheme of former affix "**ta**" is behind it. [For "**ṭṭha**" function, refer to Sutta 573]

- Yiṭṭho-(is) sacrificed. *sl.* [wa] yaja+ta
- yiṭṭhā-(are) sacrificed. ***pl.*** [wa] yaja+ta

ṭṭhe'ti kimatthaṁ?
What is the word "ṭṭhe" for?
To show that the example shown below is inapplicable as it lacks a **ta**-morpheme "**ṭṭha**" in it.
* Yajanaṁ-act of sacrifice. [wa] yaja+yu

६११, ६०८. हचतुत्थानमन्तानं दो धे

611, 608. **Ha-catutthāna'mantānaṁ do dhe.**

[Ha-catutthānaṁ+antānaṁ+do+dhe. 4 words]

[V] **Ha**-catutthānaṁ dhātva'ntānaṁ **d**o-ādeso hoti **dhe** pare.

The last component consonants "**ha, dha, bha**" of the roots "**naha, kudha, yudha, sidha, labha, rabha**" etc. change into "**da**" when a morpheme "**dha**" of former affix "ta" is being present behind. [Refer to Sutta 576 for "dha" morpheme]

(1) • Sannaddho-well-tied. [**ha** changes into **da**]
[wa] Saṁ√naha+ta

(2) • kuddho-(was) angry. [wa] kudha+ta

(3) • yuddho-fought. [wa] yudha+ta

(4) • siddho-accomplished. [wa] sidha+ta
[In example 2, 3, 4, **dha** changes into **da**]

(5) • laddho-obtained. [wa] labha+ta

(6) [a] • āraddho-exerted. [wa] ā√rabha+ta. [In 5,6, **bha** changes into **da**]

[b] pleased [wa] ā√radha+ta (Different root for this meaning).

Note: Catuttha (fourth) means those which are fourth in the vagga group. Especially, **dha** from ta-group, **bha** from **pa**-group. They are to be changed into "**da**" by function of this Sutta.

६१२, ६१५. डो ढकारे

612, 615. Ḍo ḍhakāre. [Ḍo+ḍhakāre. 2 words]

[V] **Ha**-catutthānaṁ dhātva'ntānaṁ **ḍo**-ādeso hoti **ḍha**kāre pare.

The last component consonants "**ha, ḍha**" of the root "daha, waḍha" change into "**ḍa**" when a morpheme "**ḍha**" of the former affix "**ta**" is being present behind. [Refer to Sutta 576 regarding the function of "**ḍha**"]

(1) Dayhatī'ti [Dayhati+iti] Dayhati-(is) burnt. iti • daḍḍho-burnt. [Kamma-sādhana] [wa] daha+ta

(2) Vaḍḍhatī'ti [Vaḍḍhati+iti] Vaḍḍhati-(it) grows. iti • vuḍḍho-grown, increased. [Kattu-sādhana] [wa] vaḍha+ta

ḍhakāre'ti kimatthaṁ?

What is the word "ḍhakāre" for?

To show that the example below is inapplicable as it does not have a morpheme "ḍha" in it.

* Dāho-act of burning, the heat. [wa] daha+ṇa

६१३, ५८३. गहस्स घर णे वा
613, 583. **Gahassa ghara ṇe vā.**

[Gahassa+ghara+ṇe+vā. 4 words]

[V] **Gaha**-iccetassa dhātussa sabbassa **gharā**'deso hoti vā **ṇa-**paccaye pare.

The entire root "**gaha**" sometimes changes into "**ghara**" when the affix "**ṇa**" follows after it.

- Gharaṁ-house. *ns.* [wa] gaha+ṇa+si
- gharāni also ghrāṇi-houses. *np.* [wa] gaha+ṇa+yo

Vā'ti kimatthaṁ? What is the word "vā" for?
To show that the example shown below is inapplicable as restricted by the word "vā".
* Gāho-act of grabbing such as one's view, notion etc.[wa] gaha+ṇa

६१४, ५८१. दहस्स दो ळं
614, 581. **Dahassa do ḷaṁ.**

[Dahassa+do+ḷaṁ. 3 words]

[V] **Daha**-iccetassa dhātussa **da**kāro **ḷa**tta'māpajjate vā **ṇa-**paccaye pare.

The component letters "**da**" of the root word "**daha**" sometimes changes into "**ḷa**" when affix "**ṇa**" is applied after it. [da=**ḷa**>**ḷa**ha> after Vuddhi procedure of "a", it becomes> **ḷāha=pari ḷāha**]

Paridahanaṁ-act of burning, • pariḷāho-burning (as with heat, desire, anger, sorrow etc.).[Bhāva-sādhana ED] [wa] pari√daha+ṇa

Vā'ti kimatthaṁ?
What is the word "vā" for?
To show that the example shown is inapplicable as restricted by the word "vā"
* Paridāho-burning. [wa] pari√daha+ṇa

६१५, ५८६. धात्वन्तस्स लोपो क्विम्हि

615, 586. **Dhātva'ntassa lopo kvimhi.**

[Dhātu-antassa+lopo+kvimhi. 3 words]

[V] Dhātva'ntassa byañjanassa lopo hoti kvimhi paccaye pare.

The last component consonant of the root is to be elided after the affix "**kvi**" is applied after the root.

(1) Bhujena gacchatī'ti • bhujago. (Re: Sutta 530)

(2) Urena-by chest, gacchatī'ti • urago-the creature which goes crawling by means of chest. a reptile, snake [Both Kattu-sādhana] [wa] ura-saddūpapada-gamu+kvi

(3) • turago-the creature which goes by means of dashing speed. a horse. [wa] tura-saddūpapada-gamu+kvi

(4) • saṅkho. (Re: Sutta 530)

६१६, ५८७. विदन्ते ऊ

616, 587. **Vida'nte ū.** [Vida-ante+ū. 2 words]

[V] **Vida**-iccetassa dhātussa ante **ū**kārā'gamo hoti **kvi**mhi paccaye pare.

There should come an "**ū**" after the root word "**vida**" when a "**kvi**" affix is applied after it. [This affix is later deleted]

Lokaṁ-the world, vidati jānātī'ti [jānāti+iti] jānāti-knows, iti • lokavidū-the one who knows the world. **i.e.** Buddha. [Kattu-sādhana ED] [wa] Loka-saddūpapada-vida+kvi

Note: Both verbs "**vidati**" and "**jānāti**" in ED are synonyms. The first verb "vidati" is explained by means of another verb of the same meaning. The purpose is to affirm the meaning of the root "**vida-to know**" as it has other different meanings such as "**to feel, to get**". In this instance, only this meaning "to know" is applicable.

६१७, ६३३. न म क रानमन्तानं नियुत्ततम्हि

617, 633. **Na, ma, ka, rāna'ma'ntānaṁ ni'yuttatamhi.**

[Na, ma, ka,rānaṁ+antānaṁ+na+iyutta-tamhi. 4 words]

[V] **Na**kāra, **ma**kāra, **ka**kāra, **ra**kārānaṁ dhātva'ntānaṁ lopo na hoti **i**-kārayutte ta-paccaye pare.

The last component consonants "**n, m, k, r**" (of the roots "**hana, gamu, ramu, saka, kara**" etc.) are not to be elided in "**ta-**affixed" words when "**an inserted i**" is already in place. [Refer to Sutta 605 for "**i**"]

Summary: This Sutta enjoins not to elide the last consonants of the root in the "**ta-affixed words**" when an inserted "**i**" have been already applied in the word.

What does this injunction mean?

It means that to form a very simple word-structure and word-form of "**ta**-affixed" verbs and verbal nouns, is only to apply the affix "**ta**" and insert an "**i**" between the root and affix. **There is no need either to elide the last consonant of the root nor to do any other specific morphological change if these two functions have been already applied on such words.**

See the examples carefully to clarify this. Throughout Pāli texts, such words are found aplenty. It is a very simple word-form of **ta**-affixed words. It should be noted that even though it is generally said in Sutta as "**tamhi**-ta-affixed", **all ta-containing affixes are also applicable** in view of a wider usage of such examples found in the Pāli texts.

Q: What kind of **ta**-containing affixes are applicable then?

A: They are, **tabba, tuṁ, tvā and tvāna,** etc.

["**tuna, tave, tāye, tavantu, tāvi** and **teyya**" affixes are inapplicable. **Please see** the morphological structure of each word shown in **the first square bracket** before WA to clarify the rule of this Sutta.

(1) • Hanituṁ-to kill. [hana+i+tuṁ] [wa] hana+tuṁ

(2) • gamito-gone. [gamu+i+ta] [wa] gamu+ta

(3) • ramito-rejoiced. [ramu+i+ta] [wa] ramu+ta

(4) • sakito-honored. [saka+i+ta] [wa] saka+ta
(5) • sarito-remembered. [sara+i+ta] [wa] sara+ta
(6) • karitvā-having done. [kara+i+tvā] [wa] kara+tvā

ni'yuttatamhī'ti kimatthaṁ?
What is the word "niyuttatamhi" for?
To show that in the examples shown below, there is no "**i**" in them. So, the last component of the root is elided.
By word "vā", it means that restriction placed by this Sutta, is not always applied except in some instances of words where an "**i**" is already present with a "**ta-affix**" applied behind the root.
* Gato-gone. [wa] gamu+ta * sato-remembered. [wa] sara+ta

६१८, ५७१. नकगत्तं चजा ण्वुम्हि

618, 571. **Na ka, gattaṁ ca, jā ṇvumhi.**

[Na+ka, gattaṁ+ca, jā+ṇvumhi. 4 words]

[V] **C**akāra, **ja**kārā **ka**kāra, **ga**kārattaṁ nā'pajjante **ṇvu**mhi paccaye pare.

The function of changing the last component consonants "**c, j**" of the roots into "**ka, ga**" is inapplicable when a "**ṇvu**" affix follows.
Summary: This Sutta debars the function of Sutta 623 in words with a "ṇvu" affix having already been applied.
Why?
Because it is a very consistent pattern of the language for any ṇvu-affixed word to change into an "**aka**" as per Sutta 622. There is no other morphological procedure affecting on "ṇvu-affixed words" except the "**aka**" function and a Vuddhi process where necessary.

(1) Pacatī'ti [pacati+iti] pacati-(One) cooks. iti • pācako-the one who cooks, chef. [wa] paca+ṇvu
(2) Yajatī'ti [Yajati+iti] Yajati-(One) sacrifices. iti • yājako-the one who performs sacrifices.[All are Kattu-sādhana EDs] [wa] yaja+ṇvu

६१९, ५७३. करस्स च तत्तं तुस्मिं

619, 573. **Karassa ca tattaṁ tusmiṁ.**

[Karassa+ca+tattaṁ+tusmiṁ. 4 words]

[V] **Kara**-icce'tassa dhātussa antassa **ra**kārassa **ta**kārattaṁ hoti **tu**-paccaye pare.

The component consonant "**r**" of the root "**kara**" changes into "**t**" when a "**tu**" affix is applied after it.

(1) Karotī'ti [karoti+iti] karoti-(One) does. iti • kattā-the one who does, doer. *ns* [wa] kara+tu+si

(2) Karontī'ti [karonti+iti] karonti-(ones) do. iti • kattāro-those who do, doers. *np.* [Both are Kattu-sādhana] [wa] kara+tu+yo

६२०, ५४९. तुंतुनतब्बेसु वा

620, 549. **Tuṁ, tuna, tabbesu vā.**

[Tuṁ, tuna, tabbesu+vā. 2 words]

[V] **Kara**-icce'tassa dhātussa antassa **ra**kārassa **ta**kārattaṁ hoti vā **tuṁ, tuna, tabba**-icce'tesu paccayesu.

The component consonant "**r**" of the root "**kara**" sometimes changes into "**t**" when "**tuṁ, tuna, tabba**" affixes are applied. [That "**t**" shown in bold, is to be added to those affixes. See the examples carefully. The second example in each pair is inapplicable]

(1) • Ka**t**tuṁ, * kātuṁ-to do. [wa] kara+tuṁ

(2) • ka**t**tuna, * Kātuna-having done. [wa] kara+tuna

(3) • ka**t**tabbaṁ, * kātabbaṁ-(It) should be done. [wa] kara+tabba

६२१, ५५३. कारितं विय णानुबन्धो

621, 553. **Kāritaṁ viya ṇā'nubandho.**

[Kāritaṁ+viya+ṇa-anubandho. 3 words]

[V] **Ṇ**akārā'nubandho paccayo kāritaṁ viya daṭṭhabbo vā.

Any "**ṇ**-conjoined affix" is sometimes to be formally named as "**kārita-affix**".

Note: "**ṇa, ṇya, ṇvu, ṇī, ṇuka**" affixes are called **ṇ-conjoined** affixes.

[**ṇa**-affixed words]

- Dāho-burning. [wa] daha+ṇa
- deho-body. [wa] diha+ṇa
- vāho-mode of conveyance (such as horses, elephants, mules and chariots etc.), vehicle. [wa] vaha+ṇa
- bāho-arm. [wa] baha+ṇa
- cāgo-charitable giving, sharing. [wa] caja+ṇa
- vāro-turn. [wa] vara+ṇa
- cāro-strolling, ambling. [wa] cara+ṇa
- parikkhāro-accessories. [wa] pari√kara+ṇa

[**ṇvu**-affixed words]

- dāyako-donor. [wa] dā+ṇvu
- nāyako-leader. [wa] nī+ṇvu
- lāvako-cutter. [wa] lū+ṇvu
- bhāvako-the ariser, the developer. [wa] bhū+ṇvu

Note: There is always an "**aka**" function in every word affixed with "ṇvu" affix in addition to having a vuddhi-vowel.

[**ṇī**-affixed words]

- kārī-the one who used to do. [wa] kara+ṇī
- ghātī-the one who used to kill. [wa] hana+ṇī
- dāyī-the one who used to give. [wa] dā+ṇī

Vā'ti kimatthaṁ?

What is the word "vā" for?

To show that the example below is an exception to the rule as restricted by "vā" of this Sutta. It is inapplicable to formally regard the applied "ṇ" affix in it as a Kārita, because there is no need to perform a "vuddhi function" for that word. [Please note that the purpose of function of this Sutta is to initiate a "vuddhi" procedure necessary for completion of some words]

* Upakkharo-act done in proximity, intimate act, help.
[wa] upa√kara+ṇa

६२२, ५७०. अनका युण्वूनं

622, 570. **Ana'kā yu, ṇvū, naṁ.**

[Ana, akā+yu, ṇvū, naṁ. 2 words]

[V] **Yu, ṇvu**-icce'tesaṁ paccayānaṁ **ana, aka**-icce'te ādesā honti.

The affix "**yu**" changes into "**ana**" and the affix "**ṇvu**" changes into "**aka**". [See the functions shown in bold, underlined]

- Nand**<u>ana</u>**ṁ-joy. [wa] nanda+yu
- kār**<u>ak</u>**o-doer. [wa] kara+ṇvu

Note: This Sutta shows a universal pattern of "**yu, ṇvu-affixed**" words by stating that yu-affixed words has to end in an "**ana**" while "ṇvu-affixed" words usually end in an "**aka**" function.

६२३, ५५४. कगा चजानं

623, 554. **Ka, gā ca, jānaṁ.**

[Ka, gā+ca, jānaṁ. 2 words]

[V] **Ca, ja**-icce'tesaṁ dhātva'ntānaṁ **ka**kāra, **ga**kārā'desā honti **ṇā**'nubandhe paccaye pare.

The last component consonant "**c**" of the root "**paca**" etc. changes into "**k**" and also last component consonant "**j**" of the root "**yaja**" etc. changes into "**g**" when an affix "**ṇa**" is applied after the roots. ["**c**">"**k**", "**j**">"**g**"]

- Pāko-cooking. [wa] paca+ṇa (Here, "c" changes into "k")
- yogo-act of tying up, engaging, effort.
  [wa] yuja+ṇa (Here, "j" changes into "g")

Iti kibbidhānakappe pañcamo kaṇḍo.
The Fifth Section of Kita ends.

Kitakappo niṭṭhito.
Kita Chapter ends.

8. Uṇādi Kappa
Uṇādi Chapter

Chaṭṭha Kaṇḍa
The Sixth Section of Kita

६२४, ५६३. कत्तरि कित

624, 563. **Kattari kitā.** [Kattari+kitā. 2 words]

[V] **Kattu**-icce'tasmiṁ atthe **kita**-paccayā honti.

All the "kita" affixes have a sense of Kattu (doer, agent).

- Kāru-maker, doer, an artisan such as carpenter etc. [wa] kara+ṇu
- kāruko-same meaning as the first word. [wa] kara+ṇuka [Refer to Sutta 536 for similar affix]
- kārako-doer. [wa] kara+ṇvu
- pācako-the cook. [wa] paca+ṇvu [Refer to Sutta 527]
- kattā-doer. [wa] kara+tu
- janitā-that which causes something, the cause, the father. [wa] jana+tu
- pacitā-the cook. [wa] paca+tu
- netā-the carrier. [wa] nī+tu [Refer to Sutta 527 for similar affix]

Note: WA of most examples are shown before.

६२५, ६०५. भावकम्मेसु किच्चक्तक्खत्था

625, 605. **Bhāvakammesu kicca, kta, kha'tthā.**
[Bhāvakammesu+kicca, kta, kha-atthā. 2 words]

[V] Bhāvakamma-icce'tesva'tthesu **kicca, kta, khattha**-icce'te paccayā honti.

All the **kicca** affixes and **kta, kh**-conjoined **a** suffixes have senses of **bhāva and kamma.**

Examples of Kicca affix "tabba & anīya"

(1) Upasampādetabbaṁ-should be ordained.
[wa] upa√saṁ√pada+tabba

(2) • upasampādanīyaṁ-should ordain. bhavatā-by your Honorable. **i.e.** Your honorable should get be ordained (as a novice or as a monk) [wa] upa√saṁ√pada+anīya

(3) • sayitabbaṁ-should sleep. bhavatā. **i.e.** Your honorable should sleep [wa] si+tabba

(4) • kattabbaṁ-should do. bhavatā. [wa] kara+tabba

(5) • bhottabbo-should eat. odano-the rice, bhavatā, [wa] bhuja+tabba

(6) • asitabbaṁ-should eat. bhojanaṁ-meal, bhavatā. [wa] asa+tabba

Examples of the affix "ta"

(7) • asitaṁ-eaten. bhavatā, [wa] asa+ta

(8) • sayitaṁ-slept. bhavatā, [wa] si+ta

(9) • pacitaṁ-cooked. bhavatā, [wa] paca+ta

(10) • asitaṁ-ate. asanaṁ-food. bhavatā, [wa] asa+ta

(11) • sayitaṁ-slept. sayanaṁ-bed. bhavatā, [wa] si+ta

(12) • pacito-cooked. odano-rice. bhavatā, [wa] paca+ta

Examples of kh-conjoined "a" affix.

(13) • kiñcissayo-little sleep, sleeping a little. [wa] kiñci-saddūpapada-si+a

(14) • īsassayo (same meaning) [wa] īsaṁ-saddūpapada-si+a

(15) • dussayo-bad sleep, sleeping badly. [wa] du-√si+a

(16) • sussayo-good sleep, sleeping well. bhavatā. [wa] su-√si+a

Note: The affix for examples 1,2.3.4,5,6, are shown in Sutta 540. The affix for 7-12 are shown in 555, 556, 557. The affix for 13-16, are shown in Sutta 560.

६२६, ६३४. कम्मनि दुतियायं क्तो

626, 634. **Kammani dutiyāyaṁ kto.**

[Kammani+dutiyāyaṁ+kto. 3 words]

[V] Kamma-icce'tasmiṁ atthe dutiyāyaṁ vibhattiyaṁ kattari **kta**-paccayo hoti.

The affix "**kta**" is applied in the context of a kamma (object).

Note: This affix (क्त) is indeed a Sanskritized affix. It is similar to "ta" affix in the Kita section. So, it can be regarded as such.
However, if it is taken as kta-affix, "k" has to be elided by 517. This affix is referred to sometimes as a k-conjoined "ta" affix by Pāli scholars. Also see Sutta 643 regarding this affix.

(1) Dānaṁ-alms, • dinno-gave. [Re Sutta 582] devadatto-Devadatta, **i.e.** Devadatta gave alms. [wa] dā+ta (Shown before)
(2) sīlaṁ-moral precept, • rakkhito-observed. devadatto. **i.e.** Devadatta observed precept. [wa] rakkha+ta
(3) bhattaṁ-food, • bhutto-ate. devadatto. **i.e.** Devadatta ate food. [wa] bhuja+ta (Shown before in Sutta 578)
(4) garuṁ-to the teacher, • upāsito-cared or approached. devadatto. **i.e.** Devadatta approached or cared the teacher. [wa] upa√ āsa+ta

६२७, ६५२. ख्यादीहि मन म च तो वा

627, 652. **Khyā'dīhi mān, ma ca to vā.**

[Khī-ādīhi+mān+ma+ca+to+vā. 6 words]

[V] **Khi, bhī, su, ru, hu, vā, dhū, hi, lū, pī, ada,** ice'va'mādīhi dhātūhi **man-**paccayo hoti, **M**assa ca **t**o hoti vā.

The affix "**man**" is applied after such roots as "**khi, bhī, su, ru, hu, vā, dhū, hi, lū, pī, ada** etc." and the "**m**" of affix changes into a "**t**" in the word "**attā**-self".

(1) Khīyanti-(are) exhausted. upaddavā-dangers, etthāt'i[ettha+iti] ettha-here, iti-therefore, • khemo-safe place. **i.e.** Nibbāna where dangers are exhausted (disappeared). [Adhikaraṇa-sādhana ED] [wa] khī+man
(2) [a] bhāyitabbo'ti [bhāyitabbo+iti] bhāyitabbo-should fear. iti • bhemo-something to fear, fearful. [Kamma-sādhana ED] [b] bhāyanti-(are) afraid of, etasmā'ti [etasmā+iti] etasmā-from this (shocking) object, iti vā • bhemo-shocking thing from which people fear. [Apādāna-sādhana ED] [wa] bhī+man

Note: There are two EDs for this word shown in two Sādhanas.

(3) raṁsiyo-the rays, abhissavetī'ti [abhissaveti+iti] abhissaveti-(causes) to radiate. iti • somo-the moon which radiates the rays. [Hetu-kattu-sādhana ED] [wa] su+man

(4) ravati gacchatī'ti [gacchati+iti] gacchati-(it) comes up. iti • romo-hair. [Kattu-sādhana] [wa] ru+man

(5) huvati juhvati-sacrifices. etenā'ti [etena+iti] etena-by this offering. iti • homo-offerings by means of which a sacrifice is performed. [Karaṇa-sādhana] [wa] hu+man

(6) [a]paṭilomavasena-by being opposite of the right side. Vāti gacchatī'ti, gacchati-goes, (happens). iti • vāmo-left side which goes or happens as the opposite of right.

[b]Lāmakavasena-by being lower mode. vāti gacchati pavattatī'ti [pavattati+iti]. pavattati-happens. vā. iti • vāmo-the left side (which happens as lower mode as per ancient belief). [Kattu-sādhana] [wa] vā+man [2 EDs for this word based on two different meaning of the root word "vā"]

(7) dhunāti kampatī'ti. kampati-(it) shakes. • dhūmo-smoke which shakes, (is unstable). [Kattu-sādhana] [wa] dhū+man

(8) seṭṭhabhāvena-by being the best, hinoti pavattati-happens. cittaṁ-mind, thought, etasmin'ti [etasmiṁ+iti] etasmiṁ-in this object (**i.e.** gold), iti • hemo-gold, where (human) mind happens to view it as the best (of all possessions). [Adhikaraṇa-sādhana] [wa] hi+man

(9) [a] Lunitabbo'ti [Lunitabbo+iti] Lunitabbo-should shave, cut. iti • Lomo-the hair which should be shaved or cut. [Kamma-sādhana]

[b] maṁsacammāni-flesh and skins, lunāti chindatī'ti [chindati+iti] chindati-cuts. iti vā • Lomo-the hair which cuts through flesh and skins when it grows. [Kattu-sādhana] [wa] lū+man

(10) [a] piyanaṁ-act of loving, • pemo-love, [Bhāva-sādhana]

[b] piyāyitabbo'ti [piyāyitabbo+iti] piyāyitabbo-should love, iti vā • pemo-love. [Kamma-sādhana.2 EDs] [wa] pī+man

(11) [a] sukhadukkhaṁ-pleasure and pain, adati bhakkhatī'ti bhakkhati-consumes. iti • attā-the body which consumes

both pleasure and pain (even though the mind doesn't like pain). [Kattu-sādhana] [wa] ada+man

[b] jātijarāmaraṇā'dīhi-by birth, old-age and death etc. adīyate-is taken. bhakkhīyate'ti [bhakkhīyate+iti] bhakkhīyate-(is) devoured. iti vā • attā, * ātumā-the body devoured by birth, old-age and death etc. [Kamma-sādhana] [wa] ada+man

६२८, ६५३. समादीहि थमा

628, 653. **Samā'dīhi tha, mā.** [Samu-ādīhi+tha, mā. 2 words]

[V] **Samu, damu, dara, raha, du, hi, si, bhī, dā, yā, sā, ṭhā, bhasa-**icce'va'mādīhi dhātūhi **tha, ma,** paccayā honti.

The affixes "**tha, ma**" are applied after roots "**samu, damu, dara, raha, du, hi, si, bhī, dā, yā, sā, ṭhā, bhasa**" etc.

(1) Sametī'ti [sameti+iti] sameti-(it) calms the mind. iti • samatho-the samatha which calms the mind. [Kattu-sādhana] [wa] samu+tha

(2) [a] damatī'ti [damati+iti] damati-(it) tames, trains. iti • damatho- taming, training. [Kattu-sādhana] [wa] damu+tha

[b] damanaṁ-act of taming, training. vā • damatho-taming, training. [Bhāva-sādhana]

[c] damitabbo'ti damitabbo-should train. vā • damatho-something or someone to be domesticated, or trained. [Kamma-sādhana.3 EDs]

(3) daratī'ti [darati+iti] darati (it) exhausts. iti • daratho-anxiety, stress. [Kattu-sādhana] [wa] dara+tha

(4) [a] jiṇṇabhāvaṁ-to state of degeneration, rahissati gaṇhissatī'ti [gaṇhissati+iti] gaṇhissati-(it) will take up. iti • ratho-the chariot which will take up degeneration process (in the future). [Kattu-sādhana] [wa] raha+tha

[b] dabbasambhāre-component parts (such as wheels, axles, etc.), rahati gaṇhātī'ti [gaṇhātīi+iti]. gaṇhāti-takes up. iti vā • ratho- chariot (which takes up various components to build it). [Kattu-sādhana]

(5) [a] davati gacchatī'ti [gacchati+iti] gacchati-(it) comes up.
• dumo-tree which shoots up when growing. [Kattu-sādhana]
[wa] du+ma

[b] davati-grows. vuddhi viruḷhi-to the state of thriving and flourishing. gacchati-goes. pavattatī'ti [pavattati+iti] pavattati- happens. uddhaṁ-upward. iti vā dumo-tree which grows, happens upward when thriving. [Kattu-sādhana]

(6) pathavī, pabbatādīsu-on earth and mountain etc. gacchati patatī'ti [patati+iti] patati-falls. iti • himo-the snow, which falls on the earth and mountains and so on. [Kattu-sādhana]
[wa] hi+ma

(7) [a] kammavācāya-by formal kammavācā. bandhati-binds, demarcated. etthā'ti [ettha+iti] ettha-here. iti • sīmā-an ordination hall (where boundaries) are demarcated by means of formal recitation of kammavācā and declaration of boundaries. [Adhikaraṇa-sādhana] [wa] si+ma

[b] Bandhitabbā'ti.Bandhitabbā-should be demarcated. iti vā • sīmā- an ordination hall (which should be) demarcated by means of formal recitation of kammavācā . [Kamma-sādhana]

(8) Bhāyanti etasmā'ti • bhīmo-the object from which people fear. (Refer to 627) [Apādāna-sādhana] [wa] bhī+ma

(9) [a] satte-beings. avakhaṇḍenti nivārenti-prevents. etenā'ti [etena+iti] etena-by this. iti • dāmo-preventive barrier of flower hedge. [Karaṇa-sādhana] [wa] dā+ma

[b] mūsikādīhi-by animals such as rat and so on. Khādīyati avakhaṇḍīyatī'ti [avakhaṇḍīyati+iti] avakhaṇḍīyati-(is) bitten. iti vā • dāmo-floral works, [Kamma-sādhana]

(10) yāti gacchatī'ti gacchati-(it) passes. iti • yāmo-the phases of night which passes. [Kattu-sādhana] [wa] yā+ma

(11) paresaṁ-of others. cittaṁ-mind. gaṇhituṁ-to take. samatthetī'ti [samattheti+iti] samattheti-(is) able. iti • sāmo-golden complexion of skin, which can attract other's mind. [Kattu-sādhana] [wa] sā+ma

(12) tiṭṭhanti-stand. etenā'ti etena-by this. • thāmo-energy by which people stand, [Karaṇa-sādhana] [wa] thā+ma

(13) bhasati bhasmīkarīyatī'ti [bhasmīkarīyati+iti]

bhasmīkarīyati- makes it so as to become ash, pulverize into ash. iti • bhasmā-ash. [Kattu-sādhana, Re: original verb "**bhasati**"] [wa] bhasa+ma

६२९, ५६९. गहस्सु'पधस्से वा

629, 569. **Gahassu'padhasse' vā.**

[Gahassa+upadhassa+e+vā. 4 words]

[V] **Gaha**-icce'tassa dhātussa **upadha**ssa **a**kārassa **e**ttaṁ hoti vā.

The penultimate vowel "**a**" of initial consonant "**ga**" of the root "**gaha**" sometimes changes into "**e**". [Look at example word to clarify the function of Sutta. It is quite simple and clear.]

Dabbasambhāraṁ-building material. gaṇhātī'ti [gaṇhāti+iti] gaṇhāti-takes up. iti • gehaṁ, * gahaṁ-house (which takes up various building materials to build). [Kattu-sādhana] [wa] gaha+a

Note: Upadhā=penultimate syllable is called "upadhā". [**upa**-near by, closely+**dhā**-kept, located. A near-by vowel is called "upadhā"].

६३०, ६५४. मसुस्स सुस्स च्छरच्छेरा

630, 654. **Masussa sussa cchara, ccherā.**

[Masussa+sussa+cchara, ccherā. 3 words]

[V] **Masu**-icce'tassa pāṭipadikassa **su**ssa **cchara, ccherā**'desā honti.

The "**su**" of pāṭipadika word "**masu**" changes into "**cchara, and cchera**".

Maccharatī'ti [Maccharati+iti] Maccharati-is jealous of. iti
• maccharo-jealousy. [wa] masu+kvi
evaṁ-similarly,
• macchero-jealousy. [Kattu-sādhana] [wa] masu+kvi
[Masu is not a root, a pāṭipadika. WA of both are the same]

Note: A crude form of word without any applied vibatti, paccaya in it, but which has its own specific meaning in a morphologically uncompleted state is called "**Paṭipadika**" which means an individual word separate from the completed word. [pati+pada+ika]

६३१, ६५५. आपुब्बचरस्स च

631, 655. **Āpubbacarassa ca.** [Āpubbacarassa+ca. 2 words]

[V] Āpubbassa **cara**-icce'tassa dhātussa **cchariya, cchara, ccherā**'desā honti, **ā**pubbassa ca **rasso** hoti.

The root "**cara**" prefixed with an upasagga "**ā**" changes into "**cchariya, cchara, cchera**". In addition, the prefix Upasagga "**ā**" is shortened as "**a**".

Ābhuso-intensely, very much, caritabban'ti. caritabbaṁ-should be treated, wondered. **i.e.** something which occurs in an amazing way and treated with awe, and disbelief.

• acchariyaṁ-wonderful. Both ***kn & adj*** [Kamma-sādhana]

Evaṁ

• accharaṁ, • accheraṁ-wonderful. [wa] ā√cara+kvi

Caggahaṇena **masu**ssa **su**ssā'pi **cchariyā**'deso hoti.

By the word "Ca", the "**su**" of the word "**masu**" also changes into "**cchariya**".

• Macchariyaṁ-jealousy. [wa] masu+kvi

६३२, ६५६. अल कल सलेहि ल या

632, 656. **Ala, kala, salehi la, yā.**

[Ala, kala, salehi+la, yā. 2 words]

[V] **Ala, kala, sala**-icce'tehi dhātūhi **la, ya**-paccayā honti.

The "**la, ya**" affixes are applied after the roots "**ala, kala and sala**".

(1) Alati samatthetī'ti, smattheti-is able. iti • allaṁ-wet. [Kattu-sādhana] [wa] ala+la

(2) Kalitabbaṁ saṅkhyātabban'ti [saṅkhyātabbaṁ+iti] saṅkhyātabbaṁ-should count as being fit. iti • kallaṁ-suitable, fit, appropriate (adj). [Kamma-sādhana] [wa] kala+la

(3) Salati gacchati pavisatī'ti pavisati-(it) enters (piercing.)

• sallaṁ-arrow, thorn etc. (which pricks or pierces). [Kattu-sādhana] [wa] sala+la

Evaṁ

• alyaṁ-wet. [wa] ala+ya
• kalyaṁ-suitable, fit. [wa] kala+ya
• salyaṁ-arrow, thorn etc. [wa] sala+ya

६३३, ६५७. याण लाणा

633, 657. **Yāṇa, lānā.** [Yāṇa, lānā. 1 word]

[V] Tehi **kala, sala**-icce'tehi dhātūhi **yāṇa, lāna**-paccayā honti.

The "**yāṇa, lāna**" affixes are applied after those "**kala, sala**" roots respectively.

(1) Kalitabbaṁ saṅkhyātabban'ti [Re: 632] • kalyāṇaṁ-good. [Kamma-sādhana] [wa] kala+yāṇa

(2) Gaṇato-from the crowd, paṭikkamitvā-having left, salanti-stays. etthā'ti ettha-here, iti • paṭisallānaṁ-quiet place,(where one stays alone leaving crowd or friends). [Adhikaraṇa-sādhana] [wa] pati-√sala+lāna

Evaṁ

• sallāno (See the next word for meaning). [wa] sala+lāna
• paṭisallāno-quiet place of seclusion or such an act. [wa] pati√sala+lāna

६३४, ६५८. मथिस्स थस्स लो च

634, 658. **Mathissa thassa lo ca.**

[Mathissa+thassa+lo+ca. 4 words]

[V] **Matha**-icce'tassa dhātussa **thassa lā**'deso hoti.

The component word "**tha**" of the root "**matha**", changes into "**la**".

Aññamaññaṁ-mutually, one against another, mathati viloḷatī'ti [viloḷati+iti] viloḷati-wrestles. iti • mallo, • mallaṁ-wrestler, boxer. [Kattu-sādhana] [wa] matha+a (Both are the same)

Caggahaṇena lato ko ca āgamo hoti.

By the word "Ca", an additional "ka" is to be added after the "la".

• Mallako, • mallakaṁ-wrestler, boxer.
[wa] matha+a (Both are the same)

६३५, ५५९. पेसातिसग्गपत्तकालेसु किच्चा

635, 559. Pesā'tisagga, pattakālesu kiccā.

[Pesa, atisagga, pattakālesu+kiccā. 2 words]

[V] **Pesa, atisagga, pattakāla**-icce'tesva'tthesu **kicca**paccayā honti.

The "**kicca**" affixes are applied to express "**pesa**-command, **atisagga**-permission, **pattakāla**-telling the due time to do something".

Summary: This Sutta shows where and when the suffixes shown in the examples are used. Even though it is referred generally as Kicca, there is more relevancy to "**tabba and anīya**" as these are two affixes widely used as verbs of the said meaning.

(1) • Kattabbaṁ-should be done . kammaṁ-work, bhavatā-By your honorable, [wa] kara+tabba

Three meanings as per the rule of this Sutta

(a) Your honorable must do work. [**pesa,** command].
(b) Your honorable can do work [**atisagga,** permission].
(c) Work should be done by your honorable [**pattakāla,** expressing the due time and obligation].

(2) • karaṇīyaṁ-should do. kiccaṁ-the matter, case, bhavatā, [wa] kara+anīya
i.e. The matter should be carried out by your honorable.

(3) • bhottabbaṁ-should eat. bhojanaṁ-meal, bhavatā, [wa] bhuja+tabba
i.e. The meal should be consumed by your honorable.

(4) • bhojanīyaṁ-should eat. bhojanaṁ bhavatā, [wa] bhuja+anīya
i.e. The meal should be eaten by your honorable.

(5) • ajjhayitabbaṁ-should recite. ajjheyyaṁ-the thing to recite. bhavatā, [wa] adhi-√i+tabba
i.e. It should be recited by your honorable.

(6) • ajjhayanīyaṁ-should recite. ajjheyyaṁ bhavatā.
[wa] adhi-√i+anīya
i.e. the text should be recited by your honorable.

६३६, ६५९. अवस्सकाधमिणेसु णी च

636, 659. **Avassakā'dhamiṇesu ṇī ca.**

[Avassaka, adhamiṇesu+ṇī+ca. 3 words]

[V] **Avassaka, adhamiṇa**-icce'tesva'tthesu **ṇī**-paccayo hoti. kiccā ca.

When expressing a sure action or event and a debt owed to someone, a "**ṇī**" affix as well as other **kicca** affixes can also be applied.

Avassake tāva–(Examples) in expressing sure action:

(1) • kārī'si [kārī+asi] kārī-doer. asi-(you) are [Refer to Sutta 496 for understanding this word]. me-my. kammaṁ-work. avassaṁ-surely.
i.e. You are surely to do my work. [wa] kara+ṇī

(2) • hārī'si [hārī+asi] hārī-carrier. asi me bhāraṁ-load or burden. avassaṁ-surely. **i.e.** You are surely to carry my burden or load. [wa] hara+ṇī

Adhamiṇe–(Examples) in the expression of debt:

(1) • dāyī'si [dāyī+asi] dāyī-giver. asi me sataṁ-hundred. iṇaṁ-debt, **i.e.** You are to pay a hundred debt of mine. [wa] dā+ṇī

(2) • dhārī'si [dhārī+asi] dhārī-carrier. asi me sahassaṁ-thousand. iṇaṁ-debt. **i.e.** You carry (**i.e.** owe) a thousand debt to me. [wa] dhara+ṇī

Kiccā ca–The examples of kicca-affixes:

(1) • dātabbaṁ-should pay. me-my. bhavatā sataṁ iṇaṁ.
i.e. My one hundred debt should be paid by your honorable.
[wa] dā+tabba

(2) • Dhārayitabbaṁ-should carry. me bhavatā sahassaṁ iṇaṁ,
i.e. You should be carrying my one thousand debt by your honorable. [So, you are obliged to pay back it to me.]
[wa] dhara+tabba

(3) • kattabbaṁ-should do. me bhavatā gehaṁ-house.
i.e. My home should be done by your honorable (Please build a home for me now). [wa] kara+tabba
(4) • karaṇīyaṁ-should do. me bhavatā kiccaṁ-matter,
i.e. My matter should be done by your honorable (Do it for me). [wa] kara+anīya
(5) • kāriyaṁ-should do (prepare). me bhavatā sayanaṁ-bed.
i.e. My bed should be made by your honorable (Please prepare bed for me). [wa] kara+ṇya

६३७, ०. अरहसक्कादीहि तुं

637,...Araha, sakkādīhi tuṁ.

[Araha, sakka-ādīhi+tuṁ. 2 words]

[V] **Araha, sakka, bhabba**-icce'vamādīhi payoge sati sabbadhātūhi **tuṁ**-paccayo hoti.

The affix "**tuṁ**" is applied after all roots in the contexts of **araha**-worthiness, **sakka-**ability and **babba-**possibility, likelihood and so on, to express those meanings.

Examples used in context of "**araha-**being deserved, worthiness"
(1) Arahā-deserves. bhavaṁ-your honorable. • vattuṁ-to speak,
i.e. Your honorable deserves to speak (You should speak). [wa] vada+tuṁ
(2) arahā bhavaṁ • kattuṁ-to do, [wa] kara+tuṁ
i.e. Your honorable deserves to do (You should do).

Examples used in context of "**sakka-**ability and capacity"
(1) sakkā-is able. bhavaṁ • hantuṁ-to kill,
i.e. Your honorable is able to kill . [wa] hana+tuṁ
(2) sakkā bhavaṁ • janetuṁ, • janituṁ, [wa] jana+tuṁ (Both the same) • bhavituṁ-to let it happen, [wa] bhū+tuṁ
i.e. Your honorable is able to let it happen (You can make it happen).
Note: janetuṁ, janituṁ and **bhavituṁ** have the same meaning.
(3) sakkā bhavaṁ • dātuṁ-to give,
i.e. Your honorable is able to give (You can give it). [wa] dā+tuṁ

(4) sakkā bhavaṁ • gantuṁ-to go,
i.e. Your honorable is able to go (You can go). [wa] gamu+tuṁ

Examples in context of "babba-possibility, likelihood and future prospect"

(1) babbo-is likely. bhavaṁ • janetuṁ-to cause it happen.
i.e. Your honorable is likely to cause it happen. [wa] shown icce'va'mādi.

६३८, ६६०. वजादीहि पब्बज्जादयो निप्पज्जन्ते

638, 660. **Vajā'dīhi pabbajjā'dayo nippajjante.**

[Vaja-ādīhi+pabbajja-ādayo+nippajjante. 3 words]

[V] **Vaja**-icce'vamādīhi dhātūhi, upasaggapaccayādīhi ca pabbajjā'dayo saddā nippajjante.

The words "**pabbajjā**" etc., which has the root "**vaja-**to go, prefixed with **pa**" and other words with various affixes and Upsagga prefixes, can be duly completed by means of this Sutta.

Examples with "ṇya" affix:

(1) Paṭhama'meva [Paṭhamaṁ+eva] Paṭhamaṁ eva-the first only. vajitabbā'ti [vajitabbā+iti] vajitabbā-should go. iti • pabbajjā-spiritual life such as monastic life etc. which should be first in significance. [Kamma-sādhana] [wa] pa√vaja+ṇya

(2) iñjanaṁ-trembling. • ejjā-trembling. [wa] iji+ṇya

(3) samajjanaṁ-moving in joyous manner. • samajjā-entertainment show, festival. [wa] Saṁ-√aja+ṇya

(4) nisīdanaṁ-sitting. • nisajjā-sitting. [wa] ni√sada+ṇya

(5) vijānanaṁ-knowing. • vijjā-knowledge. [wa] vida+ṇya

(6) visajjanaṁ-answering. • visajjā-answer. [wa] vi√saja+ṇya

(7) padanaṁ-going. • pajjā-going. [wa] pada+ṇya

(8) hananaṁ-killing. • vajjhā-killing. [wa] hana+ṇya

Note: The root "hana" has to be changed into "vadha" by Sutta 592 and later completed by this Sutta.

(9) esanaṁ-wanting. • icchā-wish, desire. [wa] isu+ṇya

(10) atiesanaṁ-wanting very much [**ati**-very much+**esanaṁ**-wanting]. • aticchā-strong, excessive wish. [wa] ati-√isu+ṇya

(11) sadanaṁ-being fatigued. • sajjā-fatigue., [2-11, All are Bhāva-sādhana EDs] [wa] sada+ṇya

(12) sayanti-lie down. etthā'ti [ettha+iti] ettha-here. iti • seyyā-bed where people lie down. [Adhikaraṇa-sādhana] [wa] si+ṇya

Examples with "kvi" affix:

(13) sammā-well. cittaṁ-the mind. nidheti-keeps. etāyā'ti [etāya+iti] etāya-by this faith. iti • saddhā-faith by which one can keep one's mind well convinced. [Karaṇa-sādhana]
[wa] Saṁ-√dhā+kvi

(14) caritabbā-should practice. • cariyā-the practice, conduct. [Kamma-sādhana] [wa] cara+kvi

Example with "ṇya" affix:

(15) karaṇaṁ-act of doing. • kiriyā-action. [Bhāva-sādhana]
[wa] kara+ṇya (this word has other affix in Sutta 554)

Examples with "cha" affix:

(16) rujanaṁ-afflicting. • rucchā-affliction with ailment.
[wa] ruja+cha

(17) padanaṁ-reaching. • pacchā-reaching. [wa] pada+cha

(18) riñcanaṁ-retiring to be alone. • ricchā-retirement from crowd.
[wa] rica+cha

(19) tikicchanṁ-curing. • tikicchā-cure [wa] kita+cha

(20) saṁkocanaṁ-withholding. • saṁkucchā-withholding.
[wa] saṁ√kuca+cha

(21) madanaṁ-being mad. • macchā-madness. [wa] mada+cha

(22) labhanaṁ-obtaining. • lacchā-attainment. [All Bhāva-sādhana]
[wa] labha+cha

(23) [a] raditabbā'ti [raditabbā+iti] raditabbā-should etch. iti • racchā-road (which looks like an etched line on the surface of the earth). [Kamma-sādhana]

[b] radanaṁ vilekhanaṁ-etching. vā • racchā-etching. [Bhāva-sādhana] [wa] rada+cha

(24) adhobhāgena-by lower portion (with one's body being downward). gacchatī'ti [gacchati+iti] gacchati-goes. iti • tiracchā, • tiracchāno-the animal (which goes with one's belly horizontally downward). [Kattu-sādhana] [wa] tira+cha

(25) ajanaṁ-strolling. • acchā-stroll, [Bhāva-sādhana] [wa] aja+cha

Example with "kha" affix:

(26) titikkhatī'ti [titikkhati+iti] titikkhati-(He) bears. iti • titikkhā-patience. [Kattu-sādhana] [wa] tija+kha

Examples with "cha" affix:

(27) saha-together. āgamanaṁ-coming. • sāgacchā-coming together, congress. [wa] Saha-saddūpapada, ā√gamu+cha

Note: "Saha" becomes "sa". **sa**-togeher+**ā-gacchā**-coming.

(28) duṭṭhu-badly. bhakkhanaṁ-eating. • dobhacchā-bad eating. [wa] du√bhasa+cha

(29) duṭṭhu-bad. rosanaṁ-harassing. • durucchā-bad harassment. [wa] du√rusa+cha

(30) pucchanaṁ-questioning. • pucchā-question. [wa] puccha+cha

(31) muhanaṁ-being confused. • mucchā-confusion. [wa] muha+cha

(32) vasanaṁ-staying. • vacchā-stay, [wa] vasa+cha

(33) kacanaṁ-shining. • kacchā-shine, [wa] kaca+cha

(34) saha-together. kathanaṁ-talking. • sākacchā-discussion. [wa] saha-saddūpapada+Katha+cha ["Saha" becomes "sā"]

(35) tudanaṁ-poking. • tucchā-poking, [wa] tuda+cha

(36) visanaṁ-entering. • vicchā-entry, [wa] visa+cha

Example with "chilla" affix:

(37) pisanaṁ-crushing. • picchillā-crushed. [27 to 37 are Bhāva-sādhana EDs] [wa] pisa+chilla

Example with "cha" affix:

(38) sukhadukkhaṁ-happiness and suffering. mudati bhakkhatī'ti [bhakkhati+iti] bhakkhati- consumes. iti • macco-a living being who has to consume (**i.e.** bear) pleasure and pain (of life). [Kattu-sādhana] [wa] muda+cha

Example with "tyu" affix:

(39) sattānaṁ-of beings. pāṇaṁ-life. museti-snatches. cajetī'ti [cajeti+iti] cajeti-causes to abandon. iti • maccu-death which

snatches and takes away the life of beings. [Kattu-sādhana]
[wa] musa+tyu

Examples with "tya" affix:

(40) satanaṁ-being perpetually true. • saccaṁ-truth. [Bhāva-sādhana, Neuter gender word] [wa] sata+tya

(41) uddhaṁ-upward, on and on. dhunāti kampatī'ti [kampati+iti] kampati-flutters, agitated. • uddhaccaṁ-restlessness of mind. [Kattu-sādhana] [wa] u√dhu+tya

Note: This word can also be a Bhāva-taddhita word with affix "ṇya". The base structural pattern is **Uddhata**-being restless+**ṇya**-the state of. **Uddhata** is a Kita-noun,[u√dhara+ta].**u**-upward,on and on, **dhara**-to be carried away+**ta**-past perfect suffix.**i.e.**restlessness]

(42) naṭanaṁ-dancing. • naccaṁ-dance. [Bhāva-sādhana] [wa] nata+tya

(43) nitanaṁ-being perpetual. • niccaṁ-always, perpetually (adj). [Bhāva-sādhana] [wa] niti+tya

Example with "cha" affix:

(44) tathanaṁ-being true. • tacchaṁ-true. [Bhāva-sādhana] [wa] tatha+cha

icce'va'mādi.

६३९, ५८५. क्विलोपो च

639, 585. **Kvilopo ca.** [Kvilopo+ca. 2 words]

[V] Kvilopo hoti. Puna ca nippajjante.

The affix "**kvi**" is to be elided (so that all other necessary morphological procedures can be carried out for the completion of "kvi-affixed" words).

(1) [a]Vividhehi-various. sīlādiguṇehi-by virtues such as Sīla etc. bhavatī'ti [bhavati+iti] bhavati-is, becomes. iti • vibhū-the one who becomes a Supreme being by means of various virtues. **i.e.** Buddha.

[b]visesena-specially. vā bhavatī'ti • vibhū-the one who specially happens or arises. [wa] vi-√bhū+kvi [Re: Sutta 530]

(2) sayaṁ attanā-oneself. bhavatī'ti • sayambhū-self-enlightened Buddha. [wa] sayam-saddūpapada-bhū+kvi

(3) abhibhavitvā-having overcome (all obstacles). bhavatī'ti • abhibhū-the one who arises (emerges) by overcoming all obstacles. [wa] abhi√bhū+kvi

(4) saṁ suṭṭhu-well. dhunāti-shakes. kampatī'ti • sandhū-something that shakes well. [wa] saṁ√dhu+kvi

(5) visesena bhāti-shines. dibbatī'ti [dibbati+iti] dibbati-shines. iti • vibhā-specially shining light. [wa] vi√bhā+kvi

(6) nissesena-thoroughly. bhāti dibbatī'ti • nibhā-thoroughly shining light. [wa] ni-√bhā+kvi

(7) pakārena-variously. bhāti dibbatī'ti • pabhā-variously shining light. [wa] pa√bhā+kvi

(8) saha-together. bhāsanti-speak. etthā'ti ettha-here in this meeting. • sabhā-conference where people talk together. [Adhikaraṇa-sādhana ED] [wa] saha-saddūpapada+bhāsa+kvi

Note: "saha" changes into "sa".

(9) ā bhuso-very much. bhāti-shines. dibbatī'ti • ābhā-intense light. [wa] ā√bhā+kvi [Here, Upasagga particle "ā" is intensifier]

(10) bhujena kuṭilena-by being twisted, in zigzag. gacchatī'ti • bhujago. [Re: Sutta 530]

(11) turitaturito-speedily. gacchatī'ti • turago-horse which goes by galloping speed. [wa] tura-saddūpapada-gamu+kvi

(12) saṁ suṭṭhu-well. pathaviṁ-earth. khanatī'ti [khanati+iti] khanati-digs, burrows. • saṅkho-conch. [Re: Sutta 530]

(13) visesena yamati-abstains. uparamatī'ti [uparamati+iti] uparamati-abstains. • viyo-special abstinence. [wa] vi√yamu+kvi

(14) suṭṭhu-well. manati-knows. jānatī'ti [jānātī'ti] jānāti-knows. iti • sumo-a person so-named or the wise person. [wa] su√mana+kvi

(15) pari samantato-from all around. tanoti-extends. vitthāretī'ti [vitthāreti+iti] vitthāreti-spreads. iti • parito-the width all across, diametrically. [All, except 8, are Kattu-sādhana EDs] [wa] pari√tanu+kvi

Note: Normally, this word is an indeclinable which means "from all around". An Upasagga "Pari" which is affixed with indeclinable affix

"to". (Re: Sutta 248).
icce'va'mādi.

६४०, ०. सचजानं कगा णानुबन्धे

640,...Sa, ca, jānaṁ ka, gā ṇā'nubandhe.

[Sa, ca, jānaṁ+ka, gā+ṇa-anubandhe. 3 words]

[V] **Sa, ca, jā**naṁ dhātūna'mantānaṁ **ca, jā**naṁ **ka, gā**'desā honti yathāsaṅkhyaṁ **ṇā'**nubandhe paccaye pare.

The root-end consonants "**c, j**" of certain roots, change into "**k, g**" respectively when an **ṇ**-conjoined affix is applied after the roots. [Similar function with Sutta 623]

- Oko [Re Sutta 528]. • pāko [Re: Sutta 529, 623],
- Seko-pouring. [wa] sica+ṇa
- Soko-sorrow. [wa] suca+ṇa
- Viveko-quiet solitude. [wa] vi-√vica+ṇa
- Cāgo [Re: Sutta 529, 621]. • Yogo [Re: Sutta 623],
- Bhogo-That which should be properly used, wealth. [wa] bhuja+ṇa
- Rogo [Re: Sutta 528] • Rāgo [Re: Sutta 590],
- Bhāgo [Re: Sutta 529],
- Bhaṅgo • Raṅgo • Saṅgo [Re: Sutta 607 for these three examples].

६४१, ५७२. नुदादीहि युण्वून मनानानाकाननका सकारितेहि च
641, 572. Nudā'dīhi yu,ṇvūna'manā'nanā'kā'nanakā sakāritehi ca.

[Nuda-ādīhi+yu, ṇvūnaṁ+ana, ānana, aka, ānanakā +sakāritehi+ ca. 5 words]

[V] **Nuda, sūda, jana, su, lū, hu, pu, bhū, ñā, asa, samu**-icce'va'mādīhi dhātūhi, **phanda, citi, āṇa**-icce'va'mādīhi sakāritehi ca **yu, ṇvū**naṁ paccayānaṁ **ana, ānana, aka, ānanakā**'desā honti yathāsaṅkhyaṁ kattari, bhāvakaraṇesu ca.

The "**yu, ṇvu**-affixes" which have senses of Kattu, Bhāva and Kraṇa, being applied after the root "**nuda, sūda, jana, su, lū, hu, pu, bhū, ñā, asa, samu**" etc. and other roots such as "**phanda, citi, āṇa**", which also have causative affixes, change into "**ana, ānana, aka** and **ānanaka**" respectively.

Note: This Sutta changes "**yu, ṇvu**-affixes" into "**ana, ānana, aka** and **ānanaka**". Please carefully note the systematic order of functions to be applied. Usually the functions applied in 3, 4(See below) will be either hetu-kattu or Hetu-Kamma Sādhana, a very special combined type of Sādhana. Below is the order of functions to be applied according to the applied affixes.

(1) The "yu" affix (applied in the sense of Kattu, bhāva or Kraṇa) >**ana.**

(2) The "ṇvu" affix (applied in the sense of Kattu, bhāva or Kraṇa) >**aka.**

(3) The "yu" affix plus a causative suffix>**ānana.**

(4) The ordinary "ṇvu" affix plus a causative suffix> **ānanaka.**

Kattari tāva–(Examples with "yu" affix) in the sense of Kattu **(doer, agent),** in **ana**-function:

(1) panudatī'ti [panudati+iti] panudati-extracts. iti • panūdano-extractor. [Kattu-sādhana] [wa] pa√nuda+yu

Evaṁ

(2) • sūdano-something which flows. [wa] suda+yu
(3) • janano-maker. [wa] jana+yu
(4) • savaṇo-listener. [wa] su+yu
(5) • lavano-cutter. [wa] lū+yu
(6) • havano-sacrificer. [wa] hu+yu
(7) • pavano-purifier. [wa] pu+yu
(8) • bhavano-something which arises, ariser. [wa] bhū+yu
(9) • ñāṇo-something which knows, knowledge. [wa] ñā+yu
(10) • asano-eater. [wa] asa+yu
(11) • samaṇo-calmer, the one who is calm, monk. [wa] samu+yu

Bhāve ca–Examples with "yu" affix in the sense of Bhāva **(action) :**
(1) panudate-act of extraction. • panūdanaṁ-extraction. [Bhāva-sādhana]

Evaṁ

(2) • sūdanaṁ-flowing.
(3) • jananaṁ-arising.
(4) • savaṇaṁ-listening.
(5) • lavanaṁ-cutting.
(6) • havanaṁ-sacrificing.
(7) • pavanaṁ-purification.
(8) • bhavanaṁ-arising.
(9) • ñāṇaṁ-knowing.
(10) • asanaṁ-eating.
(11) • samaṇaṁ-being calm.

Note: WA of these examples are the same as foregoing ones except the neuter gender ending of these words.

Examples of "**yu+causative**" affix, in **ānana**-function:
(12) • sañjānanaṁ-causing to know well, educating .
[wa] saṁ√ñā+yu
(13) • kuyate-sounding. • kānanaṁ-act of sounding.
[All Bhāva-sādhana] [wa] ku+yu

Kārite ca–Examples with "**causative** ṇāpe-affix", "yu" affixes in **Bhāva sense**", **ana**-function:

(1) phandāpīyate-causing to shake • phandāpanaṁ-causing to shake. [Bhāva-sādhana] [wa] phadi+"ṇāpe+yu" [dual affixes]

(2) cetāpīyate-causing to incite. • cetāpanaṁ-inciting. [wa] citi+"ṇāpe+yu" [two affixes]

(3) āṇāpīyate-causing to command • āṇāpanaṁ-command. [wa] āṇa+"ṇāpe+yu" [Bhāva-sādhana] [two affixes]

Karaṇe– Examples with "yu" affix in the sense of **Karaṇa (Instrument, supporting cause) ana**-function:

(1) nudanti-extract. anenā'ti [anena+iti] anena-by this. iti
• nūdanaṁ-that by which things are extracted. [Karaṇa-sādhana] [wa] nuda+yu

Evaṁ

(2) • sūdanaṁ-that by which it flows. **i.e.** the source of flow.

(3) • jananaṁ-that by which it arises. **i.e.** the cause of something.

(4) • savaṇaṁ-that by which one listens. **i.e.** the source of hearing.

(5) • lavaṇaṁ-that by which it is cut. **i.e.** the sickle etc.

(6) • havanaṁ-that by which one sacrifices. **i.e.** the food or flower etc.

(7) • pavanaṁ-that by which one is purified. **i.e.** act of penance etc.

(8) • bhavanaṁ-that by which it arises. **i.e.** the cause.

(9) • ñāṇaṁ-that by which one knows. **i.e.** knowledge.

(10) • asanaṁ-that by which one eats. **i.e.** the hand etc.

(11) • samaṇaṁ-that by which one calms. **i.e.** the meditation etc.

Note: WA of these examples are the same as foregoing ones except the neuter gender ending of these words. Keep in mind that the words "that by which" are literalized interpretations reflective of Karaṇa sādhana.

Puna kattari– Again, examples with "ṇvu" affix in the sense of Kattu, **aka**-function:

See the underlined verbs of EDs which signifies a **Kattu-sādhana** before each example. The verbs of ED are affixed in invisible "a" affix of Kattu-sense in the present tense. That is why it is called **Kattu-sādhana** EDs).

(1) <u>nudatī</u>'ti [nudati+iti] nudati-(one) extracts.
• nūdako-extractor.[wa] nuda+ṇvu

(2) sūdatī'ti [sūdati+iti] sūdati-(It) flows. iti • sūdadhako-that which flows. [wa] sūda+ṇvu

(3) janetī'ti [janeti+iti] janeti-(it) causes, or causes to born (causative verb). iti • janako-a cause, father . [wa] jana+ṇvu

(4) suṇotī'ti [suṇoti+iti] suṇoti-(one) listens. iti • sāvako-the one who obeys guidance. A disciple, a follower. [wa] su+ṇvu

(5) lunātī'ti [lunāti+iti] lunāti-cuts (crops). iti • lāvako-harvester, cutter. [wa] lū+ṇvu

(6) juhotī'ti [juhoti+iti] juhoti-(one) sacrifices. iti • hāvako-sacrificer. [wa] hu+ṇvu

(7) punātī'ti [punāti+iti] punāti-(it) purifies. iti • pāvako-purifier, fire. [wa] pu+ṇvu

(8) bhavatī'ti [bhavati+iti] bhavati-(it) arises. • bhāvako-something which arises, developer, [wa] bhū+ṇvu

(9) jānātī'ti [jānāti+iti] jānāti-(one) knows. iti • jānako-someone who knows, knower. [wa] jana+ṇvu

(10) • asatī'ti [asati+iti] asati-(one) eats. iti • asako-consumer. [wa] asa+ṇvu

(11) upāsatī'ti [upāsati+iti] upāsati-(one) closely follows. iti • upāsako-follower, devotee. [wa] upa√asa+ṇvu

(12) sametī'ti [sameti+iti] sameti-(it) calms. iti • samako-that which calms. [All Kattu-sādhana] [wa] samu+ṇvu

Kārite tu–Examples with causative "ṇāpaya" and "ṇvu" affix in sense of causative Kattu voice (**Causative Agent), aka-**function**:** (The examples shown below are very unique as there are causative affixes in verb of ED and example. They are formally called "**Hetu-Kattu** sādhana", a rare form of Sādhana. Causative verbs of ED[1] and finished words of Hetu-kattu sādhana[2] are shown in superscript numbers.)

(1) phandāpayatī'ti [phandāpayati+iti] [1]phandāpayati-(is) caused to be shaken. iti • [2]phandāpayako-something causing to be shaken, the shaker. [Hetu-Kattu-sādhana]

[wa] phadi+"ṇāpaya+ṇvu" [Two affixes]

Evaṁ

(2) • [2]āṇāpayako--something causing to be commanded, the command-giver. [wa] āṇa+"ṇāpaya+ṇvu"

(3) • [2]cetāpayako--something causing to be incited, the instigator. [wa] citi+"ṇāpaya+ṇvu"

Examples of **ānanaka**-function with **causative+ṇvu** affixes:

(4) • [2]sañjānanako--something or someone causing to know, enlightener or an educator. [wa] saṁ√ñā+"ṇāpe+ṇvu"

६४२, ५८८. इ य त म किं एसानमन्तस्सरो दीघं क्वचि दिसस्स गुणं दो रं स क्खी च

642, 588. **I,ya, ta, ma, ki, e, sāna'mantassaro dīghaṁ kvaci disassa guṇaṁ do raṁ sa,kkhī'ca.**

[I,ya, ta, ma, ki, e, sānaṁ+antassaro+dīghaṁ+kvaci+disassa+guṇaṁ+do+raṁ+sa, kkha, ī+ca. 10 words]

[V] **I, ya, ta, ma, ki, esa**-icce'tesaṁ sabbanāmāna'manto saro dīgha'māpajjate, kvaci.
disa-icce'tassa[51] dhātussa **i**-kāro [52]**guṇa**'māpajjate. **da**kāro **ra**kāra'māpajjate.

---

[51] **dusa-icce'tassa dhātusassa u-kāro guṇa'māpajjate** (These are originally found words in earlier texts which seems like a corrupted text. This might had happened due to copyist's errors over many years during which time the copies of text are manually copied. There is no root "dusa" in the Sutta but the root "**disa**-to see, to view" in the Sutta).
disa-iccetassa dhātusassa i-kāro guṇa'māpajjate (The edited text, which is relevant and reflective of the words "disassa guṇaṁ" contained in the Sutta). The meaning of these words in this sentence do not carry much significant weight in expounding any additional particular injunction of Sutta as it only reiterates the third function of changing "sa" of the root into "ī".

[52] This Sutta is the only place where usage of the term "guṇa" is found. Here, Guṇa merely means "times increase in the metrical nature". This term "guṇa" as well as the grammatical concept of a "guṇa" is seldom found as an applied grammatical concept in the Kaccayana Pāli grammar like the way it is widely applied in the Sanskrit grammars. Instead, Pāli grammarians apply "vuddhi" as the applied concept in matters of morphology. To see the difference and to compare, refer to Sutta 406, 407 of Kaccāyana and Pāṇinī Sutta 1-1-1

dhātva'ntassa **sa**ssa ca **sa, kkha, ī**-icce'te ādesā honti yathāsambhavaṁ.
Ete saddā sakena sakena nāmena yathā'nuparodhena Buddhasāsane pacchā puna nippajjante.

The component vowels "**i, ya, ta, ma, ki, e, sa**", which are parts of their respective Sabbanāma nouns change into dīgha (long vowels).
The vowel "i" of the root "disa" changed into a guṇa "ī".
The letter "**d**" of the root "**disa**" changes into an "**r**" and the component consonant "**s**" of the root "**disa**" changes into "**sa, kkha, ī**".
Each of these words are to be morphologically completed not contravening the prevalent usage in Pāli texts.

Explanation

On Parts of Sabbanāma Nouns and Three Functions of Sutta

I is part of **ima** (this). **ya** is part of **ya** (which). **ta** is part of **ta** (that). **ma** is part of **amha** (me). **ki** is part of **kiṁ** (What, interrogative). **e** is part of **eta** (that). **sa** is part of **samāna** (same, similar).

(1) Of all these, all **"i, a"** vowels in each sabbanāma-words except "e" of "eta", are to undergo the "dīgha" process of lengthening. Thus, each is lengthened as "**ī, yā, tā, mā, kī, sā**".

(2) The "**d**" of the root word "**disa**" changes into an "**r**".

(3) "**s**" of "**disa**" changes into "**sa, kkha, ī**". [Changing "s" of "disa" into "s" is a redundant function of affirmation]

Note: There is a hidden function not shown the Vutti of Sutta. It is to change "**amha**" into "**ma**", "**eta**" into "**e**" and "**samāna**" into "**sa**" by this Sutta and to lengthen inherent vowels into dīgha. In **Rūpasiddhi**, it is said:
"**ma**-iti nipātanena **amha**saddassa mādeso.
e-iti nipātanena **eta**saddassa ekāro.
sa-iti nipātanena **samāna**saddassa sādeso. ta'dantassa vā dīgho".

(वृद्धिरादैच) and 1-1-2(अदेङ गुणः).

(Rūpasiddhi Grammar, Sutta 588)

There is also a Sutta (समानेदं किमदः सेक्यामू) in the **Mugdhabhoda** Sanskrit grammar with somewhat similar function which changes "samāna" into "sa", "idam" into "ī", "kiṁ" into "kī" and "ada" into "amū".

The following are examples where the lengthening procedure of dīgha process takes place in the initial vowels excluding "e" of "eta". Only one function is applied in these examples.

(1) Ima'miva [imaṁ+iva] imaṁ iva-like this person. naṁ-to that person. passatī'ti [passati+iti] passati-(he) sees. iti • īdiso-such-like person or such-kind-of person.
[wa] ima-saddūpapada-disa+kvi

(2) ya'miva [yaṁ+iva] yaṁ iva-like any person. naṁ passatī'ti • yādiso-any-kind-of person. [wa] ya-saddūpapada-disa+kvi

(3) ta'miva [taṁ+iva] taṁ iva-like that person. naṁ passatī'ti • tādiso-that-kind-of person. [wa] ta-saddūpapada-disa+kvi

(4) ma'miva [maṁ+iva] maṁ iva-like me. naṁ passatī'ti • mādiso-me-like person. or a person like me.
[wa] amha-saddūpapada-disa+kvi

(5) kim'iva [kiṁ+iva] kiṁ iva-like who. naṁ passatī'ti • kīdiso-which kind of person. [wa] Kiṁ-saddūpapada-disa+kvi

(6) eta'miva [etaṁ+iva] etaṁ iva-like that person. naṁ passatī'ti • ediso-that-kind-of person. [wa] eta-saddūpapada-disa+kvi

Note: "eta" changes into "e" by this Sutta. If this function is not applied, then the lengthening procedure is applicable thereby resulting in the word form "etādiso", which is also widely found in the Pāli texts.

(7) samāna'miva [samānaṁ+iva] samānaṁ iva-like same person. naṁ passatī'ti • sādiso-similar-kind-of person. [All Kattu-sādhana EDs] [wa] Samāna-saddūpapada-disa+kvi

In the following examples, besides a dīgha process in the initial vowels, "d" of the root "disa" also changes into "r". However, the meanings and ED of each example and WA are the same. See all the examples carefully to clarify two applied functions.

(1) Ima'miva naṁ passatī'ti • īriso.

(2) ya'miva naṁ passatī'ti • yāriso.

(3) ta'miva naṁ passatī'ti • tāriso.

(4) ma'miva naṁ passatī'ti • māriso.

(5) kim'iva naṁ passatī'ti • kīriso.

(6) eta'miva naṁ passatī'ti • eriso.
[one "r" changing function only, no dīgha function]

(7) samāna'miva naṁ passatī'ti • sāriso. [All Kattu-sādhana]

In the following examples, apart from a dīgha process in the initial vowels, "s" of the root "disa" changes into "kkh". The meanings and all EDs of each example and WA are the same though.

(1) Ima'miva naṁ passatī'ti • īdikkho.

(2) ya'miva naṁ passatī'ti • yādikkho.

(3) ta'miva naṁ passatī'ti • tādikkho. [Kattu-sādhana]

Evaṁ

(4) • mādikkho,

(5) • kīdikkho,

(6) • edikkho,

(7) • sādikkho.

In the following examples, besides dīgha process, "sa" of " the root "disa" changes into an "ī". The meanings and ED of each examples and WA are the same.

(1) • īdī. (2) • yādī. (3) • tādī. (4) • mādī. (5) • kīdī. (6) • edī.
(7) • sādī.

Caggahaṇena tesa'meva saddānaṁ **i, ya,** icce'va'mādīna' manto ca saro **Kvaci** dīghatta'māhu.

By means of the word "Ca" in Sutta, those initial vowels of "i, ya, etc." are said to be made into a "dīgha".

This function is already shown in the main Sutta. Hence, it seems like redundant. Note that there is no "dīgha" process in four examples shown with this asterisk mark * [WA of each example is the same as shown before]

(1) • īdikkho. (2) • yādikkho. (3) • tādikkho.

(4) • mādikkho. (5) • kīdikkho. (6) *• edikkho.

(7) • sādikkho-same-kind-of-person.
[wa] Samāna-saddūpapada-disa+kvi
(WA of 2, 3, 4 below are the same as this)

(1) • īdiso. [wa] ima-saddūpapada-disa+kvi.

No dīgha in three examples below.

(2) *• sadiso-same-kind-of-person.

(3) *• sariso-same-kind-of-person.

(4) *• sarikkho-same-kind-of person.

६४३, ६३५. भ्यादीहि मति बुधि पूजादीहि च क्तो

643, 635. **Bhyā'dīhi mati, budhi, pūjā'dīhi ca kto.**

[Bhī-ādīhi+mati, budhi, pūja-ādīhi+ca+kto. 4 words]

[V] **Bhī**-icce'va'mādīhi dhātūhi, **mati, Budhi, pūjā**'dito ca **kta**-paccayo hoti.

The affix "**kta**" is applied after the roots "**bhī, mana** (**mati** refers to the root word "**mana**-to know), **budha** (**budhi** refers to the root **budha**-to know), **pūja**" etc.

(1) Bhāyitabbo'ti [Bhāyitabbo+iti] Bhāyitabbo-should fear. iti • bhīto-feared. [wa] bhī+ta

(2) supitabbo'ti [supitabbo+iti] supitabbo-should sleep. iti • sutto-slept. [wa] supa+ta

(3) mijjitabbo sinehetabbo-should like or admire. iti • mitto-friend that should be liked. [wa] mida+ta

(4) [a] sammannitabbo-should acknowledge well. iti • sammato-well-acknowledged, well-recognized.

[b] saṁ suṭṭhu-well. mānitabbo pūjetabbo-should honor. iti • sammato-well-honored.

[c] sammānīyitthā'ti [sammānīyittha+iti] sammānīyittha-well adored. iti • sammato-well-adored. [wa] saṁ√mana+ta

(5) [a] saṁkappīyate-well thought. iti • saṅkappito-well thought,

[b] saṁkappīyitthā'ti [saṁkappīyittha+iti] saṁkappīyittha-well thought. iti • saṅkappito-well thought.

[wa] saṁ√kappa+ta

Note: In ED (a), an Ākhyāta verb in Kamma sense is used. In (b), the past tense mode is employed. All similar EDs should thus be noted.

(6) [a] sampādīyate-well provided. iti • sampādito-well provided,

[b] sampādīyitthā'ti [sampādīyittha+iti] • sampādito-well provided. [wa] saṁ√pada+ta

(7) [a] avadhārīyate-is limited. iti • avadhārito-limited, restricted,

[b] avadhārīyitthā'ti [avadhārīyittha+iti] • avadhārito-limited.
[wa] ava√dhara+ta

(8) bujjhitabbo ñātabbo-should know. iti • buddho-something which should know. [wa] budha+ta

Note: "ñātabbo" is synonymous kita-verb of "bujjhitabbo".

(9) [a] ajjhayitabbo-should recite, or learn. iti • ito-something which should be recited or learnt.

[b] etabbo gantabbo-should go. iti • ito-somewhere which should be gone. [wa] i+ta

Note: Though of the same root, these two words have different meanings. In **(9-a),** the root means to study, to recite **(ajjāyana'ttha),** In **(9-b),** it means to go, to move. **(gaty'attha).**

(10) viditabbo ñātabbo-should know. iti • vidito-known, famous.
[wa] vida+ta

(11) takkīyate-(is) thought out. iti • takkito-thought.
[wa] takka+ta

(12) [a] pūjīyate-(is) honored. iti • pūjito-honored.

[b] pūjīyitthā'ti [pūjīyittha+iti] pūjīyittha-is honored. iti • pūjito-honored. [wa] pūja+ta

(13) apacāyitabbo-should be respected. iti • apacāyito-respected.
[wa] apa√caya+ta

(14) mānitabbo pūjetabbo-should honor, or adore. iti • mānito-honored, adored. [wa] māna+ta

(15) apacīyate-(is) respected. iti • apacito-respected.
[wa] apa√ci+ta

(16) [a] vandīyate-is bowed. iti • vandito-bowed,

[b] vandīyitthā'ti [vandīyittha+iti] • vandito-had bowed.
[wa] vanda+ta

(17) [a] sakkarīyate-(is) adored, is well treated with respect and devotion. iti • sakkārito-adored,

[b] sakkarīyitthā'ti [sakkarīyittha+iti] • sakkārito-adored.
[All are Kamma-sādhana EDs]
[wa] saṁ√kara+ta or sakkara+ta

Note: Even though the affix is mentioned as "kta" in Sutta, it is shown as "ta" in WA so as to be in conformity with prevalent usage in the canonical texts and the main grammatical principle of being "jinavacanayutta".

६४४, ६६१. वेपु सी दव वमु कु दा भूह्वादीहि थुत्तिम णिमा निब्बत्ते
644, 661. **Vepu, sī, dava, vamu, ku, dā, bhū,hvā'dīhi thu, ttima, ṇimā nibbatte.**

[Vepu, sī, dava, vamu, ku, dā, bhū, hu-ādīhi+athu, ttima, ṇimā+ nibbatte. 3 words]

[V] **Vepu, sī, dava, vamu, ku, dā, bhū, hu**-icce'va'mādīhi dhātūhi yathāsambhavaṁ **athu, ttima, ṇima**-paccayā honti nibbatta'tthe.

The affixes "**athu, ttima, ṇima**" are applied after the roots "**vepu, sī, dava, vamu, ku, dā, bhū, hu**" and so on, in the sense of "caused by, or originated from".

Note: There are two EDs for each example shown by numbers. The first is called minor-ED which precedes final major ED of example. It is not an example of Sutta but a related one, necessary to make the examples much easier to understand. The WA of minor ED is shown for enriching the grammatical knowledge and broadening the grammatical skill of the students. The second is major, complete ED of the word.

(1) [1]Vepanaṁ-shaking. vepo-tremor or involuntary motion of the body. [Bhāvasādhana, Minor ED] [wa] vepu+ṇa
[2]Tena-by that shaking. nibbatto-(it) arises. • vepathu-ailment which occurs by shaking of body (like that of Parkinson's). [Major, final ED] [wa] vepu+athu

(2) [1]sayanaṁ-sleeping. sayo-sleep. [wa] si+ṇa
[2]Tena nibbatto • sayathu-disease characterized by abnormal sleepiness. [wa] si+athu

(3) [1]davanaṁ-heating. davo-the heat, [wa] dava+a
[2]Tena nibbatto • davathu-illness characterized by body heat (high temperature). [wa] dava+athu

(4) [1]Vamanaṁ-vomitting. vamo-act of vomiting. [wa] vamu+a
Tena nibbatto • vamathu-disease marked by vomitting. [wa] vamu+athu

(5) [1]Kutti-creating. karaṇaṁ-act. [wa] kara+yu
[2]Tena nibbattaṁ • kuttimaṁ-something created artificially, not naturally. [wa] kara+ttima

(6) [1]Dāti-giving. dānaṁ-giving. [wa] dā+yu
[2]Tena nibbattaṁ • dattimaṁ-something received by giving. [wa] dā+ttima

(7) [1]Bhūti-arising. bhavanaṁ-arising. [wa] bhū+yu
[2]Tena nibbattaṁ • bhottimaṁ-something that occurs by arising. [wa] bhū+ttima

(8) [1]Avahuti-sacrificing. avahanaṁ-sacrificing.
[wa] ava-√hu+yu
[2]Tena nibbattaṁ • ohāvimaṁ-things meant for sacrifice or left over after sacrifice. [wa] ava-√hu+ṇima

६४५, ६६२. अक्कोसे नम्हानि

645, 662. **Akkose namhā'ni.** [Akkose+namhi+āni. 3 words]

[V] **Akkosa**-icce'tasmiṁ atthe **na**mhi paṭisedhayutte **āni**-paccayo hoti dhātūhi.

To express reviling or cursing, an affix "**āni**" is applied after the roots in the context of the negative particle "**na**" barring the action.

(1) Na-not. gamitabbaṁ-should go. • agamāni-should not go. te-by you. jamma-bad guy! desaṁ-to the location, **i.e.** You should not be going there, bad guy! [wa] na-saddūpapada-gamu+āni

(2) na kattabbaṁ-should not do. • akarāṇi-should not do. te jamma kammaṁ-work. **i.e.** You should not be doing that deed, bad guy! [wa] na-saddūpapada-kara+āni

Namhī'ti kimatthaṁ?
What is the word "namhi" for?
To show that the examples shown below are inapplicable as there is no negative nipāta "na" used in the context. Hence, no "āni" affix applied.

(1) * Vipatti-be ruined! te-for you. jamma-mean guy! **i e.** Be ruined to you mean (lowly) guy! [wa] vi-pada+ti

(2) * vikati-be broke! te jamma-mean guy! **i.e.** Be broke to you mean guy! [wa] vi-kara+ti

Akkose'ti kimatthaṁ? What is the word "akkose" for? To show that the example shown below is inapplicable as it doesn't mean "akkosa-to revile". Hence, no "āni" affix is applied.

Na gantabbā-should not go. * agati-any partial act. te-by you. **i.e.** You should not go to any partial, biased action.
[wa]agati=na-saddūpapada-gamu+ti

Note: The words with this **"āni"** affix used in this context are seldom found in the Tipiṭaka canonical texts.

६४६, ४१९. एकादितो सकिस्स क्खत्तुं

646, 419. **Ekā'dito sakissa kkhattuṁ.**

[Eka-ādito+sakissa+kkhattuṁ. 3 words]

[V] **Ekā**'dito **saki**ssa **kkhattuṁ** hoti.

The Nipāta particle "**sakiṁ**-times" applied after numerical nouns "**eka**" etc. changes into "**kkhattuṁ**"

Note: When expressing "one time", the "**kkhattuṁ**" affix denoting time and frequency, is suffixed after numerical words and (other words) like "**eka-one**" etc. It is an indeclinable affix without gender. It rather serves as an adverb of frequency or times in a sentence.

(1) Ekassa-of one. padatthassa-the meaning of word. sakiṁ-one time. vāraṁ-one turn. **i.e.** The meaning of one word for one-time as well as one-turn. • ekakkhattuṁ-is called "ekakkhattuṁ" which means "once, one time". [wa] eka+kkhattuṁ (**eka** etc. is not the root, but numeral noun)

(2) dvinnaṁ-of two. padatthānaṁ-the meaning of words. sakiṁ vāraṁ • dvikkhattuṁ-twice, two times, [wa] dvi+kkhattuṁ

(3) tiṇṇaṁ-of three. padatthānaṁ sakiṁ vāraṁ • tikkhattuṁ-thrice, three times, [wa] ti+kkhattuṁ

evaṁ

(4) • catukkhattuṁ-four times. [wa] catu+kkhattuṁ

(5) • pañcakkhattuṁ-five times. [wa] pañca+kkhattuṁ

(6) • chakkhattuṁ-six times. [wa] cha+kkhattuṁ

(7) • sattakkhattuṁ-seven times. [wa] satta+kkhattuṁ
(8) • aṭṭhakkhattuṁ-eight times. [wa] aṭṭha+kkhattuṁ
(9) • navakkhattuṁ--nine times. [wa] nava+kkhattuṁ
(10) • dasakkhattuṁ-ten times. [wa] dasa+kkhattuṁ

Icce'va'mādayo saddā yojetabbā.
Such words should be applied.

Note: According to prevalent view of the Pāli grammarians, this morpheme, "**kkhattuṁ**" should be regarded as an indeclinable affix denoting frequency or times which does not have gender. The "**kkhattuṁ**-affixed word" usually plays the role of an adverb in the sentence.

६४७, ६६३. सुनस्सुनस्सोण वानुवानू नुनखुनाना

647, 663. Sunassu'nasso'ṇa vānu, vānū nu'nakhu'nānā.

[Sunassa+unassa+oṇa, vāna, uvāna, ūna, unakha, una, ā, ānā. 3 words]

[V] **Suna**-icce'tassa pāṭipadikassa **una**ssa **oṇa, vāna, uvāna, ūna, unakha, una, ā, ānā**'desā honti.

The "**una**" of the Pāṭipadika word "**suna** (dog) ", changes into "**oṇa, vāna, uvāna, ūna, unakha, una, ā** and **āna**".
[This Sutta changes "una" of the word "suna" into "**oṇa, vāna, uvāna, ūna, unakha, una, ā** and **āna**". See examples]

(1) Sāmikassa-of owner. saddaṁ-voice. suṇātī'ti [suṇāti+iti] suṇāti-listens, obeys. iti • soṇo-the animal which obeys the voice-command of the owner, the dog.
[Kattu-sādhana, **Ona**-function example]
[wa] suna+si [No affix, but nominative singular "si"]
(2) sāmikassa saddaṁ suṇātī'ti • svāno-the dog. [**Vāna**-function]

Evaṁ

- suvāno-the dog [**uvāna**-function] • sūno [**ūna**-function]
- sunakho [**unakha**-function] • suno [**una**-function]
- sā [**ā**-function] • sāno-dog [**āna**-function] (All the same meaning).

६४८, ६६४. तरुणस्स सुसु च

648, 664. **Taruṇassa susu ca.** [Taruṇassa+susu+ca. 3 words]

[V] **Taruṇa**-icce'tassa pāṭipadikassa **susu**-ādeso hoti.

The Pāṭipadika word "**taruṇa**" changes into "**susu**".

• Susu-youth. kāḷakeso-who has black hair. **i.e.** The black-haired youth. [wa] taruṇa+si [No affix, but nominative singular "si"]

Note: The word "taruṇa" is also a Pātipadika word, not a root, with a noun-vibatti "si" applied after it.

६४९, ६६५. युवस्सुवस्सुवुवानु नूना

649, 665. **Yuvassu'vassu'vu vānu'nūnā.**

[Yuvassa+uvassa+uva, uvāna, una, ūnā. 3 words]

[V] **Yuva**-icc'etassa pāṭipadikassa **uvassa uva, uvāna, una, ūnā**'desā honti.

The component letters "**uva**" of Pāṭipadika word "**yuva**", change into "**uva, uvāna, una** and **ūna**". [This Sutta changes "uva" of the word "yuva" into "**uva, uvāna, una,** and **ūna**"]

• Yuvā, • yuvāno, • yuno, • yūno-youth. (all of the same meaning). [wa] yuva+si [No affix, but nominative singular "si"]

Note: "yuva" is also a Pātipadika word, not a root, with a noun-vibatti "si" applied after it. That "si" later changes into ''ā" by Sutta 152.

६५०, ६५१. काले वत्तमानातीते ण्वादयो

650, 651. **Kāle vattamānā' tīte ṇvā'dayo.**

[Kāle+vattamānā-atīte+ṇu-ādayo. 3 words]

[V] Kāle vattamāna'tthe ca atīta'tthe ca **ṇu, yu, ta**-paccayā honti.

The affixes "**ṇu, yu, ta**" are applied in the sense of present and past.

(1) [1] Akāsi-did, [2] karotī'ti [karoti+iti] karoti-does. iti • kāru-an artisan or carpenter who did, and is doing his craft or carpentry. [wa] kara+ṇu

(2) [1] agacchi-gone, [2] gacchatī'ti [gacchati+iti] gacchati-goes. iti. • vāyu-the wind which has gone blowing and goes blowing in both past and present. [wa] vā+yu

(3) [1] abhavi-it was, [2] bhavatī'ti [bhavati+iti] bhavati-it is. iti • bhūtaṁ-creature (big and small) which have been and which still are). [All are Kattu-sādhana] [wa] bhū+ta

Note: In the EDs, there are two numbered verbs which signify a specific tense of the past and present according to the structure of verbs.

६५१, ६४७. भविस्सति गमादीहि णी घिण

651, 647. **Bhavissati gamā'dīhi ṇī, ghiṇ.**

[Bhavissati+gamu-ādīhi+ṇī, ghiṇ. 3 words]

[V] Bhavissatikāla'tthe **gamu, bhaja, su, ṭhā**-icc'e'va'mā'dīhi dhātūhi **ṇī, ghiṇ**-paccayā honti.

In the sense of future, the affixes "**ṇī, ghiṇ**" are applied after the roots "**gamu, bhaja, su, ṭhā**" etc.

(1) Āyatiṁ-in the future. gamituṁ-to go. sīlaṁ-(is the) habit. yassa- whose, so-that person. hotī'ti • gāmī-one who will go habitually. [wa] gamu+ṇī

(2) āyatiṁ bhajituṁ-to share. sīlaṁ yassa, so hotī'ti • bhājī-one who will share (the portions) habitually. [wa] bhaja+ghiṇ

(3) āyatiṁ passāvituṁ-to listen. sīlaṁ yassa, so hotī'ti • passāvī-one who will listen habitually. [wa] pa√su+ghiṇ

(4) āyatiṁ paṭṭhāyituṁ-to stand. sīlaṁ yassa, so hotī'ti • paṭṭhāyī-one who will stand habitually. [All are Kattu-sādhana] [wa] pa√ṭhā+ṇī

Note: Compare the words like "Evaṁbhāvī-will be thus" which are expressive of future process [Nava Sivathika-pabba Section, Mahā Satipaṭhāna Sutta] This Sutta enjoins to apply two affixes in the sense of future. Actually, the affix "**ṇī**" alone is sufficient to complete these words used in the context of future sense in this Sutta. The examples affixed with "**ghiṇ-affix**" are found to be very much the same like "**ṇī**". As a matter of fact, it could be a redundant affix as it is very much similar to "**ṇī**" affix shown in Suttas 532(Kita chapter), 636. To clarify this, there is an affix "घिनुण" which seems strikingly similar to "**ghiṇ-affix**" of this Sutta found in Kridanta affixes section, Sutta Numbers 3121, 3122, 3123, 3124, 3125 of **Siddhanta-Kaumudi Sanskrit Grammar,** PP 129-131. Some of the examples shown in those Sutta are: **Damī (दमी)** -the one who is tamed, **Pamādī**-(प्रमादी) the one who is mad or forgetful or negligent etc.

६५२, ६४८. क्रियायं ण्वु तवो

652, 648. **Kriyāyaṁ ṇvu, tavo.** [Kriyāyaṁ+ṇvu, tuvo. 2 words]

[V] Kriyāya'matthe **ṇvu, tu**-icc'ete paccayā honti bhavissatikāle.

When expressing an impending action of future, the "**ṇvu, tu**" affixes are applied in the sense of future. (The affix is already shown in Sutta 527 except distinctive sense of future tense expression)

(1) "Karissan" ti [Karissaṁ+iti] "Karissaṁ-I will do". iti-thinking thus. • kārako-would-be doer. vajati-goes, [wa] kara+ṇvu

(2) "bhuñjissan" ti [bhuñjissaṁ+iti] "bhuñjissaṁ-I will eat" iti • bhottā-would-be eater. vajati. [Kattu-sādhana] [wa] bhuja+tu

६५३, ३०६. भाववाचिम्हि चतुत्थी

653, 306. **Bhāvavācimhi catutthī.**

[Bhāvavācimhi+catutthī. 2 words]

[V] Bhāvavācimhi catutthīvibhatti hoti bhavissatikāle.

The Catutthī vibhatti (dative case) is applied after nouns which signifies "**Bhāva**-action" in the sense of the future. (Each example word is shown by two EDs by means of a future and Bhāva action in its EDs. See two numbered verbs in each EDs)

(1) [1] Pacissate-will cook, [2] pacanaṁ-cooking. vā **pāko**-Cooking. [Here, a bhāva-sādhana mini ED in the sense of future or Bhāva as shown in ED]

• pākāya-in order to cook. vajati-(he) goes. [Here, dative case in the sense of future or Bhāva is applied and changed into an "**āya**" by Sutta 109. This function "**āya**" itself signifies an infinitive]

i.e. He goes with the intention to cook.
[wa] paca+ṇa+sa

(2) [1] Bhuñjissate-will eat, [2] bhojanaṁ-eating. vā **bhogo**-eating. [Here, a bhāva-sādhana mini ED] • bhogāya-in order to eat. vajati. [Here, dative case in the sense of future or Bhāva is applied] **i.e.** He goes with the intention to eat. [wa] bhuja+ṇa+sa

(3) [1] Naccissate-will dance, [2] naccanaṁ-dancing. vā **naccaṁ**. [Here, a bhāva-sādhana mini ED] • naccāya-in order to dance. vajati. **i.e.** He goes with the intention to dance.
[wa] nata+ṇa+sa

Note: The dative case applied through injunction of this Sutta clearly defines the meaning of each word in dative case by showing as **an infinitive**. The result or purpose of such word is a possible intended-action of the future which is about to take place.

६५४, ६४९. कम्मनि णो

654, 649. **Kammani ṇo.** [Kammani+ṇo. 2 words]

[V] Kammani upapade **ṇa**-paccayo hoti bhavissatikāle.

The "**ṇa**" affix is applied in context of a near-by **kamma** word in the sense of future.

(1) Nagaraṁ-city. karissati-will create. • nagarakāro-the would-be city-planner. vajati-goes. **i.e.** "I will create the city", thinking thus, the would-be city-planner goes.
[wa] nagara-saddūpapada-kara+ṇa

(2) sāliṁ-barley. lāvissati-will harvest. • sālilāvo-the would-be barley-harvester. vajati. [wa] sāli-saddūpapada-lū+ṇa

(3) dhaññaṁ-grain. vapissati-will sow. • dhaññavāpo-the would-be grain-planter. vajati. [wa] dhañña-saddūpapada-vapa+ṇa

(4) bhogaṁ-wealth. dadissati-will give. • bhogadāyo-the would-be wealth-sharer. vajati. [wa] bhoga-saddūpapada-dā+ṇa

(5) sindhuṁ-the water of Sindhu river. pivissati-will drink.
• sindhupāyo-the would-be water-drinker. vajati.
[wa] sindhu-saddūpapada-pā+ṇa

६५५, ६५०. सेसे स्सं न्तु मानाना

655, 650. **Sese ssaṁ, ntu, mānā'nā.**

[Sese+ssaṁ, ntu, māna, ānā. 2 words]

[V] **Sesa**-icce'tasmiṁ atthe **ssaṁ, ntu, māna, āna**-icce'te paccayā honti bhavissatikāle kammū'papade.

When expressing as yet unfinished action, the affixes "**ssaṁ, ntu, māna, āna**" are applied in the sense of future tense in the context of a near-by Kamma-word.

(1) Kammaṁ-work. karissati-will do. kammaṁ-work.
• karissaṁ-while doing. [wa] kara+ssaṁ

evaṁ-similarly,

(2) kammaṁ • karonto [wa] kara+ntu

(3) kammaṁ • kurumāno [wa] kara+māna

(4) kammaṁ • karāno-while doing. vajati-(he) goes.
[wa] kara+āna

(1) Bhojanaṁ-food. bhuñjissati-will eat. bhojanaṁ
• bhuñjissaṁ- while eating. [wa] bhuja+ssaṁ

evaṁ

(2) bhojanaṁ • bhuñjanto. [wa] bhuja+ntu

(3) bhojanaṁ • bhuñjamāno. [wa] bhuja+māna

(4) bhojanaṁ • bhuñjāno-while eating. vajati-(he) goes.
[wa] bhuja+āna

(1) Khādanaṁ-dessert. khādissati-will munch. khādanaṁ
• khādissaṁ-while munching, [wa] khāda+ssaṁ

evaṁ

(2) khādanaṁ • khādanto. [wa] khāda+ntu

(3) khādanaṁ • khādamāno [wa] khāda+māna

(4) khādanaṁ • khādāno-while munching. vajati.
[wa] khāda+āna

(1) Maggaṁ-the road. carissati-will go. maggaṁ • carissaṁ-while going. [wa] cara+ssaṁ

evaṁ

(2) maggaṁ • caranto, [wa] cara+ntu
(3) maggaṁ • caramāno, [wa] cara+māna
(4) maggaṁ • carāno vajati. [wa] cara+āna

(1) Bhikkhaṁ-food. bhikkhissati-will beg. bhikkhaṁ
• bhikkhissaṁ-while begging. [wa] bhikkha+ssaṁ

evaṁ

(2) bhikkhaṁ • bhikkhanto, [wa] bhikka+ntu
(3) bhikkhaṁ • bhikkhamāno. [wa] bhikkha+māna
(4) bhikkhaṁ • bhikkhāno-while begging. vajati.
[wa] bhikkha+āna

Note: There are differing views regarding the affixes of Sutta. According to the current version of Kaccāyana text and its examples, there will be four affixes.

(a) In the second opinion of Rūpasiddhi in Sutta 650, it is said "**ssantu**-iti eko'va paccayo daṭṭhabbo". [Trans] It should be regarded **ssantu** as one complete affix, not **ssaṁ** and **ntu** separately.

But Rūpasiddhi accepted the affix "māna and āna" without any different opinion.

(b) *Tha-bye-kan* Sayadaw, one of the most respectable Pāli scholars of Burma, is of the opinion that the actual affixes applicable by this Sutta in all likelihood should be **"ssantu, ssamāna and āna"** affixes. He has strong reasons for having this view based on his wide knowledge of the Sanskrit grammar texts.

(c) In Moggalāna Pāli grammar, Khādikaṇḍa section, there is a Sutta "Te ssapubbā'nāgate, တေ ဿပုဗ္ဗာ·နာဂတေ", with its two examples shown as "ṭhassanto, ṭhassamāno". See the double **"ss"** in the affix-position carefully.

(d) In Kātantra Grammar, Krita chapter, the fourth section, there is a Sutta titled " शन्त्रानौ स्यसंहितौ शेषे च ", with the examples shown as "करिश्यन व्रजति, करिश्यमाणो व्रजति, Karissaṁ vajati, Karissamāno vajati".

In the light of these facts, the affixes applicable by this Sutta are more likely **"ssantu, ssamāna and āna"**. In this case, the examples will have to reflect the affixes such as "**(a)** Karissaṁ, Karissanto, Karissamāno, Karāno, **(b)** Buñjissaṁ, Buñjissanto, Buñjissamāno, Buñjāno" and so forth.

The words in these affixes are sometimes called "future participles" according to their contextual position in a sentence. Except in the case of **āna**-affixed example, it is a common pattern of language to have an **"i"** after the root and a double **"ss"** in the affix or verb-termination in such words of simple structure when denoting the future.
The words in affix "**āna**" are frequently found in the Pāli texts such as "sayāno, anupādiyāno, Jigīsāno, esāno" and so on.

६५६, ६६६. छदादीहि त त्रण

656, 666. **Chadā'dīhi ta, traṇ.** [Chada-ādīhi+ta, traṇ. 2 words]

[V] **Chada, ci, ti, su, nī, vida, pada, tanu, yata, ada, mada, yuja, vatu, mida, mā, pu, kala, vara, ve, pu, gupa, dā-** icce'va'mādīhi dhātūhi **ta, traṇ**-icce'te paccayā honti yathāsambhavaṁ.

The affixes "**ta, tran**" are accordingly applied after the roots "**chada, citi, su, nī, vida, pada, tanu, yata, ada, mada, yuja, vatu, mida, mā, pu, kala, vara, ve, pu, gupa, dā**" etc.

Note: The words affixed with "**tran-**affix" are seldom found in the Pāli texts except the word "Cittraṁ".

(1) Ātapaṁ-the heat. chādetī'ti [chādeti+iti] chādeti-covers. iti • chattaṁ, • chatraṁ-the umbrella which covers the heat. [Kattu-sādhana] [wa] chada+ta [wa] chada+tran

(2) [a] Ārammaṇaṁ-the object. cintetī'ti [cinteti+iti] cinteti-awares. iti • cittaṁ, • citraṁ-the mind which is aware or thinks the object. [Kattu-sādhana]

[b] Cintenti-aware. sampayuttadhammā-concomitant mental states. ethenā'ti [etena+iti] etena-by this mind. vā • cittaṁ, • citraṁ-the mind by which all concurring mental states are aware of the objects. [Karaṇa-sādhana] [wa] citi+ta [wa] citi+tran

(3) [a] Atthe-the meanings. abhissavetī'ti [abhissaveti+iti] abhissaveti-causes to flow, presents. iti • suttaṁ, • sutraṁ-Sutta or grammatical principle (aphorisms) which presents (explains) the meanings.

[b] Atthe sūcetī'ti [sūceti+iti] sūceti-exposes, clarifies. iti vā • suttaṁ, • sutraṁ-Sutta (a discourse) or a grammatical principle which exposes the meaning. [Kattu-sādhana]
[wa] su+ta [wa] su+tran

(4) [a] Satte-beings. netī'ti [neti+iti] neti-leads or guides. iti • nettaṁ, • netraṁ-eye which guides beings. [Kattu-sādhana]

[b] Satte icchitaṭṭhānaṁ-the intended place. nenti etenā'ti [etena+iti] etena-by this eye. iti vā • nettaṁ, • netraṁ-the eye by which living beings are guided to (reach) intended place. [Karaṇa-sādhana] [wa] nī+ta [wa] nī+tran

(5) [a] Pakārena-in various ways. vidatī'ti [vidati+iti] vidati-knows. • pavittaṁ, • pavitraṁ-various knowledge.
[wa] pa√vida+ta [wa] pa√vida+tran

[b] Vividhena-by various. ākārena-manner. maṅgaṁ pāpaṁ-bad things. punāti-cleanses. sodhetī'ti [sodheti+iti] sodheti-clears. • pavittaṁ, • pavitraṁ (पवित्रं) -the pure, the sacred and the sinless.

Note: According to this ED, the root of this word is not "vida", but "**pu**-to cleanse" [wa] pu+ta [wa] pu+tran

[c] Sucibhāvaṁ-to the state of purity. vā pāpuṇātī'ti [pāpuṇāti+iti] pāpuṇāti-reaches. iti • pavittaṁ, • pavitraṁ-the pure and sacred which reaches to the state of purity. [Kattu-sādhana] [wa] pa√vida+ta [wa] pa√vida+tran

(6) [a] Padati-goes. pāpuṇātī'ti pāpuṇāti-reaches. • patto, • patro- pedestrian. [Kattu-sādhana] [wa] pada+ta.
[wa] pada+tran

[b] Āhārā-foods. patanti-fall (when put in). ettha-here. bhājane'ti [bhājane+iti] bhājane-in the bowl. iti • pattaṁ, • patraṁ-the bowl where foods fall. [Adhikaraṇa-sādhana].
[wa] pata+ta [wa] pata+tran

Note: According to this ED, the root is "**pata**-to fall, not **pada**".

[c] Padati pavattatī'ti [pavattati+iti] pavattati-(food) arises. Vā • pattaṁ, • patraṁ-bowl where food is. [Kattu-sādhana]
[wa] pada+ta [wa] pada+tran

(7) [a] Tanoti-extends. vitthāretī'ti [vitthāreti+iti] vitthāreti-spreads. iti • tantaṁ, • tantraṁ-thread on the loom which extends or spreads. [Kattu-sādhana]

[b] tanitabbaṁ vitthāretabban'ti [vitthāretabbaṁ+iti] vitthāretabbaṁ-should spread. iti vā • tantaṁ, • tantraṁ-thread on the loom which should be spread. [Kamma-sādhana]

[wa] tanu+ta [wa] tanu+tran

(8) [a] Yatatī'ti [Yatati+iti] Yatati-exerts effort. • yattaṁ, • yatraṁ-effort. [Kattu-sādhana]

[b] Yatati-exerts. vīriyaṁ karoti-makes effort. etenā'ti [etena+iti] etena-by this mental energy. vā • yattaṁ, • yatraṁ-effort. [Karaṇa-sādhana]

[c] Yatanaṁ-attempting. vā • yattaṁ, • yatraṁ-effort. [Bhāva-sādhana] [wa] yata+ta [wa] yata+tran

(9) Sukhadukkhaṁ adati bhakkhatī'ti • attā, • atrā-body. [Re Sutta 627] [Kattu-sādhana] [wa] ada+ta [wa] ada+tran

(10) Madatī'ti [madati+iti] madati-inebriates.iti • mattaṁ, • matraṁ-intoxicated. [Kattu-sādhana] [wa] mada+ta [wa] mada+tran

(11) Vatthuṁ-things. yujjanti-tied. etenā'ti [etena+iti] etena-by this rope. • yottaṁ, • yotraṁ-rope by which things are tied up. [Karaṇa-sādhana] [wa] yuja+ta [wa] yuja+tran

(12) Vattatī'ti [Vattati+iti] Vattati-(It goes) rolling. iti • vattaṁ, • vatraṁ-a ball, or any spherical object which rolls. [Kattu-sādhana] [wa] vatu+ta [wa] vatu+tran

(13) [a] Midati-moistens. sinehaṁ-love. karotī'ti[karoti+iti] karoti-does. **i.e.** It moistens (softens the mind) and creates love. iti • mittaṁ. • Mitraṁ-friendly relationship which moistens (softens) (**i.e.** goodwill). [Kattu-sādhana]

[b] Midati sinehati-loves. etāyā'ti [etāya+iti] etāya-by this spirit. iti • mettā, • metrā-mettā by which one loves (others. **i.e.** the spirit of love). [Karaṇa-sādhana]

[wa] mida+ta [wa] mida+tran

(14) [a] Pari samantato-from all around. sabbā'kārena-by all manner. minanti-measure. etāyā'ti [etāya+iti] etāya-by this measurement. iti • mattā, • matrā-measuring yardstick or

ruler by which all-around dimensions of things are measured. [Karaṇa-sādhana]

[b] Mānanaṁ-act of measuring. vā • mattaṁ, • matraṁ-measuring. [wa] mā+ta [wa] mā+tran

(15) Attano-of oneself. kulaṁ-family race. punāti-cleanses. sodhetī'ti [sodheti+iti] sodheti-clears. • putto, • putro-son, who cleanses and clears family lineage. [Kattu-sādhana]
[wa] pu+ta [wa] pu+tran

(16) Kalitabbaṁ saṅkhyātabban'ti [Re Sutta 632] • kalattaṁ, • kalatraṁ (कलत्रं) -wife, whom one should count (as family). [Kamma-sādhana] [wa] kala+ta [wa] kala+tran

(17) Saṁ suṭṭhu-well. vāreti-prevents. etenā'ti [etena+iti] etena-by this. iti • varattaṁ, • varatraṁ-leather-strap by which it prevents dress from slipping. [Karaṇa-sādhana]
[wa] vara+ta [wa] vara+tran

(18) Vepati kampatī'ti [kampati+iti] kampati-shakes. • vettaṁ, • vetraṁ-rattan vine which is shaken by winds etc. [Kattu-sādhana] [wa] vepu+ta [wa] vepu+tran

(19) Gopitabbaṁ-should be protected. rakkhitabban'ti [rakkhitabbaṁ+iti] rakkhitabbaṁ-should be guarded. iti • guttaṁ. • Gutraṁ, • gottaṁ, • gotraṁ-family race which should be protected. [Kamma-sādhana] [wa] gupa+ta [wa] gupa+tran

(20) Dāti avakhaṇḍati-cuts. etenā'ti [etena+iti] etena-by this sickle. iti • dāttaṁ, • dātraṁ-sickle by which grain-crops are cut (when harvesting). [Karaṇa-sādhana]
[wa] dā+ta [wa] dā+tran

icce'va'mādi.

६५७, ६६७. वदादीहि णित्तो गणे

657, 667. **Vadā'dīhi ṇitto gaṇe.**

[Vada-ādīhi+ṇitto+gaṇe. 3 words]

[V] **Vada, cara, vara**-icce'va'mā'dīhi dhātūhi **ṇitta**-paccayo hoti **gaṇa**'tthe.

The affix "**ṇitta**" is applied after the roots "**vada, cara, vara**" etc. in expressing collective grouping. [**gaṇa**-group]

(1) Vāditānaṁ-of musical instrument players. gaṇo-group.
• vādittaṁ- the group of instrument players, Orchestra.
[wa] vada+ṇitta

Evaṁ

(2) • cārittaṁ-group of ethical precepts or rules. Moral codes.
[wa] cara+ṇitta

(3) • vārittaṁ-group of legal injunctions, Legal codes.
[wa] vara+ṇitta

icce'va'mādi.

६५८, ६६८. मिदादीहि त्ति तियो

658, 668. **Midā'dīhi tti, tiyo.** [Mida-ādīhi+tti, tiyo. 2 words]

[V] **Mida, pada, ranja, tanu, dhā**-icce'va'mādīhi dhātūhi **tti, ti**-icce'te paccayā honti.

The affixes "**tti, ti**" are applied after the roots "**mida, pada, ranja, tanu, dhā**" etc.

(1) Midati sinehatī'ti [Re Sutta 656] • metti-love. [Kattu-sādhana]
[wa] mida+tti

(2) padati gacchatī'ti [gacchati+iti] gacchati-goes. • patti-pedestrian, infantry soldier etc. which goes on foot. [Kattu-sādhana]
[wa] pada+tti

(3) ranjati-craves. etthā'ti [ettha+iti] ettha-at this night time. iti
• ratti-The night when craving arises in beings. [Adhikaraṇa-sādhana]
[wa] ranja+tti

(4) [a] tanoti vitthāretī'ti [vitthāreti+iti] [Re Sutta 656] • tanti-lineage.
[b] attano-of oneself. kulaṁ-family. tanoti-extends. vitthāretī'ti vā • tanti-lineage which extends one's family line. [Both Kattu-sādhana] [wa] tanu+ti

(5) [a] paresaṁ-of other. itthīnaṁ-women. puttaṁ-child. dhāretī'ti [dhāreti+iti] dhāreti-carries. iti • dhāti-foster-mother who carries to raise other woman's child.
[b] khīraṁ-milk. dhāretī'ti vā • dhāti-foster-mother who carries (**i.e.** suckles) milk (for other's child).

[c] attano-of itself. sabhāvaṁ-nursing nature. dhāretī'ti vā
• dhāti-foster-mother who carries one's nursing nature.
[All three Kattu-sādhana] [wa] dhā+ti

icc'e'va'mādi.

६५९, ६६९. उसुरन्जदंसानं दंसस्स दड्ढो ढठा च

659, 669. **Usu, ranja, daṁsānaṁ daṁsassa daḍḍho ḍha, ṭhā ca.**

[Usu, ranja, daṁsānaṁ+daṁsassa+daḍḍho+ḍha, ṭhā+ca. 5 words]

[V] **Usu, ranja, daṁsa**-icce'tesaṁ dhātūnaṁ **daṁsa**ssa **daḍḍhā'**deso hoti. **ḍha, ṭha**-paccayā ca honti.

The affixes "**ḍha, ṭha**" are applied after the roots "**usu, ranja, daṁsa**". Besides, the word "**daṁsa**" changes into "**daḍḍha**". [Two functions]

(1) Usīyate-heating • uḍḍho-heat or heated. [Bhāva-sādhana] [wa] usu+ḍha

(2) ranjanti-clings (as with desire). etthā'ti [ettha+iti] ettha-Here in this land. • raṭṭhaṁ-the country or kingdom (where kings or rulers cling to as with fervent attachment to maintain authority & control). [Adhikaraṇa-sādhana] [wa] ranja+ṭha

(3) daṁsīyate'ti [daṁsīyate+iti] daṁsīyate-(is) bitten. iti • daḍḍho- bitten (as by snake etc.). [Kamma-sādhana] [wa] daṁsa+kvi

६६०, ६७०. सूवुसान मूवुसान मतो थो च

660, 670. **Sū, vu, sāna'mū, vu'sāna'mato tho ca.**

[Sū, vu, asānaṁ+ū, u, asānaṁ+ato+tho+ca. 5 words]

[V] **Sū, vu, asa**-icce'tesaṁ dhātūnaṁ **ū, u, asā**naṁ **atā**'deso hoti, **tha**paccayo ca.

The "**ū, u, asa**" of the roots "**sū, vu, asa**" changes into "**ata**". Besides, the affix "**tha**" is also applied. [Two functions]

(1) Savati hiṁsati-hurts. etenā'ti [etena+iti] etena-by this weapon.
• satthaṁ-weapon by which one is hurt. [Karaṇa-sādhana]
[wa] sū+tha

(2) hiro'ttappaṁ-the modesty. saṁvarati-protects. etenā'ti. etena-by this dress. • vatthaṁ-cloth by means of which one's modesty is protected. [Karaṇa-sādhana] [wa] vu+tha

(3) saddā'nurūpaṁ-in accordance with the word. asati bhavatī'ti bhavati-it is. iti • attho-the meaning (which happens or which has to be interpreted in accordance with the structural pattern of the original word). [Kattu-sādhana] [wa] asa+tha

६६१, ६७१. रन्जुदादीहि धदिद्दकिरा क्वचि जदलोपो च

661, 671. **Ranju'dā'dīhi dha, di'dda, kirā kvaci ja, da, lopo ca.**

[Ranja, uda-ādīhi+dha, da, idda, ka, irā+kvaci+ja, da, lopo+ca. 5 words]

[V] **Ranja, uda, idi, cadi, madi, khuda, chidi, rudi, dala, susa, suca, vaca, vaja**-icce'va'mādīhi dhātūhi **dha, da, idda, ka, ira**-icce'te paccayā honti. kvaci **ja, da,** lopo ca. Puna nippajjante.

The affixes "**dha, da, idda, ka, ira**" are applied after the roots "**ranja, uda, idi, cadi, madi, khuda, chidi, rudi, dala, susa, suca, vaca, vaja,**" etc. At some instances of words, the component words "**ja, da**" of some roots are elided. [Two Functions]

Note:(1) After the root **ranja="dha-**affix" is applied.
(2) After **uda, idi, cadi, madi, khuda, chidi, rudi=da**-affix
(3) **dala=idda-**affix**.**
(4) **susa, suca, vaca=ka-**affix.
(5) **vaja=ira-**affix.

(1) [a] Rañjitabban'ti [Rañjitabbanṁ+iti] Rañjitabbaṁ-to get colored or get stuck to. iti • randhaṁ-hole.
[b] ranjayitthā'ti [ranjayittha+iti] ranjayittha-painted, stuck. iti vā • randhaṁ-hole. [Both Kamma-sādhana. In this example, the component consonant "**j**" is elided]
[wa] ranja+dha

Note: The word "Randha" has various meanings: (a) an opening of a hole (b) A fault, shortcoming (as a figurative expression) (c) the cooked food.

[Reference texts] (a-b) R*andhaṁ na passanti* (Theragāthā Pāli, Mahākappinathera Gāthā verse No.547)
(c) R*andhaṁ rājā aloṇakaṁ* (Mūgapakkha Jātaka, Jātaka Pāli, Verse No.85)

(2) attani-in oneself. sannissitānaṁ-to those dependent on. macchamakārānaṁ-fish, shark and sea animals. pīti, somanassaṁ-joy and happiness. undati-increases. pasavati-multplies. janetī'ti [janeti+iti] janeti-causes. iti • samuddo-ocean which causes joy and happiness to all sea-creatures which are dependent on it. [Kattu-sādhana] [wa] saṁ√uda+da

(3) [a] indati paramī'ssariyaṁ-highest authority. karotī'ti [karoti+iti] karoti-makes. • indo-the celestial king named "Indra" who makes (**i.e.** asserts) the highest authority on his underlings.

[b] indattaṁ adhipatibhāvaṁ-the lordship. karotī'ti vā • indo-the celestial king named "Indra" who makes the lordship on other celestial beings. [Both Kattu-sādhana] [wa] idi+da

(4) canditabbo icchitabbo'ti [icchitabbo+iti] icchitabbo-should be wished. iti • cando-moon wished (by beings to bring light at night time). [Kamma-sādhana] [wa] cadi+da

(5) [a] mandati hāsetī'ti [hāseti+iti] hāseti-should be amused. iti • mando-the young one which should be amused or keep entertained. [Kattu-sādhana]

[b] maditabbo hāsetabbo'ti [hāsetabbo+iti] hāsetabbo-should be amused. iti vā • mando-the young one. [Kamma-sādhana] [wa] madi+da

(6) khudati pipāsetī'ti [pipāseti+iti] pipāseti-causes thirst. iti • khuddo-thirst, thirsty. [Kattu-sādhana] [wa] khuda+da

(7) chinditabbo'ti [chinditabbo+iti] chinditabbo-should cut. iti • chiddo-the hole which should be cut. [Kamma-sādhana] [wa] chidi+da

(8) rudati hiṁsatī'ti [hiṁsati+iti] hiṁsati-hurts. iti • ruddo-rude person who hurts (others). [Kattu-sādhana] [wa] rudi+da

(9) dalati duggatabhāvaṁ-to the state of being poor. gacchatī'ti [gacchati+iti] gacchati-gets. • daliddo-destitute person who reaches to the state of being poor. [Kattu-sādhana]
[wa] dala+idda

(10) sussatī'ti [sussati+iti] sussati-(it) dries. iti • sukkaṁ-any dried thing or dry (adj). [Kattu-sādhana] [wa] susa+ka

(11) sucatī'ti [sucati+iti] sucati-worries. iti • soko-sadness, worry. [Kattu-sādhana] [wa] suca+ka

(12) vacitabban'ti [vacitabbaṁ+iti] vacitabbaṁ-should utter. iti • vakkaṁ-speech which should be uttered. [Kamma-sādhana]
[wa] vaca+ka

(13) appaṭihato-unobstructed. hutvā-being. vajati-goes. gacchatī'ti [gacchati+iti] gacchati-goes. • vajiraṁ-thunderbolt, which goes being unobstructed. It also means "diamond". [Kattu-sādhana] [wa] vaja+ira

icc'eva'mādi.

६६२, ६७२. पटितो हिस्स हेरण हीरण

662, 672. **Paṭito hissa heraṇ, hīraṇ.**

[Paṭito+hissa+heraṇ, hīraṇ. 3 words]

[V] **Paṭi**-icce'tasmā **hi**ssa dhātussa **heraṇ, hīraṇ**-ādesā honti.

The root word "**hi**" prefixed with "**paṭi**" changes into "**heraṇ, hīraṇ**".

Paṭipakkhe-the opponents. madditvā-having crushed. gacchati pavattatī'ti [pavattati+iti] pavattati-happens. iti • pāṭiheraṁ, • pāṭihīraṁ-the act of miracle which happens (as if to dispel doubt of the opponent skeptics). [Kattu-sādhana] [wa] pati√hi+kvi
[wa] pati√hi+kvi

६६३, ६७३. कढयादीहि को

663, 673. **Kaḍyā'dīhi ko.** [Kaḍi-ādīhi+ko. 2 words]

[V] **Kaḍi, ghaḍi, vaḍi, karaḍi, maḍi, saḍi, kuṭhi, bhaḍi, paḍi, daḍi, raḍi, taḍi, isiḍi, caḍi, gaḍi, aḍi, laḍi, meḍi, eraḍi, khaḍi**-icce'va'mādīhi dhātūhi **ka**-paccayo hoti.
Saha paccayena ca nippajjante yathāsambhavaṁ.

An affix "**ka**" is applied after the roots "**Kaḍi, ghaḍi, vaḍi, karaḍi, maḍi, saḍi, kuṭhi, bhaḍi, paḍi, daḍi, raḍi, taḍi, isiḍi, caḍi, gaḍi, aḍi, laḍi, meḍi, eraḍi, khaḍi**" etc.
[This "ka" affix is elided later on]

(1) Kaṇḍitabbo chinditabbo'ti [chinditabbo+iti] chinditabbo-should be cut. iti • kaṇḍo-section, chapter which should keep cut and separated. [Kamma-sādhana] [wa] kaḍi+ka

(2) ghaṇḍitabbo ghaṭetabbo'ti [ghaṭetabbo+iti] ghaṭetabbo-should be struck. iti • ghaṇḍo-bell. [Kamma-sādhana] [wa] ghaḍi+ka

(3) vaṇḍanti-gather. etthā'ti [ettha+iti] ettha-here. • vaṇḍo-stem where all fruits and flowers gather(grow). [Adhikaraṇa-sādhana] [wa] vaḍi+ka

(4) karaṇḍitabbo bhājetabbo'ti [bhājetabbo+iti] bhājetabbo-should be put in portions. iti • karaṇḍo-small cups and mini food-containers. [Kamma-sādhana] [wa] karaḍi+ka

(5) maṇḍīyate vibhūsīyate-(is) adorned. etenā'ti [etena+iti] etena-by this. • maṇḍo-beauty products. [Karaṇa-sādhana] [wa] maḍi+ka

(6) saṇḍanti gumbanti-gather together. etthā'ti [ettha+iti] ettha-here. iti • saṇḍo-group, multitude. [Adhikaraṇa-sādhana] [wa] saḍi+ka

(7) aṅgamaṅgāni-bodily parts. kuṇṭhati chindatī'ti [chindati+iti] chindati-cuts. iti • kuṭṭhaṁ-leprosy which cuts bodily parts. [Kattu-sādhana] [wa] kuṭhi+ka

(8) bhaṇḍitabban'ti [bhaṇḍitabbaṁ+iti] bhaṇḍitabbaṁ-should argue or fight for. iti • bhaṇḍaṁ-possession for which people argue or fight. [Kamma-sādhana] [wa] bhaḍi+ka

(9) paṇḍati-goes. liṅgavekallabhāvaṁ-to the state of having deviant gender (sexual nature). gacchatī'ti [gacchati+iti] gacchati- goes or happens. iti • paṇḍako-gay who goes to the state of having deviant gender (sexual nature). [Kattu-sādhana] [wa] paḍi+ka

(10) Daṇḍati-punishes (the offender). āṇaṁ-the executive order. karoti- makes. etenā'ti [etena+iti] etena-by this. iti • daṇḍo-punishment or fine meted out (by authorities as a way of punishing and imposing law and order on the offenders & wrong-doers). [Karaṇa-sādhana] [wa] daḍi+ka

(11) raṇḍati hiṁsatī'ti [hiṁsati+iti] hiṁsati-hurts (himself and others). iti • raṇḍo-drunkard, an alcoholic who hurts (himself and others). [Kattu-sādhana] [wa] raḍi+ka

(12) visesena-specially. taṇḍati cāleti-shakens. paresaṁ-other. viññūnaṁ-scholars. hadayaṁ-heart. kampetī'ti [kampeti+iti] kampeti-shakens. iti • vitaṇḍo-opposite views which agitates the heart of scholars. [Kattu-sādhana] [wa] vi-√taḍi+ka

(13) isiṇḍati-dominates. paresaṁ-the opposing party. maddatī'ti [maddati+iti] maddati-overwhelms. iti • isiṇḍo-A king named "isiṇḍa". [Kattu-sādhana] [wa] isiḍi+ka

(14) caṇḍati caṇḍikkabhāvaṁ-to the state of being cruel. karotī'ti [karoti+iti] karoti-creates. • caṇḍo-cruelty which by itself creates a state of being cruel. [Kattu-sādhana] [wa] caḍi+ka

(15) gaṇḍati sannicayati-(it) collects. samūhaṁ-collection. karoti- makes. etthā'ti [ettha+iti] ettha-in this side of the mouth. iti • gaṇḍo-each lateral side of the mouth, (where some people used to keep food for chewing while they eat). [Adhikaraṇa-sādhana] [wa] gaḍi+ka

(16) aṇḍīyati-laid. nibbattīyatī'ti [nibbattīyati+iti] nibbattīyati-(is) caused. iti • aṇḍo-The egg laid and caused (produced) by hen. [Kamma-sādhana] [wa] aḍi+ka

(17) laṇḍitabbo jigucchitabbo'ti [jigucchitabbo+iti] jigucchitabbo-to be detested. iti • laṇḍo-feces, and animal droppings. [Kamma-sādhana] [wa] laḍi+ka

(18) meṇḍati-goes. kuṭilabhāvaṁ-to the state of being crooked. gacchatī'ti [gacchati+iti] gacchati-goes. • meṇḍo-the goat

which goes (moves) in a non-straight way. [This ED is a bit ambiguous] [Kattu-sādhana] [wa] meḍi+ka

(19) eraṇḍati-fights. rogaṁ-disease. hiṁsatī'ti [hiṁsati+iti] hiṁsati-fights. iti • eraṇḍo-caster oil plant, also called jatropa [Ricinus Communis] which fights disease (as it contains some curative, medicinal properties). [Kattu-sādhana] [wa] eraḍi+ka

(20) khaṇḍitabbo chinditabbo'ti [chinditabbo+iti] chinditabbo-should be cut. iti • khaṇḍo-section or portion of jaggery (molasses). [Kamma-sādhana] [wa] khaḍi+ka

icce'va'mādi.

६६४, ६७४. खादामगमानं खन्धन्धगन्धा

664, 674. **Khādā'ma,gamānaṁ khandhan'dha-gandhā.**

[Khāda, ama, gamānaṁ+khandha, andha, gandhā. 2 words]

[V] **Khāda, ama, gamu**-icce'tesaṁ dhātūnaṁ **khandha, andha, gandhā**'desā honti, **ka**-paccayo ca hoti.

The roots "**khāda, ama, gamu**" change into "**khandha, andha, gandha**" respectively while an affix "**ka**" is also applied at the end of some words. [Two functions]

(1) Jātijarāmaraṇā'dīhi-by birth, old-age and death etc. saṁsāradukkhehi-sufferings of Saṁsarā. khāditabbo'ti [khāditabbo+iti] khāditabbo-consumed. iti • khandho-body or aggregates which is consumed (devoured) by sufferings of Saṁsarā such as birth, old-age and death etc. [Kamma-sādhana] [wa] khāda+kvi

(2) [a] amati aṅga'maṅgassa-of (certain) bodily part. rujjanabhāvaṁ-to the state of being afflicted. gacchatī'ti [gacchati+iti] gacchati-goes. iti • andho-blindness in which a certain bodily part called "eye" goes to the state of being afflicted and inapplicable. [Kattu-sādhana]

[b] cakkhunā-by way of the eye. amati rujjatī'ti [rujjati+iti] rujjati-is afflicted. iti vā-another method of ED. • andho-blindness by which the eye is afflicted by it. [Kattu-sādhana] [wa] ama+kvi

(3) taṁ-to that. taṁ-to that. ṭhānaṁ-place, **i.e.** here and there. vātena-by means of wind. gacchatī'ti. gacchati-goes. iti • gandho-smell or scent which travels to here and there by means of wind. [Kattu-sādhana] [wa] gamu+kvi

Evaṁ-in same manner, are the examples where "**ka**" affix is applied after the word.

(1) • khandhako-five aggregates, the body. [wa] khāda+ka

(2) • andhako-blindness, the blind. [wa] ama+ka

(3) • gandhako-the smell or scent. [wa] gamu+ka

६६५, ६७५. पटादीह्यलं

665, 675. **Paṭā'dīhya'laṁ.** [Paṭa-ādīhi+alaṁ. 2 words]

[V] **Paṭa, kala, kusa, kada, bhaganda, mekha, vakka, takka, palla, sadda, mūla, bila, vida, caḍi, pañca, vā, vasa, paci, maca, musa, gotthu, puthu, bahu, maṅga, baha, kamba, samba, agga-**icceva'mā'dīhi dhātūhi pāṭipadikehi ca uttarapadesu **ala-**paccayo hoti, pacchā puna nippajjante.

An affix "**ala**" is applied after roots "**Paṭa, kala, kusa, kada, bhaganda, mekha, vakka, takka, palla, sadda, mūla, bila, vida, caḍi, pañca, vā, vasa, paci, maca, musa, gotthu, puthu, bahu, maṅga, baha, kamba, samba, agga** and also after some **pāṭipadika** words.

(1) Paṭe-in being useful. alan'ti [alaṁ+iti] alaṁ-is fit or suitable. iti • paṭalaṁ-layer or slab which is fit to be used. [wa] paṭa+ala

(2) kale-in being muddy. alan'ti [alaṁ+iti] alaṁ-is fit or suitable. iti • kalalaṁ-mud. [wa] kala+ala

(3) [a] pāpake-the evil. akusale dhamme-unwholesome mental states. kusati chindatī'ti [chindati+iti] chindati-cuts. iti • kusalaṁ-merit or wholesome mental state which cuts evil and unwholesome mental states. [Kattu-sādhana]

[b] kusabhūte-those vile things termed Kusa (कुश).

yathāsabhāvadhamme-in the naturally bad things. alan'ti vā. alaṁ-is able to remove. • kusalaṁ-able in removing naturally vile things called Kusa.

[c] kuse uddissa-being specifically focused. dāne-in giving alms. alan'ti vā • kusalaṁ-wholesome meritorious goodwill by which one can give alms.

[d] kuse sañcaye dhammasamudāye-group of unwholesome mental states. alan'ti vā • kusalaṁ-the wholesome things which can overwhelm collective group of unwholesome mental states. [wa] kusa+ala

(4) kadde madde-in being intoxicated. alan'ti • kadalaṁ-banana (Refers to Bananas which are being fermented). [wa] kada+ala

(5) [a] bhagande secane-in dripping of bodily fluid. alan'ti • bhagandalaṁ-fistula disease.

[b] bhagande muttakarīsaharaṇe-in discharging of stool and urine. alan'ti vā • bhagandalaṁ-Fistula which makes discharge of bodily waste quite a problem. [wa] bhaganda+ala

(6) mekhe kaṭivicitte-in adorning the waist. alan'ti • mekhalaṁ-belt which adorns the waist (in a practical sense), belt. [wa] mekha+ala

(7) vakke rukkhatace-in being a tree-bark. alan'ti • vakkalaṁ-tree-bark, fibrous matter of the plant. [wa] vakka+ala

(8) takke rukkhasilese-in being tree sap, alan'ti • takkalaṁ-tree sap. [wa] takka+ala

(9) palle ninnaṭṭhāne-in low sloping areas. alan'ti • pallalaṁ-muddy clay. [wa] phalla+ala

(10) sadde harite-in being green. alan'ti • saddalaṁ-greenery. [wa] sadda+ala

(11) mūle patiṭṭhāne-in being established. alan'ti • mulālaṁ-the stem of lotus which makes it established. [wa] mula+ala

(12) biḷe nissaye-in being reliable (as a resource). alan'ti • bilālaṁ-sea-salt. [wa] bila+ala

(13) vide vijjamāne-in being present. alan'ti vidalaṁ-visible object. [wa] vida+ala

(14) caṇḍe-in hard and dirty works. alan'ti • caṇḍālo-manual laborer, or a person of lowest caste in ancient India. [wa] caḍi+ala

(15) pañcannaṁ-of the five. rājūnaṁ-kings. alan'ti • pañcālo-the region so-named which is so wide that it fits to be ruled by five

separate kings. [wa] pañca+ala

(16) vā gatigandhanesu-in being mobile and binding. alan'ti
• vālaṁ-tail. [wa] vā+ala

(17) vā padagamane-in being able to move on foot. alan'ti vā
• vāḷo-wild animal. [wa] vā+ala

Note: Example 16,17 are two different words with different "l".

(18) vase acchādane-in hiding, covering up one's faults. alan'ti
• vasalo-a person of mean conduct and mentality who used to cover up one's own faults. [wa] vasa+ala

(19) pace vitthāre-in amplifying things to be this and that. alan'ti
• pacalo-fickle person who used to make a fuss. [wa] paci+ala

(20) mace corakamme-in act of stealing. alan'ti • macalo-thief. [wa] maca+ala

(21) muse theyye-in stealing, muse pāṇacāge-in being fatal when struck with. vā alan'ti • musalo-pestle or a club. [wa] musa+ala

(22) gotte vaṁse siṅgālajātiyaṁ-in being included in the species as a fox. alan'ti • gotthulo-fox or hyena. [wa] gotthu+ala

(23) puthumhi vitthāre-in being broad. alan'ti • puthulo-broad, huge (adj). [wa] puthu+ala

(24) [a] bahumhi-much. saṅkhyāne-in counting. alan'ti
• bahulo-many (adj).

[b] bahumhi vuddhimhi-in being numerous. alan'ti vā
• bahulo-numerous, many (adj). [wa] bahu+ala

(25) maṅgamhi gamane-in going auspicious. alan'ti
• maṅgalaṁ-blessing. [wa] maṅga+ala

(26) bahumhi vuddhimhi-in being grown. alan'ti • bahalaṁ-solidly grown, thick (adj). [wa] baha+ala

(27) kambamhi sañcalane-in being portable, alan'ti
• kambalaṁ-carpet or woolen coat. [wa] kamba+ala

(28) Sambamhi maṇḍane-in adorning and providing. alan'ti
• sambalaṁ-provisions for the journey, viaticum (शंबलं). [wa] samba+ala

(29) agge gatikoṭille-in going roundabout. alan'ti • aggaḷaṁ-door-latch (अर्गलः). [wa] agga+ala

Icce'va'mādayo aññe'pi saddā bhavanti.
And other example words in similar affix too are applicable.

६६६, ६७६. पुथस्स पुथु पथा मो वा

666, 676. **Puthassa puthu, pathā'mo vā.**

[Puthassa+puthu, pathā+amo+vā. 4 words]

[V] **Putha**-icce'tassa pāṭipadikassa **puthu, pathā**'desā honti, kvaci **ama**-paccayo hoti.

The pāṭipadika word "**putha**" changes into "**puthu, patha**". In some words, an affix "**ama**" is applied.

(1) Puthu-vast. hutvā-having being. jātan'ti [jātaṁ+iti] jātaṁ-occurred. iti • puthavī-earth which occurred (as a vast expanse of land mass). [wa] putha+kvi

(2) pathame-in the beginning. jāto-happens. • pathamo-the first. [wa] putha+ama
• pathavī-earth. • paṭhamo-first. vā. [wa is the same as the first pair of example]

(3) puthu-various. kilese-defilements. janetī'ti [janeti+iti] janeti-causes. iti • puthujjano-An unenlightened commoner, worldling who still causes defilements (in his mind). [Kattu-sādhana]
[wa] puthu-saddūpapada-jana+kvi (Putha is also possible word)

(4) puthu hutvā jātan'ti • pathavī, • paṭhavī-earth. (Different in terms of **tha** & **ṭha**) vā. [wa] puthu+kvi

६६७, ६७७. सस्वादीहि तु दवो

667, 677. **Sasvā'dīhi tu, davo.** [Sasu-ādīhi+tu, duvo. 2 words]

[V] **Sasu, dada, ada, mada**-icce'va'mādīhi dhātūhi **tu, du**-icce'te paccayā honti.

The affixes "**tu, du**" are applied after the roots "**sasu, dada, ada, mada**" etc.

(1) Aññe-other. satte-beings. sasati hiṁsatī'ti [hiṁsati+iti] hiṁsati-hurts. iti • sattu-enemy who harms others. [Kattu-sādhana] [wa] sasu+tu

(2) dukkhaṁ-trouble. dadātī'ti [dadāti+iti] dadāti-gives. iti
• daddu- the itch which gives trouble. [Kattu-sādhana]
[wa] dada+du

(3) [a] dukkhena-with pain. adati bhakkhati-eats. etthā'ti ettha-here. • addu-prison where one is consumed by pain. [Adhikaraṇa-sādhana]

[b] dukkhaṁ-suffering. adati anubhavati-undergoes. jano-people. etenā'ti. etena-by this. iti vā • addu-prison by which people undergo suffering. [Karaṇa-sādhana]

[c] dukkhaṁ-of trouble. bhājanaṁ ādhāraṁ-as place of origin. bhāvatī'ti. bhavati-is. vā • addu-prison which is like a place of the origin of troubles. [Kattu-sādhana]
[wa] ada+du

(4) [a] madati-inebriates. ummattaṁ-a state of being mad. karotī'ti. karoti-creates. iti • maddu-narcotics which can intoxicate or create a state of being crazy (to the user). [Kattu-sādhana]

[b]madati maddabhāvaṁ-a state of overwhelming. karotī'ti vā • maddu-narcotics which overwhelms (the reasoning capacity and the sane mind of) the user. [Kattu-sādhana]
[wa] mada+du

६६८, ६७८. च्यादीहि ईवरो

668, 678. **Cyā'dīhi īvaro.** [Ci-ādīhi+īvaro. 2 words]

[V] **Ci, pā, dhā**-icce'va'mādīhi dhātūhi **īvara**-paccayo hoti.

An affix "**īvara**" is applied after the roots "**ci, pā, dhā**" etc.

(1) Cīyatī'ti [Cīyati+iti] Cīyati-(is) sewn or stitched. iti
• cīvaraṁ-the robe which is stitched by tailor. [Kamma-sādhana]
[wa] ci+īvara

(2) [a]pivatī'ti [pivati+iti] pivati-drinks. iti • pīvaro (पीवर) fat or corpulent person who becomes fat by drinking or eating much. [Kattu-sādhana] [wa] pā+īvara

[b]pātabbaṁ rakkhitabban'ti [rakkhitabbaṁ+iti] rakkhitabbaṁ-should be protected. iti vā • pīvaraṁ-the fat person whom should be protected from falling down etc.

[Kamma-sādhana] [wa] pā+īvara

(3) Dhāreti-carries. dhāretvā-having carried (fishing net). jīvitaṁ-living. kappetī'ti [kappeti+iti] kappeti-makes. • dhīvaro, • dhīvaraṁ-(धीवर) fisher-man who carries fishing net, who makes a living having carried it. [Kattu-sādhana] [wa] dhā+īvara

६६९, ६७९. मुनादीहि चि

669, 679. **Munā'dīhi ci'.** [Muna-ādīhi+ca+i. 3 words]

[V] **Muna, yata, agga, pata, kava, suca, ruca, mahāla, bhaddāla, mana**-icce'va'mādīhi dhātūhi, pāṭipadikehi ca **i**-paccayo hoti.

An affix "**i**" is applied after the roots "**muna, yata, agga, pata, kava, suca, ruca, mahāla, bhaddāla, mana** and also after some pāṭipadika words.

(1) Atthā'natthaṁ-what is beneficial and not beneficial. munāti-knows, ñeyyadhammaṁ-things that should be known. lakkhaṇā'divasena-by understanding the characteristics etc. vā-also. jānātī'ti [jānāti+iti] jānāti-knows. iti • muni-sage who knows what is beneficial and not beneficial, the one who also knows things that should be known by understanding the characteristics etc. [Kattu-sādhana] [wa] muna+i

(2) yatati-exerts. vīriyaṁ-effort. karotī'ti karoti-makes. • yati-an ascetic who makes effort. [Kattu-sādhana] [wa] yata+i

(3) aggati kuṭilabhāvaṁ-to the state of being twisted in motion. gacchatī'ti [gacchati+iti] gacchati-goes. • aggi-fire which goes in zigzag course (such as the flames and smoke in its motion). [Kattu-sādhana] [wa] agga+i

(4) patati seṭṭho-dominant. hutvā-having. purato-at front. gacchatī'ti • pati-husband who goes at the front by being dominant in the position (in the family & households in the ancient patriarchal societies). [Kattu-sādhana] [wa] pata+i

(5) [a] kavyaṁ-poem and poetic expression. bandhatī'ti [bandhati+iti] bandhati-composes. iti • kavi-the poet who composes poems or poetic expressions. [Kattu-sādhana]

[b] kantaṁ-pleasant. manāpavacanaṁ-charming word. vadatī'ti vadati-speaks. vā-also, as other method of ED.
• kavi-the wise who speaks charming words, eloquent speaker. [Kattu-sādhana] [wa] kava+i

(6) Sucati-cleans. parisuddhaṁ-being pure. bhavatī'ti. bahavati-is. • suci-the pious who is clean and pure. [Kattu-sādhana] [wa] suca+i

(7) rucati-shines. dibbatī'ti. dibbati-shines. • ruci-the light which shines. [Kattu-sādhana] [wa] ruca+i

(8) mahantaṁ-great. vibhavaṁ-wealth. bhogakkhandhaṁ-the collection of possession. lātī'ti [lāti+iti] lāti-takes. iti • mahāli-a person named "mahāli" who takes great collection of wealth, rich. [Kattu-sādhana] [wa] mahāla-pātipadika+i,
(also) mahā-saddūpapada+lā+i [**mahā**-great+**lā**-to take+**i**]

Note: According to ED, the word "mahāli" means the one who take great amount of wealth. However, it is only an explanation of the the word **mahāli** dividing it into two components "**mahā** and **lā**" from grammatical point. The actual condition of the person may not reflect ED as he may be a poor man or just a person of ordinary social status.

(9) bhaddaṁ-good. yasaṁ-fame. lātī'ti • bhaddāli-a person named **bhaddāli** who takes good fame. [Kattu-sādhana] [wa] bhaddāla-pātipadika+i, (also),badda-saddūpapada+lā+i [**badda**-good+**lā**-to take+**i**]

(10) manaṁ-the mind. tattha ratane-in that jewel. nayatī'ti. nayati- carries. • maṇi-Ruby which carries the fantasy of people (as it is quite precious and glamorous to own and wear). [Kattu-sādhana] [wa] maṇa+i

६७०, ६८०. विदादीह्यूरो

670, 680. Vidā'dīhyū'ro. [Vida-ādīhi+ūro. 2 words]

[V] **Vida, valla, masa, sida, du, ku, kapu, maya, udi, khajja, kura,** icce'va'mādīhi dhātūhi, pāṭipadikehi ca **ūra**paccayo hoti.

An affix "**ūra**" is applied after the roots "**vida, valla, masa, sida, du, ku, kapu, maya, udi, khajja, kura**" and also after some pāṭipadika words.

(1) [a] Viditum̐-to get. alan'ti. alaṁ-not easy, not able. [Re: Sutta 665 on usage of this word "alaṁ"] iti. • vidūro-distant place,

Another possible and applicable meaning:

[a] Viditum̐-to know. alan'ti. alaṁ-is capable. iti. • vidūro-the one who is capable of knowing, **i.e.** the wise person.

[b] vidūraṭṭhāne-in a distant place. jāto-(is) born. • vedūro-one who was born in a distant place. [wa] vida+ūra

Note: The second ED is possibly a Taddhita ED which is irrelevant for WA.

(2) [a] vallati vallabhāvena-as cover. bhavatī'ti. bhavati-happens. iti • vallūro-a leafy shelter, a bower which serves as a shelter. [Kattu-sādhana]

[b] vallati aññamaññaṁ-one on one, mutually. bandhatī'ti bandati-ties up, entangles. vā • vallūro-a thicket. [Kattu-sādhana] [wa] valla+ūra

Note: valla (वल्ल) is a covering of thickly grown vines or bushes serving as a canopy. Vallūro (वल्लूर) is such a place. In some instances, it also means dried meat.

(3) āmasitabbo'ti [āmasitabbo+iti] āmasitabbo-should rub. iti • masūro-pulses such as lentil. [Kamma-sādhana] [wa] masa+ūra

(4) [a] sindati siṅgārabhāvaṁ-to a state of being glamorous. gacchatī'ti • sindūro-glamor.

[b] sindati virocatī'ti. virocati-looks glamorous. vā • sindūro-glamor. [Both are Kattu-sādhana] [wa] sida+ūra

(5) gamituṁ-to travel. alaṁ-not suitable. anāsannattā'ti [anāsannattā+iti] anāsannattā-for reason of being not near. iti • dūro-The distant, far away place which is not fit to travel as it is not near. [wa] du+ūra

(6) kuti saddaṁ-the cracking sound. karotī'ti. karoti-makes. • kūro- dried cooked-rice, which makes a cracking sound (when roasted or fried). [Kattu-sādhana] [wa] ku+ūra

(7) [a] attano-of its own. gandhena-by smell. aññaṁ-other. gandhaṁ-scent. kapati hanati-rids. hiṁsatī'ti. hiṁsati-

overwhelms. • kappūro-camphor which overwhelms other smells.

[b] kappati rogā'panayane-in removing some ailments. samatthetī'ti. samattheti-is able. vā • kappūro-camphor which can remove (cure) some ailments. [Both Kattu-sādhana] [wa] kapu+ūra

(8) [a] mahiyaṁ-on the earth. ravatī'ti. ravati-sounds, or sings. iti • mayūro-peacock which makes sound on earth.

[b] mahiyaṁ yāti-goes. gacchatī'ti. gacchati-goes. iti • mayūro-peacock which moves on earth. [Both Kattu-sādhana] [wa] maya-pātipadika+ūra

Note: This is a grammatical ED for this word. Actually, other creatures also move and make sounds while moving on the surface of earth.

(9) paṁsuṁ-the soil. undati pasavatī'ti [pasavati+iti] pasavati-increases (when burrowing). iti • undūro-rat or any rodent. [Kattu-sādhana] [wa] unda-pātipadika+ūra

(10) khajjitabbo khāditabbo'ti [khāditabbo+iti] khāditabbo-should be eaten (as a dessert snack). iti • khajjūro-date (Phoenix Dactylifera). [Kamma-sādhana] [wa] khajja+ūra

(11) kurati akkosatī'ti [akkosati+iti] akkosati-curses uttering abusive words, reviles. iti • kurūro-rude person. [Kattu-sādhana] [wa] kura+ūra

६७१, ६८१. हनादीहि नु णु तवो

671, 681. **Hanā'dīhi ṇu, nu, tavo.**

[Hana-ādīhi+ṇu, nu, tuvo. 2 words]

[V] **Hana, jana, bhā, ri, khanu, ama, ve, dhe, dhā, si, ki, hi**-icce'va'mādīhi dhātūhi **ṇu, nu, tu**, icce'te paccayā honti.

The affixes "**ṇu, nu, tu**" are applied after the roots "**hana, jana, bhā, ri, khanu, ama, ve, dhe, dhā, si, ki, hi**" etc.

(1) Bhojanaṁ-food. hanati hiṁsati-grinds and chews. etenā'ti etena-by this bodily part. iti • haṇu-jaw by which food is chewed. [Karaṇa-sādhana] [wa] hana+ṇu • hanu vā-It is also found in ordinary "**n**" as "**hanu**".

(2) Gamanaṁ-act of moving. janetī'tī. janeti-(it) causes. • jāṇu-knee through which moving is caused. [Kattu-sādhana]
[wa] jana+ṇu.
Note: In some texts, the word "jānu" is also found in ordinary "n" which is also applicable.

(3) bhāti-(it) shines. dibbatī'ti. dibbati-shines. • bhāṇu-the sun which shines. [Kattu-sādhana] [wa] bhā+ṇu

(4) nivāte-in the air-less(air-tight) place. riti-wafts. gacchatī'tī. gacchati-goes. • reṇu-dust which falls even in air-less place. [Kattu-sādhana] [wa] ri+ṇu

(5) khaṇitabbo-should be dug. avadāritabbo'ti [avadāritabbo+iti] avadāritabbo-should be cut. iti • khāṇu-tree stump which should be dug out and cut. [Kamma-sādhana] [wa] khanu+ṇu

(6) Aṅgamaṅgassa-of bodily part. rujjanabhāvaṁ-to the state of penetration. amati gacchatī'ti. gacchati-goes. • aṇu-atomic particles which penetrates even into bodily parts. [Kattu-sādhana]
[wa] ama+ṇu

(7) [a] veti tantasantāne-in the fibrous row of fibers. bhavatī'tī bhavati-occurs. iti • veṇu-bamboo which has fibrous content. [Kattu-sādhana]

[b] bahisāre-in outer layer only. alan'ti [alaṁ+iti] alaṁ-fit to use. iti vā • veṇu-bamboo which is usable only in outer part (as it lacks core hard-wood). [wa] ve+ṇu

(8) vacchaṁ-calf. dheti pāyetī'tī [pāyeti+itī] pāyeti-suckles. itī • dhenu-cow which suckles her calf. [Kattu-sādhana]
[wa] dhe+ṇu

(9) [a] atthaṁ-meaning. dhāretī'tī [dhāreti+itī] dhāreti-carries. itī • dhātu-the root of verb which carries its meaning. [Kattu-sādhana]

[b] gamana, pacanā'dikaṁ [gamana, pacana+ādikaṁ] gamana, pacana, ādikaṁ-going, cooking and so on. kriyaṁ-the action. dhāretī'tī [dhāreti+itī] dhāreti-carries. itī vā
• dhātu-the root of verb which carries (explains) various actions such as going and cooking etc. [Kattu-sādhana] [wa] dhā+tu

(10) sīyatī bandhīyatī'tī [bandhīyati+itī] bandhīyati-(is) tied up. iti • setu-bridge which is to be tied up (by various materials such as nails and timber etc.). [Kamma-sādhana] [wa] si+tu

(11) uddhaṁ-upward. gacchati-goes. pavattatī'tī [pavattati+iti] pavattati-happens. iti • ketu-banner, flag which flutters up through the winds. [Kattu-sādhana] [wa] ki+tu

(12) attano-of itself. phalaṁ-result. hinoti-causes. pavattatī'ti [pavattati+iti] pavattati-happens. iti • hetu-reason or cause which gives rise to its result. [Kattu-sādhana] [wa] hi+tu

६७२, ६८२. कुटादीहि ठो

672, 682. **Kuṭā'dīhi ṭho.** [Kuṭa-ādīhi+ṭho. 2 words]

[V] **Kuṭa, kusa, kaṭa**-icce'va'mādīhi dhātūhi, pāṭipadikehi ca **ṭha**-paccayo hotī.

An affix "**ṭha**" is applied after the roots "**kuṭa, kusa, kaṭa**" and pāṭipadika words.

(1) Aṅgamaṅgaṁ-parts of body. kuṭati chindatī'ti. chindati-cuts. • kuṭṭhaṁ-leprosy which cuts some parts of the body such as fingers and toes and so on as it advances. [Kattu-sādhana] [wa] kuṭa+ṭha

(2) dhaññena-by grain. chādetabbo-should be covered. pūretabbo'ti [pūretabbo+iti] pūretabbo-should be filled. iti • koṭṭho-grain-storage or grain-silo which should be filled with grain. [Kamma-sādhana] [wa] kusa+ṭha

(3) kaṭitabbaṁ madditabban'ti [madditabbaṁ+iti] madditabbaṁ- should be split. iti • kaṭṭhaṁ-wood which should be split (for any purpose such as timber or fire-wood). [Kamma-sādhana] [wa] kaṭa+ṭha

६७३, ६८३. मनुपूरसुणादीहि उस्स, णुसिसा
673, 683. **Manu, pūra, suṇā'dīhi ussa, ṇusi'sā.**

[Manu, pūra, suṇa-ādīhi+ussa, ṇusa, isā. 2 words]

[V] **Manu, pūra, suṇa, ku, su, ila, ala, maha, si, ki-** icce'va'mādīhi dhātūhi pāṭipadikehi ca **usa, nusa, isa,** icce-te paccayā honti. Puna nippajjante.

The affixes "**usa, ṇusa, isa**" are applied after the roots "**manu, pūra, suṇa, ku, su, ila, ala, maha, si, ki**" and also after some pāṭipadika words.

Note: In the Sutta, both "Manu, pūra, suṇā'dīhi" and "Mana, pūra, suṇā'dīhi" are two possible and applicable texts. If the word is taken as "manu", then it will be a pāṭipadika which means someone named **manu**-an early ancestor of mankind so named. If taken as "mana", it is the root which means "to know, to understand". The latter matches with all three EDs of the two example words "manusso, mānusso" as all EDs use an ākhyāta verb "manati" which comprises the root "mana". In light of three EDs which uses the two verbs "**manati**" and its synonymous verb "**jānati**", it could be the root "**mana**-to know" in the word "manusso". It also matches with the Sutta number 10,(मनेरूष्यः) the six pāda, Uṇādi Vritti text.

(1) [a] Kusalā'kusale [Kusala+akusale] Kusalā'kusale dhamme-

(both) wholesome and unwholesome things. manati-knows. jānātī'ti [jānāti+iti] jānāti-knows. iti • manusso, • mānusso-a human being who knows both wholesome and unwholesome things (the knower of good and bad things).

[b] Kāraṇā'kāraṇaṁ [Kāraṇa+akāraṇaṁ] Kāraṇā'kāraṇaṁ-(both) reason and non-reason. manati jānātī'ti vā • manusso, • mānuso-a human being who knows both reason and non-reason. **i.e.** the one who can distinguish between what is reasonable and what is unreasonable.

[c] Atthā'natthaṁ [Attha+anatthaṁ] Atthā'natthaṁ-(both) things of benefit and non-benefit. manati jānātī'ti vā • manusso, • mānuso-a human being who knows both beneficial and non-beneficial things. [All three are Kattu-sādhana EDs] • manusso [wa] manu or mana+usa

• mānuso [wa] manu or mana+ṇusa

(2) [a] Mātāpitūnaṁ-of mother and father. hadayaṁ-heart. pūretī'ti [pūreti+iti] pūreti-fills (with joy). iti • puriso-male-offspring or son who fills the heart of mother and father (with joy and pride).

[b] attano-of oneself. manorathaṁ-the mind's chariot, **i.e.** desire. pūretī'ti vā • puriso-male person who fulfils one's wishes. [wa] pūra+isa

[c] pūretī'ti vā • poso-man. [All Kattu-sādhana] [wa] pūra+isa

(3) [a] sasurehi-by in-laws. suṇitabbā hiṁsitabbā'ti [hiṁsitabbā+iti] hiṁsitabbā-is bothered. iti • suṇisā-daughter-in-law who is (sometimes) bothered or pestered by in-laws.

[Kamma-sādhana]

[b] dvinnaṁ-of two. jānānaṁ-people (wife's side and husband's side). kulasantānaṁ-the family lineage. karotī'tīti. karoti-creates to increase. vā iti. • suṇisā-daughter-in-law who increases the family lineage of two persons (wife and husband). [Kattu-sādhana] [wa] suṇa+isa

(4) kucchitabban'ti [kucchitabbaṁ+iti] kucchitabbaṁ-is to be detested. iti • karīsaṁ-feces which is detested. [Kamma-sādhana] [wa] ku+isa

(5) [a] gabbhaṁ-dark cloud cover. vimocetī'ti [vimoceti+iti] vimoceti-releases (removes). iti • suriso-Sun which removes dark clouds. [wa] su+isa

[b]tamandhakāravidhamanena

[tama+andhakāravidhamanena=**tama**-darkness+**andhakāra**-invisibility-causing, **vidhamanena**-by removing]

tama'ndhakāravidhamanena-by removing darkness which causes invisibility. sattānaṁ-of beings. bhayaṁ-fear. surati hiṁsatī'ti [hiṁsati+iti] hiṁsati-kills, or removes. iti • sūriyo-Sun which kills or removes fear of beings by removing darkness. [Both Kattu-sādhana] [wa] su+isa

(6) rogaṁ-(certain) ailment. hiṁsatī'ti. hiṁsati-kills or cures. iti • sirīso-Rain tree which can kill or cure some disease (by its medicinal curative properties). [Kattu-sādhana] [wa] su+isa

(7) [a] ilati kampatī'ti [kampati+iti] kampati-trembles. iti • illiso-A person named "**illiso**" who trembles (a fickle person).

[b] taṇhāya-due to craving. dubbalo-weak. hutvā-having being. ilati kampatī'ti vā • illiso-a person named "**illiso**" who fickles in the face of temptations due to craving, capricious. [Both Kattu-sādhana] [wa] ila+isa

(8) pāpakaraṇe-in doing unwholesome things. alati-is able. samatthetī'ti. samattheti-is able. iti • alaso-The idle person (lazy man) who is prone to do unwholesome things. [Kattu-sādhana] [wa] ala+isa

(9) mahitabbo pūjetabbo'ti [pūjetabbo+iti] pūjetabbo-is honored. iti • mahiso-Buffalo which is honored (in some tribal societies). [Kamma-sādhana] [wa] maha+isa

Note: The word is also found spelled as "mahiṁso" in the majority of texts. It should be noted as an "ṁ" is inserted in such case of word.

(10) sīyati bandhīyatī'ti [bandhīyati+iti] bandhīyati-is tied up. iti • sīsaṁ-Head which is tied up (by head-band etc.) [Kamma-sādhana] [wa] si+isa

(11) kitabbaṁ hiṁsitabban'ti [hiṁsitabbaṁ+iti] hiṁsitabbaṁ-is hurt. iti • kisaṁ-emaciated person (who is hurt or is vulnerable by possible onset of infections or diseases etc.) [Kamma-sādhana] [wa] ki+isa

icce'va'mādi-and so on.

Iti kibbidhānakappe uṇā'dikappo chaṭṭho kaṇḍo.
The Sixth Uṇādi Section of Kita ends.

Uṇā'dikappo niṭṭhito.

Uṇādi Chapter ends.

Kaccāyanapakaraṇaṁ [53]niṭṭhitaṁ.

Kaccāyana's Pāli Grammar ends.

---

[53] In the earlier versions of the text such as those of M.E. Senart and Mahābodhi editions, there is a following colophon:

Yāni sippāni lokasmiṁ, Aṇuṁ thūlāni vijjare
Tāni sabbāni sippāni, Sayaṁ Sijjā bhavantu me.

Here is translation of the verse:

"Whatever branch of knowledge in the world, be it trivial or significant one,
May all those knowledges be self-manifest to me".

Nigama-gāthāyo

The Concluding Verses

(These verses are not from the original text, but composed by the translator as a record for the posterity)

Aho gambhīracittatā, niruttaññuno desanā!
yathā'nusiṭṭhaṁ caranto, sukhāpeti sukhesinaṁ!

Māgadhikāya Sambuddho, niruttipadakovido
saddhammaṁ suṭṭhu desayi, pāpento amataṁ pajaṁ.

Tassā vyākaraṇasatthaṁ, Kaccāyanena vihitaṁ
anuvyā'haṭaṁ vi'yākataṁ, **Englisā**'nukūlato.

[54]**Sajjana-**nāmadheyena, **Mramma**jaccena bhikkhunā
saddhammavuḍḍikāmena, saddhāpamukhacetasā.

"Ayaṁ gantho sukhaṁ detu, sādhujane mahītale
sukhena niruttiñāṇam, saṁvaḍḍhento puna'ppunaṁ
Buddhapāvacanaseṭṭhaṁ, ñāpayaṁ sampamodayaṁ"

Puññenā'nena katena, mā'ha'massaṁ bālo sayaṁ
bālenā'pi na saṁvase, na kare pāpajamminaṁ.

Attaparahitaṅkaro, tikkhagambhīrañāṇavā
Dhammakāmī dhammagaru, dhmmaññū ca susīlavā.

Pāpabālehi ajeyo, bahūnaṁ sukhadāyako
attapaṇidhisampanno, paññājīvī dukkha'ntagū.

---

[54] **Sajjana(सज्जन)** is a correctly spelt Pāli name of the translator, an equal term for "Thitzana" which is spelled as per Myanmar phonetics.

Appendices

SAMPLE MORPHOLOGY

Note: Studying morphological procedure is an important part of grammar study in the ancient times. It helps students learn how a word is evolved till it becomes a complete word after a series of procedures as prescribed in relevant Suttas are being carried out. It is in fact an active process of grammatical dynamics pursued by ancient students which is both interesting and enriching. **Studying the meaning of various Suttas and relevant examples alone is not enough** for a serious student as it may seem like quite a quiescent process. It has tremendous impact in the development of grammatical knowledge and in gaining the mastery of the language effectively in the process. A few samples of systematic morphological procedures are shown below. Keep in mind that there are different steps for each word according to their grouping as a noun, or compound noun, or a Taddhita-affixed noun, or an Ākhyāta verb, or Kita and Uṇādi-affixed words. [Morphological procedures for Sandhi are already shown in the Sandhi chapter]

Noun Words

Steps of the procedures:

(1) Set up the base according to its natural ending category of the vowel.

(2) Apply the applicable vibatti(case-ending) after it.

(3) Perform necessary functions till it becomes a complete word.

(a) **Puriso**-man. (Nominative Singular) [Re: Sutta 104]

[1] Set up the base as **Purisa** [This is a crude noun-form]

[2] Apply a nominative, singular "si" after it> **purisa+si**

[3] Change "si" into "o" by 104 >**Purisa+o**

[4] Elide the last "a" of purisa and keep it as it is by 83 > **puris+o** (It thus becomes a complete word)

(b) **Purisā**-men (Nominative Plural) [Re: Sutta 107]

[1] Set up the base as **Purisa**

[2] Apply a nominative plural "yo" after it>**Purisa+yo**
[3] Change "yo" into "ā" by 107 > **Purisa+ā**
[4] Elide the last "a" of Purisa and keep it as it is by 83 >**Puris+ā** (It becomes a complete word)

Ākhyāta Verbs

Steps of the procedures:
(1) Set up the root as a base.
(2) Declare the relevant meaning of the root and formally name it as a root by 457.
(3) Elide the last vowel of the root as necessary by 521.
(4) First, apply applicable Vibatti after the root and then apply an applicable affix between the root and vibatti.
(5) Perform any necessary morphological procedure till it becomes a complete verb.

(a) **Gạcchati**-(He) goes. [Re: Sutta 476] (An Ākhyāta verb, in present tense, third person singular "ti" termination)
[1] **Gamu**-*gatimhi*-to go.
[2] Elide the last vowel of the root "u" by 521>**gam**
[3] Apply a verb termination in present tense, third person singular "ti" by 414 after the root >**gam+ti**
[4] Then, apply an affix "a" in the sense of a Kattā (active voice) right after the root by Sutta 445 >**gam+a+ti**
[5] Change "m" of the root into "cch" by 476>**ga+cch+a+ti** (It becomes a complete word).

(b) **Gacchanti**-(They) go. [Re: Sutta 410] (An Ākhyāta verb, in present tense, third person plural "anti" termination)
[1] Gamu-gamane-to go.
[2] Elide the last vowel of the root "u" by 521>**gam**
[3] Apply a verb termination in present tense, third person plural "anti" by 414 after the root>**gam+anti**
[4] Then, apply an affix "a" in the sense of a Kattā (active voice) right after the root>**gam+a+anti**
[5] Change "m" of the root into "cch" by 476. >**ga+cch+a+anti** (Remember, one "a" is still needed to be elided).

[6] Elide the affix “a” by 510>**ga+cch+anti** (The completed word)

Kita-affixed words

Steps of the procedures:
(1) Set up the root as a base.
(2) Declare relevant meaning of the root and name it as a root.
(3) Elide the last vowel of the root as necessary.
(4) Apply applicable affix after the root.
(5) Perform any necessary morphological procedure.
(6) When all is done, formally recognize it as a noun
(7) Apply a noun vibatti case-ending after it and do all necessary further morphological procedures as those prescribed in normal noun words.

Note: There are two stage-procedures:
(a) **Step 1-5** are Kita-morphological procedures.
(b) **The remaining steps** are noun procedures.
The procedure for uṇādi-affixed words are similar to that of Kita-affixed words.

(a) **Cāgo**-charitable giving, sharing [Re: Sutta 529]
[1] **Caja**-*cāge*-to share generously
[2] Elide the last vowel of the root>**caj**
[3] Apply a “ṇa” affix after the root by 529>**caj+ṇa**
[4] recognize the ṇ-containing affix as a Kārita by 621
[5] Then elide that “ṇ” by 523>**caj+a**
[6] Then apply a “vuddhi” function on the first “a” of “caj” by 483>**cāja** (It becomes an “ā” as a result of Vuddhi function)
[7] Change “j” into “g” by 623>**cāga**
[8] Recognize this almost-finished word “cāga” in transit as a noun by 601
[9] Apply a noun-vibatti in nominative singular “si” after it >**cāga+si**
[10] Change “si” into “o”> **cāga+o**. Next apply step 4 procedure as mentioned in Puriso. (It becomes a complete word “cāgo”.)

(b) **Buddho**-The one who knows truth, who awakened. [Re Sutta 557]
[1] **Budha**-*ñāṇe*-to know, *jāgaraṇe*-to wake up.
[2] Elide the last vowel of the root>**Budh**

[3] Apply a "ta" affix after the root by 557>**Budh+ta**
[4] Change the affix "ta" applied after dh-ending root into "dha" by 576.>**Budh+dha**
[5] Then, change "dh" of the root into "d" by 611>**Bud+dha**
[6] Recognize this almost-finished word "Bud+dha" in transit as a noun by 601.
[7] Apply a noun-vibatti in nominative singular "si" after it >**Buddha+si**
[8] Change "si" into "o">**Buddha+o**. Next apply the step 4 procedure as mentioned in Puriso. ("Buddho" completed.)

Uṇādi-affixed words

(a) **Samatho**-that which calms the mind, Samatha meditation. [Re: Sutta 628]
[1] **Sama**-*upasame*-to calm
[2] Apply a "tha" affix after the root by 628>**Sama+tha** (No need to elide the last vowel of the root)
[3] Recognize this word "Sama+tha" in transit as a noun by 601.
[4] Apply a noun-vibatti in nominative singular "si" after it. >**Samatha+si**
[5] Change "si" into "o">**Samatha+o**.
[6] Next apply the step 4 procedure as mentioned in Puriso. (It becomes a complete word "Samatho".)

(b) **Gehaṁ**-home [A neuter gender word in nominative singular, Re: Sutta 629]
[1] **Gaha**-*gahaṇe*-to take.
[2] Elide the last vowel of the root>gah
[3] Apply an "a" affix after the root by 527>**Gah+a**
[4] Then apply the function of changing the near-by first vowel "a" of "Gah" into "e" by 629>**Geha**
[5] Recognize this half-finished word "Geha" in transit as a noun by 601.

[6] Apply a noun-vibatti in nominative singular "si" after it. >**Geha+si**

[7] Then, change "si" into "aṁ" by Sutta 219>**Geha+aṁ.**

[8] Next apply step 4 procedure as mentioned in Puriso. (It thus becomes a complete word "Gehaṁ")

Compound Nouns

Steps of the procedures:

(1) Set up all component words in crude-forms as a base.

(2) Apply a vibatti after each base-word.

(3) Perform any necessary morphological procedure as shown in nouns chapter till it becomes a complete ED with coherent and relevant meaning.

(4) Then, declare the meaning of ED and name it as a compound noun. Also give a relevant specific name of compound.

(5) Delete all the applied vibatti and all morphological traces of change till it returns to its initial crude-stage of the base.

(6) Then, recognize it as a noun and apply any necessary procedure as explained below until it becomes a complete word.

Rājaputto-the king's son, **i.e.** the prince.

[1] Set up the two base words as "**Rāja+Putta**"

[2] Then apply genitive singular "sa" after rāja and nominative singular "si" after putta>**rāja+sa, Putta+si.**

[3] (a) Change rāja together with the applied vibatti "sa" into "**rañño**" by 135. (b) also change the nominative singular vibatti "si" applied after putta into "o">putta+o. Then elide the preceding "a" by 83>**putto**.>**rañño putto.**

[4] After this basic procedure is done, it becomes a complete *viggaha* sentence (ED) as "**Rañño putto**" which has a coherent and relevant meaning as "the king's son" [**rañño**-of king, p**utto**-son]

[5] Then, as this ED sentence has coherent and relevant meanings to each other, it is declared and formally named as Chaṭṭhī-Tappurisa by Sutta 327.

[6] Then, elide all vibattis and its concomitants (noun-case-endings "sa" and "si" along with their traces of morphological

procedure such as newly changed word-forms "rañño putto") by Sutta 317. >**rājaputta**. In addition, keep it as it is by Sutta 318.

[7] Then, this word "rājaputta" in transit is to be recognized as noun by means of Sutta 601.

[8] Apply a nominative singular "si" after rājaputta >**rājaputta+si**

[9] Then, change "si" into "o" by Sutta 104>**Rājaputta+o**.

[10] Apply elision procedure on the last "a" of the rājaputta by Sutta 83 (It becomes a complete word.)

Noun in Taddhita-affix

Steps of the procedures:

(1) Set up the word and applicable additional words such as "apacca" etc. as a base according to specific category of Taddhita.

(2) Apply a vibatti after each base-word.

(3) Perform any necessary morphological procedure as shown in the nouns chapter till it becomes a complete ED with coherent and relevant meaning.

(4) Then, declare the meaning of ED and apply a relevant affix as necessary.

(5) Wipe out the applied vibatti and all morphological traces of change till it returns to its initial crude-stage of the base.

(6) Then, recognize it as a noun and apply any necessary procedure as explained below until it becomes a complete word.

Vāsiṭṭho-Vasiṭṭha's son.

[1] Set up the base as **Vasiṭṭha+apacca**

[2] Apply genitive singular "sa" after vasiṭṭha>**Vasiṭṭha+sa** and add one more "s" to the front of "sa" by means of Sutta 61. >**vasiṭṭhassa**

[3] Apply a nominative singular "si" after apacca>apacca+si. Besides, change that "si" into "aṁ" by Sutta 219. >**apacca+aṁ.** Then, elide the preceding "a" by means of 83>apaccaṁ. Thus, it becomes a complete ED sentence as "**Vasiṭṭhassa apaccaṁ**" which has relevant meaning.

[4] **Vasiṭṭhassa**-of someone named "vasiṭṭha", **apaccaṁ**-son. When this meaning signifying patronymic is implied by this ED,

an affix "ṇa" is applied between two words by 344. It will then look like this>**vasiṭṭhassa+ṇa+apaccaṁ.**

[5] Then, by means of the word "tesaṁ" in Sutta 317, all the applied vibatti, traces of morphological procedures as well as the word "apacca" are to be deleted>**vasiṭṭha+ṇa.**

[6] Elide the "ṇ" of the affix by means of Sutta 396. >**vasiṭṭha+a.**

[7] Keep it as it is by Sutta 318.

[8] Then, by rule of Sutta 400, perform a vuddhi function on the front "a" at Vasiṭṭha>**Vāsiṭṭha+a.** Then, elide the second "a" by Sutta 83.

[9] Recognize this word "**vāsiṭṭha**" as noun by Sutta 601 and apply a nominative "si" after it>**Vāsiṭṭha+si**

[10] Then, change that applied "si" into "o" by Sutta 104. >**Vāsiṭṭha+o.**

[11] Apply elision procedure by Sutta 83 on the last vowel "a" of Vāsiṭṭha>**Vāsiṭṭh+o.** (It thus becomes a complete word.)

Note: Performing morphological procedures for Samāsa and Taddhita words require a strong and thorough knowledge and understanding of Nāma, Ākhyāta and Kita chapters. Thus, this branch of study of the structural morphology of Pāli words can broaden and enrich the grammatical insight of the student in many ways and lead to a more profound in-depth mastery of the language.

KĀRAKA AND SĀDHANA

Sādhana means that by which a specific word suffixed with a ***Kita*** or an ***uṇādi*** affix is completed or brought to completion. It refers to various kinds of Kita and Uṇādi affixes through application of them words are brought to completion as perfect words. The completed words carry the specific subtle meanings such as those grammatically defined terms of Kattu, Kamma and so on. The grammatical concept of Sādhana is originally based on the nature of affix being applied after the root and its relevant EDs. There are certain Suttas, such as *Bhāvakammesu ta (*556), K*attukaraṇapadesesu ca* (548) and so on, which directly show a specific affix to be applied in a particular sense of Sādhana. Besides, the EDs of such words are also to be in concordant with relevant Sādhanas. For example, if the affix of the word is applied in the sense of Kattu sādhana, then the ED of that word has to be a Kattu Sādhana ED.

For the ease and convenience of students, the name of specific Sādhana of EDs are shown in both Kita and Uṇādi chapters. Though studying and understanding the Sādhanas and their general aspect and characteristics can help to develop a more thorough grammatical knowledge and skill, it is not essential for beginners. However, for the benefit of developing such a skill, all relevant information will be briefly explained. [Sādhiyate nipphādiyate anenā'ti sādhanaṁ. **sadha**-*nipphattiyaṁ*-to complete+**yu**]

The Role of Kāraka & Sādhana

Though Kāraka and Sādhana share somewhat similar implications, the role they can play in the grammar and actual sentence structure of the practical language application are quite different.

(a) The six Kārakas in individually assigned case-endings as per the relevant Suttas in the Kāraka chapter, can definitely play their own specific roles such as the subject (for Kattu-kāraka) or the object (for Kamma-kāraka) and so forth.

(b) On other hand, most of the **Sādhanas do not have this kind of significant role**. However, out of seven Sādhanas, **Kattu, Kamma and Bhāva, have some significant role in affecting the voice of a verb and the structure of a sentence.**

For example, a Kattu-affixed word may affect the voice of sentence to be an active voice. Kamma-affixed word and Bhāva-affixed words will affect as passive voice and impersonal voices respectively. Shown below are some sample sentences structured with such words as examples.

Example sentence of Kattu-Sādhana-affixed words.

Note: The verbs with Kattu-sādhana affix are shown underlined.

(1) Dānaṁ Dinno devadatto [dā+ta] (Sutta 626, Kaccāyana text, Uṇādi chapter) Devadatta gave alms. (Active voice)

(2) Kumaro antepuraṁ gato [gamu+ta] (Mahāpadāna Sutta, Mahāvagga Pāli) The prince went into the palace. (Active voice)

(3) So bhagavā sayam'pi cattāri saccāni Buddho [Budha+ta] (Cūla-Saccaka Sutta commentary, Mūlapaṇṇāsa Pāli texts) That glorious Buddha knew four truths by himself too. (Active voice)

Example sentence of Kamma-sādhana affixed words

Note: The verbs with Kamma-sādhana affix are shown underlined.

(1) Buddhena dhammo desito [disa+ta] The Dhamma is taught by Buddha. (Passive voice)

(2) Bhotabbo odano bhavatā [bhuja+tabba] (Sutta 625, Uṇādi chapter, Kaccāyana text) The rice is to be eaten by your honorable. (Passive voice)

Example sentence of Bhāva-sādhana affixed word.

Note: The verbs with Bhāva-sādhana affix are shown underlined.

(1) Tassa Gītaṁ [ge+ta] (Sutta 556, Kita chapter) Of that person (**i.e.** His) singing, His singing.

(2) Sayitabbaṁ bhavatā [si+tabba] (Sutta 625, Uṇādi chapter) Eating by your honorable. (Impersonal voice)

General Aspects of Sādhana.

Keep in mind that the remaining four Sādhanas, namely **Karaṇa, Sampadāna, Apādāna and Adhikaraṇa, do not have any significant role** except that of an ordinary noun in a sentence. The meaning of words affixed in each of the seven Sādhanas have their own subtle meanings which are clearly and simply translated below. See an ordinary translation and then a bit detailed explanatory note shown in parenthesis which reflect their respective Sādhana and the ED in Pāli. In order to understand a Sādhana and relevant ED of each Sādhana, a student needs to know the sense of affix and the general structural aspect of each ED which are distinctive from each other. Please read notes carefully which explains general aspects of the EDs of each Sādhana. As a matter of fact, it requires a very firm foundation of thorough study and grammatical knowledge to understand all aspects of Sādhana and EDs.

1. **[Kattu]** Nāyako-the leader (who leads) (Sutta 527)
   [ED in Pāli] Netī'ti Nāyako. [neti+iti]
   Note: Here, Kattu-sādhana is signified by means of the Ākhyāta verb "neti" which in itself is an active-voice verb in Kattu-sense. Also note the word "iti" is included to indicate the reason (*Vacana-hetu*).
2. **[Kamma]** Kammaṁ-work (which is being done) (531)
   [ED in Pāli] Karīyate tan'ti Kammaṁ. [karīyate taṁ+it]
   Note: Here, Kamma-sādhana is signified by means of the Ākhyāta verb "Karīyate" which in itself is a passive voice verb with the affix "ya" in Kamma-sense. Also note the word "iti" is included to indicate the reason.
3. **[Bhāva]** Cāgo-generosity (act of giving, sharing) (529) [ED in Pāli] Cajate, Cajanaṁ vā Cāgo (**vā** indicates another possible ED)
   Note: Here, Bhāva-sādhana is signified by means of twin verbs of two applicable EDs, the first "Cajate" being an Ākhyāta verb in Bhāva voice and the second Kita word "Cajanaṁ" in Bhāva affix "yu". Here, the verbs which in themselves are expressive of Bhāva-sense. Also note that there is no "iti" at all. This is the only Sādhana where there is no "iti" required in its ED.

4. **[Karaṇa]** Vinayo-the discipline (by which one is trained) (527) [ED in Pāli] Vineti etenā'ti Vinayo. [etena+iti]
Note: Here, Karaṇa-sādhana is signified by means of a Sabbanāma-noun word "eta" in instrumental case which by itself is a Karaṇa. Also note the word "iti" is included to indicate the reason.
5. **[Sampadāna]** Dānīyo-the recipient monk (to which alms should be given) [ED in Pāli] Databbo Assā'ti Dānīyo. [assa+iti]
Note: Here, Sampadāna-sādhana is signified by means of the Sabba-nāma word "Ta" in dative case which by itself is a Sampadāna. Also note the word "iti" is included to indicate the reason.
6. **[Apādāna]** Bhemo-the fearsome object (from which people fear) (627) [ED in Pāli] Bhāyanti etasamā'ti Bhemo. [etasmā+iti]
Note: Here, Apādāna-sādhana is signified by means of Sabbanāma noun "eta" in ablative case which by itself is an Apādāna. Also note the word "iti" is included to indicate the reason.
7. **[Adhikaraṇa]** Ṭhānaṁ-the place (where people stand) (548) [ED in Pāli] Tiṭṭhanti Tasmin'ti Ṭhānaṁ [tasmiṁ+iti]
Note: Here, Adhikaraṇa-sādhana is signified by means of Sabbanāma noun "ta" in locative case which by itself is an Adhikaraṇa also called Padesa or Okāsa. Also note the word "iti" is included to indicate the reason.

By taking a careful look at the above explanation, it is hoped that the students will clearly understand how Kāraka and Sādhana play their inherent parts in the structure of Pāli words and its sentences.

THE LIST OF SIMILAR SUTTAS
found in Pāṇinī & Kaccāyana.

Sanskrit Sutta (SS) and Kaccāyana Sutta (KS) are shown here alongside in transliterated Romanized characters to show different or similar physical structure of each Sutta found in both grammatical texts. Numbers after Suttas indicate the book, chapter and serial sequence of each respectively. **Being similar does not necessarily mean to be identical in terms of function and physical structure.** Most Suttas, except a few, have only partial similarity and affinity in terms of the implied function, physical structure of wording and sentence make-up. The transliterated words of each Sutta will attest to the fact that Kaccāyana's work can not be unilaterally averred as a complete copy of its cousin grammars, but a work borne out of shared linguistics which have deeply-rooted ancestry in the ancient Indo-Aryan civilization. [55]There are 3925 or 3996 Suttas in Pāṇinī while Kaccāyana comprises only 673 or 675 if two more Suttas from earlier versions are included. The ratio and margin of similarity is not much substantial in relation to the amount of Suttas in the Sanskrit texts as it was assumed by some scholars. Below is a list of Suttas which have some similarities, being prepared after careful research of the relevant texts.

---

[55] This number of Sutta is as practically found in the alphabetical index of Suttas in "Aṣṭādhyāyī of Pāṇinī", translated by Sumitra M. Katre. In Wikipedia online encyclopedia, it is found as 3996 Suttas which needs verification.

(1) तत्पुरुषः समानाधिकरणः कर्मधारयः (1-2-42)

[SS] Tatpuruṣa: samānādhikaraṇa: karmadhāraya:
[KS] Dvipade tulyā'dhikaraṇe kammadhārayo

(2) सरूपाणमेकशेष एकविभ्क्तौ (1-2-64)

[SS] Sarūpānamekaśeṣa ekavibaktau
[KS] Sarūpāna'mekasesva'sakiṁ

(3) भूवादयो धातवः (1-3-1)

[SS] Bhūvādyo dhātava:
[KS] Bhūvādayo dhātavo

(4) भावकर्मणोः (1-3-13)

[SS] Bhāvakramaṇo
[KS] Attanopadāni bhāve ca kammani

(5) शेषात कर्त्तरि परस्मैपदम (1-3-78)

[SS] Ṡeshāt kratri prasamepadaṁ
[KS] Kattari parassapadaṁ

(6) यूस्त्रयाख्यो नदी (1-4-3)

[SS] Ūsatrayākhyo nadī
[KS] Nadā'dito vā ī

(7) संयोगे गुरु (1-4-11)

[SS] Saṁyoge guru
[KS] Dumhi garu

(8) दीर्घञ्च (1-4-12)

[SS] Dīrghañca.
[KS] Dīgho ca

(9) ध्रवमपायेऽपादानम (1-4-24)

[SS] Dhravamapāye pādānaṁ
[KS] Yasmā'dapeti, bhaya'mādatte vā ta'dapādānaṁ

(10) साधकतमं करणम (1-4-42)

[SS] Sādhakatamaṁ karaṇaṁ
[KS] Yena vā karīyate taṁ karaṇaṁ

(11) आधारोऽधिकरणम (1-4-45)

[SS] Ādhāro dhikaraṇaṁ

[KS] Yo'dhāro ta'mokāsaṁ

(12) कर्तुरीप्सिततम कर्म (1-4-49)

[SS] Kraturīpsitatamaṁ krama

[KS] Yaṁ karoti taṁ kammaṁ

(13) लः परस्मैपदम (1-4-99)

[SS] La: Parasmepadaṁ

[KS] Atha pubbāni vibattīnaṁ cha parassapadāni

(14) तङानावात्मनेपदम (1-4-100)

[SS] Taṅāvātatmanepadaṁ

[KS] Parāṇya'ttanopadāni

(15) तिङस्त्रीणि त्रीणि प्रथम मध्यमोत्तमाः (1-4-101)

[SS] Tiṅ catrīṇi trīṇi prathama, mdhyamottamā:

[KS] Dve dve paṭhama, majjimu'ttamapurisā

(16) युष्मद्युपपदे समानाधिकरणे स्थानिन्यपि मध्यमः(1-4-105)

[SS] Yuṣmadyūpapade samānādhikaraṇe sthāninyapi madyaṁ

[KS] Tumhe Majjimo

(17) अस्मद्युत्तमः (1-4-107)

[SS] Asmdyutttama:

[KS] Amhe Uttamo

(18) शेषे प्रथमः (1-4-108)

[SS] Seṣe prathama:

[KS] Nāmamhi payujjamāne'pi tulyādhikaraṇe paṭhamo

(19) संख्यापूवो द्विगु (2-1-52)

[SS] Saṅkhyāpūvo dvigu

[KS] Saṅkhyāpubbo digu

(20) अनेकमन्यपदार्थे (2-2-24)

[SS] Anekamanyapada artthe

[KS] Aññapada'tthesu bahubbīhi

(21) चार्थे द्वन्द्वः (2-2-29)
[SS] Carthe dvandva:
[KS] Nāmānaṁ samuccayo dvando
(22) कर्मणि द्वितिया (2-3-2)
[SS] Kramaṇi dvitiyā
[KS] Kama'tthe dutiyā
(23) कालाध्वनोरत्यन्त संयोगे (2-3-5)
[SS] Kāladhvanoratyanta saṁyoge
[KS] Kāla'ddhāna'maccantasaṁyoge
(24) कर्मप्रवचनीययुक्त्ते द्वितिया (2-3-8)
[SS] Krāmpravacanīyayukte dvitiyā
[KS] Kamma'ppavacanīyayutte
(25) चतुर्थी संप्रदाने (2-3-13)
[SS] Caturtthī saṁpradāne
[KS] Sampadāne catutthī
(26) येनङ्गविकारो (2-3-20)
[SS] Yenaṅgavikāro
[KS] Yena'ṅgavikāro
(27) अपादाने पञ्चमी (2-3-28)
[SS] Apādāne Pañcamī
[KS] Apādāne Pañcamī
(28) यस्य च भावेन भावलक्षणम (2-3-37)
[SS] Yasya ca bhāvena bhāvalakhaṇaṁ
[KS] Kālabhāvesu ca
(29) षष्ठी चानादर (2-3-38)
[SS] Ṣhaṭṭī cā nādāre
[KS] Anā'dare ca
(30) स्वामिश्वाराधिपति दायाद साक्षिप्रतिभूप्रसुतैश्च(2-3-39)
[SS] Svāmisvārādhipati dāyāda sākhi pratibhū prasutesca
[KS] Sāmi'ssarādhipatidāyādasakhīpatibhūpasuta kusalehi ca

(31) यतश्च निर्द्धारणम (2-3-41)

[SS] Yatas ca nirdhāraṇaṁ
[KS] Niddhāraṇe ca

(32) प्रसितउत्सुकाभ्यं तृतिया (2-3-44)

[SS] Prasitautsukābyaṁ tritiyā
[KS] Maṇḍitu'ssukesu tatiyā

(33) संबोधने च (2-3-47)

[SS] Saṁboddhane ca
[KS] Ālapane ca

(34) द्विगुरेकवचनम (2-4-1)

[SS] Dvigurekavacanaṁ
[KS] Dvigusse'kattaṁ

(35) स नपुंसकम (2-4-17)

[SS] Sa napuṁsakaṁ
[KS] So napuṁsakaliṅgo

(36) असते भूः (2-4-52)

[SS] Asate bhū:
[KS] Asabbadhātuke bhū

(37) प्रतययः (3-1-1)

[SS] Pratyaya:
[KS] Dhātuliṅgehi parā paccayā

(38) गुपतिजकिदभ्यः सन (3-1-5)

[SS] Gupatijakidbya: san
[KS] Tija, gupa, kita, mānehi kha, cha, sā vā

(39) उपमानादाचारे (3-1-10)

[SS] Upamānā dācāre
[KS] Āya nāmato kattū'pamānā'dācāre

(40) कर्त्तरि शप (3-1-68)

[SS] Kratri śap
[KS] Bhū'vādito a

(41) दिवादिभ्यः श्यन (3-1-69)

[SS] Divādibya: Ṡyan

[KS] Divā'dito yo

(42) श्रुव शृ च (3-1-74)

[SS] Ṡruva ṡri ca

[KS] Svā'dito ṇuṇā, uṇā ca.

(43) रुधादिभ्यः श्नम (3-1-78)

[SS] Rudhādibya: Ṡnaṁ

[KS] Rudhā'dito niggahitapubbañ'ca

(44) तनादिकृञ्भ्यः उ (3-1-79)

[SS] Tanādi kriñbya: u

[KS] Tanā'dito o, yirā

(45) कयादिभ्यः श्ना (3-1-81)

[SS] Krayādibya: ṡnā

[KS] Ki'yādito nā

(46) तव्यत्तव्यानीयरः (3-1-96)

[SS] Tavyat tavyānīyara:

[KS] Bhāvakammesu tabbā'nīyā

(47) नन्दिग्रहिपचादिभ्यो ल्युणिन्यचः (3-1-134)

[SS] Nandi, grahi, pacādibhyo lyuṇinya ca:

[KS] Nandā'dīhi yu

(48) कर्मण्यण (3-2-1)

[SS] Kramaṇyaṇ

[KS] Dhātuyā kammā'dimhi ṇo

(49) क्विप च (3-2-76)

[SS] Kvip ca

[KS] Kvi ca

(50) परोक्षे लिट (3-2-115)

[SS] Parokhe lit

[KS] Apaccakkhe prokhā'tīte

(51) कुधमण्डार्थेभ्य श्च (3-2-151)

[SS] Kudhamaṇḍartthebya ṡca

[KS] Sadda, kudha, cala, maṇḍattha, rucā'dīhi yu

(52) मतिबुद्धिपूजार्थेभ्य श्च (3-2-188)

[SS] Mati, budhi, pūjārtthebya ṡa

[KS] Bhyā'dīhi mati, budhi, pūjādīhi ca kto

(53) तुमुनण्वुलौ क्रियायं क्रियार्थायाम (3-3-10)

[SS] Tumun ṇvulau kriyāyaṁ kriyārthayāṁ

[KS] Kriyāyaṁ ṇvutavo

(54) भाववचनाश्च (3-3-11)

[SS] Bhāvavacanās ca

[KS] Bhāvavācimhi catutthī

(55) अण कर्मणि च (3-3-12)

[SS] Aṇ kramaṇi cā

[KS] Kammani ṇo

(56) पदरुजविशस्पृशो घञ (3-3-16)

[SS] Pada, ruja, viṡa, spriṡo ghañ

[KS] Visa, ruja, padā'dito ṇa

(57) भावे (3-3-18)

[SS] Bhāve

[KS] Bhāve ca

Note: There is another Sutta (4-4-144) with identical structure like KS, but with rather different function.

(58) स्त्रियं क्तिन (3-3-94)

[SS] Striyaṁ ktin

[KS] Itthiya'matiyavo vā

(59) आकोशे नञ्यनिः (3-3-112)

[SS] Ākroṡe nañyani:

[KS] Akkose namhā'ni

(60) ईषददुःसुषुकृच्छाकृच्छर्थेषु खल (3-3-126)

[SS] Īshad, du, sushu, krichākrishattheshu khal

[KS] Īsaṁ, du, sūhi kha

(61) समानकर्तृकेषु तुमुन (3-3-158)

[SS] Samānakratrikeṡu tumun

[KS] Icchatthesu samānakattukesu tave,tuṁ vā

(62) पेषातिसर्गप्राप्तकालेषु कृत्याश्च (3-3-163)

[SS] Peṡātisraggaprāptakāleṡu krityā ṡva

[KS] Pesā'tisaggapattakālesu kiccā

(63) अवश्यकाधमर्ण्ययो र्णिनी (3-3-170)

[SS] Avṡyakādhamaṇyryo ṇirnī

[KS] Avassakā'dhamiṇesu ṇī ca

(64) माङिलुङ (3-3-175)

[SS] Māṅi luṅ

[KS] Māyoge sabbakāle ca

(65) समानकर्तृकयोः पूर्वकाले (3-4-21)

[SS] Samānakratrikayo: pūrvakāle

[KS] Pubbakāle'kakattukānaṁ tuna, tvāna, tvā vā

(66) कर्तरि कृत (3-4-67)

[SS] Kratari krit

[KS] Kattari Kitā

(67) तयोरेव कृत्यक्तखलर्थाः (3-4-70)

[SS] Tayoreva kritya, kta, kkhal, ratthā

[KS] Bhāvakkamesu Kicca, kta, kkha'tthā

(68) तिङशितसार्वधातुकम (3-4-113)

[SS] Tiṅṣita sarvadhātukaṁ

[KS] Hiyyattanī, pañcamī, vattamānā sabbadhātukaṁ

(69) तस्यापत्यम (4-1-92)

[SS] Tasyā patyaṁ

[KS] Vā ṇā'pacce

(70) तेन रत्तं रागात (4-2-1)

[SS] Tena Rattaṁ rāgāt

[KS] Ṇa rāgā tass'eda'maññatthesu ca

(71) ग्रामजनबन्धुसहायोभ्यस्तल (4-2-43)

[SS] Grāma, jana, bandhu, sahāyobyastal

[KS] Gāma, jana, bandhu, sahāyā'dihi tā

(72) द्वेस्तियः (5-2-54)

[SS] Dvestiya:

[KS] Dvitīhi tiyo

(73) इदमो हः (5-3-11)

[SS] Idamo ha:

[KS] Imasmā ha, dhā ca

(74) सर्वैकान्यकिंयत्तदः काले दा (5-3-15)

[SS] Sravekānyākiṁyatād: kāle dā

[KS] Kiṁ, sabbaññe'ka, ya, ku, hi dā, dācanaṁ

(75) इदमो र्हिल (5-3-16)

[SS] Idamo rahil

[KS] Imasmā rahi, dhunā, dāni ca

(76) प्रकारवचने थाल (5-3-23)

[SS] Prakārvacane thāl

[KS] Sabbanāmehi pakāravacane tu thā

(77-78) (a) इदमस्थमुः (5-3-24)

(b) किमश्च (5-3-25)

[SS] Idamsathamu:

[SS] Kiṁ ṣaca

[KS] Kimi'mehi thaṁ

(79) प्रश्यस्य श्रः (5-3-60)

[SS] Praṡyasya ṡra:

[KS] Pasatthassa so ca

(80) वृद्धस्य च (5-3-62)

[SS] Vriddhasya ca

[KS] Vuddhassa jo iye'tthesu

(81) अन्तिकबाढयो र्नेदसाधो (5-3-63)

[SS] Antikabādḍayor nedasādho

[KS] Antikassa nedo

[KS] Bālhassa sādho

(82) युवाल्पयोः कनन्यतरस्याम (5-3-64)

[SS] Yuvālapyo kanyatarasyaṁ

[KS] Yuvānañ'ca

[KS] Appassa kaṇ

(83) वीन्मतो र्लुक (5-3-65)

[SS] Vīnmatorluk

[KS] Vantu,mantu,vīnañ'ca lopo

(84) तत्प्रकृतवचने मयद (5-4-21)

[SS] Tatprakritavacane myad

[KS] Ta'ppakativacane mayo

(85) धनुष श्च (5-4-132)

[SS] Dhanuṡa ṡca

[KS] Dhanumhā ca

(86) पुर्वोभ्यासः (6-1-4)

[SS] Purvo byāsa:

[KS] Pubbo'bbhāso

(87) इको यणचि (6-1-77)

[SS] Iko yaṇci

[KS] Ivaṇṇo yaṁ navā

(88) आटश्च (6-1-90)

[SS] Āttañṡca

[KS] Āttañ'ca (Only Sutta's wording is identical. Function is totally different)

(89) स्त्रियाः पुंवद्भाषितपुंस्कादनूङ समानादिकरणे स्त्रियमपूरणी पियादीषु (6-3-34)

[SS] striyā: puṁvatbhāṣitapuṁsakādanūṅ samānādhikaraṇe striyamapūrṇī piyādīṣu

[KS] Itthiyaṁ bhāsitapumitthī pumā'va ce

(90) पुंवत्कर्मधारयजातियदेशियेषु (6-3-42)

[SS] Puṁvat karmadhāraya jātiyadesiyeṣu

[KS] Kammadhārayasaññe ca

(91) इदंकिमोरीशकी (6-3-90)

[SS] Idakimo rīṣakī

[KS] Iyatamakiṁetānamantassaro dīghaṁ kvaci disassa guṇaṁ do raṁ sakhī' ca

(92) कोः कत्तत्पुरुषेऽचि (6-3-101)

[SS] Ko: kat tatpuruṣe aci

[KS] Kad Kussa

(93) ईषदर्थे (6-3-105)

[SS] īṣadrathe

[KS] Kā'ppatthesu ca

(94) अत उत्सार्वधातुके (6-4-110)

[SS] Ata Utsarvadhātuke

[KS] Karassā'kāro ca

(95) श्नसोरल्लोपः (6-4-111)

[SS] Śna sorallopa:

[KS] Sabbatthā'sassā'dilopo ca

(96) युवोरनाकौ (7-1-1)

[SS] Yuvo ranākau:

[KS] Ana'kā yu,ṇvūnaṁ

(97) अतोऽम (7-1-24)

[SS] Ato'm

[KS] Siṁ'

(98) समासे नञपूर्वे क्त्वो ल्यप (7-1-37)

[SS] Samāse nyañpūrve ktvo lyap

[KS] Sabbehi tunā'dīnaṁ yo

(99) त्वाहौ सौ (7-2-94)

[SS] Tavāhau sau

[KS] Tva'mahaṁ simmhi ca

(100) तुभ्यमह्यौ ङयि (7-2-95)

[SS] Tubyamahyau ṅayi

[KS] Tuyhaṁ mayhañ'ca

(101) तवममौ ङसि (7-2-96)

[SS] Tava mamau ṅasi

[KS] Tava mama se

(102) किमः कः (7-2-103)

[SS] Kima: Ka:

[KS] Sesesu ca

(103) तदोः सः सावनन्त्ययो (7-2-106)

[SS] tado: sa: sāvanantyayo:

[KS] Etatesaṁ so

(104) इदोऽय पुंसि (7-2-111)

[SS] Ido'ya puṁci

[KS] Anapuṁsakassā'yaṁ siṁmhi

(105) अनाप्यकः (7-2-112)

[SS] Anāpayaka:

[KS] Ani'mi nāmhi ca

(106) तद्धितेष्वचामादेः (7-2-117)

[SS] Taddhiteṣvacāmāde:

[KS] Vuddhā'disarassa vā'saṁyogantassa saṇe ca

(107) इषुगमियमां छः (7-3-77)

[SS] Iṣugamiyamāṁ cha:

[KS] (a) Gamissa'nto cho vā sabbāsu

(b) Isu, yamūna'manto cho vā

(108) पाघ्राधमास्थाम्नादाणदृश्यर्तिसार्तिशदसदां पिबजिघ्रधमतिष्ठ मनयच्छपश्यऋच्छधौशीयसीदाः (7-3-78)

[SS] Pā, ghrā, dhamā, sṭhā, manā, dāṇ, driṣi, arti, sarti, sada, sadaṁ piva, jighra, dhama, tiṣṭha, mana, yaccha, paṣya, riccha, dhau, sīya. sīdā:

[KS] (a) Pā pivo (b) ṭhā tiṭho (c) Disassa passa, dissa, dakkhā vā (d) Sadassa sīdattaṁ (4 Suttas)

(109) शाजनो र्जा (7-3-79)

[SS] Jñā, janor jā

[KS] ñāssa jā, jaṁ, nā

(110) बहुवचने झल्येत (7-3-103)

[SS] Bahuvacane jhalayet

[KS] Suhisva'kāro e

(111) वचः उम (7-4-20)

[SS] Vaca: uṁ

[KS] Vacassa'jjattanimhi'makāro o

(112) ह्रस्वः (7-4-59)

[SS] Hrasva:

[KS] Rasso

(113) कुहो श्चु (7-4-62)

[SS] Kuho ṣcu

[KS] Kavaggassa cavaggo

(114) युष्मदस्मदोः षष्ठी-चतुर्थी-द्वितीयास्थयोर्वान्नावौ (8-1-20)

[SS] Yuṡmadasmado: ṡaṡṭhī caturthī dvitiyīyā sthayorvānnāvau

[KS] Padato dutiyā, catutthī, chaṭṭhīsu vo, no

(115) बहुवचनस्य वस्नसौ (8-1-21)

[SS] Bahuvacanasya vasanasau

[KS] Bahuvacanesu vo, no

(116) तेमयावेकवचनस्य (8-1-22)

[SS] Temayāvekavacanasya

[KS] Te, me'kavacanesu ca

(117) तवामौ द्वितियायाः (8-1-23)

[SS] Tavāmau dvitiyāyā:

[KS] Tvaṁ mama'mhi

(118) संयोगन्तस्य लोपः (8-2-23)

[SS] Saṁyogantasya Lopa:

[KS] Vyañjano ca visa'ññogo

(119) मो नुस्वारः (8-3-23)

[SS] Mo nusvāra:

[KS] Aṁ Vyañjane niggahitaṁ

(120) मय उञो वो वा (8-3-33)

[SS] Maya uño vo vā
[KS] Va'mo'du'dantānaṁ

(121) रषाभ्यां नो णः समानपदे (8-4-1)

[SS] Raṡābyaṁ no ṇa: samānapade
[KS] Ra,hā'dito ṇa

Total: 121

The List of Similar Suttas
found in Kātantra & Kaccāyana.

There are about 1401 Suttas in Kātantra grammar and 399 Suttas in Uṇādi Vritti. Those shown below are a list of Suttas from both texts which share some partial or total similarities in terms of function or structural wording although not all of them bear a complete resemblance. However, there are quite a few Suttas which are almost identical.

सन्धि (Sandhi)

(1) ते वर्गा पञ्च पञ्च पञ्च

[SS] Te vraggā pañca pañca pañca

[KS] Vaggā Pañcapañcaso mantā

(2) अं इत्यनुस्वारः

[SS] Aṁ itya nusvāra:

[KS] Aṁ iti niggahitaṁ

(3) व्यञ्जनमस्वरं परं वर्ण नयेत

[SS] Vyañjana masvaraṁ paraṁ vraṇṇa nayet

[KS] Naye paraṁ yutte

(4-5) (a) अवर्ण इवर्णे ए [SS] Avraṇṇa-ivraṇṇe e.

(b) उवर्णे ओ [SS] Uvraṇṇe O. [2 Suttas]

[KS] Kvacā'savaṇṇaṁ lutte

(6) इवर्णो यमसवर्णे न च परो लोप्यः

[SS] Ivraṇṇo yamasavraṇṇe na ca paro lopya:

[KS] Ivaṇṇo yaṁ navā

(7) वमुवर्णः

[SS] Vamu vraṇṇa:

[KS] Va'mo'du'dantānaṁ

(8) ए अय E aya

(9) ओ अव O ava (These Suttas which are identical with Kaccāyana Suttas, are found in Ākhyāta verbs chapter in the Kaccāyana text)

(10) अनुपदिष्टश्च

[SS] Anupadiṡtañṡca

[KS] Anu’padiṭṭhāhaṁ vuttayogato

(11) मोऽनुस्वारं व्यञ्जने

[SS] Mo nusvāraṁ vyañjane

[KS] Aṁ byañjane niggahitaṁ

(12) वर्गे तदवर्गपञ्चमं वा

[SS] Vragge tadvraggapañcamaṁ vā

[KS] Vaggantaṁ vā vagge

नाम (Nāma)

(1) तस्मात्परा विभत्तयः

[SS] Tasmā Taprā Vibaktaya:

[KS] Tato ca vibattiyo

(2) आमन्त्रिते सिः संबुद्धि

[SS] Āmantrite si: saṁbuddhi

[KS] Ālapane si gasañño

(3) द्वन्द्वस्थाच्च

[SS] Dvandvasṭṭhā cca

[KS] Dvandaṭṭhā vā

(4) नायत सार्वनामिकम

[SS] Nāyat sārvanāmikaṁ

[KS] Nā’ññaṁ sabbanāmikaṁ

(5) बहुव्रीहौ

[SS] Bahuvrīhau

[KS] Bahubbīhimhi ca

(6) त्वमहम सौ सविभक्त्योः

[SS]Tvamahaṁ sau savibaktayo:

[KS] Tvamahaṁ simhi ca

(7) तुभ्यम मह्यम ङयि

[SS]Tubyaṁ mayhaṁ ṅayi

[KS] Tuyhaṁ mayhañca

(8) तव ममङसि

[SS]Tavamama ṅasi

[KS]Tava mama se

(9) किम कः

[SS]Kiṁ ka:

[KS] Sesesu ca

कारक (Kāraka)

(1) अव्ययीभावादकारन्ताद्विभक्तीनाम मपञ्चम्याः

[SS] Avyayībhāvādakārantād vibaktīnā'ṁ' mapañcamyā:

[KS] Aṁ vibattīna'makārantā abyayībhāvā

(2) अन्यस्माल्लुक

[SS] Anyasmālluk

[KS] Aññsmā lopo ca

Note: In Kaccāyana grammar, these two Suttas are found in the Samāsa chapter which is more relevant.

(3) यतोऽपैति भयमादत्ते वा तदपादानम

[SS] Yatopeti bhaya mādatte vā tadpādānaṁ

[KS] Yasmā'dapeti bhaya'mādatte vā ta'dapādānaṁ

(4) इप्सितं च रक्षार्थानाम

[SS] Ipsitaṁ ca rakhāratthānaṁ

[KS] Rakkhaṇatthāna'micchitaṁ

(5) यस्मै दित्सा रोचते धारयते वा तत समप्रदानम

[SS] Yasme ditsā rocate dhārayate vā tat sampradānaṁ

[KS] Yassa dātukamo rocate, dhārayate vā.
tam sampradānaṁ

(3) प्रकृतिश्च स्वरान्तस्य

[SS] Prakriti śca svarāntasya

[KS] Pakati ca'ssa sara'ntassa

(4) पदे तुल्याधिकरणे विझेयः कर्मधारयः

[SS] Pade tulyādhikraṇe viñeya: krammadhārya:

[KS] Dvipade tulyādhikaraṇe kammadhārayo

(5) संख्यापुर्वो द्विगुरिति ज्ञेयः

[SS] Saṅkhyāpurvo dviguriti ñeya:

[KS] Saṅkhyāpubbo digu

(6) तत्पुरूषावुभौ

[SS] Tatpurūshā vubho

[KS] Ubhe tappurisā

(7) विभ्त्तयो द्वितियाद्य नाम्ना परपदेन तु स्मस्यन्ते समासो हि झेयस्तत्पुरुषः स च

[SS] Vibaktayo dvitiyādya nāmnā parapadena tu smassayante samāso hi ñyeya statpurusha: sa ca

[KS] A'mādayo parapadebhi

(8) स्यातं यदि पदे द्वे तु यदि वा स्युर्बहून्यपि। तान्यन्यस्य पदस्यार्थे बहुव्रीहिः

[SS] Syātaṁ yadi pade dve tu yadi vā syurbahūnyapi,
Tānyan'yasya padasyaratthe bahuvrīhi.

[KS] Aññapada'tthesu bahubbīhi

(9) द्वन्द्वः समुच्चयो नाम्नोर्बहूनां वापि यो भवेत

[SS] Dvandva: samuccayo nāmanorabahūnaṁ vā'pi yo bhavet

[KS] Nāmānaṁ samuccayo dvando

(10) स नपुंसकलिङ्गं स्यात

[SS] Sa napuṁsakaliṅgaṁ syāt

[KS] So napuṁsakaliṅgo

(11) पुंवद्भाषितपुंस्कानूङ्पूरण्यादिषु स्त्रियां तुल्याधिुरणे

[SS] Puṁvadbhāshita puṁskānūṅpūraṇyādishu striyaṁ

tulyādhikraṇe
[KS] Itthiyaṁ bhāsitapumi'tthī pumā'va ce
(12) कर्मधारयसंज्ञे तु पुंवद्भावो विधीयते
[SS] Krammadhārayasaññe tu puṁvadbhāvo vidhīyate
[KS] Kammadhārayasaññe ca
(13) कोः कत
[SS] Ko: Kat
[KS] Kad kussa
(14) का त्वीषदर्थेऽक्षे
[SS] Kā tvīshadratthe khe
[KS] Kā'ppatthesu ca

तद्धित (Taddhita)

(1) वा णपत्ये
[SS] Vā ṇa patye
[KS] Vā ṇā'pacce
(2) तत्वौ भावे
[SS] Tatvau bhāve
[KS] Ṇyattatā bhāvesu
(3) तदस्यास्तीति मन्त्वन्त्वीन
[SS] Tadasyā stīti mantvantvīn
[KS] Satyā'dīhi mantu.
Guṇadito Vantu
Tadassatthīti vī ca (3 Suttas in Kaccāyana text)
(4) संख्यायाः पूरणे डमो
[SS] Saṅkhyāyā: Pūraṇe imo
[KS] Saṅkhyāpūraṇe mo
(5) द्वेस्तीयः
[SS] Dvestiya:
[KS] Dvitīhi tiyo

(6) इदमो हः

[SS] Idamo ha:

[KS] Imasmā ha, dhā ca (Found in the Nāma, Nouns chapter in Kaccāyana text)

(7) इदमो र्ह्यधुनादानिम

[SS] Idamo rahya, dhunā, dānim

[KS] Imasmā rahi, dhunā, dāni ca (Found in Nāma, Nouns chapter in Kaccāyana text)

(8) दादानिमौ तदः स्मृतौ

[SS] Dā, dānimau tad: smritau

[KS] Tamhā dāni ca (Found in Nāma, Nouns chapter in Kaccāyana text)

(9) प्रकारवसने तु था

[SS] Prakāravacane tu thā

[KS] Sabbanāmehi pakāravacane tu thā

(10) इदमकिम्भ्यां थमुः कार्य्यः

[SS] Idam, kiṁbyāṁ thamu: kāriyya:

[KS] Ki'mimehi thaṁ

(11) वृद्धिरादौ सणे

[SS] Vriddhi rādau saṇe

[KS] Vuddhā'disarassa vā'saṁyogantassa saṇe ca

(12) न य्वोः पदाद्योर्वृद्धिरागमः

[SS] Na yvo: padādyor vriddhirāgama:

[KS] Mā yūna'māgamo thāne

आख्यात (Ākhyāta)

(1) अथ परस्मैपदानि नव

[SS] Atha prasmepadāni nava

[KS] Atha pubbāni vibattīnaṁ cha parassapadāni

(2) नव पराण्यत्मने

[SS] Nava prāṇyatmane

[KS] Parāṇy'attanopadāni

(3) त्रीणि त्रीणि प्रथम मध्य मोत्तमा

[SS] Trīṇi trīṇi prathama, madhya'moktamā

[KS] Dve dve paṭhama, majjimu'ttama, purisā

(4) युगपदवचने परः पुरुषणाम

[SS] Yugapadavacane pra: purushaṇāṁ

[KS] Sabbesa'mekābhidhāne paro puriso

(5) नाम्नि प्रयुज्यमानेऽपि प्रथमः

[SS] Nāmani payujjamāne'pi prathama:

[KS] Nāmamhi payujjamāne'pi tulyādhikaraṇe paṭhamo

(6) युष्मदि मध्यमः

[SS] Yushamadi mdhyama:

[KS] Tummhe majjimo

(7) अस्मद्युत्तमः

[SS] Asmadyuttama:

[KS] Ammhe Uttamo

(8) काले

[SS] Kāle

[KS] Kāle

(9) सम्प्रति वर्तमाना

[SS] Samprati Vrattamānā

[KS] Vattamānā paccuppanne

(10) परोक्षा

[SS] Prokhā

[KS] Apaccakkhe prokhā'tīte

(11) पञ्चम्यनुमतौ

[SS] Pañcamya numatau

[KS] Āṇaty'āsiṭṭhe anuttakāle pañcamī

(12) मायोगेऽद्यत्तीन

[SS] Māyogedyattīn

[KS] Māyoge sabbakāle ca

(13) षडाद्याः सार्वधातुकम
[SS] Ṣaḍādyā: sravadhātukam
[KS] Hiyyattanī, sattamī, pañcamī, vattamānā sabbadhātukaṁ

(14) प्रतययः परः
[SS] Pratyaya: pra:
[KS] Dhātuliṅgehi parā paccayā

(15) गुप्तिजकिद्भ्यः सन
[SS] Guptija kidbya: san
[KS] Tija, gupa, kita, mānehi kha, cha, sā va

(16) धातोर्वातुमन्तादिच्छतिनैककर्तृकात
[SS] Dhātorvā tumantādicchati neka katrikāt
[KS] Bhuja, ghasa, hara, su, pā’dīhi tu’micchatthesu

(17) नाम्न आत्मेच्छायं यिन
[SS] Nāmna ātme’cchāyaṁ yin
[KS] Nāmammhā’tticcha’the

(18) उपमाना दाचारे
[SS] Upamānā dācāre
[KS] Āya nāmato kattūpamānā’dācāre

(19) चुरादेश्च
[SS] Curāde śca
[KS] Curā’dito ṇe, ṇayā

(20) अन विकरणः कर्त्तरि
[SS] An vikarana: kattari
[KS] Bhūvādito a

(21) दिवादेर्यन
[SS] Divāde ryan
[KS] Divā’dito yo

(22) नुः स्वादेः
[SS] Nu: svāde:
[KS] Svādito ṇuṇā, uṇā ca

(23) ना कयादेः

[SS] Nā Kryāde:

[KS] Ki'yādito nā

(24) आत्मनेपदानि भावकर्मणोः

[SS] Atmanopadāni bhāvakrammaṇo:

[KS] Attanopadāni bhāve ca kammani

(25) शेषात कर्त्तरि परस्मैपदम

[SS] Ṡeshāt katri prasamepadaṁ

[KS] Kattari parassapadaṁ

(26) द्विर्वचनमनभ्यासस्यौकस्वरस्याद्यस्य

[SS] Dvirvacanamanabyāsasyaukasvarasyādysya

[KS]Kvcādivaṇṇāna mekasarānaṁ dvebhāvo

(27) पूर्वोऽभ्यासः

[SS] Pūrvo byāsa:

[KS] Pubbo'bbhāso

(28) द्वितियचतुर्थयो प्रथमतृतियौ

[SS] Dvitiya, caturthayo prathama, tritiyo

[KS] Dutiya, catutthānaṁ paṭhama, tatiyā

(29) हो जः

[SS] Ho ja:

[KS] Hassa jo

(30) कवर्गस्य चवर्गः

[SS] Kvragasya ca vraga:

[KS] Kavaggassa cavaggo

(31) ह्रस्वः

[SS] Hrasva:

[KS] Rasso

(32-33) (a) भवतेरः (b) सन्यवर्णस्य

[SS] (a) Bhavatera: (b) Sanya vraṇasya [2 Suttas]

[KS] Antassi'vaṇṇā'kāro vā

(34) अस्योकारः सार्वधातुकेऽगुणे

[SS] Asayokāra: sārvadhātuke guṇe

[KS] Karassā'kāro ca

(35) अस्तेरादेः

[SS] Asaterāde:

[KS] Sabbatthā'sassā'dilopo ca

(36-37) (a) गोहेरूदुपधायाः (b) दुषेः कारिते

[SS] (a) Gohe rūdupdhāyā (b) Dushe kārite [2 Suttas]

[KS] Guha, dusānaṁ dīhaṁ

(38) अस्ते र्भूरसार्वधातुके

[SS] Asater bhūr sārvadhātuke

[KS] Asabbadhātuke bhū

(39) गमिष्यमां छः

[SS] Gamishyamāṁ cha:

[KS] Gamissanto ccho vā sabbāsu

(40) पः पिबः

[SS] Pa: piva:

[KS] Pā pivo

(41) स्था स्तिष्ठः

[SS] Sṭhā stiṭha:

[KS] ṭhā tiṭho

(42) दृशोः पश्यः

[SS] Driśo: Paśya:

[KS] Disassa passa, dissa, dakkhā vā

(43) ज्ञाश्च

[SS] ñā śca

[KS] ñāssa jā jaṁ nā

(44) अणिवचेरोदुपधायाः

[SS] Aṇivacerodupadhāyā:

[KS] Vacassa'jjatanimhi'makāro o

कित (Kita)

(1) तव्यानीयौ

[SS] Tavyā nīyau

[KS] Bhāvakammesu tabbā'nīyā

(2) ते कृत्या

[SS] Te krityā

[KS] Te Kiccā

(3) नन्द्यदेर्युः

[SS] Nandyāderyu:

[KS] Nandā'dīhi yu

(4) कर्मण्यण

[SS] Kramma ṇyaṇ

[KS] Dhātuyā kammādimhi ṇo

(5) क्विप च

[SS] Kvip ca

[KS] Kvi ca

(6,7,8) (a) कर्मण्युपमाने त्यदादौ दृशष्टकसकौ च

(b) इदमी (c) किम की

[SS] (a) Kramaṇyupamāne tydādau drishathakaskau ca

[SS] (b) Ida mī (c) Kima kī

[KS] I, ya, ta, ma, kiṁ, esāna'mantassaro dīghaṁ kvaci disassa guṇaṁ do raṁ sakhī ca

(9) ञ्यनुबन्धमतिबुद्धिपूजार्थेभ्यः क्तः

[SS] ṅyanuvandha, mati, vuddhi, pūjārthabya: kta:

[KS] Bhyā'dīhi mati, budhi, pujā'dīhi ca kto

(10) भविश्यतिगम्यादयः

[SS] Bhaviśyati gmyādya:

[KS] Bhavissati gamā'dīhi ṇī, ghiṇ

(11) वुणतुमौ कियायं कियार्थायम

[SS] Vuṇ tumau kriyāyaṁ kriyarāthāyaṁ

[KS] Kiriyāyaṁ ṇvu, tavo

(12) भाववाचिनश्च

[SS] Bhāvavācinañśca

[KS] Bhāvavācimhi catutthī

(13) कर्मणि चाण

[SS] Krammaṇi cāṇ

[KS] Kammani ṇo

(14) शन्त्रानौ स्यसंहितौ शेषे च

[SS] Śantrānau syasaṁhitau śeshe ca

[KS] Sese ssantu, mānā'nā

(15) पदरुजविशस्पृह शोचां घञ

[SS] Padarujaviśaspriha śocāṁ ghañ

[KS] Visa, ruja, padādito ṇa

(16) भावे

[SS] Bhāve

[KS] Bhāve ca

(17) स्त्रियां क्ति

[SS] Striyāṁ kti

[KS] Itthiya'matiyavo vā

(18) इच्छार्थेष्वेककर्तृकेषु तुम

[SS] Icchārtthe shaveka krattrikeshu tuṁ

[KS] Icchatthesu samānakattukesu tave, tuṁ vā

(19) अवश्यकाधमिणयो णि

[SS] Avaśykā dhamiṇayo ṇi

[KS] Avassakā'dhamiṇesu ṇī ca

(20) कर्तारि कृतः

[SS] Krattari krita:

[KS] Kattari kit

(21) भावकर्मणो कृत्यत्तखलर्थाः

[SS] Bhāva krammaṇo kritya, kta, khalara'tthā:

[KS] Bhāvakammesu kicca, kta, kkha'tthā

(22) समासे भाविन्यनञः त्तवो यप

[SS] Samāse bhāvinyañ ktvo yap
[KS] Sabbehi tunādīnaṁ yo

(23) चजोः कगौ घुडघानुबन्धयौः

[SS] Cajo: kagau ghuḍaghānuvandhayau:
[KS] Ka, gā ca, jānaṁ

उणादि (Uṇādi)

(1) खर्जिकृपिमसिपिञ्जालादिभ्यः ऊरोलौ

[SS] Khrajikripimasipiñcālādibya ūrolau
[KS] Vidā’dīhihū’ro

(2) सर्वधातुभ्ये मन

[SS] Sarvadhātubye man
[KS] Khyā’dīhi man, ma ca to vā

(3) प्रथेरमः

[SS] Prathe rama:
[KS] Puthassa puthu, pathāmo vā

(4-5) (a) मनेरूष्यः (b) मानेरूषः

[SS] (a) Mane rūshya: (b) Māne rūsha:
[KS] Manupūrasuṇā’dīhi usa, ṇusi’sā

(6) मडिकुडिमङिगाभ्येऽलः

[SS] Maḍi, kuḍi, maṅgibyo la:
[KS] Paṭādīhya’laṁ

Total: 142.

KACCĀYANA DHĀTVĀ'VALI

The Index of Roots in Kaccāyana Text

Note: The roots are like the basic building blocks of various Pāli words. One can multiply various verb-forms and nouns by using different verb-terminations and applicable affixes. Therefore, it is quite important to have some basic knowledge of the roots. Below is an alphabetical order of the roots in the list. (a) The root called *Dhātu* is shown in bold. (b) Its meaning called ***Dhātvattha-pavedanā*** is shown in italicized Pāli followed by English. (c) The Sutta numbers where example word of the root are found, are shown alongside. [**dhātvattha-dhātu**-the root+ **attha**-meaning+**pavedanā**-letting it be known, **i.e.** declaration.]

Usually, ***dhātvatthapavedanā*** is a kita-affixed noun in Locative singular case-ending which may be affixed with one of **yu, ṇa, a** or **ti** affixes.

(1) When it is affixed in "**yu**", it will end in "**ane, aṇe, āne, āṇe**". e.g. Kath**ane**, sar**aṇe, dāne,** ñ**āṇe** .

(2) When affixed in **ṇa** or **a**, it will end in just an "e" with or without a *vuddhi* function in the word. e.g. P**ā**k**e**, Nay**e**.

(3) When affixed in "**ti**", it will be just plain "ti" ending in **yaṁ** or **mhi.** e.g. gatiyaṁ, gatimhi. (**yaṁ** and **mhi** are derivative morpheme of locative singular "smiṁ". Refer to Sutta 216, 99)

A *dhātvatthapavedanā* usually declares the meaning of the root as **an action** (*kriya'ttha*) such as "to go, to speak" and so on. But in some rare instances, there are a few roots which may mean **the substance** (*dabba'ttha*) rather than being an action. e.g., **palla**-*ninnathāne*-in being low-lying area.

Please note that generally some roots may have one single meaning but there are roots with more than one meaning. Some of the roots may even change their original meaning in many distinctive ways when prefixed with various *upasagga* particles.

Also note that any root having the meaning of "**gati**-to move, to go" may even mean "to know, to be or to reach" which is a bit like English verb "get" which has a rich variety of meanings in various contextual usages. All of the roots are drawn from Ākhyāta, Kita and Uṇādi chapters totaling 273.

[a]

The numbers inside parenthesis indicate the Sutta numbers.

agga-*gatikoṭille*-to move in a non-straight way. (665)
aja-*gatimhi*-to go (638)
ada-*bhakkhaṇe*-to consume, to eat (627)
aḍi-*aṇḍatthe*-to lay the egg. (663)
apa-*pāpuṇe*-to reach (448)
ama-*roge*-to afflict,(664)
aya-*gatimhi*-to go, to be (528)
ala-*sāmatthe*-to be able to, (632)
asa-*bhuvi*-to be (492-494) bhakkhaṇe-to eat (641). (9)

[ā]

āsa-*upavesane*-to approach, to devote (540) (1)

[i]

i-*gatiyaṁ*-to go, to move (when prefixed with "adhi", it means to learn, to recite (635).
ikkha-*pekkhane*-to look to, to see (277)
iji-*kampane*-to shake (638)
idi-*paramissariye*-to lord over (661)
ila-*kampane*-to tremble, (673)
isiḍi-*avamaddane*-to press down, to crush (663)
issa-*issāyaṁ*-to be jealous of. (277)
isiḍi-*vimaddane*-to press. (663)
isu-*icchāyaṁ*-to want (522) (9)

[u]

uca-*samavāye*-to manifest together (640).
viyattiyaṁ vācāyaṁ-to articulately speak (580)
udi-*pasavane*-to increase. (661)
udha-*usagge*-to discard, to throw (441)
usu-*dāhe*-to burn (659)
usūya-*usūyāyaṁ*-to be envious of. (277) (5)

[e]

eraḍi-*hiṁsāyaṁ*-to torture, (663) (1)

[ka]

kaca-*dittiyaṁ*-to shine (638)
kaṭa-*maddane*-to thrash (672)
katha-*kathane*-to speak (564)
kaḍi-*chedane*-to cut (663)
kada-*madde*-to inebriate (665)
kappa-*takkane*-to think (643)
kapi-*calane*-to shake (533)
kapu-*hiṁsā, takkala, gandhesu*-to torture, in being the smell of tree sap (670)
kamu-*padavikkhepe*-to move steps, to go (458).
(also) *icchāyaṁ*-to want (524)
kamba (also) **kabi**-*sañcalane*-to shake (665)
kara-*karaṇe*-to do (451)
karaḍi-*bhājane*-to distribute as in small cups (663)
kala-*saṅkhyāne*-to count (632)
ki-*hiṁsāyaṁ*-to torment (673)
ki, kī-*dabbavinimaye*-to sell, to trade (449)
kita-*rogāpanayane*-to cure as diseases. *kaṅkhāyaṁ*-to doubt (433)
kira-*vikiraṇe*-to spread, to cast all over (581)
ku-*sadde*-to sound. (670) *kucchite*-in being disgusted (673)
kuca-*saṁkocane*-to hesitate (638)
kuṭa-*chedane*-to cut. (672)

kuṭhi-*chedane*-to cut (663)
kudha-*kopane*-to be angry (533)
kura-*akkose*-to revile (670)
kusa-*akkose* (498) *chedana, bhūta, dāna, sañcayesu*-to cut, to be, to give, to accumulate (665) *acchāda, pūraṇe*-to cover, to fill up (672) (23)

[kha]

khajja-*bhakkhaṇe*-to eat (670)
khaḍi-*chedane*-to cut (663)
khanu-*avadāraṇe*-to dig (586)
khamu-*sahane*-to bear, to put up with (584)
khādha-*bhakkhane*-to eat, to munch (664)
khida-*khede*-to be weary, to tire out (582)
khī-*khaye*-to run out of, to have no more (627)
khuda-*pipāsāyaṁ*-to be hungry (661) (8)

[ga]

gaṭi-*ghaṭṭane*-to strike (663)
gaḍi-*sannicaye*-to gather
gamu-*gatimhi*-to go, to move (476)
garaha-*nindāyaṁ*-to censure (544)
gaha-*upādāne*-to cling to, to grab, to take (450)
gāhu-*viloḷane*-to mess up (589)
gupa-*nindāyaṁ*-to censure, also, *gopane*-to protect (433)
guha-*rakkhaṇe*-to protect, to hide (486)
ge-*sadde*-to sound, to sing (608) (9)

[gha]

ghaṭa-*cetāyaṁ*-to incite (484)
ghaḍi-*ghaṭṭane*-to strike as a bell (663)
ghasa-*bhakkhaṇe*-to eat (434)
ghusa-*sadde*-to sound, *ghosane*-to say loudly (533) (4)

[na]

naṭa-*gattavikkhepe*-to dance, to sway the body (571)
namu-*paṇāme*-to bow as in respect (Begininng Verses)
nanda-*nandane*-to be pleased (547)
ninda-*nindāyaṁ*-to censure, to chide (562)
naha-*bandhane*-to bind, to entangle (589)
niti-*nicce*-in being eternal (638)
nī-*naye*-to carry (514)
nuda-*panūdane*-to extract, to pull out, *khepe*-to throw, to rid of (641) (8)

[pa]

paca-*pāke*-to cook. (445)
paci-*vitthāre*-to extend, to enlarge. (665)
paṭa-*gatimhi*-to move (309)
paṭha-*viyattiyaṁ vācāyaṁ*-to speak articulately, to recite (445)
pata-*gatimhi, patane*-to move or to fall (669)
pada-*gatimhi*-to move (also) -*pavattane*-to be (656)
paḍi-*liṅgavekalle*-in being sexually deviant (663)
palla-*ninnathāne*-in being low-lying area (665)
phala-*nipphattiyaṁ*-to bear fruit, to accomplish (443)
pisa-*sañcuṇṇe*-to pulverize, to crush to become powder (638)
piha-*sinehe*-to love, to admire,(277)
pā-*pāne*-to drink (469) *pālane*-to protect.
pī-*tappane*-to enrapture, to be pleased with (627)
pu-*pavane*-to purify (449)
puccha-*pucchāyaṁ*-to question (573)
putha-*vitthāre*-to stretch (665)
pūra-*pūraṇe*-to fill (581)
pūja-*pūjāyaṁ*-to honor, to worship (583) (18)

[pha]

phadi-*calane*-to shake (533)
phusa-*phusane*-to touch, to come in contact (528) (2)

[ba]

bhaḍi-*bhaṇḍane*-to argue, to quarrel (663)
baha-*vuddhimhi*-to grow (589)
bahu-*saṅkhyāne*-to count (665)
bila-*nissaye*-in being a dependent base (665)
budha-*ñāṇe*-to know (557) (5)

[bha]

bhaganda-*secane*-to pour, to drip (665)
bhaja-*vibhāge*-to distribute (651) (also)
bhanja-*avamaddane*-to press down, to crush (573)
bhaṇa-*kathane*-to speak (227)
bhamu-*anavaṭhāne*-to be unable to stand firmly, to be fickle, to spin around just as a top (584)
bhasa-*bhasamīkaraṇe*-to pulverize, to make into ash as in burning (628) *bhakkhaṇe*-to eat (638)
bhā-*dittiyaṁ*-to shine (671)
bhāsa-*kathane*-to speak (533) *jutiyaṁ*-to shine.
bhikkha-*yācane*-to beg (535)
bhidi-*dvidhākaraṇe*-to divide into two, to break (582)
bhī-*bhaye*-to fear (627)
bhuja-*bhakkhaṇe*-to eat. (also) *pālane*-to protect (578)
bhū-*sattāyaṁ*-to be (445)
bhūsa-*alaṅkāre*-to adorn, to beautify (533)
brū-*viyattiyaṁ vācāyaṁ*-to speak (520) (15)

[ma]

maca-*core*-to steal (665)
maja-*parimajjane*-to massage, to rub all over (441)
maṅga-*maṅgale*-in being auspicious. (665)
manta-*guttabhāsane*-to whisper as in private talk or discussion (452)
matha-*vilolane*-to mess up (502)
mada-*ummāde*-to inebriate, in being mad, (544)
madi-*hāse*-to amuse (661)

maḍi-*maṇḍane*-to adorn, to beautify (663)
mana-*ñāṇe*-to know (444)
mara-*maraṇe*-to die (505)
masa-*āmasane*-to caress, to fondle, to rub (670)
maha-*pūjāyaṁ*-to honor (502)
mā-*māne*-to measure (502)
māna-*vīmaṁsāyaṁ*-to analytically think (also) *sammānane*-to adore (433)
mida-*sinehe*-to adore, to love (658)
mekha-*kaṭivicitte*-to adorn waist as with a belt.
meḍi-*kuṭile*-in being not straight as horns of an animal
muna-*ñāṇe*-to know (449)
musa-*theye*-to steal (665) *pāṇacāge*-to give up on life, to die (638) *vināse*-to lose, to disappear
muha-*vecitte*-to be confused.
mūla-*patiṭhāyaṁ*-to take root, to establish (665) (21)

[ya]

yaja-*pūjāyaṁ*-to offer sacrifice to, to honor (503)
yata-*payatane*-to exert effort (656)
yamu-*viratiyaṁ,* or *uparamaṇe*-to abstain from (522)
yā-*gatiyaṁ*-to move, to go (628)
yuja-*yoge*-to tie up, to yoke, to bind (544)
yudha-*pahāre*-to strike, to hit (447) (6)

[ra]

rakkha-*rakkhaṇe*-to protect, to guard.
raḍi-*hiṁsāyaṁ*-to torture, to hurt as a drunkard
rabha-*ārambhe*-to exert effort (600)
ranja-*rāge*-to dye as with color, to lust for (578)
ramu-*ratiyaṁ*-to enjoy (587)
raha-*upādāne*-to cling to (628)
rādha-*saṁsiddhiyaṁ*-to accomplish (277)
ri-*gatiyaṁ*-to move (671)
ru-*gatimhi*-to move,(also) sadde-to sound (627)

ruca-*rocane*-to shine (454)
ruja-*roge*-to pain, to be afflicted. (528)
ruda-*rodane*-to lament, to cry as in sadness (582)
rudi-*hiṁsāyaṁ*-to torture, to harm (661)
rudha-*āvaraṇe*-to obstruct (446)
ruha-*ārohaṇe*-to go up as on a tree or building (589)
rusa-*rosane*-to harass (638) (16)

[la]

laḍi-*jegucche*-in being disgusted as excrement.
labha-*lābhe*-to get, to obtain (497)
lipa-*lepane*-to anoint, to smear (580)
lū-*chedane*-to cut, to clip (449) (4)

[va]

vakka-*rukkhattace*-in being tree-bark (665)
vaja-*gatimhi*-to move (638)
vatu-*āvattane*-to turn round,(also) p*avattane*-to be (656)
vada-*viyattiyaṁ vācāyaṁ*-to speak (Ākhyāta verse)
vaḍi-*saṅghāte*-to gather collectively as in a bunch (663)
vaḍḍha-*vaḍḍhane*-to grow, to thrive (533)
vanda-*vandane*-to bow as in a show of respect (597)
vamu-*uggīraṇe*-to vomit (584)
vapa-*bījanikkhepe*-to cast the seed, to sow (654)
vara-*saṁvaraṇe*-to protect (656)
valla-*bandhane*-to bind, to entangle (670)
vasa-*nivāse*-to dwell (487) a*cchādane*-to cover up (665)
vaha-*pāpuṇe*-to arrive at, *vāhane*-to carry (487)
vā-*gatimhi*-to go (650)
vica-*viveke*-to be alone, to dissociate from (578) v*icaye*-to analyze.
vida-*ñāṇe*-to know (616) *anubhavane*-to feel (553) s*attāyaṁ*-to be (665) *lābhe*-to obtain (670)
vidha-*vijjhane*-to penetrate, to pierce into (444)
visa-*pavesane*-to enter (528)

vu-*saṁvaraṇe*-to protect (448)
ve-*bahisāre*-in being external essence (671),
(also) *tantasantāne*-to weave fabrics as a weaver (524).
vepu-*kampane*-to shake (644) (21)

[sa]

saka-*sāmatthe*-to be able to (583)
sata-*sātacce*-in being eternal, to endure always (638)
sada-*nisīdane*-to sit (609) *visādane*-to tire,(638)
sadda-*sadde*-to sound (533) *harite*-in being lush green (665)
saḍi-*gumbatthe*-in being clusters (663)
sanja-*saṅge*-to cling to (578)
sapa-*akkose*-to revile, *upalabbhe*-to swear in order to win trust.
sama-*upasame*-to calm (628)
samu-*upasame*-to calm (584) *nivāse*-to dwell, *khede*-to be tired.
samba (sabi) -*maṇḍane*-to adorn (665)
sara-*saraṇe*-to remember (512)
sala-*gatiyaṁ*-to go (632)
sasu-*hiṁsāyaṁ*-to torture (667)
sā-*sāmatthe*-to be able to (628)
sāsa-*anusiṭṭhimhi*-to instruct, to teach (556)
si-*bandhane*-to bind (628)
sida-*siṅgāre*-in being serene and romantic (670)
sidha-*saṁsiddhimhi*-to accomplish, to succeed (611)
sica-*secane*-to pour liquid on (580)
silāgha-*thutiyaṁ*-to praise (277)
sivu-*sibbane*-to sew, to stitch (447)
si, sī-*saye*-to sleep, to lie down (644)
su-*savaṇe*-to listen to (434) *abhisave*-to flow (656)
gabbhavimocane-in being cleared of clouds (673)
*hiṁsāyaṁ (*673)
suca-*soke*-to be sad,(661)
suṇa-*hiṁsā, kulasantānesu*-to harass, to prolong family lineage (673)
supa-*soppe*-to fall sleep (559)

subha-*pahāre*-to strike, to hit (446)
susa-*sosane*-to dry, to wither (583)
sū-*pīḷane*-to torment (660)
sūca-*vibhāvane*-to clarify (656)
sūda-*paggharaṇe*-to drip, to ooze (641) (31)

[ha]

hana-*hiṁsāyaṁ*-to torture (586)
hara-*haraṇe*-to carry over (434)
hasa-*hasane*-to smile (556)
hansa-*pahaṁsane*-to be happy (573)
hā-*cāge*-to abandon, to dump (464)
hi-*gatiyaṁ (*628)
hu-*pūjāyaṁ*-to offer sacrifice (464)
hū-*sattāyaṁ*-to come into being, to be (480) (8)

Index

Note: The index is arranged in a chapter-wise, alphabetical order for easy access. **S** means Sutta while **P** means page.

Introduction

A quick study guide of Samāsa P, 40
Kaccāyana and his identity P, 11
Pāli Grammar Study Guide P, 35
Rūpasiddhi P, 45
Sub-Units of grammar Study P, 41
The Components of a Sutta P, 32
The Steps of Effective Learning P, 30
Three Kinds of EDs P, 42
Types of Sandhi P, 35
Types of Vidhi P, 34
WA (Word Analysis) P, 44

1 Sandhi

Aghosa(surds) S.9/P, 124
Akkharā (Alphabet) S.2/P, 118
Asarūpa (Non-homogenous vowel) S.13/P, 129
Asavaṇṇa S.13/P, 129
Byañjana (Consonant) S.6/P, 121
Dīgha (Long vowel) S.5/P, 120
Dvebhāvo (act of doubling, Reduplication) S.28/P, 149
Ghosa(sonant) S.9/P, 124
Niggahita (an upper dot of nasal sound which is placed on top of three short vowels) S.8/P, 123
Pakati procedure S.23,24/P, 143
Rassa (Short vowel) S.4/P, 120
Sara (vowel) S.3/P, 119
Sarūpa (Homogenous vowel) S.13/P, 129
Savaṇṇa S.13/P, 129
Suttavibhāga (Split-Sutta procedure) S.20/P, 138

Table of Reduplication with Dissimilar Consonants S.29/P, 151
Table of Reduplication with Similar Consonants S.28/P, 150
Upasagga **particles** S.51/P, 177
Vagga (Group of five consonants classified as a vagga-group) S.7/P, 122
Vagganta-Function (changing an upper dot into one of five nasal stops, 157
Vagganta-the end consonants of the group, sometimes referred as "nasal stops" S.7/P, 122
Visaññoga procedure (Changing conjunct into non-conjunct) S.41/P, 169
Yutte (Applicability) S.11/P, 126

2 Nāma

"ā" and "ī" "inī" affixes signify feminine gender. S.237, 238, 240/P, 351
20 Upasagga Words S.221/P, 322
Adhikāra (governing rule) S.52/P, 183
Akatarassa (Natural short vowel) S.96/P, 229
Alutta Samāsa S.77/P, 209
Avadhāraṇa (Limitation) S.79/P, 211
āya(Infinitive form of nouns) S.109/P., 240
Bhāvaniddesa (abstract wording of Sutta) S.90/P, 224
Detailed Meanings of Upasagga Particles S.221/P, 324
Different Usages of vocative form "Bhavanta" S.243/P, 355
Jinavacanayutta S.52/P, 183
Kāranta (ending vowel of nouns) S.55/P, 189
Liṅga(Gender) S.53/P, 184
Nipāta Particles S.221/P, 341
Ntu affixes S.92/P, 225
Recognition of **nta-affix** as an equal of **ntu-affix** S.187/P, 302

Recognition of **"smā"** vibatti as **"nā"** S.270/P, 370
Salient characteristic of Mano-group nouns S.183/P, 296
saṁ, sā function S.179, 293
santa (saint) changes into "**sa**" S.185/P, 299
Saralopo Sutta & two major functions S.83/P, 216
Tabbiparita (reversal procedure) S.79/P, 211
Temporary Terms For Some Endings S.55/P, 190
Three functions debarred in Sabbanāma nouns S.110/P, 242
Three kinds of Upasagga particles S.221/P, 323
to, ti, tā function S.127/P, 255
Traces of vibatti-forms S.220/P, 320
ve, vo function S.116/P, 247
Vibatti (14 noun case-endings) S.54-55/P, 186
vo, no function S.147,151/P, 267, 271
yā function S.112/P, 244
Yogavibāga (split-Sutta procedure) S.80/P, 213

3 Kāraka

Ablative of reason S.296/P, 421
Accantasaṁyoga(on-going condition) S.298/P, 422
Accusative case in Genetive sense S.306/P, 431
Accusative in Instrumental S.307/P, 431
Accusative in Locative S.307/P, 432
Ādhāra, Locative (of four kinds) S.278/P, 408
Ālapana(vocative) S.285/P, 413
Anā'dara S.305/P, 428
Anā'dara-Catukka S.305/P, 429
Aṅgavikāra(Defective body part) S.291/P, 416
Apādāna(Ablative) S.271/P, 373
Avuta Kattā (non-principal subject in a passive voice) S.288/P, 415
Binnā'dhikaraṇa Visesana S.292/P, 417
Genitive in Ablative S.309/P, 434
Genitive in Accusative S.309/P, 434

Genitive in Instrumental S.308/P, 432
Genitive in Locative S.308/P, 433
Hetu Kattā or **Causative subject** S.282/P, 412
Instrumental in the Locative sense S290/P, 416
Instrumental of reason S.289/P, 416
Kamma, the Object S.280/P, 410
Kamma'ttha-chaṭṭhī (Object-genitive or patient genitive) S.309/P, 434
Kammappavacanīya (Kamma-enhancer particle) S.299/P, 423
Karaṇa, the instrumental S.279/P, 410
Kattu or Kattā (subject), 411
Katv'attha-Chaṭṭhī (Subject-genitive or Agent genitive) S.308/P, 433
Lakkhaṇa S.313/P, 437
Locative in Ablative S.312/P, 436
Locative in Accusative S.310/P, 435
Locative in Dative S.311/P, 436
Locative in Instrumental S.310/P, 435
Locative of reason (also called absolute or nimitta sattamī) S.310/P, 435
Niddhāraṇa(Selection) S.304/P, 426
Niddhāraṇa-Catukka S.304/P, 427
Okāsa or **ādhāra** S.278/P, 408
Sāmī (the owner, possessive) S.283/P, 413
Sampadāna(Recipient) S.278/P, 391
Six Kāraka and Applicable Vibattis S.273/P, 374
Ta'dattha Sampadāna S.277/P, 401
Tulyā'dhikaraṇa Visesana S.292/P, 417
Tumattha Sampadāna S.277/P, 402
Visesana S.292/P, 417

4 Samāsa

Abyayībhāva (the nature of) S.319/P, 446
Aññapadattha S.328/P, 460

Bahubbīhi (the nature of) S.328/P, 459
Digu (Characteristic of) S.325/P, 455
Dvanda (the nature of) S.329/P, 481
Elision of vibatti(case-endings) and related things S.317/P, 444
Endings of Abyayībhāva Compound S.343/P, 493
Gender and number of Digu S.321/P, 448
Gender of abyayībhāva S.320/P, 448
Kammadhāraya (The characteristic of) S.324/P, 454
Pakati procedure for compound nouns and Taddhita nouns S.317/P, 445
Tappurisa (the nature of) S.327/P, 457
Ubhe tappurisa S.326/P, 456
Yutattha, (being related and relevant) S.316/P, 444

5 Taddhita

"e, o"(Vuddhi-substitute vowels) S.401/P, 561
Absolute grammatical rule vs. conditional grammatical rule as per common usage pattern and relevant applicability S.352/P, 518
Abyaya Taddhita (indeclinables) S.397-399/P, 557
Ādesa Procedure S.404/P, 570
Āgama Procedure S.404/P, 568
Ane'ka'ttha Taddhita S.350-353/P, 506
Apacca Taddhita (nouns in patronymic affix) S.344-349/P, 495
Bhāva Taddhita (abstract condition) S.360,361,362/P, 528
ivaṇṇa S.405/P, 571
koṭi(crores) to infinity S.395/P, 556
Lopa Procedure S.404/P, 567
Name of Twelve Months S.352/P, 516
ṇ-containing affixes S.396/P, 557
Samūha Taddhita S.354-355/P, 523
Saṅkhyā Taddhita S.373-395/P, 539

Ta'dassa'tthi Taddhita (quality or possession) S.364-370/P, 532
Ta'dassaṭhāna Taddhita(source or cause) S.356/P, 525
Ta'ppakati Taddhita (made up of, crafted with) S.372/P, 538
Tabbahula Taddhita (prominent nature) S.359/P, 527
Taddhita (the nature of noun-enhancers) S.344/P, 495
Tannissita Taddhita (dependent nature or source) S.358/P, 527
Upamā Taddhita (analogious similitude) S.357/P, 526
uvaṇṇa S.405/P, 571
Vikāra Procedure S.404/P, 568
Viparīta Procedure S.404/P, 569
Visesa Taddhita (superlative) S.363/P, 531
Vuddhi (the definition of)) S.405/P, 571
Vuddhi Procedure S.404/P, 566
vuddhi-function Sutta S.400/P, 560

6 Ākhyāta

"**ya**" affix S.440,447/P, 629
Abbhāsa (extra syllable), 645
Ajjatanī (Aorist) S.428/P, 591
Anuvuddhi (follow-up procedure of Vuddhi) S.513,514,515/P, 660
Asabba dhātuka vibatti (See footnote) S.431/P, 592
Asaṁyoganta (non-conjunct) S.483/P, 660
atha (various meanings of) S.406/P, 575
Attanopada S.407/P, 577
Bhavissanti (Future) S.429/P, 591
CAUSATIVE VERBS P., 608
Deleting "**ṇ**" of all causative **kārita** affixes S.523/P, 683
Deleting the last vowel in multi-stem roots S.521/P, 681
Dhātu (root) S.457/P, 643
Dhātu-paccaya also **Dhātu niddiṭṭha affixes** S.455/P, 642
Eight Ākhyāta verb-groups S.445-452/P, 636
Eight Modes of verbs S.414-422/P, 583

Eight Vibattis(verb-terminations) S.423-430/P, 588
Formative System of Pāli Verbs P., 594
Hiyyattanī (Past perfect) S.427/P, 590
Impersonal voice P., 615
Kālātipatti (Conditional) S.430/P, 592
Kārita Paccaya, or causative affixes S.438/P, 626
kha, cha, sa (Desiderative verb affixes) S.434/P, 622
Mahāsutta (Great Sutta of all morphological functions) S.391,517,404,571/P, 677
Nāma-dhātu kiriyā nominal-stem verbs S.435,436,437,439/P, 623
Onomatopoetic verb affixes S.435-437/P, 623
paccaya-the affixes S.432/P, 619
Pañcamī (The imperative) S.424/P, 588
Parassapada S.406/P, 576
Paro puriso (Applicable rule in a sentence of multiple persons as subjects) S.409/P, 579
Parokkhā (Past imperfect) S.426/P, 590
PLAIN VERBS (Active voice) P., 601
PLAIN VERBS (Passive Voice) P., 606
Pubbarūpa (assimilation of affix to the root-end consonant) S.443/P, 634
Purisa (three persons) S.408/P, 578
Reduplication procedure of certain verbs S.458/P, 644
Reversal of Attanopada into Parassapada procedure S.518/P, 678
Rules of Active Voice Sentence P., 612
Rules of Passive Voice Sentence P., 614
Sabbadhātuka vibatti S.431/P, 593
Sattamī (the optative) S.425/P, 589
The Affix and its impact on verb-form P., 599
Two kinds of ya-affixed verbs S.440/P, 630
Two main groups of verbs S.406,407/P, 577
Uttamapurisa (The high or last person) S.412/P, 582
Vattamāna-termination (Present Indicative) S.423/P, 588

VIBATTI TABLE P., 597
Vikaraṇa Paccaya affixes S.445-452/P, 636
Voice of attanopada-group verbs S.453/P, 640
Voice of prassapada-group verbs S.456/P, 642
Vuddhi procedure on verbs S.483,484,485/P, 660

7 Kibbidhāna

Garu (types of) S.602, 603/P, 747
Kārita-affix Recognition Procedure S.621/P, 759
kha affix S.560/P, 715
Kicca affixes S.545/P, 706
Kita'ntogadha(a hybrid of Kita & compound noun) S.524/P, 687
Kita-affixes S.546/P, 706
List of r-containing affixes S.539/P, 700
List of r-containing functions S.539/P, 700
māna , anta (present participle affix) S.565/P, 718
Recognition as noun procedure S.601/P, 746
Sādanas & their roles P., 685
ta affix, its tenses & uses S.556,557/P, 713
ta, tavantu, tāvī affixes S.555/P, 712
tabba, anīya affixes S.540/P, 701
Tassila(habitual pattern) etc, S.532/P, 694
tave, tuṁ affix S.561,562,563/P, 716
tuna, tvāna, tvā (gerund or absolutive affixes) S.564/P, 717

8 Uṇādi

ghiṇ-affix S.651/P, 796
Guṇa vs. Vuddhi S.642, 406, 407/P, 785
Hetu-Kattu Sādhana S.641/P, 784
Pāṭipadika P., 769, 816, 818, 819, 823, 824
ssantu, māna, āna (future participle affixes in the context of a Kamma) S.655/P, 799

Three meanings of tabba, anīya-affixed words S.635/P, 772
Upadhā, (A nearby word, penultimate syllable) S.629/P, 769

ABOUT PARIYATTI

Pariyatti is dedicated to providing affordable access to authentic teachings of the Buddha about the Dhamma theory (*pariyatti*) and practice (*paṭipatti*) of Vipassana meditation. A 501(c)(3) non-profit charitable organization since 2002, Pariyatti is sustained by contributions from individuals who appreciate and want to share the incalculable value of the Dhamma teachings. We invite you to visit www.pariyatti.org to learn about our programs, services, and ways to support publishing and other undertakings.

Pariyatti Publishing Imprints

Vipassana Research Publications (focus on Vipassana as taught by S.N. Goenka in the tradition of Sayagyi U Ba Khin)

BPS Pariyatti Editions (selected titles from the Buddhist Publication Society, co-published by Pariyatti in the Americas)

Pariyatti Digital Editions (audio and video titles, including discourses)

Pariyatti Press (classic titles returned to print and inspirational writing by contemporary authors)

Pariyatti enriches the world by

- disseminating the words of the Buddha,
- providing sustenance for the seeker's journey,
- illuminating the meditator's path.